Crisis Response and Management and Emerging Information Systems:

Critical Applications

Murray E. Jennex
San Diego State University, USA

Information Science
REFERENCE

Senior Editorial Director:	Kristin Klinger
Director of Book Publications:	Julia Mosemann
Editorial Director:	Lindsay Johnston
Acquisitions Editor:	Erika Carter
Development Editor:	Hannah Abelbeck
Production Editor:	Sean Woznicki
Typesetters:	Mike Brehm, Keith Glazewski, Natalie Pronio, Jennifer Romanchak
Print Coordinator:	Jamie Snavely
Cover Design:	Nick Newcomer

Published in the United States of America by
Information Science Reference (an imprint of IGI Global)
701 E. Chocolate Avenue
Hershey PA 17033
Tel: 717-533-8845
Fax: 717-533-8661
E-mail: cust@igi-global.com
Web site: http://www.igi-global.com/reference

Library of Congress Cataloging-in-Publication Data

Crisis response and management and emerging information systems: critical
applications / Murray E. Jennex, editor.
    p. cm.
 Includes bibliographical references and index.
  Summary: "This book provides a comprehensive, cross disciplinary look at the
advancing and understanding of organizational, technical, human, and cognitive
issues associated with the use of information systems in responding and
managing crises of all kinds"--Provided by publisher.
  ISBN 978-1-60960-609-1 (hbk.) -- ISBN 978-1-60960-610-7 (ebook) 1.
Emergency management--Information services. 2. Emergency communication
systems. I. Jennex, Murray E., 1956- II. Title: Crisis response and
management and emerging information systems.
 HV551.2.C755 2011
 363.34'80684--dc22
                                2011014954

British Cataloguing in Publication Data
A Cataloguing in Publication record for this book is available from the British Library.

Table of Contents

Detailed Table of Contents

Chapter 1

    John R. Harrald, Virginia Polytechnic Institute and State University, USA

A significant body of social science research has concluded that improvisation in distributed, collaborative, open systems is the key to success in responding to and recovering from extreme events. The evolution of emergency management in the United States since the 9-11 attacks has emphasized the development of doctrine, process, and structure. In earlier work I concluded that both the agility desired by the social sciences and the discipline created by the professional practitioners are essential. This article explores how agility can be developed within a disciplined system and concludes that the keys are the development of outcome based goals, adaptive leadership, and technology that supports collaborative sense-making and decision making in open, organizational systems.

Chapter 2

    Murray Turoff, New Jersey Institute of Technology, USA
    Starr Roxanne Hiltz, New Jersey Institute of Technology, USA
    Connie White, New Jersey Institute of Technology, USA
    Linda Plotnick, New Jersey Institute of Technology, USA
    Art Hendela, New Jersey Institute of Technology, USA
    Xiang Yao, New Jersey Institute of Technology, USA

Emergency preparedness, planning, and response suffer from shortcomings that impede the potential for effectiveness. In this article, we provide an overview of Emergency Preparedness and Management that is based upon our research, including insights into the shortcomings of current practices, a discussion of relevant theories (e.g., High Reliability Organizations, muddling through) and recommendations to promote more effective planning, management, and response. Our recommendations include system support for the principles of High Reliability Organizations and muddling through, rethinking risk analysis to have a longer-term view and reflect more than just monetary loss, creating ways to better inform and involve the public, and encouraging collaboration and collective intelligence through such means as a dynamic Delphi voting system.

Chapter 3

The introduction of information systems and the humanitarian reform process are both having a tremendous impact on the way that humanitarian assistance is delivered – yet the two processes are extremely weakly connected. As a result, the humanitarian community is failing to realise the potential that information technology has to support key aspects of the reform process, but also failing to recognise that technology is likely to render many of the discussions around reform moot. The balance of knowledge is shifting towards those affected by disaster, implying that they will become increasingly empowered by technology to more effectively cope with the impact of those disasters. Traditional actors in the humanitarian community must incorporate these realities into its own processes or risk being overtaken by newer and more agile institutions which may not be so concerned with humanitarian principles.

Chapter 4

The early designs for crisis management decision support systems used data-based or model-based methodologies and architectures. We argue that the complexity of crisis management situations means that a greater emphasis on collaboration is needed. Moreover, modern interactive Web 2.0 technologies allow group decision support to be offered to geographically dispersed teams. Given that crisis management often requires teams to be drawn together from a number of organisations sited at different locations, we reflect upon the potential of these technologies to support the early stages of crisis management without the need to draw the team together at a common location. We also report on a small scale experiment using GroupSystems ThinkTank to manage an emerging food safety event. We conclude that such systems have potential and deserve more careful evaluation.

Chapter 5

Past experience has shown that introducing new Information Technologies can have unintended and undesirable consequences, such as new forms of errors and a narrowing of data search activities. Eight Incident Commanders (ICs) took part in a simulated disaster response exercise to determine how the availability of real-time image feeds from a UAV impact on situation assessment and decision-making. The exercise simulated the video feed from an unmanned aerial vehicle (UAV) that allows incident command centers to monitor developments at a crisis site. The results showed that information from the video image channel dominated information available from other channels or in other forms. Nearly all of the ICs failed to detect important changes in the situation that were not captured in the imaging channel but that were available via other, more traditional data sources. The dominance of the image feed resulted in ICs narrowing their data search activities and reducing cross-checking across diverse data sources. This study confirms anecdotal reports that users can over-rely on video feeds from UAVs.

Chapter 6

    Monika Büscher, Lancaster University, Denmark
    Preben Holst Mogensen, University of Aarhus, Denmark
    Margit Kristensen, The Alexandra Institute Ltd., Denmark

In this article we use the formative evaluation of a prototype 'assembly' of pervasive computing technologies to specify design implications for emergency virtual teamwork tools. The prototype assembly, called "Overview", was implemented in collaboration with police, fire and medical emergency services as part of the real life event management during the Tall Ships' Races 2007 in Denmark. We describe how the emergency teams used the technologies for collaboration between distributed colleagues, to produce shared situation awareness, to manage efforts and resources and respond to minor emergencies. Trust in technology is a key need virtual teams identify in their endeavours to dovetail innovative technologies into emergency work. We show how practices of working up trust are supported by the PalCom open architecture (which was used to build Overview), and delineate design guidelines to enable the productive integration of pervasive computing.

Chapter 7

    Aviv Segev, KAIST, Korea

In a crisis, the problem of the lack of a shared platform or similar communication methods among the collaborators usually arises within a few hours. While a crisis requires rapid response of emergency management factors, ontology is generally represented in a static manner. Therefore, an adaptive ontology for crisis knowledge representation is needed to assist in coordinating relief efforts in different crisis situations. This chapter describes a method of ontology modeling that modifies the ontology in real time during a crisis according to the crisis surroundings. The method is based on modeling a basic predefined multilingual ontology while allowing the expansion of the ontology according to the crisis circumstances and the addition of other languages within the crisis time limitations. An example of ontology use based on a sample Katrina crisis blog is presented. Motivation for multilingual ontology use is supplied by the Boxing Day tsunami crisis.

Chapter 8

    Mark Gaynor, Saint Louis University, USA
    Sarah Friedeck, Saint Louis University, USA
    Alan Pearce, Information Age Economics, USA
    Scott Brander, Harvard University, USA
    Ken Post, Alert Systems Inc., USA

The chapter suggests and supports a public policy in which the Federal Communications Commission (FCC) should seize a unique opportunity to resolve some of the nation's critical communications problems in times of crises with the allocation of a portion of the spectrum at 700 MHz (specifically, the D band) for the deployment of a nationwide interoperable emergency broadband wireless network built by a public-private partnership. It then presents a convincing theoretical model that advocates that an open and/or neutral, as opposed to a closed, network will add greater efficiency, greater choice, while advancing public safety along with the deployment of new and valuable technologies, applications, and services.

Chapter 9

The focus of this chapter is the design and development of Information and Communication Technologies that support collaborative work and processes in command and control teams, more specifically, in joint emergency response operations. The unique contexts and varying circumstances of response operations have an impact on how collaborative work and interactions among commanders emerge, as well as on the extent to which Information and Communication Technologies are used. This emergence of response operations poses specific methodological complications and demands on how to study command and control teams, and also how to approach high-level design problems. The chapter demonstrates how such analysis can be performed. It presents a study of scenario-based role-playing simulation with professionals – emergency management commanders – as participants. The study documents the work practice of a team of commanders from the Swedish local and regional emergency response organizations responding jointly to an emergency, a medium size forest fire. The study also identifies areas and/or activities that may be enhanced by command and control tools. A combined set of bottom-up data driven and top-down methods – topical episode analysis, communicative roles, socio-metric status and communication modelling – are used to assess communication and interactions among the commanders. The findings indicate that the studied commanders used informal arrangements within the established formal command and control structures, and took informal functions and communicative roles across organizational and domain boundaries to handle diverse incidents and so called pseudo-problems. This identified adaptive and improvised behaviour of the commanders – and the team as whole – was identified as a critical characteristic for effective command and control work in joint response operations. Cross-domain and cross-organizational knowledge was found to be the most important feature of this type of capability to adapt and improvise. The study, further, highlights the significance of employing bottom-up, data driven methods for analysis of design and development processes, as well as important methodological challenges related to this type of analysis.

Chapter 10

In this chapter, we explore design foundations and conceptualize a design approach to examine the socio-technical knowledge that crisis organizations have about crisis management Information Systems. We use findings from a case study across four crisis organizations to illustrate how the network of knowledge, information management, and integration of technology and information were interpreted by stakeholders during a large wild fire in 2006. The design approach illustrates that design foundations of crisis management Information Systems encompass: a network of knowledge, IT management, and information integration. We argue that the design foundation is promising for analysis and explanation of the enrolment of actors, adaptation of technology/processes, and stabilization of crisis management Information Systems.

Chapter 11

Crisis response involves handling information intensive processes, and coordination of large quantities of information from and for different relief-response organizations. The information needs and responses of such organizations are closely related to the situations and roles these organizations are involved during a crisis relief-response process. The information seeking and retrieval processes associated with crisis situations influence the affectivity of response vigor and the coordination of relief-response activities. To provide an effective solution for a European Main Port's crisis response needs, a role-based situation-aware information seeking and retrieval conceptual framework is formulated. The conceptual framework, the design approach, and the implementation in a prototype are presented as an approach to design future crisis response for information seeking and retrieval services.

Chapter 12

Warnings to the broad population in an emergency situation, irrespective of location and condition, are a public policy responsibility. Public wireless networks offer now the opportunity to deliver emergency warnings in this way with explanations, because in many countries, the mobile penetration rates and coverage are higher than any other access form. This chapter summarizes the analysis of the selection process between short messaging services (SMS) and Cell Broadcast (CB) messaging in the context of Denmark based on end user requirements, stakeholder roles and case-based analysis. It demonstrates the many technical, cost-benefit, and other trade-offs needed in supporting the population now with a dependable and wide-spread technology. This research is the basis for a national policy.

Chapter 13

Most organizations face difficult challenges in managing knowledge for crisis response, but it is crucial for response effectiveness that such challenges be overcome. Organizational members must share the knowledge needed to plan for emergencies. They also must be able during an emergency to access relevant plans and communicate about their responses to it. This article examines the role and relevance of knowledge management (and knowledge management systems therein) in support of crisis response. We begin by discussing what knowledge management and crisis response mean. We move on to suggest why crisis response efforts within an organizational context, might benefit from knowledge management initiatives. Specific examples of how knowledge management efforts have supported crisis response in the past are then presented. We end by offering researchers with some suggestions for future research work in light of this subject domain.

Chapter 14

Eli Rohn, New Jersey Institute of Technology, USA
Denis Blackmore, New Jersey Institute of Technology, USA

Managers of emergencies face challenges of complexity, uncertainty, and unpredictably. Triadic constraints imply requisite parsimony in describing the essence of the emergency, its magnitude and direction of development. Linguistic separation increases as the crisis management organization is more complex and made up of diverse constituents. Therefore, a standard objective emergency scale is vital to quantify and unambiguously communicate the nature of any emergency. Previous work laid the foundations for an objective measurable emergency event scale. This article proposes a unified emergency scale based on a mathematical model, accompanied by several examples spanning local to national events.

Chapter 15

Gunter Zeug, European Environment Agency, Denmark
Dominik Brunner, Fraunhofer Institute of Optronics, Germany

Today, the added value of geoinformation for crisis management is well known and accepted. However, experiences show that disaster management units on local administrative levels in the developing world often lack the use of Geographic Information Systems for analysing spatial interrelations and making their own maps. Various studies mention the shortage of financial resources, human capacity, and adequate knowledge as reasons for that. In recent years publically available virtual globes like Google Earth™, Microsoft® Bing™ Maps 3D or Nasa World Wind enjoy great popularity. The accessibility of worldwide high resolution satellite data, their intuitive user interface, and the ability to integrate own data support this success. In this chapter, the potential of these new geospatial technologies for supporting disaster preparedness and response is demonstrated, using the example of Google Earth™. Possibilities for the integration of data layers from third parties, the digitization of own layers, as well as the analytical capacities are examined. Furthermore, a printing module is presented, which supports the production of paper maps based on data previously collected and edited in Google Earth™. The efficiency of the proposed approach is demonstrated for a disaster management scenario in Legazpi, a Philippine city exposed to several natural hazards due to the vicinity to Mayon volcano and the annually occuring typhoons in the region. With this research, current technological trends in geospatial technologies are taken up and investigated on their potential for professional use. Moreover, it is demonstrated that by using freely available software general constraints for using GIS in developing countries can be overcome. Most importantly, the approach presented guarantees low cost for implementation and reproducibility, which is essential for its application in developing countries.

Chapter 16
Tricia Toomey, San Diego State University, USA
Eric Frost, San Diego State University, USA
Murray E. Jennex, San Diego State University, USA

Emergency management is a diverse field. Effective disaster management involves knowledge of various subjects as well as work experience in all aspects related to mitigation, planning, response, and recovery efforts. One field not being fully exploited by disaster management is the use of geospatial tools in the form of Geographic Information Systems (GIS), cartography, and geovisualization. One reason for this is that many emergency managers are not fully aware of the assistance GIS can lend to effectively manage disaster situations. All functions of emergency management have a strong geographic component. Where is the earthquake epicenter? Where is the damage? Where does the dam inundation run and who/what is in that path? Where is the area of road closures? The questions asking "where" are endless in effective emergency management and range from the mitigation stage through to the recovery stage. For example, a tsunami may inundate only a certain portion of the region, therefore, it is important to have mitigation and planning efforts concentrated in those regions. It is also important to know what businesses, housing, and populations are in the affected areas. The integration of geospatial tools for risk assessment, mitigation, planning, response, and recovery efforts is emerging as an effective and potentially invaluable resource for answering such questions in regards to emergency management.

Chapter 17
Ahmad Kabil, Lawrence Technological University, USA
Magdy Kabeil, Sadat Academy for Management Sciences, Egypt

The National Crisis Decision Support System NCDSS represents special type of mission critical systems highly responsive enough to face a national crisis. The value of a NCDSS is assessed according to its impact on the value of surviving a national crisis. Such systems should have common initial requirements associated with their common conceptual design. A conceptual design representing basic modules of NCDSS is developed. The conceptual design provides a general foundation that can be transferred to a detailed design and implementation of an application. The proposed concept of NCDSS meets the initial specifications that are validated using a case scenario. The relative percentage of the total score that each module contributes to the design is evaluated using the Analytical Hierarchy Process (AHP) and the Quality Function Deployment (QFD) technique.

Preface

IMPLEMENTING SOCIAL MEDIA IN CRISIS RESPONSE USING KNOWLEDGE MANAGEMENT

Welcome to *Crisis Response and Management and Emerging Information Systems: Critical Applications!* This book expands upon articles presented in the first volume of the International Journal of Information Systems for Crisis Response and Management, IJISCRAM, and is the first volume in an annual series of books that I expect to become an invaluable resource for crisis response and management researchers, practitioners, and students. The journal and this volume are focused on providing cutting edge research and advances in the crisis response discipline. Authors are a mix of established senior researchers, those beginning their academic careers, and some in between.

To introduce the book, this first chapter will explore two technical innovations that made headlines in disasters and crises, starting with Hurricane Katrina. The first innovation is social media, and individuals have been using it with great success to save themselves or others. The second is cloud computing, which is a fairly recent name for the innovation trend that has included open source, software as a service, and service oriented architecture. The chapter proposes that for organizations to use these innovations successfully they should use knowledge management to guide their implementation.

OVERVIEW

Organizations need to be prepared to respond to crises. Traditionally, organizations prepare themselves for crisis response through planning, preparing response procedures and a crisis response system, and performing at least basic overview training to expected crisis responders. Crisis planning involves identifying potential crisis scenarios and determining what resources and actions will be needed to mitigate them (Raman, et al., 2010). Crisis response procedures provide direction to responders on how to recognize the crisis, what immediate actions to take, what communications to make, what long term actions are to be taken, and how to end the crisis (Jennex, 2004, 2008). Crisis response systems support communications, data gathering and analysis, and decision-making. Crisis response systems are rarely used but when needed, must function well and without fail. Designing and building these systems requires designers to anticipate what will be needed, what resources will be available, and how conditions will differ from normal. A standard model for a crisis response system is from Bellardo, Karwan, and Wallace (1984) and identifies the components as including:

- Database
- Data analysis capability
- Normative models
- User interface.

This model has been modified by Jennex (2004, 2008) using experience with the Year 2000, Y2K, response, Hurricane Katrina, the Strong Angel III and Golden Phoenix exercises, and the 2007 San Diego Wildfires to add:

- Trained users (where users are personnel using the system to respond to or communicate about the emergency)
- Dynamic and integrated (yet possibly physically distributed) methods to communicate between users (responders, concerned citizens, and victims) and between users and data sources
- Protocols/ontology to facilitate communication
- Geographical information systems
- Processes and procedures used to guide the response to and improve decision making during the crisis.

The goals of the expanded crisis response system model are to:

- Facilitate clear communications
- Improve data, information, and knowledge transfer
- Improve the efficiency and effectiveness of decision-making
- Manage data, information, and knowledge to prevent or at least mitigate information overload.

Finally, crisis response training prepares expected responders to use the crisis response system and respond effectively to the crisis. Training can take several forms, from table top exercises to full blown dress rehearsals. Also, it can be done once, annually, or at some other interval as determined by the organization (Patton & Flin, 1999; Turoff, 2002; Andersen, Garde, & Andersen, 1998; Lee & Bui, 2000; Fischer, 1998; Renaud & Phillips, 2003).

Unfortunately, crises can happen at any time making it difficult for organizations to have appropriate resources (responders, expertise, and material) where and when they are needed. Additionally, most organizations have little to no experience with real emergencies. These organizations need to take advantage of all available experience and technologies to support the decision making needed in fast paced and high stress/tension circumstances. Finally, the complexity of communicating, collaborating, and decision making processes in the context of crisis response efforts should not be underestimated or trivialized.

To mitigate the unpredictability of crises and the complexity of crisis response, affected individuals and first responders are using new technologies, particularly social media, to help themselves. Examples include:

- Concerned citizens used a wiki after Hurricane Katrina to organize, collaborate, and rapidly create the PeopleFinder and ShelterFinder systems (Murphy & Jennex, 2006).
- Citizens affected by the 2007 San Diego Wildfires used a wiki to pool knowledge on which homes burned and which survived when the local media failed to support their needs (this has not been

previously reported in the literature but was an activity performed by my students during the event).

- Mumbai citizens used Twitter to report their status, let others know where to find friends, relatives, etc., and to solicit blood donations following the 2008 Mumbai terrorist attacks (Beaumont, 2008).
- Victims trapped by falling debris during the 2010 Haiti earthquake used texting and/or Facebook to alert their friends/family to their location and condition (Boodhoo, 2010).

These anecdotes provide evidence of the value of social media to individuals in responding to crisis. However they do not indicate that organizations can benefit from the use of social media during crisis response. This paper provides a process and reason for incorporating social media into organizational crisis response planning and systems. The process is based on using knowledge management, KM, as the guiding approach to implementing social media as a technology for improving connectivity and knowledge transfer among crisis response teams.

The inspiration for this comes from the disputed 2009 Iranian elections. Plotnick and White (2010) and the Wikipedia summaries on this election include several references discussing how protesters used social media such as Twitter and Facebook to organize and manage the protests. This is interesting, but not the inspiration for the paper. The inspiration comes from the possible use of KM by the protest organizers to create a coordinated protest. The author knows of this from his role as editor in chief of the International Journal of Knowledge Management. Approximately nine months prior to the election protests, the author received a request for a copy of his knowledge management success model paper from an Iranian academic colleague. I queried the colleague on why they wanted the paper and the response was that they were researching how to create autonomous, self-organizing youth teams. I found this an odd application at the time but sent them the paper. It wasn't till the election protests nine months later that it became apparent what the possible use of the autonomous, self-organizing youth teams was. While I cannot verify that this is what the research was for, it did get me thinking on the problem of finding applications for social media and initiated my research into using KM as the process for creating the strategy and process for incorporating social media into organizations for their crisis response.

SOCIAL MEDIA AND KNOWLEDGE MANAGEMENT

Plotnick and White (2010) describe social media as generally being attributed to the collaborative applications supported by Web 2.0 technologies. These include, but are not limited to, Twitter, Facebook, MySpace, wikis, and blogs. Blogs, wikis, and MySpace were the first applications becoming popular in the early 2000s, while Facebook and Twitter are more recent creations. While popular with the public, organizations have struggled to find business uses for social media. Wikis have been the first social media adapted by organizations as they have been found to be very useful in supporting collaboration within teams and work groups. Facebook, Twitter, and blogs are not always looked at favorably by organizations. Many consider them information leaks and venues for dissatisfied employees and/or customers to vent their complaints.

Jennex (2010) summarized KM as being about using knowledge and experience gained from past events and activities as an aid in making current and future decision making. Knowledge management systems, KMS, provide tools and repositories for acquiring, storing, searching, manipulating, displaying, and transferring knowledge. KM/KMS focuses on two issues:

- Leveraging what the organization "knows" so that it can better utilize its knowledge assets, and
- Connecting knowledge generators, holders, and users to facilitate the flow of knowledge through the organization

Jennex and Raman (2009) (appearing later in this book) have discussed how KM can be used to support crisis response. They consider a crisis response system as a form of a KMS. This chapter expands on Jennex and Raman (2009) by applying KM to the specific issue of how organizations can incorporate social media into their crisis response plans. This is done using Jennex and Olfman's (2006) investigation of what was necessary for KM/KMS success and the identification of twelve critical success factors, CSFs. Among these are having a knowledge strategy and an integrated technical infrastructure. These two CSFs can be used to align social media with organizational based crisis response.

An integrated KM technical infrastructure includes networks, databases/repositories, computers, software, KMS experts (Alavi & Leidner, 1999; Cross & Baird, 2000; Davenport, et al., 1998; Ginsberg & Kambil, 1999; Jennex & Olfman, 2000, 1998; Sage & Rouse, 1999; Yu, et al., 2004). Social media assists in several ways. As it is Web 2.0 based, social media operates over a global integrated network. Wikis, blogs, You Tube, and social networking sites all provide repositories that can be harnessed for crisis response. Additionally, these same applications provide methods of connecting to experts. Overall, social media provides a good solution to the need for an integrated technical infrastructure.

KM strategy identifies users, user experience level needs, sources, where knowledge needs to flow, knowledge processes, storage strategy, knowledge, and links to knowledge for the KMS (Ginsberg & Kambil, 1999; Holsapple & Joshi, 2000; Jennex, Olfman, & Addo, 2003; Koskinen, 2001; Sage & Rouse, 1999; Yu et al., 2004). This CSF is critical for assessing how to use social media in the organizational setting. KM strategy drives the organization to plan the use of social media. KM strategy guides the organization in finding/identifying crisis response knowledge sources as well as those needing this knowledge to assist in their crisis response. KM strategy also drives the organization to plan the storage of knowledge by driving the organization to taxonomy and ontology as well as storage formats. Social media provides methods for storing and organizing unstructured knowledge such as video, audio, victim stories, lessons learned, et cetera. Social networking applications such as Facebook provide methods for creating and communicating networks of links to expertise, as well as methods for connecting experts. Overall, preparing a crisis response KM strategy guides the organization into planning the adoption and implementation of social media into their crisis response plans.

To summarize, these two CSFs (KM Strategy and Integrated Technical Infrastructure) and the focus on connecting knowledge generators, holders, and users drive the adoption of social media as a KM technology. Social media provides technology that links KM participants and KM strategy is what helps the organization determine how to use social media.

However, social media suffer from three significant weaknesses. The first is managerial control. Organizations found it very difficult to control how members used social media and what they posted online. This lack of controls has resulted in reluctance in implementing social media applications. Second, social media also has had reliability issues. This relates to the control issue as organizations found that since they did not control the social media infrastructure they could not control version releases, reliability of accessibility, overall access to the application, and security of data, information, and knowledge placed in social media repositories. Thirdly, social media has a trust issue with respect to postings and content. Due to the aforementioned lack of control, postings and content could be posted by anyone with no quality or truthfulness control being applied. This was an initial concern with Wikipedia as the initial thought that the power of crowds would monitor content, and postings did not work as well or as quickly as expected. The issue has been mitigated by the use of expert editorial review boards reviewing and approving content updates prior to their posting.

The advent of cloud computing is mitigating some of the reliability concerns. Wikipedia describes Cloud computing as Internet-based computing, whereby shared resources, software, and information are provided to computers and other devices on-demand, like the electricity grid. Highly reliable server farms hosted by companies providing cloud services provide reliable data, information, and knowledge storage as well as reliable Web and Web application hosting. Other benefits include the abundance of open source software. Crisis response software is available to organizations at little to no charge. Of course, the issue of control is not mitigated by the cloud or open source software.

Can and should organizations be concerned with control and truthfulness/accuracy of data, information, and knowledge? Of course they should be concerned. Data, information, and knowledge are critical resources that need to be protected. Access and/or misinformation by unauthorized persons during a crisis can cause confusion and intentional interference affecting the organization's ability to respond. Can KM assist organizations in addressing these issues? Again, of course, Jennex and Zygier (2007) addressed incorporating security into KM. Jennex and Zyngier (2007) utilized the National Security Telecommunications and Information System Security Committee model (NSTISSC 1994), commonly known as the CIA (confidentiality, integrity, availability) model, to incorporate security into KM. Security in KM involves incorporating security processes into KM strategy. KM strategy should incorporate the use of risk management to identify threats with corresponding risks (consequence and probability) to crisis response data, information, and knowledge and includes the identification of security policies for mitigating these threats and risks. These security policies should address access control, technologies for storing, transmitting, and processing data, information, and knowledge, and processes regulating the update, use, and ultimate archiving of crisis response data, information, and knowledge.

To summarize, social media provides a rapid response and collaboration tool set that can be utilized by organizations for crisis response. It is proposed that a KM strategy for crisis response can be used to guide the adoption of social media for crisis response in organizations. Jennex (2004a) outlines the critical issues that an organization faces in creating a KM strategy. These are summarized for crisis response as follows:

- Identifying users of the KMS: Without knowing who is expected to use the KMS and for what purpose, designers do not know what knowledge or level of context needs to be captured.
- Having an overall organizational KM strategy: Without an overall organizational KM strategy many organizations tend to fail in implementing a crisis response specific KM initiative.
- Identifying a representation strategy: Crisis responders tend to be a transient workforce with a regular rate of turnover, this generally drives the organization to codify into computerized knowledge repositories as much data, information, and knowledge as possible. Also, new workers tend to need to talk to knowledge holders providing a driver to capturing as many links to knowledge as possible. Additionally, given the variety of formats that knowledge is created and used in organizations must specify how they will manage long term storage of data, information, and knowledge.

- Flooding the KMS with content: Information overload is a real issue in crisis response (Jennex and Raman, 2009). Knowledge strategy has to identify that data, information, and knowledge necessary to support crisis response decision making and focus on capturing, storing, and displaying this data, information, and knowledge.
- Inadequate search capabilities for the KMS: Crisis responders need data, information, and knowledge when they need it and cannot be expected to spend much time searching. Knowledge needs to be stored and organized in a format and with labels/tags that facilitates search and retrieval.
- Senior Management Support: Crisis response needs sensitive data, information, and knowledge that without top management support for encouraging knowledge sharing and for allocating resources, will not be available.
- Security: KM processes need to ensure critical crisis response data, information, and knowledge is secure
- Maintaining currency of knowledge: Crisis response data, information, and knowledge must be accurate and relevant temporally for users to use the KMS
- KM Goals and Purpose: Crisis response KM initiatives need a clearly identified and communicated set of goals and purpose so that the impact of the initiative can be measured.
- An Organizational Learning Culture: Organizations, and specifically the crisis response organization, need a strategy that fosters a learning organization including incentives to share and use knowledge

While addressing the above crisis response KM strategy issues, an additional set of issues need to be addressed before an organization adopts social media for crisis response:

- What technologies should be used?
- Who should use the technologies?
- What data, information, and knowledge should be made available for response?
- What security policies should be implemented?

The following section discusses how to resolve these issues.

IMPLEMENTING SOCIAL MEDIA FOR CRISIS RESPONSE

What Technologies Should be Used?

Technologies should be adapted based on their ability to integrate/interface with the organization's existing technical infrastructure. Additionally, the organization should conduct a crisis response needs analysis and select technologies that meet that analyzed need and assessed capability of the technology to meet that need. Some general guidelines for social media:

Wikis are excellent for collaborative authoring and storage, organization, and dissemination of documents, processes, and solutions. Wikis are appropriate for crisis planning, training, response, and recovery (Raman et al., 2010; Jennex & Raman, 2009). The key advantage is support for distributed expertise to collaborate synchronously or asynchronously. Additionally, secure wiki technology is being made available in organizational applications such as Sharepoint which are useful for internal collaboration between organizational experts. Non-secure wikis available via open source or as a service are useful for collaboration with external experts, victims, and the general public as well as for dissemination of data, information, and knowledge to the public. External wikis from partner organizations should be identified and vetted before use. Knowledge management should also be used to identify data, information, and knowledge to be collected and made available. Finally, KM should be used to determine the format for storing the collected data, information, and knowledge.

Blogs are an excellent communication tool. As illustrated by the 2010 Gulf oil spill, blogs can be used to get an organization's message out to the public, to affected persons, and to internal members. It should also be noted that blogs are easy to set up and be used by external participants, some of whom may not be sympathetic to the organization's response.

Twitter and instant messaging applications are excellent for keeping responders statused or calling for specific needs or responses. Implementations should have specific users subscribed and the organization should monitor and manage the subscriber list.

Facebook and other social networking sites can be used much like blogs to post public information, updates for internal responders, as an instant messaging system, and to build a sustainable community (Belblidia, 2010). Users should be screened to those on the response team or in the organization for organizational sites. Public sites can be open to all subscribers.

Google map mashups can be used to create custom crisis response maps for responders, crisis management, and victims. Examples include:

- British Blizzard of 2009 where twitter was used to allow users to post snow conditions that were then published on the mashup map (Lang & Benbunan-Fich, 2010)
- The 2007 San Diego wild fires where map mashups were generated to help direct fire response and to alert victims and the public where the fire was, what houses were destroyed, what areas were still under evacuation (Toomey, et al., 2009, appearing later in this book).
- Haiti earthquake of 2010 where a map was generated fusing aerial photography with street maps so that refugee camps could be identified to relief workers so they could deliver emergency food and water supplies (unpublished research from work done in the San Diego State University Visualization Laboratory, article currently under review).

Open source software and software as a service are good choices if from established crisis response support organizations. Two such organizations are Sahana (http://sahanafoundation.org/) and InRelief (www.inrelief.org). Sahana is an open source initiative that provides a full service crisis response system free to users. Users are allowed to tailor the software as needed and can provide changes back to Sahana. InRelief is a data, information, and knowledge service based on Google technology, provided by a registered non-government organization, NGO, and managed by San Diego State University. Both recognize the need for security and access control and provide those features while also allowing for open collaboration between organizations. Both also have a track record of success. Sahana has been used in major crises since 2005 and InRelief has been used to support earthquake response in Haiti and Mexico, the 2010 Gulf oil spill, and was tested by the United States military and other civilian organizations during Exercise 24 conducted at San Diego State University in September, 2010. Finally, both are KM repositories as both provide lessons learned and history from previous crises.

A concluding consideration is what computer/communication technology to utilize. Experience is showing that dedicated crisis response equipment becomes obsolete very quickly (Jennex, 2004, 2008).

It is better to utilize the computer/communication tools used by responders and other crisis response personnel on a daily basis. While wireless enabled laptop computers have been the technology of choice for the last few years, the trend is towards the use of Internet enabled cell phones with large built in memories and using data services and away from wireless laptops. This suggests that organizations should move towards hand held mobile computer/communication as it is what the responders will be accustomed to using.

Who Should Use the Technologies?

Knowledge management processes should be used to identify knowledge sources and users. Social network analysis tools can be used with KM to identify data, information, and knowledge flows. It should be noted that KM analysis usually finds that data, information, and knowledge flows usually do not follow organizational hierarchies. While crisis leadership can be appointed as the organization requires, data, information, and knowledge flows work best if they are designed to fit the actual organizational social networks, including the identified knowledge gate keepers.

What Data, Information, and Knowledge Should be Made Available for Response?

Knowledge management success is defined as capturing the right knowledge, getting the right knowledge to the right user, and using this knowledge to improve organizational and/or individual performance. KM success is measured by using the dimensions: impact on business processes, impact on strategy, leadership, and knowledge content (Jennex, Smolnik, & Croasdell, 2009). As previously discussed, KM strategy is the process for determining the right data, information, and knowledge to capture and store, where this data, information, and knowledge is located, who needs it, and how to get it to them. Organizations need to appoint a KM leader for this strategic effort. Jennex and Olfman (2006) caution that not all data, information, and knowledge can be captured in a computer based repository. Linkages to data, information, and knowledge also need to be identified and captured for that which cannot be extracted from a source and captured in a repository. Typical data, information, and knowledge needed to be capture includes:

- Resource data and information (type, amount, location of resources)
- Expertise needed for response such as process, equipment, risk, and personnel knowledge as well as specialized skills and capabilities knowledge
- Response procedures and processes
- Lessons learned from previous events
- Environmental, geographical, and demographic data and information
- Industry data and information
- Regulatory data and information

Useful tools for identifying critical data, information, and knowledge includes table top exercises and scenario walkthroughs, analysis of previous events, and participation in and analysis of large scale crisis response exercises.

What Security Policies Should be Implemented?

The previous discussions provide the analysis for this activity. The organization needs to identify the response team and expert sources as well as organization sensitive data, information, and knowledge. Access control is applied by selecting the appropriate technology, secure wikis for collaboration and social networking tools/sites that allow the tool/site owner to manage access control lists. Organizations then need to implement a process for vetting and authorizing membership to the social media source. This is fairly simple prior to a crisis, but organizations need to include this process during the crisis to manage adding membership under crisis pressure and where it may need to be done very quickly. A short list of recommended security policies for crisis response follows:

- Access Control (internal and external personnel)
- Initial Hiring including Background Investigation
- Termination
- Communication/Encryption
- Acceptable Use
- Data, Information, and Knowledge Storage and Maintenance
- Software Vendor Qualification
- Application Development and Maintenance
- Data, Information, and Knowledge Validation (internal and external sources)

CONCLUSION

Social media are being implemented by individuals during a crisis. Usually, this is a self organizing activity without any organizational control or management. However, organizations can also take advantage of social media for their crisis response as long as they take precautions to maintain the integrity of their proprietary data, information, and knowledge and manage access to these resources to those vetted appropriate. This book proposes the use of knowledge management strategy incorporating security to assist in this analysis and specifically warns against just adopting social media for crisis response without first considering its impact on and risk to the organization and its members.

The remaining chapters will support readers in determining these impacts and risks. It is my hope that readers will get sufficient knowledge and tools from these chapters to support their crisis response management researches and/or initiatives.

Murray E. Jennex
San Diego State University, USA

REFERENCES

Alavi, M., & Leidner, D. E. (1999). *Knowledge management systems: Emerging views and practices from the field*. 32nd Hawaii International Conference on System Sciences, IEEE Computer Society.

Andersen, H. B., Garde, H., & Andersen, V. (1998). MMS: An electronic message management system for emergency response. *IEEE Transactions on Engineering Management, 45*(2), 132–140. doi:10.1109/17.669758

Beaumont, C. (2008, November 27). Mumbai attacks: Twitter and Flickr used to break news. *The Telegraph.* Retrieved on December 2, 2010 from http://www.telegraph.co.uk/news/worldnews/asia/india/3530640/Mumbai-attacks-Twitter-and-Flickr-used-to-break-news-Bombay-India.html

Belblidia, M. S. (2010). Building community resilience through social networking sites: Using online social networks for emergency management. *International Journal of Information Systems for Crisis Response and Management, 2*(1), 24–36. doi:10.4018/jiscrm.2010120403

Bellardo, S., Karwan, K. R., & Wallace, W. A. (1984). Managing the response to disasters using micro-computers. *Interfaces, 14*(2), 29–39. doi:10.1287/inte.14.2.29

Boodhoo, N. (2010, January 18). Earthquake confirms value of social media. *Miami Herald.* Retrieved November 28, 2010 from http://www.miamiherald.com/2010/01/18/1432022/earthquake-confirms-value-of-social.html

Cross, R., & Baird, L. (2000). Technology is not enough: Improving performance by building organizational memory. *Sloan Management Review, 41*(3), 41–54.

Davenport, T. H., DeLong, D. W., & Beers, M. C. (1998). Successful knowledge management projects. *Sloan Management Review, 39*(2), 43–57.

Fischer, H. W. (1998). The role of the new Information Technologies in emergency mitigation, planning, response, and recovery. *Disaster Prevention and Management, 7*(1), 28–37. doi:10.1108/09653569810206262

Ginsberg, M., & Kambil, A. (1999). *Annotate: A Web-based knowledge management support system for document collections.* 32nd Hawaii International Conference on System Sciences, IEEE Computer Society Press.

Holsapple, C. W., & Joshi, K. D. (2000). An investigation of factors that influence the management of knowledge in organizations. *The Journal of Strategic Information Systems, 9*, 235–261. doi:10.1016/S0963-8687(00)00046-9

Jennex, M. E. (2004). Emergency response systems: The utility Y2K experience. *Journal of Information Technology Theory and Application, 6*(3), 85–102.

Jennex, M. E. (2004a). Knowledge management strategy: Critical issues. *Global Journal of E-Business and Knowledge Management, 1*(1), 35–44.

Jennex, M. E. (2008). A model for emergency response systems . In Janczewski, L., & Colarik, A. (Eds.), *Cyber warfare and cyber terrorism* (pp. 383–391). Hershey, PA: Information Science Reference.

Jennex, M. E. (2010). Preface: Why knowledge management? In Jennex, M. E. (Ed.), *Ubiquitous developments in knowledge management: Integrations and trends* (pp. xviii–xxix). Hershey, PA: Information Science Reference.

Jennex, M. E., & Olfman, L. (2000). *Development recommendations for knowledge management/ organizational memory systems*. Information Systems Development Conference 2000.

Jennex, M. E., & Olfman, L. (2006). A model of knowledge management success. *International Journal of Knowledge Management*, *2*(3), 51–68. doi:10.4018/jkm.2006070104

Jennex, M. E., Olfman, L., & Addo, T. B. A. (2003). *The need for an organizational knowledge management strategy*. 36th Hawaii International Conference on System Sciences, HICSS36, IEEE Computer Society.

Jennex, M. E., & Raman, M. (2009). Knowledge management is support of crisis response. *International Journal of Information Systems for Crisis Response and Management*, *1*(3), 69–82. doi:10.4018/ jiscrm.2009070104

Jennex, M. E., Smolnik, S., & Croasdell, D. T. (2009). Towards a consensus knowledge management success definition. *VINE: The Journal of Information and Knowledge Management Systems*, *39*(2), 174–188.

Jennex, M. E., & Zyngier, S. (2007). Security as a contributor to knowledge management success. *Information Systems Frontiers: A Journal of Research and Innovation, 9*(5), 493-504.

Koskinen, K. U. (2001). *Tacit knowledge as a promoter of success in technology firms*. 34th Hawaii International Conference on System Sciences, IEEE Computer Society.

Lang, G., & Benbunan-Fich, R. (2010). The use of social media in disaster situation: Framework and cases. *International Journal of Information Systems for Crisis Response and Management*, *2*(1), 11–23. doi:10.4018/jiscrm.2010120402

Lee, J., & Bui, T. (2000). A template-based methodology for disaster management Information Systems. *Proceedings of the 33rd Hawaii International Conference on System Sciences*.

Murphy, T., & Jennex, M. E. (2006). Knowledge management, emergency response, and Hurricane Katrina. *International Journal of Intelligent Control and Systems*, *11*(4), 199–208.

NSTISSC. (1994). *National training standard for information systems security (INFOSEC) professionals*. (NSTISSI No. 4011). National Security Telecommunications and Information Systems Security Committee. Retrieved on March 1, 2006, from http://niatec.info/pdf/4011.pdf

Patton, D., & Flin, R. (1999). Disaster stress: An emergency management perspective. *Disaster Prevention and Management*, *8*(4), 261–267. doi:10.1108/09653569910283897

Plotnick, C., & White, L. (2010). A social media tsunami: The approaching wave. *International Journal of Information Systems for Crisis Response and Management*, *2*(1), i–iv.

Raman, M., Ryan, T., Jennex, M. E., & Olfman, L. (2010). Wiki technology and emergency response: An action research study. *International Journal of Information Systems for Crisis Response and Management*, *2*(1), 49–69. doi:10.4018/jiscrm.2010120405

Renaud, R., & Phillips, S. (2003). Developing an integrated emergency response programme for facilities: The experience of Public Works and Government Services Canada. *Journal of Facilities Management*, *1*(4), 347–364. doi:10.1108/14725960310808051

Sage, A. P., & Rouse, W. B. (1999). Information Systems frontiers in knowledge management. *Information Systems Frontiers, 1*(3), 205–219. doi:10.1023/A:1010046210832

Toomey, T., Frost, E., & Jennex, M. E. (2009). Strategies to prepare emergency management personnel to integrate geospatial tools into emergency management. *International Journal of Information Systems for Crisis Response and Management, 1*(4), 33–49. doi:10.4018/jiscrm.2009071003

Turoff, M. (2002). Past and future emergency response Information Systems. *Communications of the ACM, 45*(4), 29–32. doi:10.1145/505248.505265

Westfall, A., Jennex, M. E., Dickinson, S., & Frost, E. (2009). Event report: Golden Phoenix 2008. *International Journal of Information Systems for Crisis Response and Management, 1*(2), 72–79. doi:10.4018/jiscrm.2009040106

Wikipedia. (2010). *2009–2010 Iranian election protests*. Retrieved on November 25, 2010, from http://en.wikipedia.org/wiki/2009%E2%80%932010_Iranian_election_protests

Wikipedia. (2010). *Cloud computing*. Retrieved on November 25, 2010, from http://en.wikipedia.org/wiki/Cloud_computing

Wikipedia. (2010). *Iranian presidential election*, 2009. Retrieved on November 25, 2010, from http://en.wikipedia.org/wiki/Iranian_presidential_election,_2009#cite_note-gulfnews_facebookblock-87

Yu, S.-H., Kim, Y.-G., & Kim, M.-Y. (2004). *Linking organizational knowledge management drivers to knowledge management performance: An exploratory study*. 37th Hawaii International Conference on System Sciences, HICSS36, IEEE Computer Society.

Chapter 1
Achieving Agility in Disaster Management

John R. Harrald
Virginia Polytechnic Institute and State University, USA

ABSTRACT

A significant body of social science research has concluded that improvisation in distributed, collaborative, open systems is the key to success in responding to and recovering from extreme events. The evolution of emergency management in the United States since the 9-11 attacks has emphasized the development of doctrine, process, and structure. In earlier work I concluded that both the agility desired by the social sciences and the discipline created by the professional practitioners are essential. This article explores how agility can be developed within a disciplined system and concludes that the keys are the development of outcome based goals, adaptive leadership, and technology that supports collaborative sense-making and decision making in open, organizational systems.

WITHOUT AGILITY: BUREAUCRACY AND FAILURE

It was my honor to be a keynote speaker at IS-CRAM 2005, where I discussed "Supporting Agility and Discipline When Preparing for and Responding to Extreme Events". This talk grew out of my concern that, since the attacks of 9-11, the U.S. government has focused on strengthening the doctrine and structure of the nation's emergency management system, while neglecting or even negating the factors that have historically fostered creative and adaptive problem solving actions by emergency managers when faced with unexpected situations. Taking terms from software and systems engineering (Boehm and Turner, 2004), I identified the implementation of doctrine and structure as "discipline" and the ability to foster creative, adaptive, improvisation skills as "agility". Leading social scientists (Drabek and McEntire, 2002, Tierney et al. 2006) have criticized the increased emphasis on command and control by the US Department of Homeland Security, and have urged a return to a more collaborative and coordinat-

DOI: 10.4018/978-1-60960-609-1.ch001

ing approach based on decades of social science research (Dynes and Quarantelli, 1968, 1976, Dynes, 1994). Practitioners, however, continue to develop structural and doctrinal solutions to response management problems. The major point of my ISCRAM presentation was that agility and discipline are both needed for successful disaster management, and that thinking of them as alternatives approaches presents a false choice. I concluded with the prediction that, by increasing doctrine and structure without also enhancing agility, the US response system was becoming more bureaucratic and procedural and would not function well when faced with the unexpected complexities of an extreme event.

Four months after ISCRAM 2005, Hurricane Katrina struck the U.S. Gulf Coast and flooded the city of New Orleans. Faced with extreme needs that overwhelmed local and state resources, the response of the U.S. government was slow, bureaucratic and inadequate. The Director of the Federal Emergency Management Agency (FEMA) was fired and much of the pre-designated structure was abandoned or modified. I have discussed my observations on the failure of the Federal system in other documents (Harrald, 2007). My intent in this article is to discuss in greater detail how a response system can be created that preserves needed structure and doctrine while also enabling the system to adjust more nimbly to the unexpected

Since Hurricane Katrina, the U.S. Government has made additional changes to the National Response System. The Post Katrina Reform act directed a reconfiguration and strengthening of the Federal Emergency Management Agency. Much of the emphasis continues to be on doctrine: the National Response Plan was revised and reissued as a National Response Framework with a greatly expanded focus on preparation and planning for potential catastrophic events. FEMA has attempted to define the nation's response needs by issuing a Target Capabilities List and a Universal Task List (available from www.fema.gov). Some of these actions taken will also contribute to enhancing

agility. Regional response and leadership capabilities have been strengthened, deployable national Incident Management Assist Teams with skills and resources have been created, and investments have been made in information systems to support situational awareness and decision making.

In the remainder of this article, I will discuss three elements that I believe are essential for the creation of an agile, but disciplined, response system. These elements are:

1. Managing for success. Defining outcome based goals and management strategies for achieving these goals, thereby freeing managers from managing to procedure based rules and empowering them to be creative in reaching goals.
2. Developing adaptive leaders capable of establishing and communicating a vision of success and empowering those they lead to make that vision a reality.
3. Enhancing distributed decision making in open organizational systems, recognizing that the pre-designated nodes will not be the only or even the optimal location for strategic and operational decision making.

MANAGING FOR SUCCESS, THE IMPORTANCE OF VISION AND METRICS

Reviews of the response to Hurricane Katrina concluded that FEMA and the Department of Homeland Security (DHS) failed (White House 2006, Senate Homeland Security and Government Affairs Committee 2006, Department of Homeland Security Inspector General 2006). What set of outcomes would have led the same reviewers to conclude that the response was a success? What set of measurable outcomes should FEMA and DHS leaders have established as their vision as they mobilized resources in anticipation of the hurricane strike? Interestingly enough, there is no

Figure 1. Existing disaster metrics

Event	Physical Impact	Socio-Economic Impact
Hurricane	Building damage	Deaths
-Wind Speed	Critical Facility damage	Displaced people
-Category	Infrastructure damage	Injuries
-Storm Surge		Insured losses
		Estimated losses
Earthquake		
-Magnitude		
-Intensity		
-Ground Acceleration		
-Ground Velocity		
Tornado		
-Saffer-Simpson		
-Wind Speed		
Flood		
-Flood Stage		
-Water Height		

> **Metrics describing event are more precise than metrics describing physical impact.**
>
> **Socio-Economic impacts drive response and recovery—metrics are incomplete and inadequate and have not been linked to physical impacts**

a priori standard for success in disaster management. Success or failure is typically determined by the reaction of the media and the public after the fact, leading to political attempts to influence or "spin" the inevitable evaluation. The reason assessing success is difficult is that we do not have a good methodology for measuring the social and economic impacts of an extreme event, and therefore have no way of determining if our actions are minimizing these impacts.

As shown in Figure 1, we can apply relatively precise metrics to define the physical phenomena of an extreme event and given time can assess the physical damage caused by the event. The social and economic impact, however, is a function of both the physical impact and the pre-disaster social and economic vulnerability of the affected area. Our surrogate measures of impact—deaths, injuries, people displaced, insured losses, are incomplete and inadequate metrics for disaster management.

As a result, the response to a disaster is often guided by managing inputs and activities which can be directly evaluated and counted. During a response, measuring outputs and outcomes requires the collection and analysis of time critical situational data from the field as shown in Figure

2. One objective of current planning for catastrophic events is to establish output, or capacity goals, through using sophisticated impact and loss estimation models (Hester et al., 2008). The existence of output and capacity goals and a assessment of current capabilities and capacities enable planners to conduct a gap analysis and to influence subsequent investment strategies.

Without a shared vision of desired outcomes, the establishment of the analysis capability required to provide outcome measures to decision makers is not a priority. This issue has not been widely addressed by either practitioners or researchers. James Miskel, a former FEMA and DHS official has attempted to develop a minimal set of outcomes for a response to a catastrophic disaster in his recent book, *Disaster Response and Homeland Security* (2008). Miskel's proposed critical outcome measures are:

- Claims for Federal disaster assistance payments are processed rapidly and applicants are not forced to wait extended periods of time to apply for assistance
- Few if any disaster victims remain stranded in life-threatening situations or without

Figure 2. Disaster management metrics

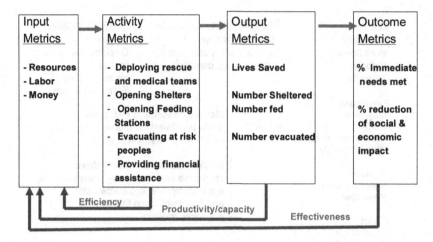

urgent medical attention for more than a few hours

- Few if any disaster victims are left without adequate shelter, food, or water for more than twenty four hours
- Individuals seeking to evacuate are able to do so
- Electricity, water, and communications utilities are restored to the vast majority of people in the affected area within twenty-four to thirty six hours.

I made an attempt at defining success as the basis for planning in two environments—oil spills of national significance (a post Exxon Valdez project funded by the Coast Guard, see Harrald and Mazzuchi, 1993) and international complex emergencies (a post Rawanda project funded by the IFRC, see Harrald and Stoddard, 1998). I used Rockhart's critical success factor approach (Rockhart 1979, 1981, Rockhart and Bullen, 1982) and scenario based exercises in workshops to assist senior operational managers to define successful operational outcomes prior to defining planning goals. I found it interesting that the managers were able to consistently and coherently articulate the criteria for success, yet these criteria were absent from their own doctrine

and plans. While success factors may be out of the leader's control—they must be communicated. If the definition of success is not communicated to media and public, the media cannot be expected to agree that success has been achieved or even to use same definition of success.

Equally important to visualizing final outcomes is the recognition that a disaster response goes through distinct phases, as shown in figure 3. Each phase has distinct critical success factors that must be achieved, critical decisions that must be made, and information that must be obtained. As discussed in detail in Harrald, 2006, success (or failure) cascades from one phase to the next. Operational leaders must be focused on achieving the short term success factors in order to reach the envisioned outcomes.

Achieving agility is, therefore, impossible without a clear vision of desired outcomes. Improvisation is not an objective, it is a means to achieving defined goals in the face of unexpected circumstances. Constraining creativity within the context of achieving a goal is operationally essential. Improvisation without a clear sense of direction and purpose can lead to increased chaos and confusion. The definition of outcome measures and expression of goals in terms of observable and measurable quantities, as discussed

Figure 3. Phases of a disaster response

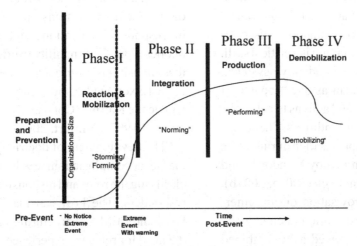

Definition of success, decisions and actions change over time.
Success or failure cascades.
Leadership is most critical during transitions.

above, provides the guiding constraints to improvisation and creativity. Managing the unexpected under extreme conditions requires leaders with the wisdom and skill to be both agile within a disciplined context and the development and use of tools that support their sense-making and decision needs.

LEADERSHIP, THE NEGLECTED DIMENSION

An important product of the development of structure and doctrine is the identification of positions where leadership must be exercised. One of the failures of the Hurricane Katrina response is that people in critical positions (DHS, FEMA, State, and local organizations) did not have the basic skills, knowledge, or experience required to perform adequately under the conditions that they faced. (Baughman 2006, Harrald 2006). The Post Katrina Reform Act of 2006 addressed this issue at the Federal level by requiring the FEMA Director to have prior emergency management experience, and directing FEMA to develop qualifications and

training for Federal Coordinating Officers and Primary Federal Officials. Although role definition, selection, and training are essential, they are not sufficient condition for effective leadership during a disaster. Three critical leadership capabilities must also be present:

- The ability to create and lead an adaptive, creative management team when faced with the unexpected
- The ability to manage organizational change and transition
- The ability to manage in a open, dynamic organizational system

Disaster researchers have noted the importance of adaptive, creative leadership. Karl Weick in his study of the Mann Gulch fire (Weick 1996a, 1996b) and in his books *Managing the Unexpected: Assuring High Performance in an age of Complexity (2001)* and *Sensemaking in organizations* (1995*).* Weick makes the case that a primary task of leadership is the fostering of improvisation and collaboration, but notes that the theoretical and practical focus on management control impedes our ability to understand creativity and innovation (Weick, 1998). Muhren, Van Den Ede and van de Wall (2008) note that in crisis situations, discontinuity is the rule and sensemaking is a critical skill. Comfort focuses on complex adaptive systems, defining an adaptive system as one "capable of reallocating its resources and actions to achieve a stated goal under changing conditions. The cognitive dimensions of the improvisation during crisis situations has been examined by Mendonca and Wallace (2004) and, Mendonca (2007a, 2007b). Mendonca defines improvisation during emergency response as "Improvisation in emergency response has long been viewed as a combined cognitive, behavioral and social activity in which creativity is exercised under time constraint in order to meet response objectives." (Mendonca et al., 2007c). He points out that this improvisation may be focused on coping with unexpected decision/task oriented, new or expanded roles, or new or unexpected personal and organizational relationships. The important dimension of role improvisation has bee described by Webb (2004).

The task and organizational environment evolves during a response as shown if Figure 3 above. The initial response phase (which may begin before the event actually occurs if it is for an event with warning such as a hurricane or riverine flood) requires the simultaneous rapid response with available resources and the mobilization of the extensive resources that will be required. As these resources are deployed, and as local resources and organizations emerge, they must be integrated into an effective response organization. This integration must be completed as soon as possible so that the human needs resulting from the disaster can be met. At some point response forces can be demobilized and the needs of the population are best met by transitioning to a recovery focused organization. I identified critical success factors and critical decisions and actions for each of these phases in an earlier paper (Harrald, 2006). The important thing to note is that there is a significant re-focusing of objectives as a response evolves,

and that a crucial function of leadership is to recognize the need for transition and to ensure that the response organization adapts to the new phase of operations. The inability to effectively manage these transitions contributed to the failed responses to the Exxon Valdez spill, Hurricane Andrew, and Hurricane Katrina (Cohn et al., 1991, Carley and Harrald 1997, Comfort, 2005).

The development of doctrine and structure in the US, accomplished since 9-11, has succeeded in clarifying the roles and responsibilities of Federal responders. The Post Katrina Reform Act and DHS and FEMA restructuring have emphasized the need for relevant experience in key positions. No matter how extensive their experience, leaders will still be faced with the unexpected in the aftermath of an extreme event. There is a critical need to develop leaders with the emotional intelligence, intuition, creativity necessary to improvise under stress. While the military services in the US have a history of trying to incorporate emerging leadership theory in their training and education programs, the emergency management community has not. There would be great value, in my opinion, in creating a viable knowledge transfer between the academic leadership community that is developing new theory applicable to leadership and management in complex environments and the emergency management community. The James MacGregor Burns Academy of Leadership at the University of Maryland, for example is attempting to develop a new framework for leadership that would be very applicable to the environments faced by emergency managers. This framework (available at www.academy.umd.edu/Research_Centers/TLC:researchAgenda.html) is based on principles such as:

- Support of reflective individual and group leadership practice, including self awareness, cognitive complexity, emotional and narrative intelligence, paradigm vigilance and vision driven, rather than problem focused, theories and models of change

- Foster the creative capacities needed to successfully navigate change, to innovate, and to shift the stories we live to ensure a greater quality of life individually and collectively
- Demystify the dynamics of change processes and of complex interdependent systems, groups, organizations, networks and coalitions, and social movements.
- Develop awareness of unconscious processes that determine deeply held values and a sense of calling, but which also, if not made conscious, can lure people into negative shadowy, counterproductive behaviors.
- Assist leaders in working with, not against, natural processes and peoples essential gifts and commitments and in taking a positive, win/win approach in order to more efficiently achieve desired results
- Develop the capacity for life long individual and group learning and of using communication skills to inspire and motivate others.

The Academy's goal is to produce a leadership model that promotes respectful interdependence, genuine dialogue, intuition, and creativity and supports the shift from command and control hierarchies to coalitions and networks. This is a very accurate description of the needs of the emergency management community.

MANAGING IN AN OPEN SYSTEM

A disaster response may start with a pre-defined closed organization structure (e.g. the National Incident Management System defines structure and roles for the national response). However, as the response evolves, unexpected situations stress this organizational discipline and the organizational structure and procedures may be forced to change. The structure defined by the National Contingency Plan lasted 3 days after the Exxon Valdez spill (Cohn et al., 1991), the structure defined by the Federal Response Plan lasted less than a week after Hurricane Andrew (Carley and Harrald, 1997), and the structure defined by the National Response Plan and the National Incident Management System survived but was significantly modified during the response to Hurricane Katrina (Harrald, 2007. The doctrine and structure were designed to operate the response organization as a closed organizational system. The reality of the response, as shown in Figure 4, is an open organizational system consisting of key participants who were not part of the planning and preparedness phase, but have been recruited as a result of the disaster itself.

In a phenomenon observed for decades (Dynes and Quarantelli, 1976), organizations and individuals within the impacted area engage in problem solving behavior resulting in emergent groups. These ad hoc groups may become large operations. They must be integrated into the response effort, or if their behavior is unsafe, ineffective, or inappropriate, convinced to terminate their operations. The emergency manager must have the vision of outcomes that defines success and the leadership skills to create and manage collaborative networks to make this occur.

Managing in an open system, however, challenges the ability to share and analyze information. Information has a cultural context and language. For example, most citizen groups cannot penetrate the sea of acronyms used by professional emergency managers. Information technology developed for emergency managers assumes that the sharing of information will be restricted to a closed organizational system. As a result, in an actual event such as the Katrina response technology can constrain, not enable, essential collaboration.

Muhren et al. describe case studies demonstrating that the phenomena of sensemaking as the key to understanding how decision makers deal with uncertainty and discontinuity. They make the

Figure 4. Is the national response system a closed system?

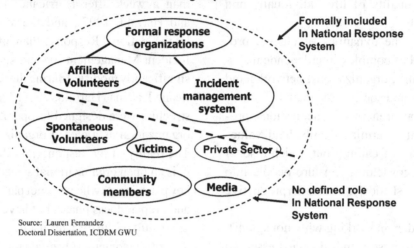

A system is a collection of inter-related components that work together to accomplish a common goal. Where is the system boundary? The national Response System excludes critical groups.

Source: Lauren Fernandez
Doctoral Dissertation, ICDRM GWU

case that information technology design must take sensemaking needs into account: "If IS are not capable of supporting sensemaking, the making of sense runs the risk of being disrupted. And then the situation collapses, unravels or disintegrates; the metaphorical bridge falls down." (p. 321) The need to develop technology that can be used to support sensemaking in collaborative, distributed decision making environment is discussed in more detail in Jefferson and Harrald (2007). Key research funded by US National Science Foundation career awards will play a big part in the development of this technology. Mendonca (2007) is studying the cognitive process of improvisation and developing decision support technologies that will support this process. Paylen and her colleagues (2008a, 2008b, 2008c) are investigating the phenomena of technology enhanced social networking and its emergency as a disaster related phenomena, which they classify as disaster informatics. The work of Mendonca and Paylen demonstrates that the technology will soon be available, if it does not already exist, to support agile, networked collaboration involving new actors faced with unexpected circumstances.

CONCLUSION

The premise of this article is that agility can be achieved without sacrificing discipline, and that both are essential to success. The achievement of this agility will, however, require a significant change in how we prepare for and respond to extreme events. This change will have three dimensions—strategic, individual, and systemic. The strategic dimension will require us to develop a vision for response and recovery based on measurable outcome goals. Our selection, training, and education systems must be able to produce leaders capable of enabling creative improvisation within networked, collaborative environments. Both the vision and the leadership will operate in an open organizational environment with organizations and individuals entering and leaving the system in unanticipated ways. Our technology must support this environment and the cognitive processes required to enable the system to collaboratively and effectively engage in sensemaking and decision making.

REFERENCES

Baughman, Bruce. 2006. Testimony to US Senate Homeland Security and Government Affairs Committee Hearing: Hurricane Katrina—Recommendations for Reform. March 8 2006

Boehm, B., & Turner, R. (2004). *Balancing Agility and Discipline: A Giode fpr the Perplexed.* Boston, MA: Addison-Wesley, Pearson Education.

Carley, K. M., & Harrald, J. R. (1997). Organizational Learning under Fire: Theory and Practice. *The American Behavioral Scientist, 40*(3), 310–332. doi:10.1177/0002764297040003007

Cohn, R. E. W. A. Wallace, and J. R. Harrald. 1991. "Organizing for Response: The Unresolved Problem. *Proceedings, 1991 International Oil Spill Conference.* American Petroleum Institute. Washington, DC. Pp 29-33.

Comfort, L. K. (1999). *Shared Risk: Complex Systems in Seismic Response.* Pittsburgh, PA: Pergamon Press.

Comfort, L. K. 2005. "Fragility in Disaster Response: Hurricane Katrina, 29 August 2005" *The Forum,* Vol 3, Issue 3, Article 1.

Drabek, T. E., & McEntire, D. A. (2002). Emergent Phenomena and Multiorganizational Coordination in Disasters: Lessons from the Research Literature. *International Journal of Mass Emergencies and Disasters, 20,* 197–224.

Dynes, R. R. (1994). Community Emergency Planning: False Assumptions and Inappropriate Analogies. *International Journal of Mass Emergencies and Disasters, 12,* 141–158.

Dynes, R. R., & Quarantelli, E. L. (1968). "Group Behavior under Stress" A Required Convergence of Organizational and Collective Behavior Perspectives. *Sociology and Social Research, 52,* 416–429.

Dynes, R. R., & Quarantelli, E. L. (1976). *Organizational Communications and Decision Making During Crises. Preliminary Paper #17.* Disaster Research Center. University of Delaware.

Harrald, John.R. and T. Mazzuchi "Planning for Success: A Scenario Based Approach to Contingency Planning Using Expert Judgment" 1993. *Journal of Contingencies and Crisis Management* 1:4. pp. 189-198

Harrald, J. R. and Linda Stoddart. 1998. "Scenario Based Identification and Structuring of Information Needs for the Response to Complex International Crises *Proceedings, Fifth Annual Conference of The Emergency Management Society.* Washington, D.C. pp. 295-306.

Harrald, J. R. (2006). Agility and Discipline: Critical Success Factors for Disaster Response. *The Annals of the American Academy of Political and Social Science, 604,* 256–272. doi:10.1177/0002716205285404

Harrald, J. R. 2007. "Emergency Management Restructured: Intended and Unintended Consequences of Actions Taken Since 9/11/01", Chapter 6. *Emergency Management: The American Experience 1900-2005.* Claire B. Rubin, Editor. Public Entity Risk Institute, Fairfax, VA.

Hester, N. C. J. Wilkinson, S.P.Horton, T. I Jefferson. 2008 "Integration of Information Systems for Port Earthquake Research Response. *Proceedings of the 5ᵗʰ International ISCRAM Conference,* F. Fiedrich and B. Van de Walle eds. pp. 362-367.

Jefferson, Theresa. and J. Harrald. (2007). Collaborative Technology: providing agility in response to extreme events. *International Journal of Electronic Governance, 1*(1), 79–93. doi:10.1504/IJEG.2007.014344

Kendra, J., & Wachtendorf, T. (2002). *Preliminary Paper #324. Disaster Research Center, University of Delaware.* Creativity in Emergency Response After the World Trade Center Attack.

Mendonca, D. (2005in press). *Decision Support for Improvisation in Response to Extreme Events: Learning from the Response to the 2001 World Trade Center Attack.* Decision Support Systems.

Mendonça, David., J. Harrald and T. Jefferson. (2007). Emergent Interoperability: Collaborative Adhocracies and Mix and Match Technologies in Emergency Management. *Communications of the ACM, 50*(3), 45–49. doi:10.1145/1226736.1226764

Mendonça, D. (2007). Decision Support for Improvisation in Response to Extreme Events. *Decision Support Systems, 43*(3), 952–967. doi:10.1016/j.dss.2005.05.025

Mendonca, D., & Wallace, W. A. (2004). Studying Organizationally-situated Improvisation in Response to Extreme Events. *International Journal of Mass Emergencies and Disasters, 22*(2), 5–29.

Mendonça, David and W. A. Wallace, 2007. "A Cognitive Model of Improvisation in Emergency Management," *IEEE Transactions on Systems, Man, and Cybernetics: Part A,* Vol #7 (4). Pp 547-561.

Miskel, J. (2008). *Disaster Response and Homeland Security: What Works, What Doesn't.* Stanford University Press.

Muhren, W. G. Van Den Eede, B. Van de Walle. 2008. "Sensemaking as a Methodology for IS-CRAM Research: Information Processing in an Ongoing Crisis. *Proceedings of the 5ᵗʰ International ISCRAM Conference,* F. Fiedrich and B. Van de Walle eds. pp. 315-323.

Palen, L., Vieweg, S., Sutton, J., Liu, S., & Hughes, A. 2007a. "Crisis Informatics: Studying Crisis in a Networked World". Proceedings of the Third International Conference on E-Social Science, Ann Arbor, MI, Oct 7-9,

Palen, Leysia and Sophia B. Liu, 2007b. "Citizen Communications in Crisis: Anticipating a Future of ICT-Supported Participation", Proceedings of the ACM Conference on Human Factors in Computing Systems CHI 2007, 727-736.

Rockhart, J. R. (1979). Chief Executives Define Their Own Data Needs. *Harvard Business Review, 57*(2), 81–93.

Rockhart, J. R. (1981). The Changing Role of the Information System Executive: A Critical Success Factor Perspective. *Sloan Management Review,* 15–25.

Rockhart, J. R. C. V. Bullen, 1982. *A Primer on Critical Success Factors, MIT Center for Information Systems Research,* Cambridge, MA.

Sutton, J., Palen, L., & Shklovski, I. 2008. "Backchannels on the Front Lines: Emergent Use of Social Media in the 2007 Southern California Fires". *Proceedings of the 5ᵗʰ International IS-CRAM Conference,* F. Fiedrich and B. Van de Walle eds. pp. 624-631.

The White House/ 2006. *The Federal Response to Hurricane Katrina: Lessons Learned.* Washington, D.C. -06-32 March 2006

Tierney, Kathleen. and C. Bevc. 2007. "Disaster as War: Militarism and the Social Construction of Disaster in New Orleans." In D. Brunsma and S. Picou (eds.) *The Sociology of Katrina: Perspectives on a Modern Catastrophe.* Lanham, MD: Rowman and Littlefield.

Tierney, Kathleen J., C. Bevc, and E. Kuligowski. (2006). Metaphors Matter: Disaster Myths, Media Frames, and Their Consequences in Hurricane Katrina. *The Annals of the American Academy of Political and Social Science, 604*(March), 57–81. doi:10.1177/0002716205285589

U.S. Department of Homeland Security Inspector General. (2006). *A Performance Review of FEMA's Disaster Management in Response to Hurricane Katrina*. Washington, D.C.

U.S. Senate Homeland Security and Government Affairs Committee. 2006. *Hurricane Katrina: A Nation still Unprepared.* Washington, DC

Webb, G. R. (2004). Role Improvising during Crisis Situations. *International Journal of Emergency Management, 2*, 47–61. doi:10.1504/IJEM.2004.005230

Weick, K. (1995). *Sensemaking in Organizations*. CA: Sage Publications.

Weick, K. (1996). Prepare your organization to fight fires. *Harvard Business Review*, (May): 1.

Weick, K. E. (1996). Drop Your Tools: An Allegory for Organizational Studies. *Administrative Science Quarterly, 41*, 301–313. doi:10.2307/2393722

Weick, K. E. (1998). Improvisation as a Mindset for Organizational Analysis. *Organization Science, 9*(5), 543–555. doi:10.1287/orsc.9.5.543

Weick, K. E., & Sutcliffe, K. M. (2001). *Managing the Unexpected: Assuring High Performance in an Age of Complexity*. San Francisco: Jossey-Bass.

This work was previously published in International Journal of Information Systems for Crisis Response and Management, Volume 1, Issue 1, edited by Murray E. Jennex, pp. 1-11, copyright 2009 by IGI Publishing (an imprint of IGI Global).

Chapter 2
The Past as the Future of Emergency Preparedness and Management

Murray Turoff
New Jersey Institute of Technology, USA

Linda Plotnick
New Jersey Institute of Technology, USA

Starr Roxanne Hiltz
New Jersey Institute of Technology, USA

Art Hendela
New Jersey Institute of Technology, USA

Connie White
New Jersey Institute of Technology, USA

Xiang Yao
New Jersey Institute of Technology, USA

ABSTRACT

Emergency preparedness, planning, and response suffer from shortcomings that impede the potential for effectiveness. In this article, we provide an overview of Emergency Preparedness and Management that is based upon our research, including insights into the shortcomings of current practices, a discussion of relevant theories (e.g., High Reliability Organizations, muddling through) and recommendations to promote more effective planning, management, and response. Our recommendations include system support for the principles of High Reliability Organizations and muddling through, rethinking risk analysis to have a longer-term view and reflect more than just monetary loss, creating ways to better inform and involve the public, and encouraging collaboration and collective intelligence through such means as a dynamic Delphi voting system.

INTRODUCTION

It is our intent in this article to provide an overview of Emergency Preparedness and Management that is based upon our prior work in this area. To start with, we first summarize the findings of a major

U.S. government study on Disaster Preparedness because they are very relevant to the motivation of our work (Turoff et al. 2004a, 2004b) and the observations and recommendations that follow. The purpose of this report was to identify the key areas needing improvement throughout the U.S. for improving Emergency Preparedness and Management. We will first itemize these concerns

DOI: 10.4018/978-1-60960-609-1.ch002

in terms of words taken directly form the initial summary of findings study (pages 3 to 6):

Planning is essential for any region or community likely to be affected by a disaster, in order to determine what preventive and protective measures can and should be taken before and at the time of a disaster. Planning requires cooperation from all levels of government... To be confident that disaster planning is preparing government officials, volunteers, and the public to cope better with disasters, such plans must be exercised and evaluated.

Vulnerability analysis is a prerequisite to effective disaster preparedness. The variety in types and frequency of natural disasters and the differences in effect and damage make it clear that an assessment of vulnerability must be made for each community as a first step in formulating regulations, plans, and programs to reduce hazards and prepare for disasters.

The reduction of hazards and preparedness for disasters are government responsibilities as well as the concerns of every citizen. For this purpose there must be... appropriate *disaster legislation* for all levels of government.

Public awareness of the threats posed by the various natural disasters is essential to preparing for them and reducing their destructive effects.

The value of past investment in *prediction and warning capabilities* is clearly demonstrable. Despite the increasing property losses, there has been a notable decline in lives lost when such capabilities have been established and used.

The objective of *mitigation* is to find ways to reduce the vulnerability of people and property to damaging effects.... there is a need for a national program involving Federal, State, and local jurisdictions in avoiding the mistakes of the past and in gaining fuller consideration of natural hazards in regulating land use and construction.

The main focus of *emergency response* to major disasters should be: (1) to expand routine emergency services, such as police, firefighting and sanitation; (2) to provide those things which the individual citizen takes care of by himself in normal times but which have been interrupted by the disaster, such as food, housing, and personal welfare; and (3) to make special provisions for medical care.... There is a favorable benefit-cost ratio in taking early measures when a disaster is imminent.

Research on the causes and characteristics of natural disasters and for the protection of people and property holds great promise and is a national imperative. The most immediate need is to apply the scientific and technological knowledge already existing. The sheer number and variety of disaster related research activities in the government and private sectors now make it difficult to coordinate and integrate these activities.

This report to the US Congress, titled Disaster Preparedness, was published by the Office of Emergency Preparedness (OEP) in the Executive Office of the President in January 1972. This extensive report was inspired by General George A. Lincoln who was director of OEP, an executive office agency which was scheduled for elimination in 1973 along with the Office of Science and Technology. The final quote included is a few words from the director's letter to the U.S. Congress.

The main thrust of this report points to the need for improvement in disaster preparedness at all levels.... Disaster preparedness is a task never completed. It represents an unbroken chain stretching from the prevention though ultimate recovery and requires continuous effort at all levels of government.

The words of this report, with the inclusion of man-made disasters as well as natural ones, appear to be just as true today as they were in 1972. Within the context of the above requirements the authors are going to review some of the recent work that addresses these concerns, roughly following the topics in the report as summarized above. We will review the continuous planning cycle for emergency response, including the applicability of "muddling through" as a management philosophy for this field. Then we will discuss a scaling method that we have devised that can be helpful for assessing vulnerability. After briefly reviewing disaster legislation in the U.S., which provides the context for the current disjointed situation, we discuss the need for public awareness and community involvement in mitigation and other phases of the planning process. Our emphasis in moving to information systems for emergency response is on providing collaboration tools for communities of practice.

PLANNING

This is the foundation on which everything rests and it involves integration of the plans across all the ongoing objectives of planning or what is loosely termed the phases of emergency management. What is not clear to all is that these objectives of planning are part of a continuous process:

Planning (for all the objectives below)

- Mitigation (long term reduction of risk or vulnerabilities)
- Training (for all actions)
- Detection and Warning (for all disaster types)
- Preparedness (pre disaster event readiness)
- Responders, volunteers, community, organizations, press, etc.
- Response (to a disaster event usually short term, but not always)
- Recovery (restoring what was normal)
- Evaluation and Process improvement
- What went wrong and how to correct it for the future?

Good planning requires good communications and good information. Both today are a problem. Disasters or emergencies cross political, geographical, or organizational boundaries. The fragmentation of participation by existing human-determined boundaries and the presumption that these divisions are appropriate for planning and dealing with an emergency have been principal reasons why we have not seen major improvements in many of these areas since 1972.

- Lack of commonality with respect to interface design, visualization, and decision support, making it difficult for practitioners to master a range of very different systems necessary to their concerns (Carver and Turoff, 2007).
- The separation of threats by source (terrorism, natural disasters, and man made disasters) with very different priorities for different phases and dissimilar activities.
- Lack of major integration requirements across organizations.

The above properties result from a web of deeper problems that tend to prevent the actions and developments that are needed. For example the common perception is that the response phase of an emergency will only last a week or two. However, this was not the case with the Anthrax emergency in the US and clearly the response phase of hurricane Katrina was far in excess of what usually occurs in urban areas. If we ever encounter a true pandemic, the response phase will last years. Fundamental issues of this sort greatly impact the design of information systems to deal with all the phases that can occur in any of these events.

In this article we raise a number of such issues that need to be more explicitly exposed, investigated, and treated to make sure information systems can deal with likely future occurrences as well as past ones. We also suggest associated future R&D objectives. The characteristics that have changed considerably since 1972 are those associated with the evolution of the Web and the opportunities, applications, and problems that it now makes possible. (See Chapter 16 in Van de

Walle, Turoff and Hiltz, 2009, for more details). These issues include:

- Lack of an integrated structure and ethical policy for dealing consistently with all types of disasters, at least in the U.S.
- The problem of information overload for emergency management professionals
- The critical processes of Cooperation, Coordination, and Collaboration on a wide area and national basis
- Recognition of the planning, policy analysis, and decision process of "muddling through"
- Social Computing, Community Involvement, and Citizen Participation as the future road to successful emergency preparedness and management.

Muddling Through

Trying to plan also presumes one is aware of how decisions are made in any of the disaster phases. Recent writings have argued that High Reliability Theory (HRT) and Sensemaking are the foundations of what should underlie good decision making practices (Weick and Sutcliffe, 2001). HRT has evolved from organizations dealing with physical systems such as nuclear power plants and does make a lot of sense; however, it turns out there is an earlier theory that does not require the existence of any physical systems. This is commonly known as mudding through and also as a form of incrementalism. This was originally proposed as the way in which important government policy decisions should be made. In 1959 Lindblom wrote a classic paper about the concept of making decisions by "the science of muddling through" rather than by a "scientific" process of setting goals and deducing logical resulting actions. The following summarizes and contrasts the two views of decision making discussed:

1. Scientific deductive decision making with complete knowledge of all relevant variables and values from which an optimization can be made by use of resulting obvious criteria for the decisions.
2. The subjective comparison of a limited number of alternatives relying heavily on experts and their past experience and expertise, where they are focusing on a judgment based upon a few of the most important values.

This might be an over-simplification of a superb paper proposing a different form of decision making for governmental decisions at all levels. However, it strikes us that in the context of the unexpected such as occurs in disasters and emergencies, "The Science of Muddling Through" should be required reading for practitioners, designers, and researchers concerned with Emergency Preparedness and Management. Furthermore it is a foundation for the approach to collaborative decision processes that we have taken in most of our writings in this area, producing a 'collective intelligence' where the group will produce a better outcome than any individual member of the group would have.

Ill structured, wicked events call for flexibility in decision-making as well as improvisation with the available assets to best accommodate a situation to lessen the chances for the worst outcome and increase chances of the best. Traditional management styles of one or two people in charge of making all the decisions must be replaced by the expertise of the group and defer to that expertise during the response efforts. As the magnitude of an event grows, so too does the group of people to manage. It has been suggested that implementing an incident command system as a hierarchical network is the best solution for managing a large and unknown situation, allowing for flexibility for those in charge (Moynihan 2007). We differ very much with this view and offer the challenge of how to turn a large scale team of professionals into an instant HRO (High Reliability Organization, Weick and Sutcliffe, 2001), networking even when they have never worked together before.

In 1979 Lindblom published a follow-up paper restating the concepts of muddling through in a comparative analysis of different types of "incrementalism." In that paper he listed the stratagems for muddling through that could also be termed as "disjointed incrementalism." What is startling for our purposes is how much they seem like the concepts underlying High Reliability Organizations and concepts of "sense making" which are increasingly popular in Emergency Management operations (Van de Walle and Turoff, 2008). Quoting Lindblom from his 1979 paper:

1. A greater analytical preoccupation with ills to be remedied than positive goals to be sought;
2. A sequence of trials, errors, and revised trials;
3. Analysis that explores only some, not all, of the important possible consequences of a considered alternative;
4. Fragmentation of analytical work to many (partisan) participants in policy making (e.g. stakeholder analysis and community participation).

Determining what went wrong and getting that corrected for the future by changes to the process was top priority for "muddling through" and later for HRT (High Reliability Theory). This incremental series of changes based upon understanding the past is a critical human process in making improvements to any situation. In terms of policies, plans and practices, Lindblom, (1979) also observed:

A fast-moving sequence of small changes can more speedily accomplish a drastic alternation of the status quo than can an only infrequent major policy change. (page 520)

The above seems to be the way practitioners have to actually plan and execute responses and recovery in this field. It also seems that emergencies or disasters are the time when changes can be more easily made in local, state, or federal government agencies; the term emergency in Korean also means "opportunity." It should also be a time to uncover mistakes and take action to eliminate them from any of the phases in the future. Today we have too many fears and inhibitions about allowing these errors to be exposed and corrected. In addition, there are the following weaknesses in the current process, in the U.S.:

*   We don't create the working team until the emergency occurs.
*   We don't really integrate volunteer organizations or community groups into the command and control structure.
*   The command structure does not allow integration across levels of government, organizations, and various man made boundaries (Chen et al, 2009).
*   We isolate the public and the press and really do not always offer an accurate picture of what is taking place.
*   The people who do the planning are not the people who have to execute the plans, making them difficult to communicate and lacking detail on local conditions (Byrne, 2008).
*   Unprotected organizations are reluctant to expose errors because of liability and public reaction (Lee et al, 2006).
*   Too many sources are trying to be the official source for materials critical to locals for dealing with emergencies and the result is information overload.

The technology available today offers solutions for many of these problems and will be discussed later in this article when we deal with collaboration and community involvement.

VULNERABILITY AND RISK ANALYSIS

A Risk Analysis done by the method of cost benefit studies has two prime fallacies. A risk study is an examination of relative truths in the sense that it compares various risks and tries to determine their relative importance. Therefore the process follows the Kantian philosophy of science (Mitroff and Turoff, 1975). However, cost benefit studies translate everything to dollars which linearizes the relationships between the causes of risks and the consequences of them. However many risk situations are non linear in their relationships and the comparison of risks really needs to be done based upon the physical parameters/variables in the real world (deaths, buildings destroyed, number of accidents, etc.) underlying their occurrences and consequences.

The second related fallacy is the application of discounting (applying time dependent discount factors to measures of performance or costs) in the cost benefit model. This assumes there is no memory of consequences in the model as to when (in what year in the future) a value or cost would be gained and they are independent in any year (Linstone, 1972). For example, if there is a slow leak in a nuclear reactor which would not accumulate a deadly level in the surrounding area for over 100 years, the typical cost benefit study would show that available money should be spent on other threats more likely to produce deaths next year. Even a 2% discount rate would bring the costs a hundred years from now down to almost nothing. Essentially, discounting destroys any impact of a variable change in one year propagated or compounded into other years.

A recent action by the Environmental Protection Agency (CBS News, Washington, July 10, 2008) reduced the value of a human life by one million dollars. This has the impact of making increased regulations to reduce deaths in the future far more costly to implement than the value of the lives saved. The current wisdom is

the ratio must be greater than one to implement stiffer regulations. When decisions of this sort are reduced to thresholds based upon arbitrary modeling decisions, games can always be played. In emergency management the reality of this is the growing age of our infrastructure as the decrease in maintenance or replacements of bridges, sewers, water systems, etc is seen by politicians as a way to reduce budgets; but eventually, "tomorrow" comes and the bridges fail.

The older term used in 1972 of "Vulnerability Analysis" of specific situations and locations was much more clearly understood as referring to studies of the physical variables that characterize the risk rather than financial abstractions. In Emergency Preparedness it is not the financial damage that is important before the event or immediately after. It is measures like the expected causalities, injuries, and requirements for shelter, food, water, power, transportation, etc.

Students in a recent graduate course in Emergency Management Information Systems were asked to use the Delphi Method (Linstone and Turoff, 1975) to determine the relative importance of different dimensions for measuring the impact of a disaster before and during the event, to aid the Emergency Management function (Plotnick, Gomez, White, and Turoff, 2007). The lowest values for informative purposes were the two that are most often reported (financial loss and recovery costs). What citizens who might be involved in the disaster want to know are the other variables in the Thurstone's scale shown in Table 1 that was derived as a group result from the individual preference rating. Note the top rated dimensions of *Causalities and Fatalities* is 2000 to 1 more important, as rated by the class, than the last which is *Financial Recovery Costs*. Clearly the latter may become more significant after the disaster is over.

Many of these variables are better estimated by local citizens with experience in prior similar disasters or local experts familiar with things like local building codes and practices. Using na-

Table 1. A Thurstone scale for the relative importance of measures of disaster impact (Plotnick et al, 2007)

Scale	Value	Disaster Damage Dimensions	Value	Disaster Damage Dimensions
20	20.00	Casualties and Fatalities		
19				
18	18.00	Utilities Impact		
17				
16	16.60 15.90	Potential to Spread Ability of local response adequacy		
15	15.43 15.40	Loss of Command and Control Infrastructure Damage	15.40 15.38	Resources for Aid or Containment Time needed for response
14	14.82	Duration of Disaster		
13	13.09	Public Reaction		
12	12.96	Geographic Impact		
11				
10	10.07	Time to Return to Normal		
9				
8	8.61	Chance of imminent reoccurrence		
7				
6				
5				
4	4.70	Financial Loss		
3				
2				
1	0.01	Financial Recovery Costs		

tional estimates does not give informative estimates when the threat is on the way nor does it aid the management processes of insuring the availability of current resources. One needs local estimates of each variable on this scale. That local estimate and measurement will change dynamically from the initial detection of the threat, through the occurrence and response, and into the recovery.

Each of the dimensions below can have a local scale of the degree of damage estimated by the local community "experts" on a continuous basis from the earliest detection of the current threat right up to its actual occurrence, and then afterwards as actual damage assessment occurs.

This estimation process also points out the difference in understanding of the situation when one is looking at the status of each of these dimensions or just the total of potential financial loss as one would do in a cost-benefit study.

If we are going to take many types of extreme events seriously we need to do much more about meaningful citizen involvement, as they are the true first responders (Palen, Hiltz, and Liu 2007). The area that has the greatest payoff for handling extreme events is the more complete involvement of the communities and their citizenry in all phases of disaster preparedness and response. This should be our first line of defense.

DISASTER LEGISLATION AT ALL LEVELS OF GOVERNMENT

A real difficulty that planners have today is that there is no commonly understood ethic of what any level of government feels is its explicit responsibility for responding to the needs of communities and citizens. U.S. citizens cannot say what the local, state, or federal government will take responsibility for in the case of a disaster. Once upon a time (until the mid 1970s) there was a federal ethic that expressed the philosophy behind most of the disaster legislation passed by congress:

Insofar as possible citizens and business should be restored to the state they were in prior to the disaster; however, no one should profit from a disaster.

This had its problems since one could not spend federal funds to build a better bridge if the bridge went out in a flood. Rarely did local communities or states add money to build a better bridge. However, the lack of explicit knowledge on just what different government agencies will do in a given situation leaves the planner in emergency management in a rather difficult situation. How do the local planners plan either response or recovery when they don't know what the state and federal governments provide? There needs to be more transparency for the public and associated organizations.

PUBLIC AWARENESS AND COMMUNITY INVOLVEMENT

Even in classical management we have seen the evolution of concepts such as Stakeholder Analysis to overcome the shortcomings of the typical monetary approach to Risk Analysis. A formal approach to Stakeholder Analysis is more useful for integrating the large spectrum of concerned planners, responders, and decision makers. This would mix the key people in different levels of government (federal, state, local) and other national or even international organizations concerned with any of the disaster phases. There are also in various communities severe problems in communications because non governmental groups are not regular members of the command and control system used during disasters. For example in many urban areas there is no active linkage between community organizations providing emergency health services and the general social support system in that community (Turoff and Hiltz, 2008). As a result, someone coming out of a hospital care situation after a disaster is not in any database that would interface to the community organizations that might help them further with such basic problems as shelter, food, and other forms of help.

In any case, what is clear is the following needs for emergency preparedness based risk analysis (Hendela et al, 2006; Turoff et al, 2002, 2004a, 2004b, 2008; White et al, 2007a, 2007b, 2008, Yao and Turoff, 2007):

1. Determining what has worked and what has not worked in past experience.
2. The participation collaboratively of a large multidisciplinary community of practice with members who are familiar with the local area and its vulnerabilities.
3. An information based knowledge structure able to accept, organize, and provide a community and organizational memory for experiences, plans, resources, and other critical items for Emergency Preparedness and Response.
4. The ability for the community citizens and professionals to continually and dynamically contribute their knowledge and wisdom and to be able to evaluate and expose problems and disagreements for discussion and resolution.

This would be in essence a community recommender system for the community decision makers in local government, private companies, non profits, and other community organizations.

Mitigation and Improved Emergency Response

The community as a whole should provide the opportunity for participation in building and maintaining a community disaster plan. Today most plans come down as templates from the federal government and are not highly tailored to the local community. The usual government members are not made up of the professionals who have the background knowledge to be able to assess details such as engineering vulnerabilities in the infrastructure. The CERTs (Civilian Emergency Response Teams) are a positive concept but really limited to civilian training for only the response phase and do not encourage contributors to any of the other critical phases such as planning and mitigation. Also there is no easy way for leadership in the community to be actively involved except for an occasional table top exercise. This might happen once every six to twelve months, never get to a professional level of detail, be conducted face to face only, and rarely have a detailed result except for some top level insights by the leadership, who may not come back to a second exercise.

Local severity and probability risk assessment could well serve as a first motivational tool. This should be generated and compiled on an asynchronous basis much as in an online Dynamic Delphi, allowing continuous input and discussion by members of the community as well as collective ratings of risks. The results of such an approach could well serve as a collaborative process for the community and leadership to determine the important planning details and preparation for having the necessary resources and equipment.

A new variant of Wikipedia (http://www.wikimapia.org) allows people to link information to specific points or areas on a map, which can utilize detailed maps of a given area as the knowledge structure. This means a lot of community information and viewpoints can be linked to the potential location of a risk, problem, resource, etc. The Wikimapia system is available online and is accessible anywhere there is Internet connectivity and a browser.

There have been other recent calls for the use of modern web technology to create a 911 system that would integrate all the community activities in emergency management at the local, regional, state, and federal level. It would cut across all the different physical devices available to community members (Shneiderman and Preece, 2007). The name suggested has been "911.gov" in the United States and it would provide a variety of applications tied to any phase of emergency preparedness and it would provide for open access to all citizens.

Involving the public and other organizations in the planning process as well as the other aspects will lead to many important benefits for all the phases of emergency preparedness and management. Once the public feels it is getting reliable information from all levels of government, efforts to improve mitigation of future disasters or emergencies will be a lot easier to accomplish. Carrying out emergency response will be much easier when virtual representations of response plans and especially evacuation processes can be viewed and understood by any concerned citizen.

Collaboration and Collective Intelligence

When disasters cross political boundaries, emergency response teams are often partially or fully distributed virtual teams. Virtual teams have been an area that has seen a great deal of prior work at NJIT, with teams involved on such tasks as software development and project management (Hiltz, Fjermestad, Ocker, and Turoff, 2006). A partially distributed virtual team is a hybrid team whereby there are some individuals collocated in subgroups, and the subgroups are distributed from one another (Huang and Ocker, 2006). In an emergency, people from each organization that is involved in the response may form such distributed collocated subgroups. The challenge is for the subgroups to form an effective team. A communication/ information system must enable the teams to overcome the inherent difficulties of working in such teams. For example, collocated members may tend to have "collocation blindness" (Bos, Olsen, Nan, Shami, Hoch, and Johnston, 2006) whereby they will resist reaching out to distributed members even when the best expertise lies outside of the collocated group. Deferring to Expertise (HRO theory) is something too often lacking in extreme events.

Lindblom in his book, The Intelligence of Democracy, (1965) put it in very clear terms: "that people can coordinate with each other without anyone's coordinating them (Lindblom, 1965, p. 3)." In disaster planning and response it is full scale collaboration that is needed and we would extend the above quote to encompass coordination, cooperation, and collaboration.

ELEMENTS OF A DYNAMIC RESPONSE INFORMATION SYSTEM

Real-time, effective decisions are required of experts collaborating on management and response. Without effective response, outcomes can be catastrophic, with more dire consequences than expected or experienced previously. Errors in management and decision making can exacerbate the situation and result in greater injury, loss of life, or a disastrous financial toll. Lessons learned from past experiences include the need for a feedback mechanism in a support system so that the processes of an event can be critiqued and further utilized to promote learning from failures. Characteristics or values of success need to be identified and integrated into the information system. Expecting the unexpected and managing disasters effectively calls for a system with dynamic features conducive to support group collaboration on a large scale.

Thurstone's Law of Comparative Judgment helps to reflect best a group's opinion by breaking complex situations down to a manageable set of characteristics (Thurstone, 1927a, 1927b, 1928; Torgerson, 1858). We have made a major theoretical modification to Thurstone's method that allows complete dynamic voting and the introduction of new items with a fluctuating number of contributing voters possible on any subset of preference items in the list (White, Turoff, and Van de Walle 2007a; White, Plotnick, Turoff, and Hiltz 2007b). The critical contribution is a new measure of uncertainty that provides a separate Thurstone scale that shows the greatest possible uncertainty condition that results from some items having only a few votes and others having a lot more. This results in a second Thurstone's scale that can be lined up with the first scale to show the potentially large variations that can occur for items that are new and/or have currently only a small number of evaluations.

The approach provides two separate visualizations based upon the interval scales generated by the Thurstone method. If two alternatives are at the same point this means that half of the individuals who are voting on that comparison prefer A to B and the other half prefer B to A. The linear distance between the two is the current vote. Thus, $P(A>B) = P(B>A) = .5$ is the zero difference point between the two options. In the second scale those not voting but who indicate they are likely to vote at some point are assumed to be able to drive the vote back in the opposite direction and this gives a new version of the scale that measures the uncertainty when compared to the original scale. The first votes cast are meant to expose any disagreements so they can be brought out and discussed by everyone focusing on the particular problem, quickly bypassing areas of agreement and saving precious time. With this method anyone can change their vote at any time based upon the discussion that has occurred about what appears to be meaningful disagreements. The interval scale provides a visual measure of the degree of agreement on the relative preference of any two items. With this feedback, and the visual information provided by the second scale that shows the uncertainty as previously mentioned, experts have a more complete understanding of the level of agreement and status of opinions for decision making. People may choose to vote via "paired comparisons," rank order, "yes," "no," "no judgment," or "no judgment at this time," the latter showing other participants their intention to vote in the future. The feedback mechanisms of the voting scheme allow participants to see just how many vote changes have occurred for any one item in the list. We are adapting the standard Delphi design practice of only encouraging those who are confident in their judgment to express a preference (Linstone and Turoff, 1975).

Thus, this new method allows for providing a group reflection of individual experts to vote, revote, or not vote at all on a given situation, depending upon the relevance of the decision to the experts' domain of knowledge. These subsets of experts can then work more effectively given the dynamic nature of the event, and with the aid of Internet technology, from anywhere, anytime, and asynchronously. Prior research supports implementing the following list of characteristics into a distributed group support system to aid the decision making process so that better solutions are produced (Linstone and Turoff, 1975, Turoff 2002, White, Turoff, and Van de Walle 2007):

- Anytime, anywhere participation in decision processes
- Ability to vote on an issue, not vote, wait for more information to vote, or change a vote based on the changes in merit from evolving information input
- Visual feedback on real time vote status
- Anonymous voting
- Total vote changes on any item and histogram of recent vote changes over time
- Contribution to any part of the decision process by any team member

Anyone can participate in any part of the process at any time; this is crucial as the experts can change their minds, change a vote on a given decision based on the changes in merit of the arguments. Discussion is stimulated by disagreements made salient to the participants by a visual voting feedback system. This discussion amongst experts furthers understanding of a given situation and lessens ambiguity. In many cases the individuals converging on a specific problem will have different professional backgrounds and represent different viewpoints. In such situations the quick recognition of differences in meaning (ambiguity) is critical to reaching the stage where the more difficult issue of uncertainties can be dealt with.

Thus, expertise is used when it is most needed. Teams of experts should be in a standby mode ready to respond anytime when disaster strikes. However, the system must be used by the contributors in the interim because having a history of using the system regularly will promote ease of use. Waiting until a disaster to use a system impedes making full use of its capabilities. Only when a system is used on a day to day basis will the experts and teams be able to interact efficiently and effectively use it as a means to communicate and solve problems. This means that the thousands of people involved, who come from a great many different organizations and affiliations, must have access to the system between emergencies. This is for the purpose of replacing the need for a physical system as the basis for an HRO (e.g. nuclear power plant, aircraft carrier) with a virtual command and control system which can be fine tuned and used for training on a continuous basis (Turoff, Chumer, and Hiltz 2006). They can become part time participants in virtual organizations (Mowshowitz, 2002) where they can also develop the social relationships and other factors necessary to evolving a team and developing trust in each others' capabilities necessary to allow for the sharing of roles and responsibilities in any event with an unknown duration.

This approach allows those who feel confident through experience and/or expertise to self choose the problems to which they believe they can contribute. The shared motivation to reduce or mitigate the harm occurring in an emergency or crisis and the trust that only those that feel qualified to contribute are enough to eliminate the problems we usually fear in group collaboration due to Arrow's paradox. What we hope can be accomplished in this type of collaborative process is "collective intelligence" (Hiltz and Turoff, 1978, 1993) where the group result is better than any one member would have reached working alone and where decision making can occur as quickly as a single individual seeking to collect and consider carefully all the available information that might influence the process.

Accessibility to an easy to use management system can also create a bank of experts in which subsets can dynamically come together and handle unforeseen situations with the best outcome given the set of events. Such dynamically formed groups of experts need a system to support making fast decisions based on merit. No one can predict the composition of the perfect teams needed for problems that cannot be predicted ahead of time. What is needed is a system that is open to all the participants and provides the necessary information and alerts for individuals to find the problems they feel they can contribute to at any given moment or place in the response activity.

A Dynamic Emergency Response Management Information System (DERMIS) has been proposed by Turoff et al. (2004a, 2004b, 2006) which will provide for supporting dynamically changing teams of experts as they respond to or plan for extreme events. By focusing on roles, changes in personnel assigned to those roles can occur seamlessly and not adversely impact the effectiveness of the team. Each individual needs to have access to information that is relevant for an effective response. Flexibility, robustness and a dynamic nature are keys to effective handling of such emergencies. It is proposed (White, Plotnick, Adams-Moring, Turoff, and Hiltz, 2008) that a dynamic voting Delphi- like process can further increase effectiveness and ameliorate some of the problems that are inherent in rapidly changing, critical environments.

Other benefits of consistent use of a system are that users will meet one another and have a means of building trust within a virtual social network (Turoff et al., 2004a). On the other hand, during large scale or unexpected events, numerous participants in the command, control and analysis process may not have interacted before or have a plan that fits the circumstances. The secret for planning in emergencies is to have a process that works and known resources that can be commanded, not in designing decisions ahead of time. Trust may need to develop quickly as swift trust, and/or have challenges not present in more static, well-defined situations (Iacono and Weisband, 1997; Coppola, Hiltz, and Rotter, 2004). A person in a decision role may be reluctant to hand over that role to someone they do not know well enough to trust to carry out the role as well as they do. This is what leads to individuals working until exhaustion becomes a problem where it concerns making reliable decisions. Roles have to function on a 24 hour, 7 day basis. This also requires systems that track accurately the status of any response so that those taking over roles can have all the information dealing with an open response event. Familiarity with a system is a critical factor, especially when the participants in a crisis are further challenged with duress from psychophysical symptoms (Turoff et al, 2004a) such as the Threat-Rigidity Syndrome. Even during down times, it is important for participants to stay abreast of the situation so that when they come back on shift, they are aware of any drastic changes and can seamlessly continue the teamwork as an effective member.

ALLEVIATING INFORMATION OVERLOAD IN COMMUNITIES OF PRACTICE

When experts work collaboratively with a goal of learning from one another about a common interest, a Community of Practice (Wenger, McDermott, and Snyder 2002) can emerge; this strengthens the likelihood of good performance in situations of great stress. If the system has been used previously and is well understood, attention can be focused on the emergency and not diverted to issues of system use.

The history of the U.S. federal government in Emergency preparedness and management has resulted in numerous and diverse sources of information for communities of practice. There is no single source of collaboration among all those involved including the state and local governments and no single source for the collection and dissemination of plans and best practices for any or all of the many phases of the emergency preparedness process. Instead, there are numerous fragmented sources in specific areas, where some organizations or agencies have many more resources than others. The result for the practitioners is a proliferation of diverse documents that is not handled in any systematic approach and which has lead to practitioners in all areas and phases of emergency preparedness and management being overwhelmed with information they cannot adequately find, filter, or utilize (Turoff and Hiltz, 2008).

While there are significant efforts in the medical emergency area to overcome this information overload problem, even there the primary current emphasis from an information science viewpoint is on classical information retrieval utilizing largely academic sources of literature. There are no systematic attempts to collect best practices, working plans, case studies, and other sources of what is commonly called the "gray literature." A search on the web for "emergency management" or "emergency preparedness" turns up about nine million hits. A recent study of the behavior of practitioners in this area clearly identifies the conviction of practitioners that they all feel the problem of information overload. Just joining a few of the relevant message lists produces hundreds of new documents every week. Many emergency practitioners feel these documents might have something useful, but they have no time to skim anywhere near that number of documents. Their feeling that something is there that might improve their performance but which they have not seen is very real (Turoff and Hiltz, 2008). There is no library type organization that takes the role of integrating all this material into an integrated index relevant to all the different concerns, in the U.S. or internationally.

The resulting design for the emergency response community to attempt to solve their information overload problem involves interpreting their requirements to create a new type of information recommender system controlled by the practitioners themselves. Such a system would have to allow vetted practitioners in Emergency Preparedness and Management to:

1. Nominate documents to be included
2. Retrieve and skim or read these documents
3. Comment on the usefulness of a given document.
4. Vote on the usefulness if they are vetted professionals in a specific area.
5. Be able to view very useful documents rated as such by others who are in the same specific areas of EP&M as themselves.
6. Provide visualizations of document clusters on an interval scale such as provided by Thurstone's law of comparative judgment.
7. Allow them to change their vote or viewpoint based upon the information provided by others.
8. Allow for collaborative tagging to let the community keep the indexing tags for documents current and evolving with the latest changes in knowledge.

9. Provide vote summaries broken down by the types of professionals that voted on any particular document (medical, fire, hazards, etc).

This would represent a system supporting a "community of practice" to accumulate and acquire their own knowledge base of what they consider the most current and useful material for their field of endeavor (White, Plotnick, Turoff and Hiltz, 2007; White, Plotnick, Adams-Moring, Hiltz and Turoff, 2008; White, Hiltz, and Turoff, 2008). But all the above is somewhat foreign to the classic approach to information retrieval and would bypass the current journal industry. Essentially a recommender system for a community of practice would take the control of the literature out of the hands of journals, reviewers, and the publication industry, reduce costs greatly, and allow total control of the process by the actual users themselves. It would be the ultimate "open access" system (Poynder, 2008). It would still require vetting the contributors to insure they are active and knowledgeable professionals in some particular aspect of Emergency Preparedness and Management. Also, there would still be a need for editors in specific areas to look for anomalies of strong disagreements among professionals that should be investigated. Even Wikis today now have roles for editors for given pages to assess changes and conflicts.

FINAL OBSERVATIONS

Currently the process of bringing bottled water to a disaster site by the federal government is a very complex one which requires going up a significant number of governmental layers and engaging in outsourcing to a contractor that will actually acquire and supply the bottled water (Byrne, 2008), no doubt at a higher cost than one would expect. Local authorities and clearances between local emergency managers in a region

and sources of bottled water from local established stores would require very few agreements and a few phone calls to have such deliveries made to a point of need within hours, if in fact we had the right sort of agreements and command and control structure integrating all the local or regional parties involved.

The fragmentation of participation by existing human-determined boundaries and the presumption that these divisions are appropriate for planning and dealing with an emergency has been a principal reason why we have not seen major improvements in many of these areas since 1972.

- Lack of commonality with respect to interface design, visualization, and decision support, making it difficult for practitioners to master a range of very different systems necessary to their concerns.
- The separation of threats by source (terrorism, natural disasters, and man made disasters) with very different priorities for different phases and dissimilar activities.
- Lack of major integration requirements across organizations.

The above properties result from a web of deeper problems that tend to prevent the actions and developments that are needed. For example the common perception is that the response phase of an emergency will only last a week or two. However, this was not the case with the Anthrax emergency in the US and clearly the response phase of hurricane Katrina was far in excess of what usually occurs in urban areas. If we ever encounter a true pandemic, the response phase will last years. Fundamental issues of this sort greatly impact the design of information systems to deal with all the phases that can occur in any of these events.

There is a very dedicated community of professionals in emergency management in the US and elsewhere in the world. They have often faced terrible examples of mismanagement and lack of influence in the processes associated with many recent disasters. They need to be better integrated with those developing and implementing the systems needed to address the problems they face. They need to be part of a continuous community of practice that integrates across all local organizations and has the resources to involve all the local community, agencies, organizations, and individuals that want to participate in any phase of the Emergency Preparedness process. There is a significant element of truth in the unofficial motto they have expressed in the IAEM (International Association of Emergency Managers) message list in recent years:

We, the willing, led by the incompetent to do the impossible for the ungrateful, have done so much for so long with so little, we are now capable of doing practically anything with nothing.

REFERENCES

Bos, N., Olsen, J. S., Nan, N., Shami, N. S., Hoch, S., & Johnston, E. (2006) 'Collocation Blindness' in Partially Distributed Groups: Is there a Downside to Being Collocated? *Proceedings of the CHI 2006*, Montreal, Quebec, 2006.

Byrne, M. And Not a Drop to Drink, Water: an Alternative Test for Emergency Managers," *Homeland Security Affairs* IV, no. 2 (June 2008), http://www.hsaj.org/ ? article =4.2.2

Carver, L., & Turoff, M. (2007). Human Computer Interaction: The Human and Computer as a Team in Emergency Management Information Systems. *Communications of the ACM*, (March): 33–38. doi:10.1145/1226736.1226761

Chen, R., Sharman, R., Rao, H. R., Upadhyaya, S. J., & Cook-Cottone, C. P. (in press) Coordination of Emergency Response: An Examination of the Roles of People, Process, and Information Technology, in Information Systems for Emergency Management, (Van de Walle, B., Turoff, M., and Hiltz S.R. eds) in the Advances in Management Information Systems monograph series (Zwass, V. editor-in-chief), Armonk, NY: M.E. Sharpe Inc. Anticipated 2009.

Coppola, N., Hiltz, S. R., & Rotter, N. (2004). Building Trust in Virtual Teams. *IEEE Transactions on Professional Communication*, *47*(2), 95–104. doi:10.1109/TPC.2004.828203

French, S., & Turoff, M. (2007). Decision Support Systems. *Communications of the ACM*, *50*(3), 39–40. doi:10.1145/1226736.1226762

Hendela, A., Yao, X., Turoff, M., Hiltz, S. R., & Chumer, M. (2006) Virtual Emergency Preparedness Gaming: A follow up study, *Proceedings of ISCRAM06*, May 14-17, NJIT, Newark NJ, ISBN 90-9020601-9

Hiltz, S. R., Fjermestad, J., Ocker, R., & Turoff, M. (2006) Asynchronous Virtual Teams: Can Software Tools and Structuring of Social Processes Enhance Performance? In Volume II: Human-Computer Interaction in Management Information Systems: Applications, Dennis Galletta and Ping Zhang, editors, Armonk, NY: M. E. Sharpe, Inc., 119- 142.

Hiltz, S. R., & Turoff, M. (1993). The Network Nation: Human Communication via [Addison Wesley, MIT Press.]. *Computer*, 1978.

Huang, H., & Ocker, R. (2006) Preliminary Insights into the In-Group/Out-Group Effect in Partially Distributed Teams: An Analysis of Participant Reflections, *Proceedings of SIGMIS-CPR '06*, Claremont, California.

Iocono, C. S., & Weisband, S. (1997) Developing Trust in Virtual Teams, IEEE Proceedings, 30th Hawaii International Conference on System Sciences (HICSS) Volume 2: Information Systems Track - Collaboration Systems and Technology. Washington DC: IEEE Computer Society.

Lee, J. S., Lee, S. L., Damon, S. A., Geller, R., Janus, E. R., Ottoson, C., & Scott, M. J. (2006) Risk Communication needs in a chemical event, *Journal of Emergency Management*, 4, 2, 37-43, full report http://www.wetp.org/ wetp/ public/ has1_get_blob. cfm?ID=1051

Lindblom, C. (1959). The Science of Muddling Through. *Public Administration Review*, 79–88. doi:10.2307/973677

Lindblom, C. (1965). *The Intelligence of Democracy*. Free Press.

Lindblom, C. (1979). Still muddling, not yet through. *Public Administration Review*, (November/December): 517–526. doi:10.2307/976178

Linstone, H., & Turoff, M. (1975) The Delphi Method: Techniques and Applications, Addison Wesley Advanced Book Program, 1975 (available online at http://is.njit.edu/ turoff). Available at http://is.njit.edu/ turoff, last access 18 August 2007.

Linstone, H. A. (1973). On discounting the future. *Technological Forecasting and Social Change*, 4, 335–338. doi:10.1016/0040-1625(73)90074-7

Mitroff, I., & Turoff, M. (1973). Technological Forecasting and Assessment: Science and/or Mythology? *Journal of Technological Forecasting and Social Change*, 5, 13–134.

Mowshowitz, A. (2002). *Virtual Organizations*. Quorum Books.

Moynihan, D. (2006) From forest fires to Hurricane Katrina: Case Studies of Incident Command Systems, Networks and Partnerships Series, IBM Center for The business of Government.

Palen, L., Hiltz, S. R., & Liu, S. (2007). Citizen Participation in Emergency Preparedness and Response. *Communications of the ACM, 50*(special issue), 3, 54–58. doi:10.1145/1226736.1226766

Plotnick, L., Gomez, E. A., & White, C. (2007) Furthering Development of a Unified Emergency Scale Using Thurstone's Law of comparative Judgment: A progress Report, *Proceedings of ISCRAM 2007, 4ᵗʰ International Conference on Information Systems for Crisis Response and Management*, Delft, the Netherlands, May 13-16, Brussels University Press.

Poynder, R. (2008), Open Access: Doing the Numbers http://poynder.blogspot.com/ 2008/ 06/ open-access-doing-numbers.html, Open and Shut Blog, Wednesday, 11 June 2008.

Thurstone, L. L. (1927a). A Law of Comparative Judgment. *Psychological Review*, 34, 273–287. doi:10.1037/h0070288

Thurstone, L.L., (1927b). The Method of Paired Comparisons for Social Values. Journal of Abnormal and Social Psychology, 21, 384:400.

Thurstone, L. L. (1928). Attitudes Can Be Measured. *American Journal of Sociology, XXXIII*(4), 529–554. doi:10.1086/214483

Torgerson, W. S. (1958). *Theory and Methods of Scaling*. John Wiley & Sons, Inc.

Turoff, M. (2002). Past and Future Emergency Response Information Systems. *Communications of the ACM, 45*(4), 29–33. doi:10.1145/505248.505265

Turoff, M., Chumer M., Hiltz, R., Klashner, R., Alles, M., Vararheyi, M., and Kogan, A., (2004b) Assuring Homeland Security: Continuous Monitoring, Control & Assurance of Emergency Preparedness, *Journal of Information Technology Theory and Application, (JITTA)*, 6, 3, 1-24.

Turoff, M., Chumer, M., & Hiltz, S. R. (2006) Emergency Planning as a Continuous Game. *Proceedings of the 3rd International ISCRAM Conference, Newark, NJ.*

Turoff, M., Chumer, M., Van de Walle, B., and Yao, X., (2004a) The Design of a Dynamic Emergency Response Management Information System (DERMIS). *Journal of Information Technology Theory and Application, (JITTA),* 5:4, 1-35.

Turoff, M., and Hiltz, S. R., (2008) Information Seeking Behavior and Viewpoints of Emergency Preparedness and Management Professionals Concerned with Health and Medicine, Report to the National Library of Medicine, February, 2008. (Will be Web accessible)

Turoff, M., Hiltz, S. R., Cho, H.-K., Li, Z., & Wang, Y. (2002) Social Decision Support Systems. *Proceedings of the 35th Hawaii International Conference of System Sciences.*

Van de Walle, B., & Turoff, M. (2008). Decision Support for Emergency Situations. In Burstein, F., & Holsapple, C. (Eds.), *Handbook on Decision Support Systems, International Handbook on Information Systems Series, Springer-Verlag, (This chapter will be open on the Web).*

Van de Walle, B., Turoff, M., & Hiltz, S. R. (in press). (expected 2009). Information Systems for Emergency Management. In the Advances in Management Information Systems monograph series (Editor-in-Chief: Vladimir Zwass). Armonk, NY. *M.E. Sharpe Inc.*

Weick, K., & Sutcliffe, K. (2001). *Managing the Unexpected: Assuring High Performance in an Age of Complexity.* Jossey-Bass Publishers.

Wenger, E., McDermott, R., & Snyder, W. (2002). *Cultivating communities of practice: a guide to managing knowledge.* Boston, Mass.: Harvard Business School Press.

White, C., Plotnick, L., Aadams-Moring, R., Turoff, M., & Hiltz, S. R. (2008) Leveraging a Wiki to Enhance Virtual Collaboration in the Emergency Domain, Proceedings *of the 41st HICSS.*

White, C., Plotnick, L., Turoff, M., & Hiltz, S. R. (2007b) A Dynamic Voting Wiki, *Proceedings of 13th Americas Conference on Information Systems.*

White, C., Turoff, M., & Van de Walle, B. (2007a). A Dynamic Delphi Process Utilizing a Modified Thurstone Scaling Method: Collaborative Judgment in Emergency Response. *Proceedings of 4th Information Systems on Crisis Response Management.*

Yao, X., & Turoff, M. (2007) Using Task Structure to Improve Collaborative Scenario Creation, *Proceedings of ISCRAM 2007, 4th International Conference on Information Systems for Crisis Response and Management,* Delft, the Netherlands, May 13-16, Brussels University Press.

This work was previously published in International Journal of Information Systems for Crisis Response and Management, Volume 1, Issue 1, edited by Murray E. Jennex, pp. 12-28, copyright 2009 by IGI Publishing (an imprint of IGI Global).

Chapter 3
Only Connect:
Problem Sciences, Information Systems and Humanitarian Reform

Paul Currion
humanitarian.info, UK

ABSTRACT

The introduction of information systems and the humanitarian reform process are both having a tremendous impact on the way that humanitarian assistance is delivered – yet the two processes are extremely weakly connected. As a result, the humanitarian community is failing to realise the potential that information technology has to support key aspects of the reform process, but also failing to recognise that technology is likely to render many of the discussions around reform moot. The balance of knowledge is shifting towards those affected by disaster, implying that they will become increasingly empowered by technology to more effectively cope with the impact of those disasters. Traditional actors in the humanitarian community must incorporate these realities into its own processes or risk being overtaken by newer and more agile institutions which may not be so concerned with humanitarian principles.

INTRODUCTION: PROBLEM SCIENCE 101

In his book on the limits of science, Impossibility, Barrow (1998) suggests that:

When their activities become very expensive and have no direct technological or military relevance to the state, then [scientist's] continued support will be determined by other great problems that confront society. In the future, we might expect the development of what we will call the "problem sciences" —those studies needed to solve the great environmental, social, and medical problems that threaten humanity's continued existence and well-being.

This article takes as its starting point the idea that, while the state – and particularly the military – continues to play a large role in the development of new technology, the first seeds of the problem sciences could already be seen at

DOI: 10.4018/978-1-60960-609-1.ch003

the end of the twentieth century. The appropriate technology movement of the 1970s identified the need for "trailing edge" technology to meet the needs of poorer communities, preferably rooted in innovation that emerges from those communities themselves, rather than wholesale adoption of existing "rich world" technology.[1] This fits with the "Shock of the Old" thesis, in which Edgerton (2007) introduced "the concept of creole technologies to suggest that the technology poor world cannot be reduced either to its stock of rich world technologies, or traditional, local technologies, or hybrids between the two. A new technological world of technologies derived and adapted from those of the rich world in complex ways, and then often entering into hybrids, are some of the complexities the term seeks to capture."[2]

These creolization processes must be viewed in light of another significant trend – the "remarkable acceleration of the speed at which technologies trickle down from leaders to followers during the postwar period" (Comin & Hobijn, 2003). Comin & Hobijn attribute this primarily to changes in governance, regulation and capital, with little discussion of how radical shifts in mass communication have affected the diffusion of other technologies. Three key trends – the spread of personal computing, internet access and mobile telephony – are particularly significant in this respect, gradually converging all around the world to create entirely new modes of sharing information. While information technology is not usually thought of as "appropriate", the personal computer as a "universal machine" is ideally placed for creolization. This is reflected in its relatively rapid uptake in developing countries, the main constraint being that:

high levels of educational attainment are important determinants of computer-technology adoption, even after controlling for a variety of other macroeconomic variables... The effect is quantitatively substantial... a one-percentage-point increase in

the fraction of the labor force who have better than primary education leads to an increase in computer investment per worker of roughly 1%. (Caselli and Coleman, 2000)

This in turn has a strong effect on limiting internet access (as well as limiting demand for internet access), which projects such as the Simputer and One Laptop Per Child (OLPC) XO[3] are intended to redress. Although there is an ongoing debate about the role of computers in basic education (especially given other constraints on education in many developing economies), these low-cost laptops can be viewed as part of the first wave of "appropriate IT". However more recent developments suggest that computer access will not be the main determinant of internet access in future:

The information-poverty of developing countries has helped make the impact of mobile all the more powerful, as mobile penetration... has increased even more rapidly in poor countries... The importance of mobile communications in the information-poor context of developing countries enhances their potential contribution in disasters, even greater than in the developed world with its richer infrastructure. (Coyle, 2005)

This vision of mobile telephones as the primary means of mobilising resources to support the individual or community response to disaster has been supported by research carried out by the UK Department For International Development, which found that:

The most substantial value of the telephone in terms of livelihoods is in its impact on overall vulnerability, particularly in emergencies. The telephone here has exceptional added value compared with other communications media, in particular because of its immediacy, interactivity and ability to secure assistance from afar. (Souter et al., 2005)

These trends are important because they represent a shift in the global balance of knowledge – and knowledge is power. It is hardly credible that the information revolution will grind to a halt, and as a result the empowerment of people around the world is likely to have a significant impact on every aspect of human society – including how we respond to disasters.

In terms of identifying solutions for the problems of disaster response, it is useful to divide them into two levels. The first is the most obvious: *how can individuals, communities and institutions meet the challenges posed by disasters?* This requires researchers to look for solutions to critical problems raised by disasters, and frame them in such a way as to make the findings practically useful for the end users. The second level is less obvious, but in many ways more important: *how can the capacity of individuals, communities and institutions to meet the challenges posed by disasters be increased?* It is vital to note the key difference between these two levels – the oft-quoted difference between giving a man a fish and teaching him to fish.

Information systems are not in themselves a response to disaster; instead they operate at the second level of the problem sciences, focused on increasing our collective capacity to respond. What is exciting about this area of endeavour is that the information revolution has fundamentally altered the way in which knowledge is produced, disseminated and accessed; it has given us extremely powerful tools that can increase that capacity, offering an entirely new paradigm for capacity building – albeit one which has not yet been fully realised. The reasons for this are complicated, but are embedded in the nature of the humanitarian community.

Disasters, Old and New

The effects of natural and manmade emergencies are being felt ever more strongly around the world. One of the key documents in the humanitarian reform movement of the new century was Ambiguity and Change, a research and mapping exercise commissioned by a group of leading humanitarian Non Governmental Organisations (NGOs), which began by pointing out that:

The conflation of environmental degradation, climate change, globalization, and retrenching governments will lead to many more complex and cascading emergencies, especially in the urban environment. (Walker, Minear et al., 2004)

While questions are valid concerning how impartial such analysis is (given that the flow of funding to the NGOs that commissioned the report depends on the continued incidence of disasters) so far this trend has been confirmed by the evidence. It is also supported by other academic research, particularly around social complexity and community resilience, suggesting that as social structures become more complex they also become more fragile, and consequently vulnerable to shocks (Homer-Dixon, 2005).[4]

Conceptually it is most useful to class disasters according to the level, nature and source of inputs that they mobilise, rather than the type of disaster itself. It makes sense to think of resource mobilisation moving outwards depending on the scale of the disaster – like a rock dropped in a pool, the impact of the disaster spreads further depending on its size, visualised as per Figure 1.

Each successive layer usually becomes involved only if the resources available to those occupying the next layer inwards on the diagram are insufficient. It is clear that increasing the capacity of each layer will limit the need for additional resources, with the greatest return on investment provided by increasing capacity towards the centre. Thus the primary question in disaster management is *how to ensure that individuals and (more frequently) communities mobilise sufficient resources to withstand shocks.*

In an ideal world, sufficient resources would always be available at the lowest level, in the

Figure 1. Impact levels of disaster

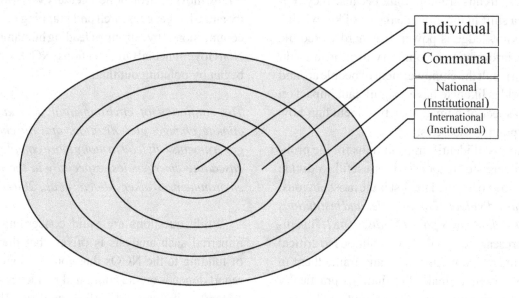

Individual

Communal

National
(Institutional)

International
(Institutional)

context of resilient communities that are able to withstand shocks with little if any external support. Realistically this is unlikely to happen for most communities around the world in the foreseeable future, and so the requirement for external inputs will continue. The secondary question is therefore *how to mobilise resources successfully between one level and the next to mitigate the impact of shocks.*

With regard to the primary question, the obvious focus for information systems should be to help actors at any given level to mobilise the resources that they need – most obviously information resources. Far from being trivial, the International Federation of the Red Cross and Red Crescent Societies (IFRC) has reported that:

Information is also a vital form of aid in itself. People need information as much as water, food, medicine or shelter. Information can save lives, livelihoods and resources. It may be the only form of disaster preparedness that the most vulnerable can afford. (IFRC, 2005)

As the World Disasters Report goes on to point out, however, this aspect of humanitarian assistance is "very much neglected", since most of the institutions involved in disaster response focus on "gathering information for their own needs and not enough on exchanging information with the people they aim to support." (IFRC 2005) These institutions - the loosely organised set of organisations that includes the Red Cross movement, United Nations (UN) family and a large body of NGOs[5] - form the humanitarian community. Essentially this community is focused on addressing the secondary question rather than the primary question, seen clearly in the role played by services such as the Humanitarian Information Centres (HICs) and UN Joint Logistics Centre (UNJLC), whose work is geared towards supporting other humanitarian organisations.

There have been some efforts to improve information sharing with communities. There are some examples in the area of early warning, where community outreach is the primary focus (Samarajiva, 2005). The NGO Telecoms Sans Frontieres (TSF) was founded with the objective of providing disaster survivors with three-minute phone calls, primarily to reunite them with their families.[6] Another example is the use of text messaging by the World Food Programme (WFP) to alert Iraqi refugees in Syria to food distributions, the first time SMS has been used in such a situation; whether this will prove to be the beginning of more widespread community notification community notification remains to be seen, however (Kincade and Verclas, 2007).

These exceptions prove the rule that the humanitarian reform process – particularly its attempts to mainstream information and communications technology – continues to focus on improving communication within the community (whether intra- or inter-organisational), rather than external outreach and accountability to beneficiary populations. According to a post-tsunami United Nations Development Programme (UNDP) report, represents a tremendous missed opportunity:

A good communications strategy will not fix a fundamentally misconceived project, hide problems that emerge as it progresses, or gloss over defects in government policy. But information flow to communities almost always enhances projects, contributing considerably to a good working relationship with beneficiaries and higher satisfaction levels. Effective outreach for service-based projects also increases uptake of services. Transparency in projects is recognized and appreciated by communities and rewarded with increased credibility and trust. (Wall, 2006)

Given such a wide range of potential benefits, it is unclear why agencies have not already developed such mechanisms. One answer lies in another problem endemic in the community, that of accountability. Since funding does not come from the affected communities but from external stakeholders (mainly large public institutions and individual charitable donations), agencies do not have incentives to invest in relationships with beneficiaries beyond that which is necessary to deliver the assistance paid for by those stakeholders[7].

This essentially negative prognosis is offset by the growing understanding "that emergencies are not aberrant phenomena but reflections of the ways that societies structure themselves and allocate resources." (Walker, Minear et al, 2004) This holds out the promise that it will be possible to re-structure societies and re-allocate resources in ways which improve the resilience of those societies. In order to support these restructuring processes the humanitarian community will need to reform its own approach in such a way as to make this possible while retaining its core values.

Technology Overtaking Reform

It is obvious that the information revolution must play a critical role in any such reform; but it should also be equally obvious that the impact of the information revolution on the wider society also needs to be taken into account in this reform process. While the first point has been recognised by "traditional" humanitarian actors, the second point – with a few exceptions – has not. Rather than improving relationships between institutions and their beneficiaries, technology in the humanitarian reform process has focused on improving relationships between institutions – without question an important endeavour, but one which runs the risk of undermining the entire humanitarian enterprise.

Co-ordination remains the critical issue in humanitarian response, and has been one of the specific areas of focus for the Humanitarian Reform process lead by the UN over the last three years. Emergency Telecommunications has been established within the Cluster approach, but responsibility for it was split between three different organisations: the Office for Co-ordination of Humanitarian Affairs (OCHA) has overall responsibility; WFP deals with security communications (in practice, radio) and UNICEF with data communications (in practice, satellite communications). While there were concerns that the cluster might be less effective as a result of this three-way split, this has proved not to be the case. However the Cluster is almost solely concerned with improving existing ways of communicating rather than innovation, and has no interest in what communications are being used for.

This interest is dealt with by an Information Management Working Group, rather than a Cluster, but information management has been placed within the cluster approach and is more clearly visible now than at any previous point.

As a starting point for looking at Cluster/Sector capacity, it is interesting to note the increased level of visibility that information management as a Cluster / Sector function in itself appears to be gaining. While there was relatively little discussion of IM per se within the Cluster Appeal for 2006-7, in the 2007-8 Appeal for Building Global Humanitarian Response Capacity, all clusters have explicitly included information. (Larsen, 2007)

However this visibility at the global level has not translated into activity in the response itself; in the Cyclone Nargis response in Myanmar, only two of the clusters fielded dedicated information management staff as part of their initial surge; and at the global level there are visible discrepancies in levels of investment between different clusters. This carries with it the potential danger that some clusters will be better-equipped than others to handle their own intra-cluster information—which in turn has negative implications for inter-cluster information management, which is obviously the key to the success of the overall response.

There is also a commitment "to ensure that information management activities support national information systems, standards, build local capacities and maintain appropriate links with relevant Government, State and local authorities" (OCHA, 2007), a commitment which starts to move towards the questions of capacity building raised earlier. However this commitment is not substantial; there is limited guidance or support available for staff in the field, and no way of measuring progress towards meeting this objective.

Within the various organisations comprising the humanitarian community, there has certainly been significant progress in improving the way in which technology is used. Increasingly private sector management techniques are being imported, particularly into NGOs, with many senior IT staff being recruited from the private sector. However the differences between private and public – even at the international level – are sufficiently large that there have been numerous problems with this. In some cases the introduction of technology to the humanitarian community has suffered from misunderstandings about the nature of the community by those approaching from the outside. The bad news is that this has seen multiple failures in the sector, which has made it more difficult to generate interest in the technology; the good news is that there is a rapid learning curve, and that second or third iterations of these projects seem to do much better than the first.

A good example of both of these is the Helios software developed by the Fritz Institute, a non-profit foundation created specifically to bring logistics expertise from the private sector.[8] The earliest version was developed for the IFRC and, despite some problems with implementation, met their needs – but this could not be easily transferred horizontally to other organisations that did not share the IFRC's particular organisational (and particularly logistics) structure. Taking it back to the drawing board, Fritz emerged with a much more robust piece of software which is now being piloted by multiple NGOs, although it will take more time before it is clear what the outcome of this pilot scheme is, and more time yet to find out whether other organisations not specifically targeted by Fritz for the pilot can easily adopt the software.[9]

In some ways Helios is symptomatic of the problems faced by the humanitarian community in introducing new technology. The community has been slow to adopt new technology for three reasons. First, technology is not the main focus of most organisations, so there are limited resources for exploring and exploiting new developments. Second, since they have not traditionally used return on investment (ROI) as a basis for making decisions, communities have failed to identify where and how new technology can save their resources. Third, the decentralised nature of many organisations mean that innovation in one location (whether a country, region or headquarters) is not easily transferred to other locations. The danger of these natural obstacles is that the humanitarian community has been overtaken by technology on more than one occasion; in areas such as mobile telephony (over radio) and neogeography (over Geographic Information Systems, or GIS).

Mobile Phones

Humanitarian organisations, used to operating in remote areas, previously relied on radio networks for their communications, and as a result there is a clearly understood radio network structure and a complete set of protocols for radio use. However this set-up was largely imported from the military, and was not developed for the specific requirements of the humanitarian community. While well-developed, is not necessarily the best fit with the needs of (for example) a small international NGO or with the budgets of a national NGO, leading to persistent gaps in radio networks.[10] In addition ensuring compliance with telecommunications guidelines has always been a problem even where there are serious security concerns.

The growth of mobile telephony meant that staff had access to a cheaper, simpler and more direct means of communication, even in areas that were previously considered remote. Organisations increasingly found that radio networks were not being used, and where they were being used, were being used incorrectly. This is a problem because mobile phone networks are significantly less secure and reliable than radio networks, meaning that they are unsuitable for security communications. Balanced against that is the fact that mobile telephones are more inclusive – for example, local government officials are unlikely to have access to the radio network but will have mobile phones (Currion, 2006).

This places the humanitarian community in a difficult position. Radio remains the backbone of security communications, but mobile telephones simply work better for staff. As mobile coverage grows, mobile networks become more resilient and mobile communications become richer, it is likely that radio will become obsolete except in particularly remote or particularly dangerous areas; and this in turn will raise questions about whether the relatively large amount of investment that radio networks require is worth it for humanitarian organisations.

Neogeography

The biggest revolution in information management has been the introduction of geospatial technologies to the humanitarian community. The application of geographic information systems combined with remote sensing imagery has had tremendous impact on the way in which humanitarian organisations visualise their operations – although not as much impact as their most enthusiastic proponents have hoped for, leading one analyst to comment that "More than any other GIS user group, the humanitarian sector appears to be the least progressive in exploiting the analytical potential of GIS technology" (Verjee, 2007).

Given that the utility of GIS was officially recognised by the UN at least eight years ago (Brahimi et al., 2000), there has been much discussion amongst practitioners as why this should be the case. The general consensus amongst those involved with geospatial technology is that the community is stuck in a vicious circle (Currion, 2005). The value of GIS has yet to be conclusively demonstrated through application in a critical process, so humanitarian organisations are understandably wary of allowing GIS to take too central a role; yet this wariness prevents GIS practitioners from finding the opportunity to conclusively demonstrate its value. In the background, there has been important progress in terms of building a UN Spatial Data Infrastructure (SDI),[11] but this will be of limited utility if the community is unable or unwilling to build anything on top of that infrastructure.

However this discussion is being rapidly overtaken by neogeography, a phrase coined to describe the explosion of accessible mapping lead by Google Maps and Google Earth. These new services, delivered over the internet, have been made possible by the declassification of remote sensing data and the lifting of Global Positioning System (GPS) restrictions. However the reasons for their success (judged at least in terms of public visibility and popularity) is due to the completely different approach which emphasises the improvised, contingent and communal aspects of maps and the mapmaking process. In many ways this approach fits better with the fluid situations that characterise disaster response, and so neogeography is likely to continue to grow – at the expense of GIS.

The common thread between these two examples is the nature of the new technology vs the old. Mobile telephony and neogeography emphasise person-to-person connections, are more accessible and usable, and require less training. Some see this as the logical next step in disaster management, applying the reasoning behind Web2.0[12] to improve the effectiveness of disaster response; when they discuss this improvement, they mean making information more accessible, primarily to victims of disaster. This fits with the broader social trends identified at the start of this article which have seen a shift in the balance of knowledge, and suggest that this shift is occurring even within our organisations, usually unnoticed.

Change or Die

The information revolution offers new possibilities for enriching the humanitarian community. The danger of continuing to focus mainly (if not solely) on their internal information systems is that humanitarian organisations will miss the opportunities created by new technologies to work more closely with and deliver services more effectively to beneficiaries. However the costs of these changes to humanitarian organisations are potentially high, and need to be accounted for. These costs will be incurred because the humanitarian community and its constituent organisations will need to change the way they work, and the way that they structure themselves to do that work. For example, even the biggest organisations will need to become flatter if they are to operate successfully, as technology leads to an increasingly peer-to-peer environment.

A more interesting shift will come in the ways that organisations deal with each other. Coordination already involves multiple actors, who generally cannot rely on their own organisation's internal systems to interact with partners, since those partners are not allowed access to those internal systems. This creates a huge problem which goes largely unnoticed at the organisational level (since the organisation cannot "see" the problem) but is keenly felt at the individual level. Previously there were no solutions to this, but in recent years there have been numerous collaboration spaces established outside the walls and not linked to organisation systems, using services such as Yahoo! Groups. More than other sectors, the humanitarian community is built on partnerships – with Cluster partners, donors, contracting organisations, working groups – and agencies need to accommodate this reality in their information systems to function effectively.

The cost of this will be a blurring of organisational lines, which will be difficult to manage for organisations that are unable to adapt to this new approach. In addition, openness is a much more difficult proposition in many of the environments in which these organisations work, as political sensitivities – particularly in peace operations, but also in natural disasters where governments are failing to deliver to their citizens – can be much harder to manage. The questions of when and how to offer particular partners access to organisational information is one with which agencies will have to grapple repeatedly. Yet if these are public organisations, funded by public money, collecting public information in the name of a public good, it is hard to argue that they should continue as they have in the past, making it inaccessible either through neglect or intent.

The truly radical change, however, goes far deeper than this. Organisations will also need to become more open not just to partners, but to donors and beneficiaries as well. The general public will have access to more information about relief work than previously (thanks to the increase in blogs, wikis and similar user-driven content) and successful fundraising will need to be based on richer, more interactive relationships than previously. In time, individual contacts between donors and beneficiaries will start to replace the highly-mediated relationships that aid agencies currently rely on. This has already started to happen in the development sector (through projects such as Kiva, which connects lenders with small businesses in developing countries through existing microfinance institutions), but we have seen how the information revolution has made it easier for diaspora groups to mobilise resources in response to disasters.

It was argued above that one of the factors that disempowers beneficiaries is their lack of access to information; the information revolution has and will continue to improve that access, and agencies can either ignore this reality or accommodate it. Few organisations have recognised this, particularly at the UN level; one of the few is Save the Children, whose CIO Ed Granger-Happ wrote in 2001:

In order to connect with the world's poorest communities, in order to create a true virtual village, two things need to happen: First, the people in these communities need access to the basic health, education and other information available via *the Internet-- or be left behind a widening digital chasm. Second, donors should to be able to enter the indigent world, to connect directly with the information, programs and people in the local community and by the local community-- to hear and see the conditions and the successes from the source. (Granger-Happ, 2001)[13]*

The simple fact is that those affected by disaster are likely to have more information about the response in future, irrelevant of whether aid agencies help them to access that information or not. The same mobile phones that are used by fishermen to improve efficiencies in their trade (Jensen, 2007) could be used to leverage response during emergencies (Souter et al., 2005) The SMS notifications of food distributions by WFP described above ran into many problems; since it was a novel situation made possible only by a recent technological development, both sides of the transaction were improvising. However beneficiaries are frequently smarter than aid agencies and will generally find ways to game the system to serve their interests – for example, co-ordinating family members via SMS to cluster at multiple aid registration points.

This raises questions about ownership of the information itself. Who owns information about refugees, for example? Certainly the organisations that collect that information have a stake in it; certainly the organisations that use that information have a stake in it; but it is difficult to see how they can claim ownership of it in any meaningful sense. If agencies are serious about empowering communities, enabling them to mobilise their own resources – including information resources – then refugees should be the owners of information about themselves. What this means in practice must be negotiated on a case-by-case basis depending on the particular circumstances – but it seems clear that the only option available to humanitarian organisations is to embrace the information revolution rather than fight it.

CONCLUSION

With increasing attention being paid to what can loosely be called the "problem sciences", and with the information revolution reshaping the ways that human society responds to disaster, the humanitarian community needs to radically reform the way in which it deals with information. In particular, the community needs to extend its information systems as far as possible into the affected communities with which it works, as well as more effectively managing the changes wrought by technology within their own organisations.

While these are not simple challenges, neither are they optional. These changes – and more like them – will come whether agencies plan for them or not. If they are serious about their commitment to empowering beneficiaries, about building community resilience, about being more transparent and more accountable, about collaborating more effectively – all those issues which are the focus of the humanitarian reform process, in fact – they must start taking technology more seriously, ensuring that their information systems serve their humanitarian objectives as much as any other part of their organisations.

There is no blueprint for success in this area, and each organisation must find its own solutions to the questions raised by technology. In terms of the evolution of the sector, clearly the best approach is to encourage experimentation, allowing for the possibility of failures but ensuring that we learn from those failures. The framework outlined at the start of this article offers a way of thinking about the challenges both for agencies providing assistance and for developers providing information systems. In particular:

1.   Agencies need to view information as a resource that beneficiaries seek to mobilise in the same way as other resources, and ensure that they do their best to provide that information. However they also need to recognise that beneficiaries will increasingly have access to information of their own, and ensure that their other programmatic responses take that into consideration.

2.   Developers should bear in mind that information systems operate at the secondary level of the problem sciences, that of increasing capacity to respond. Research and development should be embedded into the capacity building question, while at the same time using technology to help organisations towards new configurations that can better manage the impact of the information revolution.

The humanitarian community as we know it is relatively young – perhaps 60 years old – yet in its short history it has been through many changes. The current humanitarian reform process is yet another change, as is the introduction of novel information technology; the key to surviving the next 60 years is to bring them together successfully.

REFERENCES

Barrow, J. (1998). *Impossibility: The Limits of Science and the Science of Limits*. Oxford: Oxford University Press.

Brahimi, L. (2000). *Report of the Panel on United Nations Peace Operations (United Nations A/55/305?S/2000/809)*. New York: United Nations.

Calamard, A. (2001). *Why humanitarian accountability? Contextual and operational factors*. Geneva: Humanitarian Accountability Project.

Caselli, F., & Coleman, W. J. (2001). *Cross-Country Technology Diffusion: The Case of Computers*. CEPR Discussion Paper No. 2744.

Coyle, D., & Childs, M. B. (2005). *The Role of Mobiles in Disasters and Emergencies*. GSM Association.

Currion, P. (2006). *Better the Devil we Know: Obstacles and Opportunities in Humanitarian GIS*. London: humanitarian.info.

Currion, P. (2006). *Information and Technology Requirements Initiative: Assessment Report*. Washington, DC: Emergency Capacity Building Project.

Edgerton, D. (2007) *Creole technologies and global histories: rethinking how things travel in space and time*, in Journal of History of Science and Technology Vol.1, 75-112.

Emergency Telecommunication Cluster, W. F. P. (2008). *Security Telecommunication Assessment Mission – Liberia*. Rome: World Food Programme.

Fink, S. (2007, November). *The Science of Doing Good*. Scientific American Magazine.

Granger-Happ, E. (2001). *Wiring the Virtual Village*. Connecticut: Save the Children.

Hobijn, B. and Comin, D. (2003). *Cross-Country Technology Adoption: Making the Theories Face the Facts*. FRB NY Staff Report No.169.

Homer-Dixon, T. (2007). *The Upside of Down: Creativity, Catastrophe and the Renewal of Civilisation*. London: Souvenir Press.

International Federation of Red Cross and Red Crescent Societies. (2005). *World Disasters Report 2005*. Geneva: IFRC.

Jensen, R. (2007). *The Digital Provide: Information (Technology), Market Performance and Welfare in the South Indian Fisheries Sector*, in The Quarterly Journal of Economics, Vol.CXXII, Issue 3, 879-924.

Kincade, S., & Verclas, K. (2008). *Wireless Technology for Social Change: Trends in Mobile Use by NGOs. Washington, DC and Berkshire*. UK: UN Foundation – Vodafone Group Foundation Partnership.

Larsen, L. (2007). *Strengthening Humanitarian Information Management: A Status Report*. Geneva: OCHA Field Information Services Unit.

OCHA. (2007). *Operational Guidance on Responsibilities of Cluster / Sector Leads & OCHA in Information Management v2.0*. Geneva: OCHA Field Information Services Unit.

Samarajiva, R. (2005) *Mobilizing information and communications technologies for effective disaster warning: lessons from the 2004 tsunami*, in New Media & Society, Vol 7(6): 731–747.

Souter, D. (2005). *The Economic Impact of Telecommunications on Rural Livelihoods and Poverty Reduction: A study of rural communities in India (Gujarat), Mozambique and Tanzania*. London: Commonwealth Telecommunications Organisation and Department for International Development.

Verjee, F. (2007). *An Assessment of the Utility of GIS-based Analysis to Support the Coordination of Humanitarian Assistance*. Washington: The George Washington University, Dept. of Engineering Management and Systems Engineering.

Walker, P., & Minear, L. (2004). *Ambiguity and Change: Humanitarian NGOs Prepare for the Future*. Massachusetts: The Feinstein International Famine Center, Tufts University.

Wall, I. (2006). *The Right to Know: The Challenge of Public Information and Accountability in Aceh and Sri Lanka*. New York: Office of the UN Secretary General's Special Envoy for Tsunami Recovery.

ENDNOTES

[1] Contemporary examples of this can be found on the Afrigadget blog (http://www.afrigadget.com/).

2   However Edgerton goes on to say that, "while the term ['creole technologies] is very suggestive, it reaches the end of its usefulness when confronted with some technological novelties in the poor world" – essentially, that we do not yet have a sufficient framework for discussing technology globally.

3   More information on these projects is available at http://www.simputer.org/ and http://ww.laptop.org.

4   This was seen most recently and unexpectedly in the food riots that broke out across the world at the beginning of 2008, generally seen as presaging further social disruptions as fuel prices rise.

5   As opposed to what might be referred to as emergency management, which is largely a domestic concern; and also a serious consideration only in countries above a certain level of economic development.

6   While TSF continues to provide this service, however, its growth since its creation in 1998 seems to have been funded primarily by providing telecommunications services to the UN and other international organisations.

7   There are a wide range of issues around humanitarian accountability; an overview of the development of these issues can be found in Callamard, 2001.

8   More information is available at http://www.fritzinstitute.org/prgTech-HELIOS.htm.

9   It is also worth noting that the Fritz Institute have diversified from simply developing software to offering a range of services, including certification in humanitarian logistics – an indication that information systems must be seen in the context of an entire organisation, not as standalone projects.

10   A recent Security Telecommunication Assessment Mission to Liberia found that the NGO community suffered from "absence or limited access to the security telecommunication system... Where NGOs have access to the security telecoms network, they do not use standard call sign structure" due to unfamiliarity with standard procedures. (WFP, 2008)

11   The Logistics Cluster is most advanced in this area, developing an SDI for Transport which can be downloaded at http://www.unjlc.org/mapcenter/unsdi.

12   Broadly speaking, Web 2.0 refers described "the trend in the use of World Wide Web technology and web design that aims to enhance creativity, information sharing, and, most notably, collaboration among users." (http://en.wikipedia.org/wiki/Web_2)

13   This realisation led Granger-Happ and Save the Children to take the lead in founding NetHope (www.nethope.org), one of the few groups committed to addressing these issues.

This work was previously published in International Journal of Information Systems for Crisis Response and Management, Volume 1, Issue 1, edited by Murray E. Jennex, pp. 29-40, copyright 2009 by IGI Publishing (an imprint of IGI Global).

Chapter 4
Web–Based Group Decision Support for Crisis Management

Simon French
Manchester Business School, UK

Clare Bayley
Manchester Business School, UK

Nan Zhang
Manchester Business School, UK

ABSTRACT

The early designs for crisis management decision support systems used data-based or model-based methodologies and architectures. We argue that the complexity of crisis management situations means that a greater emphasis on collaboration is needed. Moreover, modern interactive Web 2.0 technologies allow group decision support to be offered to geographically dispersed teams. Given that crisis management often requires teams to be drawn together from a number of organisations sited at different locations, we reflect upon the potential of these technologies to support the early stages of crisis management without the need to draw the team together at a common location. We also report on a small scale experiment using GroupSystems ThinkTank to manage an emerging food safety event. We conclude that such systems have potential and deserve more careful evaluation.

INTRODUCTION

In this article we explore current developments in web-based group decision support systems (wGDSS), asking how and whether they can support the development of strategy for teams of geographically dispersed crisis managers. Our concern is that the use of any group decision support system (GDSS), web-enabled or not, requires a common understanding of the system and shared mental models so that the group can interact consistently and draw the same messages to inform the crisis management process. Will this be possible if the group are spatially dispersed and perhaps have never met face-to-face? In the following we discuss these issues in greater detail and describe an exploratory experiment in which

DOI: 10.4018/978-1-60960-609-1.ch004

we simulated the management of a crisis relating to food safety using a *w*GDSS.

When Gorry and Scott Morton (1971) first defined decision support systems (DSS) *per se*, they recognised that some systems would support unstructured decision making: DSS were "interactive computer-based systems, which help decision makers utilise data and models to solve unstructured problems". Notwithstanding this, the majority of early DSS focused on supporting well structured operational decisions[1]. They were built on data-based information providing or model-based prediction, simulation and evaluation architectures, both of which do little to support decision making in highly unstructured circumstances (for examples of such architectures see, e.g., Mallach, 2000). However, foreshadowed by decision analysts working to support strategic decisions, often the responsibility of groups of decision makers, more flexible, less structured, group enabled DSS tools were developed (see, e.g., Clemen & Reilly, 1996; DeSanctis & Gallupe, 1987; Eden & Ackermann, 1998; Eden & Radford, 1990; Nunamaker, Briggs, Mittleman, Vogel, & Balthazard, 1996; Phillips, 1984). Some of these tools were designed to work with groups in plenary decision conferences; others allowed individual group members to interact via networked computers sited in group decision support rooms (French & Xu, 2004; Morton, Ackermann, & Belton, 2003). Currently the use of web-technologies is enabling the development of group decision support for dispersed groups of decision makers facing unstructured strategic decisions.

Individuals working together divide their efforts between three cognitive processes (Nunamaker et al., 1996):

- **Information processing:** storing, retrieving analyzing and summarizing the data needed to support group deliberations.
- **Communication:** people devote their attention to choosing words, behaviours, images, and artefacts, and presenting them

through a medium to the others in the group.
- **Deliberation:** people devote cognitive effort to forming intentions toward accomplishing a goal, including clarifying and formulating the problem, developing and evaluating alternatives, choosing, monitoring, and so on.

When responding to a crisis, a team must bring together the right information, expertise, and leadership ability, and work under time pressure (Briggs, Nunamaker, & Sprague, 1997/1998). In the public sector, crisis teams are often drawn together from several organizations and thus at the outset of an incident, have to come together and form before they can function effectively (Carter & French, 2005). These people must continuously develop and evaluate possible courses of action in response to the unfolding situation – a situation which by its very nature may be entirely unanticipated, very complex and require creative solutions if it is to be managed effectively. This suggests that collaborative systems that support dispersed teams of decision makers could have a significant role in managing crises. Web 2.0 technologies offer many opportunities for developing such support. *ThinkTank* developed by *GroupSystems* is a *w*GDSS offering support for these processes. *ThinkTank* employs a Web 2.0 architecture to support techniques such as brainstorming, organizing ideas, voting on alternatives, prioritizing, building consensus, etc. It also creates a clear, custom output of the content created during the innovation process for alignment on action or for future reference.

In the next section we review general GDSS in a little greater detail before discussing current developments in *w*GDSS. We emphasise some the benefits and challenges that relate the behavioural aspects of groups. Following that we discuss an experiment based on the use of *ThinkTank* to support a dispersed team of managers dealing with a simulated unstructured food safety event. We close with a discussion of future work needed to ensure that *w*GDSS really can usefully support crisis management.

A BRIEF REVIEW OF GDSS AND WEB-BASED COLLABORATION

Early work indicates that using GDSS to support co-located teams within organizations facing complex problems can increase productivity and reducing elapsed hour to reach decisions: Field studies have shown average labour savings of 50% to 70%, and reductions in project cycle time averaging 90% (e.g. Fjermestad & Hiltz, 1998-1999; Grohowski, McGoff, Vogel, Martz, & F., 1990; Post, 1992). Proper use of GDSS can lead to greater group cohesiveness, better problem definition, a wider range of alternative solutions, and stronger buy-in to the final decisions. Features such as parallel input and anonymity can overcome process losses such as production blocking and evaluation apprehension, and thus help the individuals participate more equally and produce more contributions of higher quality (A. R. Dennis, Valacich, & Nunamaker, 1990; Gallupe, Bastianutti, & Cooper, 1991). Anonymity has been long suggested to be helpful in divergent thinking needed for exploring and understanding issues (Linstone & Turoff, 1978; Nunamaker et al., 1996). Working anonymously can encourage group members to view their own ideas more objectively, i.e. the group can separate ideas from the politics behind them and see criticism as a signal to suggest other ideas. Moreover, anonymity frees people to participate without fear of retribution from peers or superiors so that they will reduce the reluctance to contribute information. Production blocking occurs when there are things preventing people's verbalization of ideas, and results in negative influence on idea generation: One may forget an idea while waiting for a turn to speak, or may devote efforts to remembering an idea and become distracted to generate new ones. GDSS enables

parallel input, i.e. the ability of group members to enter information simultaneously, so that participants do not need to wait for others to finish before making their input. Hence, working with GDSS permits groups to collaborate than would otherwise be possible, and many studies report higher quality outcomes and higher satisfaction for groups using GDSS, particularly when they are used as supplementary tools in face-to-face meetings.

Initially GDSS were built on local networking technologies and confined to an organisation and perhaps a specific GDSS room; modern web-technologies allow collaborative participation to take place beyond organisational boundaries. With the advent of web-technologies, it has become possible for the decision makers to be dispersed both in geographic and organisational terms. All they need is access to a web-browser to engage in the deliberation. Although this technology allows for groups to discuss issues, debate objectives, formulate problems, access data and analyse models, vote, decide and implement actions all via virtual meetings with no need for face-to-face meetings, alone it may not be sifficient to make distributed collaboration viable (French, Rios Insua, & Ruggeri, 2007). In organisations with a common culture and common working practices, these tools are proving very successful. But for crisis teams coming from disparate backgrounds, without much experience of working together this may not be true. Moreover, performance of using GDSS to support distributed group collaboration have not been entirely consistent across studies (Bui & Sivasankaran, 1990; A.R. Dennis & Gallupe, 1993; Fjermestad & Hiltz, 1998-1999). Seeking to answer the question whether such a tool can be used in crisis management, we need to keep in mind that technology is only one of many elements of social context that influence patterns of behaviours (Barley, 1986; Orlikowski, 1992). The larger context of human actors, technology, and task properties needs to be considered. Technology is socially constructed by the users in their contexts of use through the different meanings they attach to it and the various features they emphasize and use. A system of high quality should support users in performing their task related activities, meanwhile users need to manipulate and reshape their systems to accomplish tasks and fit in the particular social contexts they work with (Goodhue, 1995; Goodhue & Thompson, 1995).

- **Technology:** Distributed teams often suffer from serious problems because communication through *w*GDSS is limiting and frustrating compared with the conventional face-to-face meetings. Firstly, feedback from others working geographically separately often comes slower than from those working in the same place. Participants can feel alone on the system if they do not receive immediate feedback. They may question whether there is really any value in making contributions, and choose to be observers rather than participants. Secondly, communication with *w*GDSS in a distributed mode is less capable of providing concurrent feedback, i.e. body languages, gestures, expressions and grunts. Such feedback plays an important role in communication and team formation. Team formation is a core stage of collaboration establishing member roles, enabling trust, and helping to create a common language for effective knowledge sharing and communication. The absence of nonverbal communication will reduce social presence and can result in reduced accuracy of communication and increased time to complete a task. Additionally, people working in a distributed mode are more prone to distraction than those who work in the same room. What a virtual team can accomplish depends heavily on getting participants engaged in the process and then maintaining that involvement throughout (Romano, Nunamaker, Briggs, & Vogel,

1998). Lack of such focus can lead the group to disjointed ideas, separate often hidden agendas, and information overload, which may outweigh any possible benefits of them working in a distributed mode.

- **People:** In many countries crisis management is by undertaken by multi-organizational teams (Carter & French, 2005; Niculae, French, & Carter, 2004). The early uses of *w*GDSS have generally been entirely within single organisations; thus the teams concerned have shared common objectives, cultures and working practices. In particularly, they will have been trained in the specific *w*GDSS being used and will use in a variety of situations. Group dynamics and politics can be very different in a crisis management team: No predetermined hierarchical relationships exist within the team. They may lack of commonality in terms of objective, culture, and working practices. There is also a risk for the widely dispersed users, without enough training or support, to misunderstand and misuse the technology. Even if they have used *w*GDSS before, they may have used different systems with different conventions. For groups who work on risk/crisis issues in public sectors, the issue of learning to work together using a particular *w*GDSS might outweigh the gains of not needing to meet face-to-face, even if the system could support all the activities they might need to analyse and manage the situation. In other words, most groups in making public decisions have little prior experience with the *w*GDSS tools, unfamiliar with how to apply the *w*GDSS structures to the task they face. A facilitator can improve group performance by encouraging effective task and relational behaviours (Bostrom, Anson, & Clawson, 1993). Therefore the need for facilitation would be high to providing training to help the group understand how to work together using *w*GDSS. The facilitator also needs to design a structured process to constrain the way in which participants can use the *w*GDSS, so that they are more likely to adapt the *w*GDSS structures in the way intended. Although the art of facilitation in a face-to-face meeting has been long practised and well established, the literature of facilitating virtual meetings where the groups work in separated time or space is minimal (Macauley & Alabdulkarim, 2005; Szerdy & McCall, 1997). Such concerns make the timeliness and effectiveness of using *w*GDSS in virtual meetings more questionable (Carter & French, 2005; Niculae et al., 2004).

• **Task:** Major crisis management and response provides, perhaps, the most unstructured of circumstances in which we have to make decisions. The emergency services are well attuned and trained for dealing with common daily emergencies such as house fires or road accidents. But crises, by which we mean rare events with significant negative impacts that are managed by processes outside those used in normal working, require the managers to develop strategy to deal with novel, dreadfully immediate circumstances. Niculae and French (2005) argue that model-based and data-based GDSS are inappropriate for such major incidents, although many of the current GDSS for crisis management have been developed on such architectures. Rather one needs methods that encourage creative thinking, the exploration and sharing of ideas and perceptions. Thus they argued for the inclusion of many more collaborative technologies in the design of such crisis management systems ideas (see also French, Carter, & Niculae, 2007).

Based upon the discussion above, we ask whether *w*GDSS has a place in risk/crisis management in public sectors. Within the context of a larger experiment within the RELU-Risk project which seeks to investigate how a wider range of stakeholders might participate in the decision making processes (Shepherd et al., 2006), we have tested how a *w*GDSS, *GroupSystems' ThinkTank*, might be used to support deliberation between distributed participants. We report on two small scale experiments using *ThinkTank*. Two scripted food risk/crisis scenarios were utilized to demonstrate the viability of using *ThinkTank* for distributed groups to manage such situations. The first experiment was for trial purposes, and it enabled us to explore some features of *ThinkTank* and to learn how to work with it. The second related to a food safety crisis, and it was to simulate the use of *ThinkTank* in real situation.

EXPERIMENTS

Protocol

Previously we have designed and validated a structured process for conventional face-to-face stakeholder workshops. This protocol has been re-used in the two experiments we conducted with *ThinkTank*, but with modified questions to fit with the current case study. The agenda consists of several stages:

1. **Initial Assessment** to familiarise participants with the problem situation.
2. **Risk identification** to identify the risks along the food chain.
3. **Risk mitigation** to develop possible strategies for managing the problem situation.

At the end, the stakeholders arrived at a mutual agreement on most important strategies that need to be taken to manage the risk/crisis situation. We also collect questionnaires asking people's thoughts at different stages of the process so that their mental models can be analysed and compared.

Experiments

The trial experiment was based on a food safety case study about campylobacter in chicken. The objectives were, firstly, to test how *w*GDSS can be used to support public decision making process, particularly with distributed participants in asynchronous situation; and, secondly, to gain experience in the use of *ThinkTank* in order to plan the next experiment for crisis management situation. 12 postgraduate students were involved in this trial test. The exercise was to inform the participants of the case study and get them engaged in a decision making process to develop and prioritise the risk mitigation strategies in order to reduce the incidence of campylobacter in chicken.

The results from the *ThinkTank* experiment were similar to those from earlier conventional workshops in terms of that all agreed that education at the consumer end of the food chain should be the most important strategy. While the trial experiment seemed to be successful and gives us the confidence to assess *Thinktank* in the pressurised circumstances of a crisis, the process was fraught with challenges that could be improved for future practice: Although the use of *ThinkTank* was limited to several simple operations and most participants had used *ThinkTank* before, it still took quite some time for the participants to get used to the software environment and kicked off the discussion. The trial experiment also suffered problems from getting the participants to focus on the task, particularly in the asynchronous sessions. That could be partly due to the virtual teams lacking feedback mechanisms and nonverbal cues than those who work in the same place at same time as we discussed earlier. In addition, the participants were recruited from students, who were not real problem owners and did not have a direct interest in the task itself. An individual's contribution could not be specifically identified in the experiment due to anonymity. As a result, the participants were more prone to distraction, and were easily engaged in multiple unrelated tasks (See Zhang, Bayley, & French, 2008 for further details on this trial experiment).

In the second experiment, we presented the information of a crisis management case study to a group of participants. The case study has already been used in the face-to-face stakeholder workshops the RELU-Risk project. See Figure 1 for the timeline of the scenario, which evolves into three different stages as information becomes available to the group on a potential food safety issue. The story starts from a report of increased chick mortality and morbidity of chickens, reduced growth rate, ataxia and neck oedema on a broiler farm for over two weeks and another report of a sudden drop in egg production in laying flock. The case study develops to the next stage as chicken samples are submitted for further testing and similar signs are found in other farms. A feed company soon reports to FSA an incident involving probable contamination of poultry feed, which establishes the possibility of the dioxin incident. At the final stage, we present a feed test report conducted by FSA to confirm the cause of the incident and require a communication strategy for press release to the public. The task itself is complex enough to simulate real-world problem solving which involves a small group of key stakeholders, conflicting values, plurality of perspectives, multiple strategies and high levels of uncertainty.

On the basis of the lessons learnt from the trial study, we made several design decisions in developing this second experiment. Firstly, a short pre-training session was carried out before starting the discussion on the real issue so that the participants could get to know the software operation and other participants they were working with. The participants were asked to assume that they were a group of people brought together by the UK Food Standards Agency (FSA) to investigate and offer advice on the incident. They

Figure 1. Timeline of the case study

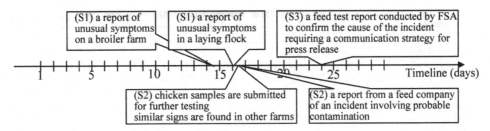

role-played different stakeholders and represented their interests and concerns in the discussion. Each role represented different knowledge and experience from the experts and stakeholders in the real situation and had a vested interest in the outcome, i.e. scientists, retailers, farmers and consumers. To complete the task requires special knowledge not generally available to the public, thus several information packages were prepared about general background of the key stakeholder roles. They were also asked to use aliases to indicate their roles in the discussion so that their contribution could be identified.

Seven postgraduate students and one visiting professor took part in the experiment. The participants were asked to fill in a short questionnaire about their demographic information before the experiment. Among the eight participants, half of them were female, and half among the age of 25 to 35 (two under 25, two above 45). They were all heavy computer users, who connected to the internet at least several times per week. Only one of them had experience using *w*GDSS before but for different conventions, and none of them had used *ThinkTank* before. Nor did any of them have prior experience managing risk/crisis situations involving food-related public issues. Different roles were assigned to each participant according to the subjects they were studying and the relevant prior working experience. The participants did not know each other and had never worked together before the experiment, which to some extent stimulates the real situation that often happens.

The experiment was run in a distributed mode for three hours. The protocol was re-used in this experiment with modified questions to fit with the current case study. The process of initial assessment, risk identification and risk mitigation was repeated at each stage. We started by asking questions about what they needed to know about the situation and who they wanted to ask, what they thought was going on, who they thought were key stakeholders, what actions should/could be taken at that stage, and what they told the stakeholders and general public about the situation. See Figure 2 for a screen shot of the *ThinkTank* interface at this stage. We encouraged divergent thinking among the participants by encouraging them to bring out as many unique ideas as they could in a short periods of time. Often with the help of the facilitator, the ideas were then converged to a reduced number by eliminating those with the same meaning or by abstracting multiple specific concepts into a more general one. The summarised information was then extracted to the following sessions for further analysis techniques, i.e. stakeholder plots and risk assessment. Stakeholder plots help the group identify and prioritise attention on relevant stakeholders (O'Brian & Dyson, 2007). The participants were asked to vote on two 10-point Likert-scale criteria of 'power/influence' and 'stake' for each stakeholder groups they identified. The power/influence dimension refers to the degree to which a party can affect what happens, whereas the stake dimension refers to the degree to which they are affected by what happens. The results were shown in a two dimensional plot. See

Figure 2. A screen shot of the ThinkTank interface - initial assessment

Figure 3. A screen shot of ThinkTank interface - stakeholder plot

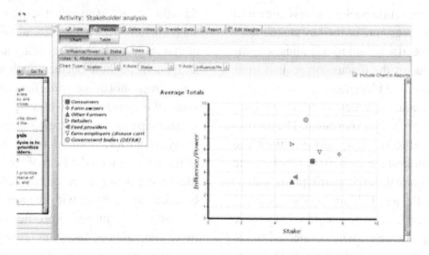

Figure 3. Such analysis influences how decision makers may consider dealing with the relevant stakeholders. The risk assessment technique applied in the experiment was similar to the stakeholder plot. The two defined dimensions which the participants voted on for each risk they identified were likelihood of occurrence and severity of any impact. Such assessment techniques allowed the group to prioritise the key issues and to identify areas of consensus and disagreement so that the group could focus their discussion. Finally, they reached an agreement on the importance of the management strategies by voting based upon different criteria, i.e. feasibility, cost, and effectiveness. The participants were asked to continuously refine their thoughts and judgments in response to the evolving situation, and to make decisions under time pressure. Questionnaires were sent out after each stage of the story asking the participants to write down all their thoughts about the situation, which should include everything in their minds regardless of whether they thought it was relevant or not. The results were used to compare and analyse their mental models.

EVALUATION

We employed a qualitative approach to evaluate this *ThinkTank* experiment based upon the analysis of both the transcript of the discussion and the result of the questionnaires gathered at each stage of the experiment. We assessed several criteria including user-friendliness of the interface, different aspects of the deliberation process associated with the goals of competence, fairness, representativeness, and clarity, and user perceptions of the participation process, i.e. perceived usefulness, perceived ease of use, perceived enjoyment, and user satisfaction.

- **User-friendliness of *ThinkTank* interface:** All the participants used computer and internet in their everyday work and thus we could assume that they had high computer efficacy. Although none of them had experience using *ThinkTank* before, a short pre-training session was carried out before starting the discussion on the real issue. The observation of the process indicated that all the participants were actively expressing their views and commenting on others, thus it seemed that *ThinkTank* interface was user-friendly and all the participants managed to interact with the software very well. The results of the evaluation questionnaire gathered after the experiment showed that most of the participants thought it was easy and flexible to use *ThinkTank* and handle the task. However, several participants noted the low processing efficiency of the system, which could be due to low response efficiency of the web server. They pointed out that their screen froze several times and they had to log out and log in again to make the programme work. One participant was affected so badly that she missed part of the exercise (see the following quotation from a participant's feedback), but she happened

to be the only participant who missed the pre-training session due to late attendance.

I had huge problems using the ThinkTank software and had to constantly log out and log in again. I couldn't cast votes at first because of a lack of responsiveness and it took me a while to figure out that I had to re-boot to get it to work. It was also a problem to read some of the supplementary info. As a result I ended up falling behind and was not able to comment on what I wanted to or to read some comments.

- **Process quality of the task:** Although the exercise was based upon a hypothetical case study and the participants were all students who role-played the stakeholders, we still took some steps to ensure that the decisions were informed with the best available knowledge in order to achieve high competency of the process. Firstly, an information package was sent out to each participant a few days before the experiment to feed him/her with the general background knowledge about his/her role in the experiment. Secondly, two PhD students with strong relative scientific background were assigned the role of scientists and were asked to provide neutral views on the issue based upon their expertise. Thirdly, a vet and a scientist from the RELU-Risk group were invited to the experiment to contribute their scientific knowledge to the participation by providing factual and technical answers arose in the discussion, but they were not allowed to express their personal views. The questionnaire results also suggested that the participants by large thought the information generated in the experiment was in high quality and supportive for them to handle the task. The fairness of the process was reflected in the analysis of the transcript by the number of comments that came out from each participant: 6 participants proposed 25-35 comments, whereas one extreme with 47, the other 15. Though it is worth noting that the participant who only contributed 15 comments was the one who did not manage to work well with *ThinkTank* and claimed to have fallen behind the agenda. We also asked the participants in the questionnaire about their opportunities to express their own views and listen to the others. All the participants thought that they could easily put forward their ideas but two participants pointed out that sometimes they could not get their point across as the conversation easily moved away from the original point it started with. Different interests and concerns, e.g. public health, economic loss, environmental impact, legal issues, were discussed several times in the experiment. The participants also widely agreed different views were presented fairly in the process although one participant argued that the interests of some stakeholder groups might be under-represented because some participants were not playing their roles. The highly-structured protocol which has been used in other workshops we did in the RELU-Risk project was refined and reused in this experiment. The agenda and instructions could be read all the time throughout the discussion process to ensure the transparency of the process. The participants also claimed that the process was clear and supportive for the task, and some suggested that the protocol could be used to support this kind of risk management tasks in future practice. However, some participants did question whether consensus was built too quickly in voting on different ideas. They argued that the discussion needed to be more extensive and elaborative before and/or after prioritisation of the actions.

• The participant's internal beliefs on the usefulness, ease of use and enjoyment of the participatory process and *ThinkTank* groupware were measured by several 5-point Likert scales close-ended questions. As shown in Table 1, the mean value of all the internal beliefs were higher than the neutral value of 3, which indicated that the users generally perceived their experience of the experiment as useful, easy to use and enjoyable. Additionally, the participants' average perceived enjoyment of the experiment was relatively higher than their other beliefs. The participants who experienced problem of using *ThinkTank* rated each of the question items the lowest in the group, which might suggest the user-friendliness of a system could affect one's perceptions of usefulness, ease of use and enjoyable.

We asked an open question in the evaluation questionnaire about whether participants were satisfied with the exercise in terms of the participatory process, the outcome and *ThinkTank* in supporting the task. Not surprising, the participant who claimed *ThinkTank* not easy to use was least satisfied with her experience in the experiment. The other participants were both satisfied with the deliberation process and the interaction with *ThinkTank*. See the following quotations from the questionnaires.

I am dissatisfied only because of the software and the problems I experienced with it. I missed out on participating as much as I would have liked to.

Yes, because many a times one can write more than one can talk about ideas. The opposite also exists but today was one of the former type of discussions. Lots of ideas and critical thinking. ThinkTank is a good way of bringing people of different areas and physically present at different locations together.

Table 1. Descriptive statistics of the variables assessing the user's internal beliefs

Questions	Min	Max	Mean	Std. Dev.
Overall do you feel that a participatory process like this is useful in similar public decision making situations?	2.00	4.00	3.25	.71
Overall do you think that the group support systems like *ThinkTank* are useful to support public participation in similar situations?	1.00	5.00	3.38	1.19
Did you find it easy to get involved in such a participatory process?	2.00	5.00	3.38	.92
Did you find *ThinkTank* easy to use?	1.00	5.00	3.38	1.27
Did you find it enjoyable to be involved in such a participatory process?	3.00	5.00	3.88	.64
Did you find it enjoyable to interact with *ThinkTank*?	1.00	5.00	3.75	1.28

Given that the experiment was based upon a hypothetical scenario and the participants were not potential problem owners, we did not assess its impact, e.g. educational and psychological influence on the participants and the genuine impact on final decision. However, results from analysis of their mental models did suggest that the participants better understood and learned more about the issue after each stage of the experiment.

DISCUSSION

One of us (SF) was quite surprised at the success of the experiment. For the reasons, given earlier in the article, he expected that the lack of history and previous collaboration of the 'team' together with their inexperience would mitigate against their completing the task. However, not only did they complete the task, their solution and performance was similar to that of face-to-face teams who had addressed the issue, including one drawn entirely from FSA members. Clearly, it is impossible to draw any general conclusions from this single experiment, but the findings in *this particular case* indicate that *ThinkTank* provides a medium that can efficiently and effectively facilitate decision making tasks under time pressure in a crisis situation, even when the task at hand is complex and the participants have no prior experience using the software, have not worked together before, have no expertise in the problem domain and are distributed

geographically. For a small group as we had in the experiment, the participants contributed equally to the process and listened to the others. Different ideas were fairly represented. A preliminary comparison of the results of this experiment and our earlier experiments in which the same crisis was managed by a group working face-to-face suggests that the face-to-face workshop seems to be more effective in intense discussion and building consensus, whereas the *w*GDSS seems to be more effective in expanding the discussion and bringing out new ideas in a short-period of time. But obviously all of our conclusions are based upon a very limited experience and are only indications of hypotheses that further research needs to investigate much more carefully.

Our experiments and other experience also suggest some guidelines for these if the teams are to have a fair chance of using the system to its potential. A pre-training session seems helpful in familiarising the users the interface before they enter into discussion of the issue. A non-anonymous approach might be more appropriate where the group is small and the possibility of the occurrence of evaluation apprehensions is low so that the participant's contribution can be identified to improve the trust in the information source that can be easily traced. A facilitator is needed to set up the agenda, organise the session, shape down the ideas and help the participants with difficulties they might face using the system.

CONCLUSION

Given this success, there is clearly a need to perform many more trials and evaluate the effectiveness of *w*GDSS tools for crisis management. However such trials turn out, it seems vital to us that such a programme of investigations *is* carried out. There are cost and time pressures on crisis management teams to adopt such tools. But to do so without full prior evaluation risks mismanagement of the response. We would also emphasise that while we believe that data-based and model-based decision support tools are by themselves insufficient for crisis management (French, Carter et al., 2007; Niculae et al., 2004), equally we would not expect that *w*GDSS will of themselves be sufficient. The three different functionalities – data-based information provision; model-based prediction and evaluation; and collaboration and interaction support – need to be merged into a common architecture to support the *whole* crisis response process.

ACKNOWLEDGMENT

We are grateful to Research Councils UK for funding the RELU-Risk and our partners in that project at the Universities of Leeds and Surrey, the Central Science Laboratory, York, and the Institute of Food Research, Norwich. We thank Gary Barker, John Maule, Andy Hart, Gwendolyn Kolfshoten, Nadia Papamichail and Richard Shepherd for many discussions and help in this work.

REFERENCES

Barley, S. R. (1986). Technology as an Occasion for Structuring: Evidence from Observations of CT Scanners and the Social Order of Radiology Departments. *Administrative Science Quarterly*, *31*(1), 78–108. doi:10.2307/2392767

Bostrom, R., Anson, R., & Clawson, V. (1993). Group facilitation and group support systems. In Jessup, L., & Valacich, J. (Eds.), *Group Support Systems: New Perspectives* (pp. 146–168). New York, NY: Macmillan.

Briggs, R. O., Nunamaker, J. F., & Sprague, R. H. (1997/1998). 1001 unanswered research questions in GSS. *Journal of Management Information Systems*, *14*(3), 3–21.

Bui, T., & Sivasankaran, T. R. (1990). *Relation between GDSS use and group task complexity.* Paper presented at the Proceedings of the Twenty-Third Hawaii International Conference on Systems Sciences, Hawaii

Carter, E., & French, S. (2005). *Nuclear emergency management in Europe: a review of approaches to decision making.* Paper presented at the ISCRAM 2005: Information Systems for Crisis Response and Management, Brussels.

Clemen, R. T., & Reilly, T. (1996). *Making Hard Decisions with Decision Tools* (2nd Edition ed.). Pacific Grove, CA: Duxbury, Thomson Learning.

Dennis, A. R., & Gallupe, R. B. (Eds.). (1993). *A history of GSS empirical research: Lessons learned and future directions*. New York: Macmillan.

Dennis, A. R., Valacich, J. S., & Nunamaker, J. F. (1990). An experimental investigation of small, medium and large groups in an electronic meeting system environment. *IEEE System. Man and Cybernetics*, *25*, 1049–1057. doi:10.1109/21.59968

DeSanctis, G., & Gallupe, B. (1987). A foundation for the study of group decision support systems. *Management Science*, *33*, 589–609. doi:10.1287/mnsc.33.5.589

Eden, C., & Ackermann, F. (1998). *Making Strategy: the Journey of Strategic Management*. London: Sage.

Eden, C., & Radford, J. (Eds.). (1990). *Tackling Strategic Problems: the Role of Group Decision Support*. London: Sage.

Fjermestad, J., & Hiltz, S. R. (1998-1999). An assessment of group support systems experimental research: Methodology and results. *Journal of Management Information Systems*, *15*(3), 127–149.

French, S., Carter, E., & Niculae, C. (2007). Decision Support in Nuclear and Radiological Emergency Situations: Are we too focused on models and technology? *Int. J. Emergency Management*, *4*(3), 421–441. doi:10.1504/IJEM.2007.014295

French, S., Maule, A. J., & Papamichail, K. N. (2008). *Decision Making: Behaviour, Analysis and Support*. Cambridge: Cambridge University Press.

French, S., & Niculae, C. (2005). Believe in the Model: Mishandle the Emergency. *Journal of Homeland Security and Emergency Management*, *2*(1). doi:10.2202/1547-7355.1108

French, S., Rios Insua, D., & Ruggeri, F. (2007). e-participation and decision analysis. *Decision Analysis*, *4*(4), 1–16. doi:10.1287/deca.1070.0098

French, S., & Xu, D.-L. (2004). (in press). Comparison study of multi-attribute decision-analytic software. *Journal of Multi-Criteria Decision Analysis*.

Gallupe, R. B., Bastianutti, L., & Cooper, W. H. (1991). Unblocking brainstorms. *The Journal of Applied Psychology*, *76*(1), 137–142. doi:10.1037/0021-9010.76.1.137

Goodhue, D. L. (1995). Understanding user evaluations of information systems. *Management Science*, *41*(12), 1827–1844. doi:10.1287/mnsc.41.12.1827

Goodhue, D. L., & Thompson, R. L. (1995). Task-technology fit and individual performance. *Management Information Systems Quarterly*, *19*(2), 213–236. doi:10.2307/249689

Gorry, A. G., & Scott-Morton, M. S. (1971). A framework for management information systems. *Sloan Management Review*, *13*, 55–70.

Grohowski, R. B., McGoff, C., Vogel, D. R., & Martz, W. B., & F., N. J. (1990). Implementation of group support systems at IBM. *Management Information Systems Quarterly*, *14*(4), 369–383. doi:10.2307/249785

Linstone, H. A., & Turoff, M. (1978). *The Delphi Method: Techniques and Applications*. London: Addison- Wesley.

Macauley, L., & Alabdulkarim, A. (2005). *Facilitation of e-Meetings: State-of-the-Art Review*. Paper presented at the IEEE International conference on e-technology, e-commerce and e-service, Hong Kong.

Mallach, E. G. (2000). *Decision Support and Data Warehouse Systems*. Boston: McGraw Hill.

Morton, A., Ackermann, F., & Belton, V. (2003). Technology-driven and model-driven approaches to group decision support: focus, research philosophy, and key concepts. *European Journal of Information Systems*, *12*(2), 110–126. doi:10.1057/palgrave.ejis.3000455

Niculae, C., French, S., & Carter, E. (2004). Emergency Management: Does it have a sufficiently comprehensive understanding of decision-making, process and context? *Radiation Protection Dosimetry*, *109*, 97–100. doi:10.1093/rpd/nch257

Nunamaker, J. F., Briggs, R. O., Mittleman, D. D., Vogel, D. R., & Balthazard, P. A. (1996). Lessons from a Dozen Years of Group Support Systems Research: A Discussion of Lab and Field Findings. *Journal of Management Information Systems*, *13*(3), 163–207.

O'Brian, F. A., & Dyson, R. G. (Eds.). (2007). *Supporting strategy: frameworks, methods and models*. Chichester: John Wiley and Sons, Ltd.

Orlikowski, W. J. (1992). The Duality of Technology: Rethinking the Concept of Technology in Organizations. *Organization Science, 3*(3), 398–427. doi:10.1287/orsc.3.3.398

Phillips, L. D. (1984). A theory of requisite decision models. *Acta Psychologica, 56,* 29–48. doi:10.1016/0001-6918(84)90005-2

Post, B. Q. (1992). *Building the business case for group support technology.* Paper presented at the the Twenty-Fifth Annual Hawaii International Conference on System Sciences., Los Alamitos, CA.

Romano, N. C., Nunamaker, J. F., Briggs, R. O., & Vogel, D. R. (1998). Architecture, design, and development of an HTML/JavaScript web-based group support system. *Journal of the American Society for Information Science American Society for Information Science, 49*(7), 649–667. doi:10.1002/(SICI)1097-4571(19980515)49:7<649::AID-ASI6>3.0.CO;2-1

Shepherd, R., Barker, G., French, S., Hart, A., Maule, J., & Cassidy, A. (2006). Managing food chain risks: integrating technical and stakeholder perspectives on uncertainty. *Journal of Agricultural Economics, 57*(2), 313–327. doi:10.1111/j.1477-9552.2006.00054.x

Simon, H. (1960). *The New Science of Decision Making.* New York: Harper and Row.

Szerdy, J., & McCall, M. R. (1997). How to Facilitate Distributed Meetings Using EMS Tools. In Coleman, D. (Ed.), *Groupware: collaborative strategies for corporate LANs and intranets.* Upper Saddle River, NJ: Prentice Hall.

Zhang, N., Bayley, C., & French, S. (2008). *Use of Web-based Group Decision Support for Crisis Management.* Paper presented at the IS-CRAM2008, Washington DC.

ENDNOTE

[1] For discussions of the differing characteristics of strategic, tactical and operational decision maker, see, e.g., Simon (1960) or French *et al.* (2008).

Chapter 5
Incident Command Situation Assessment Utilizing Video Feeds from UAVs:
New Risks for Decision Making Breakdowns

John McGuirl
The Ohio State University, USA

Nadine Sarter
University of Michigan, USA

David Woods
The Ohio State University, USA

ABSTRACT

Past experience has shown that introducing new Information Technologies can have unintended and undesirable consequences, such as new forms of errors and a narrowing of data search activities. Eight Incident Commanders (ICs) took part in a simulated disaster response exercise to determine how the availability of real-time image feeds from a UAV impact on situation assessment and decision-making. The exercise simulated the video feed from an unmanned aerial vehicle (UAV) that allows incident command centers to monitor developments at a crisis site. The results showed that information from the video image channel dominated information available from other channels or in other forms. Nearly all of the ICs failed to detect important changes in the situation that were not captured in the imaging channel but that were available via other, more traditional data sources. The dominance of the image feed resulted in ICs narrowing their data search activities and reducing cross-checking across diverse data sources. This study confirms anecdotal reports that users can over-rely on video feeds from UAVs.

DOI: 10.4018/978-1-60960-609-1.ch005

INTRODUCTION

Decision-makers in complex, naturalistic settings are faced with numerous challenges, including time stress, solving ill-structured problems with limited sometimes unreliable or ambiguous information, and high costs for failure (Klein et al., 1986). In the case of incident command in emergency response and related fields of practice (Davis, 2002; Gilchrist, 2000; Demchak et al., 2007), new technologies are being used to support decision-making by increasing the flow of timely data through new sensors on robotic platforms that provide real-time image streams to decision-makers (e.g., feeds from one or more unmanned aerial vehicles). It is assumed that the video feed from this channel will help incident commanders develop timely situation assessments and allow incident commanders to closely track the activities of responders on the scene as they develop response strategies as they confront various challenges on the ground (Demchak et al., 2006; Rodriguez et al., 2006; MacKenzie et al., 2007; Bergstrand and Landgren, 2009).

However, previous research has shown that introducing new technology into complex fields of practice changes what is expertise, how practitioners coordinate activities, and how systems are able to adapt to surprise and change (Woods and Hollnagel, 2006). This chapter describes a study that examines the consequences of one point of technology change - the introduction of real-time video feeds into emergency management through the use of unmanned aerial vehicles (UAVs). The availability of sensors on UAVs allows incident command centers to monitor developments at the crisis site remotely (McCurdy et al., 2005).

The goal of the study was to assess how this new data channel changes data gathering, integration, and sense making of emergency management decision-makers. Command centers find access to real time images from the scene of interest to be very compelling, but anecdotal reports and observations from exercises and deployments

suggest the new image data channel may be too compelling and lead command decision makers to focus only on information from this one data channel.

In the study the data gathering and sensemaking activities of eight actual incident commanders were tracked as they manage a simulated crisis (petro-chemical plant fire) with access to a real-time video feed of the crisis site. The crisis management exercise evolved in ways designed to challenge incident command decision-making and, in particular, to reveal if the incident commanders over-relied on information coming in through the image data stream and under-utilized information available from other data channels.

The results showed that information from the video channel dominated information available from other channels or in other forms. Nearly all of the ICs failed to detect important changes in the situation that were not captured in the imaging channel but that were available via other data sources. The dominance of the image feed evidenced in how ICs narrowed their data search activities and reduced cross-checking activities across the diverse data sources available to them. This study confirms anecdotal reports that users can over-rely on video feeds from UAVs, and it demonstrates how this over-reliance can distort decision-making. The results suggest new forms of representation are needed to balance information integration across diverse, valuable data sources.

Challenges in Incident Command

Emergency operations management is a classic case of "multi-threaded work" (Woods and Hollnagel, 2006) in which the practitioner must assess the situation by gathering and integrating multiple data sources, detect anomalies in the evolution of events, and exercise authority over a distributed, multi-level organization. In particular, the Incident Commander (IC) must maintain an up-to-date working model of the situation by monitoring incoming data about the evolving threats/disturbances and about how various kinds of resources are needed or being deployed to respond to the threats/disturbances. As the situation and responses evolve, the decision-maker is as "extracting data from disparate sources and combining them in meaningful ways to create a veridical, holistic view of an environment" (Shattuck et al. 2000, p. 478). In incident command status reports arrive from multiple sources at different times and in different formats. As a result, they are stripped of context, parsed, and only contain information about a subset of the overall situation. Their contents must be then transferred and integrated into representations such as maps, white boards, and personal notebooks to place the data into context.

Ideally, ICs would be able to gather this information via direct observation, which would allow them to apply their expertise to draw meaning from the raw data in real-time. However, the physical size of many incidents often limits the IC's ability to directly observe the entire situation. Instead, the majority of the information used by the IC consists of verbal or text-based messages from remote team members. Utilizing data available in these forms of communication can be labor intensive, and result in limited, sometimes inaccurate data exchange. For example, verbal communications between non co-located team members require turn taking between the participants in order to establish and maintain "common-ground" (Clark and Brennan, 1991). While vital for reducing ambiguity, this context building requires continuous effort in a highly dynamic, multi-task environment. Similarly, receiving text-based data from multiple sources can require significant cognitive work to integrate into a cohesive framework. This in turn limits the IC's ability to assess the situation, re-plan, and manage the overall response operation (Brehmer and Allard, 1991; Johansson et al., 2002; Klein, 2007).

Delays in feedback can contribute to the creation of a "buggy model," i.e., an incomplete and/ or erroneous understanding of the situation. This result can undermine a decision-maker's ability to anticipate how the crisis will evolve and be prepared to deal with changes, contingencies, and surprises (Johansson et al, 2002; Woods et al, 2010; Woods and Branlat, 2010). The goal of anticipating events, rather than reacting to them, often drives the IC's desire for more direct, and immediate feedback (Danielsson and Ohisson, 1999).

Supporting Data Analysis and Sense-Making

The dynamic information requirements of the IC can outstrip the availability of data in the course of managing an incident response. The goal then is to enhance the ability of the IC and their staff to quickly obtain relevant information needed to understand the nature and scope of the crisis, to assess the effect of response activities, and to project how the incident may evolve.

One potential solution to the challenges of limited data and feedback delays is to provide the IC and command center personnel with real-time imaging of the incident scene. A key advantage of image-based data over verbal and text-based information is that it transforms the cognitively demanding task of creating and updating a mental model of spatial and temporal relationships into a less demanding perceptual task (Norman, 1993). Video would also allow ICs to observe the dynamics of a crisis in real-time and would therefore enable them to better project how it may develop and how best to respond to those developments. MacKenzie et al. (2007) demonstrated that imaging data could support collaboration between on-site responders and command center personnel. In their study, both mobile and fixed ground level platforms provided still and video imaging to explosives experts at several remote locations during a bomb threat training exercise. They found that by using these imaging tools, the remote experts were able to quickly assess the situation and provide valuable input to the on-site responders. Their analysis showed that different data formats were used for different tasks and in a complementary manner. The higher resolution still images allowed the experts to discern local details that were important for planning purposes, but were not visible in the video, while the live video was preferred for guiding activities such as extricating victims from the scene.

While these results are promising, the ground-based cameras were limited in their field of view. To overcome this problem, some emergency management agencies have begun to employ unmanned aerial vehicles (UAVs) to provide live imaging and video during large-scale emergency responses, such as during wildfires or flooding events (Claessens et al., 2005). The overhead perspective afforded by a UAV is expected to enable ICs to quickly develop a global perspective of the situation and thus support the development of a response strategy (Rodriguez et al., 2006).

Research Objectives

To date, much of the work in this area has focused on how video and imaging data channels can support cooperative work and sense-making. But in practice a new concern has emerged, ironically, perhaps because of the value of the live video feed. Reports from the field comment that the video feeds from UAVs are very compelling to command personnel. So compelling that anecdotal evidence from the field suggests that decision-makers may fixate on the real-time imaging rather than use it to compliment other data sources.

A similar bias has been observed with the use of some automated decision support systems in which there can be a "tendency to use automated cues as a heuristic replacement for vigilant information seeking and processing" (Mosier & Skitka, 1996, p. 205). As a result of this bias, information that conflicts or is inconsistent with what an automated decision aid is presenting is discounted or missed, which leads to failures to revise assessments, hy-

potheses, and plans (Lee & Moray, 1992; Smith et al., 1997; Sarter & Schroeder, 2001; McGuirl & Sarter, 2006). In other words, there is the potential that the ICs may fail to seek out and process cues that conflict with what the video indicates.

This study, rather than establish the potential gains, examined new risks of decision errors as the compelling nature of the video feed from UAVs could narrow data search, reduce corroboration and cross-checking across data sources, and distort situation assessments under certain conditions.

METHODOLOGY

A simulation exercise was developed based on the 1994 accident at the Octel facility in Cheshire, England. The use of an actual event as the basis for the simulation helped to ensure its face validity, which is an important factor in eliciting authentic performance from experienced practitioners (Johansson et al, 2002). This particular event was chosen because of (a) its level of complexity, (b) the availability of post-event analysis and reference materials (Davis, 2002; HSE, 1996), (c) the expectation that, due its location (the UK) the participants would likely not be familiar with the details of this event, and (d) the scenario could not be understood and managed properly if one over relied on data just from the image channel. This last characteristic allowed the scenario to be designed as a *garden path* problem (Johnson et al., 1988; DeKeyser and Woods, 1990; Woods and Hollnagel, 2006) where the early, highly salient cues point to a plausible, but incomplete, or incorrect assessment, while later, less salient cues point to the correct assessment (see Figure 3). In this class of problems, decision makers can fail to revise their situation assessment due to narrow information search, reduced cross checking to corroborate assessments, or discounting information inconsistent with the initial assessment (Patterson et al., 2001; Elm et al., 2005; Grossman et al. 2007).

Figure 1. Workstation setup

Figure 2. Screen capture of imaging

Participants

Eight volunteers were recruited from fire services and emergency management agencies in three different counties in Ohio, USA. All were experienced ICs, with between 2 and 16 years (mean = 6.1 yrs) of experience in incident command.

Set-Up

The simulation exercise was conducted at the Butler County, OH Emergency Management Agency's Operations Center. This facility provided all of the standard sources of information used to manage a crisis of this nature. They included a geographical map of the facility and surrounding area, a facility-layout map, a status board, used to indicate the number and type of assets available and on-site, and material safety data sheets (MSDS), which provide the nature, associated hazards, and recommended tactics to address spills of various chemicals. Weather updates, which included the ambient air temperature, wind speed and direction, and cloud and precipitation conditions were available every 10 minutes.

In addition, a 21" monitor was placed on the left side of the workstation to present the simulated imaging feedback from the UAV (see Figure 1). The UAV imaging was created by digitally enhancing a high-resolution photo of the facility using

Fire Studio 3.0 (Digital Combustion) to produce a video-like presentation (see Figure 2). Due to limitations in the simulation software, the imaging data was limited to a fixed view. However, the participants were only informed of this limitation if they asked to modify the vantage point during the simulation.

Procedure

Prior to beginning the exercise, the participants were given time to ensure they were familiar with the equipment and resources available for conducting the operation. They were informed that they could request any additional information they needed, including details on the facility, the chemical processes, and surrounding areas. A series of data cards (see Table 1) were prepared which contained detailed information on the processes and chemical hazards at the facility. The data cards were used to make the ICs data search and integration processes externalized for the research analysis and is a classic technique. Note that H5 – H8 relate to potential complications and hazards associated with the presence of liquid ethyl chloride or EC (HCL is hydrochloric acid; BLEVE refers to boiling liquid expanding vapor explosion). Answers to queries outside this data set were provided by the experimenter relayed to the IC through the confederate.

Table 1. Data cards

Facility data	Hazard data
F1: Chemicals on site	H1: EC reactor contents
F2: Description of surrounding area/population	H2: Vapor hazards
F3: Fire protection systems (cladding, suppression)	H3: EC exposure standard
F4: Types of chemical & processes on site	H4: EC handling
F5: Chlorine storage area description & location	H5: Boiling point of EC
F6: Number of employees	H6: HCL hazard
F7: Hydrology of area	H7: Liquid EC hazards
	H8: BLEVE conditions
	H9: EC environmental effects

At the start of the simulation, a confederate gave the IC a verbal briefing and hardcopy report of the events leading up to that point in time. The confederate also mediated communications and requests between the IC and the simulated on-site responders, facility employees, and outside agencies. The simulation ran for approximately 90 minutes. It should be noted that it ran in real-time, with no "time-outs" or artificial advances in time. A 30-minute debriefing provided an opportunity to further probe any observations from the simulation session and to capture the subjects' thoughts on the use of the new imaging data.

Simulation Scenario

The ICs assumed command of a HAZMAT event at a large petro-chemical processing facility that produces motor fuel anti-knock compounds. There were approximately 300 employees on-site and a residential development 250 meters from the southwest boundary of the facility. A large vapor cloud was clearly visible in the UAV imaging and was reported to be enveloping an ethyl chloride (EC) processing plant. The second hazard was a large pool of liquid EC collecting near the container tank. However, it was obscured from

view by the vapor. The vapor would breach of the facility boundary at the 70-minute mark and if it was not addressed, the liquid EC would ignite and flash back to the storage tank at the 85-minute mark. Figure 3 shows the timeline of key events in the simulation.

Tasks

The ICs had three main tasks during the simulation: diagnose the threat(s), manage the operation, and conduct three verbal staff briefings. The simulation was not paused while the IC conducted the briefing i.e., events, including changes in the smoke pattern or fires, continued to be displayed in real-time on the monitor.

Diagnose Hazards

The main task was to identify any and all hazard(s) at the facility and to develop a response to contain and minimize the threat(s) to the surrounding population and property.

Manage Operations

As in an actual crisis, the diagnostic task was conducted while also responding, in real-time, to externally-driven events, such as new developments in the situation and fulfilling requests from on-site responders for information, decision-input, or for additional resources (Woods and Hollnagel, 2006). These events were communicated via "injects" which were read to the IC and then presented as a text message by a confederate. Note that the diagnosis and operations management tasks had to be performed concurrently, in that operational demands would occur throughout the simulation. However, while they often represented a source of work, many of the operational events also provided information that could be incorporated into a diagnosis.

There were 22 scheduled update reports and 22 requests from the field requiring a response.

Figure 3. Simulation timeline

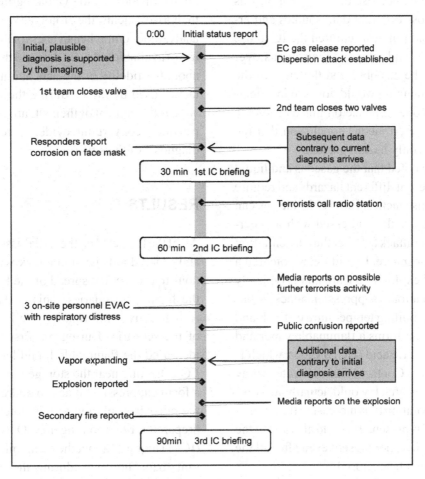

As much as possible, the scenario was adapted to account for the participant's decisions by discarding a pre-planned message if it became irrelevant as a result of an earlier decision. The ICs had the option of verbalizing their responses, recording them on the message form, or both.

Verbal Briefings

The ICs were required to give three, 3 minute verbal assessment reports as if they were updating the center staff on the state of the event and response, at 30, 60, and 90 minutes into the exercise. The reports needed to include a review of the current state and nature of the hazard(s), the planned response(s) (including resource manage-

ment recommendations), and how they expected the situation to evolve until their next briefing in 30 minutes.

Performance Standard

Although there was no single prescribed sequence of actions for properly managing this scenario, a performance standard was developed based on feedback from several subject matter experts. The standard detailed what could be expected from a proficient IC who had been provided with the tools and information contained in the exercise.

All of the information necessary to detect and correctly diagnose the liquid EC hazard, as well as the threat that it presented, was available to the ICs. However, because this information was distributed across different data sources and arrived at different times, it required the IC to use multiple sources and integrate their inputs over time. Because the gas obscured the view of the liquid EC, the imaging would not help in detecting it. Thus an over-reliance on this data source could lead to the erroneous conclusion that the EC gas was the only hazard present.

It should be noted that the gaseous and liquid forms of EC present different hazards and require different response tactics. Ethyl chloride gas can be toxic and is usually addressed with a water-based dispersion attack to lower the concentration level in the atmosphere. Liquid EC is potential a flammable and explosive hazard and is typically addressed with a foam suppression attack. It has a relatively low boiling temperature of 54° F and as it evaporates, it forms a flammable vapor and mist of hydrochloric acid (HCL) vapor, which is highly corrosive. Contact with the water spray from a dispersion attack would actually increase the rate of evaporation thus increasing the amount of flammable gas present. It would also add to the amount of visible vapor present even after all the source valves had been closed.

One verbal report the ICs received from the field stated that after attempting to close one of the main valves responsible for the leaking gas, one of the facility personnel had to be assisted from the area due to corrosion on their face shield. Knowledge of both the boiling point of EC and the new hazard created from its evaporation were important in the simulation because the ambient air temperature rose from 43° F to 54° F during the course of the scenario.

Data Collection and Analysis

Audio and video recordings were made of each session. Verbal and behavioral protocols from these recordings were then used to develop a process trace of each IC's performance (Woods, 1993; Dekker, 2002; Woods et al., 2010; Patterson et al.,

2010). In addition to evaluating the accuracy of their assessments, the protocols were also used to analyze the comprehensiveness of the participants' use of available/relevant data and their skepticism about the fidelity of the data and its source. The tactics used by the IC during the simulation, as well as the content of their situation assessments, provided converging evidence regarding their diagnosis of the situation.

RESULTS

All of the ICs acted on the initial assessment report and ordered a dispersion attack with water cannons to prevent the spread of the EC gas beyond the facility boundaries. This is the appropriate response given information available at the start of the scenario. During his first briefing IC#4 identified the flammable liquid hazard from the EC collecting near the storage unit, and initiated a foam suppression attack to address it. None of the other ICs referred to this potential threat or prepared for this contingency. Only one other IC (IC#1) inquired about the availability of suppressant foam; however, during the debriefing, he indicated that this was a precautionary measure only and not tied to any identified threat. This surprising result suggests that none of the remaining ICs found information or detected any anomalies in the evolution of the crisis that would indicate the need to modify the initial assessment of the situation.

Patterns in Data Search Strategies

A review of the ICs' data requests was performed in order to determine if any patterns existed that correlate to their performance in the diagnosis task. Tables 2 and 3 show which of the facility and hazard data cards each of the ICs selected. The subjects are grouped according to which cards they selected with IC#4's selections highlighted for comparison. Clearly the fact that an IC did

Table 2. Facility data card requests

Facility data	Subject number							
	4	1	5	2	7	3	6	8
F1: Chemicals on site	♦	♦	♦	♦	♦	♦	♦	♦
F2: Description of surrounding area and population	♦	♦	♦	♦	♦	♦	♦	♦
F3: Fire protection systems	♦	♦	♦	♦	♦	♦	♦	♦
F4: Description of the chemical processes at plant	♦	♦	♦	♦	♦	♦	♦	♦
F5: Description of the chlorine storage area	♦	♦	♦					
F6: Number of employees at facility						♦	♦	♦
F7: Hydrology of area								

not request a specific piece of information does not necessarily mean that they did not possess it through some other means, i.e., prior experience. Therefore it was important to analyze these results in the context of the planning and assessments as described below.

Table 2 shows that IC#4's facility data requests were not unique. In fact, details about the on-site chemicals, processes, and fire protection systems as well as the surrounding population (F1 through F4) were universally selected. ICs 1, 4, and 5 also requested additional information on the nature of the chlorine storage facility and its location (F5).

Table 3 shows a more interesting difference between IC#4's data requests and the rest of the ICs with regards to the search of chemical hazard data. Only IC#4 requested information about the boiling point of EC and the potential hazards of liquid ethyl chloride (H5 and H7).

A separate review was also conducted to elicit any patterns specific to the use of the imaging, including the timing and relative frequency of sampling and if it was coordinated with other data sources. Although eye tracking data was not collected, analysis of the behavioral protocols indicates that IC#4 sampled the imaging less frequently and he tended to sample it only during relatively low tempo periods, i.e., when no updates or external demands had recently been received. In contrast, the other ICs would often reference

Table 3. Chemical hazard data card requests

Facility data	Subject number							
	4	1	2	5	3	8	6	7
H1: EC reactor contents	♦	♦	♦	♦	♦	♦	♦	♦
H2: EC vapor hazards	♦	♦	♦	♦	♦	♦	♦	♦
H3: EC exposure standard		♦	♦	♦			♦	
H4: EC handling procedure	♦	♦	♦	♦				
H5: Boiling point of EC	♦							
H6: Hazards associated with HCL		♦						♦
H7: Hazards associated with liquid EC	♦							
H8: BLEVE conditions								
H9: Environmental impact of EC								

Table 4. Protocol excerpt from IC#4 assessment #1

Actions / **Dialogue**	**Commentary**
Requests updates from the plant and local hospitals. "Do we have any casualties reported?"	The requested information aids in assessing the scope and scale of the situation.
Initially looks at display, then refers to the facility map to orient, then back to monitor. "OK, its just the cloud. Looks like it's headed…what direction is that? OK, east towards the town.	Coordinating the map and imaging compass headings and establishing reference points.
Turns from the monitor and reviews the listing of chemicals used and processes conducted at the plant. Requests updates from the site and facility information. "It's a chlorine plant, wow, chlorine is the worst. That's going back to the fire liaison for information about how those (chemicals) can affect each other and if the chlorine has been affected at this point..."	Gathering data from multiple sources to model and anticipate possible interactions and future developments.
Sweeps hand over the monitor in the direction of the town "We'll need to evacuate that area. I'll have my HAZMAT guy determine the area (to evacuate)".	Establishes a plan of action for the current threat. Defers to staff member to work out details.

the monitor when a verbal update arrived and attempt to locate the position of the event being reported on the screen.

Situation Assessments

Situation assessment in incident command is an example of inferential analysis in which the decision-maker must often develop a suitable explanation for uncertain, incomplete, and contradictory information, and adopt a course of action that is as flexible, adaptive, and robust as possible (Patterson et al., 2001).

A review of the protocols from the twenty-four verbal reports indicates that none of the ICs except #4 revised their situation assessments to include additional hazards beyond the toxic gas release. This is indicated by the lack of any direct references to additional potential hazards, but also in the preparations and contingency plans they developed. A review of IC#4's protocols, as shown in Table 4, also reveals that although there was significant overlap in the data requested, he consistently requested verification of the data as well as the underlying assumptions associated with it (particularly if it did not originate from fire service personnel). For example, while referencing the MSDS (material safety data sheets) to verify the response strategy employed by the

facility personnel, he noted the low boiling point of liquid EC. Although the presence of liquid EC was not indicated in the initial briefing, this cross-check of the response strategy yielded data that, in conjunction with other information, supported another hypothesis and line of reasoning.

Table 5 provides an excerpt from IC#3's final assessment but it provides a sample of the type of dialogue observed in the other ICs' (except #4) reports. It suggests that the ICs' tended to focus more on the physical and spatial relationships to a greater degree than IC#4. In contrast, IC#4 appears to have focused more on the functional

Table 5. Protocol excerpt from IC#3 assessment #3

Actions/**Dialogue**	**Commentary**
Sweeps hand over the center of the display "I've got the plant evacuated" *Pulls hand away from monitor* "My firefighters are backed off" *Sweeps hand around the monitor* "The community has been evacuated"	Appears focused on spatial relationships with the monitor as the sole reference.
Points to the site of the EC leak at lower right hand corner of the display "I've got water going on the leak and on the tanks"	
"Looks like we're spreading…is that another fire?"	Observes a new fire near the EC leak and terminates report.

relationships and interactions between elements in the EC processing system.

Methodological Considerations

Some limitations in the present study warrant discussion. This study was exploratory in nature, with the goal of determining if the phenomena that had been reported in the field could be duplicated. As such, it lacked a baseline condition, which would have allowed for the measurement of the effects this new technology had on performance.

It is possible that the novelty of the imaging feed could have made the ICs more likely to use information available through the video feed in developing their assessment and planning activities. On the other hand, they have much more experience using more traditional data sources. In addition, the image source (the simulated UAV) was not controllable. If the ICs had the ability to change views, they could have been drawn more deeply into the 'picture' provided by that source to the exclusion of information available only through other channels.

DISCUSSION

The main tasks in the exercise were to correctly identify all of the hazards and to apply the appropriate responses as quickly as possible. Only one of the ICs maintained a broad data search strategy and revised the initial, erroneous assessment that only one hazard was present.

As indicated in Table 3, IC#4 referenced key data regarding the properties and hazards associated with liquid EC that the other ICs did not. This suggests that he was pursuing an alternate hypothesis from the gas cloud hazard that the other ICs followed. Additionally IC#4 spent less time observing the video, even when highly salient cues were being displayed on the monitor.

He also questioned the accuracy of incoming data more often by comparing it to other relevant indicators, even during high tempo periods i.e., when multiple updates were arriving. This comparative exercise, also known as crosschecking, can often reveal inconsistencies between data sources, which may indicate flaws in the current analysis (Patterson et al., 2004; Elm et al., 2005; Grossman et al., 2007). Recall that the initial assessment provided by the facility staff indicated that a toxic vapor release had occurred, which, while not erroneous, was an incomplete description of the problem. The imaging supported this incomplete assessment not only by highlighting the vapor hazard, but also by masking other relevant cues, such as a pool of liquid EC at the base of the processing plant. Therefore, additional sources of information needed to be accessed to obtain the correct and complete assessment of the incident.

The remaining ICs did not pursue as broad of a search strategy and as a result, they failed to incorporate important facts that were available from other sources into their working hypothesis of the nature of the hazard. They also appear to have spent more time observing the monitor than IC#4. In fact, during the staff briefings, several of the ICs used the monitor as a substitute for a paper map when discussing their strategy and the deployment of assets.

The results corroborate the reports from the field that video images from UAVs are compelling and tend to dominate information search and situation assessment. The next question becomes—why does the video feed dominate other data sources?

Seeing is Believing?

Due to the nature of their work, and their extensive field experience, ICs typically place a high level of trust in visual evidence and in their ability to evaluate a situation based on direct, visual observation (Page, 2005). It has also been suggested that the fire service's emphasis on a "hands on approach" engenders a belief that "seeing is believing" (Gilchrist, 2000; Page, 2005). Therefore it is possible that the more familiar format of the imagining garnered greater trust, than the other sources of information data.

In addition to being a new source of visual data, the overhead view provided by the simulated UAV feed also gave the IC a "global" perspective that is unavailable from ground-based resources. This unique perspective, along with the use of a large, high-resolution monitor may have contributed to the perceived fidelity of the imaging and consequently, to a perception as a highly reliable means to see the overall situation.

Also, compared to verbal messages, which are transient in nature, and text-based data, which can be obscured or misplaced at a workstation, the real-time imaging was continuously available to the IC and easily observable. Thus, it could be argued that the imaging was a more salient cue in the environment relative to the other available information sources.

However, while it afforded the ability to see spatial relationships, it did not reveal functional relationships and therefore, did not contain all of the necessary information. It is possible that the principle of "seeing is believing" led to a "surface/deep" oversimplification in which an emphasis is given to the interpretation afforded by surface cues, when in reality, a deeper search is required to uncover important cues (Feltovich et al, 1997). With an unprocessed image, the task of detecting the relevant cues from the context-rich, detailed background is left to the observer, as IC#4 comments:

"I found it distracting to corroborate this (map of the facility) and the video - both because they're not to scale and they differ. It was simpler to look at the map because it's all theory; it's all strategy". – IC #4

The terms "theory" and "strategy" seem to refer to the sparse, abstract nature of the line drawing map, which allowed greater focus on the relevant relationships directly related to certain tasks, which in this case was the planning of a potential evacuation.

Timing is Everything

In highly dynamic environments, the perceived value of information is highly correlated with its currency, or as one IC commented: "newest equals best". In other words, the latest updates provide the most relevant information. It is clear that in order to define a problem in a dynamic environment, the decision-maker needs information about any changes in the world that may impact the validity of their model and redefine what viable options exist. For example, physical maps of the incident area are typically used to plan the routing and positioning of resources relative to the area of interest. However, because they depict conditions prior to the incident, local operators must often adapt or even discard their initial plans due to unforeseen circumstances, such as restricted access or other unexpected hazards.

The reasonable assumption made by the ICs was that the real-time imaging addressed this deficiency and was accurately reflecting the current state of the situation. As summarize in this debriefing comment:

"The (paper) map obviously wasn't accurate. Once that gets to a certain point, it becomes distracting. This (the monitor) was accurate; you can't dispute that." The video can never be obsolete." – IC#6

The perceived value of the imaging data, and thus its dominance in framing the problem for the ICs, may have been due to its immediacy. It provided current information directly to the IC in an environment where information often arrives slowly and is dependent on mediation through (several) other individuals.

However, most of the ICs did not balance their information search across all data channels and missed important information. Also they did not crosscheck their assessment sufficiently using other data channels. While video can support the discovery and exploration of a solution space, it does not contain all of the necessary information and, as this study has shown, it can potentially obscure important features in that space.

This study provides the first empirical confirmation of the observations and reports from the field that command center personnel can become fixated on the video feeds from UAV resources and over-rely on the information available from that source and undervalue or miss information only available from other sources. The study indicates that the new technological resource, while providing benefits, also creates new vulnerabilities (Woods et al., 2010). The challenge is to preserve the benefits while providing new visualizations or other mechanisms that help incident command to balance information search over all of the data channels/information resources available (Woods and Sarter, 2010), to better cross-check sources and findings in order to revise assessments (Patterson et al., 2001), and to avoid premature narrowing in on one assessment or hypothesis (Woods and Hollnagel, 2006).

Future work should develop and test new representations that can support a broad utilization of data from all sources and support hypothesis generation, evaluation and revision (Norman, 1993; Elm et al., 2005). For example, new visualizations could encourage a more balanced monitoring across multiple data sources, new analytic tools can suggest areas where cross-checks may be needed or fruitful. One example of this approach is the Wireless Internet Information System for Medical Response in Disasters (WIISARD) (Demchak et al, 2006, 2007). The system consolidates multiple data feeds regarding such things as patient location, status, and the location of hot zones, to create information overlays which can then be combined with a video image, or a map to provide context for the command center personnel. The result is a display in which the video image is merely the framework in which the context is supported.

The Liveresponse system (Bergstrand and Landgren, 2009), also incorporates video into a larger display that includes map services with GPS data. This system was tested during a series of actual responses to major traffic accidents, with the on-site IC broadcasting live video feed from a hand held camera. In the debriefings, the command center personnel stated that viewing the video data improved their ability to gauge resource requirements and enhanced their understanding of the nature and the extent of the incident. The ICs considered it important that the command center personnel were able to see what they were seeing, which is consistent with the concept of maintaining "common ground". However, while a live broadcast was always available to the command center personnel, their tasks often did not allow them to view it in real-time. Instead, they reviewed it "near live", i.e., within minutes of being broadcast, and used it to develop their action plans, which involve a longer time horizon than that of the on-site responders.

Another visualization approach is to provide new perceptual interfaces that support perspective shifts (McCurdy et al., 2005; Morison et al., 2009). While the simulated UAV in this study only provided a single perspective of the scene of interest, actual UAV and sets of sensors can provide multiple perspectives. New interfaces for perspective taking can help commanders stay close to the scene of action via some perspectives while also allowing them to smoothly step back to take a more global view that supports strategic analysis. Image overload from one or more sensor feeds is becoming the critical bottleneck in seizing the opportunity provided by new sensing technology. New perceptual and attentional interfaces may be needed to overcome this form of data overload (Woods and Sarter, 2010).

While improved interfaces and representations can support sense-making and data search, other approaches are also relevant. One is use interactive critiquing technology to encourage the exploration of alternative hypotheses and enhance anomaly detection (Smith et al., 1997). The scenario simulation/garden path problem itself could serve as the basis for a training module designed to help incident commands practice better information search and integration by confronting some of the vulnerabilities that could trap them. And many researchers are searching for aids to support sense-making (Klein and Moon, 2006).

CONCLUSION

This study provides empirical evidence to support the anecdotal reports that real-time, image-based feeds can dominate other sources of data in command decision making. Second, the study shows that this characteristic of the video feed distorts the data search, situation assessment and revision processes. The dominance of data available from the video feed back can result in a premature narrowing of both data search activities and the exploration of a solution space can have an adverse effect on data search and analysis activities. The results suggest that this new resource, while holding promise for supporting information analysis, can also have a strong framing effect, which can result in a premature narrowing of both data search activities and the exploration of a solution space. Similar risks of premature narrowing have been identified in related studies of data overload in intelligence (Patterson et al., 2001; Zelik et al., 2010).

While the results document a new vulnerability, they should not be interpreted as undercutting the value of new sensors that connect distant commanders to the scene of interest. Rather the results show the need for continued innovation of new visualizations and interfaces to seize the opportunity created by the new technologies and to avoid predictable negative side effects of this episode of technology change.

ACKNOWLEDGMENT

We wish to thank all of the study participants for their time, efforts and valuable feedback. Special thanks also go the Butler County Emergency Management Agency for its support of this project. This research was prepared, in part, through collaborative participation in the Advanced Decision Architectures Consortium sponsored by the U. S. Army Research Laboratory under the Collaborative Technology Alliance Program, Cooperative Agreement DAAD19-01-2-0009, and through support from the Eddowes Memorial Endowment, The Ohio State University.

REFERENCES

Bergstrand, F., & Landgren, J. (2009). Information sharing using live video in emergency response work. *Proceedings of the 6th International ISCRAM Conference.*

Brehmer, B., & Allard, R. (1991). Dynamic decision-making: The effects of task complexity and feedback delays. In Rassmussen, J., Brehmer, B., & Leplat, J. (Eds.), *Distributed decision making: Cognitive models for cooperative work* (pp. 319–334). New York, NY: Wiley.

Claessens, M., Lewyckyj, N., Biesemans, J., & Everarerts, J. (2005). Pegasus, a UAV project for disaster management. *Proceedings of the 2nd International ISCRAM Conference* (pp. 233-236).

Clark, H. H., & Brennan, S. (1991). Grounding in communication. In Resnick, L., Levine, J., & Teasley, S. (Eds.), *Socially shared cognition*. Washington, DC: American Psychological Association. doi:10.1037/10096-006

Danielsson, M., & Ohisson, K. (1999). Decision-making in emergency management: A survey study. *International Journal of Cognitive Ergonomics, 3*, 91–99. doi:10.1207/s15327566ijce0302_2

Davis, D. (2002). Fire commander. In Flin, R., & Arbuthnot, K. (Eds.), *Incident Command: Tales from the hot seat* (pp. 88–104). Burlington, VT: Ashgate Publishing Ltd.

De Keyser, V., & Woods, D. D. (1990). Fixation errors: Failures to revise situation assessment in dynamic and risky systems. In Colombo, A. G., & Saiz de Bustamante, A. (Eds.), *Systems reliability assessment*. Dordrechts, The Netherlands: Kluwer Academic.

Dekker, S. W. A. (2002). *The field guide to human error investigations*. Burlington, VT: Ashgate Publishing Ltd.

Demchak, B., Chan, T. C., Griswold, W. G., & Lenert, L. (2006). Situation awareness during mass-casualty events: Command and control. *AMIA Annual Symposium Proceedings* (p. 905).

Demchak, B., Griswold, W. G., & Lenert, L. A. (2007). Data quality for situational awareness during mass-casualty events. *AMIA Annual Symposium Proceedings* (pp. 176-180).

Digital Combustion, Inc. (2004). *Fire Studio 3.0* (computer software).

Elm, W., Potter, S., Tittle, J., Woods, D., Patterson, E., & Grossman, J. (2005). Finding decision support requirements for effective intelligence analysis tools. *Proceedings of the Human Factors and Ergonomics Society 49th Annual Meeting* (pp. 297-301).

Feltovich, P. J., Spiro, R. J., & Coulson, R. L. (1997). Issues of expert flexibility in contexts characterized by complexity and change. In Feltovich, P. J., Ford, K. M., & Hoffman, R. R. (Eds.), *Expertise in context: Human and machine*. Menlo Park, CA: AAAI/MIT Press.

Gilchrist, I. (2000). *An analysis of the management of information on the fire service incident ground*. (Unpublished doctoral dissertation). University of Manchester, UK.

Grossman, J., Trent, S., Patterson, E. S., & Woods, D. D. (2007). Supporting the cognitive work of information analysis and synthesis: A study of the military intelligence domain. *Proceedings of the Human Factors and Ergonomics Society 51st Annual Meeting* (pp. 348-352).

HSE. (1996). *The chemical release and fire at the Associated Octel Company Ltd*. Sudbury, MA: HSE Books.

Johannson, B., Hollnagel, E., & Granlund, A. (2002). The control of unpredictable systems. In C. Johnsson (Ed.) *Proceedings of the 21st European Annual Conference on Human Decision Making and Control*. GIST Technical Report G2002-1, Department of Computing Science, University of Glasgow, Scotland.

Johnson, P. E., Moen, J. B., & Thompson, W. B. (1988). Garden path errors in diagnostic reasoning. In Bolec, L., & Coombs, M. J. (Eds.), *Expert system applications*. New York, NY: Springer-Verlag.

Klein, G., Moon, B., & Hoffman, R. R. (2006, July/August). Making sense of sensemaking 1: Alternative perspectives. *IEEE Intelligent Systems*, 22–25.

Klein, G. A. (2007). Flexecution as a paradigm for replanning, part 1. *Intelligent Systems, 22*(5), 79–83. doi:10.1109/MIS.2007.4338498

Klein, G. A., Calderwood, R., & Clinton-Cirocco, A. (1986). Rapid decision making on the fire ground. *Proceedings of the Human Factors Society 30th Annual Meeting*, (pp. 576-580).

Lee, J., & Moray, N. (1992). Trust and the allocation of function in the control of automatic systems. *Ergonomics, 35*, 1243–1270. doi:10.1080/00140139208967392

MacKenzie, C., Fu-Ming Hu, P., Fausboll, C., Nerlich, M., Benner, T., & Gagliano, D. (2007). Challenges to remote emergency decision-making for disasters or Homeland Security. *Cognition Technology and Work, 9*, 15–24. doi:10.1007/s10111-006-0051-y

McCurdy, N. J., Griswold, W. G., & Lenert, L. A. (2005). Reality fly through: Enhancing situational awareness for medical response to disasters using ubiquitous video. *AMIA Annual Symposium Proceedings* (pp. 510-514).

McGuirl, J. M., & Sarter, N. B. (2006). Supporting trust calibration and the effective use of decision aids by presenting dynamic system confidence information. *Human Factors, 48*(4), 656–665. doi:10.1518/001872006779166334

Morison, A. (2009). Integrating diverse feeds to extend human perception into distant scenes. In McDermott, P. (Ed.), *Advanced decision architectures for the Warfighter: Foundation and technology*. Alion Science.

Mosier, K. L., & Skitka, L. J. (1996). Human decision makers and automated decision aids: Made for each other? In Parasuraman, R., & Mouloua, M. (Eds.), *Automation and human performance: Theory and applications* (pp. 201–220). Mahwah, NJ: Lawrence Erlbaum Associates, Inc.

National Research Council. (2006). *Facing hazards & disasters: Understanding human dimensions*. Washington, DC: National Academy Press.

Norman, D. A. (1993). *Things that make us smart: Defending human attributes in the age of the machine*. Reading, MA: Addison-Wesley Publishing.

Page, D. (2005). Seeing is believing. *Fire Chief*, September, 2005. Retrieved from http://firechief.com/tactics/command_camera_092305/

Patterson, E. S., Cook, R. I., Woods, D. D., & Render, M. L. (2004). Examining the complexity behind a medication error: Generic patterns in communication. *IEEE SMC Part A, 34*(6), 749–756.

Patterson, E. S., Roth, E. M., & Woods, D. D. (2001). Predicting vulnerabilities in computer-supported inferential analysis under data overload. *Cognition Technology and Work, 3*, 224–237. doi:10.1007/s10111-001-8004-y

Patterson, E. S., Roth, E. M., & Woods, D. D. (2010). Facets of complexity in situated work. In Patterson, E. S., & Miller, J. (Eds.), *Macrocognition metrics and scenarios: Design and evaluation for real-world teams*. Aldershot, UK: Ashgate.

Rodriguez, P. A., Geckle, W. J., Barton, J. D., Samsundar, J., Gao, T., Brown, M. Z., & Martin, S. R. (2006). An emergency response UAV surveillance system. *AMIA Annual Symposium Proceedings* (p. 1078).

Shattuck, L. G., Graham, J. M., Merlo, J. L., & Hah, S. (2000). Cognitive integration: A study of how decision makers construct understanding in evolving contexts. In *Proceedings of the Human Factors Society 44th Annual Meeting*, (pp. 478-482). Santa Monica, CA: Human Factors and Ergonomics Society.

Smith, P. J., McCoy, C. E., & Layton, C. (1997). Brittleness in the design of cooperative problem-solving systems: The effects on user performance. *IEEE Transactions on Systems, Man, and Cybernetics, 27*, 360–371. doi:10.1109/3468.568744

Woods, D. D. (1993). Process-tracing methods for the study of cognition outside the experimental psychology laboratory. In Klein, G. A., Orasanu, J., Calderwood, R., & Zsambok, C. E. (Eds.), *Decision making in action: models and methods* (pp. 228–251). Norwood, NJ: Ablex Publishing Corporation.

Woods, D. D., & Branlat, M. (2010). How adaptive systems fail. In Hollnagel, E., Paries, J., Woods, D. D., & Wreathall, J. (Eds.), *Resilience engineering in practice*. Aldershot, UK: Ashgate.

Woods, D. D., Dekker, S. W. A., Cook, R. I., Johannesen, L. L., & Sarter, N. B. (2010). *Behind Human Error* (2nd ed.). Aldershot, UK: Ashgate.

Woods, D. D., & Hollnagel, E. (2006). *Joint cognitive systems: Patterns in cognitive systems engineering*. Boca Raton, FL: Taylor & Francis. doi:10.1201/9781420005684

Woods, D. D., & Sarter, N. B. (2010). Capturing the dynamics of attention control from individual to distributed systems. *Theoretical Issues in Ergonomics*, *11*(1), 7–28. doi:10.1080/14639220903009896

Zelik, D. Patterson. E. S., & Woods, D. D. (2010). Measuring attributes of rigor in information analysis. In E. S. Patterson & J. Miller (Eds.), *Macrocognition metrics and scenarios: Design and evaluation for real-world teams*. Aldershot, UK: Ashgate.

Chapter 6

When and How (Not) to Trust It?
Supporting Virtual Emergency Teamwork

Monika Büscher
Lancaster University, Denmark

Preben Holst Mogensen
University of Aarhus, Denmark

Margit Kristensen
The Alexandra Institute Ltd., Denmark

ABSTRACT

In this article we use the formative evaluation of a prototype 'assembly' of pervasive computing technologies to specify design implications for emergency virtual teamwork tools. The prototype assembly, called "Overview", was implemented in collaboration with police, fire and medical emergency services as part of the real life event management during the Tall Ships' Races 2007 in Denmark. We describe how the emergency teams used the technologies for collaboration between distributed colleagues, to produce shared situation awareness, to manage efforts and resources and respond to minor emergencies. Trust in technology is a key need virtual teams identify in their endeavours to dovetail innovative technologies into emergency work. We show how practices of working up trust are supported by the PalCom open architecture (which was used to build Overview), and delineate design guidelines to enable the productive integration of pervasive computing.

INTRODUCTION

Pervasive computing technologies have great potential to augment the work of distributed 'virtual' emergency teams. Experimental R&D shows that interactive maps, mobile and wearable devices, sensor-networks, location tracking, and ambient technologies (e.g. CCTV) could support en route sense-making (Landgren, 2005), risk assessment, resource allocation and communication (Jiang, Hong, Takayama & Landay, 2004), reasoning about conditions on the ground (Betts, Mah, Papasin, del Mundo, McIntosh & Jorgensen, 2005), reconnaissance and navigation (Denef, Ramirez, Dyrks, Stevens 2008), and in-field patient triage and tracking (Lorincz, Malan, Fulford-Jones,

DOI: 10.4018/978-1-60960-609-1.ch006

Nawoj, Clavel, Shnayder, Mainland, Welsh & Moulton, 2004). However, in practice, the potential of pervasive computing is hard to unlock. Erika Frischknecht Christensen, Medical Director of Pre-hospital care, Central Denmark Region, pinpoints why:

... everybody talks about wireless monitoring, but I haven't seen it work so far. I think one of the things is ... how do I identify the patients, am I sure that what I see on the screen is actually that patient and not that patient? (Discussion, December 2007)

Frischknecht identifies a key need virtual teams encounter in dovetailing innovative technologies into safe emergency work practices: People must be able to trust their technologies.

This is a 'Catch 22' challenge. Trust in technology is 'accepted dependability' (Avizienis, Laprie, Randell & Landwehr, 2004). It grows as technologies become more dependable and familiar, but to become dependable and familiar technologies must be tested in use when they cannot (yet) be trusted. This is particularly difficult in emergency work, where only controlled leaps of faith, combining 'graceful augmentation' (Jul, 2007) with safe levels of redundancy in experimental but realistic use of new technologies will allow innovations to be adopted. This strategy is currently ill supported by many pervasive computing technologies.

In his pioneering vision for 'ubiquitous' computing, it was Mark Weiser's 'highest ideal to make a computer so imbedded, so fitting, so natural, that we use it without even thinking about it." (http://www.ubiq.com/ubicomp/). Weiser's call to make the computer 'invisible' has been enthusiastically interpreted, most often literally. For all the right reasons – e.g. to protect responders from additional work and complexity overload – designers seek to hide computing by embedding it in devices, environments (Lorincz et al, 2004), even clothing (Rantanen, Impiö, Karinsalo, Malmivaara, Reho, Tasanen & Vanhala, 2002), by making it

'autonomous' (Fiedrich, 2000), self-healing, and context-aware (Lorincz et al, 2004). While we value the power of these approaches, we also believe that they can – paradoxically – hamper what they seek to support. This is because Weiser's main concern was not invisibility *per se*, but 'invisibility-in-use', synonymous with the phenomenological notion of 'ready-to-hand', meaning that users are able to focus on their work rather than on their technologies. In this process, trust is not a state of mind, or once-and-for-all accepted dependability, but an ongoing practical achievement. Just as people come to trust other people because they continuously (often precognitively) observe and probe their behaviour in different situations (Boden & Molotch, 1994), people work up trust in technologies through ongoing practical engagement with them (Clarke, Hardstone, Rouncefield & Sommerville, 2006). However, if the technologies are designed to hide their states and processes, people have no basis on which to build their trust. In a conceptual framework for 'palpable computing' we argue that in order to understand and trust technologies people must be able to sense what these technologies are doing or could do for them (Kyng, 2007). To this aim, we have developed an open software architecture and prototype technologies that support people in making computing palpable (Andersen, 2007).

In what follows, we describe a key stage in this endeavour: the experimental deployment of a prototype assembly of pervasive computing technologies – the *'Overview'* – during the Tall Ships' Races 2007 (TSR), in Aarhus, Denmark. In collaboration with police, fire and medical emergency services we enabled the flexible integration and interrogation of existing and prototypical pervasive computing technologies as part of the real life event management, utilizing the PalCom open architecture. The main purpose was to evaluate a) the usefulness of *Overview*, and b) the usefulness of the PalCom architecture. When, and more practically *how*, (not) to trust the technologies emerged as a crucial issue for end users and developers. We discuss how the emergency virtual teams used the technologies for collaboration between distributed colleagues, to produce shared situation awareness, to manage efforts and resources and respond to minor emergencies. Our three examples show how trust in technologies was practically achieved and provide important lessons for design. To sum up, we describe three key implications for design and argue that attention to these challenges could facilitate the productive integration of pervasive computing technologies in emergency virtual teamwork.

BACKGROUND

Design for palpability and trust demands a fundamental re-orientation of pervasive computing principles and this is our primary concern. But such 'large' design aims are best achieved through ethnographically informed, experimental and iterative participatory design (Büscher, 2006; Kristensen, Kyng & Palen, 2006; Büscher, Kristensen & Mogensen, 2007). In a 4 year research project called PalCom (http://ist-palcom.org) we have used a nested participatory design approach, developing a range of pervasive computing application prototypes as a vehicle for the design of more fundamental architectural support (Büscher, Christensen, Hansen, Mogensen & Shapiro 2008). *Overview* has been developed close to 'product stage', aimed to support emergency responders, and through its experimental deployment during TSR we explore key use requirements in emergency virtual teamwork. Apart from trust in technology, the most significant problems – and opportunities – for design that this long-term collaboration with first responders has identified centre on:

Collaboration, coordination and improvisation. Crises require collaboration and unified management, but make their ongoing achievement difficult (Wachtendorf & Kendra, 2005). The need to establish priorities through inter/intra-

organizational communication is often frustrated through disrupted or inoperable communication infrastructures (The White House, 2006). As these are patched with temporal solutions, interoperability and resilience become a concern. Speedy, reliable communication is also key to integrating capabilities provided by the military, volunteers, or the public (Palen & Liu, 2007). Support for accountable and collaborative improvisation is lacking.

Overview and Situation awareness. The ability to gather and use reliable information to make decisions and project future developments is crucial for accurate overview, comprehension and communication of what has happened (Endsley, Bolté & Jones, 2003). Speed is important, but appropriateness of response ranks even higher. First responders often receive multiple reports from several sources and experience complex 'symptoms' at multiple sites under great pressure to act immediately (Greater London Authority, 2006; Martin & Bowers, 1997). This hampers the production and communication of accurate assessments of the incident, its causes and unfolding effects.

Overview seeks to support collaboration, coordination, improvisation and the production of overview and shared situation awareness. The prototype and the set-up at TSR 2007 are described in the next section.

OVERVIEW AT THE TALL SHIPS' RACES 2007

From July 5th – 8th 2007 over 100 sailing ships docked in Aarhus harbour, before setting off for a race. Many were open to the ca. 500,000 people who attended the event. In addition, over 50 restaurants, bars, shops, and entertainments were set up in the 3 km² harbour area. *Overview* allows professionals to utilize pervasive computing devices and services to produce a dynamic overview of the situation on the ground. It integrates

Figure 1. Overview display in Topos™ in 3D mode

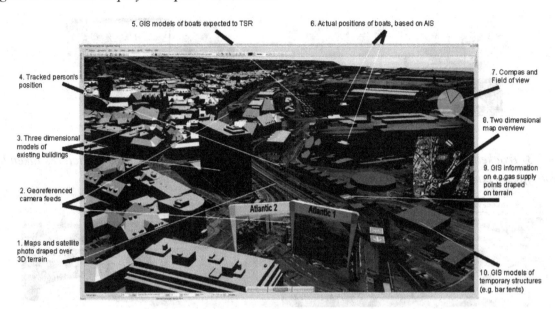

Topos™ with PalCom-enabled services, where PalCom-enabled means that resources utilize the PalCom open architecture (Andersen, 2007) and can, therefore, be interrogated, inspected and combined with other PalCom services. Figure 1 shows an *Overview* screenshot one day before the start of the event.

Satellite photography is draped over the 3D terrain (Figure 1, item 1), so that real surfaces, existing buildings and vegetation are visible. Users can switch GIS data draping and map overlays on or off (9). Models and GIS information for permanent and temporary structures are inserted (3, 10). A GIS inspector enables users to search tabular GIS information. The boat-shaped models (5) indicate where ships are supposed to dock. Live tracking of GPS positions of different resources (Automatic Identification Systems (AIS) (6), mobile phones (4), fire trucks or patrol vehicles), makes it possible to see the actual positions and movements of people and objects. In Figure 1, for example, two ships are arriving (6). Live streaming of video and still pictures taken by GPS tracked mobile phones are shown at geo-referenced positions (2). Users can sketch e.g. poten-

tial access routes, and a 2D map overview (8), where one's current position is marked, supports navigation.

Overview devices and services were installed around the harbour. In the command centre, established in the strategically located old customs house, staff used Topos™ on a large interactive display (Figure 2), to view, discuss and interrogate data from external devices, including:

- five web cameras fixed onto high buildings
- a remotely controllable dome-camera fixed onto a corner of the main stage
- four Nokia N95 GPS enabled phones carried by different officers on patrol in the event area (Figure 3)
- one Nokia N95 phone carried by the rescue divers on their boat patrolling the harbour (Figure 3)
- more than 100 AIS transponders (existing, standard equipment on ships)

Officers used the phones to photograph issues they wanted to report or discuss with colleagues in

Figure 2. The command centre with Overview during TSR

Figure 3. Tracked officer (Jens Fonseca) and tracked boat with rescue divers. Right: Pictures taken by patrol officers can be viewed in the context in which they were taken within the model

the command centre. Figure 3 shows pictures and their locations that were discussed in managing the event (see also Example 1). In addition to the devices directly used by the emergency personnel, three computers were used by developers to monitor the status of devices and services within *Overview* (seen in the background of Figure 2). ´

EXAMPLES OF USE AND EVALUATION

In this section we present three examples of how *Overview* and the PalCom open architecture were used during TSR. As part of long-term ethnographically informed participatory design process these technologies are designed to support collaboration, coordination, improvisation and the production of overview and shared situation awareness. In addition, they respond to the fact that in order to realize this potential, people need to be able to build trust in these technologies. This latter requirement is largely intuited by the researchers, but clearly important. Trust, like agreement in conversations, is often implicit.

Explicit statements like Frischknecht's are rare, especially when actually trying to use the technologies. Rather, trust (or distrust) is documented through continued (or discontinued) use. In the examples below we describe how trust in technologies was practically achieved and seek to draw out important lessons for design and implementation.

Example 1

This example explores how the personnel work to trust (or distrust) technologies: Christian, the fire service team leader, asks two patrol officers to carry one of the tracked Nokia phones. They receive less than one minute of instructions, during which a picture is taken, which duly shows up in Topos™ on the doorstep of the command centre (the last position recorded by the GPS, which only works outdoors). As the patrol set off, their movements are tracked. We see them at Pier Three, then, half an hour later, at Pier Two. Christian's mobile phone rings: the officers have spotted a car parked on an emergency access route. Christian asks them for the registration number. Writing it on a notepad, he asks them to take a picture, then

Figure 4. The patrol officers 'AABR-vagt' document a wrongly parked car

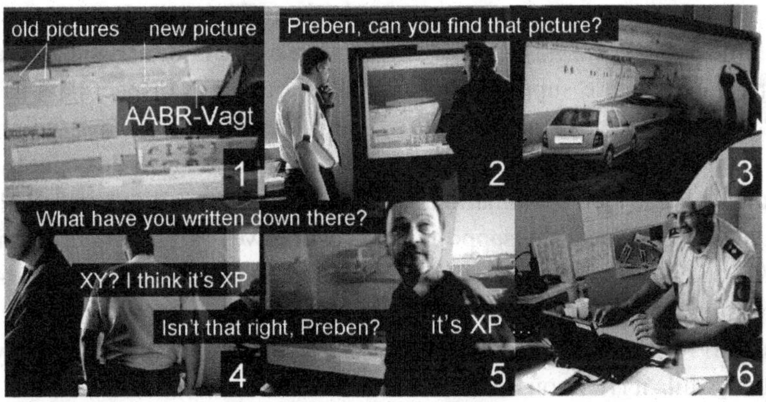

shouts the registration number across the room to a police officer who begins a search on the police database to find the phone number of the car owner in order to get the car moved. Christian walks to the Topos™ screen, where Preben, one of the computer scientists, is demoing *Overview* to a visiting emergency chief. Christian asks: 'Preben can you find that picture that just came up?' (Figure 4). Preben, who had also been monitoring the patrol, notes a new picture along their path and opens it in its host application (Figure 4). He gives Christian time to see the registration number, before continuing the demo.

Christian walks to the police desk. Looking at the police officer's note pad, Christian notes a mistake 'What have you written down here? XY? I think it's XP' (Figure 4.4). Preben overhears this and pulls the picture to the front (4.5), just as Christian says 'Isn't that right Preben?'. Preben reads the registration number out. The police officer re-enters the number in the database and now finds the owner's telephone number.

Lessons Learned

The phones used at TSR often ran out of battery, which meant last known, 'frozen' positions were shown in Topos™. Everyone knew that the representations of positions should be regarded with healthy distrust. However, in the above ex-

ample, Christian is evidently confident that all concerned are talking about the same car, whose actual position is known. A closer look reveals different methods in the ongoing working up of trust, including:

- triangulating shown positions with people's descriptions of where they were/are, (Christian knew from the phone conversation that the officers were on Pier Two)
- seeing the label, representing the phone, wobble (which it does due to fluctuations in GPS accuracy, even when the phone carried is not moved), which means that we are receiving live signals from it
- seeing the label move as the person carrying the phone moves
- seeing that the representation of the officers' position was close to where the new picture showed up
- noting that what is shown on the picture matches the reported position (a car next to a large ship, on a known emergency access route)
- knowing that developers are confident things are working

Any single one of these methods would not ensure that the reported positions were correct, but the different indications in combination provide

Christian with sufficient assurance to trust that the technologies support accurate risk assessment and decisions about the parked car.

The PalCom open architecture supports the assembly of the GPS and the camera in the phones with services that display their output in a way that supports these methods and their combination (Andersen, 2007; Kyng, 2007). We call this support for *flexible redundancy*. As we will elaborate in Example 3, there are multiple layers of inspection. But the value of support for flexible redundancy also lies in the fact that, while it is obvious that the individual technologies' reliability could be substantially improved (e.g. through better batteries), with so many devices, services, connections, etc. in play, some of them will always fail. Multiple, flexible indicators are, therefore, crucial to allow people to combine different means of assessing the trustworthiness of the reported state of affairs.

Another important means for working up trust is *quick and implicit experimentation*. The rapid sequence of taking a test picture and seeing it appear in the expected position, before going out on the patrol, is one such experiment. It relies on – and documents – the functioning of *Overview*. Moreover, the *flexible interaction* with *Overview* provides means to ensure the different actors that they are assessing the situation correctly. Christian and Preben's ability to either open the image in its host application (Figure 4a.3), or bring the image to the front (Figure 4b.5), or go to the geo-positioned image of the issue at hand and see it in its context allows users to inspect data as part of different activities (enquiries into the matter, checking a detail, demo-ing). It does not by itself show how such small enquiries supported development of trust. However, throughout TSR innumerable such interaction experiments were carried out, and we observed how they fostered trust in, and ever more extensive use of, the technology.

Example 2

This example shows how multiple sources of situation accounts and technologically mediated evidence can support the production of situation awareness and collaborative accountable improvisation: 7:40 pm Saturday: Paul, an untracked fire service officer, calls: 'I'm behind the stage (marked X in Figure 5.1). It's chaos here. I need Jens'. People queuing for a concert are creating a dangerous situation, blocking vehicles from accessing the ferry port (5.2). Paul wants the duty police officer's (Jens') opinion. The call taker in the command centre – Peter – looks at *Overview* (5.1): 'Jens is on the corner of Pier Three, near you'. This completes the radio conversation and Paul goes looking for Jens. Meanwhile, the

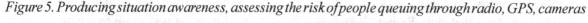

Figure 5. Producing situation awareness, assessing the risk of people queuing through radio, GPS, cameras

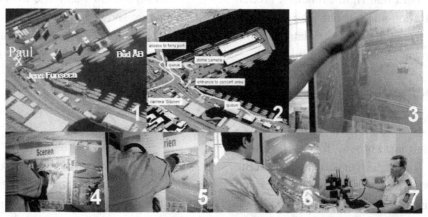

police commander, Amrik, has asked one of the developers, who is already looking at the concert area using the dome video camera mounted on the stage, to turn it to look at the entrance (5.3). As the camera reveals a view, Amrik says 'There's no pressure [no problem] here' (5.4). He asks the developer to switch to the camera overlooking the crossing close to the concert area (Sibirien) and remarks 'But they're queuing all the way down here,' (5). There is no camera with a view onto the ferry port access road. Now Paul calls again: 'I can't find Jens'. Amrik asks the developer 'Can I take over?' and switches to the 'home' position to see Jens' position (5.6). Peter looks at it and tells Paul: 'But he is there' (5.7). When Paul and Jens finally meet, Jens requests back-up, saying 'You know where I am', and they resolve the situation.

Lessons Learned

The use of *Overview* in this situation affords the emergence of new virtual teamwork practices. Paul, Peter, Amrik, and Jens are enabled to form a shared picture of the situation on the ground. Amrik initially treats Paul's report with scepticism, not because he does not trust Paul, but because he knows that being embroiled in a situation on the ground can make things look more dramatic than they are. He checks, making full use of the technology to inspect the trouble through evidence from different sources (radio report, map and model, two different camera angles) and leads the collaborative risk assessment and response. Such flexible access to *multiple sources of situational evidence* supports *distributed collaboration* in the production of situation awareness. Moreover, it opens up possibilities for *accountable and collaborative improvisation*. Current systems often fail to integrate real-time capability and asset tracking, and bureaucratic demands slow down fast and flexible utilization of available resources and capabilities (The White House, 2006). Using the methods outlined in Example 1, the emergency staff here confidently rely on the technologies.

This enables publicly visible collaborative improvisation: Peter and Amrik can see where Jens is (and trust that this is live information) and work with Paul, Jens and eventually a patrol car crew to address the situation. It is easy to imagine how an expanded assembly – with more cameras, and tracking devices for every officer and patrol car, as well as mobile (simplified) Topos™ displays of *Overview* carried by every officer – could expand the capacity for such improvisation. It would be accountable in two senses: First, capabilities and resources would 'account' for where they are as they move. Second, it is possible to record and replay movements. While this may create dilemmas for professional accountability if analyses with hindsight are used to critique in situ decision making, such records – if used responsibly – could be an invaluable learning resource. Indeed, some recordings made during TSR were used for debriefing sessions after the event.

Example 3

This example shows that there are multiple layers and multiple practices of inspection: The fire service patrol officers drop into the command centre to pick up a new charged phone. They ask one of the developers (Jesper) if they could see the pictures they took on their last round (Figure 6.1). He opens the last picture displayed in Topos™. It shows the window sill of the command centre (where the developers charge the phones) (6.2)! This is unexpected. Reading the picture's full file name, which includes the phone's name (N95_3) and a time stamp (6.4), Jesper sees that it was taken just before the officers set off. He inspects whether a heartbeat is received from the phone and what happened to the 'missing' picture(s), utilizing a range of PalCom supported means for tracing communication among devices and services (Andersen, 2007), which allows them to reconstruct the pictures' journeys.

They find that the pictures the patrol officers describe taking after setting off had been taken,

Figure 6. Making sure N95-3 is connected properly into the assembly

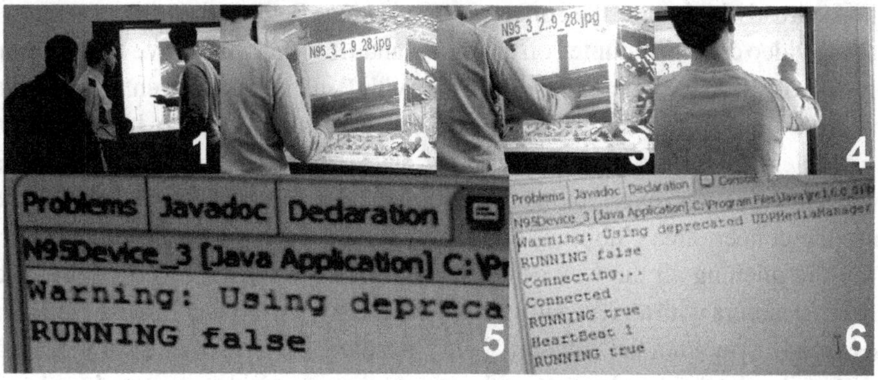

tagged with their position, sent and saved at the command centre, just not sent to and displayed in Topos™. Restarting the gateway service to re-establish lost connections makes the missing pictures appear in their correct positions.

Lessons Learned

Most of the work in this example was done by developers using low level interfaces and tools. The PalCom open architecture provides the possibility to inspect traffic along incoming and outgoing connections and the live 'primitives' produced, received and passed on by each assembled device and service (e.g. GPS coordinate strings, data packets) (Figure 7). Such facilities for *inspection of states, processes and connection* greatly enhanced the developers' ability to build trust in the technologies.

But inspecting not only helped the developers to pinpoint points of failure and fix parts of the assembly. It also helped them to explain to the professionals what was going on and demonstrate that they were in control – enabling one of the methods of establishing trust on the professionals' part: knowing that technicians are (justifiedly) confident that things are working (or know why they aren't). There are thus multiple *layers of inspection* and *multiple practices of inspecting*.

Figure 7. Screenshot of a PalCom Visual Browser showing active/inactive devices, services and connections in Overview with details of some devices and services unfolded (right) (Andersen 2007)

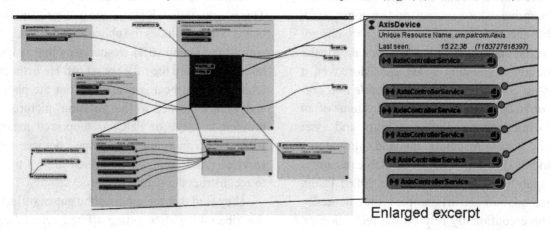

Enlarged excerpt

While the PalCom architecture in its current state makes crucial fundamental mechanisms for inspection available, it is obvious that more thoroughgoing awareness of, and trust in pervasive computing technologies assemblies could be further supported. This make us turn to a discussion of design implications.

DESIGN IMPLICATIONS FOR PERVASIVE COMPUTING FOR EMERGENCY VIRTUAL TEAMS

Pervasive Computing technologies could extremely productively support the work of emergency virtual teams. However, a professional leap of faith is made difficult by a design philosophy that seeks to hide the inner workings of the technologies involved. In this article we have presented examples and reflections from experimental deployment of a prototype assembly of existing and prototypical pervasive computing technologies (*Overview*), built upon the PalCom open architecture (Andersen, 2007), during the Tall Ships' Races in Aarhus 2007. These technologies embody a different design philosophy, one that explicitly seeks to enable people to 'look under the hood' of pervasive computing. One of the main drivers for this shift in design philosophy is the recognition that people need to be able to trust their technologies.

Through three examples of how *Overview* and the PalCom open architecture were used as part of the event management during TSR, we have demonstrated that trust is not a state of mind, or once-and-for-all accepted dependability, but practically, and often collaboratively achieved. We show how users build up trust in *Overview*, identifying a set of methods that can be actively supported through design. Drawing on our TSR experience, we can sketch out key implications for pervasive computing design for emergency virtual teamwork.

First, our attention must turn towards the process of innovation. Developing, and developing trust in, new technologies – generally – is inextricably entangled with developing, and developing trust in, new ways of working. Design should seek synergy with everyday innovation, because in order to anticipate and design for future practices, designers need the critical insight from professionals and from non-discursive embodied and tacit innovation. This can be achieved through experimental deployment of prototypes as part of as-realistic-as-possible real world work. In emergency virtual teamwork, such a participatory approach to innovation can help facilitate the realization of technological potential by balancing technologically ambitious design with 'graceful augmentation' (Jul 2007) and safe levels of redundancy.

Second, our experience with *Overview* and the PalCom open architecture suggests a range of design challenges for a fundamental re-orientation towards actively supporting methods of building trust in the design of pervasive computing technologies for emergency teamwork, including support for:

- *flexible redundancy* with regard to the methods of working up trust
- *flexible interaction* modes to suit multiple motivations and forms of inspection
- *quick and implicit experimentation* which allows quick probing of cause-effect relations in complex, distributed systems
- *inspection of states, processes and connections* to make it possible to examine what is going on, all the way down to the 'primitives' of computational processes, such as GPS strings or data being sent or received
- *multiple layers and practices of inspection* to enable different users to understand and trust technologies.

Our examples show that there were many different users during TSR with many different motivations, competencies and practices for working up trust and inspection (the different emergency responders, basic end-users, super-users and researchers/technical systems-supporters). Our final challenge is perhaps the most difficult: how to enable different users to translate complex live system information about computational operations into information they can understand. This clearly is not a matter just for 'once and for all' interface design, but a matter of (1) inventing new forms of collaboration between technical experts and end-users, (2) creating new professional roles and positions for technology management and (3) designing support for the assembly of relevant and appropriate accounts of technological states, processes and connections.

Third, the way in which the experimental deployment of *Overview* and the PalCom open architecture 'forced' a future in which professionals could begin to utilize pervasive computing technologies for real world work, provides insight into emergent future virtual emergency teamwork practices. It becomes clear that situation awareness (like trust) is not a purely cognitive state, produced by individual minds processing information, but a practically, collaboratively produced dynamic and at least partially public understanding. Through combining *multiple sources of situation evidence* the professionals begin to develop practices of *distributed collaboration* (e.g. in determining the troublesome-ness of a wrongly parked car, or the level of chaos caused by a queue) and enable *accountable, collaborative improvisation* (such as brokering meetings between colleagues who are in close proximity but cannot see each other, or sending resources to colleagues whose location is known without the need for description).

Clearly, our own design efforts are beginning to address these challenges, but leave much room for improvement – for example, rolling out (simplified) Topos™ displays of *Overview* to personnel on the ground, in vehicles, and remote locations (such as hospitals). Having had the possibility to implement *Overview* and the PalCom open architecture in real use settings, where real end-users – the emergency responders – used it for several days has given us invaluable input to our research and design. We hope that the challenges and opportunities we have identified can contribute to the further unlocking of the potential of pervasive computing technologies for emergency virtual teamwork.

ACKNOWLEDGMENT

We thank our colleagues in the different emergency agencies in Aarhus and in the PalCom project, and the anonymous ISCRAM reviewers for their insightful comments.

REFERENCES

Andersen, P. (Ed.). (2007). Deliverable 54: Open architecture. Retrieved October 20, 2008 from http://www.ist-palcom.org/publications/deliverables/Deliverable-54-%5B2.2.3%5D-open-architecture.pdf

Avizienis, A., Laprie, J.-C., Randell, B., & Landwehr, C. (2004). Basic Concepts and Taxonomy of Dependable and Secure Computing. *IEEE Transactions on Dependable and Secure Computing*, *1*(1), 11–33. doi:10.1109/TDSC.2004.2

Betts, B. J., Mah, R. W., Papasin, R., Del Mundo, R., McIntosh, D. M., & Jorgensen, C. (2005). Improving Situ-ational Awareness for First Responders via Mobile Computing. Published by *National Aeronautics and Space Administration Ames Research Center* Moffett Field, California. NASA/TM-2005-213470. Retrieved March 9, 2008 from http://ntrs.nasa.gov/archive/nasa/casi.ntrs.nasa.gov/20060000029_2005249624.pdf

Boden, D., & Molotch, H. (1994). The compulsion to proximity. In Friedland, R., & Boden, D. (Eds.), *NowHere. Space, time and modernity*. Berkeley: University of California Press.

Büscher, M. (2006). Interaction in motion: Embodied conduct in emergency teamwork. In: Mondada L. (ED.). Online Multimedia *Proceedings of the 2nd International Society for Gesture Studies Conference 'Interacting Bodies'*, 15-18 June 2005, Lyon, France. Retrieved October 20, 2008 from http://gesture-lyon2005.ens-lsh.fr/article.php3?id_article=221

Büscher, M., Christensen, M., Hansen, K. M., Mogensen, P., & Shapiro, D. (2008). Bottom-up, top-down? Connecting software architecture design with use. In Voß, A., Hartswood, M., Ho, K., Procter, R., Rouncefield, M., Slack, R., & Büscher, M. (Eds.), *Configuring user-designer relations: Interdisciplinary perspectives*. New York: Springer Verlag.

Büscher, M., Kristensen, M., & Mogensen, P. (2008). Making the future palpable: Notes from a major incident Future Laboratory. *International Journal of Emergency Management, 5*(1/2), 145–163. doi:10.1504/IJEM.2008.019911

Clarke, K., Hardstone, G., Rouncefield, M., & Sommerville, I. (2006). *Trust in Technology: A Socio-Technical Perspective (Computer Supported Cooperative Work)*. New York: Springer-Verlag.

Denef, S., Ramirez, L., Dyrks, T., & Stevens, G. (2008). Handy Navigation in Ever-Changing Spaces. An Ethnographic Study of Firefighting Practices. *Proceedings of DIS2008*. February 25–27, 2008. Cape Town, South Africa. forthcoming

Endsley, M., Bolté, B., & Jones, D. G. (2003). *Designing for Situation Awareness: An Approach to User-Centred Design*. London: Taylor & Francis.

Fiedrich, F. (2000). An HLA-based multi-agent system for the search and rescue period after strong earthquakes. *Proceedings of the International Conference on Multiagent Systems* (ICMAS 2000) Workshop on RoboCup Rescue: Multi-Agent Approaches to the Simulation and Management of Major Urban Disasters, Boston, MA.

Greater London Authority. (2006). *Report of the 7 July Review Committee*. ISBN 1 85261 8787.

Jiang, X., Hong, J. I., Takayama, L. A., & Landay, J. A. Ubiquitous computing for firefighters: Field Studies and prototypes of large displays for incident command. *Proceedings of the international conference on Computer-Human Interaction* (CHI) 2004, pp. 279-686.

Jul, S. (2007). Who's Really on First? A Domain-Level User, Task and Context Analysis for Response Technology. *Proceedings of the 4th International Conference on Information Systems for Crisis Response and Management ISCRAM2007* (Eds. B. Van de Walle, P. Burghardt & C. Nieuwenhuis), 2007, pp. 139-148.

Kristensen, M., Kyng, M., & Palen, L. (2006). Participatory Design in Emergency Medical Service: Designing for Future Practice, *Proceedings of the ACM Conference on Human Factors in Computing Systems* (CHI 2006), 161-170.

Kyng, M. (Ed.). (2007). PalCom External Report no 52: Revised conceptual framework for palpable computing Section I. Retrieved October 20, 2008 from http://www.ist-palcom.org/publications/deliverables/Deliverable-37-%5B2.1.2%5D-palpability-revised-SectionI.pdf

Landgren, J. (2005). Supporting fire crew sensemaking enroute to incidents. *International Journal of Emergency Management, 2*(3), 176–188. doi:10.1504/IJEM.2005.007358

Lorincz, K., Malan, D.J., Fulford-Jones, T., Nawoj, A., Clavel, A., Shnayder, V., Mainland, G., Welsh, M. & Moulton, S. (2004). Sensor Networks for Emergency Response: Challenges and Opportunities. *Pervasive Computing* October - December 2004, pp. 16-23.

Martin, D., Bowers, J. & D. Wastell. The interactional affordances of technology: An ethnography of human-computer interaction in an ambulance control center. *Proceedings of HCI'97*, 263-281.

Palen, L., & Liu, S. (2007). Citizen Communications in Crisis: Anticipating a Future of ICT Supported Participation, *Proceedings of the ACM Conference on Human Factors in Computing Systems* (CHI 2007), 727-736.

Rantanen, J., Impiö, J., Karinsalo, T., Malmivaara, M., Reho, A., Tasanen, M. & Vanhala, J. Smart Clothing Prototype for the Arctic Environment, *Personal and Ubiquitous Computing*, Vol. 6, Issue 1, Jan. 2002. New York: Springer-Verlag.

The White House. (2006). *The Federal Response to Hurricane Katrina: Lessons Learned*. Washington, D.C.: The White House.

Wachtendorf. T. & Kendra, J.M. (2005). Improvising disaster in the city of jazz: Organizational response to hurricane Katrina. Understanding Katrina: Perspectives from the social sciences, Retrieved October 20, 2008 from http://understandingkatrina.ssrc.org

This work was previously published in International Journal of Information Systems for Crisis Response and Management, Volume 1, Issue 2, edited by Murray E. Jennex, pp. 1-15, copyright 2009 by IGI Publishing (an imprint of IGI Global).

Chapter 7
Multilingual Crisis Knowledge Representation

Aviv Segev
KAIST, Korea

ABSTRACT

In a crisis, the problem of the lack of a shared platform or similar communication methods among the collaborators usually arises within a few hours. While a crisis requires rapid response of emergency management factors, ontology is generally represented in a static manner. Therefore, an adaptive ontology for crisis knowledge representation is needed to assist in coordinating relief efforts in different crisis situations. This chapter describes a method of ontology modeling that modifies the ontology in real time during a crisis according to the crisis surroundings. The method is based on modeling a basic predefined multilingual ontology while allowing the expansion of the ontology according to the crisis circumstances and the addition of other languages within the crisis time limitations. An example of ontology use based on a sample Katrina crisis blog is presented. Motivation for multilingual ontology use is supplied by the Boxing Day tsunami crisis.

INTRODUCTION

Rapid response in a situation, such as a crisis, usually entails bringing down physical as well as logical barriers to allow fast transfer of critical information. Knowledge Representation is generally used to refer to representations intended

for processing by computers, and in particular, representations consisting of explicit objects and of assertions about them. The representation of knowledge in such explicit form enables computers to draw conclusions from knowledge already stored. However, during a crisis there exists a massive amount of information relating to new concepts not yet represented. To provide a rapid response it is necessary to build a new

DOI: 10.4018/978-1-60960-609-1.ch007

knowledge representation system sometimes in a matter of hours.

According to the Munich Research Group (Munich, 2005) website, most definitions of the term "crisis" include ten characteristics: 1) an unusual volume and intensity of events, 2) 'change of state' in the flow of international political actions, 3) disruptive interactions between two or more adversaries, 4) abrupt or sudden change in one or more basic system variables, 5) change in the external or internal environment, 6) threat to basic values, 7) high probability of involvement in military hostilities, 8) awareness of finite time for response, 9) surprise, and 10) uncertainty.

Based on these definition characteristics, knowledge representation during rapid response situations will be influenced by the mass production of information relating to multiple events. Communication will be limited in scope between the participants. Chaos and lack of official chain of control and decision making can be expected in this situation. Furthermore, the most critical aspect might be the time limitation.

Figure 1 shows a blog entry posted by a New Orleans resident at the beginning of the U.S. Katrina crisis (The survival of New Orleans Weblog, http://interdictor.livejournal.com, 8:54 am, August 30th, 2005). The request in the text to receive relevant information can be viewed as a simple query posted in natural language. The request for information presented in the figure requires a knowledge representation relevant to crisis that can be expanded and matched to specific incidents and locations.

Figure 1. Sample blog posting during Katrina Crisis: August 30th, 2005

Right now, it's a matter of survival. There are 3 important aspects to surviving this: you need food/water/medicine, you need personal protection, and you need the means to conduct personal hygiene in such a way that you're not creating more of a problem than you're solving. For any media out there reading this, it would be very helpful for you to post guidelines for survivalist hygiene.

The chapter presents a model for designing an ontology-based knowledge representation during a situation with time constraints. The chapter describes the steps and the resources required to build a satisfactory solution which can serve as a basis for setting up the rescue and support systems under these time constraints.

The rest of the chapter is organized as follows. The next section provides related work, followed by a section which presents the concept of crisis ontology. The sections after describe the ontology design and the aspects of the ontology implementation. Then a discussion and implementation of ontology for the Katrina crisis and the Boxing Day Tsunami crisis are presented, followed by the conclusion and further research.

RELATED WORK

A common definition of an ontology considers it to be "a specification of a conceptualization" (Gruber, 1993), where conceptualization is an abstract view of the world represented as a set of objects. The term has been used in different research areas, including philosophy (where it was coined), artificial intelligence, information sciences, knowledge representation, object modeling, and most recently, eCommerce applications. In his seminal work, Bunge defines Ontology as a world of systems and provides a basic formalism for ontologies (Bunge, 1977), (Bunge, 1979). Typically, ontologies are represented using Description Logic (Borgida & Brachman, 1993), where subsumption typifies the semantic relationship between terms.

The realm of information science has produced an extensive body of literature and practice in ontology construction, e.g., (Vickery, 1966). Researchers in the field of knowledge representation have studied ontology interoperability, resulting in systems such as Protégé (Noy & Musen, 2000). An adaptive ontology model that allows the ontology to evolve quickly during the crisis timeline is proposed here.

Previous efforts to utilize ontology for crisis response include the OpenKnowledge system, which supports and enhances the sharing and effective use of information and services among different actors (Vaccari et al., 2006). Previous work also focused on blogs and the collaborative tagging approach (Ziesche, 2007). Other work analyzed the availability of information and information sharing in emergency management in hierarchical and network teams (Schraagen et al., 2010). An analysis of the building blocks of an effective response system (Ansell et al., 2010) emphasizes the need of the response system to operate 'robustly' across boundaries and in different scales. However, the present work takes ontology for crisis management further and enables real-time extension of the ontology.

Ontology merging has been researched from various aspects. The groundwork for ontology merging appeared in Stumme and Maedche (2001) which described merging ontologies following a bottom-up approach that offers a structural description of the merging process. Further ontology expansions on ontology evolution were discussed in Noy and Klein (2003). Improving the quality of the ontology using a transformation approach was presented in Mostowfi and Fotouhi (2006). In Tolk et al. (2007) various layered composability approaches are presented along with their derived implications and requirements for ontologies. Similar ideas are incorporated in the expanding the ontology section.

Although it is possible to create metadata documents semi-automatically, a more precise approach requires human intervention. Much of the information that can be usefully specified for a resource simply cannot be extracted without some kind of human interpretation. Also, the metadata to be recorded about a resource is often derived from a vocabulary of interesting categories that are relevant for subsequent processes. These vocabularies, called ontologies, can be required

to adhere to standards that can only be applied by humans. There are two competing models by which we can express metadata. Web Ontology Language (OWL) / Resource Description Framework (RDF) (Smith et al., 2004) is a World Wide Web Consortium (W3C) recommendation and by design is meant to form the base of the W3C's vision of the Semantic Web. Topic Maps (Gashol & Moore, 2006) is an International Organization for Standardization (ISO) standard, and although developed independently of the W3C, it has several properties that make it an alternative to OWL/ RDF. Currently there are attempts to integrate both models (Pepper, 1999; Pepper & Grønmo, 2001). The model described in the present chapter can be implemented using both of these techniques.

CRISIS ONTOLOGY

In the quest to identify frameworks, concepts, and models for crisis ontologies the term 'Open Ontology' was addressed in Di Maio (2007). 'Open Ontology' refers to a given set of agreed terms, in terms of conceptualization and semantic formalization, that has been developed based on public consultation and that embodies, represents, and synthesizes all available valid knowledge thought to pertain to a given domain and necessary to fulfill a given functional requirement.

The Sphere handbook (Sphere Project, 2004) is designed for use in disaster response and may also be useful in disaster preparedness and humanitarian advocacy. It is applicable in a range of situations where relief is required, including natural disasters and armed conflict. It is designed for use in both slow- and rapid-onset situations, rural and urban environments, developing and developed countries, anywhere in the world. The emphasis throughout is on meeting the urgent survival needs of people affected by disaster, while asserting their basic human right to life with dignity.

Analysis of the Sphere handbook index, displayed in Figure 2, indicates that it meets many

Figure 2. Index of Humanitarian Charter and Minimum Standards

cooking
   fuel supplies 158, 159, 234, 235-6
   environmental impact 123, 159
   stoves 234, 235
   utensils
      access 163, 164
      initial needs 233, 242
   water supplies 64
coordination
   food aid 109, 113-14
   health services 255, 261-3, 263-4
   information exchanges 30, 33-4, 35
   shelter programmes 209-10
crude mortality rates (CMR)
   baseline 260-1
   calculations 301
   documentation 32-3, 259, 271
   maintenance 259, 260
cultural practices
   data gathering 38
   housing 207, 219, 220, 221, 222, 240
   normality 291, 293

...

   transmission 76, 77-9
vitamins
   A
      deficiencies 187
      measles vaccination 275
   daily requirements 189
   deficiencies 137-8, 140
   supplies 137
vulnerable groups
   clothing needs 231
   construction tasks 237
   definitions 9-10, 57-8, 110, 210
   economic needs 215
   fuel supplies 235-6
   hygiene promotion 61
   nutritional support 142-6, 164
   personal hygiene 232
   protection 10-13
   social needs 215
   washing facilities 70, 71
   water supplies 57-8, 66

initial assessments 92
on-site soak pits 87-8
planning 86, 87
slopes 88, 218
surface topography 216, 218
surface water 86
drugs
   donated 266
   essential lists 266, 268
   management 269
   reserve stocks 280

earthquakes, injuries 257, 286
eating utensils 233-4
employment
   food production 128-30
   remuneration 128, 129-30, 131
environment
   erosion 228
   impact
      fuel supplies 123, 234, 235, 242
      settlements 227-9, 241
      protection 13, 227-8

people per outlet 65-6
quantities 63, 64
queuing times 63, 66
vulnerable groups 57-8, 66
women
   see also vulnerable groups
   birth attendants 262
   equal rights 12
   gender-based violence 288, 289-90
   health services 255
   laundry facilities, privacy 70
   menstruation 75, 232, 233
   pregnant, nutrition 142
   reproductive health 285, 288-9
   safety
      exploitation 40-1
      shelter 220
      toilets 73, 75
   sexual coercion 37, 41, 225
      food supplies 113
   shelter programmes 209, 225
   water collection 56, 66

requirements of Open Ontology. Thus, the current index can be defined as an Index Ontology. Generic top level requirements for an Open Ontology according to Di Maio (2007) include:

- Declaring what high level knowledge (upper level ontology) it references. The Index Ontology primary concepts can be identified by the outer level keywords in the index. These keywords serve as a high level framework defining the primary topics of the Crisis Ontology.
- The ontology allows reasoning / inference based on the index. For example, according to Figure 2 the concept *fuel supplies* is related to the class of *cooking* and also related to the concept *impact*, which is related to the concept *environment*. It is also related to the concept *vulnerable groups*.

The relational index structure supplies the initial structure of the Index Ontology.

- Natural language queries can be supported by simple string matching of words from the query against the Index Ontology concepts. The request to receive relevant information appearing in Figure 1 which shows a blog entry posted by a New Orleans resident displays an example of a textual natural language query which could be analyzed using the Index Ontology. Simple string matching between the text and the Index Ontology can identify relevant topics such as: *food/water/medicine* and *personal hygiene*, which appear in the Index. The relevant page numbers of the index topics can supply immediate relevant information delivered in response to the query in any of the above topics. These could include a short description and possible values required to maintain minimal standards in areas such as *personal hygiene*. A simple Web interface could support an online connection between the blog and the Index Ontology, allowing immediate response.
- Use of the Index Ontology supplies an easy-to-understand mechanism with which most users are familiar. The skills required to utilize the ontology are minimal and can be implemented by any ontology tool, such as Protégé (Noy & Musen, 2000) or Topic Maps Ontopia (Pepper, 1999).
- The 'high level knowledge' represented by the Index Ontology can easily be linked to classes representing required actions such as: status updates, email notification of current crisis situation, resources required for the survivors, and critical locations where immediate intervention is required. The current ontology representation already includes values that can be represented as properties such as measuring acute malnutrition in children under five years and other age groups.

- The implementation of the ontology is independent of any ontology language. It can be implemented in any currently used ontology language such as OWL/DARPA Agent Markup Language (DAML) and due to its simplicity can be implemented by alternative ontology languages such as Topics, Associations, and Occurrences (TAO) of topic maps.
- The adoption of an Index Ontology allows a flexible approach to ontology creation and adoption. As the following section describes, the ontology can be expanded using additional Index Ontologies or alternatively direct links to information on the Web.
- Finally the basic ontology and the knowledge it represents are already defined in multiple languages, allowing multiple viewpoints of similar information in multiple languages. Furthermore, it allows information in multiple languages to be directed to identical ontology concepts.

ONTOLOGY DESIGN

This section presents the ontology design process. The first section shows how concepts are extracted from predefined research presented in a book or on-line documentation to construct the ontology layout. The following section displays how to extract the concept relations. Next, the section depicts how the ontology can be expanded and similar documents based on similar concepts can be added to the ontology. The last section shows how the ontology can function in a multilingual environment.

Extracting the Ontology Layout

Based on the Sphere Handbook index (Sphere Project, 2004), an initial ontology can be constructed using existing hierarchical and semantic relations. Furthermore, data linking to additional information can be stored as class properties. Figure 3 displays a sample of the Index Ontology created from the Sphere Handbook index (Figure 2). The class defined as *cooking* is defined as a super-class of four subclasses: *fuel supplies, environmental impact, water supplies,* and *stoves.* However, *fuel supplies* is a subclass of two additional classes: *vulnerable groups* and *impact.* Similarly, *water supplies* is a subclass of both *cooking* and *vulnerable groups.* The properties of the class *personal hygiene* can match the class with additional information regarding hygiene in the Sphere Handbook, such as full description pages or relevant values. Additionally, external

Figure 3. A sample of the extracted indexOntology

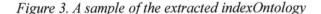
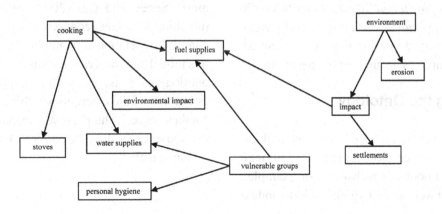

Figure 4. Ontology concept relations based on document sections

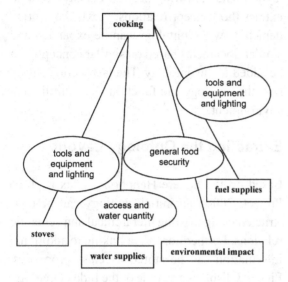

Figure 5. Possible concepts expansion based on Wikipedia indexing

Hygiene

Contents
1. Personal hygiene
2. Food and cooking hygiene
3. Medical hygiene
4. Personal service / served hygiene
5. History of hygienic practices
     5.1 Europe
6. Grooming
7. Hygiene Certification
8. Academic resources

information extracted from other resources can be matched with the extracted Index Ontology.

Extracting the Concept Relations

The ontology concept relations can be extracted in a similar technique, using the book index. The binary relation is defined as the chapter title shared by each of two concepts. For example, in the Sphere Handbook, for each two concepts appearing in the Index Ontology, the chapter title which connects the two can be defined as the relation.

Figure 4 displays an example of the relations of the *cooking* concept with another four concepts. In the example it can be seen that the relation of *tools and equipment and lighting* describes both *cooking* and *fuel supply* and *cooking* and *stoves*. The relation that can be automatically extracted in this case supplies an appropriate description.

Expanding the Ontology

The ontology can be expanded using external information from other resources such as additional data based on books or websites. For example, the Wikipedia website for hygiene includes index

information which could be added to the current Index Ontology using similar class definitions. Figure 5 displays index information from the Wikipedia *hygiene* index (Hygiene, 2008) that can be used as concepts for possible ontology expansion. Notice that the concept *personal hygiene* is a subclass of hygiene according to this definition. Figure 6 displays the ontology expansion based on the Wikipedia *hygiene* entry. Alternatively, additional index books considered fundamental in the field can be added to the ontology. For example, the Merck Manual of Medical Information (Beers, 2003) index can be used for medical class expansion.

There are multiple approaches to merging ontologies such as the Formal Concept Analysis described in Stumme and Maedche (2001). Possible merging operations for the ontology engineer are presented in (Noy and Klein, 2003). Furthermore, Segev and Gal (2007) proposed using (machine generated) contexts as a mechanism for quantifying relationships among concepts. Using this model has an advantage since it provides the ontology administrator with an explicit numeric estimation of the extent to which a modification "makes sense." The present research adopts the method of expanding the ontology based on context mechanism.

Figure 6. Ontology expansion based on Wikipedia

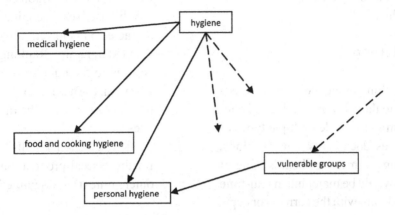

Multilingualism

An ontology-based model for multilingual knowledge management in information systems has been proposed in Segev and Gal (2008). The unique feature was a lightweight mechanism, dubbed context, which is associated with ontological concepts and specified in multiple languages. The contexts were used to assist in resolving cross-language and local variation ambiguities. The technique can be adopted to build an ontology where each concept can be represented in multiple languages.

The technique presented here is different from the previous model since it requires the ability to create and modify the ontology in real-time as the crisis arises and continues to evolve. This requirement necessitates having a basic predefined multilingual ontology while allowing the expansion of the ontology according to the crisis circumstances and the addition of other languages within the crisis time limitations. The technique can be adopted to build an ontology where each concept can be represented in multiple languages and can be expanded for use in crises, such as the Boxing Day Tsunami.

The Sphere handbook (Sphere Project, 2004) is designed for use in disaster response and was translated into 37 languages. Thus it supplies a top level ontology that can be used concurrently in multiple languages. Since each high level In-

dex Ontology concept is represented in multiple languages, there is faster ontology adaptation in crisis situations. A sample of a multilingual ontology in English, French (F), Tamil (T), and Sinhala (S) is presented in Figure 7.

UTILIZING THE ONTOLOGY

The question arises of how the Index Ontology can support agencies and groups involved in a crisis. The answer can be divided into two separate tasks: to enable the information flow during the crisis to be matched with relevant ontology concepts and

Figure 7. A sample of the extracted multilingual ontology

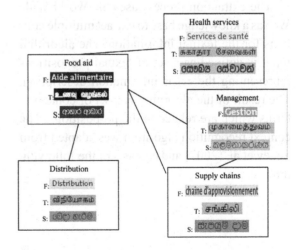

to direct the relevant information to the correct agency or individual.

Ontology Matching

The ontology matching process directs the crisis information flow to the relevant ontological concepts. The crisis might include multiple types of information such as documents, emails, blogs, and update postings in message boards. One of the difficult tasks would be matching in real-time each information datum with the correct concepts without the usual training process required in ontology adjustment and usually performed over a long period of time.

To overcome the time limitation required to process ontology for optimal information flow the following method is proposed. Let O_1, O_2, ..., On be a set of ontologies, representing either the Index Ontology or each representing different domain knowledge. A simplified representation of an ontology is $O \equiv <C, R>$, where $C = \{c_1, c_2, ..., c_n\}$ is a set of concepts with their associated relation R.

To analyze the crisis information flow a context extraction algorithm can be used. To handle the different vocabularies used by different information sources a comparison based on context comparison is used in addition to simple string matching. The context is extracted for each document and then compared with the ontology concept.

The extraction process uses the World Wide Web as a knowledge base to extract multiple contexts for the textual information. The algorithm input is defined as a set of textual propositions representing the crisis information description. The result of the algorithm is a set of contexts - terms which are related to the propositions. The context recognition algorithm was adapted from Segev et al. (2007) and consists of the following three steps:

1. Context retrieval: Submitting each token to a Web-based search engine. The contexts are extracted and clustered from the results.
2. Context ranking: Ranking the results according to the number of references to the keyword, the number of Web sites that refer to the keyword, and the ranking of the Web sites.
3. Context selection: Finally, the set of contexts for the textual proposition, defined as the outer context, is assembled.

To evaluate the matching of the concepts with the information and its context, a simple string-matching function is used, denoted by $\textbf{\textit{match}}_{str}$, which returns 1 if two strings match and 0 otherwise. $\textbf{\textit{I}}$ is defined as the information, and $\textbf{\textit{D}}^I$ is the information descriptor. Also, $\textbf{\textit{n}}$ is defined as the size of $\textbf{\textit{D}}^I$.

The match between the concept and the information is defined as the sum of the concept matching values:

$$match(I, c_j) = \sum_{t_i \in D^I} match_{str}(t_i, c_j)$$

The overall match between the ontology and the information is defined as a normalized sum of the concept matching values:

$$match(I, O_i) = \frac{1}{n} \sum_{c_j \in O_i} \sum_{t_i \in D^I} match_{str}(t_i, c_j)$$

Directing the Crisis Information Flow

The Index Ontology can serve as a knowledge base for directing crisis information flow. An information system deployed in a crisis can use the Index Ontology as an immediate knowledge representation that can be accessed by emergency forces. Civilians in a crisis can access such a system to link to relevant information or to provide real-time information that will be matched immediately with concepts predefined in the ontology.

All rescue forces will be able to utilize the Index Ontology directly or indirectly. New, uploaded information will be mapped to the relevant ontology concepts. Each rescue force will be able to include communication means which will alert them to new relevant information regarding specific concepts. Using such a mechanism, email or text messages can be delivered to handheld devices on the scene. Relevant information can be extended to include geographical information systems. Consequently, ontology concepts can be identified with geographical location resulting in concepts such as *flooding* being identified with locations in the New Orleans area.

Each on-site crisis actor can constantly update rescue and management decision making forces. The information can be automatically classified according to the ontology matching algorithm described previously. Using crisis actors who can deliver information in real-time allows the amount of accessible information to be increased at a very low information delivery cost when an automatic Index Ontology is used.

Rescue forces can supply the crisis population with relevant information according to relevant concepts. Users with Web access can select relevant information when needed. Users can always access the Sphere Handbook as default information that is specific information on limited concepts. Rescue and management forces will be able to add updates to all relevant concepts for all civilians in need.

DISCUSSION AND IMPLEMENTATION

In a crisis, people put different types of relevant information online – documents, emails, blogs, and posts in message boards. Much of this information can be channeled to real-time updates for both rescue personnel and people suffering the crisis.

The example, presented in Figure 1, is a sample blog posting from the U.S. Katrina crisis during the initial stages in August 2005. The example depicts a request for additional information relevant to personal hygiene. The blog was one of the few websites that continually supplied information during the crisis. Mapping the relevant request would identify a similar concept in the ontology itself. The Index Ontology includes a *personal hygiene* concept as a subclass of the *vulnerable groups* concept. Linking the blog request to the relevant information using relevant index pointers would allow the user to receive information relevant to the request. Figure 8 shows an immediate response that includes most of the relevant information and can be posted to supply the user with the requested relevant information to assist in the crisis.

Analysis of the Katrina crisis request using the ontology relations which appear in Figure 4 provides additional information which can be directed toward the blog request. The request for information regarding water can be answered using the *water supplies* and *cooking* concepts. Similarly, the request for information regarding food can be answered with the *cooking* and *environmental impact* concepts. These concepts and the associated information can supply specific variables for the minimal survival requirements.

This ontology can be set up in the initial time frame of the crisis allowing information to be sent in multiple languages using the same framework. The example of the Boxing Day Tsunami shows the relevance of such an ontology. For instance, an email or a blog web-site requesting *food aid* in the civilians' local language such as Tamil or Sinhala could be collected with all of the incoming *Food Aid* requests from all of the crisis locations to the relevant concept. Consequently, management teams can make decisions based on the information associated with the *Management* concept and its related concepts (Figure 7).

CONCLUSION

The chapter presents work in the field of developing an adaptive method for crisis ontology design which can be used to represent knowledge in rapid response situations. The technique extends the ontology during a crisis and tailors it to the needs of the ongoing crisis. The implementation of the ontology within an information system will enable the mapping of the crisis information flow. The described Index Ontology allows multidirectional flow of data between different rescue forces, from rescue forces to the civilian population, and from the civilian population to rescue and reporting organizations. The real life crisis examples evaluated using the ontology hold promise for future crisis information flow management.

REFERENCES

Ansell, C., Boin, A., & Keller, A. (2010). Managing transboundary crises: Identifying the building blocks of an effective response system. *Journal of Contingencies and Crisis Management, 18*(4). doi:10.1111/j.1468-5973.2010.00620.x

Beers, M. (Ed.). (2003). *The Merck manual of medical information* (2nd ed.). Merck Research Laboratories.

Borgida, A., & Brachman, R. J. (1993). Loading data into description reasoners. In *Proceedings of the 1993 ACM SIGMOD International Conference on Management of Data*, (pp. 217–226). New York, NY: ACM Press.

Bunge, M. (1977). *Treatise on basic philosophy, the furniture of the world, ontology I* (*Vol. 3*). New York, NY: D. Reidel Publishing Co., Inc.

Bunge, M. (1979). *Treatise on basic philosophy: vol. 4, ontology II: A world of systems*. New York, NY: D. Reidel Publishing Co., Inc.

Di Maio, P. (2007). An open ontology for open source emergency response system. *Open Source Research Community*, January 2007.

Garshol, L. M., & Moore, G. (2006). *Information Technology - Document description and processing languages - Topic maps - XML syntax*. ISO. (ISO 13250-3).

Gruber, T. R. (1993). A translation approach to portable ontologies. *Knowledge Acquisition, 5*(2). doi:10.1006/knac.1993.1008

Hygiene. (2008, October 15). In *Wikipedia, The Free Encyclopedia*. Retrieved October 15, 2008, from http://en.wikipedia.org/w/index.php?title=Hygiene&oldid=245367616

Livejournal. (2005). *The survival of New Orleans Weblog*. Retrieved from http://interdictor.livejournal.com

Mostowfi, F., & Fotouhi, F. (2006) Improving quality of ontology: An ontology transformation approach. In *Proceedings of the 22nd International Conference on Data Engineering Workshops* (p. 61). Atlanta, GA.

Munich Research Group. (2005). *Node 2*. Retrieved May 30, 2005, from http://www.lrz-muenchen.de/~ua352bm/webserver/webdata/Will/node2.html

Noy, F. N., & Musen, M. A. (2000) PROMPT: Algorithm and tool for automated ontology merging and alignment. In *Proceedings of the Seventeenth National Conference on Artificial Intelligence* (AAAI-2000), (pp. 450–455). Austin, TX.

Noy, N., & Klein, M. (2003). Ontology evolution: Not the same as schema evolution. *Knowledge and Information Systems*, 5.

Pepper, S. (1999). Navigating haystacks, discovering needles. *Markup Languages: Theory and Practice, 1*(4). MIT Press.

Pepper, S., & Grønmo, G. O. (2001). *Towards a general theory of scope*. Retrieved from http://www.ontopia.net/topicmaps/materials/scope.htm

Schraagen, J. M., Huis in 't, V. M., & de Koning, L. (2010). Information sharing during crisis management in hierarchical vs. network teams. *Journal of Contingencies and Crisis Management, 18*(2). doi:10.1111/j.1468-5973.2010.00604.x

Segev, A., & Gal, A. (2007). Puzzling it out: Supporting ontology evolution with applications to e-government. In *Proceedings of IJCAI-Workshop on Workshop on Modeling and Representation in Computational Semantics*.

Segev, A., & Gal, A. (2008). Enhancing portability with multilingual ontology-based knowledge management. *Decision Support Systems, 45*(3). doi:10.1016/j.dss.2007.07.011

Segev, A., Leshno, M., & Zviran, M. (2007). Context recognition using Internet as a knowledge base. *Journal of Intelligent Information Systems, 29*(3). doi:10.1007/s10844-006-0015-y

Smith, M. K., Welty, C., & McGuiness, D. L. (2004). *OWL Web ontology language guide*. W3C recommendation. Retrieved from http://www.w3.org/TR/owl-guide/

Sphere Project. (2004). *Humanitarian charter and minimum standards in disaster response*. Geneva, Switzerland: The Sphere Project.

Stumme, G., & Maedche, A. (2001). Ontology merging for federated ontologies on the Semantic Web. In *Proceedings of the International Workshop for Foundations of Models for Information Integration*. Viterbo, Italy.

Tolk, A., Diallo, S. Y., & Turnitsa, C. D. (2007). Applying the levels of conceptual interoperability model in support of integratability, interoperability, and composability for system-of-systems engineering. *Journal of Systemics. Cybernetics and Informatics, 5*(5), 65–74.

Vaccari, L., Marchese, M., Giunchiglia, F., McNeill, F., Potter, S., & Tate, A. (2006). *OpenKnowledge deliverable 6.5: Emergency response in an open Information Systems environment*.

Vickery, B. C. (1966). *Faceted classification schemes. Graduate* New Brunswick, NJ: School of Library Service, Rutgers, the State University.

Ziesche, S. (2007). Social-networking Web systems: Opportunities for humanitarian information management. *Journal of Humanitarian Assistance*.

Chapter 8
Open Infrastructure for a Nationwide Emergency Services Network

Mark Gaynor
Saint Louis University, USA

Sarah Friedeck
Saint Louis University, USA

Alan Pearce
Information Age Economics, USA

Scott Bradner
Harvard University, USA

Ken Post
Alert Systems Inc., USA

ABSTRACT

The chapter suggests and supports a public policy in which the Federal Communications Commission (FCC) should seize a unique opportunity to resolve some of the nation's critical communications problems in times of crises with the allocation of a portion of the spectrum at 700 MHz (specifically, the D band) for the deployment of a nationwide interoperable emergency broadband wireless network built by a public-private partnership. It then presents a convincing theoretical model that advocates that an open and/or neutral, as opposed to a closed, network will add greater efficiency, greater choice, while advancing public safety along with the deployment of new and valuable technologies, applications, and services.

DOI: 10.4018/978-1-60960-609-1.ch008

INTRODUCTION

Traditional economic markets cannot – and do not – always meet all of the needs of society (Pearce, 2006). Public Safety is one example where business and government must cooperate for the overall benefit of society. With correct public policy and open infrastructures, business can thrive while society receives immeasurable gains. Because of new threats to society, along with an apparent increase in the number of so-called natural disasters, there is need for new thinking and new solutions in order to deal with these potentially catastrophic emergencies. The 2008 FCC auction of the nationwide D band (758-763 MHz and 788-793 MHz) (FCC, 2007) presented a unique opportunity to resolve some of the nation's communications problems in times of crises.

This chapter is an extended and updated version of a conference and journal paper (Gaynor, Pearce, & Bradner, 2008; Gaynor, Pearce, Bradner, & Post, 2009) presented at the 5th International Conference on Information Systems for Crisis Response and Management (ISCRAM) and then published in International Journal of Information Systems for Crisis Response Management (IJISCRAM) that proposes an infrastructure based on open standards to be built by a public/private partnership would best serve the needs of the Nationwide Emergency Services Network (NESN). Our proposed infrastructure will allow distributed management to promote innovation leading to the introduction of new devices, applications, and services, along with centralized control for nationwide crisis management. In the proposed architecture, local entities such as first responders (i.e., ambulance, fire, and police) are able to develop and deploy emergency services with applications and services that they urgently need. Many of these applications and services are not currently available or not affordable to individual agencies. Too often the results are unnecessary loss of life and property with recovery costs amounting to billions of dollars annually.

Devices manufactured by any vendor should be able to interoperate on this "open" NESN, quickly amounting to trillions of dollars over time. An "open" NESN will encourage the promotion of innovation and provide economic opportunities for a wide variety of device manufacturers, service providers, and application developers. At the same time, it will promote greater public safety by enabling more effective and efficient communications at lower costs. We briefly present and discuss a model that in a future version of this paper will be used to prove theoretically that openness in application, services, and devices are critical to maximize the benefits of any NESN.

Public safety mobile communications networks in the United States are in dire straits. Almost a decade after the September 11, 2001 terrorist attacks on New York City, Washington, D.C., and Pennsylvania (9/11), and five years after Hurricane Katrina, the public safety community still lacks the resources to build a robust and interoperable nationwide network to serve public safety and national law enforcement agencies (Lipton, 2006; Pearce, 2006). First responders lack the basic voice and data communications services that they need to confront terrorism, natural disasters, chemical spills, and other emergencies that threaten life and property and cost the nation multiple billions of dollars annually.

One example of local emerging interoperability of emergency networks is the Capital Wireless Information Net (CapWIN) organization (CapWIN, 2007). CapWIN was created in the Washington D.C. area because communication networks of fire, police, and other emergency services were not interoperable between departments, and were not interoperable across municipal boundaries. Police from this area did not have effective communications with their counterparts in Virginia and Maryland. By building a local, interoperable network, CapWIN will enable communication between organizations across geographic areas. This idea should be replicated throughout the country.

PUBLIC SAFETY BROADBAND SPECTRUM

In 2007, the FCC allocated the 700 MHz public safety broadband spectrum, which consists of 10 MHz (763-768 MHz and 793-798 MHz), to public safety providers. Shortly after, the Public Safety Spectrum Trust (PSST), a non-profit 501(c)(3) entity, was selected to be the Public Safety Broadband Licensee (PSST, 2010).

On May 12, 2010, the Federal Communications Commission (FCC) released an order conditionally approving 21 public safety jurisdictions waiver petitions to develop interoperable statewide, regional, or local Public Safety Broadband Networks (PSBNs) in the 700 MHz public safety broadband spectrum, which is a step towards a fully nationwide interoperable public safety network. These entities will coordinate with the FCC's Emergency Response Interoperability Center to ensure technical compatibility and interoperability (FCC, 2010a).

Waiver recipients must comply with "technical, operational, and governance conditions … [and must] submit to the Public Safety and Homeland Security Bureau (Bureau) … a detailed plan for achieving interoperability with other PSBNs" (Interoperability Showing) (FCC, 2010d, p. 1). Waiver recipients also must enter a "long term de facto spectrum transfer lease with the PSST" (FCC, 2010c, p. 1). On August 11, 2010, the PSST's budget was approved by the Bureau (FCC, 2010b). On August 17, 2010, in order to allow wavier recipients more time to develop their Interoperability Showings, the 60-day deadline was tolled (FCC, 2010e).

The D band spectrum at 700MHz ideally fits the needs of an NESN because this spectrum is nationwide, unencumbered, and has good physical propagation properties. As we have previously suggested, several bills supporting the additional allocation of the D block to public safety agencies have been introduced, including the "First Responders Protection Act of 2010"

(S. 3625, 2010), the "Public Safety Spectrum and Wireless Innovation Act," (S. 3756, 2010) and the "Broadband for First Responders Act of 2010" (H.R. 5081, 2010). All three of these bills have been referred to appropriate committees (i.e., the U.S. Senate Commerce, Science, and Transportation Committee, or the U.S. House Committee on Energy and Commerce). The Public Safety Spectrum and Wireless Innovation Act, in particular, supports building the networks to open standards, which also coincides with our beliefs and recommendations.

Combined with the FCC proposed regulations concerning network build out and performance parameters, the D band could help meet the nation's needs for effective communications in critical situations. This spectrum is unique because of its nationwide coverage. Previous users of this spectrum were required to vacate by 2009. Due to the propagation properties of this spectrum, the infrastructure will be relatively inexpensive to build, and will work with devices behind walls and in buildings. The D block offers a rare opportunity to build a robust and comprehensive NESN network.

OPENNESS OF NESN

A wireless network can be open to devices, applications, services, and transport. It can also be closed, which means that the network operator or owner determines what devices, applications and services are to be offered and what are rejected. Openness means that any manufacturer can build a device, subject to open technical specifications and standards that can be used by any end user, on any network. Openness in the context of applications and services means that any end users can pick any application or service they desire, and use them over the open network. Finally, openness in the context of transport services means that the transport network service provider must sell bandwidth at a wholesale cost to others that also wish to provide competitive and/or alternative transport services.

Openness can be complex. A transport network provider may require a certification process to use a device, or run an application or service over the network. This certification process may be complex and expensive, which can be a barrier to entry for potentially competitive or emerging companies. Organizations may claim that they support openness, but may take actions that do not promote it. An example is complex document standards. The complexity of some standards makes it too expensive for some organizations to compete effectively. This is particularly a problem for innovators in the public services product arena where the market is relatively small.

There is a fine line between applications and services. Voice over Internet Protocol (VoIP) can be both an application and a service. Using Session Initiation Protocol (SIP), two end users can talk over the Internet with a complete end-2-end architecture (described later); only the two end devices know that a voice conversation is occurring. Clearly, this is an application. However, the same protocol, SIP, can be used to create a service where a SIP proxy provides a VoIP service. To a user, the application and service may appear identical.

Prior to the FCC's 700 MHz auction, Google proposed that the C band of the 700MHz spectrum have the following open requirements:

- "Open applications: consumers should be able to download and utilize any software applications, content, or services they desire;
- Open devices: consumers should be able to utilize a handheld communications device with whatever wireless network they prefer;
- Open services: third parties (resellers) should be able to acquire wireless services from a 700MHz licensee on a wholesale

basis, based on reasonably nondiscriminatory commercial terms; and
- Open networks: third parties (like internet service providers) should be able to interconnect at a technically feasible point in a 700 MHz licensee's wireless network." (Whitt, 2007).

Since recommending these requirements, Google has claimed that it still believes that there should be equal access regarding the wired Internet. However, Google is now siding with Verizon Communications (its new cell phone partner) that this same access should not apply to cellular Internet phones. This could mean carriers having the ability block certain applications from mobile phones or being able to charge more for access to specific applications; some believe that this would eventually make certain services inaccessible / unaffordable for some consumers (Kang, 2010; Helft & Miller, 2010).

To be truly "open", 700 MHz system issues must also be considered in context – a unified incident command / decision support (UIC/DS) system that includes:

1. Sensors including human intelligence (e.g., CIA, FBI, 911 calls) and pre-analyzed work product (e.g., weather forecasts, food recalls, infectious disease detection) providing situational awareness.
2. Communications network including connectivity with critical infrastructure providers.
3. Information technology / incident command tools that facilitate the core processes of Unified Incident Command System efforts, specifically:
   a. Data Gathering
   b. Information Management
   c. Knowledge Formation
   d. Knowledge Dissemination
4. 'Last-mile' warning, mobilization and public information channels.

5. Devices and terminals used for public warning, external resource mobilization, local interagency notification, and temporary 911 services.
6. Tactical 'last-mile' communications channels.
7. Devices and terminals providing tactical capabilities – communications of all types, control of robots, personnel safety sensors, data terminals.
8. Ancillary systems and tools including those that consider responder family issues.

All UIC/DS elements need to be tightly coupled for maximum responsiveness and effectiveness. Openness here requires transparency for all functions.

ESN INFRASTRUCTURE

In order to achieve the maximum benefits to society, an NESN must follow at least the first three of Google's original openness requirements: open devices, applications, and services. We believe that wholesaling basic transport service would provide a more open and vibrant marketplace, but we do not think that all is lost if wholesaling is not included, as long as the other three openness requirements are present. Openness is designed to create an environment where device manufacturers can innovate with new devices, where application developers have opportunities to discover novel applications, and where successful applications can become services that match the uncertain needs of first responders. This environment is conducive to innovation and must also promote enough management structure to meet the needs of emergency responders in chaotic environments. 9/11 and Hurricane Katrina have taught us many lessons, including how traditional communication networks can quickly become overwhelmed with traffic during and after a crisis.

Standards Based

The Internet has taught us that a rich eco system does develop around open networks built from standards. Under the direction of the Internet Engineering Task Force (IETF), the Internet has become a model of how voluntary standards can build an interoperable infrastructure. In turn, this infrastructure promoted the emergence of many successful ventures for devices, applications, and services. Examples of these successes include devices such as Personal Digital Assistants (PDAs) and Internet-enabled cell phones, applications like e-Bay and Amazon.com, and services such as those offered via VoIP by Vonage, among others.

A degree of centralized control and management will benefit an NESN because of the importance of maintaining a robust network that is not overwhelmed with traffic. Wholesaling transport services on an NESN does not seem to be an absolute requirement in order to create an eco system of vendors, applications developers, and service providers as long as they can use their devices, applications, and services on the NESN, but it would likely increase the number of players as well as the variety of services.

We agree with the report, "Communications Issues for Emergency Communications Beyond E911" (NRIC VII Focus Group 1D, 2005), that IP should be the underlying standard for the NESN. We also believe that there must be no network-specific functions that would inhibit the ability for any IP-based application to operate fully. This is also in line with the all "IP mantra" for Third Generation (3G) wireless services that most wireless service providers have adopted. The IP protocol has demonstrated the flexibility of an unreliable datagram service for building a vast array of different network applications and services. Using IP will enable the NESN to interoperate with existing IP networks, including the current Internet, and will increase the physical transport options for the NESN. The use of IP will also mean that NESN deployment can take place in parallel at the same time on existing infrastructures and on the infrastructures that will be deployed as a result of the 700 MHz auction, thus maximizing the speed of deployment.

End-2-End

An end-2-end infrastructure for an NESN is preferred because it has spurred the innovation that underlies the success of the Internet and the World Wide Web (Web) and provides many valuable lessons for designers of flexible infrastructures. The end-2-end principle states that networks should provide only the simplest of services (Saltzer, Reed, & Clark, 1984; Isen, 1998). The end systems should have responsibility for all applications and any state information required by the application. By providing the basic building blocks, instead of complex network services, the network infrastructure will not constrain future applications. Services with end-2-end architecture, by definition, have a distributed structure because they push complexity to the endpoints of the network. The idea is to keep the network simple, and build any needed complexity into the ends, or edges, of the network. Applications that are end-2-end are generally unknown, or neutral, to the network infrastructure. This means that changes to the network, or permission to add new end-2-end services, are not necessary, because nothing within the network inhibits or constrains a new service. The end-2-end structure is one of increased innovation, and the proof of its validity is the success of the Internet and World Wide Web. The network does need to provide support for some middleware services including authentication and access control. However, the services themselves should be distributed with local entities responsible for their users wherever they are accessing the network.

End-2-end also guarantees that services offered by the underlying network infrastructure must be as simple as possible. If a carrier were to try to anticipate the services that applications will need,

the carrier is likely to be wrong, and as a result might inhibit new applications by constraining them with services that do not serve the needs of the public. The IP protocol in the Internet is a good example of this philosophy—it is simple, only offering the most basic type of network service, i.e., the unreliable datagram service. This simple core protocol has allowed immense innovation at the transport and application layers. Different application modules can utilize the transport protocols that match their needs, yet all of them are built over IP, which has become the glue holding the Internet together. The success of the Internet is partially due to the simplicity of IP, which validates the end-2-end argument.

By permitting applications at the user level, much more experimentation is enabled. Since end-2-end applications do not require modification of the network infrastructure or permission to experiment, users can and do innovate by creating and developing new services. Consider the creation of the World Wide Web. Tim Berners-Lee (Berners-Lee, 1999) was not a network researcher searching for innovative ways to utilize the Internet. Rather, he was an administrator trying to better serve his users. He developed the Web to allow the scientists in his organization to share information across diverse computers and networks. It just so happened that his solution, the Web, met many other user needs far better than anything else at the time. This illustrates one powerful attribute of the end-2-end argument - you never know who will think of the next great idea, it could be anybody and with end-to-end services, anyone could deploy the new idea for the entire world.

Just as end-2-end argument promoted innovation in the Internet, the value of open infrastructure is greatest when uncertainty is high and users are able to experiment with new devices, applications, and services. Sometimes, as Hippel (1998) shows, users are best suited to solve their own problems and end-2-end infrastructure enables user innovation.

Modified End-2-End

We believe in a modified end-2-end structure for the NESN. It is important to promote innovation with devices, applications, and services while maintaining the ability to dictate what is used when on the network and when. In the Internet anybody can try anything; for example we can try to launch a distributed denial of service attack on any user we desire. Clearly this is not desirable on the NESN. This boils down to some limited types of admissions and authorization control systems to determine who can do what, and when.

Given that we believe the NESN must be based on open standards, vendors can build devices and develop applications and services. However, they should not be able to deploy these new devices/applications/services without explicit permission from the organizations that use the NESN. The combination of end-2-end thinking and admission control should serve society best because it will promote innovation while being able to deliver a network that can meet the stringent requirements of an NESN. NESN structure should be considered in the context of the unified incident command / decision support (UICDS) system as noted earlier.

NESN Governance

The NESN raises large governance questions. Who should be the overseer? Who should decide which access and operating procedures need to be set and who should set them? Who should decide which types of improvements and updates as need to be approved as science and technology evolve? Who should be able to ration network usage if a disaster limits infrastructure capacity or causes an overwhelming demand for bandwidth? Who should allocate deployment and upgrade costs?

The NESN needs a governance mechanism that is representative of the missions, responsibilities and interests of at least 9 categories of stakeholders:

1. Federal Agencies with public safety, homeland security and disaster related missions.
2. State Agencies with public safety, disaster related missions.
3. Local Agencies with emergency management missions.
4. Technology providers – equipment manufacturers, communications carriers including radio / TV media, innovators.
5. Organizations with risk & liability interests – city / county risk managers, risk pool managers, insurance firms, operators of critical infrastructure including utilities, hospitals, dams, nuclear power, and chemical plants.
6. Organizations with hazards research, education, policy missions.
7. Auxiliary services providers – Red Cross, Urban Search & Rescue, others.
8. Public & advocates for people who are deaf, elderly, or otherwise disabled.
9. Enterprises, such as universities and businesses that need to provide emergency communication for their students and employees

An umbrella governance mechanism is key to widespread NESN support and adoption. Many stakeholders insist on voice and vote on final decisions as the price for their cooperation. They cite many examples of where critical mission needs or interests have been trumped or ignored for political and other reasons. It is just as important to decide when governance is not required as it is to decide on the mechanism of governance.

The NESN governance mechanism needs specific protections against mission creep and program politicization. These program complications discourage support and participation by practitioners. The governance mechanisms should not unduly restrict the innovation environment. Shifting political interests make it near impossible to keep pace with rapid advances in science and technology. And by some estimates, the gap in the application of science and technology to public safety / disaster management infrastructure already exceeds 25 years.

To maintain focus, we suggest that the charter or bylaws of the governance mechanism include 6 key principles / operating disciplines:

1. Incident Command System (4 core processes, all functional units)
2. Agility of resources (interoperability of people and equipment)
3. Systems engineering (economics, logistics, reliability, maintenance, recovery, operational efficiency, etc.)
4. Readiness (training, human factors. all national planning scenarios)
5. Public / private partnership (engage all stakeholders, work to respective strengths of each sector)
6. Innovation (maintenance of an environment that supports innovation)

The principles / disciplines above can be factored into performance metrics that minimize factional self-interests. The metrics enable meaningful goals and measures of progress.

The NESN governance mechanism should favor practitioners as representatives of stakeholder categories. Practitioners are best able to separate the ordinary risks of respective disciplines from the extraordinary risks associated with certain technology and system feature decisions. They're generally best able to factor technology trends and new methods.

The experience of disaster management practitioners is particularly important to decisions involving NESN control. These control decisions include those that enable suspension or cannibalization of certain NESN resources during major disasters. Incident command officers are already trusted with extraordinary discretion in major disasters. They can discard federal, state and local acquisition and some labor rules when necessary to save lives, and to minimize environmental damage, economic activity losses and other disaster consequences. They should help determine NESN control mechanisms that have similar consequences.

The views of local disaster management agencies need particular attention. Because the first objective in a disaster situation is to maintain confidence in government, local officials are reluctant to discuss infrastructure problems openly. As a result, local agency views are often under-weighted. On the other hand, it is not uncommon for local agencies to not recognize their own infrastructure problems. Just as there must be a way to empower those local agencies that recognize problems to fix them there also must be a way to help local agencies to recognize problems they do not see.

Local agencies have economic, responsiveness, mutual aid, training, and logistical concerns that factor into network feature decisions. They have multi-hazard missions that dictate multipurpose solutions and cannot afford a separate system for every problem and function.

Local agency concerns favor compatibility with private sector network protocols and hardware where reasonable. This might allow public safety radio makers to take advantage of high-volume cellular handset technology to reduce radio costs. It might allow the cell-phones of search and rescue and other auxiliary service providers to be temporarily linked with the radios of 1st responders.

Many local jurisdictions lack the population base to justify dedicated NESN functionality. This economic constraint raises spectrum sharing, preemption and private sector network compatibility issues.

Intellectual Property Issues

The NESN raises intellectual property issues. Intellectual property should not be an obstacle to public safety and homeland security. The NESN governance body should favor a cross-licensing pool or other means that facilitates the application of cutting-edge science and technology.

Network Structure

Wireless networks can have either a centralized infrastructure, similar to traditional cellular networks, or a more distributed architecture, such as the emerging collection of Wi-Fi networks. Centralized networks allow better coordination, but do not promote innovation (Gaynor & Bradner, 2003). Coordination is critical in major disaster situations. To partially offset the discouragement of innovation by centralized network approaches, we suggest charter or license provisions that specifically favor innovation.

We also find merit in the idea of one of our informal reviewers, KC Chaffy at The University of San Diego, who suggested that a portion of the D band be given to local communities to allow experimentation with different wireless infrastructures. She would also like to see infrastructure enabling traffic measurement while protecting user privacy. We welcome both ideas since they promote innovation via experimentation and market selection, and encourage the collection of data to aid network researchers.

Priority Service with Admission Control

For effective emergency services, the NESN must support several types of priority services that include prioritization of communications and dynamic admission control. The NESN will carry data, voice, and video traffic from heterogeneous sources to heterogeneous endpoints. Voice and Video traffic require low latency. Communications for command and control from emergency managers needs priority over less critical information. At the very least we recommend a best effort classification for non-emergency traffic, priority classification for normal emergency communications, highest priority for management emergency traffic, and a low latency category for time sensitive data such as voice and video. That said, the design should recognize that all traffic

over the infrastructure can be important when responding to an emergency so providing priority classification for officially designated emergency traffic cannot lockout all other traffic.

General Internet traffic prioritization has two main favors: a coarse-grained packet classification strategy called differentiated services described in RFC 2475 and RFC 3260 (Black et al., 1998; Grossman, 2002) and fine-grained session level reservation methodology called integrated services discussed in RFC 2205 and 4495 (Braden et al., 1997) oriented protocols. We recommend packet level QoS such as Diffserv, which scales well and is robust because there is no per-flow meta-data within the network infrastructure. Diffserv offers best effort, expedited forwarding behavior for delay sensitive traffic, and up to 12 classes of Assured Forwarding. The scalability and robustness of class-based priority offered by the Diffserv architecture is reasonable for the NESN. Diffserv can also be configured to split the network in such a way to provide a guaranteed capacity for emergency traffic while preserving some network capacity for other traffic.

The Defense Information Systems Agency (DISA) within the Department of Defense proposed a service architecture for military telephone services, Assured Service (Baker & Polk, 2004). Multi-Level Precedence and Preemption (MLPP) (American, 1992) defines a dynamic protocol to assure that the most important calls preempt less critical communications. Multi-Level Expedited Forwarding is a partial solution to MLPP but needs a dynamic admission protocol to begin to satisfy the MLPP requirements (Baker & Polk, 2004). A proposed solution that has both call admission control with packet priority and preemption is discussed in an IETF Internet draft (Baker & Polk 2006). While current Internet protocols may not fully meet MLPP, they clearly can evolve to meet the communication needs of the NESN.

Table 1. Reserve Vs Bid Price

700MHz Auction Results			
Block	**Bidders**	**Total**	**Reserve Price**
A	Verizon, US Cellular, Cavalier, Century Telecomm	$3.96 billion	$1.8 billion
B	AT&T, US Cellular, Verizon, Century Telecom	$9.14 billion	$1.3 billion
C	Verizon	$4.75 billion	$4.6 billion
D	Qualcomm	$472 million	$1.3 billion
E	EchoStar, Qualcomm	$1.27 billion	$903 million

Table 2. Ratio of highest bid to reserve price per MHz of bandwidth

Block	MHz	Cost Per MHz (Res)	Cost Per MHz (Bid)	Bid/ Res
A	12	$151 million	$330 million	2.19
B	12	$115 million	$761 million	6.65
C	22	$211 million	$215 million	1.02
D	10	$133 million	$130 million	0.35
D+	20	$67 million	$65 million	0.35
E	6	$151 million	$211 million	1.41

VALUE OF AN OPEN ESN

There are ways to value open versus closed architecture. One model discussed in Appendix I is based on basic probability and statistical theory (Baldwin & Clark, 1999; Gaynor, 2001 & 2003; Gaynor & Bradner, 2001, 2004, & 2008) along with several assumptions about users, device manufactures, application developers and service providers. It could be used illustrates analytically how market uncertainty affects the value to EMS organizations (i.e., the users) of an NESN network. The model would predict that when uncertainty is high in the context of what devices, applications, and services emergency organizations will find valuable then an open network has greater overall value than a closed network. The greater the uncertainty and the more choices users have the greater the value of openness.

ACTION RESULTS

Overall the 700MHz spectrum auction was successful because it generated more revenue than expected. However, the D block that was set aside for a nation wide emergency network did not sell because Qualcomm the single bidder for this block did not meet the reserve price set by the FCC. Table 1 displays information about each block including the highest bid and reserve price. Table 2 normalizes this data by calculating the cost per MHz of bandwidth. Figure 1 illustrates the ratio of the highest bid compared to the reserve and Figure 2 displays the cost per MHz of bandwidth or the highest bid compared to reserve price.

Several interesting trends emerge from this data. First, the blocks without conditions (i.e. A, B, E) sold for 1.4 to over 8 times the reserve price, while the C and D blocks, each of which had restrictions on the bandwidth, either did not sell, or sold for close to the reserve price. The highest bid for the D block designated for emergency service was only .35 of the reserve price set by the FCC. Another trend is that the more regions the spectrum is divided into the greater the value of this bandwidth. The B region with 734 licenses sold for an average of $761M per MHz, compared to the low $200M range for the B and E band with 176 licenses. The C band with 12 regions[1], and D block with a single region had the lowest highest bid to reserve price.

FCC's Response to Failed Auction

The FCC is considering the following regarding the next D block auction:

Figure 1. Reserve Vs bid price

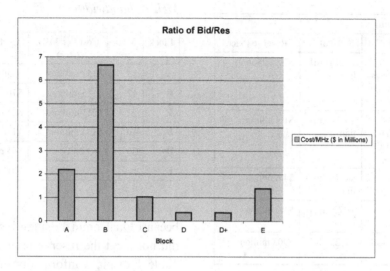

- Dropping the reserve price from $1.3B to $750M;
- Opening the auction to regional as opposed to nationwide bids;
- Increasing the build out time period from 10 to 15 years, thus significantly spreading the infrastructure costs in the hope of making the network more affordable.

At this time, the status D block auction is uncertain. We do not support such an auction because we believe the spectrum should be donated instead; however, we understand why the FCC would consider it. The above tables and graphs show that the smaller the bidding region the higher the spectrum cost. This implies that by opening up the D block to regional bidding its value would increase from the $472M that Qualcomm bid to the new reserve of $750M. The increased build

Figure 2. Reserve Vs bid price per MHz of bandwidth

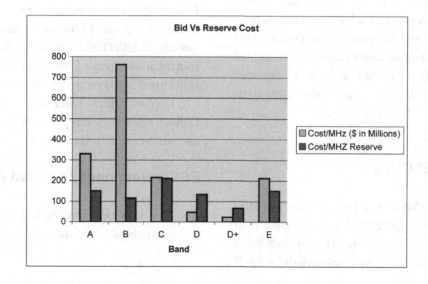

out period should also increase the value of this spectrum because it spreads out the large capital investment.

CONCLUSION

The architecture and the beginnings of a theoretical model outlined in this paper demonstrate that the risk is worth taking to demand openness in any NESN—namely that an open networks beats a closed one in terms of customer service, satisfaction, efficiency, cost, and the development and deployment of new technologies, applications and services. Furthermore, since there is a dire need for the creation of a government mandated nationwide, interoperable broadband wireless network for use of the public safety and national law enforcement agencies, this vehicle, if launched via FCC policy, could be used as a low risk experiment to test the validity of this theoretical model.

REFERENCES

American National Standards Institute. (1992). *Telecommunications, integrated services digital network (ISDN) multi-level precedence and preemption (MLPP) service capability.* (ANSI T1.619-1992- R1999).

Baker, F., & Polk, J. (2004). *Implementing MLPP for voice and video in the Internet protocol suite. Internet Engineering Task Force.* IETF.

Baker, F., & Polk, J. (2004). *MLEF without capacity admission does not satisfy MLPP requirements. Internet Engineering Task Force.* IETF.

Baker, F., & Polk, J. (2006). *Implementing an emergency telecommunications service for real time services in the Internet protocol suite (RFC 4542). Internet Engineering Task Force.* IETF.

Baldwin, C., & Clark, K. (1999). *Design rules: The power of modularity.* Cambridge, MA: MIT Press.

Berners-Lee, T. (1999). *Weaving the Web: The original design and ultimate destiny of the World Wide Web.* New York, NY: HarperCollins Publishers, Inc.

Black, S., Black, D., Carlson, M., Davies, E., Wang, Z., & Weiss, W. (1998). *An architecture for differentiated services (RFC 2475). Internet Engineering Task Force.* IETF.

Braden, R., Zhang, L., Berson, S., Herzog, S., & Jamin, S. (1997). *Resource reservation protocol (RSVP) (RFC 2205). Internet Engineering Task Force.* IETF.

Capital Wireless Information Net (CapWIN). (2007). *Capital wireless information net.* Retrieved from http://www.capwin.org

Federal Communications Commission (FCC). (2007). *Summary: Auction 72.* Retrieved from http://wireless.fcc.gov/auctions/default. htm?job=auction_summary&id=73

Federal Communications Commission (FCC). (2010a). *FCC grants conditional approval of 21 petitions by cities, counties and states to build interoperable broadband networks for America's first responders.* Retrieved from http://fjallfoss.fcc.gov/edocs_public/attachmatch/DOC-298124A1.pdf

Federal Communications Commission (FCC). (2010b). *Implementing a nationwide, broadband, interoperable public safety network in the 700 MHz band* (DA 10-1494). Retrieved from http://fjallfoss.fcc.gov/edocs_public/attachmatch/DA-10-1494A1.pdf

Federal Communications Commission (FCC). (2010c). *Public safety and homeland security bureau approves long term de facto transfer spectrum lease agreements filed by conditional waiver recipients to establish 700 MHz interoperable public safety wireless broadband networks* (DA 10-1678). Retrieved from http://fjallfoss.fcc.gov/edocs_public/attachmatch/DA-10-1678A1.pdf

Federal Communications Commission (FCC). (2010d). *Public safety and homeland security bureau offers further guidance to conditional waiver recipients on completing the interoperability showing required by the 700 MHz waiver order* (DA 10-923). Retrieved from http://fjallfoss.fcc.gov/edocs_public/attachmatch/DA-10-923A1.pdf

Federal Communications Commission (FCC). (2010e). *The FCC's public safety bureau provides 700 MHz broadband waiver recipients additional time to more fully develop and finalize their network interoperability plans* (DA 10-1540). Retrieved from http://fjallfoss.fcc.gov/edocs_public/attachmatch/DA-10-1540A1.pdf

Gaynor, M. (2001). *The effect of market uncertainty on the management structure of network-based services.* Ph.D. Thesis, Harvard University.

Gaynor, M. (2003). *Network service investment guild: Maximizing ROI in uncertain markets.* Indianapolis, IN: Wiley Publishing, Inc.

Gaynor, M., & Bradner, S. (2001). Using real options to value modularity in standards. *Knowledge Technology and Policy, Special on IT Standardization, 14*(2).

Gaynor, M., & Bradner, S. (2004). *A real options metric to evaluate network, protocol, and service architecture. Computer Communication Review.* CCR.

Gaynor, M., & Bradner, S. (2008). *A statistical model to value network neutrality.* Media Law & Policy, New York Law School.

Gaynor, M., Pearce, A., & Bradner, S. (2008). Open infrastructure for a nationwide emergency service network. *Proceedings of the 5th International ISCRAM Conference,* Washington, D.C.

Gaynor, M., Pearce, A., Bradner, S., & Post, K. (2009). Open infrastructure for a nationwide emergency service network. [IJISCRAM]. *International Journal of Information Systems for Crisis Response and Management, 1*(2). doi:10.4018/jiscrm.2009040103

Grossman, D. (2002). *New terminology and clarifications for Diffserv. Internet Engineering Task Force.* IETF.

Hipple, E. (1998). Economics of product development by user: The impact of sticky local information. *Management Science, 44*(5).

H.R. 5081: Broadband for First Responders Act of 2010, 111th Congress (2010).

Isenberg, D. S. (1998). The dawn of the stupid network. *ACM Networker, 2*(1), 24–31. doi:10.1145/280437.280445

Lipton, E. (2006). The Katrina year: The next emergency: Despite steps, disaster planning still shows gaps. *The New York Times.* Retrieved from http://www.nytimes.com/

Network Reliability and Interoperability Council VII Focus Group 1D. (2005). *Communication issues for emergency communications beyond E911, final report – Properties, network architectures and transition issues for communications between emergency service organizations, including PSAPs.*

Pearce, A. (2006). An analysis of the public safety & homeland security benefits of an interoperable nationwide emergency communications network at 700 MHz built by a public-private partnership. *Media Law & Policy Journal. New York Law School, 16*(1), 41–61.

Pierce, M., & Choi, D. (2004). *Architecture for assured service capabilities in voice over IP.* Internet Engineering Task Force (IETF) Internet draft.

Pierce, M., & Choi, D. (2004). *Requirements for assured service capabilities in voice over IP.* (Internet Engineering Task Force) IETF Internet draft.

Public Safety Spectrum Trust (PSST). (2010). *Public safety spectrum trust.* Retrieved from http://www.psst.org/index.jsp

S. 3625: First Responders Protection Act of 2010, 111th Congress (2010).

S. 3756: Public Safety Spectrum and Wireless Innovation Act, 111th Congress (2010).

Saltzer, J., Reed, D., & Clark, D. (1984). End-to-end arguments in system design. *ACM Transactions on Computer Systems*, 2(4), 277–288. doi:10.1145/357401.357402

Whitt, R. (2007). The promise of open platforms in the upcoming spectrum auction. [Web log post]. Retrieved from http://googlepublicpolicy.blogspot.com/2007/07/promise-of-open-platforms-in-upcoming.html

ENDNOTE

[1] The C block required openness as request by Google. Many feel the Google gamed this auction by biding the minimum bid to assure that the C block sold with the open network conditions. Google was willing to pay $4.6B to ensure that either it or a higher bidder would build a national open wireless network. Since Google did not try and outbid Verizon it seems clear that Google preferred an open network built and managed by others. Google wanted to insure that their services would be available on a "neutral network" (Gaynor & Bradner 2008).

APPENDIX

A Simple Probabilistic Model

This model estimates the satisfaction of EMS providers with a choice of devices compared with a single manufacture dictating what device the EMS provider must use. It illustrates that when the uncertainty of what device will function best is high, then giving EMS providers many choices has tremendous value. It seems likely that the device needs of rural EMS providers will differ from the demands of urban EMS services. Gaynor and Bradner (2004) use this probabilistic framework known as the "best of many" model to value network architecture. In this framework, the user has greater satisfaction with a device or service that better matches their needs. This model assumes that the satisfaction to the user for a particular device is a normally distributed random variable.

When device vendors do not understand what users want, they must experiment with different devices that have different form factors and different feature sets. Each experiment is seen by the user as a product and is one attempt to meet an uncertain market. The economic value of experimentation links to market uncertainty by definition - uncertainty is the inability of the experimenter to predict the value of the experiment. When uncertainty is zero, the outcome of any experiment is known with perfect accuracy. As uncertainty increases, it becomes harder to predict the success of any experiment's outcome because outcomes are more widely distributed. This means that successful devices will be well received by EMS providers, while unsuccessful products may not. This link between experimentation and uncertainty is intuitive, as long as the definition of uncertainty is consistent with the variance of results from a set of experiments.

The bottom axis represents the users satisfaction level, which is moderately happy if this satisfaction is between the average and one standard deviation (SD), happy if between 1 and 2 SDs, very happy if between 2 and 3 SDs, moderately unhappy if between the average and -1 SD, unhappy if between -1 and -2 SDs, and very unhappy if between -2 and -3 SDs from the mean. The mean of this distribution, which we denote as "V" represents the point where 50 percent of potential EMS users are at least moderately happy with the device. It would be unusual for any user to have a satisfaction level greater than 3 SDs above the mean, but likely that many potential EMS providers will be moderately satisfied with a particular device. The 68 percent of EMS users between +1 and -1 SDs are not overly happy, or unhappy with the choice. As SD increases the spread of what users are willing to pay for a service grows.

Assuming a normal distribution for the value of an experiment, Figure 3 shows what we expect to happen by attempting several parallel device experiments for a particular device. It shows the probability of experiments being a particular distance from the mean. $V = E(X)$ denotes the expected value of a particular experiment. Looking at the percentages in Figure 3, we expect that 34 percent of the devices will fall between the mean and +1 SD (moderately happy) from it, 13.5 percent between 1 and 2 SDs (happy), and 2 percent between 2 and 3 (very happy) SDs from the mean. This illustrates that finding great devices may take on the order of 1000 attempts.

Figure 3 shows *U(10)* and *U(100)*, the expected maximum of 10/100 device experiments. That is, *U(10)* is the value of the best device from a sample of 10 device experiments. This maximum is composed of two different components: first, the effect of the mean and, second, the offset from the mean. This offset from the mean (*V*) is itself composed of two parts: first, the effect of the SD and, second, the effect of the parallel experimentation. Thus, *U(n)* can be broken into these parts: $U(n) = V + Q(n)*SD$ That is, the maximum of *n* experiments equals the distribution mean plus the value of *n* experiments

Figure 3. Real option framework

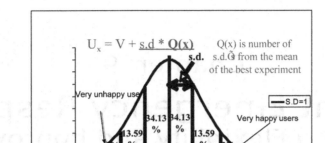

times the SD of the distribution. $Q(n)$ [14] measures how many SDs from the mean $U(n)$ is. Intuitively it makes sense that $U(n) >= V$. It follows that the probability of $U(n)$ greatly exceeding V increases as n or the variance grows.

Roughly, for $n = 2$, $Q(n) = .85$, for $n = 10$, $Q(n) = 1.5$, for $n = 100$, $Q(n) = 2.5$, and for $n = 1000$, $Q(n) = 3$. The intuition behind this is as you increase the number of device experiments, the best of these experiments has a value that grows further from the mean, but at a decreasing rate. As market uncertainty increases, so does the gain from experimentation and thus the potential for profit. This example shows that $Q(n)$ is a measure of how many SDs U is away from the mean, and the market uncertainty is the scaling factor.

This model, based on the best of many device experiments, is options-based because different players create many options for a particular device from which users select the device they like best. When only a single choice for a device exists, the expected value of this value is the distribution mean, which is lower than the value of the best of many choices. Furthermore, this difference increases as market uncertainty grows. The above illustrates how market uncertainty increases the value of giving users many choices.

Chapter 9
Resilient Emergency Response:
Supporting Flexibility and Improvisation in Collaborative Command and Control

Jiri Trnka
Swedish Defense Research Agency, Sweden

Björn J. E. Johansson
Swedish Defense Research Agency, Sweden

ABSTRACT

The focus of this chapter is the design and development of Information and Communication Technologies that support collaborative work and processes in command and control teams, more specifically, in joint emergency response operations. The unique contexts and varying circumstances of response operations have an impact on how collaborative work and interactions among commanders emerge, as well as on the extent to which Information and Communication Technologies are used. This emergence of response operations poses specific methodological complications and demands on how to study command and control teams, and also how to approach high-level design problems. The chapter demonstrates how such analysis can be performed. It presents a study of scenario-based role-playing simulation with professionals – emergency management commanders – as participants. The study documents the work practice of a team of commanders from the Swedish local and regional emergency response organizations responding jointly to an emergency, a medium size forest fire. The study also identifies areas and/ or activities that may be enhanced by command and control tools. A combined set of bottom-up data driven and top-down methods – topical episode analysis, communicative roles, socio-metric status and communication modelling – are used to assess communication and interactions among the commanders. The findings indicate that the studied commanders used informal arrangements within the established

DOI: 10.4018/978-1-60960-609-1.ch009

formal command and control structures, and took informal functions and communicative roles across organizational and domain boundaries to handle diverse incidents and so called pseudo-problems. This identified adaptive and improvised behaviour of the commanders – and the team as whole – was identified as a critical characteristic for effective command and control work in joint response operations. Cross-domain and cross-organizational knowledge was found to be the most important feature of this type of capability to adapt and improvise. The study, further, highlights the significance of employing bottom-up, data driven methods for analysis of design and development processes, as well as important methodological challenges related to this type of analysis.

INTRODUCTION

The research focus of this chapter is the design and development of information and communication technologies (ICT) that support collaborative work and processes in heterogeneous command and control teams involved in emergency response operations.

Response operations can be defined as non-routine activities that require situation-driven and problem-solving behaviour by responding organizations, teams and individuals (e.g. Comfort et al., 2001; Drabek & McEntire, 2003; Kedra & Wachtendorf, 2003). Response operations, as well as related command and control (C^2) work, are characterized by loosely defined and shifting goals, versatile situations, time pressure, high stakes and involvement of multiple actors (Orasanu & Connolly, 1993). Commanders in charge of response operations must therefore show flexibility and have the capability to adapt and improvise. They may, for example, need to shift between different work modes, thus leaving standard operational routines for situation-driven, even emergent, needs and operations. In short, commanders in emergency response need to –must – cope with high coordinative and interactive complexity.

Many organizations in the emergency response domain invest in diverse ICT to increase C^2 capabilities and/or to facilitate effective and sophisticated response when facing such challenges. ICT that are particularly relevant in this context are C^2 tools designed to enhance resource management, real-time situation assessment and communication. A key feature of modern C^2 tools is that they are intended to support teams of collaborating commanders. As these tools often lead to new work procedures, radical organizational and technological changes may appear (Woods & Dekker, 2000; Cummings, 2004).

One important issue is if, and also in what ways, these tools increase C^2 capabilities and actually facilitate enhanced response in reality. Therefore, authors working in diverse fields such as computer supported cooperative work (Schmidt & Bannon, 1992), distributed cognition (Hutchins, 1995), and cognitive systems engineering (Hollnagel & Woods, 2005), all emphasize the importance of scrutinizing the usefulness and the actual effect(s) of new tools when being applied in practice, in addition to assessment of their potential effects from a more theoretical perspective. It is, in other words, essential to empirically evaluate how an actual C^2 organization performs and how the C^2 organization's performance changes when using new C^2 tools. Taking into account the complexity of C^2 activities in emergency response, it is equally important to observe how a C^2 organization should behave as it is to notice what an actual C^2 organization does when designing new C^2 tools (Adelman, 1991; Hollnagel & Woods, 2005). It is a challenge to explore human behaviour and to gain in-depth knowledge from C^2 work in emergency response with respect to its dynamics and complexity (Killian, 2002; Stallings, 2006). Varying circumstances and the emergence of response operations pose specific methodological complications and demands (e.g., Drabek & McEntire, 2003; Mendonça & Fiedrich, 2006).

This chapter describes how such analysis of C[2] organizations can be carried out by focusing heterogeneous C[2] teams with team members distributed across different organizations. It presents an empirical study of scenario-based role-playing simulation with professionals – emergency management commanders – as participants. The study documents the work practice of a team of commanders who respond to an emergency, and identifies areas and/or activities that actually may be enhanced by C[2] tools.

BACKGROUND

Our research concerns *command and control* work conducted by *teams* of commanders, which are part of a larger emergency response *system*. Their task is to *manage dynamic, high risk situations* with possible conflicting goals under *time pressure*. In the following, we describe and discuss teams in this type of settings by combining notions of distributed decision-making (Rasmussen, Brehmer & Leplat, 1990; Cook, Noyes & Masakowski, 2007), distributed cognition (Hutchins, 1995; Garbis, 2002) and group/team communication (Hirokawa & Poole, 1996; Frey, Gouran & Poole, 1999). Other necessary notions are improvisation (Mendonça & Wallace, 2004), and command and control viewpoint (McCann & Pigeau, 2000).

Teams and Teamwork

Teamwork comprises goal oriented activities in which a number of people (team members) are engaged and clearly collaborate (Orasanu & Salas, 1993). Team members, in contrast to group members, have explicit roles and tasks. They have access to different information of various modalities from a variety of sources, and often employ special ICT (Klein & Thordsen, 1989; Artman,

2000). Team members' actions are interrelated and interdependent, and take place within the same time-framework (Orasanu & Salas, 1993; Brannick & Prince, 1997).

How team activities are organized and coordinated affects function and performance (Jones & Roelofsma, 2000). Coordination consists of continuous management of team dependencies through communication and/or team configuration (Brehmer, 1991; Fussell et al., 1998). Coordination through communication refers to the ways and forms of verbal or mediated negotiation and feedback. Coordination through team configuration refers to changes in a team's arrangement. For example, there may be team members who operate on different time scales. At the same time, however, they may sustain a certain amount of freedom-of-action to maintain their possibilities of adapting to new circumstances (Brehmer & Svenmarck, 1995).

Different team configurations, such as the level of collocation, have impact on communication (Urban et al., 1995; Artman & Persson, 2000). The quality of communication in teams with different team configurations may thus differ in a number of ways, for example quantity and content of the exchanged messages (Artman, 2000; Driskell, Radtke & Salas, 2003). Likewise, different communication settings have impact on the conditions for collaborative work and coordination within the teams (Orasanu & Salas, 1993; Johansson & Hollnagel, 2007). In other words, team configuration and communication are interrelated and have essential impact on team interaction. How work is performed, and whether a collaborative task is accomplished successfully or not, clearly reflects distributed team member accomplishments (Wertsch, 1997; Stout et al., 1999).

Command and Control Teams in Emergency Response

The teams discussed in this chapter are all engaged in "dynamic control tasks" (Brehmer & Allard,

1991; Brehmer, 1992) such as emergency response or military operations. Teams working under these circumstances are often referred to as "C^2 teams" (Jones & Roelofsma, 2000; Rasker, Post & Schraagen, 2000). C^2 teams control the progress of response operations. As the duration of response operations is time limited, it can be argued that C^2 teams exist on temporary basis as well. The fact that emergency response C^2 teams in some sense are transient has impact on the characteristics of C^2 teams, for example their initial conditions and/ or the constraints and context under which they (inter)act (Trnka, 2009).

Emergency response C^2 teams are, further, heterogeneous, temporary and task-specific. The C^2 teams are formed within minutes or hours after the occurrence of emergencies or crises, that is, on reactive basis. C^2 teams are therefore usually dimensioned and have C^2 capacity primarily based on the actual needs for every specific response operation (Cedergårdh & Wennström, 2001; Svensson et al., 2009). They are organized out of the nearest available C^2 resources of the involved organizations. This means that C^2 teams thus are configured during the initial stages of response operations, while they already carry out actual C^2 work and coordinate ongoing response efforts. The structure and size of C^2 teams, in turn, depends on the nature of emergencies, as well as the type and number of deployed resources. It should therefore be expected that C^2 teams differ from operation to operation as regards, for example, the number of commanders involved, their expertise and skills, used or employed ICT and, not least, their internal configuration and communication (Bigley & Roberts, 2001; Svensson et al., 2009).

Adaptive Behaviour and Improvisation

Response operations continuously change as a result of the development in the area of operations, implemented countermeasures, and deployed resources. C^2 teams must therefore be flexible and continuously adapt to these changes, as well as to shifting demands during entire response operations. This type of flexibility is not possible to achieve through standardized, pre-planned responses why some form of improvisation is necessary (Mendonça, Beroggi, & Wallace, 2003; Mendonça & Wallace, 2004). What is often demanded, in other words, is improvisation by individual team members, as well as improvisation of C^2 teams as whole. It can be argued that the improvisation capacity of teams actually, sometimes even directly, relates to the improvisational capability of individual team members (Vera & Crossan, 2005).

Here, improvisation refers to the identification of situations where (a) no plan or routine applies under prevailing circumstances, or (b) an applicable plan or routine cannot be executed. It may, further, refer to the development and deployment of one or several new procedures to resolve difficult or in some sense emergent situations (Mendonça & Wallace, 2007). Improvisation in this sense may thus range from modest adjustments of applicable routines to complete abandonment of all (pre-)existing plans and procedures (Moorman & Miner, 1998). It may also imply selecting and executing alternative courses of action, or taking on new roles (Mendonça & Wallace, 2007).

When improvising, C^2 teams have to deal with their short and intermediate goals simultaneously (Weick, 1998). The improvisation process thus includes various aspects of teamwork, for example internal communication and collaboration, coordination of expertise and skills within the team, or role shifting (Vera & Crossan, 2005; Mendonça & Fiedrich, 2006). The improvisation capacity of C^2 teams is, further, influenced by factors such as team cohesiveness, internal communication and coordination and, not least, the context(s) in which the teams operate (Vera & Crossan, 2005). Additional factors that are important for a teams' improvisation capacity are expectations, attentiveness and actual responses in specific situations (Hollnagel & Woods, 2005).

Absence of improvisation and adaptation signifies, in practice, teams' inability to cope with ongoing situations and/or to adjust to relevant, prevailing conditions (Hollnagel, 2006). This implies that the ability to demonstrate adaptive behaviour, and the degree to which this behaviour is successful, thus is a fundamental condition for effective C^2 work in response operations (Johansson & Hollnagel, 2007).

Constraints from Command and Control Systems

One important characteristic of C^2 teams is that they do not act in isolation but form part of larger systems, called C^2 systems. These are, in principle, distributed supervisory control systems which utilize coordination of resources, controlled by the systems themselves (Shattuck & Woods, 2000). C^2 systems are, obviously, characterized by highly complex and dynamic interactions, and medium to low coupling between their parts (Perrow, 1984).

Restrictions, limitations, regulations and other aspects relating to specific C^2 systems, such as allocation of authority, command levels and responsibilities, set different constraints on C^2 teams during response operations (Persson, 2004). Constraints, consequently, shape what and how activities are executed by C^2 teams. Not only may a teams' range of possible actions be limited; new opportunities may also be provided so that certain, initially unforeseen, actions take place (Hollnagel & Woods, 2005; Woltjer, 2009). C^2 processes can thus be seen, from the perspective of C^2 teams, as the enduring management of internal and external constraints, in order to achieve external goals defined by the C^2 systems, as well as internal goals defined by the teams themselves (Persson, 2000; Johansson, 2005). A teams' ability to manage these constraints and coordinate its actions accordingly determines if an actual C^2 team is able to accomplish its tasks and, in that case with what outcome (Woltjer, 2009).

Methodological Challenges

One significant feature of C^2 teams is distributed decision-making in practice, and that team configuration and communication is the result of assumptions and negotiations in a current situation (Artman & Waern, 1999; Johansson, 2005). Decision-making is thus context dependent and influenced by factors such as the nature of the specific response operation, available C^2 resources at specific time aspects; further, characteristics of the C^2 system that a particular C^2 team belongs to, and also the level of improvisation that a particular C^2 team must use to accomplish or complete its tasks.

The complexity of this type of decision-making is a challenge as regards the 'proper' unit for analysis, as well as its scope. It is difficult to fully exploit issues relating to C^2 work where geographically distanced commanders act under varying circumstances, and communicate through diverse ICT. Response operations are thus rarely possible to review in sufficient detail to gain insights for overall design purposes. In most studies, analyses focus on specific tasks, local usage of specific tools, consequently providing poor knowledge on how to approach higher-level or more global design problems. This raises the question how to study C^2 teams, from a more holistic perspective, in response operations acting under uncertainty and time pressure, when having access to limited resources and information.

Simulations are often proposed to be the most suitable methodology to confront and analyze C^2 work. The simulations relevant for our purposes are those that involve humans and create multi-person settings reproducing reality or parts thereof. They replicate social situations in which the participants (humans) manage tasks in real time, and where the development of the tasks can be described as dynamic (Brehmer, 1987; Crookal & Saunder, 1998). The simulation participants make decisions out of hypothetical conditions, aimed at placing the participants in vivid, demanding and realistic situations (Parsson, 1996). The simulation participants are, in other words, forced to act under uncertainty and time pressure, having access to limited resources and information.

It is, however, a rather complex task to design simulations of dynamic and non-routine situations such as emergency response, which reflect conditions and events in real response operations, and also stimulate participants to make decisions, take actions and interact with others. This type of simulations must meet the demands of research in naturalistic settings and research specifically focusing the field of simulations. Several claims are thus relevant here, for example, that the simulation may involve teams of professionals. It must, furthermore, have the possibility to employ tasks, activities and demands similar or identical to real, actual, ones. Simulations must also be scalable so that real groups, that is, C^2 teams of different sizes, can be studied appropriately, and also allow studies of work practice where various artifacts are used. The simulations must, furthermore, be repeatable in the sense that the set-up and the scenarios are replicable. The greatest methodological challenge, however, is that the simulations must allow participants to adapt, be flexible, thus permitting different work modes as well as team configurations. This increases the number of internal parameters governing simulations, consequently increasing the variations of the simulations (Crookal, Oxford & Saunders, 1987; Gestrelius, 1998; Bracken & Shubik, 2001; Crano & Brewer, 2002).

Role-playing simulations have been recognized as a suitable technique for the study of social situations where ICT are used, such as real emergency response teams, that is, dynamic, non-routine situations that are difficult to observe (Woods & Hollnagel, 2006). They are used in research dating back to the sixties and the seventies (e.g., Babb, Leslie & Van Slyke, 1966; Shubik, 1972; Cooper, 1978). The "craft" of designing and executing these simulations is therefore well known. The methodology has been recognized both by the military and the crisis management

domain (e.g., Perla, 1990; Kleiboer, 1997; Rubel, 2001; Boin, Kofman-Bos & Overdijk, 2004). Role-playing simulations have also been used to study coordination and communication, as well as to evaluate effects of ICT (e.g., Persson & Worm, 2002; Gu & Mendonça, 2005).

It is to be noted, however, that few studies use simulations with real commanders (professionals), groups (real C^2 teams), and/or constraint-bound tasks (tasks situated within a C^2 system). Mackenzie et al. (2007) focus on computer supported collaborative work between remote experts and on-site response teams. Woltjer (2006) investigates the use of information and communication technologies, as well as the coordination of critical infrastructure failure recovery. Trnka (2009) studies improvisation and information management in C^2 teams designated for crisis and disaster response operations in an international context. We argue that such studies are necessary for increasing the understanding of the processes that emerge in collaborative C^2 in emergency response operations.

METHOD

The overall focus of this work is the design and development of ICT to support collaborative work and processes in heterogeneous C^2 teams in emergency response operations. The aim is to document the work practice of a team of commanders responding to an emergency, and to identify areas and/or activities that may be enhanced by C^2 tools. To achieve this goal and to meet the methodological demands described in this chapter we use (1) a scenario-based role-playing simulation, and (2) a combined set of bottom-up, data driven methods for analysis as well as a top-down approach.

Scenario-Based Role-Playing Simulation

A scenario-based role-playing simulation here is a simulation setting which originally comes from the methodology of operational games (Shubik, 1972; Thomas, 1984) and functional exercises (Peterson & Perry, 1999; Payne, 1999). For a detailed description of simulation settings, see Trnka & Jenvald (2006).

The simulation scenario referred to in this work builds on a single self-contained event, a forest fire in central Sweden. The scenario and its size was designed to involve emergency response organizations from two neighboring counties in a joint emergency operation (see Figure 1). The task concerned a response to a forest fire located at the common border of the two counties. The location of the forest fire aimed to trigger unclear operational procedures with regard to the C^2 responsibilities. Additional incidents were included in the scenario to establish a certain context with respect to the objectives, so that we could control also the tempo of the simulation.

The simulation was a closed-room activity with seven participants forming one C^2 team. The participants were commanders from the emergency response organizations, e.g., fire and rescue, police and emergency medical services, all involved in the simulated response according to the scenario. The commanders worked and lived in the actual geographical area where the simulated event took place. All worked regularly at command posts corresponding to their assignment in the simulation. The participants were: (a) two 112/911 emergency operators, (b) two fire and rescue on-site incident commanders, (c) one fire and rescue dispatch officer, (d) one police on-site incident commander, and (e) one police dispatch officer.

The simulation took place in autumn 2005. It was launched by multiple emergency calls and lasted for two hours, simulation time being equal to real-time. For a detailed description of the simulation settings, see Trnka & Jenvald (2006).

Figure 1. Commanders participating in the simulation: ○ = *fire & rescue on-site incident commander;* □ = *fire & rescue dispatch officer;* ◑ = *police on-site incident commander;* ◨ = *police dispatch officer;* ▨ = *112/911 emergency operator;* □ *shape means the commander is physically located at a C2 center;* ○ *shape means the commander is physically located in the field*

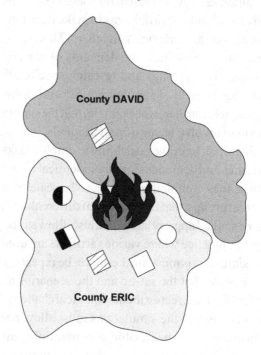

Data Collection

The main data consists of the participants' communication during the simulation. The participants were allowed to communicate with each other, as well as with the simulation staff, only through text messages. The complete communication was stored on log-files and the participants' workplaces were recorded by nine cameras. All material produced by the simulation is archived.

Following the termination of the simulation, an after-action review was conducted to support the interpretation of the data collected in the simulation. An after-action review is a professional discussion of an event, e.g., a real emergency or training session that focuses on mission and

Figure 2. An overview of the analytical process

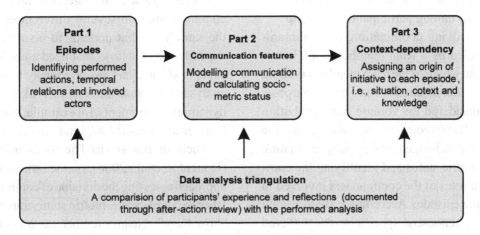

tasks performance (Scott, 1983; Downs et al., 1987; Rankin, Gentner & Crissey, 1995). Led by a facilitator, topics are debated in a moderated discussion. Here, the after-action review primarily focused information seeking, communication and data sharing and lasted for two hours. This review was recorded by two cameras. All notes made by the participants and the simulation managers during the after-action review are archived. For a more detailed description of the after-action review, see Trnka & Jenvald (2006).

Data Analysis

An issue relating to work with C² in real-life and simulated response operations is the choice of an appropriate analytic method. In other words, a method for capturing context-bound, high resolution data, describing dynamic and non-routine situations. Such empirical data require methods that allow bottom-up, data driven observations (Johansson, Artman & Waern, 2000; Stroomer & van Oostendorp, 2003). For our purpose, we combined a set of methods, that is, a bottom-up, data driven approach focusing on bits or sequences of communication and interaction called *episodes*, and participants' *communicative roles*. The top-down approach, on the other hand, consists of *socio-metric status* and *communication model-*

ling. As was pointed out previously, the analysis was complemented with data from an after-action review (see Figure 2).

A common way to examine coordination is to divide communication to subunits *pre-facto* (Svenmarck & Brehmer, 1991). This is often done when examining mission-tasks in order to create a set of categories subsequently applied to a data material. This way of structuring data, however, ignores the so called pseudo-problems, that is, problems that are not directly associated with the tasks at hand but still need attention. They commonly occur during emergency response and can, for example, be discussions if and where to establish a staging area. Problems of this type can usually not be addressed by individual team members only, and therefore require coordination within actual C² teams. To be able to address this specific issue we used *Topical episode analysis* (Korolija & Linell, 1996; Linell & Korolija, 1997) as our main method, episodes being interactional units of at least three conversational turns. From a wider perspective, Topical episode analysis was developed to capture ongoing communication and interaction in any small group consisting of at least 3-8 participants. Episodes, thus, contain processes of collaborative and collective efforts, where multiple participants jointly attend to a situation. As analytic units, episodes reflect distributed conversational, interactional and cognitive activities among participants in a group.

When studying coordination, the communication handled by a team member in a C^2 team may indicate which of the team members is doing most of the coordination work. For our purpose, we also considered the volume and distribution of the complete ongoing communication, and the content of the exchanged messages, by calculating the socio-metric status and identifying the communication roles of the commanders involved in the particular episodes. Accordingly, we were able to identify phenomena specific to the gathered material and to develop a more general account of coordination work.

Topical episode analysis. Topical episode analysis (Korolija & Linell, 1996; Linell & Korolija, 1997) divides communication to units of analysis, episodes, at a global level of dialogue. As an interactional unit, an episode contains an unbroken chain of actions internally bound together by a topical trajectory and/or a common trajectory (Korolija, 1998). Episodes thus emerge from the data and are easily seen in retrospect by any analyst (or participants themselves). This implies that episodes cannot be isolated with a pre-facto analysis of a task at hand. Further, episodes are per definition context-dependent. This means that they are grounded (begin with) something in a situation, cotext (what has previously been said), or (background, prior) knowledge (Korolija, 1998). Their links to various types of contexts are, in other words, essential for the understanding of 'what's going on in a given episode. An example of a situation is a reported forest fire, or a fire engine failure. Cotext, here, can be represented by formal grounds such as a hand over to higher command. An example of knowledge is a request for ambulance assistance as a result of previous experience from similar emergency response operations. Another advantage with Topical episode analysis is that the method captures simultaneous activities. This implies that several episodes can take place at the same time, and that the com-

municating persons manage their interaction and communication in several different episodes at the same time, but perhaps to a varying extent depending on the tasks that need attention. Topical episode analysis has previously been used in analyses of human interactions taking place in dynamic environments, for example, Aminoff, Johansson and Trnka (2007) and Trnka et al. (2009).

Socio-metric status The *socio-metric status* (Houghton et al., 2006), on the other hand, is an approach assessing the division of communication labor in detail. Socio-metric status thus measures "how busy" a team member (as a communication node) is in relation to other team members involved in an episode, and the metrics also allows a comparison of the communication distribution and load. The socio-metric status (ST) is given by the following equation:

$$ST = \frac{1}{g-1}\sum_{j=1}^{g}(x_{ji} + x_{ij})$$

where g is the total number of team members involved in communication in an episode, i and j are individual team members, and x_{ij} are the values representing the number of exchanged messages from team member i to team members j. The socio-metric status of each team member may also be compared with the *criterion of key communication agent*. The criterion (CR) is the sum of mean of socio-metric status (ST) and its standard deviation:

$$CR = \overline{ST} + \sqrt{\frac{\sum_{j=1}^{g}(ST_i - \overline{ST})^2}{g-1}}$$

If the socio-metric status value of a team member is higher than the value of the criterion, this team member has a key role for the communication in a specific episode (for a detailed description the method, see Houghton et al., 2006). Socio-metric status usually occurs in works on diverse C^2 organizations and teams (Stanton, Baber & Harris, 2008; Trnka, Granlund & Granlund, 2008; Salmon et al., 2009).

Communicative roles. Another technique to assess the division of communicative labor is to identify *communicative roles* of team members involved in particular episodes (Korolija & Linell, 1996). We used the four categories of communicative roles described by Korolija & Linell (1996) for our purposes: initiator, main speaker, main addressee and main figure. *Initiator* is the team member who initiates communication whereby a new episode begins. The initiative is usually something said, done or both – and it can even be something non-verbal (e.g. gaze in one direction). Secondly, *main speaker* is the most active team member as regards the communication throughout an episode. *Main addressee*, on the other hand, is the team member most often addressed within an episode; in our case, the team member receiving the highest number of messages. The fourth category, *main figure*, is in our work the team member responsible for the topic of concern in a particular episode according to formal C^2 doctrines. It is important to note that according to Topical episode analysis, one participant may take on different communicative roles even within the boundaries of an episode. In our data, it is obviously the case that one team member does have multiple communicative roles such as initiator, main addressee and main figure.

Communication modelling. Modelling of communication concerns the spatio-temporal distribution of the communication and connectivity of the communication acts. This method has previously been employed by, for example, Petrescu-Prahova and Butts (2005), Landgren and Nuldén (2007), and Uhr (2007).

RESULTS

This section presents the analysis and the results based on the communication data collected in the form of text messages during the simulation, including the discussion in the after-action review.

During the simulation, totally 849 messages were exchanged; 399 among the simulation participants, and 450 between the participants and the simulation managers. The messages sent between the participants and the simulation managers generally concerned communication between the commanders and the resources (simulated by the simulation management) the commanders were in control of, the emergency callers and other authorities (also simulated by the simulation management). The number of exchanged messages by the particular commanders is shown in Figure 3.

During analysis, we only focused on the exchanged messages between the simulation participants, i.e., the commanders. This implies a data set of 399 messages. Here we identified three episodes, i.e., processes where collaborative and collective efforts involving commanders from different organizations took place, for further detailed analysis:

- Episode 1: Identification and localization of the reported fire(s);
- Episode 2: Establishing a staging area;
- Episode 3: Search for lost under age children.

Episode 1: Identification and Localization of the Reported Fire(s)

This episode concerned the identification and localization of the reported fires. The episode was initiated by multiple emergency calls to the 112/911 emergency call-centers in two counties (a situation). Smoke and fires observed in the different locations in a large forest area were reported to the 112/911 emergency operators. As the 112/911 call-centers alarmed the fire and rescue services, emergency medical services and police, the 112/911 emergency operators started dialogues with (a) the police dispatch officer, (b) the fire and rescue on-site incident commander, (c) the fire and rescue dispatch officer, and (d) the police

Figure 3. Communication volume in the simulation: Number of exchanged (sent/received) messages by the particular commanders (dark grey = total number; light grey = number of messages exchanged with the other commanders only): (1) police on-site incident commander, (2) police dispatch officer, (3) fire & rescue on-site incident commander (Eric county), (4) fire & rescue on-site incident commander (David county), (5) fire & rescue dispatch officer (Eric county), (6) 112/911 emergency operator (David county), (7) 112/911 emergency operator (Eric county)

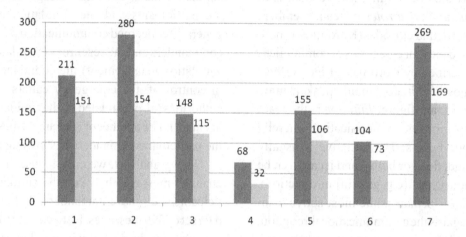

on-site incident commander. The communication involving these six commanders concerned what type of situation they were possibly facing in terms of the number, size and location of the reported fires. Another topic was, of course, the conceivable development of the situation in general.

The involved commanders exchanged 55 messages during this episode. The commander with the highest communication load was the 112/911 emergency operator in the Eric county who exchanged 37 messages with four other commanders (see Figure 4). The criterion of key communication agent (CR) was 6.2, which made the 112/911 emergency operator in the Eric county (ST=7.4) the *key communication agent* of this episode (Table 1). This 112/911 emergency operator was also the *initiator*, *main speaker*, and *main addressee* of this episode. There is, however, not any apparent *main figure* with regard to the communication and actions related to the episode. An explanation to this is that Topical episode analysis, more specifically its category main figure, more or

less demands that only one person, or one issue, is being spoken about by all participants within one an the same episode.

The 112/911 emergency operator in the Eric county had a significantly more active role than the formal description of the tasks at this post suggests. The 112/911 emergency operator is obliged to (a) receive 112/911 calls, (b) dispatch emergency medical resources (alarm, prioritize and coordinate), and (c) dispatch fire and rescue resources (alarm). The after-action review, however, revealed a tradition which has developed among the emergency response organizations, and in which the role of the main figure informally is adopted by the 112/911 emergency operators. This explains the 112/911 emergency operator's behaviour as the operator tried to make an overview of all the responding units, as well as to collect opinions and judgments from the other commanders in order to create a situation assessment – which the operator shared with the other commanders, responding units and involved

Figure 4. Commanders participating in episode 1 and the number of exchanged messages between them: ○ = *fire & rescue on-site incident commander;* □ = *fire & rescue dispatch officer;* ◖ = *police on-site incident commander;* ◧ = *police dispatch officer;* ▨ = *112/911 emergency operators;* _ _ *represents the county border;* □ *shape means the commander is physically located at a C² center;* ○ *shape means the commander is physically located in the field*

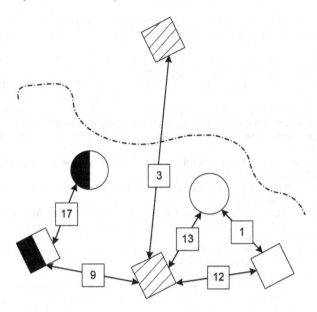

Table 1. Number of sent/received messages and socio-metric status of the six commanders involved in episode 1 (NSM = number of sent messages, NRM = number of received messages, NEM = total number of exchanged messages, ST = socio-metric status, CR = criterion of key communication agent, OIC = on-site incident commander, E = Eric county, D = David county)

	Fire & rescue OIC (E)	Fire & rescue dispatch officer (E)	Police OIC (E)	Police dispatch officer (E)	112/911 emergency operator (E)	112/911 emergency operator (D)
NSM	6	5	7	15	20	2
NRM	8	8	10	11	17	1
NEM	14	13	17	26	37	3
ST	2.8	2.6	3.4	5.2	7.4	0.6
CR	6.2					

organizations (see Excerpt 1). This partly explains why the 112/911 emergency operator had the role of initiator, main speaker, and main addressee, and also why the operator was the key communication agent in the episode.

Episode 2: Establishing a Staging Area

This episode was related to the establishment of a staging area. The episode was initiated out of the knowledge and previous experience of the

Excerpt 1. A sequence from the communication in episode 1. Note: The example is a translation of the communication, which was conducted in Swedish

11:32 CET- <u>112/911 emergency operator</u> to <u>Fire & rescue dispatch</u>: "Yes, it seems to be the same. Do you want me to alarm something more?"
11:32 CET- <u>Police on-site incident commander</u> to <u>Police dispatch officer</u>: "We wait. We do not know the extent yet but inform the commander in Low-town."
11:32 CET- <u>Police dispatch officer</u> to <u>112/911 emergency operator</u>: "What is the extent of the forest fire?"
11:33 CET- <u>Fire & rescue on-site incident commander</u> to <u>112/911 emergency operator</u>: "Do you have any opinion about the size of the fire?"
11:34 CET - <u>112/911 emergency operator</u> to <u>Police dispatch officer</u>:"None, no one is on the site yet. I'll come back to you."
11:34 CET - <u>Police dispatch officer</u> to <u>112/911 emergency operator</u>: "OK"
11:35CET- <u>112/911 emergency operator</u> to <u>Fire & rescue on-site incident commander</u>: "The answer is no. The alarm is only smoke development, unclear."
11:36 CET- <u>112/911 emergency operator</u> to <u>Fire & rescue dispatch</u>: "OK, I am waiting. Let me know if you need any help."
11:36 CET- <u>Fire & rescue on-site incident commander</u> to <u>112/911 emergency operator</u>: "Roger"
11:38 CET- <u>Police dispatch officer</u> to <u>Police on-site incident commander</u>: "So we do not know where it is. If it is OK for you I stop at the crossroad leading to Giant-mountain"
11:38 CET- <u>112/911 emergency operator</u> to <u>Fire & rescue dispatch</u>: "Do you have the possibility to repeat for me what you consider we have for a scenario, what is on the way, and if everything is OK?"
11:40 CET- <u>112/911 emergency operator</u> to <u>Fire & rescue dispatch</u>: "The ZOO park director reported smoke inside the park. Do you think it can have a connection to the previous calls?"
11:42 CET- <u>Police dispatch officer</u> to <u>Police on-site incident commander</u>: "According to the map there seems to be houses close to Giant-mountain. Unknown if there are any people. Have not heard anything from the 112/911 operator."
11:42 CET- <u>Police on-site incident commander</u> to <u>Police dispatch officer</u>: "Good"
11:45 CET- <u>Fire & rescue on-site incident commander</u> to <u>112/911 emergency operator</u>: "Seems to be very likely. Inform the ZOO park to take measures to protect the animals. Have we got any other calls"
11:46 CET- <u>112/911 emergency operator</u> to <u>Fire & rescue dispatch</u>: "No further calls"

police on-site incident commander. The topic of the episode was manifested in a dialogue among the commanders, focusing where to establish the staging area and what measures to take. The episode involved five commanders from the Eric county: (a) the police dispatch officer, (b) the fire and rescue on-site incident commander, (c) the fire and rescue dispatch officer, (d) the police on-site incident commander, and (e) the 112/911 emergency operator. One commander from the David county took part as well, the 112/911 emergency operator, meaning six commanders totally.

All in all 45 messages were exchanged in this episode (see Figure 5). The criterion of key communication agent (CR) was 5.1 (see Table 2). This means that none of the commanders had the role of key communication agent in episode 2. The *main figure* in this episode was the fire and rescue on-site incident commander. However, even if the main incident was the forest fire, the *initiative* to the discussion regarding the staging area initially came from the police, more specifically, the police

on-site incident commander. The police on-site incident commander had – besides police education and training – also fire and rescue training. This commander had experience from participating in earlier forest firefighting operations as well; his cross-domain knowledge and experience from earlier joint operations resulted in the initiative by the police on-site incident commander. The police dispatch officer was the *main speaker*, and both police commanders were *main addressees* in this episode. Obviously, these roles were influenced by the fact that the discussion regarding the staging area was held at the on-site level as well as at the command center level (see Excerpt 2).

Episode 3: Search for Lost Under Age Children

This episode describes the search for lost under age children. The episode was initiated by an emergency call to the 112/911 emergency call-center by one of the parents to the missing children.

Figure 5. Commanders participating in episode 2 and the number of exchanged messages between them: ○= *fire & rescue on-site incident commander;* □= *fire & rescue dispatch officer;* ◐ = *police on-site incident commander;* ◪= *police dispatch officer;* ▨= *112/911 emergency operators;* __ *represents the county border;* □ *shape means the commander is physically located at a C² center;* ○ *shape means the commander is physically located in the field*

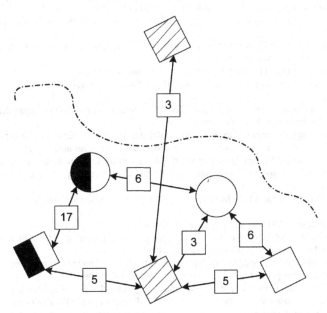

Table 2. Number of sent/received messages and socio-metric status of the six commanders involved in episode 2 (NSM = number of sent messages, NRM = number of received messages, NEM = total number of exchanged messages, ST = socio-metric status, CR = criterion of key communication agent, OIC = on-site incident commander, E = Eric county, D = David county)

	Fire & rescue OIC (E)	Police OIC (E)	Police dispatch officer (E)	112/911 emergency operator (E)
NSM	4	17	14	2
NRM	6	15	13	3
NEM	10	32	27	5
ST	3.3	10.7	9.0	1.7
CR	10.5			

The topic of the episode was a dialogue among the commanders with respect to the assessment of the ongoing situation, a review of available resources, and collection of further information for search planning (see Excerpt 3). The episode involved four commanders: (a) the police dispatch officer, (b) the fire and rescue on-site incident

commander, (c) the fire and rescue on-site incident commander, and (e) the 112/911 emergency operator in the Eric county.

In total, 35 messages were exchanged in this episode (see Figure 6). The commander with the highest communication load was the police on-site incident commander who exchanged 30 messages

Excerpt 2. A sequence from the communication in episode 2. Note: The example is a translation of the communication, which was conducted in Swedish

---

11:43 CET - Police on-site incident commander to Police dispatch officer: "Roger. This seems to be big. I want to have more units. So far I have not received anything about the staging area. For us it would suit to have it at the parking place outside the ZOO park"

11:47 CET - Police dispatch officer to 112/911 emergency operator: "To your knowledge: police on-site incident commander C. Johnson decided that the staging area for the police forces is at the parking lot at the ZOO park."

11:47 CET - Police on-site incident commander to Police dispatch officer: "Could you check with the fire & rescue dispatch so that they agree with the staging area?"

11:47 CET - Police dispatch officer to 112/911 emergency operator: "Have you got any contact with the fire & rescue on-site incident commander? Is the staging area same for everyone involved in the response?"

11:47 CET - Police dispatch officer to 112/911 emergency operator: "I'll come back to you"

11:48 CET - Police on-site incident commander to Police dispatch officer: "We do not know yet but I am going to talk to him about that right now."

11:48 CET - Police dispatch officer to fire & rescue dispatch officer: "The police on-site incident commander C. Johnson wonders if the parking lot at the ZOO park is OK for you as the staging area?"

11:48 CET – Fire & rescue on-site incident commander to 112/911 emergency operator: "The staging area for the forest fire is at the coordinates AG786, BD432. Inform all our alarmed units as well as cooperating units from other organizations."

11:48 CET - Police dispatch officer to 112/911 emergency operator: "I have informed the fire & rescue dispatch."

11:49 CET - Police on-site incident commander to Fire & rescue on-site incident commander: "Can we establish the staging area at the parking lot at the ZOO park?"

11:49 CET - Police on-site incident commander to Police dispatch officer: "I have spoken with the fire & rescue on-site incident commander and awaiting answer."

11:49CET - Police dispatch officer to 112/911 emergency operator: "Good"

11:49 CET - Fire & rescue on-site incident commander to Police on-site incident commander: "OK, if there is enough space. It could be a problem if we have to evacuate the ZOO park and get all the cars moving?"

11:50 CET - 112/911 emergency operator to Fire & rescue dispatch officer: "To your knowledge: police on-site incident commander C. Johnson decided that staging area for the police forces is at the parking lot at the ZOO park."

11:50 CET - 112/911 emergency operator to Fire & rescue on-site incident commander: "To your knowledge: police on-site incident commander C. Johnson decided that staging area for the police forces is at the parking lot at the ZOO park."

11:50 CET - Police on-site incident commander to Fire & rescue on-site incident commander: "Roger. But I could try to move some of the cars in the northern part of the parking lot. Will you instruct your incoming units to stop there?"

11:51 CET - Police on-site incident commander to Police dispatch officer: "I need additional units to empty a part of the parking lot where we will have the staging area."

---

with two other commanders. The criterion of key communication agent (CR) was 10.5, which made the police on-site incident commander (ST= 10.7) the *key communication agent* of this episode (see Table 3). The police dispatch officer was the *initiator*, while the police on-site incident commander was the *main speaker* and *main addressee*, but also the *main figure* of this episode.

DISCUSSION AND CONCLUDING REMARKS

The empirical study reported in this chapter provides important knowledge on collaborative C^2 in emergency response operations, especially as regards flexibility and improvisation. Exposing commanders to a scenario, which demands

collaboration and joint efforts beyond average day-to-day response operations, interesting conclusions can be drawn from our observations. The main findings are given in the following sections.

Informal Collaboration and Supportive Behaviour

The analysis shows that informal collaboration and supportive behaviour among the involved commanders create a common practice and essential elements in the studied response operation. Surprisingly, this informal collaboration and supportive behaviour mostly concerned incidents and what has been referred to as pseudo-problems, which could have influenced the progress and the outcome of the response efforts significantly, if not been attended to. As has been suggested,

Figure 6. Commanders participating in episode 3 and the number of exchanged messages between them: ○ = fire & rescue on-site incident commander; ◖ = on-site incident commander; ◨= police dispatch officer; ▨= 112/911 emergency operator; _ _ represents the county border; □ shape means the commander is physically located at a C² center; ○shape means the commander is physically located in the field

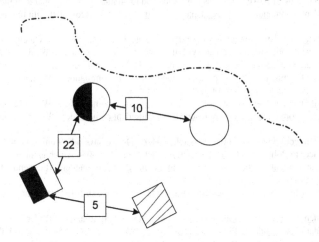

Table 3. Number of sent/received messages and socio-metric status of the four commanders involved in episode 3 (NSM = number of sent messages, NRM = number of received messages, NEM = total number of exchanged messages, ST = socio-metric status, CR = criterion of key communication agent, OIC = on-site incident commander, E = Eric county)

	Fire & rescue OIC (E)	Fire & rescue dispatch officer (E)	Police OIC (E)	Police dispatch officer (E)	112/911 emergency operator (E)	112/911 emergency operator (D)
NSM	8	7	11	12	8	1
NRM	7	6	12	12	8	2
NEM	15	13	23	24	16	3
ST	3.0	2.6	4.6	4.8	3.2	0.6
CR	5.1					

"pseudo-problems" refer to events that are not directly related to the ongoing main tasks (such as firefighting), but nevertheless could demand significant resources if not attended and handled directly (for example, establishment of the staging area; see Episode 2).

We found that commanders actively initiated diverse activities to handle this type of incidents and pseudo-problems in the simulated response operation. These activities engaged commanders from different organizations and took place across organizational and domain boundaries (e.g., fire and rescue, police, and emergency medicine). The commanders, further, supported each other on several occasions when performing these activities. Actually, through these activities, commanders even carried out various functions and communicative roles *outside* the formal C² doctrines, for example, by involving 112/911 emergency operators in very early stages of the response operation (see Episode 1).

Excerpt 3. A sequence from the communication in episode 3. Note: The example is a translation of the communication, which was conducted in Swedish

---

11:58 CET - <u>Police dispatch officer</u> to <u>Police on-site incident commander</u>: "I have one worried parent who called and reported that her day-nursery could be in the area to look at flowers. She has not succeeded to contact anyone in charge at the day-nursery."

11:59 CET - <u>Police on-site incident commander</u> to <u>Police dispatch officer</u>: "Roger. I discuss that with the fire & rescue on-site incident commander."

12:00 CET - <u>Police dispatch officer</u> to <u>112/911 emergency operator</u>: "We can have a day-nursery, which is out in the forest to observe flowers. One parent reported it. We do not have any contact with the staff from the day-nursery. We do not know which day-nursery. The parent who reported it is called Sara and has a cellular 0743789456. I need a help with which day-nursery it can be."

12:00 CET - <u>Police on-site incident commander</u> to <u>Fire & rescue on-site incident commander</u>: "We have got information that a day-nursery should be somewhere in the area. No one has got in contact with them."

12:02 CET - <u>Fire & rescue on-site incident commander</u> to <u>Police on-site incident commander</u>: "Which resources do you search for?"

12:02 CET - <u>Police on-site incident commander</u> to <u>Fire & rescue on-site incident commander</u>: "We have some, but is it safe for us to go to the area?"

12:02 CET - <u>Police on-site incident commander</u> to <u>Police dispatch officer</u>: "Do we have a K-9 unit on duty?"

12:03 CET - <u>Police dispatch officer</u> to <u>Police on-site incident commander</u>: "Yes, IRU-054 which is the only unit in North-town."

12:03 CET - <u>Fire & rescue on-site incident commander</u> to <u>Police on-site incident commander</u>: "It depends if you can get to the area from the north-east with the wind in your back."

12:03 CET - <u>Police dispatch officer</u> to <u>Police on-site incident commander</u>: "Shall we shift IRU-024 and IRU-054. I have not heard anything from the David county."

12:04 CET - <u>Police on-site incident commander</u> to <u>Fire & rescue on-site incident commander</u>: "Roger"

12:05 CET - <u>Police on-site incident commander</u> to <u>Police dispatch officer</u>: "Yes, do it. IRU-054 can search the area with dog if they can get to the area from the north-east. In other words, from Giant-mountain, but they should be careful."

12:09 CET - <u>Police on-site incident commander</u> to <u>Fire & rescue on-site incident commander</u>: "Do you have more rescue units on the way and what is the extent of the fire?"

12:09 CET - <u>Fire & rescue on-site incident commander</u> to <u>Police on-site incident commander</u>: "I am looking into that."

12:10 CET - <u>112/911 emergency operator</u> to <u>Police dispatch officer</u>: "The day-nursery is called 'The Bears'."

12:11 CET - <u>Police dispatch officer</u> to <u>112/911 emergency operator</u>: "Thanks. Is there any contact person? Will you contact them or shall we do it?"

12:11 CET - <u>Police on-site incident commander</u> to <u>Fire & rescue on-site incident commander</u>: "I am going out in the media and tell the public about what has happened and that they should not travel to the area."

Another finding was that different incidents and pseudo-problems engaged the commanders in various activities over time as the situation and the response efforts progressed. Informal functions and communicative roles were thus not stable entities but changed with new activities being initiated, ongoing ones being modified, or activities simply being concluded. Also, one commander could perform various functions and take on diverse communicative roles in different phases of the response operation, for instance, the police on-site incident commander and his involvement in Episode 2 and 3. The ability to "read" a situation, identify incidents and pseudo-problems and to take initiative to cope with them *before* they turned into major problems was found to be a crucial quality of a commander in a situation like the one presented in our study.

Communication and Information Sharing

The informal collaboration and supportive behaviour involved voluntary and self-initiated distribution of information. This distribution was based on the assumed needs of other commanders. Commanders, who obtained information that was of importance for others, "pushed" the same information to the commanders they believed were in need of it. As the supporting behaviour stretched across organizational and domain boundaries, the self-initiated distribution of information crossed these boundaries as well.

Notably, the communication trajectories concerning the pseudo-problems and incidents mentioned above did not deviate from the formal organizational structures. Communication between the commanders from the different organizations always followed the formal chain of command both within and between the involved organizations. This implies that C^2 centers only communicated with other C^2 centers, on-site commanders only with other on-site commanders, and so on. Episode 2 shows this clearly when the two police commanders wanted to discuss the possible location for the staging area. In this example the police dispatch officer communicated with the fire & rescue dispatch officer, and the police on-site incident commanders with the fire & rescue on-site incident commander. This could mean that the involved commanders were aware of the fact that deviations from formal C^2 structures actually might cause confusion among others. This observation, in turn, is essential for the analysis – and knowledge – of joint response operations, where larger C^2 teams are deployed, and C^2 structures different from day-to-day operations are used.

Adaptive and Improvisation Capability within Formal Command and Control Structures

In the scenario reported here, the informal functions and the communication roles taken by the commanders during the response efforts proved to be important conditions for success. It would have been difficult to perform efficiently if the commanders in the simulated response operation stuck strictly to their formal organizational functions, formal task assignments and predefined communication roles. This is, in itself, an observation to be noted for future work.

The documented informal collaboration and supporting behaviour indicate that commanders adapt when facing unforeseen conditions and unpredictability of tasks. At the same time this shows that there *are* functional and information needs that are not fulfilled in current, formal organizational and technological structures, that is, pre-defined communication plans, allocation of tasks and responsibilities, and pre-selected communication channels. These needs, as well

as deficiencies, were understood by all involved commanders (from the different organizations). The commanders compensated for these needs and deficiencies even without request by improvisation in terms of performing various informal functions and diverse communication roles.

The type of adaptive and improvised behaviour of the individual commanders documented in this study allowed the C^2 team – and the overall C^2 system – to function efficiently as a whole. This is an important result with respect to data collection and units of analysis for similar studies. We argue that focus on single commanders only, or organizations in joint response operations as singled-out behaviour, without understanding of collective behaviour of multiple commanders or organizations working together, may give misleading data, hence incorrect empirical conclusions.

Our work suggests, further, that adaptive and improvised behaviour can be attributed to cross-domain and cross-organizational knowledge. This is especially the case of the 112/911 emergency operators, who are used to interact with various emergency response organizations. They are in the position to foresee the needs of commanders belonging to different emergency response organizations.

Technological Aid Supporting Adaptive and Improvised Activities

Support in the form of technological aid for adaptive and improvised work is one area identified during analysis which requires attention also when designing and developing new C^2 tools. Obviously, this relates to situations when commanders handle diverse pseudo-problems and incidents. According to one of the 112/911 operators in the after-action review, C^2 tools used by commanders in their everyday work, do not always support the informal functions carried out, nor different communicative roles taken, nor the transitions of these functions and roles over time. On the contrary, such C^2 tools are often explicitly based on formal roles and even intended to be used for very specific tasks. This means that while it is necessary to optimize these tools, it is equally important to assure that they maintain a high degree of flexibility so that they are applicable also to unusual events.

Another area needing improvement as regards the design and development of C^2 tools is the support for sharing soft information among the commanders in a team. The communication in the described episodes reveals that the commanders not only share "hard" facts but also "soft" information, which concerns, for example, commanders' personal opinions, estimations and judgments about possible scenarios, and future development. Such information was also used when discussing safety and security issues, or reviewing available resources for specific activities. Soft information, in other words, partly reflects commanders' experience, cross-domain and cross-organizational knowledge. Today, this information can only be shared through voiced and in some cases -text-based communication. Future C^2 tools could support this type of information sharing by providing possibilities to spread and share sketches through virtually shared workspaces, or live video.

The kind of collaborative C^2 work described in this study demands mobile solutions; information shared by commanders should preferably be presented on portable ICT devices. Varying technological maturity of emergency response organizations is therefore an additional factor influencing the use of ICT in response operations. Changes of existing C^2 tools, or introduction of new ones providing this type of support, will therefore need to be empirically evaluated in terms of their usefulness and the actual effects on adaptive and improvisation capability of this type of teams.

Implications for Design and Development of Command and Control Tools

The results of our research show, among other things, that ICT designed and developed only on

the basis of formal C^2 doctrines and task specifications are therefore likely to inhibit parts of informal collaborative work in joint emergency response operations with multiple commanders from various organizations involved. Following formal descriptions only disguises complex interactions that emerge in situations demanding inter-organizational and cross-domain collaboration. It is, we argue, therefore absolutely necessary to realize that C^2 in joint response operations is not an entity with a predefined structure and functions; rather takes form as adaptations to unfolding situations, constraints set by the type of response operation, organizations involved, available resources, experience of involved commanders, ICT at hand, and so on. Identifying patterns of this adaptive process and mapping out interactions in collaborative C^2 work is essential to understand the problem space of collaborative C^2 work in emergency response operations.

In the scenario presented here, the distribution of communication density was not directly related to the commanding functions, nor to the type of response operation. The scenario was characterized by being a major firefighting operation. Nevertheless, the highest communication load was on the 112/911 emergency operator, police dispatch officer and police on-site incident commander in the Eric county (as shown in Figure 3). Another example is the resource allocation and availability, which had essential impact on the communication volume and the interactions of the commanders. In this case, the lack of police resources required coordination, prioritization and negotiations with other commanders of the team, resulting in high communication load on the police commanders. The last example concerns the initiative and actions taken by the police on-site incident commander as regards the establishment of the staging area in Episode 2. This was actually not a formal responsibility, but was still carried out thanks to his specific cross-domain knowledge.

In a way, we are saying that evaluation methods going beyond traditional needs analysis, requirements engineering and user-testing are demanded. It is important to take into account not only individual commanders when designing and developing C^2 tools, but also collective actions of C^2 teams which are situated in the dynamic context of emergency response. Situations such as incidents and pseudo-problems described in this chapter may confront commanders using 'traditional' C^2 tools with difficulties far beyond the ones originally envisioned by designers/developers basing their work and efforts on more conventional, role-based user scenarios or task analysis. The challenge for designers/developers of tools for collaborative C^2 is to identify this type of complex and context-bound, even 'new', situations, and also to find a balance between designing for day-to-day routine tasks, on the one hand, and situations demanding flexibility and improvisation, on the other hand. The presented study is an attempt to validate and support designers and developers when attending to this type of design problems.

Reflection on the Method of Analysis

Empirical studies of collaborative work in C^2 teams, where team members are distributed across different organizations, suffers from methodological problems because of the great complexity we have attempted to describe in this chapter. For this reason, we addressed this challenge by using a scenario-based role-playing simulation setting, and a combined set of bottom-up data driven, and also top-down, methods of analysis.

Our experience is that the methods used here are more or less necessary to document and describe adaptive C^2 work with accuracy. Our methodological stance makes it possible to study behaviour at the individual level, as well as the overall behaviour of a team. This includes information distribution and communication, collaborative processes and complex decision-making. The methodology provides a platform for realistic studies of dynamic and non-routine events, which are challenging to document in real-life settings.

Examples of such demanding situations are, for example initial stages of response operations, where (1) the most dynamic phases of emergencies take place, (2) commanders decide upon actions and coordinate activities intensively, and (3) command posts are being (or have just been) established, the C^2 organization taking its form.

The use of Topical episode analysis, as a bottom-up data driven method, provides new possibilities to identify phenomena like informal functions and communication roles among the commanders in a C^2 team – like in any group. The strength of the method is that the identified episodes do not label data in the same way as many top-down, theory-driven methods, such as those using pre-defined categorization of, for example, sequences, speech acts – or other interactional entities. However, it is imperative that the analysed data concerns communication from real response operations or simulations involving real commanders and realistic scenarios. Only by using such real situations, it is possible to capture how participants use their professional knowledge in context and constraint-bound interactions – in order to draw ecologically valid conclusions.

The method applied allowed analysis of C^2 work in this type of settings in a way that is difficult to achieve using other methods. The method described in this chapter is, in other words, appropriate for situations where we need to find out whether and how certain activities, processes and interactions take place.

CONCLUSION

This chapter highlights the design and development of ICT that support collaborative work and processes in heterogeneous C^2 teams involved in emergency response operations. It is based on, and accounts for, an empirical study aiming to document the practice of a team of commanders from the Swedish local and regional emergency response organizations, responding jointly to an emergency, (a forest fire). Further, it sets out to identify areas and/or activities that may be enhanced by C² tools.

During analysis, differences between planned and actual C² work were found. The findings indicate that commanders used informal arrangements within the established formal C² structures to handle diverse incidents and pseudo-problems. Cross-domain and cross-organizational knowledge allowed the commanders of the team to recognize the need for active engagement in diverse, joint activities, and for supporting other commanders. The commanders initiated activities and undertook informal functions and communicative roles when managing these incidents and problems. These activities, functions and roles stretched across organizational and domain boundaries. This had impact on, and was reflected in, communication and information sharing among the commanders on the team. The commanders communicated pro-actively, sharing information on a 'push-basis' across organizational boundaries, though still following formal chains of command.

In the scenario reported, the ability to allocate activities, functions and communicative roles, concerning handling of incidents and pseudo-problems across C² structures in a flexible way, was identified as a key element for success when coping with dynamic tasks such as emergency response operations. The identified adaptive and improvised behaviour of the commanders and the C² team as whole to changing conditions represents a critical characteristic of organizations that are effective in their joint response to emergencies. Cross-domain and cross-organizational knowledge was found to be the most important feature of this type of adaptive and improvisation work.

We have also identified two areas that may be supported or enhanced by C² tools. The first area concerns tools that support commanders when performing *informal* functions, for example, indications of current informal functions and communicative roles, and their development over time. The second area is related to sharing *soft*

information on, for instance, commanders' personal opinions, estimations and judgments about the possible scenarios and future development.

From a methodological point of view, this chapter points out the significance of employing bottom-up, data driven methods for analysis in the design and development process, as well as the methodological challenges related to this type of analysis. The chapter demonstrates how such analysis can be performed by using a scenario-based role-playing simulation and a combined set of bottom-up data driven and top-down methods. The study shows that the involvement of real commanders, real C² structures and constraint-bound tasks makes it possible to identify and analyze situated actions and emerging individual and team adaptations and improvisation. This type of analysis, thus, describing how commanders adapt and improvise in specific situations represents an essential input for the design and development of ICT for emergency response. From a research perspective, the study provides new insights about the interactions and processes that take place in joint emergency response operations.

Finally, knowledge on this type of complex, situated, multi-party interactions under various –even extreme – conditions, is relevant for research on teamwork and adaptive behaviour. More importantly, however, it is knowledge *essential* for design of training, or the dimensioning, of C² structures.

ACKNOWLEDGMENT

This paper is based on research funded by the Swedish Civil Contingencies Agency (MSB). The authors would like to thank Natascha Korolija, Erland Jungert, Kip Smith, Rogier Woltjer, Hedvig Aminoff and Amy Rankin for their valuable comments and reflections.

REFERENCES

Adelman, L. (1991). Experiments, quasi-experiments, and case studies: A review of empirical methods for evaluating decision support systems. *IEEE Transactions on Systems, Man, and Cybernetics, 21*(2), 293–301. doi:10.1109/21.87078

Aminoff, H., Johansson, B., & Trnka, J. (2007). *Understanding coordination in emergency response*. Paper presented at the 26th European Annual Conference on Human Decision-Making and Manual Control, Lyngby, DK.

Artman, H. (2000). Team situation assessment and information distribution. *Ergonomics, 43*(8), 1111–1128. doi:10.1080/00140130050084905

Artman, H., & Persson, M. (2000). Old practices – New technology: Observations of how established practices meet new technology. In Dieng, R., Gibson, A., Kersenty, L., & De Michelis, G. (Eds.), *Designing cooperative systems* (pp. 35–49). Amsterdam, The Netherlands: Ios Press Ohmsha.

Artman, H., & Waern, Y. (2000). Distributed cognition in an emergency co-ordination center. *Cognition Technology and Work, 1*(4), 237–246. doi:10.1007/s101110050020

Babb, E. M., Leslie, M. A., & Van Slyke, M. D. (1966). The potential of business-gaming methods in research. *The Journal of Business, 39*(4), 465–472. doi:10.1086/294887

Bigley, G. A., & Roberts, K. H. (2001). The incident command system: High-reliability organizing for complex and volatile task environments. *Academy of Management Journal, 44*(6), 1281–1299. doi:10.2307/3069401

Boin, A., Kofman-Bos, C., & Overdijk, W. (2004). Crisis simulations: Exploring tomorrow's vulnerabilities and threats. *Simulation & Gaming, 35*(3), 378–393. doi:10.1177/1046878104266220

Bracken, P., & Shubik, M. (2001). War gaming in the information age: Theory and purpose. *Naval War College Review, 54*(2), 47–60.

Brannick, M. T., & Prince, C. (1997). An overview of team performance measurement. In Brannick, M. T., Salas, E., & Prince, C. (Eds.), *Team performance assessment and measurement* (pp. 331–355). Mahwah, NJ: Lawrence Erlbaum Associates.

Brehmer, B. (1987). System design and the psychology of complex systems. In Rasmussen, J., & Zunde, P. (Eds.), *Empirical foundations of information and software science III* (pp. 21–32). New York, NY: Plenum Publishing.

Brehmer, B. (1991). Modern information technology: Timescales and distributed decision making. In Rasmussen, J., Brehmer, B., & Leplat, J. (Eds.), *Distributed decision making: Cognitive models for cooperative work* (pp. 193–200). New York, NY: John Wiley & Sons.

Brehmer, B. (1992). Dynamic decision making: Human control of complex systems. *Acta Psychologica, 81*(3), 211–241. doi:10.1016/0001-6918(92)90019-A

Brehmer, B., & Allard, R. (1991). Real-time dynamic decision making: The effects of task complexity and feedback delays. In Rasmussen, J., Brehmer, B., & Leplat, J. (Eds.), *Distributed decision making: Cognitive models for cooperative work* (pp. 319–334). New York, NY: John Wiley & Sons.

Brehmer, B., & Svenmarck, P. (1995). Distributed decision making in dynamic environments: Time scales and architectures of decision making. In Caverni, J.-P., Bar-Hillel, M., Barron, F. H., & Jungermann, H. (Eds.), *Contributions to decision making – I* (pp. 155–174). Amsterdam, The Netherlands: Elsevier Science.

Cedergårdh, E., & Wennström, O. (2002). *The elements of command & control: The general principles of command & control in fire and rescue operations*. Karlstad, Sweden: Swedish Rescue Services Agency.

Commfort, L. K., Sungu, Y., Johnson, D., & Dunn, M. (2001). Complex systems in crisis: Anticipation and resilience in dynamic environments. *Journal of Contingencies and Crisis Management, 8*(4), 208–217.

Cook, M., Noyes, J. M., & Masakowski, Y. (2007). *Decision making in complex environments*. Aldershot, UK: Ashgate.

Cooper, D. F. (1978). On the design and control of crisis games. *Omega, 6*(5), 460–461. doi:10.1016/0305-0483(78)90103-2

Crano, W. D., & Brewer, M. D. (2002). *Principles and methods of social research*. Mahwah, NJ: Lawrence Erlbaum Associates.

Crookall, D., Oxford, R., & Saunders, D. (1997). Towards a reconceptualization of simulation: From representation to reality. *Simulation /Games for Learning, 17*(4), 147-171.

Crookall, D., & Saunders, D. (1998). Towards an integration of communication and simulation. In Crookall, D., & Saunders, D. (Eds.), *Communication and simulation* (pp. 2–32). Philadelphia, PA: Multilingual Matters.

Cummings, M. L. (2004). *Designing decision support systems for revolutionary command and control domains* (Unpublished doctoral dissertation). Charlottesville, VA: University of Virginia.

Downs, C. W., Jonhson, K. M., & Fallesen, J. J. (1987). *Analysis of feedback in after action reviews* (ARI Technical Report 745). Arlington, VA: U.S. Army Research Institute for Behavioral and Social Sciences.

Drabek, T. E., & McEntire, D. A. (2003). Emergent phenomena and the sociology of a disaster. *Disaster Prevention and Management, 12*(2), 97–112. doi:10.1108/09653560310474214

Driskell, J. E., Radtke, P. H., & Salas, E. (2003). Virtual teams: Effects of technological mediation on team performance. *Group Dynamics, 7*(4), 297–323. doi:10.1037/1089-2699.7.4.297

Frey, L. R., Gouran, D. S., & Poole, M. S. (1999). *The handbook of group communication theory and research*. Thousand Oaks, CA: Sage Publications.

Fussell, S. R., Kraut, R. E., Lerch, F. J., Scherlis, W. L., McNally, M. M., et al. (1998). Coordination, overload, and team performance: Effects of team coordination strategies. In *Proceedings of the ACM Conference on Computer Supported Cooperative Work in Seattle, WA* (pp. 275-284). New York, NY: ACM.

Garbis, C. (2002). The cognitive use of artifacts in cooperative process management: Rescue management and underground line control (Doctoral dissertation). *Linköping Studies in Art and Science, 258*. Linköping, SE: Linköping University.

Gestrelius, K. (1998). *Simulation and training games: Experimental learning*. Huskvarna, Sweden: SAAB Training Systems.

Gu, Q., & Mendonça, D. (2005). Patterns of group information-seeking in a simulated emergency response environment. In B. Van de Walle, & B. Carlé (Eds.), *Proceedings of the 2nd International Conference on Information Systems for Crisis Response and Management in Brussels, Belgium* (pp. 109-116). Brussels, Belgium: SCK-CEN.

Hirokawa, R. Y., & Poole, M. S. (1996). *Communication and group decision-making* (2nd ed.). Thousand Oaks, CA: Sage Publications.

Hollnagel, E. (2006). Resilience: The challenge of the unstable. In Hollnagel, E., Woods, D. D., & Leveson, N. (Eds.), *Resilience engineering: Concepts and precepts* (pp. 9–14). Aldershot, UK: Ashgate.

Hollnagel, E., & Woods, D. D. (2005). *Joint cognitive systems: Foundations of cognitive systems engineering*. Boca Raton, FL: CRC Press. doi:10.1201/9781420038194

Houghton, R. J., Barber, C., McMaster, R., Stanton, N. A., & Salmon, P. (2006). Command and control in emergency services operations: A social network analysis. *Ergonomics, 49*(12), 1204–1225. doi:10.1080/00140130600619528

Hutchins, E. (2005). *Cognition in the wild*. Cambridge, MA: MIT Press.

Johansson, B. (2005). Joint control in dynamic situations (Doctoral dissertation). *Linköping Studies in Science and Technology, 972*. Linköping, Sweden: Linköping University.

Johansson, B., Artman, H., & Waern, Y. (2000). Technology in crisis management systems – Ideas and effects. *Document Design (Amsterdam), 2*(3), 247–257.

Johansson, B. J. E., & Hollnagel, E. (2007). Prerequisites for large scale coordination. *Cognition Technology and Work, 9*(1), 5–13. doi:10.1007/s10111-006-0050-z

Jones, P. E., & Roelofsma, P. H. M. P. (2000). The potential for social contextual and group biases in team decision-making: Biases, conditions and psychological mechanisms. *Ergonomics, 43*(8), 1129–1152. doi:10.1080/00140130050084914

Kendra, J. M., & Wachtendorf, T. (2006). *Improvisation, creativity, and the art of emergency management (Disaster Research Center Preliminary Paper 357)*. Newark, DE: University of Delaware.

Killian, L. M. (2002). An introduction to methodological problems of field studies in disaster research. In Stallings, R. A. (Ed.), *Methods of disaster research* (pp. 49–93). Philadelphia, PA: Xlibris.

Kleiboer, M. (1997). Simulation methodology for crisis management support. *Journal of Contingencies and Crisis Management, 5*(4), 198–206. doi:10.1111/1468-5973.00057

Klein, G. A., & Thordsen, M. L. (1989). *Cognitive processes of the team mind*. Yellow Springs, OH: Klein Associates.

Korolija, N. (1998). Episodes in talk: Constructing coherence in multiparty conversation (Doctoral dissertation). *Linköping Studies in Arts and Science, 171*. Linköping, Sweden: Linköping University.

Korolija, N., & Linell, P. (1996). Episodes: Coding and analyzing coherence in multiparty conversation. *Linguistics, 34*(44), 799–831. doi:10.1515/ling.1996.34.4.799

Landgren, J., & Nuldén, U. (2007). A study of emergency response work: Patterns of mobile phone interaction. In M. R. Rosson, & D. Gilmore (Eds.), *Proceedings of the SIGCHI Conference on Human Factors in Computing Systems in San Jose, CA* (pp. 1323-1331). New York, NY: ACM.

Linell, P., & Korolija, N. (1997). Coherence in multi-party conversation. In Givon, T. (Ed.), *Conversation: Cognitive, communicative and social perspectives* (pp. 167–205). Amsterdam, The Netherlands: John Benjamins.

Mackenzie, C., Hu, P. F.-M., Fausboll, C., Nerlich, M., & Benner, T. (2007). Challenges to remote emergency decision-making for disasters or Homeland Security. *Cognition Technology and Work, 9*(1), 15–24. doi:10.1007/s10111-006-0051-y

McCann, C., & Pigeau, R. (2000). *The human in command: Exploring the modern military experience*. New York, NY: Kluwer Academic/Plenum Publishers.

Mendonça, D., Beroggi, G. E. G., & Wallace, W. A. (2003). Evaluating support for improvisation in simulated emergency scenarios. In *Proceedings of the 36th Hawaii International Conference on System Sciences (HICSS'03) – Track 8 – Volume 8*. Washington, DC: IEE Computer Society.

Mendonça, D., & Fiedrich, F. (2006). Training for improvisation in emergency management: Opportunities and limits for information technology. *International Journal of Emergency Management, 3*(4), 348–363. doi:10.1504/IJEM.2006.011301

Mendonça, D., & Wallace, W. A. (2004). Studying organizationally-situated improvisation in response to extreme events. *International Journal of Mass Emergencies and Disasters, 22*(2), 5–29.

Mendonça, D., & Wallace, W. A. (2007). A cognitive model of improvisation in emergency management. *IEEE Transactions on Systems, Man and Cybernetics. Part A, 37*(4), 547–561.

Moorman, C., & Miner, A. S. (1998). Organizational improvisation and organizational memory. *Academy of Management Review, 23*(4), 698–723. doi:10.2307/259058

Orasanu, J., & Connolly, T. (1993). The reinvention of decision making. In Klein, G. A., Orasanu, I., Calderwood, R., & Zsambok, C. E. (Eds.), *Decision making in action: Models and methods* (pp. 3–20). Norwood, NJ: Ablex Publishing.

Orasanu, J., & Salas, E. (1993). Team decision making in complex environments. In Klein, G. A., Orasanu, J., Calderwood, R., & Zsambok, C. E. (Eds.), *Decision making in action: Models and methods* (pp. 327–345). Norwood, NJ: Ablex Publishing.

Parson, E. A. (1996). What can learn from a game? In Zeckhauser, R., Keeney, R. L., & Sebenius, J. K. (Eds.), *Wise choices: Decision, games, and negotiations* (pp. 233–252). Boston, MA: Harvard Business School Press.

Payne, C. F. (1999). Contingency plan exercises. *Disaster Prevention and Management, 8*(2), 111–117. doi:10.1108/09653569910266157

Perla, P. P. (1990). *The art of wargaming*. Annapolis, MD: U.S. Naval Institute.

Perrow, C. (1984). *Normal accidents: Living with high-risk technologies*. New York, NY: Basic Books.

Persson, M., & Worm, A. (2002). *Information experimentation in command and control*. Paper presented at the 2002 Command and Control Research Technology Symposium, Monterey, CA.

Persson, P.-A. (2000). Bringing power and knowledge together: Information Systems design for autonomy and control in command work (Doctoral dissertation). *Linköping Studies in Science and Technology, 639*. Linköping, SE: Linköping University.

Persson, P.-A. (2004). *Toward an understanding of the service-based command system*. Paper presented at the 9th ICCRTS Command and Control Research and Technology Symposium, Monterey, CA.

Peterson, D. M., & Perry, R. W. (1999). The impact of disaster exercise on participants. *Disaster Prevention and Management, 8*(4), 241–254. doi:10.1108/09653569910283879

Petrescu-Prahova, M. G., & Butts, C. T. (2005). *Emergent coordination in the World Trade Center disaster (Paper #36)*. Irvine, CA: Institute of Mathematical Behavioral Sciences/ University of California.

Rankin, W. J., Gentner, F. C., & Crissey, M. J. (1995). *After action review and debriefing methods: Technique and technology.* Paper presented at the 17th Interservice/ Industry Training Systems and Education Conference, Albuquerque, NM.

Rasker, P. C., Post, W. M., & Schraagen, J. M. C. (2000). Effects of two types of intra-team feedback on developing a shared mental model in command & control teams. *Ergonomics, 43*(8), 1167–1189. doi:10.1080/00140130050084932

Rasmussen, J., Brehmer, B., & Leplat, J. (1990). *Distributed decision making: Cognitive models for cooperative work.* New York, NY: John Wiley & Sons.

Rubel, R. C. (2001). War-gaming network-centric warfare. *Naval War College Review, 54*(2), 61–74.

Salmon, P. M., Stanton, N. A., Walker, G. H., & Jenkins, D. P. (2009). *Distributed situation awareness: Theory, measurement and application to teamwork.* Aldershot, UK: Ashgate.

Schmidt, K., & Bannon, L. (1992). Taking CSCW seriously: Supporting articulation work. *Computer Supported Cooperative Work, 1*(1), 7–40. doi:10.1007/BF00752449

Scott, T. D. (1983). *Tactical engagement simulation after action review guidebook (ARI Research Product 83-13).* Arlington, VA: U.S. Army Research Institute for Behavioral and Social Sciences.

Shattuck, L., & Woods, D. D. (2000). Communication of intent in military command and control systems. In McCann, C., & Pigeau, R. (Eds.), *The human in command: Exploring the modern military experience* (pp. 279–292). New York, NY: Kluwer Academic/Plenum Publishers.

Shubik, M. (1972). On the scope gaming. *Management Science, 18*(5), 20–36. doi:10.1287/mnsc.18.5.20

Stallings, R. A. (2006). Methodological issues. In Rodríguez, H., Quarantelli, E. L., & Dynes, R. R. (Eds.), *Handbook of disaster research* (pp. 55–82). New York, NY: Springer.

Stanton, N. A., Baber, C., & Harris, D. (2008). *Modelling command and control: Event analysis of systemic teamwork.* Aldershot, UK: Ashgate.

Stout, R. J., Cannon-Bowers, J. A., Salas, E., & Milanovich, D. M. (1999). Planing, shared mental models, and coordinated performance: An empirical link is established. *Human Factors, 41*(1), 61–71. doi:10.1518/001872099779577273

Stroomer, S., & Van Oostendorp, H. (2003). Analyzing communication in team tasks. In van Oostendorp, H. (Ed.), *Cognition in a digital world* (pp. 175–204). Mahwah, NJ: Lawrence Erlbaum Associates.

Svenmarck, P., & Brehmer, B. (1991). D³Fire, an experimental paradigm for the study of distributed decision making. In B. Brehmer (Ed.), *Proceedings of the 3rd MOHAWC Workshop on Distributed Decision Making in Belgirate, Italy* (pp. 47-77). Roskilde, Denmark: Risö National Laboratory.

Svensson, S., Cedergårdh, E., Måstensson, O., & Winnberg, T. (2009). *Tactics, command, leadership.* Karlstad, Sweden: Swedish Civil Contingencies Agency.

Thomas, L. C. (1984). *Games, theory and applications.* Mineola, NY: Courier Dover Publications.

Trnka, J. (2009). Exploring tactical command and control: A role-playing simulation approach (Doctoral dissertation). *Linköping Studies in Science and Technology, 1266.* Linköping, Sweden: Linköping University.

Trnka, J., Granlund, H., & Granlund, R. (2008). Using low-fidelity simulations to support design of decision-support systems for command and control applications. In M. Hirakawa, & E. Jungert (Eds.), *Proceedings of the 14th International Conference on Distributed Multimedia Systems in Boston, MA* (pp. 158-163). Skokie, IL: Knowledge Systems Institute.

Trnka, J., & Jenvald, J. (2006). Role-playing exercise – A real-time approach to study collaborative command and control. *International Journal of Intelligent Control and Systems, 11*(4), 218–228.

Trnka, J., Rankin, A., Jungert, E., Lundberg, J., & Granlund, R. (2009). *Information support in modern crisis and disaster response operations (Project Report)*. Linköping, Sweden: Linköping University.

Uhr, C. (2007). *Behind the charts – Exploring conditions for high level emergency response management in a complex environment (Report 1037)*. Lund, Sweden: Institute of Fire Safety Engineering.

Urban, J. M., Bowers, C. A., Monday, S. D., & Morgan, B. B. Jr. (1995). Workload, team structure, and communication in team performance. *Military Psychology, 7*(2), 123–139. doi:10.1207/s15327876mp0702_6

Vera, D., & Crossan, M. (2005). Improvisation and innovative performance in teams. *Organization Science, 16*(3), 203–224. doi:10.1287/orsc.1050.0126

Weick, K. E. (1998). Improvisation as a mindset for organizational analysis. *Organization Science, 9*(5), 543–555. doi:10.1287/orsc.9.5.543

Wertsch, J. V. (1997). *Mind in action*. New York, NY: Oxford University Press.

Woltjer, R. (2009). Functional modeling of constraint management in aviation safety and command and control (Doctoral dissertation). *Linköping Studies in Science and Technology, 1249*. Linköping, Sweden: Linköping University.

Woltjer, R., Lindgren, I., & Smith, K. (2006). A case study of information and communication technology in emergency management training. *International Journal of Emergency Management, 3*(4), 32–347. doi:10.1504/IJEM.2006.011300

Woods, D. D., & Dekker, S. (2000). Anticipating the effects of technological change: A new era of dynamics for human factors. *Theoretical Issues in Ergonomics Science, 1*(3), 272–282. doi:10.1080/14639220110037452

Woods, D. D., & Hollnagel, E. (2006). *Joint cognitive systems: Patterns in cognitive systems engineering*. Boca Raton, FL: CRC Press. doi:10.1201/9781420005684

Chapter 10
Exploring Socio–Technical Design of Crisis Management Information Systems

Dan Harnesk
Luleå University of Technology, Sweden

John Lindström
Luleå University of Technology, Sweden

ABSTRACT

In this chapter, we explore design foundations and conceptualize a design approach to examine the socio-technical knowledge that crisis organizations have about crisis management Information Systems. We use findings from a case study across four crisis organizations to illustrate how the network of knowledge, information management, and integration of technology and information were interpreted by stakeholders during a large wildfire in 2006. The design approach illustrates that design foundations of crisis management Information Systems encompass: a network of knowledge, IT management, and information integration. We argue that the design foundation is promising for analysis and explanation of the enrolment of actors, adaptation of technology/processes, and stabilization of crisis management Information Systems.

INTRODUCTION

The purpose of this paper is to illustrate that crisis management information systems need to be further conceptualized due to the complex mixture of socio-technical relationships that constitute

DOI: 10.4018/978-1-60960-609-1.ch010

crisis management. While mainstream design approaches to crisis management information systems concentrate on formal systems requirements (Murhen et al., 2008), the socio-technical reality of crisis management information systems has not been well researched (Comfort, 2005). For example, Turoff et al. (2004) focus on the software requirements for those planning and executing the emergency response management function. Indeed, information and communication technology is a necessity during crisis for actors at all levels, from first responders to second command line decision makers (Jennex, 2005). However, the extended information dependent crisis actor network, grounded in the hierarchy structure of crisis organizations, demands other plausible design premises than that of traditional decision science. The foremost reason is that crises are complex socio-technical environments to manage and control because they concretize discontinuity as the rule, and continuity as the exception, and crisis information systems has primary been designed according to the exception (Murhen et al., 2008).

We argue in this paper that this kind of socio-technical context needs further emphasis and clarification regarding information technology in use to understand crisis management information systems. Inspired and influenced by the socio-cognitive arguments for technological frames put forth by Orlikowski and Gash, (1994) we assemble the following three dimensions as promising ground for crisis management IS design:

- The infological dimension of information technology, which suggests that human actors can utilize IT to create and maintain knowledge in a human activity system, i.e., a network of knowledge.
- The management of information technology. This means that crisis organizations need to carefully determine, plan and evaluate alternatives of IT.
- The operational use of information technology. How information is shared between actors and why information integration is critical for successful emergency operations.

Based on the these three dimensions, we conceptualize a design approach for crisis management information systems using Actor Net-

work Theory to illustrate its applicability in the networked environment of crisis management.

The paper is structured as follows, after the introduction the seminal literature of information systems in the area of crisis management is reviewed. Next, the background to the study and methodological considerations are discussed Then follow a section in which networks of knowledge are discussed as one fundamental premise for crisis management information systems. Next, two central aspects of information management are presented that are deemed important for the understanding of technology in processes. Section six contains a discussion of the importance of integrating the flow of information in a networked crisis environment. Section seven synthesizes the above into a design approach for crisis management information systems. Finally, the conclusions from the study are presented together with suggestion for further work.

RELATED LITERATURE

The recognition of IT support during crisis management is not a new object to crisis management organizations (Comfort, 2005). In fact, there is a wide consensus in the literature that information systems are essential for crisis management (Jefferson, 2006; McDonald & Sinha, 2008; Murhen et al., 2008; Nunamaker et al., 1989; Turoff, 2002). Crisis management information systems comprise of a human activity systems that use technology to achieve defined goals, and thus need to be evaluated in the context they function in. As noted by Orlikowski & Gash (1994), *"technologies are social artefacts, their material form and function will embody their sponsors' and developers' objectives, values, interests, and knowledge of that technology"*(p. 179). To this end, Orlikowski and Gash (1994) stress the importance of local understanding of IT uses in a given setting, and found that the 'nature of technology', 'technology strategy' and 'technology in use' are domains that characterize interpretations of a certain technology. Nature of technology refers to people's images of the technology and their understanding of its capabilities and functionality. Technology strategy refers to people's views of why their organization acquired and implemented the technology. It includes their understanding of the motivation or vision behind the adoption decision and its likely value to the organization. Technology in use refers to people's understanding of how the technology will be used on a day-to-day basis and the likely or actual conditions and consequences associated with such use.

Van de Walle and Turoff (2008) point out that the context of crisis imbibes diverse and immense requirements and challenges for the design of information systems to be used in large scale emergency situations. Turoff (2002) illustrates that past and future objectives stay the same in crises, and that relevant communities in society need well designed collaborative knowledge systems to exchange information. Harrald (2006) demonstrates how the U.S. has designed and built up a national emergency response system during 30 years that did not meet the needs during the Hurricane Katrina. Harrald (2006) further discusses how researchers during this time period have documented and described the nonstructural factors such as improvisation, adaptability, and creativity that are critical to the coordination and communication and to successful problem solving. These critical nonstructural factors need to be taken into consideration when designing a crisis management system because they reflect the basic assumptions and interpretations of various stakeholders. Jennex (2008) introduces a model to be used in preparations and planning while introducing an emergency response system, describing a model to handle complex systems comprising communications, training, integration of knowledge, dynamic infrastructure etc. to be expanded with knowledge management. Knowledge management is in the model seen as

a key contributor to be able to quickly react to emergencies.

A formal design approach is presented by Turoff et al. (2004) in which principles and specifications for a dynamic response management information system where communication and information needs of first responders are addressed. The nine design principles suggested by Turoff et al. (2004) comprise of functional requirements. Among the nine principles, technical, social and contextual oriented principles are analyzed and proposed valid for design of response management systems. The criticism that could be raised towards the authors' treatment of the social and contextual principles is that they are software manifestations of the social actor and his context and not reflects human interpretations and values. This means that behavioral aspects of actors are attributable when in fact they need to be relationally oriented. Another technical design approach is taken by Meissner et al. (2002) aiming at identifying central design issues and architectural concepts for an integrated disaster management system, by means of a multi-level wireless voice and data communication infrastructure. Geographical information systems (GIS) are also important instruments for providing on-site spatial information. Cova (1999) showed that GIS applications can be used in emergency planning for evacuation and vulnerability mapping. Beside the need for communication procedures and tools there is also a great need for ability to coordinate teams involved in emergencies. Reddy et al. (2009) identify challenges with coordination of departmental teams and emergency medical teams in terms of gaining awareness, understanding of the context and the workflow between different teams. There are also successful attempts in literature to address design issues in crisis management from decision support viewpoints. For example, Comfort et al. (2001) propose a design approach for complex systems in crisis, focused on collecting, organizing, processing, and transmitting of data between University campus groups, aiming at supporting decision making. However, when considering the literature on crisis management; planning activities of crisis management seem to depend on the level of integration between different stakeholders (Comfort, 2007). For example, Palm and Ramsell (2007) point out the importance of having a network policy for sharing and coordinating recourses in case of emergencies. At the information systems level this is also significant because crisis organizations often struggle with the gap between the responsibility of information management and communication technology used in actual emergencies (Comfort & Haase, 2006). Wybo and Lonka (2002) challenge the paradox of low integration between these two aspects of information systems and conclude that they are equally important for reducing uncertainty among stakeholders during incidents and emergencies.

Notwithstanding the successful research that has been carried out in the field of crisis management, our review of the existing crisis management literature show that further research in design of crisis management information systems is needed to develop valid socio-technically based knowledge. Work done in the area mainly relate to the political policy research community and from technical traditions such as computer science or decision science.

RESEARCH METHOD

From a preparatory study to an ongoing (2008-2011) EU research project in safety and security we extracted data from four municipalities in North Sweden during two months in 2007. These municipalities have responsibility for local crisis management when emergencies hazardously impact the community. We designed a qualitative case study (Yin, 1994) and conducted interviews with practitioners concerned with operative crisis management. A theoretical sampling technique was used to find appropriate informants for the

study. According to Miles and Huberman (1994), theoretical sampling specifies that selected informants should represent the phenomenon under study. We selected actors from municipalities that work as Security Coordinators, Rescue Managers, and Municipality Directors. We chose those roles because input from different actors would nurture socio-technical insight to crisis management, encompassing operative response management as well as municipality responsibility and community aspects of crisis. We also intervened with a rescue department during a 6-hour seminar session, in which the representatives thoroughly described and explained difficulties they experienced during a large wild fire in 2006.

For the interviews, we designed questionnaire with semi-structured questions organized in themes. The themes were information management, operative information flow, and organization of crisis management. The answers we got from respondents were transcribed from paper notes and checked with the respondents afterwards. Data analysis was based on pattern search for similarities and differences between the case sites. These patterns were related to the underlying theoretical proposition that crisis management information systems capability is improved if a socio-technical design approach is favored. We also conducted a literature review, which exposed that management information systems are chiefly concerned with characteristics of the systems as such, and less concerned with the complexity of actions in relation to information aspects of crisis situations. We verified the literature review with four (4) municipality representatives with immense experience in crisis management. The interviews were semi-structured in so that the informants could give input regarding crisis management procedures. Specifically, the informants provided data for what kind of tools different implementations have used, what kind of needs first responders and second command line actors require, how they were using tools for working together, and performance of work tasks as well.

The approach of combining a literature review with semi-structured interviews increased the validity of our research concerning design issues. In so doing we aligned our research method to the concept of theoretical validity and interpretative validity (Maxwell, 1992). Theoretical validity refer to the explanation of the phenomenon studied, and not only a description of the facts or an interpretation of the underlying meaning, This type of validity is concerned with the theories or concepts used to explain the meanings of action are explicitly related to studied phenomenon. Most important is that the chosen theories can be presumed to reveal a true picture of the contextual conditions that is subject of inquiry. Interpretative validity is a meaning oriented concept and accounts for the abstractions that are employed by informants rather than theoretical abstractions. By combining these two concepts of validity we were able to create meaning of the phenomenon under study, i.e., design approach for crisis management information systems. Given the results of our data collection the analysis rendered the three overall categories: the network of knowledge, information management, and information integration. Next we present theoretical discussions of these categories with reference to the data collection.

NETWORKS OF KNOWLEDGE

Braa et al. (2004) define the notion of networks of action as *"the intention to capture the dynamics of translating, aligning heterogeneous networks of routines, technology, and learning within politically contested terrains of opposing projects and ideologies in an effort to promote sustainable, replicable changes"* (p. 342). To make these intentions institutionalized and becoming a natural part of organizational activities effective knowledge sharing between network actors is critical.

(Jennex, 2005) defines knowledge sharing, as the practice of selectively applying knowledge from previous experiences of decision-making to current and future decision making activities with the express purpose of improving the organization's effectiveness. Accordingly, one way to understand the organization of crisis management is as a network of knowledge. In the preparatory and further operative states of crisis management, several actors (nodes) will be active and contributing to recovering from the crisis. This results in what (Akrich, 1992) refers to as a scenario of action whereby organizations demonstrate their aligned purposes with collaboration. Viewing crisis management as a network also means that it could be studied with a number of different perspectives. For example, using social network analysis (Cross et al., 2001) as a lens, would produce analysis outcome displaying the complexity of communication linkages within a network. Clearly, the result of such approach would provide an outlook how an organizational network of knowledge can improve crisis management. However, a major issue in defining and setting up a network of knowledge is to draw a common cognitive map of network constituents to exploit the full potential of its knowledge (Carlsson, 2001). What would be particularly problematic in crisis management is to grasp the entanglement of human action and technology use, because crisis management is an arena of different language, cognition, technology, and routines that re-produces multiple logics of response. As a result, it is important to shape the network to become stabilized. The socio-technical way to stabilization is through an open ended set of interactions where actors interplay, rather than that of acquiring their form and attributes from pre-defined structures (Cordella & Shaikh, 2003). This ontological assumption allows us to inform the proposed design approach with Actor Network Theory, as it represents an intermediary position between technologic determinism and constructivism (Latour, 2005).

Defining the Network

Actor Network Theory postulates that a network is a concept, not a thing that humans can lay a hand on. Rather it is a tool to describe actions taken among user in a certain setting or environment. In ANT the concept of action is an effect or outcome of use patterns in the network of heterogeneous interests, irrespective whom or what carries out the action (Law & Hassard, 1999). ANT is process oriented and one of the key points in ANT is that neither social nor technical strands are privileged; rather it is a path for co-evolvement of actability. Akrich and Latour (1992) define co-evolvement as "..*the actors involved in network have to be aligned for a setting to be kept in existence or that have to be aligned to prevent others from invading the setting and interrupting its existence*" (p261). Existence of a certain setting may be interrupted by a number of reasons, e.g., new decisions of strategic nature may affect the performance of work processes in which previous and effective use patterns are established (Bijker & Law, 1992). Typically, in crisis management this means that the use patterns of action are formally predefined for first responders. For example, the police have to secure the emergency area, medical teams and fire fighters act by following protocol. The second command line of crisis actors also has its predefined routines to follow. However, these two levels may come in conflict if human action and artefacts are kept in separation. This separation induces dualism in views of the network that re-enforces the appreciation of technical merits as such, and humans as beneficiaries of the technology (Cordella & Shaikh, 2003). Clearly, the dualism reflects the manner by which information technology supplements actors during crisis management.

Our study shows that technology by all means is entangled with the objective to perform purposeful actions and task fulfilment. This view on information technology advises that the social system is concerned with the attributes of people (e.g. attitudes, skills, values). The technical system is concerned with the processes, tasks and the technology needed to transform inputs to outputs. Understanding these two areas is about understanding what the overall work systems are supposed to accomplish (Alter, 2004b). Thus, any design or redesign of a work system must deal with both systems in an integrated procedure (Avgerou et al., 2004). In IS research socio-technical studies have attempted to overcome the separation by focusing on contextual issues such as, peoples work processes and their skills, knowledge issues and coordination (Ciborra, 2002) and how these aspects are reflected in computer software. Our analysis of crisis management in the municipalities with a socio-technical lens explains the separation between management teams and first responders as tightly linked together by common goals, yet with dedicated resources. While the crisis management teams in our study wished for more social orientation in their designated work tasks due to that they needed to maintain public relations with media and so on, the organization of fire fighters subscribed to input-output system characteristics. These characteristics depend on that they move in and execute necessary operation in an emergency and move out once the tasks are accomplished. The question at hand is: To what extent could redesign of the management system be done without affecting the operative action system of fire fighters? ANT rejects the dualism of humans as one entity and technology as another entity, as both are considered entangled with each other and recursively define each others' characteristics (Cordella & Shaikh, 2003).

In conceptualizing a design approach, it is important to establish a common understanding of crisis management information systems. We subscribe to Alter's definition – "*IT-reliant work systems are work systems whose efficient and/ or effective operation depends on the use of IT*." (Alter, 2003, p. 367). Indeed, this definition is in conflict to those that underscore the IT-artefact as the core object of study in information systems research (e.g., Orlikowski & Iacono, 2001). The main question debated is in what ways IT affect a certain human setting. In hierarchy organisation, which crisis organizations are examples of, IT ideally supplements well defined work systems routines to achieve defined goals. In other human IT use situations, for example, mobile and social networking applications, technology is seen as intrinsically intertwined with human activities in which the use constitutes a hybrid collective (e.g., Hanseth, 2005). This hybrid collective of technical artefacts and human activities of performing organizational work are involved in various forms of information technology, rooms, data networks, etc., and is as such important for the ways organizational routines are created (Orlikowski, 2007). As noted by Scolaí (2008) *"..the ability by which artefacts can be carriers of practice is related to the artefacts materiality"* (p. 5). Thus, the network of knowledge relies on information systems whereby organizational contexts are influenced by different technologies that are used for fulfilment of work tasks (Lamb, 1999). From a design outlook, the challenge is to understand how decomposed organizational goals as well as individual goals in carrying out work tasks can be harmonized. In information systems research the situation is substantially investigated and reflects the perceived usefulness that humans expects from IT (Davis, 1989). In crisis management, the need for situational awareness is one example where information systems display specifics from contextual dependencies of emergencies and crisis. The purpose with such system is to manifest people, rules, procedures, technology, software, communications and allied services to support command and control. One intrinsic detail that information systems research is concerned with is how to develop software systems that are based on one common view of the world (context) and to offer standardized ways to operate. This entails a paradox that confronts insights for the importance to recognize behaviour aspects, collective actions, and cognitive apprehensions of a certain

context. Clearly, attributes of all that, is difficult to embed in software when, in fact, the nature of software is de-contextualization (Kallinikos, 1992). Hence, it is important that designers do not constraint development with rigid models that risk hampering enabling IT-infrastructures in organizations (Ciborra, 1997).

Interestingly, our study points out two major concerns for networks of knowledge. One concern is for stakeholders in the network and the other concern is the technological pattern in the network. The character of such a network is heterogeneous and dynamic, and stakeholders are involved in different processes and activities, and they are typically utilizing different information technology for their purposes (Latour, 2005). It is important to recognize that a network of knowledge in crisis management exceeds rudimentary information sharing to include information such as; information for decision making, policy based actions, injured and their relatives, media engagement, capacity and capabilities. In order for a network of knowledge to evolve, each stakeholder needs extensive understanding of the extended information flow between the nodes within the network (Braa et al., 2004). The more each stakeholder knows the more they can contribute and add value in crisis operations, i.e., external knowledge is accessible at zero marginal cost. As noted by Turoff et al. (2004), role transferability is a key problem in crisis management as it is virtually impossible to pre-define what roles actors will undertake during an emergency.

The technical pattern in a network of knowledge should ideally provide a stable secure infrastructure that supports the stakeholders in their collaborative task patterns (Landgren & Nulden, 2007). Thus, the technical stabilization may be rewarded by the procedural direction of managing information. We argue that ANT as a lens to examine the network of knowledge may assist in inscribing crisis management information systems components, that in nature are socio-technically grounded, and based on symmetry between human and non-human actors, to maintain an overall common understanding of crisis management (Callon, 1991). This approach recognizes that the IT dependent work system risks fostering divergence between formal crisis routines and the need for dynamic actions during a crisis. However, as ANT emphasizes that manifestation of technology is a process evolving over time, there is little risk to blur the analysis with object attributes, instead of process of use characteristics.

INFORMATION MANAGEMENT

Information management is herein considered as the management of information shared between humans and facilitated by information technology. A similar view is found in the literature in areas such as IT management and strategic information systems (Ward & Peppard, 2002). Our interpretation holds two outstanding directions for information management; functional information management and procedural information management. The management of information in processes of emergency and crisis environments poses a special challenge to problem solving actions during incidents. The crisis environment limits the possibility for humans to retrieve process information and disseminate information further due to complexity and uncertainty in crisis events (Comfort & Haase, 2006). Our view of information management being divided into functional management and procedural management is consistent with Comfort's (2005) emphasis on long term policy analysis as a method of detailed analysis of the characteristics of actors/agents involved in a selected system.

Functional Information Management

The central idea of the functional dimension relates to the idea of information as being a key resource for organizations (basically the information infrastructure is organized like an input-output system).

The theory of resource-based view (RBV) posits a cogent framework to evaluate the strategic value of information systems resources (Wade & Holland, 2004). As a valuable resource, information systems should serve organizational goals by maintaining a relevant information infrastructure to users involved in emergency response activities (Turoff et al., 2004). However, this is not a simple task to fulfil since emergency information is not readily available. This corresponds to the principle of *rarity* in RBV that prescribes that information as a resource needs to be maintained through ongoing organizational specific development (Wade & Holland, 2004), for example, crisis management training. Information sharing at this level of action often concerns rudimentary information that is necessary for during emergencies, for example: Emergency type, Spreading, Vicinity, Meteorological data, and Response capacity.

This type of information is certainly most important for operational efficiency in the resource based view of information management. To some extent, the municipalities we interviewed have facilities for operational and functional information sharing but they do not for example have systems they can use for crisis training. As a consequence, crisis management organizations manually have to organise and evaluate outcomes from crisis training. This kind of *instrumental orientation* (Hirschheim et al., 1996) offers to practitioners, techniques to steer development activities of system complexity, management of software, and that the quality of software systems can be maintained. Standardization of routines in management of functional information flow is requested in the municipalities so that continuous crisis planning and training can be performed. In the case of designing a crisis management system this base for information sharing contributes as an operational know-how instrument, which during crises expects to diminish the uncertainty of what collaborative actors actually direct their focus on.

Procedural Information Management

In contrast to the functional resource based view on information management, procedural information management deals with factors that relate to firm management levels and external dimensions to the firm (Segars & Grover, 1999). Among the most important factors are availability of information and information quality. Formalization and focus are typical instruments needed in crisis management. Crisis management organizations are legally required to have rules and procedures for regional responsibilities in overall crisis management. Informed by our study, municipalities are also highly focused towards integrative issues to maintain a formal structure in crisis management. To support this from the information perspective, reliable structures of information bases in functional units located at different municipality agencies must be maintained.

Ensuring these ambitions require an orientation of information management that are procedural and relational in nature. Earl (1989) identifies areas related to this approach; Strategic decisions of IT and IS-infrastructures, the role of IS, e.g., decision making, systems development issues, maintenance issues, changes in platforms and services.

In contrast to the functional resource based view, which considers information merely as a technical artefact, the procedural dimension of information management advocates for human intervention in IT based activities. The municipalities we studied did not take lightly on these issues and they stated that one of the most difficult tasks is to judge what kind information systems to implement in existing infrastructures. As noted by Turoff et al. (2004): *"...an emergency systems that is not used on a regular basis before an emergency will never be of use in an actual emergency"* (p6). Normally (hopefully), a crisis is a rare event and the systems are therefore seldom used, which means that users are not continuously updated on the functionality of the systems. In-house IT departments are usually not experts in crisis information management and therefore the external/internal relationship is not incorporated in existing IT policies, etc. A consequence of this is that an investment in crisis information systems is not only is an economic issue, but rather depending on subjective opinions of the estimated value of such systems. The economic side of information systems value is extensively investigated in literature and concern mainly the return on investment of IT. For example, Soh and Markus (1995) argue that IT-assets is something that not necessarily improve organizational performance, but if, structural factors such as, size of the organization and information intensity are taken into account, then the spending in IT may improve performance. Since the ground for performance in crisis management is operationally complex and uncertain, the fundamental subjective value approach suggested here is in what way information systems can reduce coordination costs during crises. One definition of coordination cost is "the cost of maintaining communication links (or 'channels') between actors and the cost of exchanging messages along these links" (Malone, 1987, p1319). This means that for example techniques for interaction analysis can be utilized to visualize the type and content of information shared within the network. With this procedure organizations can internally begin to shape the complex matters of crisis information, which involves both humans and information technology.

INFORMATION INTEGRATION

Information integration is a key issue to agencies for establishing a secure and trustworthy linkage between stakeholders in crisis management (Turoff et al., 2004). One fundamental task is to set up, maintain and control the IT infrastructure. The IT infrastructure should facilitate the information flow between all stakeholders ensuring availability and accountability of information in the networked human activity systems of crisis management. Three central aspects of the networked environment are cooperation, coordination and communication (Premkumar, 2000):

- Cooperation refer to the undertaking of complimentary activities to achieve mutual benefits
- Coordination is the management of interdependencies between participants.
- Communication is the formal and informal sharing or exchange of meaningful and timely information between parties facilitates the capacity of these norms to serve as a conduit between the other norms.

Crisis organizations do not operate in emergency and crisis environment without serving community obligations. The activities undertaken are clearly defined in policies and government regulations. Cooperation between stakeholders is essential and is also regulated in detailed policy documents. Turoff et al. (2004) claim the importance of information validity and timeliness by arguing for confidence in decisions by supplying the best possible up-to-date information is critical to those whose actions may risk lives and resources (p9). However, this is not always easily achieved. Lessons learned from the evaluation, made by fire brigades of the extreme wild fire in 2006 in the north of Sweden revealed several interesting aspects of cooperation, coordination, and communication between municipalities and between fire fighting teams during the events of controlling the fire. The size of the fire was 15 km² at most, several municipalities cooperated in the operation, and fire fighters were active for 32 days before the operation succeeded. The operation included many shifts of working teams, which created an interface in between fire fighters when they reported their actions. This was done entirely on manual basis, which entailed that many communication links were maintained by the team

and command and control leaders. In the actual operation of fire fighting the teams tried to use mobile phones. This was extremely troublesome since coverage of mobile signals were very low due to the geographical location of the fire. Instead communication radio equipment was used to ensure stable communication links throughout the entire operation. Overall, the results from the evaluation display only manual management of the information flow, except for the documentation phase which was accomplished by the use of computers. However, the real-time logging of activities became isolated to single individuals. Consequently, there was a great risk for information not being accountable due to reliance on face-to-face information sharing.

IT based coordination of interdependencies relies on integration between IT enabled nodes of activities (Comfort, 2007). However, it is not a simple task to set up coordination during emergencies because actions can be both planned and ad-hoc due to coincidental occurrences during the course of emergencies. Turoff et al. (2004) describe this as the 'coordination crux' of emergencies. Moreover, environmental contingencies may hamper technical infrastructures to be set up. This kind of uncertainty underpins the complexity of managing crisis seen from the management information systems perspective. Motro (1997) posits that actors should be able to qualify their confidence in the information stated, which would reduce uncertainty in any actions related to specified goals. The trustworthiness of information depends on the level of perfection/imperfection of information. If the source of information is unreliable the information gathered may become more and more misaligned as more and more people share that imperfect information. The next section deals with this contextual complexity by suggesting a three step approach for crisis management information systems.

CRISIS MANAGEMENT INFORMATION SYSTEMS APPROACH

Based on the reasoning of network of knowledge, information management, and information integration, a common ground for the use of information systems is expected to evolve among stakeholders in crisis management. Crisis management information revolves around these three different vehicles for IT matters in so that they are contributing with information systems properties to the holistic view of crisis management information systems in both an attributive and relational manner. As noted by Comfort and Haase (2006), the key in crisis management is the collaborative task by which people can add bits and pieces of information from different places, from different actors, into a common task. The relational nature of collaboration entails that crisis management expands the functional dimension of IT usage and that management should account for long term planning in information management (Comfort, 2005). That means that coordination of work tasks whether they are automated or humanly performed need to have strong communication orientation to it in order to ensure purposeful actions. To this end, the more the system characteristics are unified or overlapped the more the collaboration activities can benefit from discussions and interactive sharing of knowledge instead of just the exchange of knowledge. Murhen et al. (2008) address this through the lens of sense-making arguing that IS design deliverables should allow people 'to make sense of situations' through rich inter-personal communication, rather than storing data in different repositories.

What we want to stress in this contribution is that our view of crisis management in this paper is built upon human behaviour in cooperation with other humans, and that they have information technology at hand for both efficient and effective knowledge sharing. Apart from the choice of any suitable tools to use for collaboration support is

the issue of being mature in utilizing these tools. Normally, huge (and successful) efforts are made internally in organizations to train users with different tools. Data from our study shows that municipalities experience difficulties when the tools are being used in a network of heterogeneous stakeholders, mainly due to different strategies for adoption and adaptation of IT tools. Therefore it usually takes considerable amount of time before the tools are beneficial to clients (Turoff et al., 2004). As noted from our study, once in operation mode, the tools and the configuration of the human setting largely contribute to the networked activities through interpretation of the need for pragmatism during actions.

We argue, in line with Harrald's (2006) argument of nonstructural aspects, such as, creativity in coordination, together with the establishment of social presence among stakeholders, and formal emergency response aspects serve as a basis for crisis management information systems. Social presence is concerned with the social interactions that people undertake in order to create, maintain, and further develop the relationship with associates. Formality relates to the specific emergency actions and the need for coordination of information flow in these transactions. Thus, crisis management information systems concern the support or enabling of formal and informal information sharing (Ciborra, 2002), during the course of a crisis.

An Actor Network Theory informed design approach for crisis management information systems that deal both with social issues and technical issues can be formulated in a three phase method that in its initial state do not distinguish between the human stakeholders and technical artifacts:

Enrollment of stakeholders and or technology, or how to establish a stable network of alliances? This phase specifically focuses on the network of knowledge dimension. This is an act of agreements which specifies any role assigned to the crisis management context (Callon, 1986b). In this phase, communication norms should be defined, and also cultural, individual-collective issues needs proper attention. The engagement of stakeholders in all nodes of the network of knowledge is crucial for effectiveness in crisis management. The choice of perspective for the design of a crisis management information system is likely to affect the performance of the system. Too much reliance on technological innovations is risky if the stakeholders do not accept components of technology. On the other hand, too much focus directed towards the social setting and the stakeholders will affect the logical design of technology support. The suggested trajectory is instead to consider both technology and stakeholders as equal actors in the network (Latour, 2005), allowing for openness and trust in the configuration of the network constituents. For example, fire fighters act with a very short response time, and in such hard situations that it will be impossible to manage technology if designed in a fashion that requires switching the focus from core actions.

Technology and Process Adaptation. This phase addresses the information management dimension. Basically, this is a process of requirements elicitation and stakeholder input. Technology and crisis management processes need to be aligned and if changes occur on one side, the other have to adapt (Callon, 1986b). Hence, coordination costs in the network of knowledge need to be carefully pondered, so that uncertainty while sharing information is reduced as much as possible. Even if the organizations studied in this paper did not fully exploit information technology during emergencies due to environmental limitations such as financial strength or maturity in using technology, they were not totally hampered to make deliberate choices of information technology. However, adaptation of technology and or processes is a demanding task in terms of establishing effective communication channels between first responders and the second command line, as well as making information systems used in emergency and crisis a natural part in daily work among crisis actors. Turoff et al. (2004)

claim the necessity of information systems being used both off-line as well as during emergencies to be rendered successful. Thus, we stress the management responsibility to continuously support training and stimulating use of systems and applications, as well as aligning IT and processes based on functional and procedural information management.

Stabilization of the network of actions. Here we are concerned with information integration. The previous phases should ideally have defined the socio-technical system of crisis management. In this phase the network is in operation and functioning according to the result from initial phases, i.e., this phase is the manifest of stabilized actors and actions (Latour, 2005). This should be considered as the network of knowledge is extended and not isolated or frozen in any way (Walsham, 1997). For organizations in general, maintaining stability is costly since organizational and work processes often are moving targets. Continuous monitoring and adaptations when requirements changes over time are often needed. The integration of information flow throughout the activity chain of crisis management is vital for stability. As noticed from data of the wild fire in 2006, the activity chain indicated several gaps, which made it difficult to coordinate work tasks in the operations and gaining control of the fire. Inside the outer loop of coordination between task force leaders and second command line coordinators, the gaps were insignificant. However, this level of communication required that task force leaders took time from the operations to package the information that came from fire fighters into a form that could be sent upstream in the activity-chain.

CONCLUSION

This research set out to conceptualize a design approach for crisis management information system based on available literature in IT and information systems, and the analysis of empirical data from municipality contexts. Considering the differences in apprehension that stakeholders may have for the crisis contexts the main conclusion is that management is extremely dependent how designers as well as researchers are able to distinguish between social activities, response activities and the contingencies of information technology support to such activities (*viz.* Orlikowski & Gash, 1994). Our study has generated an integrative socio-technical approach of crisis management information systems. The design foundation that shaped our approach to crisis management information systems, contribute to the literature seeking to articulate the socio-technical dependencies that comprise crisis management information systems (e.g., Comfort & Haase, 2006; Comfort et al., 2002; Jennex, 2007; Turoff et al., 2004). In particular our study, contributes by clarifying that 'the socio' and 'the technical' largely depend on the differentiation of knowledge and information technology that is used in the domain of crisis management. Hence, our socio-technical design approach extends earlier work on crisis management information systems by empirically demonstrating that a view on crisis reflective of the operational paradigm induces problems for crisis management in contemporary crisis organizations (Van de Walle & Turoff, 2008).

Our assessment of the design approach, developed from empirical as well as theoretical sources, resulted in a holistic view of crisis management information systems, which fills a knowledge gap in the complex field of crisis management. We mainly achieved this by the conceptualization of crisis management as a network of knowledge, which serves as a base for understanding the importance of IT management and information integration issues during emergency operations. However, while our approach has advantages of being socio-technical oriented it has limitations. Our study is limited to a single case study, and in that it represent only a partial

view on crisis management information systems design. Another problem is that of distributing the theoretical assumptions underlying our approach to a community of practice. We contend that crisis management information systems in reality would gain from the view of equality between human and non-human actors that Actor Network Theory presents. However, as crisis management actors most likely are uninformed of the sociological foundations of Actor Network Theory that may thwart implementations of our suggested approach.

According to the conclusions, it is suggested that future studies in the area direct more focus on contextual aspects of crisis management. Particularly we appreciate the need to further study how elements of ANT may enable the institutionalization of crisis management information systems. This is deemed critical because contextual aspects do not only concern technological aspects, but more importantly, how technology in use supports the collaborative nature of crisis management. As noted by several IS researchers with focus on the use of IT in organizations, the gap between social and technical matters is a widespread organizational problem (e.g., Orlikowski & Barley, 2001). Our study shows that this type of situation statue the way crisis management information systems continuously are perceived by crisis organizations. However, the highly interactive nature of collaboration in crisis management, as contrasted to "normal" organizational business processes, calls for research on technologies that are embedded in the very actions performed by humans during crisis management. The action chain, from first responders to crisis managers, need access to integrated technology and information flow across different crisis organizations (Turoff et al., 2010). Therefore, we suggest that future studies preferably build the analysis on critical realist assumptions using in-depth qualitative methods.

REFERENCES

Akrich, M. (1992). The description of technical objects. In Bijker, W. E., & Law, J. (Eds.), *Shaping technology/building society: Studies in socio-technical change* (pp. 206–224). Cambridge, MA: The MIT Press.

Akrich, M., & Latour, B. (1992). A summary of a convenient vocabulary for the semiotics of human and nonhuman assemblies. In Bijker, W. E., & Law, J. (Eds.), *Shaping technology/building society* (pp. 205–224). Cambridge, MA: MIT Press.

Alter, S. (2003). 18 reasons why IT-reliant work systems should replace the IT artifact as the core subject matter of the IS field. *Communications of the AIS, 12*(23), 365–394.

Alter, S. (2004b). *Making work system principles visible and usable in systems analysis and design.* Paper presented at the the Tenth Americas Conference on Information Systems, New York.

Avgerou, C., Ciborra, C., & Land, F. F. (Eds.). (2004). *The social study of Information and Communications Technology: Innovation, actors and context*. Oxford, UK: Oxford University Press.

Bijker, W. E., & Law, J. (1992). What catastrophe tells us about technology and society. In Bijker, W. E., & Law, J. (Eds.), *Shaping technology/building society*. Cambridge, MA: MIT Press.

Braa, J. R., Monteiro, E., & Sahay, S. (2004). Networks of action: Sustainable health Information Systems across developing countries. *Management Information Systems Quarterly, 28*(3).

Callon, M. (1986b). Some elements of a sociology of translation: Domestication of the scallops and the fishermen in St. Brieuc's Bay. In Law, J. (Ed.), *Power, action and belief. A new sociology of knowledge?* (pp. 196–219). London, UK: Routledge & Kegan Paul.

Callon, M. (1991). Techno-economic networks and irreversibility. In Law, J. (Ed.), *A sociology of monsters. Essays on power, technology and domination* (pp. 132–161). London, UK: Routledge.

Carlsson, S. A. (2001). *Knowledge management in network contexts.* Paper presented at the The 9th European Conference on Information Systems.

Ciborra, C. (2002). *The labyrinths of information: Challenging the wisdom of systems*. Oxford, UK: Oxford University Press.

Ciborra, C. U. (1997). De profundis? Deconstructing the concept of strategic alignment. *Scandinavian Journal of Information Systems, 9*(1), 67–82.

Comfort, L. K. (2005). Risk, security, and disaster management. *Annual Review of Political Science, 8*, 335–356. doi:10.1146/annurev.polisci.8.081404.075608

Comfort, L. K. (2007). Crisis management in hindsight: Cognition, communication, coordination, and control. *Public Administration Review, 67*, 189–197. doi:10.1111/j.1540-6210.2007.00827.x

Comfort, L. K., & Haase, T. W. (2006). Communication, coherence, and collective action: The impact of Hurricane Katrina on communications infrastructure. *Public Works Management Policy, 10*(4), 328–343. doi:10.1177/1087724X06289052

Comfort, L. K., Sungu, Y., Johnson, D., & Dunn, M. (2002). Complex systems in crisis: Anticipation and resilience in dynamic environments. *Journal of Contingencies and Crisis Management, 9*(3), 144–158. doi:10.1111/1468-5973.00164

Cordella, A., & Shaikh, M. (2003). *Actor network theory and after: What's new for IS research?* Paper presented at the 11th European Conference on Information Systems.

Cova, T. J. (1999). GIS in emergency management. In Longley, P. A., Goodchild, M. F., Maguire, D. J., & Rhind, D. V. (Eds.), *Geographical Information Systems: Principles, techniques, applications, and management.*

Cross, R., Parker, A., Prusak, L., & Borgatti, S. P. (2001). Knowing what we know: Supporting knowledge creation and sharing in social networks. *Organizational Dynamics, 30,* 100–120. doi:10.1016/S0090-2616(01)00046-8

Davis, F. D. (1989). Perceived usefulness, perceived ease of use, and user acceptance of information technology. *Management Information Systems Quarterly, 13*(3), 319–339. doi:10.2307/249008

Earl, M. J. (1989). *Management strategies for information technology.* Prentice-Hall.

Hanseth, O. (2005). Beyond metaphysics and theory consumerism. *Scandinavian Journal of Information Systems, 17*(1), 159–166.

Harrald, J. R. (2006). Agility and discipline: Critical success factors for disaster response. *The Annals of the American Academy of Political and Social Science, 604*(1), 256–272. doi:10.1177/0002716205285404

Hirschheim, R., Klein, H. K., & Lyytinen, K. (1996). Exploring the intellectual structures of Information Systems development: A social action rhetoric analysis. *Accounting Management & Information Technology, 6*(1/2), 1–64. doi:10.1016/0959-8022(96)00004-5

Jefferson, T. L. (2006). Evaluating the role of information technology in emergency and crisis management. *The Journal of Information and Knowledge Management Systems, 36*(3), 261–264.

Jennex, M. E. (2005). What is knowledge management? *International Journal of Knowledge Management, 1*(4), i–iv.

Jennex, M. E. (2007). *Modeling emergency response systems.* Paper presented at the 40th Hawaii International Conference on System Sciences.

Jennex, M. E. (2008). A model for emergency response systems. In Janczewski, L., & Colarik, A. (Eds.), *Cyber warfare and cyber terrorism* (pp. 383–391). Hershey, PA: Idea Group.

Kallinikos, J. (1992). The significations of machines. *Scandinavian Journal of Management, 8*(2), 113–132. doi:10.1016/0956-5221(92)90020-F

Lamb, R. (1999). *Using Intranets: Preliminary results from a socio-technical field study.* Paper presented at the 32nd Hawaii International Conference on System Sciences, Hawaii.

Landgren, J., & Nulden, U. (2007). *A study of emergency response work: Patterns of mobile phone interaction.* Paper presented at the CHI 2007 San Jose, CA.

Latour, B. (2005). *Reassembling the social: An introduction to actor-network-theory.* Oxford, UK: Oxford University Press.

Law, J., & Hassard, J. (1999). *Actor network theory and after.* Blackwell Publishers/The Sociological Review.

Malone, T. W. (1987). Modelling coordination in organizations and markets. *Management Science, 33*(10), 1317–1332. doi:10.1287/mnsc.33.10.1317

Maxwell, J. A. (1992). Understanding and validity in qualitative research. *Harvard Educational Review, 62*(3), 279–300.

McDonald, S., & Sinha, R. (2008). Information communication technology: Reform of organisational crisis management during natural disasters. *International Journal of Management Practice, 3*(2), 131–149. doi:10.1504/IJMP.2008.018367

Meissner, A., Luckenbach, T., Risse, T., Kirste, T., & Kirchner, H. (2002). *Design challenges for an integrated disaster management communication and Information System.* Paper presented at The First IEEE Workshop on Disaster Recovery Networks (DIREN 2002), New York City.

Miles, M. B., & Huberman, M. A. (1994). *Qualitative data analysis.* Sage Publications.

Motro, A. (1997). Sources of uncertainty, imprecision, and inconsistency in Information Systems. In Motro, A., & Smets, P. (Eds.), *Uncertainty management in Information Systems: Needs and solutions*. Kluwer Academic Publishers.

Murhen, W., Van Den Eede, G., & Van de Walle, B. (2008). *Sensemaking as a methodology for ISCRAM research: Information processing in an ongoing crisis* Paper presented at the 5th International ISCRAM Conference Washington, DC, USA.

Nunamaker, J. R., Weber, E. S., & Chen, M. (1989). Organizational crisis management systems: Planning for intelligent action. *Journal of Management Information Systems, 5*(4), 7–32.

Orlikowski, W., & Barley, S. (2001). Technology and institutions: What can research on Information Technology and research on organizations learn from each other. *Management Information Systems Quarterly, 25*(2), 145–165. doi:10.2307/3250927

Orlikowski, W. J. (2007). Sociomaterial practices: Exploring technology at work. *Organization Studies, 28*(9). doi:10.1177/0170840607081138

Orlikowski, W. J., & Gash, D. C. (1994). Technological frames: Making sense of information technology in organizations. *ACM Transactions on Information Systems, 2*, 174–207. doi:10.1145/196734.196745

Orlikowski, W. J., & Iacono, C. S. (2001). Research commentary: Desperately seeking the "IT" in IT research - A call to theorizing the IT artifact? *Information Systems Research, 12*(2), 121–134. doi:10.1287/isre.12.2.121.9700

Palm, J., & Ramsell, E. (2007). Developing local emergency management by co-ordination between municipalities in policy networks: Experiences from Sweden. *Journal of Contingencies and Crisis Management, 15*(4), 173–182. doi:10.1111/j.1468-5973.2007.00525.x

Premkumar, G. (2000). Inter-organizational systems and supply chain management: An information processing perspective. *Information Systems Management, 17*(3). doi:10.1201/1078/43192.17.3.20000601/31241.8

Reddy, M. C., Paul, S. A., Abraham, P. J., McNeese, M., DeFlitch, C., & Yen, J. (2009). Challenges to effective crisis management: Using information and communication technologies to coordinate emergency medical services and emergency department teams. *International Journal of Medical Informatics, 78*(4), 259–269. doi:10.1016/j.ijmedinf.2008.08.003

Scolaí, P. (2008). Materialising materiality. *Proceedings of the Twenty Ninth International Conference on Information Systems*, Paris.

Segars, A. H., & Grover, V. (1999). Profiles of strategic Information Systems planning. *Information Systems Research, 10*(3), 199–232. doi:10.1287/isre.10.3.199

Soh, C., & Markus, M. L. (1995). *How IT creates business value: A process theory synthesis*. Paper presented at the 16th International Conference on Information Systems, Amsterdam, The Netherlands.

Turoff, M. (2002). On site: Past and future emergency response information systems. *Communications of the ACM, 45*(4), 29–32. doi:10.1145/505248.505265

Turoff, M., Chumer, M., Van de Walle, B., & Yao, X. (2004). The design of a dynamic emergency response management information system (DERMIS). *Journal of Information Technology Theory and Application, 5*(4), 1–36.

Turoff, M., Van de Walle, B., & Hiltz, S. R. (2010). Emergency response Information Systems: Past, present, and future. In Turoff, M., Van de Walle, B., & Hiltz, S. R. (Eds.), *Information Systems for emergency management* (pp. 369–388). New York, NY: M.E. Sharpe Inc.

Van de Walle, B., & Turoff, M. (2008). Decision support for emergency situations. *Information Systems and E-Business Management*, 6(3), 295–316. doi:10.1007/s10257-008-0087-z

Wade, M., & Holland, J. (2004). The resource-based view and Information Systems research: Review, extension, and suggestions for future research. *Management Information Systems Quarterly*, 28(1), 107–142.

Walsham, G. (1997). Actor-network theory and IS research: Current status and future prospects. In Lee, A., Liebenau, J., & DeGross, J. (Eds.), *Information Systems and qualitative research* (pp. 466–480). London, UK: Chapman Hall.

Ward, J., & Peppard, J. (2002). *Strategic planning for information systems*. Wiley.

Wybo, J. L., & Lonka, H. (2002). Emergency management and the information society: How to improve the synergy? *International Journal of Emergency Management*, 1(2), 183–190. doi:10.1504/IJEM.2002.000519

Yin, R. (1994). *Case study research*. Sage Publications Inc.

Chapter 11
Information Seeking and Retrieval Service for Crisis Response

Nong Chen
Delft University of Technology, The Netherlands

Ajantha Dahanayake
Georgia College and State University, USA

ABSTRACT

Crisis response involves handling information intensive processes, and coordination of large quantities of information from and for different relief-response organizations. The information needs and responses of such organizations are closely related to the situations and roles these organizations are involved during a crisis relief-response process. The information seeking and retrieval processes associated with crisis situations influence the affectivity of response vigor and the coordination of relief-response activities. To provide an effective solution for a European Main Port's crisis response needs, a role-based situation-aware information seeking and retrieval conceptual framework is formulated. The conceptual framework, the design approach, and the implementation in a prototype are presented as an approach to design future crisis response for information seeking and retrieval services.

INTRODUCTION

Information acquisition in the event of a crisis in a harbor infrastructure is a very complex process. Timely and effective response to an incident in a port is extremely important because escalation to

the level of a disaster can happen in minutes, as in the case of a fire in an area where millions of liters of oil and other flammable or hazardous materials are stored (Barosha & Waling, 2005). Any delay in response time can increase the number of victims of a disaster, and a fast response can reduce or prevent subsequent economic losses and social disruption (Mehrotra, Butts et al, 2004). Effective

DOI: 10.4018/978-1-60960-609-1.ch011

response to a developing disaster requires fast access to all the relevant information required to deal with the ongoing situation.

Depending on the scale of the disaster, crisis responses in a harbor infrastructure will range from dealing with a small-scale problem, in which a few organizations might be involved, to a full-scale crisis, in which multiple organizations are required to resolve and to prevent escalation of the crisis. Information relevant for a crisis response may be dispersed across heterogeneous, high volume, and distributed information resources. Such unpredictable crisis situations require the dynamic establishment of a "virtual team" consisting of the various relief-response organizations. In response to an ongoing dynamic crisis situation, membership of the "virtual team" can change accordingly depending on the type of crisis, its magnitude and how it develops. New relief-response organizations will join the "virtual team" when their services are needed, while others will leave when their response goals have been achieved. Distributed, dynamic and heterogeneous environments make it difficult for relief organizations to find and retrieve their specific organizational role and the crisis situation relevant information they require to inform their crisis relief activities.

Many harbors have built networked crisis response platforms to connect all crisis relief-response organizations, and to allow them to access, share and exchange information. One example of such a platform is called the dynamic map, which has been utilized and tested at some harbors, which allows relief-response organizations to oversee the disaster area and its surroundings, and to anticipate future developments regarding the crisis situation (Barosha & Waling, 2005). The dynamic map provides an efficient way of improving information acquisition in a distributed crisis environments, only serving to distribute uniform information to all the relief-response organizations involved in a crisis. It is difficult for an individual organization to select and retrieve information that is specifically relevant for its

role and its rescue activities, causing delays in information retrieval for its relief-response tasks. Such networked platforms are built based on the centralized design principle, which addresses inter-organizational information accesses over boundaries, is no longer the best principle to use when dealing with a dynamic crisis environment. The information needs of the relief-response organization can change dynamically, due to the unpredictable nature of a disaster throughout its course. The tasks and roles of the relief-response organizations will change, and therefore their information needs will change accordingly (Someren, Netten, et al, 2005). Some of these information needs will be short lived, and many of them will not be predictable, directly challenging the capabilities and flexibility of a centralized system design principle. The centralized design principle satisfies a user's information needs by bundling information from heterogeneous databases. Therefore, it is not capable of satisfying dynamically changing information needs since it is not feasible to predefine all information retrieval applications to meet all the information needs for each possible crisis situation. The dynamically changing nature of crisis's coupled with the diverse types of crisis's that can occur, require a complete redesign of an application to meet the information needs for each possible crisis situation.

In summary, there is a need to develop a new crisis response information system based on a more flexible design principle, which is:

1. Capable of providing relief-response organizations with a role related picture of the crises development in a time critical manner.
2. Capable of satisfying changing information needs flexibly.
3. Capable of structuring advanced technologies and available technical infrastructures in a meaningful way to realize dynamic changing user information needs during a crisis response.

4. Extendable when a relief-response organization is required to join relief-response activities.
5. Capable of dealing with a relief-response organization, when it leaves the functioning system once its task is completed.

Based on these observations, a novel design approach for a new generation of information seeking and retrieval service for crisis response systems is presented in this paper. In the next section, "Capturing Concepts," the main the concept structure that is required for designing a role-bases situation-aware information seeking and retrieval service for crisis response is presented. The "Core Meta-Model" section covers the design principle of information seeking and retrieval services' meta-model. A prototype and its implementation are presented in "The Protoype and Reflecitons on Design Decisions." The testing, evaluation and findings of the implemented prototype based on the design approach are given in "Testing, Evaluation and Conclusions."

CAPTURING CONCEPTS

The design approach for information seeking and retrieval service of the crisis response systems is based on the availability of a well founded concept structure. A well founded meta-model is considered as a comprehensive design artifact for designing stable and adaptive systems (Dahanayake, 1997). Therefore, first an informal description of main concepts and factors that influence information seeking and retrieval in crisis response domains are presented followed by meta-model representations of corresponding systems components of the service. The meta-model is formulated from the role-based situation-aware information seeking and retrieval needs and in particular for crisis response.

Role-Based Information Seeking and Retrieval Needs

The information needs and its role in information seeking and retrieval is the main factor that triggers information acquisition to fulfill a user's information needs in the domain of crisis response. Now a day's there is a deepening understanding of information needs in literature. According to Chen & Dahanayake (2007) there are three types of influencing factors used to determine user information needs: (1) user's self characteristics, e.g. user's personality, knowledge, personal interest and preferences; (2) user's roles and (work) tasks in the society, e.g. user's professional roles connected with occupied positions, and their role-related tasks; and (3) the environment, or situation.

Literature provides encouraging arguments to validate these three influence factors: Taylor (1968) & Belkin (1984) argue that user characteristics determine the information needs of users. The "situation-gap-use" model indicates that people first need to establish the context for information needs, i.e. the situation. After that they may find a gap between what they understand and what they need to make sense of the current situation. According to this theory of sense-making, information seeking and retrieval is one of the actions people will take to narrow the gap between their understanding of the world and their experience of the world (Dervin, 1999). The macro-model of information-seeking behavior proposes that information needs arise from people's environments, social roles and individual characteristics. And further, defines the work task as a central component in information behavior (Wilson, 1981). An extended model of (Wilson & Walsh, 1996) presents a complete picture of factors affecting information needs, including psychological, demographic, role-related or interpersonal, environmental and source characteristic aspects. Byström & Hansen (2005) & Taylor (1991) argue that the concept of task has gained increasing attention as it provides an important clue to help us to under-

Figure 1. Personalized information needs adopted from (Chen, 2008)

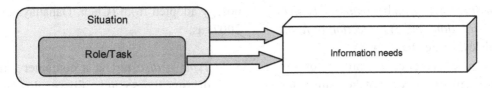

stand why people seek information, what type of information they need, and how they are going to use the information. Wilson (1981), Byström & Järvelin (1995) and Vakkari (2003) give examples relating to as a consequence, the work task has become a central factor for determining a user's information needs. Järvelin & Ingwersen (2004) argue that information retrieval research needs to be extended towards including more contexts, and that information seeking research needs to be extended to include tasks. According to (Byström & Järvelin, 1995), the model of task-based information seeking focuses on how work tasks affect the task performer's choice of information sources and information types. Vakkari (2003)'s focus is how work tasks affect information types, search strategies and relevance assessment.

The information seeking and retrieval in crisis response is a problem solving process since the purpose of information acquisition is to deal with and solve problems arising during the unfolding of a disaster. When a crisis situation is unfolding, users become aware of their role-based information needs such as the professional role they need to adopt, and the work tasks they need to execute. Information needs change during the response process as users' situation changes in response to the crisis situation, and directly influences users' judgment regarding information relevance. Individuals' personal interests and preferences do not strongly influence their information needs but their personality or knowledge may influence their search strategies. Even though different users may have different knowledge levels according to their professional role, their knowledge is inherent in the professional roles they perform within their

work situations. Assuming that the users are well trained, and that they have enough knowledge to detect their information needs based on their professional roles, users' role-based information needs in crisis response are determined by the disaster situation they perceive, and the tasks they need to execute when adopting one of their roles in their perceived situation.

Situation-Awareness (SA) in Information Seeking and Retrieval

Although today's advanced IT technology can replace a huge amount of information processing work, until now, it cannot replace a human's mental information processing process. Therefore, an information seeking and retrieval service may provide support for the users' Situation-Aware (SA) process if the situation is one of the determinant factors for determining users' information needs. SA is a concept usually applied to operational situations, especially in the fields of Artificial Intelligence, Agent-based Systems, Crisis Management, Military, etc., where people must gain SA to perform their operational tasks (Endsley, Bolte et al, 2003)

The objective of SA is to allow specific users to better perform their tasks by establishing a consistent awareness of situations. SA research focuses mainly on supporting users to be aware of their situation so that they can make an informed decision about future actions. SA is defined as "the perception of elements in the environment along with a comprehension of their meaning and along with a projection of their status in the near future" (Endsley & Rodgers, 1998). This definition breaks down SA into; a) *perception of the elements in the environment* b) *comprehension of the current situation, and* c) *projection of future status* (Endsley, Bolte et al., 2003).

These three levels reflect the process of how people become mentally aware of their situations. It is not feasible to specify all possible instances of crises situations due to the dynamic and unpredictable nature of disasters. Detecting situations based on collected historical data is required. A similar argument is made in (Endsley, Bolte et al, 2003)'s three levels of SA model, where the situation is derived from known information. To provide users' role-based, situation specific information in a crisis response, an information seeking and retrieval service system needs to provide collected historical data or information to support the different levels of users' SA processes. The question of what historical data or information is required at different levels of a SA process for realization becomes important, and leads finding what information can be used to describe and model a situation in the context of crisis response (Chen, Dahanayake et al., 2007).

Fact

During a SA process it is likely to perceive the elements present in the environment. In a crisis environment, the information elements that can be directly perceived are those that look into cover the type of disaster, place of the disaster, time the disaster happened, and Who are involved, such as what properties, i.e. hardware, buildings, docking areas, are we dealing with, etc. They describe the things that are known to have happened or to exist, i.e. facts.

Therefore, the *fact* is defined in the context of crisis response as *things that are known to have happened or to exist in a crisis environment*. The information describing those things that have happened or that exists, can be abstracted and conceptualized as type of disaster, time, place and involved objects.

This model can be explained using the terminology adopted from (Chen, Dahanayake et al., 2007) as:

- *Type of disaster*: at a container terminal, disaster types can be fire, explosion, leakage, etc.
- *Time:* There are two type of Time, i.e. a time point, e.g. 3:20pm, or a time interval, e.g. 1:00am to 2:00am, or summer. The choice of time type depends on disaster type.
- *Place*: the place is the physical location, i.e. a region, e.g. an area in the docks, on a ship.
- *Involved objects:* in the crisis situation, involved objects include personnel, properties, or a combination of these two.

A is a combination of type of disaster and any or all of the other three concepts. The possible facts observed from a disaster in a container terminal might be 'a chemical fire, at area (a), at 17:00', 'an explosion in building (n)', 'people have suffered burns', 'a person has fainted in building (n)', 'road (x) is blocked by an overturned truck', etc. The type of disaster is the key characteristic used to describe facts. The description of facts is exclusive. For instance 'a chemical fire, at area (a) at 17:00' and 'a chemical fire, at area (b), at 17:00' would be defined as two different facts although only the location of the fire differs. Facts are elementary and unique.

Scenarios to Understand the Situation

The facts are direct observations made in the crisis environment and are not narrative descriptions. Therefore, facts are not sufficient information for users to fully understand the situation. To support the comprehension of SA process, the concept of scenario is introduced.

Therefore, a *scenario* is a *short story reflecting a crisis situation*. A scenario describes known outcomes, and the casual relationship of a group of determined facts. For instance, the scenarios of the disaster example given in the previous paragraph can be described as 'a chemical fire in area (a) blocks road (x)'. 'The chemical fire causes an explosion in building (n)'. 'People were burnt because of the chemical fire', and 'the gas caused by the chemical fire has poisoned people.' Known scenarios in the crisis response are used as historical information that can be analyzed to support comprehension of the situation of SA process during a crisis response. Unknown scenarios can be detected by combining known facts from historical scenarios.

Deriving Information Needs

A problem or a group of problems that users should solve during the crisis response period indicates a situation. These problems initialize the users' information seeking and retrieval activities, determining the information needs. *Therefore, a situation is defined as a state of affairs of users' special or critical significance during the course of a crisis response with respect to their professional roles.* A situation can be derived by detecting users' professional role relevant scenarios. Direct involvement in scenarios means that users take actions during a crisis response in their professional role. Indirect involvement in scenarios means that the scenarios influence users' actions during a crisis response.

When a situation is described clearly, in the context of crisis response, users perceive the problem they need to solve. The users will take actions to solve this problem when the problem is detected and understood. A need for information arises, even before they can take any action to solve the detected problem. Therefore, *Information needs are information elements required for users to solve the problems faced in a crisis situation when performing professional roles.* For example, the problem of a fireman would be to 'extinguishing the chemical fire in area (a)'. When (s)he is

directly involved in the scenario 'the chemical fire causes an explosion in building (n)', to take any action to extinguish the fire, there is a need for information. The scenarios that constitute the situation to 'extinguish the fire' will need to know the type of chemical fire dealing with, and sort of equipment/materials should use to deal with this type of chemical fire. Indirect involvement of in the scenario 'a chemical fire in area (a) blocks the road (x)' will give rise to new information needs. The fireman needs to know how to avoid traffic to reach the disaster site. When sufficient information needs have been identified and structured in a meaningful way during a crisis response, a user will be able to take actions to solve the problem. The composition of SA process is presented the Figure 2.

Service-Orientation

A solution for building complex, dynamic and distributed information systems is by adopting a service-oriented design approach. Services are implemented with well-defined service behaviors and interfaces. Various open specifications, open source toolkits and standards can be used to implement Services (Magoulas & Dimakopoulos, 2005). It is a suitable design approach for distributed, dynamic and heterogeneous crisis response environment. The service-oriented system design approach can reconfigure dynamic crisis response systems using a composition of encapsulated, replaceable and reusable services (Stojanovic, Dahanayake et al, 2004). We regard information seeking and retrieval as a service. The design approach guides the implementation of combination of groups of services or components in a specific order based on detected situations. Figure 3 visualizes this vision.

The Service

A service has many definitions in the field of service-oriented approaches (Papazoglou, 2003;

Figure 2. SA process

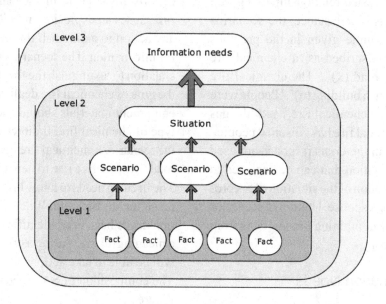

Figure 3. Service-oriented Design Approach adopted from (Chen & Dahanayake, 2008)

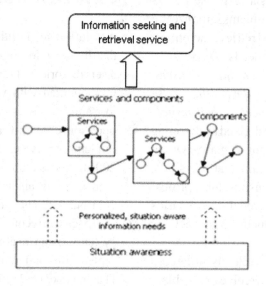

Stojanovic, Dahanayake et al., 2004; Douglas, 2003). A service is planned and designed in such a way that it has a specific functionality and it is very simple, but added together; services can perform relatively complex tasks. This informal definition offers the basic requirements for the definition of a service in the service-oriented approach.

The solution to a detected problem is constituted by a service or a combination of services. The specific functionality a service must offer is that it provides information. Therefore, in the context of this research the *services that consume information and provide information as information services*. The solution to satisfy a user's information needs is constituted by an information service or a group of information services. The information provided by a group of services is a collective outcome of all involved information services instead of a simple combination of outcomes of each service. Information services can be assembled and composed by smaller information services. The required operation and output of a simple information service is realized by grouping a specific collection of information retrieval software components. The information services are stored in a repository. Each information service has an invoke method. Each service is executed when the pre-condition is fulfilled. After execution the condition of this service is changed. This is called a post-condition.

The Task

We observed that users' information needs must be satisfied before they take any actions to solve a problem identified in crisis response. Information needs are related to insufficient information to perform their actions. The actions users need to take are conceptualized as a 'task', or a 'work task' as defined in (Byström & Järvelin, 1995; Dervin, 1999; Vakkari, 2003; Wilson, 1981).

In task-oriented information seeking and retrieval research, a task is viewed either as an abstract construction or as a concrete set of actions (Hackman, 1969; Byström & Järvelin., 1995). A task is an abstract construction, where a task is utilized as a description to enable focus on individual differences (Hackman, 1969; Byström & Hansen, 2005). We do not take individual interests and preferences into account as influencing factors to determine information needs during a crisis response in this research formulation. We take the view that a concrete set of actions can be used to define a task. A *task* is regarded *as a specific piece of work, in which a person or a group of persons undertake a series of actions in a crisis situation.* Defining a task as a piece of work indicates that it has (1) a performer; (2) a meaningful purpose; and (3) an undertaken context (Hackman, 1969;

Byström & Hansen, 2005). Similar to the definition that emphasizes the conceptualization of tasks from the actor perspective and the social context of task performance (Checkland & Hollwel, 1998).

From a social context of Crisis response, involved organizations or organizational units undertake tasks according to their professional roles in a crisis response process. Therefore *the involved organizations or organizational units are defined as actors.* The actors involved in crisis response might be firemen, police forces, and hospitals. Actor has a list of professional roles in the context of crisis response. A role is "a function or part performed especially in a particular operation or process". A role is a function relevant concept. *The professional role of an actor in a crisis response context is defined in terms of functions an actor must provide in a crisis response process.* Actors are exclusive, and are detected based on their professional roles. A task is performed when an actor adopts one of its professional roles. An actor undertakes a task is to provide required functions in a crisis situation. A task can be composed of smaller tasks.

Where an actor is required to adopt one of its professional roles, a task is performed in a situation. Therefore, tasks are distilled from the functions an actor can provide in a crisis response situation. The functions an actor can provide are relatively stable. However a situation is a dynamic concept, as supported in the SA process. It is not feasible to define task on the level of a specific situation. This is because a crisis situation may require a solution that consists of many tasks performed by many different actors, and this diversity cannot be predicted in advance. A crisis situation changes dynamically as a disaster develops, defining tasks on a set of facts are more tangible and reliable. Since a task can be composed of smaller tasks, the required tasks to solve a problem in a detected crisis situation can be composed of sub-tasks which can be identified using relevant facts. Tasks are undertaken in a process used to formulate the solution of an existing fact.

Figure 4. Meta-mode of personalized information seeking and retrieval application

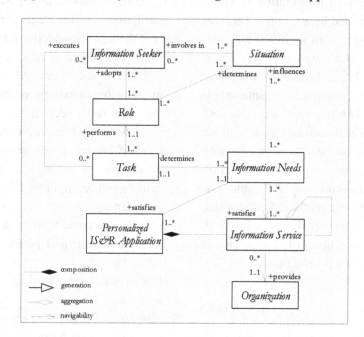

Core Meta-Model

The concepts defined in the "Capturing Concepts" section are used to formulate a meta-model for role-based situation-aware information seeking and retrieval on the basis of the service-oriented system design approach. The core of the conceptual foundation includes two meta-models (Chen & Dahanayake, 2008), a meta-model of essential concepts and relationships needed to describe *information intensive domains (D)*, and a meta-model of essential concepts and relationships needed to build personalized information seeking and retrieval applications such as for crisis response. The later is the focus of this paper.

Meta-Model of Personalized Information Seeking and Retrieval Applications

Information seekers (ISe) are individuals who work for relief-response organizational unit that deal with *information intensive domains (D)*. They

lack *information (I)* to perform their tasks when their organization adopts a *role (R)* in a specific crisis relief-response *situation (S)*. They need to be aware of their *situation (S)* before they realize the *role (R)* their organization needs to adopt, and the *tasks (T)* they need to perform. When they are clear about the *situation (S),* the *role (R)* and the *tasks (T)*, they are capable of realizing their personalized *information needs (In)*. The meta-model and the relationships between these concepts are presented in Figure 4.

The meta-models, presented in (Chen & Dahanayake, 2008), show the core concepts and relationships that are needed when designing Personalized Multidisciplinary Information Seeking and Retrieval Services (PMISRS) in *information intensive domains (D)*. The core concepts, *situation (S), information service (IS)*, and *task (T),* are defined in an abstract level. In the rest of this section, we present each concept in detail.

Figure 5. Meta-model of situation

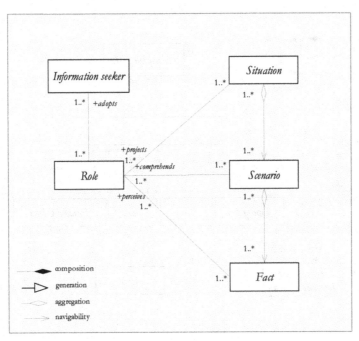

Situation (S)

A *situation (S)* can be projected and described by grouping a set of *scenarios (SC)*. However, projections of a *situation (S)* will differ depending on who makes a projection. An unknown *situation (S)* can be derived from detecting an *information seeker's (ISe)* professional *role (R)* relevant *scenarios (Sc)*, i.e. from those *scenarios (Sc)* that directly or indirectly involve the *information seeker (ISe)*. Directly involved *scenarios (Sc)* are those *scenarios (Sc)*, in which an *information seeker (ISe)* may take actions when adopting his/her *professional role (R)*. Indirectly involved *scenarios (Sc)* are those *scenarios (Sc)* that may influence an *information seeker's (ISe)* choice of *tasks (T)*. Observations from the European Port's crisis response system showed that different *information seekers (ISe)* adopting different *roles (R)* in the same *situation (S)* would perceive different levels of abstraction of information elements, i.e. different levels of abstraction of *facts (F)*. Different perceptions of *facts (F)* leads to

different comprehensions of *scenarios (Sc)*, and therefore, the projections of the *situation (S)* will differ. As a result, a description of a *situation (S)* needs to include the concepts of *roles (R)* of the *information seeker (IS)*, which will determine the abstraction levels of *facts (F)* and comprehensions of *scenarios (Sc)* respectively. We present the meta-model of situation in Figure 5.

The *facts (F)* do not supply sufficient information for an *information seeker (ISe)* to understand the *situation (S)* fully, thus the *scenario (Sc)* is defined as a short story reflecting a *situation (S)* and a collection of *facts (F)*. The concept of *scenario (Sc)* describes known outcomes, and the casual relationships between groups of detected *facts (F)* within a given time frame. The concept of *scenario (Sc)* represents the second level of an *information seeker's (ISe)* SA process (Endsley & Rodgers, 1988), i.e. understanding of the *situation (S)*. Unknown *scenarios (Sc)* can be detected by combining known *facts (F)*, and/or known *scenarios (Sc)*.

Figure 6. Meta-model of essential fact concept

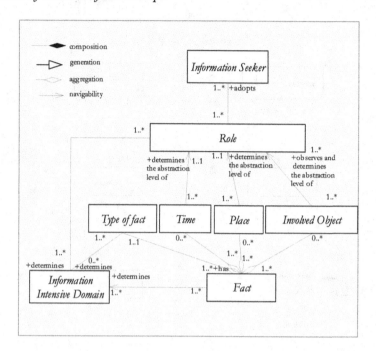

Fact (F)

The information elements perceived from the environment that describe "things that are known to have happened or to exist" [Merriam-Webster, Dictionary] is the concept *fact (F)*. The *fact (F)* represents an *information seeker's (ISe)* direct observations made in the environment, i.e. first step of an *information seeker's (ISe)* Situation Aware (SA) process (Endsley & Rodgers, 1988). Describing a fact requires 4 attributes: 1) type of fact, 2) time, 3) place, and 4) involved objects, and that these are indispensable (see "Capturing Concepts" section).

A description of a *fact (F)* should be a combination of type of fact, and any or all of the other three attributes: time, place, and involved objects, where type of fact is indispensable, but time, place, and involved objects are optional. The *roles (R)* *information seekers (ISe)* adopt determine how *facts (F)* are observed and the levels of abstraction of time and place. *Roles (R)* also differentiate the observations of objects involved in a *situation*

(S) and the level of abstraction observed. *Facts (F)* can be re-used to describe different *scenarios (Sc)*. We present the meta-model of essential *fact (F)* concept in Figure 6.

Scenario (Sc)

The concept of *scenario (Sc)* was defined as a short narrative story that reflects a *situation (S)*. Assuming that a *scenario (Sc)* can be described using a group of ordered *facts (F)*. However, a *scenario (Sc)* is not a simple combination of a group of *facts (F)*. It needs to describe the causal relationships between *facts (F)*, to follow a time sequence and the outcomes. There are two types of relationships that can be defined between two facts: *sequential relationship* (→) or *parallel relationship* (//).

Therefore, when representing a *scenario (Sc)* a *scenario-description (Sdes)* is necessary, where which *facts (F)* are relevant and what types of relationships exist between them recorded. Since the observations of relevant *facts (F)* are determined

Figure 7. Meta model of essential scenario concept

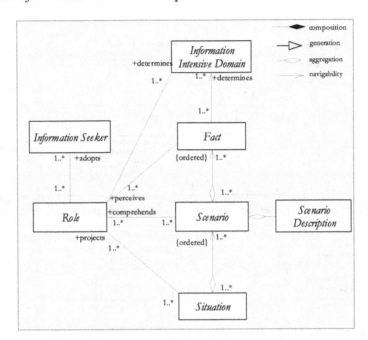

by the *roles (R) information seekers (ISe)* adopt, the same *scenario (Sc)* will be comprehended differently by different *information seekers (ISe)*, thus *scenarios (Sc)* should be explained taking into account *roles (R)*. A *scenario (Sc)* can be re-used in describing different *situations (S)*. Unknown *scenarios (Sc)* can be derived from detecting *information seekers' (ISe) role (R)*-relevant *facts (F)*. An unknown *scenario (Sc)* can also be described using a composite group of known *facts (F)* (see Figure 7).

Therefore, when representing a *situation (S)*, a situation description is necessary, in which *scenarios (Sc)* that are relevant and the types of relationships exist between the *scenarios (Sc)* should be recorded.

Situation (S)

A *situation (S)* is defined as a state of affairs of special or critical significance for an *information seeker (ISe)* when adopting a specific *role (R)*. *Situations (S)* can be projected by detecting the *in-*

formation seekers' (ISe) role (R) relevant *scenarios (Sc)*, i.e. from those *scenarios (Sc)* that directly or indirectly involve the *information seekers (ISe)*. Directly involved *scenarios (Sc)* are those *scenarios (Sc)*, in which an *information seeker (ISe)* may take actions when adopting professional *roles (R)*. Indirectly involved *scenarios (Sc)* are those *scenarios (Sc)* that may influence an *information seeker's (ISe)* choice of action(s). Since detecting and comprehension of relevant *scenarios (Sc)* are determined by the *roles (R) information seekers (ISe)* adopt, projections of the same *situation (S)* will be determined by the *roles (R)* (see Figure 8).

A simple composition of a group of *scenarios (Sc)* can not project a *situation (S)*. *Scenarios (Sc)* appearing in a *situation (S)* follow a time sequence. To project a *situation (S)*, relevant *scenarios (Sc)* and the relationships between them must be included. Two relationships: *sequential relationship* (→) and *parallel relationship* (//) are applicable in an identical manner, and can be applied with the *scenario (Sc)*.

Figure 8. Meta-model of essential situation concept

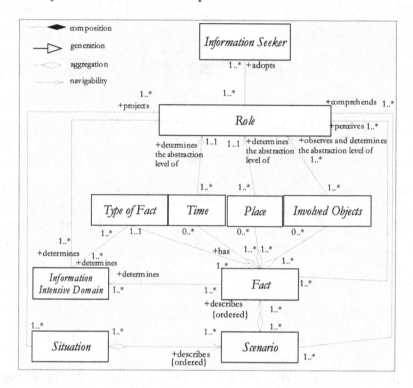

Task (T)

The concept of *task (T)* provides the clue to what *information (I)* is available, when the *information (I)* is available, and where the *information (I)* is stored. Crisis response organizations form multidisciplinary collaborations to solve a mutual problem via performing *task (T)*. The purpose of performing a *task (T)* is to carry out the function(s) an organization needs to provide when adopting a specific *role (R)* in a collaborative crisis response process. Execution of a *task (T)* produces *information (I)*, i.e. *output information*. Some tasks can be executed when, and only when, some specific *information (I)* can be provided. *Input information (II)* needed by a *task (T)* can come from *output information (OI)* produced by executing other *tasks (T)*. *Information (I)* on *task (T)* makes explicit or implicit what kinds of *information (I)* are available, and where to retrieve the *information (I)*. *Output information (OI)* satisfies the *informa-*

tion needs (In) arising from a *situation (S)*, and *input information (II)* indicates the temporal or logic order, in which *tasks (T)* need to be executed during a collaborative process.

Furthermore, organizations, which have similar lists of *roles (R)* and *tasks (T)* in a crisis response, are categorized and conceptualized as *actors (A)*. Each *actor (A)* has a list of *roles (R)*, which determine the list of *tasks (T)* they are capable of playing. Each organization belongs to an actor, and therefore, it needs to be capable of playing the list of roles of that *actor(A)*. *Tasks(T)* are provided by organizations when they adopt a specific *role (R)*. As a result, information on *actor (A)* and *role (R)* also makes explicit or implicit what kinds of *information (I)* are available, and indicates the possible directions to retrieve needed *information (I)*.

A *task (T)* needs to be executed in a context. Since the *output information (OI)* from a *task (T)* needs to satisfy the *information needs (In)*

Figure 9. Meta mode of essential task concept

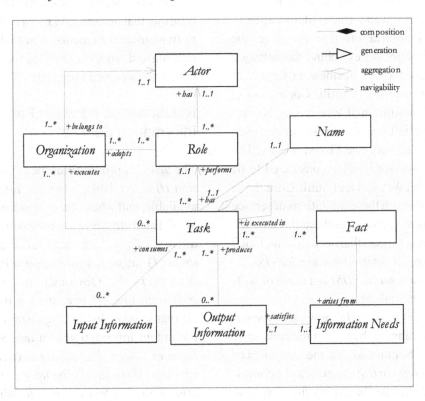

arising from a *situation (S)*, a *situation (S)* is the execution context of a *task (T)*. However, it is not possible to enumerate all possible *situations (S)* for any crisis response situation due to the dynamic and unpredictable characteristics of *situations (S)*. Therefore, it is not possible to obtain all the *information needs (In)* arising from a *situation (S)* directly. Deriving an unknown *situation (S)* from historical information, i.e. information on *facts (F)* and *scenarios (Sc)*, is the solution. *Situations (S)* are not appropriate for defining as the execution contexts of *tasks (T)*. *Information needs (In)* arising from a *fact (F)* are stable, concrete and predictable because the concept of *fact (F)* has been defined as a stable description of the things that have happened before, or that currently exists. The concept of *fact (F)* is more appropriate to be defined as the execution context of a *task (T)*. Used this way, unclear *information needs (In)* from a *scenario (Sc)* can be externalized by using

concrete *information needs (In)* arising from all the *facts (F)* that compose a *scenario (Sc)*. The same arguments can be applied to a *situation (S)*, i.e. satisfying all *information needs (In)* arising from all the *scenarios (Sc)* that compose a *situation (S)* is a prerequisite to satisfy *information needs (In)* derived from the *situation (S)* (see Figure 9).

Information Service (IS)

The services that produce *information (I)* is an information service. *Information needs (In)* can be satisfied by a group of needed *information services (IS)*.

The term service is widely used in different domains, such as the business domain, Web services or e-services. In the business domain, service is defined as some business activities that are provided by providers, and that often result in intangible outcomes or benefits (Autili,

Cortellessa et al, 2006). Many definitions of Web service exist, where Web service is defined generally as software/applications that recognize "the existence of functionalities behind the software but not the existence of business processes or business functionalities" (Autili, Cortellessa et al., 2006). This definition of Web service is comparable to the definitions of software service used in the computer science and IT community. The definition of e-service is often considered to be synonymous with Web service (Autili, Cortellessa et al., 2006). Although these definitions of service focus on different purposes in these three fields, they show several aspects that need to be included in a definition of an *information service (IS)*.

An *information service (IS)* is a piece of software entity or an application.

An *information service (IS)* provides *information (I)* as the intangible benefit in the context of crisis response. In other words, the outcomes of an *information service (IS)* are pieces of *information (I)* that need to be shared in crisis response coordination.

An *information service (IS)* is owned and provided by an organization in a service provider. Organizations build *information service (IS)* to share the *information (I)* they are willing to share during crisis response coordination. Therefore, software entities or applications that are built on top of organizations' *databases (DB)* are wrapped as *information service (IS)*. Organizations are responsible for publishing, maintaining and storing their own *information service (IS)*. *Databases (DB)* owned by organizations constitute the information resources of crisis response.

An *information service (IS)* can be accessed via the Web. An *information service (IS)* has a *service description (S-Desc)*, where information on service name, functions, providers, accessibility, service capability, etc. are recorded. The *service descriptions (S-Desc)* are published by the providers, i.e. organizations, in the *repositories (Re p)* for the future search.

Furthermore, service-orientation in design determines that *information services (IS)* are utilized as fundamental elements to build the information seeking and retrieving service for crisis response coordination (see Figure 10).

Relationships between Fact, Task And Information Service

The *tasks (T)* provide the clue as to what *information (I)* is available, when the *information (I)* is available, and where the *information (I)* is stored. We defined the *fact (F)* as the execution context of a *task (T)*. *Output information (OI)* after executing *tasks (T)* satisfies *information needs (In)* arising from *facts (F)*. Obviously, *output information (OI)* from *task (T)* execution is the *information (I)* that is provided by organizations. Wrapping the output information of a task as *information services (IS)*, and grouping needed *information services (IS)* to satisfy the *information needs (In)* arising from a *fact (F)* is a feasible solution to build a bridge between personalized *information needs (In)* arising from an unpredictable *situation (S)* and available *information services (IS)* pre-stored in the *repositories (Re p)* (see Figure 11).

A complete meta-model of information service is presented in Figure 12.

Service Description (S-Desc)

Repositories (Re p) are places, where service providers, subscribe their *information service (IS)* for the future search. *Repositories (Re p)* are not the place where *information service (IS)* are stored. They only store *service descriptions (S-Desc)* and provide indexing techniques for dealing with a queries. Therefore, defining a discoverable *service description (S-Desc)* is one of the prerequisite for the service search.

The *service description (S-Desc)* includes information regarding service name, functional description, *actor (A)*, *role (R)* and *task (T)* that represents service capability, conditions/con-

Figure 10. Meta-mode of essential information service concept

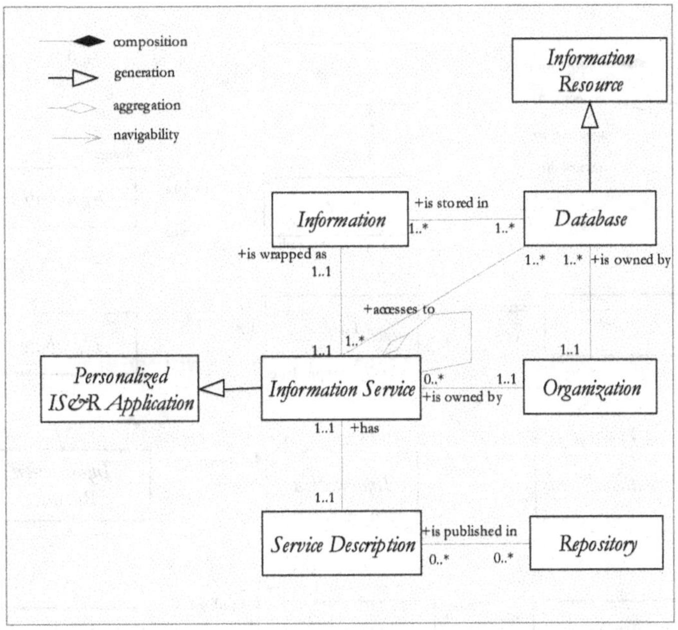

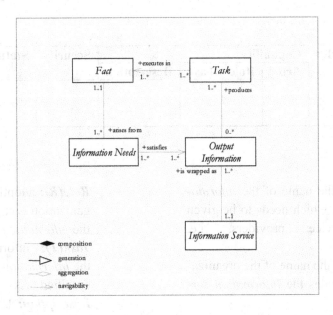

Figure 11. Relationships between fact, task and information service

straints and their corresponding service behaviors, access authorization, cost, response time, status, and location. However, the concepts of cost and response time defined in the *Quality of Service (QoS)* are not vital for inclusion in a service de-

scription. According to all these discussions and observations, a *service description (S-Desc)* is defined in Figure 13.

Figure 12. Meta model of information service in information intensive domains

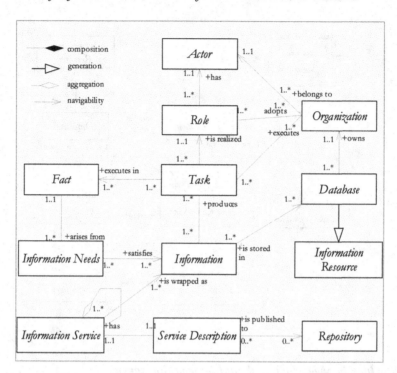

Figure 13. A service description

Service Name	Provider Name	Capability				Security	Status	Location
		Actor	**Role**	**Task**	**Description**			

- **Service name:** the name of the *information service (IS)*, which needs to be given by the service providers, i.e. organizations.
- **Provider name:** the name of the organization, which provides the *information service (IS)*.
- **Capability:**
  - *Actor(A):* which actor the organization that provides the *information service* belongs to.
  - *Role(R):* adopting which role the organization is capable of providing for the *information service*
  - *Task(T):* information provided by the *information service* comes from a specified task
  - *Description:* Domain-specific terminology needs to be used:
- to provide information on functionality and usage context.
- to describe the behavior a service provides to, or requires from, a context, and the conditions or constraints on this behavior.

Figure 14. Implementation architecture for the prototype

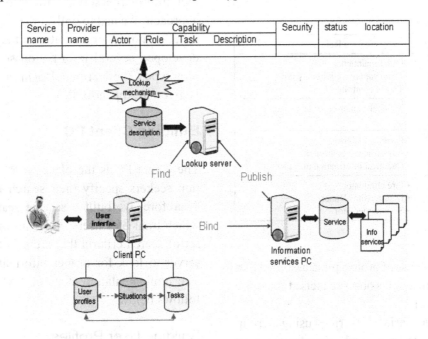

Service name	Provider name	Capability				Security	status	location
		Actor	Role	Task	Description			

- **Security:** which roles have the authorization to access to the *information service (IS)*
- **Status:** *information service (IS)* is currently available or not available
- **Location:** where the *information service (IS)* is stored. One example of location can be an URL

THE PROTOTYPE AND REFLECTIONS ON DESIGN DECISIONS

The Personalized Multidisciplinary Information Seeking and Retrieval Service (PMISRS) is a crisis response support systems' implementation based on the meta-models described in the previous section. The prototype is just one of the possible implementations built following the architecture shown in Figure 14.

Data Models

Actor and Role

As the prototype was to test the applicability of the meta-models instead of implementing a complete system, focused on collecting information on the 4 main actors: the politie (police), GHOR (medical support), DCMR (medical support and Brandweer (firefighter), and their roles (see Table 1). The other actors are: Gemeente (municipality), OV (public transport), Openbaar Ministerie (public ministry), etc.

Disaster Situation

The information elements collected in a crisis environment cover 4 aspects that describe a disaster fact: *type of disaster, time, place*, and *involved objects* with attribute that contains *property* and *personnel*. These 4 aspects were instantiated from the 4 attributes: type of fact, time, place and involved objects as defined in the meta-model of fact (see fact data model in Appendix I). To

Table 1. Main 4 actors and their roles in crisis response

Actor	Role
Politie	• Order maintainer • Legal support required by law • Traffic controller
GHOR	• Medical supporter for crisis and disaster
DCMR	• Chemical advisor • Infrastructure controller • Chemical information provider
Brandweer	• Fire eliminator • Disaster site cleaner • Service mediator

simplify the process of prototyping, assumed that all relief-response roles observe facts at the same abstraction level.

A disaster scenario is described using a group of ordered disaster facts, and a disaster situation can be described using a group of ordered disaster scenarios (see disaster scenario data model in Appendix II).

Task

Tasks in the context of crisis response are relief-response activities performed by each actor when adopting one of their roles during a collaborative process. An example of a possible task for each relief-response organization when adopting one of its roles in Table 4.1, were implemented following meta-model construct of *Task (T)*, based on the information collected (see data model of in Appendix II).

Information Service

Information shared between relief-response organizations are wrapped as information services. Since our approach is new to the field, there were no information services available for use, and relief-response organizations would not develop

their information services for us to test the design approach. We had to collect the information that relief-response organizations may share, and developed several information services for the prototype. (The data model for information service is given in Appendix IV).

Building Client PC

The Client PC is the place where the information seekers specify their search requirements. Therefore, we built a service search template, which translates users' input information into a set of search criteria that are sent to the lookup server to look for proper information services. The implementation steps of MySQL database follows below.

Building User Profiles

Information seekers need to log in before they start their information search. After login, they are provided role-based personalized information seeking and retrieval interfaces. Their role(s) and previous search behaviors influence the way the interface presents information to them, and the way retrieved information is presented. For example, their frequently accessed information services, or information services they have accessed before will be ranked at the top of a list of returned information services. Therefore, the role-based user profiles were built. Building user profiles can be a complicated process depending on how complex the user information is, they need to be linked to the information a user is allowed to access. For this purpose two simple user profiles were implemented. They are a user called Jessica, who belongs to a group that is allowed to see only the information provided by fireman and GHOR, and a user called Mary, who belongs to a group, which is allowed to see all the information.

Figure 15. Screen shot of search by fact interface

Designing User Interface

A user interface is built on the client PC, which allows information seekers to access their relevant crisis information. Three search functions on the user interface are, *search by information service, search by situation* and *search by fact.*

Search by Fact

In a crisis response, facts can be directly observed from the environment. It was an intuitive idea to utilize facts as the starting point of an information acquisition process, and it also matches a person's situation-aware (SA) process. A "fact based" search function was implemented, which provides two "search by fact" functions: search by keyword, and search by attributes, shown in Figure 15. ASP.NET was used to implement the user interface of search by fact, and C# was used to implement the two search functions.

- *Search by keyword* function was implemented based on keyword matching in fact

name and/or placeName, timeName, objectName. Facts that contain searched keyword in their attribute set will be returned for further information seeking. The search by keyword function was defined for those who are not familiar with the facts in the field. These information seekers are not capable of describing a fact using domain wide terminologies. The list of returned result can be null if the keywords selected by information seekers for a search do not match any keywords used to describe attributes of any predefined facts.

- *Search by attributes* function allows information seekers to start their information seeking process by selecting factTypeName and/or one or several other attributes of placeName, timeName, and objectName. Information seekers are not allowed to search by specifying only placeName, timeName, and objectName. factTypeName also needs to be selected. Search by attribute function is defined for those who are familiar with the facts in the field. Therefore these information seekers are capable of recognizing similar facts from factTypeName and/or one or several attributes of placeName, timeName, and objectName. The list of returned result cannot be null, although it is possible that none of the facts in the returned list is related to the fact(s) that the information seekers are seeking.

Search by Situation

The search by fact function is not suitable for a complicated disaster situation, where a myriad of different facts can be detected, and this number increase continuously. It is not a complex task for a database to record and handle such an amount of information, but it will be a demanding task for the human to extract facts relevant to themselves from those with miner differences within the returned list. Furthermore, a simple crisis can go on to become a very complicated situation, which will further increases the large number of facts that are observed. Information seekers will need to answer the following questions: What are the facts that can be utilized as a start point? And: How can we handle the inter-relationship between the observed facts? These questions may be confusing. Answers to these questions will bias the information acquisition results. The interface design of the system needs to help users to deal quickly, in a stress free manner, with this complexity.

It is more efficient to use historical information taken from past crisis situations as the starting point of the information acquisition process, i.e. to derive an unknown situation from known situations. We provided a function: *search by situation theme* by dividing historical information on situations into different categories called theme, i.e. themes of Accident, Epidemic, Fire, Natural disaster, Riot and Terrorism. Figure 16 presents the interface of this function. The search by theme allows to be immediately directed to the category of a similar situation, capable of choosing a similar situation from a situation description. The scenarios of the selected situations are retrieved from the MySQL database and displayed to select relevant scenarios according to the scenario description. The facts of the selected scenarios are then retrieved and displayed. When information seekers select relevant facts from the returned list, they start their SA processes to constitute their picture of the current situation.

Once all the facts have been selected and put in a correct order, the linkage between fact, solution and task is used to determine the required information services. The service discovery process starts after the required tasks have been identified and linked in a specific order. Tasks are used as keys to search for the required information services provided by the different organizations.

Search by Information Service

Search by information service is implemented in the prototype since information seekers might need this function when they are very clear about types of information services existing in the field, e.g. they have accessed such a service in a similar situation. Using this function will reduce the time required to find the information they need. Different algorithms, either simple or complicated, can be defined based on the attributes defined in the service description.

Generating a Service Search Template

The objective of building different search functions, i.e. search by fact, search by situation theme and search by information service mentioned previously, was to facilitate information seekers to specify their information seeking criteria. To find information services that are capable of providing relevant information, a service search template is generated at the end of each search function. It tracks a set of information seeking behaviors

Figure 16. Screen shot of user interface of service consumer

performed when interacted with the user interface to generate service search criteria.

All attributes included in the service description and their combination can be used as criteria to search for the appropriate information services. Actor, role and task are included to generate a service search template, where information on task is used as keys to search for the required information services provided by the different organizations. Other attributes, such as location, access authorization, status, etc, are included in building service search template, and more complicated algorithms are generated when necessary.

For the testing of the concepts, information on actor, role and task defined in the capability description of a service description as the criteria for searching the appropriate information services were used. Following either search by fact function or search by situation theme function, a service

search template is generated after the required tasks have been identified and linked in a specific order by the information seekers. Information on actor, role and required tasks will be obtained via ThemeManager, ScenarioManager, FactManager, TaskManager, etc. which are implemented in Controller to handle user computer interactions. Information on actor, role and required tasks will be transferred as criteria that will be filled into the service search template. Figure 17, gives a screen shot of an example of a service search template.

Send Service Search Request to Service Lookup Server

When the service search template is created, a service search request is generated that needs to be sent to the lookup server to look for the appropriate information services. We used Simple

Figure 17. Screen shot of an example of service search template

Accident > vehicle accident

Back

Search Service Template				
Actor	**Role**	**Task Description**	**Task keyword**	
Brandweer	fire eliminator	Fireman is responsible of eliminating the fire	fire eliminate	Search
Gemeente	field work	Gemeente determines the means to warn the people on the disaster site	warning means	Search
DCMR	chemical advisor	DCMR is responsible of providing advice about the dangerous dust to brandweer and citizen	advice dangerous dust	Search
GHOR	medical supporter for crisis and disaster	GHOR is responsible of suggesting medicine to help against dangerous dust	medicine dangerous dust	Search

Object Access protocol (SOAP) to implement the messages. SOAP messages are sent as the way of communications between client PC and lookup server. When the lookup server receives a SOAP message sent by the client PC, it will process the service search request contained by the SOAP message, and send the results back using anther SOAP message to the client PC.

Building Service Provider

We built several information services and implemented them as Web services using Visual C#.NET. "Chemical dust IS" is as an example of how we built the information services needed for the information provider PC.

One role DCMR needs to adopt is chemical advisor. We assumed that DCMR is willing to publish an information service that is capable of predicting the types of dangerous chemical dusts according to the color and/or smell observed in a crisis situation. Assuming that DCMR has information on all dangerous chemical dusts that is stored in a database. To share these pieces of information, DCMR needs to wrap them as an information service. For the case when DCMR wants to implement an information service as a Web service called "Chemical dust IS", a Web service of "Chemical dust IS" is built using Visual C#.NET and ASP, on a network addressable device. The interface of this Web service is presented in Figure 18. When authorized information seekers access this Web service, they can specify the color, or smell or both to obtain the information on possible types of chemical dust.

The Web service of "Chemical dust IS" is implemented in a very simple way, which only consisted of building a table that contains information on dangerous chemical dusts and building an interface to access to this table. This process of implementation indicates how an organization can build information services on the top of its existing applications. Any application can be wrapped as an information service if access authorization can be granted, and its interface can be explored.

A service description for the "Chemical dust IS" needs to be generated and the service description

Figure 18. Screen shot interface of Chemical Dust IS

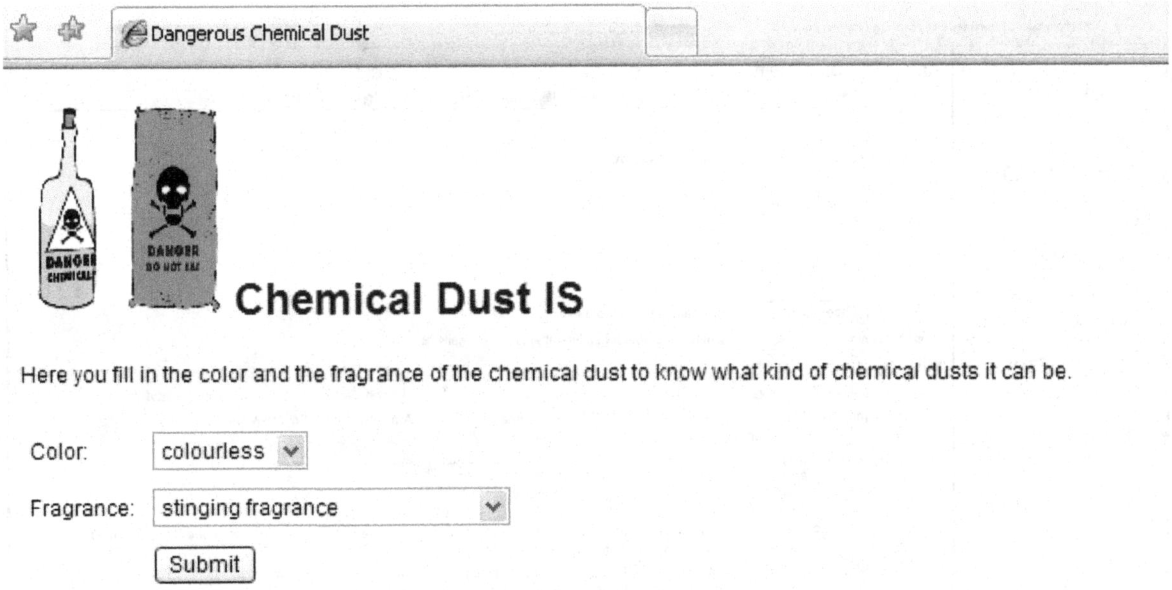

Figure 19. Service description of "Chemical dust IS"

Service name: Chemical dust IS
Provider name: DCMR
Capability
    Actor: chemical expert
    Role: chemical advisor
    Task: evacuate people because of dangerous dust
    Description: this service is capable of providing information on the type of the dangerous dust
    according to the color or smell or both observed
        Constraints: chemical dust appears but the type of it is unknown
        Behavior: provide information on type of chemical dust
Keyword: chemical dust
Security: chemical advisor and firefighter in the Netherlands
Status: available
Location: www.satyamholidays.net/chem

needs to be sent to the lookup server for the future operations. The service description of "Chemical dust IS" given in Figure 19 was subscribed to a service registry for future use.

Building Lookup Server

A lookup server was built, where service providers can register their information service. A service description database store service descriptions needed to be implemented and a service lookup mechanism needed to be built on top of this database. Both the client PC and the look up server

built in our prototype were implemented using Visual C#.NET. Intention was to ease the implementation procedure since the .NET framework is easy to use to create a web service server and a client system.

Service Description Database

To store the descriptions of information services, a description database is built on a network addressable PC, which contains a table called data-row. Figure 20 presents a screen shot of data-row, which shows part of the service descriptions stored as

Figure 20. Screen shot of table data-row in service description database

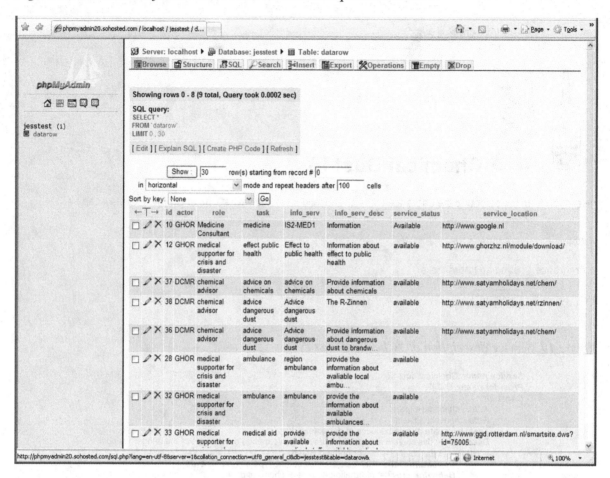

examples to explain how information service can be registered in the service description database on the service registry.

A service lookup mechanism was built to deal with the search requests from a Client PC. This lookup mechanism was built on the top of the service description database.

TESTING, EVALUATION AND CONCLUSION

Functional Testing

A set of disaster scenarios were set up to test whether the prototype was capable of handling

the information needs arising from dynamically changing disaster situations. Search by fact attribute, and search by situation are the most basic and important functions the prototype should be capable of providing to its information seekers. One example of the disaster scenarios was a fire in an area of the Port where flammable chemicals and other hazardous materials are stored. At the beginning, information needs arising from this disaster situation was an estimation of the possible development of the fire caused by known flammable chemical material (x). Information services, which are capable of providing information seekers with the information on possible hazardous development of chemical (x), are needed to be retrieved. Because it was a small scale and simple disaster situation, the information seeking process using search fact by attribute function is followed.

A chemical fire can lead to an explosion; finally the crisis might lead to a riot as local people protest that they are being subjected to a chemical hazard. Information needs arising from this disaster situation may need to be changed to knowing how to control the traffic, how to disperse personnel and how to control the riot, etc. Under these complicated circumstances, starting an information seeking process using search by situation theme is more efficient, as it shortens the search time by directing the information seeker(s) to the category of similar situations group.

The summary of the findings gathered during the functional testing using a set of pre-defined disaster scenarios, are:

- The information seekers were free to change the search functions during their information seeking process when a disaster situation changes, and/or their information needs change
- Was able to infer and construct changing information seeking needs during a crisis, although:
  - When not capable of finding facts from the prototype that were similar to the facts (s)he observed at the disaster as the start of information seeking process, the search by fact attribute will fail to retrieve appropriate information services to satisfy information seeking needs.
  - When not capable of finding disaster situations (themes), or scenarios, or facts, or tasks that were similar to the situation, or scenarios, or facts, or tasks (s)he observed at the disaster, search by situation (theme) will fail to retrieve appropriate information services to satisfy information seeking needs.

  - Appropriate information services could not found if they were not properly registered, e.g. wrong terminologies were used in their service descriptions.
- The prototype was able to support the reconfiguration of information seeking and retrieval applications flexibly to access to the required information.
- The prototype has shown that the reuse of information services in the configuration of information seeking and retrieval applications is possible. The process of selecting and configuring required information services is determined by the reuse of historical information. The exploration of an unknown situation is done through the reuse of facts and scenarios. In this situation, the data model of task supports information reuse to infer a user's role-based information needs to select services and configure them.

In summary, the prototype showed it was able to deal with dynamically changing information needs flexibly, and that future system extensions are feasible. The service-oriented design approach supports the realization of an independent service implementation and service model. Therefore, it provides for the possibility of a future systems extension when more relief-response organizations are required to join a crisis response. The meta-models, defined in the "Core Meta-Model" section, are able to provide clear guidance for a newly joined relief-response organization to share its information services and to construct its own role-based, situation-aware information seeking and retrieval services. In addition, due to the possibility to build up the interoperability between Web service, and other service-oriented standards, more commercial and scientific information software and applications can be added to the prototype if they can be implemented in one of the service-oriented standards. This is a very important and necessary improvement to support information seeking and retrieval better during a crisis response. For instance, the computational calculations for chemical pollution, which were built as a Grid based on a Web service standard, could be used and integrated into the system as information services.

EXPERT EVALUATION

The main contributions of the design approach are the meta-models, which contribute to the knowledge base of crisis response information systems. Those are design concepts needed for the designing of PMISRS artifacts in an information intensive domain. Therefore, there were two focus points for the expert evaluation:

1. To evaluate the quality of the meta-models. Experts were invited to provide their options about the *representational fidelity* of the meta-models, i.e. *accuracy, completeness, level of detail, internal consistency* of the concepts and relationships and their *semantic power and mapping power*.
2. To gain the experts' opinions about whether the information systems built, based on the meta-models, i.e. the prototype shown as an example system, is a solution that can be used to solve the problem of information overload and, which can provide flexibility and extendibility when needed.

Expert evaluations was conducted to gain insight into issues related the quality and novelty of the design approach. Five knowledgeable experts who were not involved in the process of theory development were asked to evaluate the design approach. These experts had several years working experience in the domain of crisis response, and had the knowledge of information system modeling and design, of UML in particular.

The questionnaire focused on obtaining knowledge of the expert's experience about problems of information seeking and retrieval in the domain of crisis response, and their opinions on the causes of these problems. The experts chosen had an average of 7 years working experience in crisis response in either industry or academia, which provide IT solutions for crisis response. They were regarded as experienced, knowledgeable professionals, who were capable of providing valuable comments on the design approach. According to the analysis of the questionnaire data, all the experts agreed on the novelty of the design approach. The concluding remarks reflections are summarized in the "Conclusions and reflections" section.

CONCLUSION AND REFLECTIONS

Capability of the Prototype

The capability of the prototype is tested via the functional test and expert evaluations. The experts' comments based on their observations of the functions provided by prototype and their experience in the field became important to evaluate the capability of the prototype. The results of data analysis showed a positive response to the relating questions, which concerned the prototype's capacity to satisfy personalized information needs, its flexibility and its extendibility respectively. Some experts suggested including more advanced personalized functions in the prototypes, such as including combining historical data on user information behaviors and user profiles, building role-based personalized interfaces, building location-based information search functions etc. Furthermore, some experts suggested building interfaces for modelers and /or domain specialist that could facilitate the process of system extension. All these suggestions showed that the experts perceived the potentials of the prototype and its application in the domain of crisis response to solve the problem of information overload, and to address flexibility and extendibility required to produce accurate, correct information in crisis situations.

Service-Oriented Design Approach

Some experts disputed the service-oriented design approach. In fact, all the experts agreed that applying a service-oriented architecture in building PMISRS is a novel solution that can be used to address the need for flexibility and extendibility in a dynamic environment like crisis response. The debates in this area focused in the main architecture on the service-orientation.

- A centralized system design principle is still a preferred solution for the domain of crisis response because a back office that controls and manages the quality of the information published and shared is always needed. It is not possible or very difficult to establish such a kind of centralized control point if service-oriented architecture is applied.
- A service-oriented architecture is not the only solution for the flexibility and extendibility needed. Well-defined interface specification can be implemented by advanced markup languages, such as XML, and can provide a feasible solution for the interoperability needed between software, applications and systems. Therefore, a service-oriented design principle is only one solution to connect heterogeneous software, applications and systems in a multidisciplinary environment; it is not the terminator for the centralized design principle.

No experts doubted that the design approach underpinned by a service-orientation provides a new way of building PMISRS in information intensive, multidisciplinary environments. One expert mentioned that service-oriented architec-ture is the future of system development in the domain of crisis response, and some research work has been set up especially where remote information needs to be accessed. She argued that the prototype could be a promising solution for a disaster situation where the information needed should to be pulled instead of being pushed from remote organizations. Therefore, she claimed that she observed a lot of potentials for the prototype. Moreover, some experts emphasized that a service-oriented architecture is a very valuable and feasible solution for the crisis response problem especially under circumstances where organizations only share part of their information without allowing other parties to access their databases.

Potential Use

Because of its potential, most experts thought that the prototype contributes to the domain of crisis response. Therefore, we could conclude that the design approach contribute to the domain of crisis response by providing a set of well-defined concepts and relationships needed to design and develop a PMISRS.

Generalizability of the Design Approach

The implementation of the design approach should lead to a configurable meta-modeling environment that supports the process of building PMISRS to satisfy dynamically changing, personalized needs arising from any information intensive domains. The prototype is only one instance product, which was built to test the applicability and quality of the meta-models developed to define the way of modeling, and the applicability of the way of working and controlling. Generalizability of the meta-models should be one of the major concerns of the evaluation since it refers to the validity of the meta-models in a setting different from that where the model was empirically tested and confirmed (Lee & Baskerville, 2003). In the expert evaluation session, the comments on their opinions of the potential generalizability of the meta-models, showed a positive response. Most of the experts observed that the meta-models were defined in a way that is independent of the semantics of any problem domain and that is independent of any implementation techniques. Some of them mentioned that the prototype built based on our design approach has demonstrated its potential capacity to model information from different disciplines and domains, where generic concepts are needed to link heterogeneous databases, software and applications. Therefore, our success in building such a prototype has demonstrated the generalizability of the meta-models, although our design approach was empirically tested using one case study. The experts believed that if the configurable meta-modeling environment can be fully implemented, it is capable of being used to support the design and implementation of PMISRS in many information intensive domains, such as in the domains of national defense, medical services, biochemistry research, e-commerce, etc.

REFERENCES

Autili, M., Cortellessa, V., Marco, A. D., & Inverardi, P. (2006). *A conceptual model for adaptable context-aware services*. In International Workshop on Web service Modeling and Testing.

Barosha, N., & Waling, L. (2005). *A service for supporting relief workers in the port. The final assignment in the course of Service Systems Engineering in 2004-2005*. Faculty of Technology, Policy and Management, Delft University of Technology.

Belkin, N. J. (1984). Cognitive models and information transfer. *Social Science Information Studies, 4*(2-3), 111–129. doi:10.1016/0143-6236(84)90070-X

Byström, K., & Hansen, P. (2005). Conceptual framework for task in information studies. *Journal of the American Society for Information Science and Technology, 56*(10), 1050–1061. doi:10.1002/asi.20197

Byström, K., & Järvelin, K. (1995). Task complexity affects information seeking and use. *Information Processing & Management, 31*(2), 191–213. doi:10.1016/0306-4573(94)00041-Z

Checkland, P., & Holwell, S. (1998). *Information, systems and Information Systems*. John Wiley & Sons Ltd.

Chen, N., & Dahanayake, A. N. W. (2007). Role-based situation-aware information seeking and retrieval for crisis response. In H. Zhu (Ed.), *The International Journal of Intelligent control and systems, Editorial of Special Issue on Distributed Intelligent Systems, 12*(2), 186-197.

Chen, N., & Dahanayake, A. N. W. (2008). A concept structure for designing personalized information seeking and retrieval systems in data intensive domains. In Gonzalez, R., Chen, N., & Dahanayake, A. N. W. (Eds.), *Personalized information retrieval and access: Concepts, methods, and practices*. Hershey, PA: Information Science Reference/ IGI Global. doi:10.4018/9781599045108.ch006

Dahanayake, A. N. W. (1997). *An environment to support flexible information modeling*. PhD dissertation, Technology University of Delft, Delft, The Netherlands.

Dervin, B. (1999). On studying information seeking methodologically: The implications of connecting meta theory to method. *Information Processing & Management, 35*(6), 727–750. doi:10.1016/S0306-4573(99)00023-0

Douglas, K. B. (2003). *Web services and service-oriented architectures: The savvy manager's guide*. Morgan Kaufmann.

Endsley, M. R., Bolte, B., & Debra, J. G. (2003). *Designing for situation awareness: An approach to user-centered design*. British Library Cataloging in Publication Data.

Endsley, M. R., & Rodgers, M. D. (1998). Distribution of attention, situation awareness, and workload in a passive air traffic control task: Implications for operational errors and automation. *Air Traffic Control Quarterly, 6*(1), 21–44.

Hackman, J. R. (1969). Toward understanding the role of tasks in behavioral research. *Acta Psychologica, 31*, 97–128. doi:10.1016/0001-6918(69)90073-0

Ingwersen, P., & Järvelin, K. (2005). *The turn: Integration of information seeking and retrieval in context*. Dordrecht, The Netherlands: Springer.

Lee, A. S., & Baskerville, R. L. (2003). Generalizing generalizability in information systems research. *Information Systems Research, 14*(3), 221–243. doi:10.1287/isre.14.3.221.16560

Magoulas, G. D., & Dimakopoulos, D. N. (2005). Designing personalized information access to structured information spaces. London Knowledge Lab and School of Computer Science, Birkbeck College University of London. Workshop on New Technologies for Personalized Information Access, (pp. 64-73).

Mehrotra, S., Butts, C., Kalashnikov, D., & Venkatasubramanian, N. (2004). Project rescue: Challenges in responding to the unexpected. *SPIE, 5304*, 179–192. doi:10.1117/12.537805

Papazoglou, M. P. (2003). Service-oriented computing: Concepts, characteristics and directions. In *Proceedings of the Fourth International Conference on Web Information Systems Engineering (WISE'03)*.

Papazoglou, M. P., & Georgakopoulos, D. (2003). Introduction to service-oriented computing. *Communications of the ACM, 46*(10), 24–28. doi:10.1145/944217.944233

Someren, M. v., Netten, N., Evers, V., Cramer, H., Hoog, R. D., & Bruinsma, G. (2005). A trainable information distribution system to support crisis management. In B. Carle, & B. v. d. Walle (Ed.), *Proceedings of the Second International ISCRAM Conference*, April 2005, Brussels, Belgium.

Stojanovic, Z., Dahanayake, A. N. W., & Sol, H. G. (2004). An approach to component-based and service-oriented system architecture design. In Sergio, D. C., Mark, L., & Robert, D. M. (Eds.), *Development of component-based Information Systems*. Armonk, NY: M. E. Sharpe, Inc.

Taylor, R. (1968). Question-negotiation and information-seeking in libraries. *College & Research Libraries, 29*(3), 178–194.

Vakkari, P. (2003). Task-based information searching. [ARIST]. *Annual Review of Information Science & Technology, 37*, 413–464. doi:10.1002/aris.1440370110

Wilson, T. D. (1981). On user studies and information needs. *The Journal of Documentation, 37*(1), 3–15. doi:10.1108/eb026702

Wilson, T. D., & Walsh, C. (1996). *Information behaviour: An interdisciplinary perspective*. British Library Research and Innovation Report 10. Retrieved 3 October, 2004, from http://informationr.net/tdw/publ/infbehav/prelims.html

APPENDIX A

Figure 21. Data model of fact

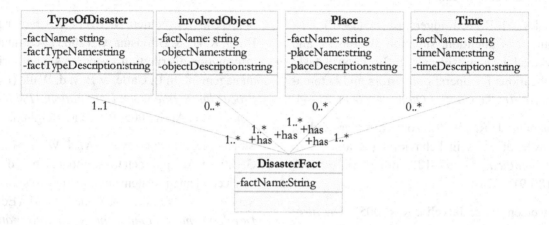

APPENDIX B

Figure 22. Data model of disaster situation

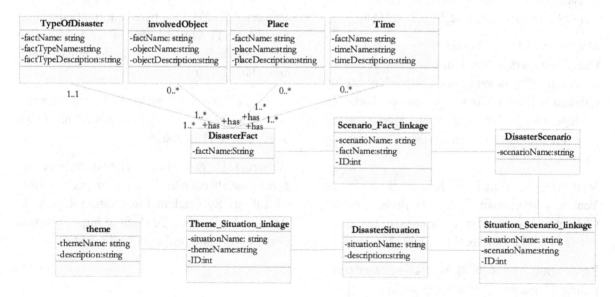

APPENDIX C

Figure 23. Data mode of task

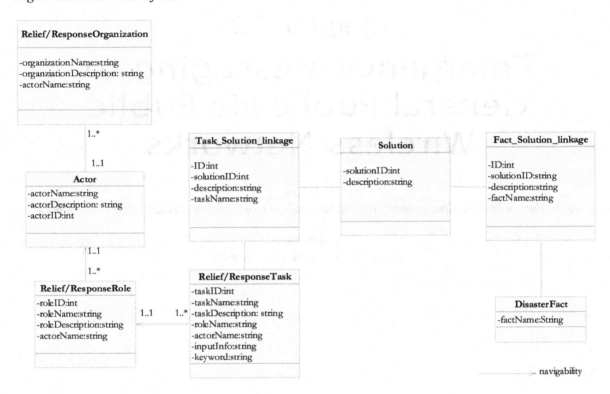

APPENDIX D

Figure 24. Data model of information service

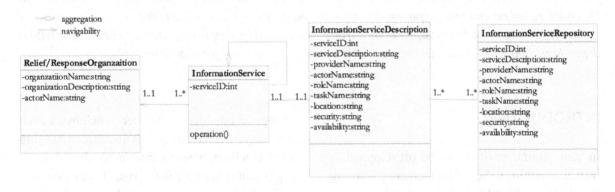

Chapter 12
Emergency Messaging to General Public via Public Wireless Networks

L-F Pau
Rotterdam School of Management, The Netherlands & Copenhagen Business School, Denmark

P. Simonsen
Accenture Denmark AS, Denmark

ABSTRACT

Warnings to the broad population in an emergency situation, irrespective of location and condition, are a public policy responsibility. Public wireless networks offer now the opportunity to deliver emergency warnings in this way with explanations, because in many countries, the mobile penetration rates and coverage are higher than any other access form. This chapter summarizes the analysis of the selection process between short messaging services (SMS) and Cell Broadcast (CB) messaging in the context of Denmark based on end user requirements, stakeholder roles and case-based analysis. It demonstrates the many technical, cost-benefit, and other trade-offs needed in supporting the population now with a dependable and wide-spread technology. This research is the basis for a national policy.

INTRODUCTION

In many countries of the world (developed as well as emerging), the basic emergency warning system to the broad population is still acoustic, with a network of static or moveable horns activated by the public authorities and ranging to groups of inhabitants in order to achieve a high coverage. A variant thereof is acoustic messaging via the radio or possibly multimedia based warnings via the public TV networks. There is however still a long way to go before Internet fixed access points, alike TV sets, will be always-on and reach a large fraction of the general population, till such acoustic warning systems will be made entirely obsolete; the implied costs born by the

DOI: 10.4018/978-1-60960-609-1.ch012

users from Internet or TV access, work patterns, mobility, as well as social factors such as age, handicap, connection behaviours, will together and for a while still prevent rather sizeable parts of the population from getting warned by Internet or TV alone when suddenly needed.

Separately, the critical analysis of public emergency situations all highlight the huge need for post-event information updates to be distributed in real time to the general population or selectively, whether people are exposed or not to the hazards, to ease rescue, evacuation, reduce panic levels, or for other tasks. Furthermore, at such post-event stages, central alarm notification is not enough, as individuals and groups need to communicate with other individuals or support points in a personalized way. This speaks in favour of personalized messaging (FICORA, 2005).

Finally, warning as well as post-event communication via resilient and redundant infrastructure should not flood communication capacity, especially if this has been reduced due to the events. Also it is not at all advised that the access terminals be made special, except for unique situations (lonely blind people, polytraumatic disabled persons etc.).

The above issues around emergency messaging to the general public is not to be confused with seamless crisis communications which is mostly carried out for public authorities, and which often uses other communications channels/technologies (e.g. in the past TETRAPOL networks, now often but not always TETRA networks).The trend, as evidenced e.g. by the 2006 European Security Research Advisory Board, is, in addition to the usual high security and dependability requirements, to add multiple data formats and advanced search. The question is rarely raised though, but should at policy level, of whether it makes always sense to separate entirely crisis communications and emergency messaging to the general public when the underlying infrastructure such as wireless networks are fully distributed and offer diverse security levels on mobile intranets with different critical nodes.

SCOPE AND BACKGROUND

This research and the resulting project therefore have first been triggered by the concept of using widely adopted modern ubiquitous personal communications and messaging facilities such as those offered by public wireless networks. Whereas wireless networks such as those based on TETRA have the same properties, they are conceived and used as private networks usually by the public authorities themselves. It should be highlighted that thanks to licensing requirements set by the national or multinational regulators, very high geographical coverage is granted in many countries, and wireless terminal penetration is very high.

The research has also been triggered by flaws found in Denmark by special interest groups in terms of the warning systems coverage in space and time, with the corresponding political and media outcry resulting from such issues being brought to the limelight. It was found that, after everything else possible had been done, there would still in Denmark be one out of thousand individuals, especially hearing impaired, who could not be warned with the planned national emergency resources (Beredskabsstyrelsen, 2005). Even if the terrain is not the issue in Denmark, just because of life behaviours, at any time 1/5 of the population are outside the range of the acoustic horns or not able to listen to radio/TV (Beredskabsstyrelsen, 2005). Also, it was found that over 60% of the population nowadays does not know the meaning of the emergency horns signals or do not react to them, as evidenced by the large flow of requests to emergency numbers after routine tests.

The scope of this paper is to summarize the findings of a policy focussed industry-academic-governmental project driven by emergency scenarios and cases, which specifies how.public wireless networks can *in the present situation at short notice* enhance and possibly replace legacy warning systems to the general public while satisfying public interest and fast deployment requests (Simonsen, 2007). More precisely, were investigated in depth the operational, technical, cost-benefit and immediate availability aspects, of public emergency messaging via SMS or Cell Broadcast (CB) standard technologies in 2G and 3G wireless networks. Was also evaluated the use of Mobile Internet, but limitations in the installed base of wireless terminals and/or user acceptance and familiarity, lead to its exclusion.

Some alternatives have been identified, such as the use of the electrical power networks, DVB-H, DBM (China), digital radio, wireless LAN hot spots, or Internet access via set-top boxes, but all were quickly disqualified for lack of penetration in the population, or incompatibility with life behaviours in view of alarm coverage and user mobility.

More precisely, if the following classification of public warning systems is considered:

- *Type A*: general warning of the largest possible part of the population in real time (such as by acoustic horns)
- *Type B*: general warning and information of the largest possible part of the population in quasi real-time (such as via radio or TV broadcasts)
- *Type C*: personalized message based warning and information of the largest possible part of the population in real time
- *Type D*: personalized message based warning and information, of specific population groups in real time (such as via fixed Internet messaging, TETRA or deaf /blind specific solutions) then the focus of this research has been on Type C solutions *for short term deployment*. The sensor and information fusion aspects for higher dependability or resilience, and better valida-

tion, can still be derived from the co-existence with other Type A, B or D systems.

WIRELESS MESSAGING TECHNOLOGIES

Short messaging service (SMS) (ETSI, 2006) allows sending in its simplest form up to 164 characters from any terminal or central node, to any single mobile subscriber, in a point-to-point manner with store-and-forward best effort delivery via SMSC (SMS Center) nodes. Enhanced SMS offers greater lengths but are exposed to much higher transmission costs; IMS messaging as standardized under 3GPP allows for very large lengths and embedded multimedia but is not much deployed yet. Cell Broadcast (CB) (Cell Broadcast Forum, 2007; Wood, 2006) is also a messaging system which allows to send in one go 93 characters from any central node, or application linked to it, to all mobile users satisfying common selection criteria; this is carried out in a point-to-multipoint manner with small delays via the CBC (CB center). CB also is unique in allowing up to 15 messages to be linked together so that they appear together once all received, i.e. in total 1395 characters.

In Denmark there were in early 2007 5.4 Million GSM wireless subscribers, and 200 000 3G subscribers, all using services compliant with GSM standards and their UMTS evolution. Short messaging systems (SMS) and CB are both mandated parts of the GSM and UMTS standards, and specified by ETSI (2006). As a result, in principle, both SMS and CB messaging services are supported in the firmware or middleware of the handsets. Whereas SMS services enjoy a phenomenal boom and represent huge revenue to the public operators, many operators decided very early on never to deploy and support CB services because of lack of commercial service revenues. Geographical coverage is 99% of the country (except in Greenland).

It is pointed out that this research has not been considering networking technologies still at the research stage, such as ad-hoc networks, distributed sensor networks, cognitive radio networks, even if their relevance to emergency networks has been hypothesized. The reason is that they do not appear yet in present day or medium term deployment plans with population wide coverage. Amateur radio service exists but does no reach the general public.

DECISION MAKING PROCESSES AND PROJECT METHODOLOGY

The adoption of messaging based systems for public emergency warnings is a national policy decision as it falls under government's decision to handle public safety. However because of the investment costs and even larger operating costs, and because of the low likelihood of the systems providing a payback as events are rare, such decisions are hard to get. On the other hand, the emergency system operators have to be neutral and positioned in such a way institutionally and legally to be able to receive all data and information needed for warning and post-event messaging, while they also must have the trust of public and government alike. Finally, the system subcontractors, such as public wireless operators, may not see at all a business case in maintaining a high degree of resilience and availability at all times, combined with randomly high traffic at alarm times. However, in such countries as Denmark, provisions were put in the mobile operator license conditions to mandate help with services of public interest, although terms and conditions had to be negotiated from case to case. It is thus necessary to take a public-private partnership business model in the role distribution and the corresponding funding schemes.

From the above description of the decision making process, the following recursive filtering and elimination methodology had to be applied:

1. Scenario analysis to characterize the range of alarm situations to be handled short-term by a wireless messaging system, on the basis of the threat categories from the Emergency Directorate (Beredskabsstyrelsen, 2005).

2. End user requirements on performance and other attributes for each scenario, and satisfaction of these requirements when the warning messaging is delivered to them using the two alternative technologies; the survey method was used to elicit the requirements so these data are primary data; secondary data are the results of the ETSI "Emergency service and civil protection communities" (www.emtel.etsi.org).

3. Engineering analysis of traffic and congestion implications.

4. Validation of the requirements from 2) from post-event debriefs from past catastrophes in Denmark and abroad, and subsequent reconciliation; such debriefs are secondary data; the two selected debrief cases are the London terrorist bombings on 07 July 2005, and the huge fireworks factory explosion in Seest, Denmark on 03 November 2004. Further validation details and sources are found in Simonsen (2007).

5. Stakeholder cost-benefit analysis of all key parties involved in the decision and operations: Information and Communications regulator ("IT & Telestyrelsen"), Emergency Directorate ("Beredskabsstyrelsen"), National Police ("Rigspolitiet"), Local Police, Police warning center ("Alarm centralen Århus"), wireless public operators (incl. TDC A/S). This analysis also involved interviews and calculations.

6. Stakeholder risk analysis for all key parties involved, this time including the end users.

7. As part of the academic-industry-governmental project, the steps 5) and 6) involved 18 structured interviews supplemented by validation questions all representing primary data and are thus not public. Interaction has

also happened with ETSI, the Cell Broadcast Forum, and CEASA which is the body specializing in warning networks with use of CB technology. The total man.month effort inside the project was for the first two years (2005-2006) of 36 man.months, with additional 18 man.months spent at all stakeholders mentioned in 5) above on specialized analysis and data collection.

WARNING OR ALARM PROCESSES

There is a differentiation between zone of operations and event location; the rescue team operates at the location of the event and has the leadership; the zone of operations encompasses a whole range of support functions (such as temporary placements for wounded persons etc) and the leadership is here by the Police. Normally, the decision to issue a warning or alarm resides with three organizations:

1. the head of the zone of operations,
2. the head of the event operations, and
3. the head of the Police district

The need to alarm goes from i. to ii. with information about the event location and type, and after feedback and confirmation to iii. who orders the public alarm via the Central alarm center. There are however exceptions where i. can request the alarm from iii. without validation, just like the watch officer in iii. can activate the alarm in extreme situations where there is not enough time to run the normal procedure. In general i. formulates the alarm message, although it may be iii. in extreme situations. The above communication is today by telefax for legal reasons, with telephone back-up and a back-up alarm center in Slagelse as well. A governmental Internet VPN will also be used.

As it is now, the watch officer at the Central alarm center in Århus (or Slagelse) activates the horns in the zone of operations, enters the warn-

ing message in the alarm system, from which it is sent to the national broadcasters DR and TV2 who produce radio/TV/Text-TV readouts; a copy is sent the Emergency Directorate and the national wire service Ritzau.

It is also allowed for the state or municipal authorities ("Kommune") with emergency handling resources to issue alarms; for the state authorities they go directly to the national alarm center in Århus, while for the others they must go via the relevant Police district. The alarm messages have a fixed format (Beredskabsstyrelsen, 2005); those analyzed in the project had an average length of approx. 1000 characters, largely because of specific orders to receivers (evacuation, physical protection, routes, etc); this length is in general too long to display on most mobile terminal displays, thus the project has recommended to send out a short version first.

REQUIREMENTS VALIDATION FROM CASES

The London case demonstrated a 2.5 hours delay between the first bomb explosion at 08:50 and the first message by the London Commissioner of Police of the Metropolis, Sir Ian Blair, at 11:15 to "go in, tune in"; this was later criticized in the July 07 Review committee report (London Assembly, 2006). The Web content on BBC referred mistakenly to electrical surges as the events. Phone calls could not be made as the networks were cut or overloaded by a factor of about ten (London Assembly, 2006). Individuals alerted others by email about the bombings from 09:30. Vodafone tells it considered sending out 15 Million SMS messages as a warning but gave up due to the added congestion and delay. City of London Police asked the wireless operator O2 to activate access overload control (ACCOLC) in a zone of 1 km around the subway stations affected by the attacks, meaning only phones with special SIM cards could use the network for about 5 hours, and O2 lost several hundred thousand calls. Many people were at work or on their way, and with no access to TV, so that lack of information made people insecure.

The Seest case (Kolding Kommune, 2005) involved a fire in the N.P. Johnsen fireworks manufacturing plant in the town of Seest in Denmark; the fire was enormous and the zone of operations had to be enlarged twice due to the broadening of all explosions. One thousand people were wounded or evacuated, on fireman died, 60 houses were burnt down totally as well as 8 fire fighting vehicles. The alarm horns were activated twice and the broadcast network DR also, 3 min after the second explosion, then the second 3 min before the largest explosions who could be heard more than hundred kilometres away. Panic spread rapidly in the population and the Police used loudspeakers from vehicles to request evacuation. The Police recognized later that the warnings by horns were not heard or understood by most people. Police had to run from house to house to request people to go to a school and register there. Detailed explanations were first given next morning on the Kolding's municipality's Web site and by the radio network DR Channel 94. During this event, the health emergency services, the firemen, the municipality's emergency resources as well as Police, all relied on the public wireless network using mobile virtual private networks in use by each party on a routine basis. The population also used the same network but with public access. It was reported that while some redialling was needed, all users got access to the network within short time, and access overload control was never used; blocking probability was also low thanks to the way the local base station network and BSC had been configured in the area.

The references Hyslop (2007), van de Walle & Turoff (2007), and Chen, Sharman, Rao, and Upadhyaya (2008) respectively provide more theoretical views from other experiences on critical information infrastructure as well as on the coordination between stakeholder organizations.

USER REQUIREMENTS AND SATISFACTION BY SMS OR CELL BROADCAST MESSAGING

The main user requirements, resulting from Steps 1-4 in the methodology Section above, are identified in the 2nd column of Table 1. The results of Steps 2 and 3 in terms of the extent to which these requirements are met by SMS and CB messaging services are featured in summary form in the two right hand columns; extensive analysis is provided in Simonsen (2007).

Template messages must be designed to both, speed up the actual editing in a specific situation, and also to help in training /exercising. An example is provided in Figure 1.

ALARM SITUATION CONGESTION TRAFFIC ANALYSIS

A full calculation model has been developped whereby Radio base system (RBS), Base system controller (BSC) and SMSC or CBC capacities over time are determined, assuming nominal capacities in signalling, storage and message traffic intensity; such capacities are specifically determined when loaded by emergency wireless messaging requests While the traffic analysis relies on standard wireless network traffic engineering (with circuit switched connections over the air interface as in 2G and 3G), the calculation is unique to emergency situations because it is time dependent and recursive.

The driving process is a person-to-person social communication network, evolving over time for a given wireless teledensity in the surroundings. At alarm time, the wireless traffic load is equal to the number of detected users in the zone of intervention or its overlapping RBS coverage area; this is determined by the active signalling channels to these RBS'es. Post alarm, any given user is assumed to call or message on behalf of other users: family, work, transporta-

Table 1. Summary of end user requirements for wireless emergency messaging, and satisfaction thereof by SMS and CB services

Number	User Requirement	SMS satisfaction	Cell Broadcast satisfaction
1	The messages must include both warnings and orders, and they must be formulated in an easy understandable language	Partially as SMS messages are too short	Yes
2	The alarms messages must be up-to-date, with possibly three categories: instant alarms, growing visible event occurrence, and expected sudden occurrence	Yes	Yes
3	Messages must be able to be sent in several languages for residents and tourists	No	Yes
4	The warning messaging system should not use any extra memory, battery or computational power in the access terminals, and thus multimedia messages including MMS are excluded	Yes	In general: yes
5	Only the population in the zone of operations and other threat areas must be warned, meaning geographical filtering is required; filtering must be from exact mapping data and not just from location names	Partially as SMSC is normally not linked to cell locations	Yes
6	Irrespective of the situation and user numbers, the maximum delay from the warning command time to receipt by end users, should be max 5 minutes	No, unless small teledensity and zone size	Yes, unless too large population and insufficient RBS capacity
7	The public warning system must operate in the whole country with all 2G and 3G public operators	Yes (99% geographical coverage in Denmark)	Yes (99% geographical coverage in Denmark)
8	The public warning system functionality must be supported in the firmware or middleware of all 2G and 3G wireless handsets	Yes	Yes
9	All persons on danish soil with a GSM or UMTS terminal must receive the warning messages without registering for the service and without specific terminal configuration	Yes	No, unless CB configuration done beforehand
10	The messaging system must include a training / exercising functionality and include provisions to distinguish alarm messages from normal text or MMS messaging	Yes	Eventually
11	Operations should not be affected when Access overload control, call gapping or other QoS features are activated	Partially	Yes
12	The system should be free of charge for end users, and operators should not charge specifically for warning messages; legislation to be introduced to enact the system under universal service obligations	Yes within tariff bundle limits	Yes
13	Deaf / blind and severely physically / mentally disabled persons should be warned by the same system, with possible additional user interfaces	Yes	Yes
14	The system should be secure and trusted with a central information control	Yes in general	Yes
15	No single point of failure in process, hardware, software or communications may exist	Yes	Yes
16	All issued warning messages, destination groups and times must be logged	Yes	Yes
17	It should be legal to build and deploy the system, and regulatory approval must be established	Yes	Yes, but operators have not activated the service in general

Figure 1. Example of template message (translated from Danish); length in Danish is 366 characters at most

----

Category: Building fire   "WARNING by Police:

A fire in (location) now produces poisonous gases: You are now in an area which this dangerous smoke may cross. Go indoors, close doors / windows / ventilators. Indoors the risk will be much reduced. Listen to DR and TV2 for more information. You will receive an update on your mobile phone when (danger is over / danger is worsened / evacuation is ordered / other).

Police Chief in (location)

----

tion assistance, health assistance. By an obvious snowball combinatorial explosion effect, each of these four message recipients from any given warning person will again generate an average of three messages or calls, of which 2 back to the person in the zone of operations. The process is set to repeat itself, at time intervals linked to an emergency event category, and once again at the possible receipt of an updated warning message from the public authorities.

Congestion happens whenever: either the calculated blocking probability exceeds some specified threshold, or when an infrastructure node is saturated because of its capacity (including on the number of active signalling channels), or when the message queue waiting length exceeds the max. 5 minutes requirements criterion. While some other theoretical research has been made on priority queuing models inside a public network, we had to develop from scratch the model described above as the call distributions assumed by queuing models usually do not apply in emergency situations.

While the full details are too extensive to be specified here, this analysis allows statistically to determine which of SMS and CB give congestion the *last,* meaning the system can be up and running longest (by either of the three congestion reasons above). SMS is shown to be strongly subject to queuing congestion except if the zone of operations has a low teledensity. A different complementary analysis method is described in Butts, Petrescu, and Cross (2007). The CB messages are sent out on the CBCH CB channel without interference from the voice traffic, unless signalling capacity is limited (Cell broadcast Forum, 2007). The effect of the RBS network planning focussing on an ideal mesh distribution is analysed in Braunstein (2006), while the reality of the uneven RBS location priorities of operators for the Danish capital and the Seest disaster area are illustrated in Figure 2. An RBS location mismatch to latent user teledensity is another additional negative factor which however was not studied in this research.

COST BENEFIT AND RISK ANALYSES

The risk analysis has been carried out by estimating for each identified event / risk category, a value at risk, and the corresponding probability; a risk priority ranking is derived by taking the product of these two numbers (Simonsen, 2007). Are determined to be factors with the highest risk: the overload of the networks, the fact that most public operators see CB as an irrelevant or not profitable technology with little compensation by the public authorities, the rarity of warnings, and the fact that the warning system implementations are not flexible enough for highly diversified risks (see e.g. Table 2).

Figure 2. RBS locations in Copenhagen and Skjern area (close to Seest disaster) Source: www.mast-edatabasen.dk; the locations are marked with a grey cube with a number or letter label

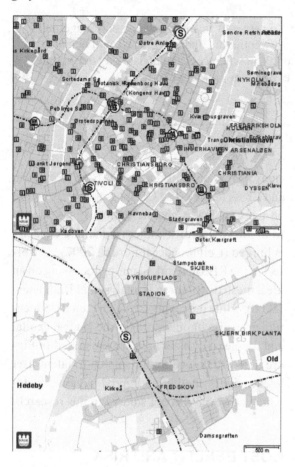

The cost-benefit analysis (Simonsen, 2007) forms the basis for a decision by policy makers about a wireless emergency network but is based on a range of assumptions and estimates which need to be revised in each concrete situation; Table 3 provides highlights in the case mentioned below.

.SMS and CB emergency messaging both represent incremental investments and operational costs to existing GSM or 3GPP1 networks; this is a favourable factor for fast adoption as the underlying basic infrastructure is already in place thanks to mobile operator investments. While 3G and HSPA/Edge may overtake GSM in the longer term as featured in Zhao, Addams-Moring, and Kekkonen (2005), the short term reality is that GSM is dominant. One cost-benefit assumption is that there are in average two emergency situations per year per zone of operations with an average of 200 000 inhabitants or guests, and that three warning messages are sent out each time (warning, post-event instructions, and end of warning); such values correspond to the average use of the horn based systems over the past 10 years (Beredskabsstyrelsen, 2005); the majority of the emergency situations are assumed from past data to be linked to dangerous smoke, water

Table 2. High risk factors and determination in CB warning case

Risk factor	Probability	Value at risk from requirements survey	Risk value
Police too slow in activating warning	0.5	0.8	0.40
Too seldom relevant warnings	0.30	0.80	0.24
Lack of system flexibility in view of unforeseen events	0.50	0.40	0.20
Overload of networks by warnings	0.9	0.8	0.72
Not all mobile operators want to participate	0.9	0.8	0.72

Table 3. Highlights from an example of cost-benefit analysis (Simonsen, 2007)

	Direct NPV of costs after 5, resp. 15 y (in M Euros)		Lives saved by system efficiencies after 5, resp. 15 y	
SMS	16	25	12	18
CB	43	74	31	54

poisoning or dangerous gas. Parametric cost-benefit assumptions deal with the benefits impact of each warning message in reducing the death count, severe injuries and light injuries by multiples of ½, 5 and 20 persons respectively. Data are also used from the Transportation and Energy Ministry (2006) about person related losses and general welfare losses for each death, major or light injury. The cost benefit present value calculation horizons are 5 or 15 years (to match residual GSM or 3GPP1 license durations) with a discounting factor of 3%.

The net present value of an SMS based emergency messaging warning system is always negative and in average about 4 times more affordable than the one for a CB based solution; also, the SMS based solution alone offers positive net cash flow except at incremental investment time (see details in Simonsen, 2007). The analysis also allows to determine the hypothetical break even situations needed to recover system investments and operating costs; for SMS messaging the needed reductions in number of deaths are at least 12 persons (for 5 years) and 18 persons (for 15 years); for CB messaging, the equivalent numbers are 31 and 54 persons.

This means that public network based emergency warning systems are strictly speaking both loss-making investments because they still do not allow in general to reduce fast enough the number of deaths and injuries. However, the SMS based solution is still the most favourable and affordable from a public benefits point of view for the normal emergencies encountered in Denmark and the possible reductions of losses within the population. Thanks to the corresponding wireless warnings, benefits seem to be achievable much faster than with CB.

REGULATORY CONSTRAINTS, SOLUTION AND IMPLICATIONS

The previous Sections have analyzed needs, stakeholders, as well as cost-benefit implications of emergency services serving public interest using public wireless services. However, even if technical feasibility (including operational deployment procedures), public interest and budget feasibility are established, key regulatory and policy issues remain to be identified.

The essence of the dilemma is that, since privatization and deregulation of public communication services, the public operators providing the needed geographical coverage (wireless, TV) are under no obligation whatsoever to provide emergency services unless contracted to do it. More precisely, according to EU regulations from 2003, so-called EU formulated "universal service obligations" on operators (for which they contribute back a share of their revenue base) did address social needs of the citizens, and not those linked to emergency situations. The reason for this is that nowadays public safety is a matter of national sovereignty not delegated to EU or to common EU regulations. Furthermore, due to deregulation, most regulatory authority on public communications operators has been assigned to independent national regulators which do not just execute orders or national laws depicted by the national parliaments. These two aspects are illustrated by Figure 3 which visualizes the flow of law and procedural controls on the stakeholders; it shows no relevant chain-of-law, other than licences and compliance to technical standards onto public operators. It also illustrates the well known dual-control on operational assets from national as well as local authorities.

However, in countries like Denmark, citizens safety and security are rooted in national constitutional obligations, thus allowing the Parliament in principle to extend the EU definition of "universal service obligations" on operators to include specific provisions to mandate, based on a government request, the provisioning of emergency based SMS or CB services as part of the national definition of "universal service obligations" which operators have to fulfil to get and keep a public license. Since almost all communication operators, have to assign a nationally regulated fraction of almost all their traffic revenues towards "univer-

Figure 3. Major stakeholders and the regulatory/policy making dependencies (in red arrows)

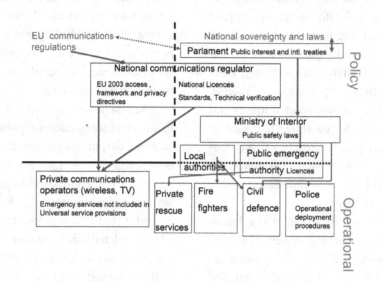

sal service obligations" based on national defini-tions, the issue is next to have the Parliament to legislate so that the national regulator can imple-ment such provisions, such also that they do not violate EU regulations. The dilemma of Parliament however is how to prioritize between social wel-fare needs under "universal service obligations" versus new emergency based provisions; fortu-nately, Denmark has been rather affluent and the budget for social needs has in effect exceeded real demands.

The estimated costs from the solution analyzed in the previous sections rely on implementing and operating SMS or CB gateways on public expense, probably reusing the staff units of the police providing the current acoustic based emergency service to be phased out. This expense would involve a mix between universal service based revenue, special investments and savings from phasing out the legacy acoustic system.

FUTURE WORK AND CONCLUSION

The first academic-industry-governmental project phase in 2005-2006 was devoted to the analy-

ses summarized above, resulting in the explicit policy change recommendation and cost-benefit study results presented in the previous Section. A subsequent phase (2007-2008) with heavier governmental and legislative participation is focussing on drafting and consensus building for the executive texts, the system specification, and the request for proposals, as well as the updates to operational procedures. The window of op-portunity comes up first in connection with the GSM license renewals, and further down the road in connection with LTE upgrades to 3G licenses.

This project has explored the short-term op-portunity offered by leveraging on existing widely used and accepted public wireless services and wireless terminals in the Danish context for emer-gency warning of the general public. The results do not preclude the fact that alternative technologies and information handling techniques (van de Walle & Turoff, 2007; Hinton, Klein & Haner, 2005) may in the future offer a better impact with same or higher access terminal adoption. It has been shown that neither SMS nor Cell Broadcast based messaging meet all user requirements, although they meet most of them. The main drawback of an SMS based solution is the high risk of not being able to warn within 5 minutes due to network congestion and recipient selection overhead. The main drawback with Cell Broadcast is that the end user must in advance have configured his/her terminal or received a configuration patch via the wireless network or at sales time. Both systems offer potentially the needed flexibility.

The risk and cost benefit analyses establish that the minimum numbers of reductions of deaths and injuries thanks to wireless warnings required for the systems to pay back over the years are likely to be met. The regulatory and policy making analysis identifies fundamental bottlenecks but offer a way forward in legislative, regulatory and budget terms by allowing to extend nationally the EU definition of universal service provisioning.

If any advice from this analysis is to be provided, the highest likelihood of meeting positive returns today in view of all the expected diverse and cumulated threats in Denmark is met by the 15 years lifetime of an SMS based solution (2G or 3G). In about 5 years, the best choice may be an SMS/IMS based solution in LTE networks resulting from a migration from SMS, possibly supplemented by Mobile Internet which offers yet other challenges. SMS also offers a known and stable platform for authorities to revisit the information content of emergency messages. Some of the reasons why Mobile Internet may not meet the basic emergency communications requirements discussed are: lack of formatting, increased difficulties in the filtering, ergonomics at input stage, even higher congestion delays, and privacy issues.

At a wider policy level, is raised the question of the full separation between wireless emergency networks and services for the general public and wireless crisis management networks and services. The EU sponsored SECRICOM project (2008-2012), as well as national projects such as the Norwegian one (Norwegian public safety radio project, 2010)are demonstrating that this may not necessarily be so, when four technologies are shared: secure encrypted mobile groups, trusted hardware nodes, improved interoperability with public wireless systems, and the introduction of distributed independent handling of requests of the various first responders involved in the emergency. After all, one essential mission is to enable to recover their communication quickly after a disaster and keep on talking / messaging to effectively coordinate services; this coordination is not only between public bodies but also with the general public and special groups.

Yet again at policy level, this tighter interoperability will be fast leveraged in operating return and cost of operations terms, as evidenced by this paper.

REFERENCES

Beredskabsstyrelsen. (2005). *Aftale om fremgangsmåden ved udsendelse af beredskabsmeddelelser* (in Danish). Retrieved from www.beredskabsstyrelsen.dk

Braunstein, B. (2006). Challenges in using distributed wireless mesh networks in emergency response. *Proceedings of the 3rd International ISCRAM Conference*, (pp 58-64). Newark, NJ, May.

Butts, C. T., Petrescu, M., & Cross, B. R. (2007). Responder communication networks in the World Trade Center disaster: Implications for modelling of communication within emergency settings. *The Journal of Mathematical Sociology*, *31*(2). doi:10.1080/00222500601188056

Cell broadcast Forum. (2007). *Cell broadcast in public warning systems*. Retrieved from www.cellbroadcastforum.org

Chen, R., Sharman, R., Rao, R., & Upadhyaya, S. (2008). Coordination in emergency response management. *Communications of the ACM*, *51*(5), 66–73. doi:10.1145/1342327.1342340

ETSI. (2006). *Analysis of the short message service (SMS) and Cell broadcast service (CBS) for emergency messaging applications*. Retrieved from www.etsi.org

FICORA. (2005). *Use of text messaging in public safety alerts*. (WG report 7/2005). Retrieved from www.ficora.fi

Hinton, D., Klein, T. E., & Haner, M. (2005). An architectural proposal for future wireless emergency response networks with broadband services. *Bell Labs Technical Journal, 10*(2), 121–138. doi:10.1002/bltj.20097

Hyslop, M. (2007). *Critical information infrastructures*. Heidelberg, Germany: Springer Verlag.

Kolding Kommune. (2005). *Spoergeskemaundersoegelse* (in Danish). Retrieved from www.kolding.dk/printpage.asp?id=31377

London Assembly. (2006). *Report of the 7th July review committee, Greater London authority*. Retrieved from www.london.gov.uk/assembly/reports/7july

Norwegian public safety radio project. (2010). *Direktoratet for noedkommunikasjon*, Oslo. Retrieved from http://www.dinkom.no/default.asp?pub=0&sub=43

SECRICOM project. (2008-2012). Retrieved from www.secricom.eu

Simonsen, P. (2007). *Katastrofevarsling til befolkningen via offentlige mobilnet* (in Danish). Cand.merc.dat thesis, Copenhagen Business school, Copenhagen.

Transport and Energy Ministry. (2006). *Key figures catalogue for use for techno-economic analyses in the transport area*, 4th ed, (in Danish). Retrieved from www.trm.dk/graphics/Synkron-Library/trafikministeriet/Publikationer/Rapporter/Noegletalskatalog%20juni%202006.pdf

van de Walle, B., & Turoff, M. (Eds.). (2007). Special issue: Emergency response Information Systems: Emerging trends and technologies. *Communications of the ACM, 50*(3), 28–65.

Wood, M. (2006). *Proposed request for comments on international cell alert via cell broadcasting channelization codes*, v3. CEASA. Retrieved from www.ceasa-int.org/channel_codes_v3.htm

Zhao, S., Addams-Moring, R., & Kekkonen, M. (2005). Building mobile emergency announcement systems in 3G networks. *Proceedings of the Communications and Computer Networks Conference*, (pp 141-148). Calgary, Canada: ACTA Press.

Chapter 13
Knowledge Management in Support of Crisis Response

Murray E. Jennex
San Diego State University, USA

Murali Raman
Multimedia University Malaysia, Malaysia

ABSTRACT

Most organizations face difficult challenges in managing knowledge for crisis response, but it is crucial for response effectiveness that such challenges be overcome. Organizational members must share the knowledge needed to plan for emergencies. They also must be able during an emergency to access relevant plans and communicate about their responses to it. This article examines the role and relevance of knowledge management (and knowledge management systems therein) in support of crisis response. We begin by discussing what knowledge management and crisis response mean. We move on to suggest why crisis response efforts within an organizational context, might benefit from knowledge management initiatives. Specific examples of how knowledge management efforts have supported crisis response in the past are then presented. We end by offering researchers with some suggestions for future research work in light of this subject domain.

INTRODUCTION

Knowledge management (KM) is about capturing knowledge created in an organization and making it available to those who need it to make decisions. Crisis response is about making decisions under stress and time pressure. While it would seem

DOI: 10.4018/978-1-60960-609-1.ch013

natural to use KM to support crisis response decision making; a review of the literature pertaining to implementation of KM and KM systems finds that the emphasis in KM research is focused on KM impacts on organizational performance and competitive enhancement (Von Krogh 1998; Hackbarth 1998; Davenport and Prusak 1998; Alavi and Leidner 2001, Jennex and Olfman, 2006, Raman et al., 2006). However, events such as the 9/11 terrorist attacks, the London subway bombings, the 2004 tsunami, and Hurricane Katrina have spurred interest in research in crisis/disaster/emergency preparation/response (henceforth referred to as crisis response). This has led to a small but growing body of research focused on examining KM and KMS support for crisis response. Accordingly, the purpose of this article is to help researchers and managers to better appreciate and understand the relationship between KM, KMS, and crisis response.

The objective of this article is to discuss how knowledge needed for crisis response can be managed more effectively by integrating KM into crisis response efforts. We offer several examples of how KM has been used to support crisis response efforts and the issues that were faced therein.

The article proceeds as follows. Section 2 examines fundamental aspects of KM and KM systems. Next we offer an overview of what crisis response is particularly with reference to the core issues involved in crisis management from a decision making perspective. Section 4 provides a brief account of the history and functions of emergency response systems, which leads to a logical discussion about how and why crisis response can benefit from KM principles. Sections 6 highlight the role of KM in different phases of a crisis situation. This is followed with several examples of prior work about KM systems applied to the context of crisis response. We end with several suggestions of future research that can be done to extend the ideas that we have presented here.

KNOWLEDGE MANAGEMENT AND KNOWLEDGE MANAGEMENT SYSTEMS

Jennex (2005) used an expert panel to generate a composite definition of KM as the practice of selectively applying knowledge from previous experiences of decision-making to current and future decision making activities with the

express purpose of improving the organization's effectiveness. Alavi and Leidner (2001, p. 114) define a KM System, KMS, as "IT (Information Technology)-based systems developed to support and enhance the organizational processes of knowledge creation, storage/retrieval, transfer, and application." They observed that not all KM initiatives will implement an IT solution, but they support IT as an enabler of KM.

The purpose of implementing KMS in organizations varies. Von Krogh (1998) takes a business perspective, stating that KMS help increase competitiveness. Hackbarth (1998) suggests that KMS lead to greater innovation and responsiveness. Davenport and Prusak (1998) provide three reasons why KMS are implemented in organizations: (i) to enhance visibility of knowledge in organizations through the use of maps, hypertexts, yellow pages; directories, etc., (ii) to build a knowledge sharing culture, i.e., create avenues for employees to share knowledge, and (iii) to develop a knowledge infrastructure, not confined to technology solely, but create an environment that permits collaborative work. Work by Hackbarth (1998) and Davenport and Prusak (1998) imply that KMS can support an organization in planning for and dealing with crises.

EMERGENCIES, DISASTERS AND CRISIS MANAGEMENT

Princeton University defines an emergency as "a sudden unforeseen crisis (usually involving danger) that requires immediate action. Another Web resource defines an emergency as "any abnormal system condition, which requires immediate manual or automatic action to prevent loss of load, equipment damage, or tripping of system elements which might result in cascading and to restore system operation to meet the minimum operating reliability criteria." The notion of disaster management can be viewed in the broader lens of crisis management. This article uses the term 'emergency' synonymous to the term 'crisis'. Majority of literature on crisis management use the term crisis to describe both emergency and disaster situations, which includes but not confined to man-made and natural disasters (Fink, 1986; Booth, 1993; Myers, 1999; Seeger et al. 2003, Herman, 1965; Miller, 2004).

Charles Herman is one of the pioneers in developing crisis management models. Herman (1965) states that any crisis situation consists of three key elements:

* "It threatens high priority values of the organization goals
* It presents a restricted amount of time in which decisions can be made and
* Is unexpected or unanticipated by the organization" (p. 64).

Herman's definition implies that crisis management is unstructured and complex in nature. This view of crisis is similar to that of Miller (2004) who defines a crisis based on nine attributes. Miller states that a crisis:

* "Suddenly occurs
* Demands quick reaction
* Interferes with organizational performance
* Creates uncertainty and stress
* Threatens the reputation, assets of the organization
* Escalates in intensity
* Cases outsiders to scrutinize the organization
* Permanently alters the organization" (p. 19).

The Institute for Crisis Management (ICM) classifies crisis situations into sixteen categories (Miller, 2004-p.21): business catastrophe, class action suits, defects/recalls, environmental damage, financial damage, labor disputes, sexual harassment, white-collar crime, casualty accident, consumer action, discrimination, executive dis-

missal, hostile takeover, mismanagement, whistle blowing and workplace violence.

Fink (1986) defines a crisis as an "unstable time or state of affairs in which a decisive change is impending - either one with the distinct possibility of a highly undesirable outcome or one with a distinct possibility of a highly desirable and extremely positive outcome" (p.15). This definition is somewhat different compared to standard definitions of emergency/crisis situations (for example Chandler and Wallace, 2004; Claremont Colleges Disaster management Plan 2004), where the notion of an emergency is often associated to a negative outcome. Fink goes on to suggest that the purpose of managing crisis is to eliminate any potential risk to the organization.

Seeger et al. (2003) offer a broader definition of organizational crisis management relative to Fink's (1986) definition. They define organizational crisis as an "unusual event of overwhelmingly negative significance that carries a high level of risk, harm and opportunity for further loss" (p.4). The authors cite spills, floods, and explosions as examples of crisis situation that can impact individual careers, health, and well being in addition to preventing organizations from resuming regular operations.

Booth (1993) suggests that every crisis is unique and cannot be accurately planned for. Fink (1986) suggests that emergency management teams in organizations ask themselves the following questions when developing a crisis management plan: "Who is responsible for notifying employees? Who is the backup? Who is responsible for notifying the media? Which local, state, or federal government agencies may need to be notified, and who will do so? Your switchboard operators are your first line of defense (or offense). What will they tell reporters or the public at large when they call? Who is responsible for briefing them? And do they need to be bilingual?" (p.60).

Chandler and Wallace (2004) studied emergency response in organizations throughout the United States. Their study compares the emergency response efforts between 2001 and 2004, with a specific focus on organizational resources devoted to disaster planning. The survey was administered at the Disaster Recovery Journal (Spring 2004) world conference. The highpoints of their study are summarized as follows. On September 11, 2001, close to 20% of companies represented in the study did not have any formally documented crisis management plan. By mid-September 2002, 66% of companies studied increased overall organizational commitment and efforts in planning for emergencies. Post 9/11, 36% of companies increased resources devoted to emergency response; 53% reported a modest increase. Only 9% said that there was no change in the organization's view of emergency response after the incident. Terror threats, bomb threats, biological hazards, and dealing with explosive materials are ranked higher in terms of risks, after 9/11. In terms of written policies, the survey respondents said that following 9/11, the emergency response/disaster recovery plans for their respective organizations now include procedures to handle "bomb threats (70%), computer crime (49%), terrorism attacks (47%), mail threats (47%), chemical release (43%) and hazardous material release (43%).

Chandler and Wallace (2004) describe four areas that should be incorporated by crisis planners in their respective policies: (i) determining guidelines and standard policies for resuming business as usual after a crisis situation, (ii) real-time tracking of implementation plans, (iii) use of simulation in training staff involved in crisis response, and (iv) prioritizing what needs to be in the organization's crisis planning process.

Myers (1999) uses the term disasters to describe a crisis. He suggests that organizations should develop a four-stage disaster response plan: (i) prevention, which includes preparedness training, (ii) development of an organized response with a focus on damage containment, (iii) protection of cash flow by using alternate procedures, and (iv) restoration of facilities by resuming normal operations. Myers identifies the essential issues, which should be part of a crisis response plan:

"Notification to employees and customers; damage assessment; rerouting incoming phone calls and/or messaging; initiating restoring computer processing capability; physical security; and relocating personnel" (p.9).

CRISIS RESPONSE SYSTEMS

Crisis Response Systems are used by organizations to assist in responding to a crisis situation. These systems support communications, data gathering and analysis, and decision-making. Crisis Response Systems are rarely used but when needed, must function well and without fail. Designing and building these systems requires designers to anticipate what will be needed, what resources will be available, and how conditions will differ from normal. A standard model for a Crisis Response System is from Bellardo, Karwan, and Wallace (1984) and identifies the components as including a database, data analysis capability, normative models, and an interface. This model is only somewhat useful as it fails to address issues such as how the Crisis Response System fits into the overall crisis response plan, Crisis Response System infrastructure, multiple organization spanning, knowledge from past emergencies, and integrating multiple systems.

To address the weaknesses of the Bellardo, Karwan, and Wallace (1984) model Jennex (2004) summarized the literature and used findings from Y2K to generate an expanded crisis response system model. These systems are more than the basic components of database, data analysis, normative models, and interface. A more complete crisis response system model includes these basic components plus trained users (where users are personnel using the system to respond to or communicate about the emergency and consist of first responders, long term responders, the emergency response team, and experts), dynamic, integrated, and collaborative (yet possibly physically distributed) methods to communicate between users and between users and data sources, protocols to facilitate communication, and processes and procedures used to guide the response to and improve decision making during the crisis. The goals of the crisis response system are to facilitate clear communications, improve collaboration between users needing to collaborate, improve the efficiency and effectiveness of decision-making, and manage data to prevent or at least mitigate information overload. Designers use technology and work flow analysis to improve system performance in achieving these goals.

Prior to the establishment of the Homeland Security Department, the task of managing information pertaining to crisis situations and crisis management in the United States was under the jurisdiction of the Office of Emergency response (OEP) (Turoff, 1972). The information requirements for the OEP were largely handled by a group of consultants from both business and academia. Over time, the OEP recognized that a system that could provide timely and relevant information to crisis responders was needed (Turoff, 1972). In 1970, twenty-five people working on crisis response were able to collaborate via a computerized Delphi system (Turoff, 1972). Computerized Delphi techniques can be administered via the web today (see for example Cho and Turoff, 2003 and Turoff and Hiltz, 1995).

In 1971, the OEP was assigned the task of monitoring a new form of crisis called the "Wage Price Freeze" (Turoff et al., 2004). This new role for the OEP included among others, to "monitor nationwide compliance, examine and determine requests for exemptions and prosecute violations" (p. 5) in relation to wage and price changes in the economy. This led to the advent of a flexible system called the Emergency Management Information System and Reference Index (EMISARI). EMISARI was a system designed to facilitate effective communication between people involved in monitoring the Wage Price Freeze situation. The system was designed to integrate people and data into a common platform that could

be updated regularly by people who were non-technical administrators (Turoff et al., 2004). The EMISARI system was flexible and enabled several hundreds of people to collaborate in responding to a crisis (see for example Rice 1987, 1990 and Turoff, 2002).

Lee and Bui (2000) documented vital observation with the use of a crisis response system during the massive earthquake that hit Kobe, Japan in 1995. Several key lessons for crisis management system designers based on Lee and Bui's work were identified. Relevant information should be included in the crisis response system prior to the actual crisis situation. This is to ensure that crisis responders have sufficient information to guide the decision-making processes in responding to a crisis. Lee and Bui (2000) imply that the task of gathering relevant information to support crisis response should be incorporated into part of the crisis response strategic initiative. Information from prior experiences should become part of the crisis management system. The system should somehow be able to capture both tacit and explicit knowledge about how prior crisis situations were dealt with. Lessons, which are learned, can be used to guide future action. Lee and Bui (2000) in this regard imply that the design of any crisis response system should support some form of organizational memory component.

In addition to designing relevant systems features to support crisis planning and response, researchers suggest that successful implementation of any crisis management system is contingent on how well people are trained to use such systems (Patton and Flin, 1999; Turoff, 1972; Lee and Bui, 2000). Patton and Flin, for instance, suggest that crisis management systems be incorporated into crisis response related activities such as training, simulations, drills, and evacuation exercises. Turoff (1972) states that crisis management systems that are not normally used will not be used when an actual crisis situation occurs.

The majority of post 9/11 literature on crisis management is confined within the realm of commercial entities (Braveman, 2003). Developments within the domain of crisis management information systems have accelerated over the past few years, particularly after the 9/11 events (Campbell et al., 2004). The authors accurately mention that issues such as resources, expertise, and personnel should be addressed at the onset, prior to designing crisis management systems within the context of local and state level communities. They call for development of "a generic set of requirements" (p.2) that can be used by both the state and local authorities to support crisis planning and response. The researchers however do not base their study on any particular theoretical foundations. Campbell and associates (2004) examine the effect of asynchronous negotiation given "a structured task and a specified negotiation sequence" (p. 3), in the context of crisis responders.

WHY CRISIS RESPONSE NEEDS KM?

Crises can happen at any time making it difficult for organizations to have the right resources where and when they are needed. Most organizations don't have experience with real emergencies so they need to take advantage of all available experience as decisions need to be made fast and under stress and high tension circumstances. The complexity of communicating, collaborating, and decision making processes in the context of crisis response efforts cannot be undermined.

The above paragraph implies that an organization's ability to survive given dynamic changes within its environment is contingent upon its ability to quickly respond to change, in a crisis mode. This includes the ability to effectively manage its knowledge resources. Burnell et al. (2004) assert that "an effective knowledge-based organization is one that correctly captures, shares, applies and maintains its knowledge resources to achieve its goals" (p.203). This echoes the view of March and Simon (1958) who state that

successful organizations are able to adapt to any dynamic environment. The information processing theory states that the role of having accurate and up to date information is vital particularly when organizations deal with a turbulent environment (Burnell et al., 2004). Integrating KM processes can support managers to proactively respond to a highly turbulent environment and will benefit an organization (Burnell et al., 2004). This would include organizations that plan and prepare for emergencies and crisis response situations (Kostman, 2004).

Figure 1 can be used to further discuss why KM can support crisis response efforts. A crisis response center (often led by a crisis response manager) deals with various stakeholders during a crisis situation. Different stakeholder groups often have different skills, resources, technical expertise, and more importantly experience in responding to a particular crisis. For any crisis response center, issues such as managing different stakeholder expectations, priorities, and the vari-

Figure 1. Complexity of emergency response

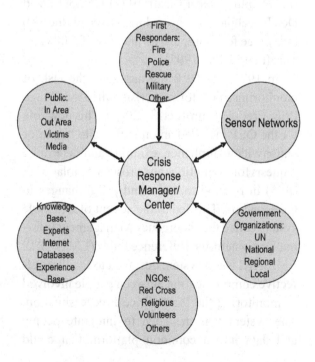

ous resource and skill sets they bring into an actual crisis response mode, is complex and dynamic. This could lead to difficulties in making accurate decisions, under time-pressured and intense situations, while responding to a particular crisis. In this context, we suggest that a KMS can be used to capture and then re-use of specific crisis response knowledge which can be used to support decision making when a crisis actually occurs. The Practice of selectively applying knowledge from previous experiences during turbulent moments of decision making, to current and future decision making activities with the express purpose of improving the organization's effectiveness, would be possible via a KMS. In addition, we further add that given the dynamic nature of crisis situations, coupled with different inputs and requirements from various stakeholder groups, a crisis response manager and centre therein, is subject to information overload, which can prevent timely and accurate decision making. A well tested and implemented KMS in this context can helps to decide what to look at, what decisions to focus on, and what decisions can be made automatically and/or in advance.

KM is an action discipline; knowledge needs to be used and applied for KM to have an impact. Crisis response relies on the use of knowledge from past situations to generate current and future response procedures. Lessons learned and the understanding of what works best in given situations (both examples of knowledge) enables emergency managers to prepare planned responses as a counter to the stress of the emergency and to ensure all relevant issues are considered during emergency response decision making.

CRISIS RESPONSE PHASES AND SYSTEMS

For the purposes of the article, crises are high stress situations that require organizations to respond in a manner that is different from their normal operating procedures (Turoff, 2002). Patton and Flin (1999) discuss these stresses on emergency managers and how to reduce them. Emergency stressors, in addition to fatigue, include dealing with a complex, unpredictable and dynamic response, time pressure, and communications, dealing with the media, and operating within an integrated crisis management context. Crises are also a series of four phases: situational analysis (SA), initial response (IR), crisis response (ER), and recovery response (RR); and five decision/hand off points: the initiating event (IE), the control event (CE), the restoration event (RE), the normalizing event (NE), and a terminating event (TE). Figure 1 (Jennex, 2007) shows the phases and decision points and includes a general plot of the amount per unit time of immediate responses and decisions that need to be made as a timeline plot following some initiating event, IE. Note that figure 1 (Jennex, 2007) is not drawn to scale and is a generic drawing of a crisis timeline. Also, a TE point is not shown. The TE is for ending the crisis and would occur if the crisis was determined to be false, or if another crisis took precedence, or any event that would cause the cessation of response to the crisis. The TE can occur in any phase and at any time so for that reason is not shown.

Figure 2 (Jennex, 2007) shows that organizations are constantly in the first crisis phase, SA, which is a data gathering and assessment phase that has a base level of activity. These base level activities are monitoring of a set of predetermined conditions, analysis of these conditions for unusual or pre-identified deviations, identification of the IE, and training and preparation of the crisis response team. A crisis begins when during the SA phase an IE is observed. This causes the IR phase to be entered. This is expected to be a very short duration phase that consists of confirming the crisis, generating early warning notices, initiating preplanned initial actions, and entering the crisis response plan. The ER phase is entered immediately upon assumption of control by the crisis response team, the CE, and generally after

Figure 2. Phases and timeline of activity level for a typical emergency

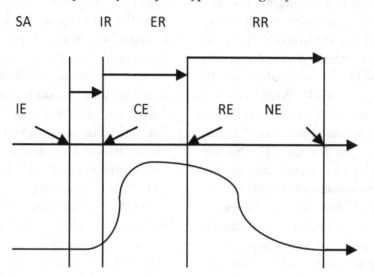

completion of the immediate response actions and early warning notifications. The ER phase implements the crisis response plan and begins coordinating responders and other resources. Additionally, this phase is the command and control phase that requires the crisis response team to monitor conditions and to coordinate response accordingly. This phase rises to the peak activity level. This phase ends with the RE. The RE is the point where the crisis response team concludes that the crisis conditions are over or are under control and crisis response actions are no longer needed and the crisis control center can cease command operations. At this point, the crisis enters the RR phase. This phase confirms the crisis is under control, controls and coordinates long term actions and reconstruction, guides the organization back to normal conditions, and identifies and captures lessons learned. This phase has a declining level of activity and concludes when the NE is announced. The NE is the point where all crisis response actions are completed, long term crisis response actions and a base level of reconstruction is completed, the crisis response team is secured, and the organization returns to normal operating procedures and the routine SA phase.

Each of these phases has their own stresses and support needs. To reduce these stresses, crisis response plans and systems should be based on operational demands, tested regularly, and have resources allocated. These plans should not be based on implicit and untested assumptions that reflect routine operational requirements and conditions as plans based on assumed capabilities are less effective than anticipated and will increase ad hoc demands on managers. Working in teams is required during crises and having a well trained, experienced team will reduce the impact of team dynamic stressor. Additionally, crises may require inter agency coordination and dealing with inter-agency conflict and terminology increases stress.

These stresses can be reduced if these agencies are integrated in their response and participants train together so that they are familiar with each other and comfortable with the integrated crisis response plan. Finally, communication systems are necessary for getting the right information to the right people, but they will not reduce stress unless participants are trained and practiced in their use. In addition to the stresses identified by Patton and Flin (1999), Bellardo, Karwan, and Wallace (1984) identify the stress of decision-making during crisis response and recommend the creation of a Crisis Response System to assist decision makers.

SPECIFIC EXAMPLES

The large number of groups that may respond to an emergency all need access to a wide range of real-time information and knowledge that requires coordination. Groups have proposed and created KM enhanced Emergency Response systems that allow for more efficient use of data and faster response. One example that has been proposed is the Information Management System for Hurricane disasters (IMASH) (Iakovou and Douligeris, 2001). IMASH is an information management system based on an object-oriented database design, able to provide data for response to hurricanes. IMASH was designed with the premise that the World Wide Web is the medium of choice for presenting textual and graphical information to a distributed community of users. This design is much more effective in the fast-changing environment of a natural disaster than the historical use of static tools which, out of necessity, have been the tools used in disaster response. Kitamato (2005) describes the design of an information management system, Digital Typhoon, designed to provide a hub of information on the Internet during a typhoon disaster.

The Digital Typhoon provides access to information from official sources (news, satellite imagery) as well as a forum for individuals to provide information (local, personal). It effectively became a hub of information, but created questions about organization, filtering, and editing. Systems used for Hurricane Katrina response realized the benefits and difficulties of these systems. Like IMASH, the systems described below use the Internet to distribute data to a community of users, and like the Digital Typhoon, the knowledge management systems described for Hurricane Katrina response became hubs of information that required data management to reduce repeti-

tion and allow for editing. Murphy and Jennex (2006) added knowledge management, KM, to the expanded Crisis Response System model proposed by Jennex (2004) and showed how it was used in open source developed systems used to aid in the response to Katrina through the implementation of the Peoplefinder and Shelterfinder systems.

These systems were unique in that they were developed independent of government support or resources. Development was through volunteers and the systems used a web interface tied to a knowledge base to gather information and knowledge on survival stories and sources of shelter. Experience with these systems showed the value of using open source, commercial tools, and wikis to build Emergency Response Systems. Success of these systems was dependent upon the interface and the quality of the knowledge stored and retrieved from the systems.

Another application of KM to emergency response is in identification of the decision/hand off points. KM is applied through the generation of guidelines, rules, and procedures that govern these points. As experience is gained and lessons learned, the criteria guiding the declaration of these points is modified to incorporate this experience. The benefit to emergency responders is that decision making with respect to these points is simplified and guided, reducing the stress on the decision maker.

Finally, future trends into emergency response systems were demonstrated during the Strong Angel III civilian-military integrated disaster response demonstration held in San Diego, California during August 2006. Demonstrations were held integrating knowledge bases into visualization systems resulting in smart displays. In particular, the use of knowledge bases within a GIS as demonstrated by the San Diego State University Visualization Laboratory illustrated the power of tying social and demographical data and knowledge to images and maps. This integration created an emergency response system that could be ad hoc queried with results displayed visually. This facilitated knowledge creation and knowledge transfer among emergency response personnel.

Wide spread emergencies such as Katrina and the 2004 Tsunami have shown the difficulty of building stand alone Emergency Response Systems (systems whose sole purpose is to respond to emergencies). These systems are expensive and it is difficult to not use them for routine activities when resources are low. Exercises preparing for a possible avian flu pandemic and for a pandemic coupled with a terrorist attack on critical infrastructure (Operation Chimera and Strong Angel III) are focusing on training large numbers of people in emergency response while using and developing open source emergency response systems (Jennex, 2006). Strong Angel III in particular focused on creating and using an emergency response system based on open source development and commercial off the shelf components. The goal is to reduce the cost, time, and effort involved in building and implementing an emergency response system while maintaining system security, especially when using the Internet and other commercial, civilian communication networks, and providing a structure for integrating diverse data and knowledge sources and bases. Additionally, Raman, et al. (2006) discusses the use of wiki technology to facilitate KM for emergency response systems. It is expected that open source technologies such as wiki technology will be used to improve connectivity and communications between diverse groups needing to communicate during an emergency. It is expected that increased use of knowledge based systems and KM will continue for emergency response. Improved KM technologies for storing, searching, and retrieving knowledge will be used to integrate KM into emergency decision making (Murphy and Jennex, 2006).

Worms like Slammer which infected 90% of all vulnerable systems connected to the Internet within 10 minutes of its release in 2003 (Panko, 2003) show the vulnerability of cyber emergency response. Currently organizations rely on intrusion detections systems, IDS, which have some alarm functions, to detect such attacks and on firewalls to protect their networks. Emergency response under these conditions is still primitive with most organizations relying on emergencies being recognized and then responded to via sets of incident response procedures. It is expected that new, fast acting emergency response systems will have to be developed that will rely on knowledge based analysis and decision support to improve emergency response times to fit emergencies such as Slammer.

In summary, there is a fusion of crisis response systems with KM. This is because decision makers, when under stress, need systems that do more than just provide data, they need systems that can quickly find and display knowledge relevant to the situation in a format that facilitates the decision maker in making decisions. It is expected that Emergency Response System evolution will continue to utilize KM concepts and approaches as experience in responding to disasters is showing that these systems are more effective than traditional Emergency Response Systems. Examples of how KM aids emergency/crisis response includes using knowledge of past disasters to design communication and data/information capture protocols and templates, capturing emergency response knowledge in procedures and protocols; incorporating lessons learned into response team training, interface and display design, and the generation of heuristics guiding decision making; and using knowledge to guide the creation of experience knowledge bases that responders can use to generate emergency response actions.

AREAS FOR FUTURE RESEARCH

KM is a relatively young field. The fusion of crisis response with KM is even younger. Thus far, only two articles on KM and crisis response have been published in the International Journal of Knowledge Management. Many questions are yet to be answered in this research domain. Cases on crisis management and how KM efforts were used or are applicable to them are always needed. This would be of value to the KM and crisis management practitioner community. Secondly, issues inherent in the context of transferring knowledge between crisis responders in all three phases of pre, during, and post crisis periods would be of interest, particularly issues involved with codification and transfer of tacit knowledge embedded within experienced crisis responders. Other areas from a more technical perspective that warrants research is in examining the role and relevance of semantic websites, use of ontologies, data fusion and visualization technologies, collaborative technologies and sense making technologies in light of crisis response efforts.

CONCLUSION

Emergency response in the United States of America, USA, is evolving from something that was locally handled to something that is standardized under Federal control. The USA implemented the National Incident Management System, NIMS, in 2004. NIMS established standardized incident management protocols and procedures that all responders are to use to conduct and coordinate response actions (Townsend, 2006). Townsend (2006) discusses lessons learned from Katrina that include communications infrastructure, knowledge about emergency response plans, integration of civilian and military response activities, and critical infrastructure and impact assessment issues. Review of these issues suggests there were failings in the emergency response systems that could have been prevented only if effective KM systems were in place.

REFERENCES

Alavi, M., & Leidner, D. E. (2001). Review: Knowledge Management and Knowledge Management Systems: Conceptual Foundations and Research Issues. *Management Information Systems Quarterly*, *25*(1), 107–136. doi:10.2307/3250961

Bellardo, S., Karwan, K. R., & Wallace, W. A. (1984). Managing the Response to Disasters Using Microcomputers. *Interfaces*, *14*(2), 29–39. doi:10.1287/inte.14.2.29

Booth, S. A. S. (1993). *Crisis management strategy: competition and change in modern enterprises*. London, New York: Routledge.

Braverman, M. (2003). Managing the human impact of crisis. *Risk Management*, *50*(5), 10–19.

Burnell, L., Priest, J., & Durrett, J. (2004). Developing and Maintaining Knowledge Management System for Dynamic, Complex Domains. In Gupta, J., & Sharma, S. (Eds.), *Creating Knowledge Based Organizations*. London: IGP. doi:10.4018/9781591401629.ch010

Chandler, R., & Wallace, D. (2004). Business Continuity Planning After September 11. *Disaster Recovery Journal*, *17*(3), 24–28.

Cho, H., & Turoff, M. (2003). Delphi Structure and Group Size in Asynchronous Computer Mediated Communication. *Paper presented at the AMCIS 2003*.

Davenport, T. H., & Prusak, L. (1998). *Working Knowledge*. Harvard Business School Press.

Fink, S. (1986). *Crisis Management. Planning for the Inevitable*. New York: American Management Association, AMACOM.

Hackbarth, G. (1998, August 1998). The Impact of Organizational Memory on IT Systems, *paper presented at the Fourth Americas Conference on Information Systems*.

Hermann, C. F. (1965). Some consequences of crisis which limit the viability of organizations. *Administrative Science Quarterly*, 8(1), 61–82. doi:10.2307/2390887

Iakovou, E., & Douligeris, C. (2001). An information management system for the emergency management of hurricane disasters. *International Journal of Risk Assessment and Management*, 2(3/4), 243–262. doi:10.1504/IJRAM.2001.001508

Jennex, M. E. (2004). Emergency Response Systems: The Utility Y2K Experience. [JITTA]. *Journal of IT Theory and Application*, 6(3), 85–102.

Jennex, M. E. (2005). What is Knowledge Management? *International Journal of Knowledge Management*, 1(4), i–iv.

Jennex, M. E. (2006). Open Source Knowledge Management. *International Journal of Knowledge Management*, 2(4), i–iv.

Jennex, M. E., & Olfman, L. (2006). A Model of Knowledge Management Success. *International Journal of Knowledge Management*, 2(3), 51–68. doi:10.4018/jkm.2006070104

Kitamato, A. (2005) Digital typhoon: Near real-time aggregation, recombination and delivery of typhoon-related information. Proceeding of the 4th International Symposium on Digital Earth. Retrieved October 26, 2005 from http://www.cse.iitb.ac.in/~neela/MTP/Stage1-Report.pdf

Kostman, J. T. (2004). 20 Rules for Effective Communication in a Crisis. *Disaster Recovery Journal.*, 17(2), 20.

Lee, J., & Bui, T. (2000). A Template-based Methodology for Disaster Management Information Systems. *Proceedings of the 33rd Hawaii International Conference on System Sciences*.

March, J. G., & Simon, H. A. (1958). *Organizations*. New York: John Wiley & Sons.

Miller, D. (2004). Exposing the Errors: An Examination of the Nature of Organizational Crisis. In *Responding to Crisis: A Rhetorical Approach to Crisis Communication*. Mahwah, NJ, London: Lawrence Erlbaum Associates.

Murphy, T., & Jennex, M. E. (2006). Knowledge Management, Emergency Response, and Hurricane Katrina. *International Journal of Intelligent Control and Systems*, 11(4), 199–208.

Myers, N. (1999). *Manager's guide to contingency planning for disasters: protecting vital facilities and critical operations*. New York: Wiley.

Panko, R. R. (2003). SLAMMER: The First Blitz Worm. *Communications of the AIS, CAIS, 11*(12).

Patton, D., & Flin, R. (1999). Disaster Stress: An Emergency Management Perspective. *Disaster Prevention and Management*, 8(4), 261–267. doi:10.1108/09653569910283897

Raman, M., Ryan, T., & Olfman, L. (2006). Knowledge Management Systems for Emergency Preparedness: The Claremont University Consortium Experience. *International Journal of Knowledge Management*, 2(3), 33–50. doi:10.4018/jkm.2006070103

Rice, R. E. (1987). Information, Computer Mediates Communications and Organizational Innovation. *The Journal of Communication*, 37(4), 65–94. doi:10.1111/j.1460-2466.1987.tb01009.x

Rice, R. E. (1990). From Adversity to Diversity: Applications for Communication Technology to Crisis Management. *Advances in Telecommunications Management*, 3, 91–112.

Seeger, M. W., Sellnow, T. L., & Ulmer, R. R. (2003). *Communication and Organizational Crisis*. Westport, CT: Praeger Publishers.

Townsend, F. F. (2006). *The Federal Response to Hurricane Katrina, Lessons Learned*. United States of America: Department of Homeland Security.

Turoff, M. (1972). Delphi Conferencing: Computer Based Conferencing with Anonymity. *Journal of Technological Forecasting and Social Change, 3*(2), 159–204. doi:10.1016/S0040-1625(71)80012-4

Turoff, M. (2002). Past and Future Emergency Response Information Systems. *Communications of the ACM, 45*(4), 29–32. doi:10.1145/505248.505265

Turoff, M., Chumer, M., Van de Walle, B., and Yao, X., (2004). The Design of a Dynamic Emergency Response Management Information System (DERMIS). *The Journal of Information Technology Theory and Application (JITTA), 5*:4, 2004, 1-35.

Turoff, M., & Hiltz, S. R. (1995). Computer Based Delphi Processes. In Adler, M., & Ziglio, E. (Eds.), *Gazing Into the Oracle: The Delphi Method and Its Application to Social Policy and Public Health* (pp. 56–88). London: Kingsley Publishers.

Von Krogh, G. (1998). Care in Knowledge Creation. *California Management Review, 40*(3), 133–153.

This work was previously published in International Journal of Information Systems for Crisis Response and Management, Volume 1, Issue 3, edited by Murray E. Jennex, pp. 69-83, copyright 2009 by IGI Publishing (an imprint of IGI Global).

Chapter 14
A Unified Localizable Emergency Events Scale

Eli Rohn
New Jersey Institute of Technology, USA

Denis Blackmore
New Jersey Institute of Technology, USA

ABSTRACT

Managers of emergencies face challenges of complexity, uncertainty, and unpredictably. Triadic constraints imply requisite parsimony in describing the essence of the emergency, its magnitude and direction of development. Linguistic separation increases as the crisis management organization is more complex and made up of diverse constituents. Therefore, a standard objective emergency scale is vital to quantify and unambiguously communicate the nature of any emergency. Previous work laid the foundations for an objective measurable emergency event scale. This article proposes a unified emergency scale based on a mathematical model, accompanied by several examples spanning local to national events.

INTRODUCTION

The American Heritage College Dictionary defines emergency as "a serious situation or occurrence that happens unexpectedly and demands immediate action" (American Heritage Dictionary 2000). There are numerous scales that attempt to define degrees of emergencies. These scales tend to describe the characteristics of the event itself rather than the consequences. Such scales are ill-suited to

DOI: 10.4018/978-1-60960-609-1.ch014

describe emergencies in a way that is meaningful for response. People assume there is a positive relationship between the magnitude of an event and the magnitude of the emergency it causes, but this is not always the case. For example, a strong earthquake in a deserted area may create a smaller emergency compared to a moderate earthquake in a densely populated area. A useful emergency scale should accurately describe the nature and magnitude of the crisis.

The need for a unified, emergency scale is vital to facilitate clear communication and mutual understanding of the nature of the emergency, by the public, government agencies, and responding organizations. It has been stated that "50% of the problems with communication are due to individuals using the same words with different meanings. The remaining 50% are due to individuals using different words with the same meanings" (Appleby, Forlin et al. 2003). They further discuss how legislation still has not provided definitions of "disaster" or "emergency", as well as the difference in impact and immediacy of response. An objectively calculable emergency scale should therefore quantify and clearly communicate the notion of "emergency". This article proposes such an emergency scale that could be understood and used at different scopes and by various clientele – internationally, nationally, regionally, at the municipality level, as well as by global companies through local organizations. Further, the proposed model satisfied all five roles of system science (Warfield 2003): it describes the physical world and portrays the results of interactions among a few of its components; it proposes a generic design; it is a constituent of "science of complexity" as it enlarges the domain of demonstrable results in the service of humanity; and, it is actionable, as it has linguistic clarity and a model that suggests clear direction of actions essential to resolve emergencies. Our model addresses several of Warfield's Twenty Laws of Complexity (Warfield 2002). It does not require humans to process more that three components at a time (triadic constraint). The model renders a parsimonious description of any

emergency. It addresses the challenge of vertical incoherence as it can show the right aggregated level to decision makers at different organizational levels. Similar to the CRISSI project (Asproth and Håkansson 2007) we consider all relevant factors of emergencies in a balanced fashion. However, while CRISSI limits itself to flooding, our abstract model can be applied to any emergency.

Related Work

Scales relating to natural phenomena that may result in an emergency are numerous. This section provides a review of emergency related scales. We concentrate mainly on weather and environmental scales that provide a common understanding and lexicon with which to understand the level of intensity and impact of a crisis. Some scales are used before and/or during a crisis to predict the potential intensity and impact of an event and provide an understanding that is useful for preventative and recovery measures. Other scales are used for post-event classification. Most of these scales are descriptive rather than quantitative, which makes them subjective and ambiguous.

1805: The Beaufort Wind Scale

One of the oldest weather related scales still in use is the Beaufort Wind Scale. It was created in 1805 by British Rear-Admiral, Sir Francis Beaufort and classifies wind based upon both its speed and the observed effects the wind has on the sea and

Table 1. Beaufort Scale (excerpt)

Beaufort scale number	Descriptive term	Units in km/h	Units in knots	Description on Land	Description at Sea
0	Calm	0	0	Smoke rises vertically	Sea like a mirror.
1 - 3	Light winds	<=19	<=10	Wind felt on face; leaves rustle; ordinary vanes moved by wind.	Small wavelets, ripples formed but do not break: A glassy appearance maintained.
5	Fresh winds	30 - 39	17-21	Small trees in leaf begin to sway; crested wavelets form on inland waters	Moderate waves, taking a more pronounced long form; many white horses are formed - a chance of some spray

land. This ranked scale, with 12 levels, goes from calm (Beaufort number 0) to Hurricane (Beaufort number 12) and thus is used in all conditions, not just emergencies. Each level has an observed effect associated with it together with a wind speed and wave height. Therefore, one can estimate the wind speed by visual inspection (NOAA 2006). This scale is used as a dimension within other emergency scales.

1931: Modified Mercalli Intensity Scale

The Modified Mercalli Intensity (MMI) scale is used to describe the intensity of visible damage by comparing the damage recorded after the event to a set scale of possibilities. The set scale of possibilities has twelve possible categories which all events must fall under. For example – *"light"*, *"moderate"*, *"violent"* (State of California 2003). The scale has no mathematical basis and therefore can vary greatly depending on the individual who is interpreting the damage (Bolt 1993).

1935: Richter Scales

The Richter Magnitude Scale developed by Charles F. Richter in 1935 (USGS 2006) is used to measure the magnitude of earthquakes. The United States Geological Survey takes great care to clearly define the differences between *intensity* and *magnitude* as there are two different scales used to determine each.

"Intensity is based on the observed effects of ground shaking on people, buildings, and natural features. It varies from place to place within the disturbed region depending on the location of the observer with respect to the earthquake epicenter" (USGS 2006).

The Intensity, as we can see above is based on observable effects, which are not calculated by the Richter scale. This differs greatly from magnitude which is based on the overall measured amplitude of the waves originating from the epicenter of the earthquake.

"Magnitude is related to the amount of seismic energy released at the hypocenter of the earthquake. It is based on the amplitude of the earthquake waves recorded on instruments which have a common calibration. The magnitude of an earthquake is thus represented by a single, instrumentally determined value (USGS 2006).

The magnitude is expressed in decimals and whole numbers. Each whole number represents a magnitude increase of 31 fold. This means that for each level of magnitude, 1, 2, 3, etc., the overall energy being released in the earthquake increases by 31 times. The magnitude of the Richter scale is calculated as follows:

$$Magnitude = \log_{10} A + (Distance\ correction\ factor)$$

where "A" is the amplitude of the seismic wave measured in millimeters. The distance correction

Table 2. Modified Mercalli Scale (excerpt)

MMI Value	Shaking Severity	Summary Damage	Full Description
V	Light	Pictures Move	Felt outdoors; direction estimated. Sleepers wakened. Liquids disturbed, some spilled. Small unstable objects displaced or upset. Doors swing, close, open. Shutters, pictures move. Pendulum clocks stop, start, change rate.
VII	Strong	Nonstructural Damage	Difficult to stand. Noticed by drivers of motor cars. Hanging objects quiver. Furniture broken. Damage to masonry D, including cracks. Weak chimneys broken at roof line. Fall of plaster, loose bricks, stones, tiles. Some cracks in masonry C

factor is included in the magnitude formula to compensate for the variation in the distance between individual seismographs and the epicenter of the earthquakes.

1969: Saffir-Simpson Hurricane Scale

The severity of a hurricane is further described by the Saffir-Simpson Hurricane Scale. The scale was initially developed by Herbert Saffir in 1969 and was based entirely on wind speed. Saffir gave the scale to the National Hurricane Center and Bob Simpson, then director of the center, added the effects of storm surge and flooding. The five category scale is defined by wind speed and describes the expected damage from the wind and storm surges. For example, a Category One hurricane has winds from 74-95mph and may cause some coastal road flooding with damage primarily limited to mobile homes and trees. A Category Five hurricane, on the other hand, is a hurricane with winds of over 155 mph and can be expected to cause complete roof failure on many residences and industrial buildings or even complete building failures (FEMA 2006).

1971: The Fujita Tornado Scale

The Saffir-Simpson Hurricane scale assignment of category is based upon current hurricane conditions. In contrast, tornados are assigned scale ratings after the fact. The Fujita scale infers tornado intensity (wind speeds) by analyzing wind damage after the tornado passed through an area (NOAA 2005). Surveyors measure the approximate path width and length of the tornado's funnel and from that assign a rank of F0 (weak) to F5 (violent). Each category in the scale has a descriptive phrase and is associated with a range of wind speed and probable damage descriptions. A weakness of this scale is that the rating is subjective and the characteristics of the tornado are inferred indirectly from the damage it left behind.

1999: Air-Quality Index

The Air Quality Index (AQI), (formerly known as the Pollutant Standards Index) was issued on July 23, 1999 by the U.S. Environmental Protection Agency (EPA) for daily air quality reporting to the public (USEPA 2008). This new index reflects revisions to the primary health-based national ambient air quality standards for ground-level ozone and particulate matter issued by the EPA in 1997. The EPA calculates the AQI and issues a daily report for five major air pollutants regulated by the Clean Air Act. The pollutants are: ground-level ozone, particle pollution (also known as particulate matter), carbon monoxide, sulfur dioxide, and nitrogen dioxide (STAPPA and ALAPCO 2006). The scale aggregates measures of those five pollutants giving a range from 0 to 500 clustered into six categories, ranging from "Good" (0 to 50) to "Hazardous" (300 and above). Each category corresponds to a different level of health concern. The AQI is also used to trigger health alerts (category 5). AQI values over 300 trigger health warnings of emergency conditions as the entire population is more likely to be affected.

2001: US Homeland Security Terror Alert Scale

Subsequent to the 9/11 Jihadists' terrorist attack, the United States Department of Homeland Security created a color-coded taxonomy of five terror alertness levels, ranging from *Low (green)* to *Severe (red)*. Each level has a short written description associated with it. The scale is nominal, even though every level is also identified by a number (DHS 2001).

2006: Emergency Scales Survey

Gomez, Rohn et. al. used a computer-mediated modified Delphi process and a survey to elicit emergency scale ideas from subjects who were knowledgeable in emergencies, yet no one was an emergency expert or a full-time first responder by training or vocation. The researchers identified three leading ordinal emergency scales (Gomez, Plotnick et al. 2007). Rohn's independent analysis of those scales revealed underlying basic dimensions that define emergency events. Those underlying basic dimensions are: Scope, Topographical Change (or lack thereof), and Rate of Change. The rest of this article articulates each dimension, proposes a unified localizable emergency scale, and discusses the characteristics and usage of the proposed scale.

Proposed Unified Emergency Scale

Any emergency can be defined using three orthogonal dimensions: (a) scope (b) topographical change (or lack thereof) and (c) speed of change. The intersection of the three dimensions provides a detailed scale for defining emergencies. Figure 3 illustrates the three dimensions and the values they may assume. The scale provides a 3D surface for professional and advanced usage, which is convertible to an equidistance numeric scale for public communications. Using an equidistance numeric scale is universally usable: it does not require meaning preservation in translation from one natural language to another as is the case with nominal scales; it eliminates misinterpretation by laic audience, as is the case with logarithmic scales, such as the Richter scale.

Scope

Scope of change varies from to small to humongous. For the purposes of this proposed scale it is a continuous variable with a lower limit of zero and a theoretical calculable upper limit. For the purposes of this scale we use only two parameters that form the scope: percent of affected humans out of the entire population, and damages, or loss, as a percentile of a given Gross National Product (GNP), which is a country's yearly output of goods and services. When used locally this could be represented by a Gross State Product (GSP) or Gross Regional Product appropriate to the entity under emergency.

The model, and specifically the scope, does not incorporate geographical size because we believe that size is not independent of the number of people affected, and should therefore not constitute an additional coordinate for scale measurements. If the phenomena happened in an isolated location its size would be rather meaningless as it has little effect on humans.

Many natural and man-made phenomena have a power law distribution. Examples are city size, income, country (state) size, word usage in corpora, ecological systems, and more (Li 1999). Other natural phenomena have logarithmic characteristics. Case in point: human hearing of sound and earthquake magnitude. Intuitively, *scope* makes a good candidate for such a power distribution. Additionally, emergencies are self-similar (Koehler 1995), where the main difference is the perception of the "size" of the emergency and the granular details. Therefore, we define scope as follows:

Figure 1. Emergency dimensions

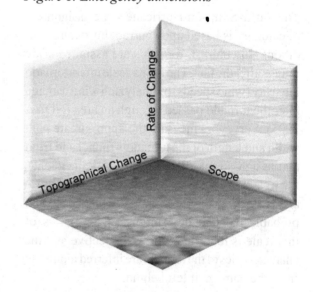

Figure 2. Scope calculations based on events

Location	Year	GNP	Population	Description	Affected Population	Losses + Rescue costs	1 - 5 scope	Data Source
US	1995	8.61E+12	260,000,000	Oklahoma City Bombing	759			NHI
US	2002	9.41E+12	275,000,000	Mississippi Nov. Storms	1,226	$ 8,296,200.00	0.01	FEMA
US	2003	1.015E+13	289,000,000	Ohio Storm	7,189	$ 752,516,100.00	0.08	FEMA
US	2005	1.241E+13	295,000,000	Huricane Katrina	1,200,000	$ 40,000,000,000.00	0.33	FEMA
Nowhere	2006	1.241E+13	300,000,000	Hypothetical Pandemic	75,000,000.00	$ 1,500,000,000,000.00	4.08	
Israel	2006	2.72E+11	6,000,000	War	1,750,000	$ 7,000,000,000.00	1.72	MFA.GOV.IL

Figure 3. Hypothetical rate of change in number of victims showing two critical points

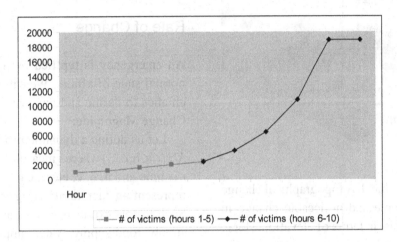

$$RawScope = \left(\frac{Victims}{Population} + \frac{\delta * Monetary\ Losses}{GNP} \right)^{\left(\frac{\ln(victims)}{\ln(losses)} \right)^{|\beta|}}$$

(1.1)

β is a coefficient which we calculated to be 1.26 ± 0.03 using sample data of US emergencies and statistics from the 2006 attack of the Hizballah on Israel, as reported by the Israeli government. δ is a financial resilience coefficient. We estimate it to be 1000 for the US, using sample data of US emergencies. We estimate it to be 600 for a country like Israel, using statistics from the 2006 aforementioned event.

$$MaxScope = \left(\frac{0.7 * Population}{Population} + \frac{0.5 * GNP * \delta}{GNP} \right)^{\frac{\ln(victims)}{\ln(losses)}}$$

(1.2)

We loosely assume that a society whose majority of the population (70% in our model)

is affected and half of its GNP is drained as a result of a calamity reaches a breaking point of disintegration. Sociologists and economists may shed light as to what a better estimate could be.

$$Scope = \left(\frac{RawScope}{MaxScope} \right) * \alpha$$

(1.3)

Where α is the normalized scale to be used. We opted for α =5, which yields a scope between zero and five.

Figure 4 shows a few examples based on real events using α =5, β = 1.26, δ=700 for Israel and δ=1000 for the United States. Note that US GNP and population are rounded estimates.

Topographical Change

This dimension indicates if the emergency has to do with some kind of a topographical change

Figure 4. Large scope high rate of change topographical emergency

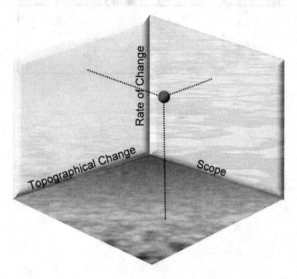

or is non-topographical. A topographical change means a measurable and noticeable change in land characteristics, in terms of elevation, slope, orientation and land coverage The later can be either natural (e.g., trees) or artificial (e.g., houses).

Topographical changes have a direct impact on the accessibility to an emergency site. Compare the 1929 stock market collapse (a form of an emergency) to that of 9/11/2001. They both happened in the same geographical area – down town Manhattan. Both claimed lives and great financial losses. One involved a major topographical change, at least on a local scale, which made the response physically more dangerous and more difficult.

For the purpose of our proposed emergency scale, topographical change is treated as a continuum ranging between 0 and 1 that gives the estimated visual fractional change in the environment. The fraction is the ratio between the geographical volume occupied before the disaster and the volume occupied after the disaster, all in relation to sea level in order to anchor the measure to a uniform constant. For example, if the volume of man-made structures, farming and natural vegetation and inanimate natural structures occupied

three cubic mile before a disaster, and only two cubic miles after a disaster occurred, then the size of the topographical change is $1-(2:3) = 1/3$. Measuring deformations by means of differential Synthetic Aperture Radar (SAR) interferometry could be a practical means to get such information quickly and reliably (Dixon 1994; Vettore, Ponte et al. 2003). ,

Rate of Change

An emergency is typified by a departure from normal state of affairs. We can use some mathematics to define and analyze a "departure", or Change Magnitude:

Let us define a dynamic process $P = \Delta x/\Delta t = X(x, t, a, b, c,...)$ where x measures an environment, t is time and a, b, c, etc. are external parameters representing factors affecting the environment. Such factors can be degree of autonomy, energy supply, food supply, water supply; "acceptable" level of political corruption, etc. $\Delta x/\Delta t$ denotes the change of the environment over time. ("Δ" is the Greek letter Delta - short for "change")

Local maximum, minimum and inflexion points occur where the graph of a function P has a horizontal tangent. Such points are called *critical points*. Some critical points can be more than that – they can be in a place where the curve has an irregular behavior such as a cusp or a point of self-intersection. Such a point is termed a *singular point*. (Anton 1988). We can view a critical point as a relatively small magnitude departure from a given state, where continuity and connectedness still exist. In contrast, a singular point is a large and sharp departure from a given state, where continuity and connectedness are not assured.

We are interested in calculating $\Delta victims/\Delta time$ and $\Delta(losses)/\Delta time$. Figure 5 illustrates a linear (1.25X/hour) growth in victims during the first five hours of an emergency, followed by an exponential growth ($x^{1.03}$/hour) in the next four hours and then zero change in the tenth hour. The change rates represent a critical point and a singular point respectively. These rates of change would typically be made for Δt small in comparison to the time increments at which the measurements are made. More precisely, if the rate of change is measured at time t_m, and the average increment between measurements is Δ_{av}, then the increments for measuring the rate of change are taken around t_m, with $\Delta t \ll \Delta_{av}$.

THE EMERGENCY SCALE MODEL

The scale is a normalized function whose variables are *Scope* (S), *Topography* (T), and *Rate of Change* (D), which may be determined by using certain clientele specific parameter values, whose relations determine the magnitude of the emergency. If one is seeking a single number to gauge the scale of an emergency (which is probably clientele specific), it should be a function of the coordinates in the proposed scale space; that is, it should be expressible in the form

$$E = Emergency = f\big(S,T,D\big), \qquad (1.4)$$

where the function *f*, which is likely to depend on the particular scope involved, needs to be specified. A reasonably good general choice would be a weighted average – with weights determined by the clientele – that can be expressed as

$$E = Emergency = f\big(S,T,D\big) = w_S S + w_T T + w_D D, \qquad (1.5)$$

where $0 \le w_S, w_T, w_D$ and $w_S + w_T + w_D = 1$. There are, of course, other simple choices for the function that can further heighten the effects of one or more of the coordinates; for example, if along with taking the last coefficient above to be significantly larger than the other two, we want to enhance the importance of the rate of change

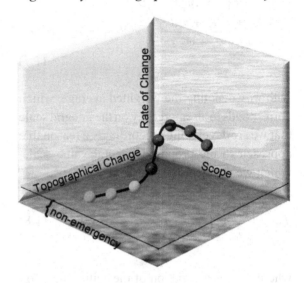

Figure 5. Dynamical graph and a critical surface

(which seems to be an appropriate approach for many applications), we could modify (1.5) as follows:

$$E = Emergency = f\big(S,T,D\big) = w_S S + w_T T + w_D D^2, \qquad (1.6)$$

or use an even larger power of *D*. This by no means exhausts the plausible choices: perhaps a particular clientele might hit upon the right choice for them by doing a bit of data analysis mixed with some intuition based upon experience.

Simplified Scale for Public Communications

In some instances, it may be preferable to have an integral scale to more simply and dramatically convey the extent of an emergency, with a range say from 1 to 10, and 10 representing the direst emergency. This can be obtained from the function *E* above in any number of ways. The following approach is as good as or better than most others: depending on the clients' perceptions, minimum values for each of the variables *S*, *T*, *D* that constitute the direst emergency can be specified and denoted as S_m, T_m, and D_m. Then we define

$$E_m := wav\left\{w_S S_m, w_T T_m, w_D D_m\right\} =$$
$$= \frac{w_S S_m + w_T T_m + w_D D_m}{w_S + w_T + w_D} = w_S S_m + w_T T_m + w_D D_m,$$

$$(1.7)$$

with *wav* denoting the weighted average, which corresponds to an emergency on the integral scale that we are developing. Accordingly a reasonable approach to the proposed integral value scale, which we denote as E_*, is to define it as

$$E_* := \left\lceil \frac{10E}{E_m} \right\rceil_{10},$$

$$(1.8)$$

where $\lceil x \rceil_{10}$ is a variation of the ceiling function defined as the smallest integer greater than or equal to the real number x, except it assumes the value 10 for all x greater or equal to 10.

The integral scale, and therefore the ceiling function, need not be confined to "10". We suggest that clientele designate ceiling values to correspond with the size of their oversight responsibility. For example, towns and cities may want to use "10", counties may want to use "50", States or their equivalent may want to use "100" while large socio-political entities such as the European Union or the United States may find it more appropriate to use "1000" for their ceiling value.

DISCUSSION

A simplistic emergency scale can be expressed as a coordinate in the *STD*-space. A more simplistic approach which might be easier to communicate to non-experts such as the public at large would be a single number. In this section we use a single real world example, hurricane Katrina, to demonstrate the usage and utility of our scale using coordinates and a single number. The next section

hints at additional utility that experts may derive from the proposed mathematical model.

Hurricane Katrina

We collected the following data about hurricane Katrina form several sources, primarily from FEMA (FEMA 2006; FEMA 2007) and NASA (NASA 2005). The hurricane affected the states of Alabama, Florida, Louisiana, and Mississippi.

Data

Number of people killed: 1800. Number of people directly affected: over 5.5 million. Estimated 400,000 jobs were lost as a result of the hurricane. About 89,000 square miles (slightly larger than the size of Great Britain) was flooded. Wind damages covered at least double that size, totaling in about 180,000 square miles. Monetary damages (as of Feb 28, 2007): individual assistance for housing and other needs: $44.28 billion; public assistance for protective measures, debris removal, road & bridges, and public buildings: $179.45 billion; national flood insurance program claims paid: $15.65 billion. Total monetary damages as of February 2007: $239.38 billion. The Gross State Product (GSP) for 2005 in billions of US dollars, as reported by (SSTI 2005) was as follows,: Alabama $132.213; Florida 595.846; Louisiana 135.362; Mississippi 69.672, totaling $933.093 billion

Scope

Using the data we calculated the raw scope to be 0.87, the max scope 2.28 and the normalized scope 0.38.

Topographical Change

Due to lack of access to volumetric topographical change data we use the ratio of the affected area to the affected states yielding 180,000/222,409=0.80; obviously this estimate could be improved greatly by the application of more sophisticated data collection techniques.

Rate of Change

Duration $= \Delta t = 13$ days. Victims $= \Delta v = 1800$ people killed. Losses – we split this up into loss of money and loss of jobs: $\Delta m = \$239.38$ billion dollars; $\Delta j = 400,000$ jobs lost. We recognize that putting a comparative value on life is ethically impossible. However, various legal systems through their courts and insurance companies do so for practical reasons, and so do we. Reckoning that loss of lives is thrice as important as loss of money, which is twice as important as loss of jobs, and that loss of life should be considered on a scale of hundreds, loss of money should be regarded on a scale of billions, while loss of jobs should be on a scale of thousands, we take the following weighted average as a measure of the rate of change:

$$D := \frac{1}{9}\left(6\frac{\Delta v}{\Delta t} + 2\frac{\Delta m}{\Delta t} + \frac{\Delta j}{\Delta t}\right) = \frac{1}{9}\left[6(18) + 2(239.38) + (400)\right] = 109.64$$

We note here that our reckoning of the relative weights of lives, money and jobs lost – as are the scales on which they are based – has been chosen somewhat arbitrarily based upon what we deem plausible reasoning. Naturally, other clients or agencies might find very different weights and scales better suited to their purposes.

Katrina Emergency Size

Using equation 1.4 we obtain Emergency $=E =$ $f(0.38, 0.80, 109.64)$. Using a cube that depicts all three orthogonal variables, the Katrina emergency would be graphed approximately at the location of the floating ball in Figure 6. In order to obtain a single value E to characterize the emergency, we would have to have the weights w_S, w_T, and w_D along with the preferred function – say (1.5), (1.6)

or some alternative. For purposes of illustration, we choose $w_S = 0.5$, $w_T = 0.25$, and $w_D = 0.25$ and select the linear form (1.5). With these choices, we compute that

$$E = (0.5)(0.38) + (0.25)(0.8) + (0.25)(109.64) = 27.80.$$

In order to compute E*, we need to decide on a reasonable value of E_m in accordance with (1.7). The following values seem plausible as thresholds for an emergency at the local (city) level: $S_m =$ 1.0; $T_m = 2.0$; and $D_m = 150$. With these values specified, we compute from (1.7) that

$$E_m = wav\left\{(0.5)(1.0), (0.25)(2.0), (0.25)(150)\right\} = 38.5.$$

Whence from (1.8) we find that

$$E_* = \left\lceil\frac{10E}{E_m}\right\rceil_{10} = \left\lceil\frac{278}{38.5}\right\rceil_{10} = \lceil 7.22 \rceil_{10} = 7.22,$$

which is certainly consistent with our perception of the magnitude of the emergency caused by Katrina at the level of a city such as New Orleans. Applying a national ceiling value of 1000, and thresholds for an emergency at the national level with $Sm = 80.0$; $Tm = 200.0$; and $Dm = 1000.0$ we find that for the US the emergency level for public communication on a national level would be:

$$E_* = \left\lceil\frac{1000E}{E_m}\right\rceil_{1000} = \left\lceil\frac{27800}{340}\right\rceil_{1000} = \lceil 81.76 \rceil_{1000} = 82\,(rounded),$$

which appears consistent with the emergency caused by Katrina at the national level, notwithstanding the news media coverage effects.

Additional Utility

If we had a more detailed timeline on all of these changes over the duration of the emergency, we could plot a graph of the losses against time (say on a daily basis) and investigate the derivative of an interpolated function as in Figure 5. This graph would then be plotted as the function

Obviously, different weights could be assigned to the various components of the rate of change. The weights could be developed using a variety of techniques, one of which is reliance on data gathered from past events.

More utility may be drawn from the scale than we have covered here, which requires additional mathematical development, and will be explored in a paper that is in progress. As emergencies are probably too complex to be completely predicted by a single number, it is more likely that a particular clientele would postulate a *critical* or *emergency surface* based upon experience and some analysis. Such a surface in $STD-$space might take the form of the locus or solution set of an equation of type

$$S_E : \quad F(S, T, D) = 0. \qquad (1.9)$$

The nature of these critical surfaces suggest that in practice they are likely to include singularities, and have projections (that would appear to play a significant role in emergency scaling) onto different coordinate planes that may exhibit standard catastrophes in the sense of Thom (Lu 1976).

If one had such a critical surface, it could be used for predicting emergencies before they happen. This might be done along the following lines. Points in the scale space would be plotted over time – using some interpolation method to join points taken at discrete times to comprise a curve (or trajectory) charting the evolution of events. Then if it is observed that a measured point is fairly close to the critical surface, one could use some standard extrapolation procedure to predict an intersection of the trajectory with S_e at some time in the near future, thereby indicating an imminent emergency and providing an opportunity to take certain necessary measures. This is better than simply noting that a point is now near the critical surface, since no matter how

close the point is the nature of the evolutionary trajectory might still show that no emergency is on the horizon. For example, suppose the critical surface is just a plane, and the trajectory is close to but also parallel to this plane.

Integration with Emergency Management Systems

The proposed emergency scale can be integrated into emergency alert systems such as the Global Disaster Alert and Coordination System (GDACS) which "provides near real-time alerts about natural disasters around the world and tools to facilitate response coordination" (United Nations and EU Civil Protection Commission 2009). The integration will necessitate the development of an emergency scale module. Alternatively, it would be possible to use an independent system that handles the input, calculations, and output of the emergency scale, and provides web services for other systems to use its capabilities. Such web services could make use of existing emergency management and collaboration schemas, such as the Common Alerting Protocol (CAP) Emergency Data Exchange Language (EDXL), the W3C Emergency Information Interoperability Framework (W3C 2005) and similar protocols and many emergency related portals surveyed by (Rohn 2007). A full working prototype of such an independent application is expected to be available towards the end of 2009.

CONCLUSION

This article proposes a unified emergency scale based on three orthogonal dimensions discovered in a previous research. The proposed scale is formulated using abstract concepts that transcend natural languages, understanding of logarithmic scales, individual organizations, counties or countries, but have the capability of integrating aspects that are sensitive to individual clientele.

The response to any given emergency is a direct derivative of these three dimensions. The model addresses some of the challenges and concerns discussed in the Emergence and Complexity literature, a feature that is entirely absent in emergency scales we have identified in the related work section. The management of an emergency event is an exercise in adaptation of complex systems to a rapidly changing environment. The adaptation process can be greatly improved by utilizing an objective measurable event scale which serves as a well grounded scaffold supporting many organizational processes and interactions that occur in an emergency.

The emergency scale is computed as a 3D surface for professional use and a single number on a simple equidistance numeric scale for public consumption, indicating the magnitude of a particular emergency, in lieu of partial, ambiguous and subjective scales that exist to date. Future mathematical development and analysis of the scale may provide sophisticated methods for emergency prediction, and may force organizations adopting it to define their tolerance to surprise changes and thresholds for emergencies during the planning phase rather than after the fact.

REFERENCES

W3C. (2005, last updated on 2008). *Emergency Information Interoperability Framework*. Retrieved 20 February, 2009, from http://www.w3.org/2005/Incubator/eiif/charter-20071203.

American Heritage Dictionary. (2000). *The American Heritage Dictionary of the English Language, Fourth Edition*. Houghton Mifflin Company.

Anton, H. (1988). *Calculus with Analitic Geometry, Third Edition*. John Weily and Sons, isbn 0-471-85045-4.

Appleby, M., Forlin, G., et al. (2003). The Law Relating to Emergencies and Disasters. *Tolley's Handbook of Disaster and Emergency Management: Principles and Practice*. R. Lakha and T. Moore, Butterworth-Heinemann, isbn 0-406-97270-2.

Asproth, V., & Håkansson, A. (2007). *Complexity Challenges of Critical Situations Caused by Flooding*. Emergence: Complexity & Organization, vol 9(1): 37-43, issn 1532-7000.

Bolt, B. A. (1993). *Earthquakes: Newly Revised and Expanded*. W.H. Freeman, New York, NY

DHS. (2001, last updated on). *Citizen Guidance on the Homeland Security Advisory System*. Retrieved 24 August, 2006, from http://www.dhs.gov/.

Dixon, T. H. (1994, last updated on). *Sar Interferometry and Surface Change Detection*. Retrieved March 26, 2007, from http://southport.jpl.nasa.gov/scienceapps/dixon/index.html.

FEMA. (2006, last updated on 27-Jul-2007). *Frequently Requested National Statistics Hurricane Katrina – One Year Later*. Retrieved 20 February, 2009, from http://www.fema.gov/hazard/hurricane/2005katrina/anniversary_factsheet.shtm.

FEMA. (2006, last updated on 09-Jun-2006). *Saffir-Simpson Hurricane Scale*. Retrieved December 12, 2006, from http://www.fema.gov/hazard/hurricane/hu_about.shtm.

FEMA. (2007, last updated on 27-Jul-2007). *Hurricane Katrina Information*. Retrieved 20 February, 2009, from http://www.fema.gov/hazard/hurricane/2005katrina/index.shtm.

Gomez, E. A., Plotnick, L., et al. (2007). *Towards a Unified Public Safety Scale*. Hawaii International Conference on System Sciences (HICSS), Waikoloa, Hawaii.

Koehler, G. A. (1995). *Fractals and Path Dependent Processes: A Theoretical Approach for Characterizing Emergency Medical Responses to Major Disasters*. What Disaster Response Management Can Learn From Chaos Theory California, USA, California Research Bureau.

Li, W. (1999, last updated on 1999). *Zipf's Law*. Retrieved 24 august, 2006, from http://myhome.hanafos.com/~philoint/phd-data/Zipf's-Law-2.htm.

NASA. (2005, last updated on 2007). *Hurricanes Katrina and Rita Storm Track Map and Animation*. Retrieved March 26, 2007, from http://www.nasa.gov/vision/earth/lookingatearth/h2005_katrina.html.

NOAA. (2005, last updated on 2005). *The Fujita Scale*. Retrieved December 12, 2006, from http://www.crh.noaa.gov/glossary.php?letter=fujita.

NOAA. (2006, last updated on 2006). *Beaufort Wind Scale*. Retrieved January, 2007, from http://www.spc.noaa.gov/faq/tornado/beaufort.html.

Rohn, E. (2007). *A Survey of Schema Standards and Portals for Emergency Management and Collaboration. The 4th International Conference on Information Systems for Crisis Response and Management (ISCRAM)*. B. Van de Walle, P. Burghardtet al. Delft, the Netherlands Retrieved Access 2007 from.

SSTI. (2005, last updated on). *Real Gross State Product by State, 2001-2005*. Retrieved March 2007, 2007, from http://www.ssti.org/Digest/Tables/061206t.htm.

STAPPA and ALAPCO. (2006, last updated on). *Air Quality Index (Aqi) - a Guide to Air Quality and Your Health*. Retrieved December 12, 2006, from http://airnow.gov/index.cfm?action=static.aqi.

State of California. (2003, last updated on 2003). *Modified Mercalli Intensity Scale*. Retrieved January, 2007, from http://www.abag.ca.gov/bayarea/eqmaps/doc/mmi.html.

United Nations and EU Civil Protection Commission. (2009, last updated on 20 Feb 2009). *The Global Disaster Alert and Coordination System* Retrieved 20 February, 2009, from http://www.gdacs.org/.

USEPA. (2008, last updated on April 22, 2008). *Air Quality Index: A Guide to Air Quality and Your Health*. Retrieved 20 July, 2008, from http://airnow.gov/index.cfm?action=aqibroch.index.

USGS. (2006, last updated on 2006). *The Richter Magnitude Scale*. Retrieved January, 2007, from http://pubs.usgs.gov/gip/earthq4/severitygip.html.

Vettore, A., Ponte, S., et al. (2003). *Space-Based Surface Change Detection with Differential Synthetic-Aperture Radar (Sar) Interferometry: Potentialities and Preliminary Investigations*. Geomatica, vol 57(3): 326-334, issn 1195-1036

Warfield, J. N. (2002). *Understanding Complexity: Thought and Behavior*. AJAR Publishing Company, Palm Harbor, Florida, isbn 0-971-6962-0-9.

Warfield, J. N. (2003). A Proposal for Systems Science. *Systems Research and Behavioral Science, 20*(6), 507–520. doi:10.1002/sres.528

This work was previously published in International Journal of Information Systems for Crisis Response and Management, Volume 1, Issue 4, edited by Murray E. Jennex, pp. 1-14, copyright 2009 by IGI Publishing (an imprint of IGI Global).

Chapter 15
Disaster Management and Virtual Globes:
A High Potential for Developing Countries

Gunter Zeug
European Environment Agency, Denmark

Dominik Brunner
Fraunhofer Institute of Optronics, Germany

ABSTRACT

Today, the added value of geoinformation for crisis management is well known and accepted. However, experiences show that disaster management units on local administrative levels in the developing world often lack the use of Geographic Information Systems for analysing spatial interrelations and making their own maps. Various studies mention the shortage of financial resources, human capacity, and adequate knowledge as reasons for that. In recent years publically available virtual globes like Google Earth™, Microsoft® Bing™ Maps 3D or Nasa World Wind enjoy great popularity. The accessibility of worldwide high resolution satellite data, their intuitive user interface, and the ability to integrate own data support this success. In this chapter, the potential of these new geospatial technologies for supporting disaster preparedness and response is demonstrated, using the example of Google Earth™. Possibilities for the integration of data layers from third parties, the digitization of own layers, as well as the analytical capacities are examined. Furthermore, a printing module is presented, which supports the production of paper maps based on data previously collected and edited in Google Earth™. The efficiency of the proposed approach is demonstrated for a disaster management scenario in Legazpi, a Philippine city exposed to several natural hazards due to the vicinity to Mayon volcano and the annually occuring typhoons in the region. With this research, current technological trends in geospatial technologies are taken up and investigated on their potential for professional use. Moreover, it is demonstrated that by using freely available software general constraints for using GIS in developing countries can be overcome. Most importantly, the approach presented guarantees low cost for implementation and reproducibility, which is essential for its application in developing countries.

DOI: 10.4018/978-1-60960-609-1.ch015

INTRODUCTION

Reliable information is an essential prerequisite for crisis-related decision making and effective disaster management. Today, the added value of geoinformation for crisis management in the form of a map is well known and accepted. Visualising information on a map makes it more understandable than spreadsheets or reports. Maps – often based on satellite imagery – are used to provide updated information in the aftermath of a natural disaster. Applications include amongst others situation assessment, evacuation planning, damage assessment, reconstruction monitoring, as well as risk and vulnerability analysis (Voigt et al., 2007). The provision of maps supports efficient decision making and hence is an important part of effective disaster response. The map providers are typically highly specialised organisations dealing with geoinformation issues or national civilian or defence mapping authorities. The move from reactive map provision to more anticipative systems, based on preparatory mapping of 'hotspots' is consistently discussed within the geo-related disaster community. This can be achieved by enhancing capacities in affected countries in using geospatial information to support the full disaster management cycle. This is for example the mission of the United Nations Platform for Space-based Information for Disaster Management and Emergency Response - UN-SPIDER (2010). However, the use of Geographic Information Systems (GIS), the software that is typically used for map making is still not widely implemented in humanitarian organisations nor at local or regional disaster management authorities, not only in developing countries (ISIS, 2003; Verjee, 2007).

Several reasons are brought up in this context: high investment cost is often mentioned as constraint for using GIS effectively (Tanser & le Sueur, 2002). This can partly be invalidated. Today decreasing costs of hardware and mass storage facilitate the use of information technologies. Due to a large community, the development of open source geospatial tools has increased in recent years. Nevertheless, their use leaves a number of obstacles, which might be poor documentation, the need for training, and difficulties of configuring or extending open source solutions. An important factor, which must not be forgotten, is the high cost of data (Currion, 2006; Tanser & le Sueur, 2002). Both, commercial datasets and the acquisition and digitization of data by the end user might be substantial expense factors especially with increasing accuracy of the data. The more accurate data are available the better can be the decisions drawn on the basis of this data. Another reason not conducive for the implementation is the comprehensive knowledge required to use today's GIS packages. According to Currion (2009) the humanitarian community is slow in adapting new technologies due to the fact that technology is not their main focus and they have failed to identify how these technologies can save their resources.

In recent years geographic information technologies made great progress also influenced by the development and provision of virtual globes, such as Google Earth™, Microsoft® Bing™ Maps 3D, Nasa World Wind or ArcGIS® Explorer. Even if their options for geospatial analysis are limited, their introduction influenced the GIS domain, and brought it forward from exclusive, expensive, and technocratic tools towards geospatial information platforms available for non-geospatial experts and due to their availability free of charge to the mass market (Miller, 2006; Sui, 2008). The integration and accessibility of worldwide high resolution satellite data, their intuitive user interface, and the ability to integrate own data combined together with a high performance support their success.

In this paper, we propose a novel, free of cost, GIS concept to support disaster management in developing countries based on virtual globes, in particular Google Earth™. We analyse its capacities and constraints with regard to data collection and analysis. For the implementation of the concept, we integrate additional freely available third party tools for KML analysis. We demonstrate the efficiency and the charateristics of the proposed approach for a disaster preparedness and response study for Legazpi, Philippines. The city is exposed to several natural hazards like volcano and earthquakes and is frequently affected by typhoons. In November 2006 the city and region of Bicol was heavily affected by supertyphoon Durian. Large lahar flows from the slopes of the volcano Mayon buried houses killing 1.399 persons. The damage of the affected areas was estimated with US $ 66.4 million (EMDAT, 2008). With this research current technological trends in geographic information technologies are taken up and investigated on their potential for professional use. Moreover it is demonstrated that by using freely available software, general constraints for using GIS in developing countries can be overcome.

This paper is organized as following. In Sec. 2, a review on the use of GIS and Google Earth™ in disaster management is conducted and demands of geoinformation for disaster related tasks are presented. Sec. 3 highlights the capacities of virtual globes and gives a short comparison of well established tools. Sec. 4 presents the proposed technical concept which addresses the challenges of using GIS in developing countries in detail. In Sec. 5, the available dataset is described, while in Sec. 6 the derived products and the conducted analysis are highlighted. Sec. 7 discusses the characteristics of the proposed concept before Sec. 8 finishes this paper with concluding remarks.

GEOINFORMATION FOR DISASTER MANAGEMENT

Geographic information technology offers tools for acquiring, managing, analysing, and visualising spatial data. GIS based spatial analysis can strongly support all phases of disaster management. Possible applications for mitigation, preparation, response, and recovery are hazard vulnerability and risk assessment, situation and damage assessment, planning and logistics, reconstruction and site planning, program evaluation and many more. The potential use of GIS in disaster management was reviewed for example by Dash (1997). Within a comprehensive compilation Cova (1999) examines the role of GIS in emergency management and its four phases: mitigation, preparedness, response, and recovery. A more recent overview of GIS and GPS use in humanitarian emergencies is given by Kaiser et al. (2003). Cutter (2003) highlights applications of GIS to emergency response, describes constraints on its utilization and suggests further GIS related research based on the needs of the disaster management communities. Pisano (2005) calls on the integration of geoinformation into integrated information management systems for crisis response. The increasing use of GIS in the humanitarian field e.g. by UN agencies and manifold non governmental organizations (NGO) is brought up by Currion (2006). Tran et al. (2008) highlight the importance of integrating local knowledge, GIS and maps into the process of local disaster management. The analysis of using information technology (IT) in general for disaster management is addressed in Stephenson and Anderson (1997) and Marincioni (2007).

Today several service providers have been established intending to process and provide mainly satellite imagery based crisis information to support disaster relief. Two service providers to be named here are the 'Center for Satellite Based Crisis Information' (ZKI) of the German Remote Sensing Data Center (DFD) of the German Aerospace Center (DLR), and UNOSAT, the UN Institute for Training and Research (UNITAR) Operational Satellite Applications Programme. Furthermore, aiming at strengthening the European capacity to respond to emergency situations the European Comission is setting up an emergency response service within its Global Monitoring of Environment and Security (GMES) programme which should become fully operational in 2014. The service will provide rapid mapping products after the disaster event and thematic reference maps to support disaster preparedness and mitigation actions.

However, despite these success stories, GIS has still not been widely implemented in humanitarian business (Currion, 2006). Personal experiences show as well, that maps and data layers provided by service providers do not reach the level where the need for up-to-date maps is greatest: namely at regional and local level of exposed countries of the developing world (see also Tran et al. 2008).

According to experts working in regional and local disaster management, several baseline datasets are sufficient for efficient preparedness planning and risk assessment (Daep, 2008). Among these are hazard maps for understanding the potential extent of the possible event. Population maps are required for determining the number of people at risk from the different hazards and for evacuation planning. Knowing which critical facilities such as hospitals, police and fire brigades and evacuation centers are most vulnerable is another prerequisite for efficient planning. This is also relevant for building and infrastructure maps. Analysing their proximity to hazard zones is useful for assessing the potential impact on the infrastructure and thus supports proactive urban planning.

In recent years it has been demonstrated that Google Earth™ is an excellent, high level visualization platform for decision makers (Nourbakhsh et al., 2006). In the field of disaster management it was successfully applied to share post-disaster imagery and other related GIS data among affected communities and response agencies. Examples are from the aftermath of Hurricane Katrina in 2005 (Mills, 2008; Nourbakhsh et al., 2006; Yarbrough, 2005), the Pakistan earthquake in the same year (Nourbakhsh et al., 2006), the Californian wildfires (Mills, 2008), and the flash floods in Sulawesi Island, Indonesia in 2007 (Priyono, 2007). During recent crisis events Google set up a web service named Google Crisis Reponse, through its philantrophic arm google.org. The website publishes latest news, photos and videos from the crisis area, a person finder application allows postings about missing persons and a donation application enables the users to donate money to relief organisations involved in the crisis response. The website is also used to make available latest satellite imagery from the crisis area which can be downloaded and further examined in Google Earth™ and professional GIS tools. For instance, in the aftermath of the Haiti earthquake in January 2010, GeoEye-1 post-event data and aerial imagery from NOAA were uploaded 1 and 5 days after the earthquake, respectivly (Google. org, 2010; NOAA, 2010). The imagery was for example further used by a crowdsourcing community to digitize a comprehensive road network of the earthquake affected area (OpenStreetMap, 2010). This is only one example of a new trend collecting "volunteered geographic information" (VGI) (De Longueville, Luraschi, Smits, Peedell, & De Groeve 2010).

THE CAPACITIES OF VIRTUAL GLOBES

During the last years the introduction of virtual globes has raised the attention and interest on geoinformation. Although the technology has been available for a long time the increase in processing power and graphic memory of modern desktop computers together with internet accessibility supported their success. The technologies quickly became a new paradigm for accessing and rendering huge amounts of image data.

A virtual globe represents a 3-dimensional model of the earth in a software environment. Users have the ability to move around and explore the virtual earth that is usually represented by high and very high resolution satellite imagery draped over the 3D earth surface. The available tools allow users to add features by digitising own datasets or by loading data and multimedia files from online repositories. The globes are applied for education, planning, and dissemination of information. More

Table 1. Comparison of well-established virtual globes

	Google Earth™	MS Bing™ Maps 3D	Nasa World Wind	ArcGIS® Explorer
Operating system	Windows, Linux, Mac OS, Android, IPhone	Platform independent (browser based)	Platform independent (Java based)	Windows
License/ cost	Freeware (for personal use)	Freeware (for non-commercial use)	Freeware Open source	Freeware
Background data	Full aerial/ satellite imagery coverage Large coverage of very high resolution imagery Street View	Full aerial/ satellite imagery coverage Large coverage of very high resolution imagery Bird's eye view	High resolution satellite imagery	Basemaps (e.g. world imagery, world streets, world topographic maps, Bing Map service) from an online database
Data formats	KML, Web Map Service (WMS), Imagery, GPS formats	GeoRSS, KML Imagery	WW XML, KML, SHP, WMS, WFS, Imagery	SHP, KML,, GDB, TXT, CSV, Imagery, WMS, GeoRSS, Client for ArcGIS® Server, ArcIMS®, ArcGIS® Online Services
Data creation and manipulation	YES	NO	YES	YES
Data sharing	YES	YES	NO	YES
GPS support	YES	NO	NO	YES
Customization	Only by integrating in web application using API	Bing™ Maps APIs and SDKs	YES (Open source)	Add-Ins, Analysis Gallery, geoprocessing tools and models published using ArcGIS Server, SDK

and more they are used for collaborative mapping of anthropogenic or natural features. Several tools exist of which Google Earth™, Microsoft® Bing™ Maps 3D, Nasa World Wind and ESRI ArcGIS® Explorer are the best known. Table 1 gives an overview and comparison of the above mentioned products.

PROPOSED CONCEPT

As communities are widely lacking financial resources, all components proposed are publicly available and do not require in depth GIS expertise. Figure 1 sketches the proposed technical concept. The setup is based on the latest available version of Google Earth™ (5.0) (Google, 2009a). It integrates self updating webservices, offers the possibility to include remote sensing imagery available in private image repositories, and provides the capabilities to create the required

information layers needed for disaster management, which can be stored and exchanged with other parties via simple text files. There are numerous toolboxes available for Google Earth™ which enhance its standard functionality. Recent developments showed the extendibility of Google Earth into a platform for online collaborative feature capturing, for instance to perform rapid mapping tasks, where many experts are working in parallel on the same dataset (Brunner, 2009). The data derived by various collaborators, which are possibly located at geographically different locations, are shared by storing the geographic features in a geodatabase connected with Google Earth™. The use of geodatabases also allows access to the spatial feature data by other GIS clients, such as gvSIG (GVSIG, 2009), providing enhanced data processing facilities. For this case study the more sophisticated setup using a geodatabase was avoided to guarantee the ease of use and replication by non-technical staff. Also the

Figure 1. System design: Google Earth™ as visualisation and data collection platform. Data analysis with freeware tools (Google Earth™ Toolbox), Printing engine to produce paper maps out of previously in Google Earth™ collected data.

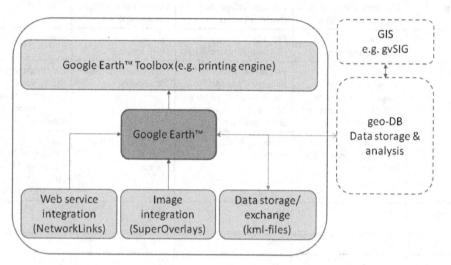

use of a professional GIS for data manipulation and retrieval is not described here but it is seen as possible extension for increasing the capacity of an overall GI architecture.

The decision to use Google Earth™ was taken due to several reasons. Google Earth™'s success is based on a big user community with numerous studies and success stories published in various internet blogs and user groups. International organizations as well as private users provide and share data layers of different concern which can be integrated into the system. One of Google Earth™'s biggest successes is the improvement in the accessibility of geospatial data which was formerly only available to geospatial professionals. A large volume of very high resolution (VHR) satellite imagery together with the possibility to include customized image products via SuperOverlays (Brunner, 2009; Lemoine & Brunner, 2007) and webservices via NetworkLinks make it even more attractive for organizations to use this tool. Note that Google Earth™ provides also a mechanism to directly import images (GroundOverlays) via the Open File menu. This mechanism is limited to 1024 by 1024 image size

and hence only the SuperOverlay mechanism is used in this concept.

The vector data created in Google Earth™ is stored in the Keyhole Markup Language (KML) (Google, 2009b), Google Earth™'s native data format, which is based on the Extensible Markup Language (XML) (W3, 2009). In 2008, KML 2.2 was approved as open coding standard by the Open Geospatial Consortium (OGC®) which supports visualising and sharing of visual geographic content in web-based online maps and virtual globes (OGC, 2008). Since KML is pure text it is very well suited to be compressed with the ZIP format, which is supported from Google Earth™ via the KMZ format.

The Google Earth™ front end provides only a fraction of capabilities professional GIS packages offer (Chow, 2008; Miller, 2006). However, this was never Google's intention for its development (Jones, 2005; Wagner, 2006). Nevertheless due to the big user community and the KML standard manifold plug-ins and tools are available converting proprietary GIS data formats into KML and supporting geospatial analysis of KML files.

For KML data conversion, processing, and analysis, public domain and stand-alone and online tools are used (see Google Earth toolbox in Figure 1). From Zonum Solutions (Zonum, 2010) the online application KML Toolbox was used to transfer KML data into SHP format. For the conversion from SHP to KML we used the Zonum tool SHP2KML. Geo Utilities provide online tools for buffering and overlay (GeoUtilities, 2010). Both tools are used to create buffer rings around points and lines as well as to overlay polygon features with polygons, points, or lines of another layer. The overlay output is a file containing the intersection points between the two layers. The software GE-Path is taken to calculate routes and distances between places (Sgrillo, 2009). A Microsoft® Excel macro-script available through the FreeGeographyTools website (FreeGeographyTools, 2010) is used to add multiple attributes to KML features.

The earth surface in Google Earth™ is represented with a growing number of VHR satellite and areal imagery from different sources. Areas not covered with very high resolution satellite imagery are represented by medium resolution Landsat data. The latest available software version (5.0) allows, as far as satellite data for the selected location are existing on the Google™ servers, to view historic satellite imagery. By moving a time slider, they can be selected and a visual change detection can be performed. Google Earth™ supports the Plate-Carree (or geographic) projection system with WGS 84 ellipsoid. Hence, all output data are projected in this projection and the data which shall be integrated needs to be provided in Plate-Carre projection. Nevertheless, the viewer also supports the display of coordinates in UTM reference system.

A feature of Google Earth™ is the integration of so called NetworkLinks. A NetworkLink enables the user to integrate Google Earth™ data hosted locally or on other servers (webservices) in the internet. The data need to be in KML format and can consist of point-, line- and polygon features as well as images. The NetworkLink can be configured to refresh automatically. Several institutions provide near-real-time hazard information as Google Earth NetworkLink. An extension to NetworkLinks is the SuperOverlay which allows the integration of large image coverages from private image repositories into Google Earth™. A SuperOverlay is a hierarchical tree-like structure of NetworkLinks of regionalized GroundOverlays, which is the standard KML element to display small georeferenced image tiles within Google Earth™. A top level KML file contains NetworkLinks to the four quad-regions of the next tiling level. The level of detail controls the visibility of each tile level in such a way that the higher resolution levels become visible when the user zooms in closer. An advantage is that SuperOverlays can also be provided on separate media for offline integration (Brunner, 2009). The tool gdal2tiles which creates SuperOverlays from georeferenced raster data is freely available with the Geospatial Data Abstraction Library (GDAL, 2008). An implementation of an algorithm to generate SuperOverlays is presented in (Lemoine & Brunner, 2007).

Further features of Google Earth™ are the import and real-time tracking of GPS data and the possibility to include multi-media information such as photographs, videos, and voice which is particularly interesting for the integration of ground observations. Google Earth™'s limitation for the need of an active internet connection for its use is restricted by its capability to run in an offline mode with locally cached imagery (FreeGeographyTools, 2009). It must be mentioned that the use of the imagery provided is restricted and data must not be extracted from the software.

Besides its analytical capacities GIS is still an important tool for creating paper maps. Google Earth™ does not support to layout hardcopy maps. The resolution of printed images is limited in the freeware version and in screenshot mode without information on the orientation, reference system or loaded KML files on top of the earth surface.

This is a drawback for professional users who need to provide printed information e.g. for field trips or if the information needs to be provided to decision makers who cannot be expected to be familiar using Google Earth™. For that reason the printing engine was developed which is a web based tool implemented in Java, using the Google Maps API (GoogleMaps, 2009) and the Google Web Toolkit (GoogleWebToolkit, 2009). It supports the print of customized maps in A3 and A4 format containing north-oriented Google Maps™ data content together with ancillary KML layers, a legend and a map frame indicating latitude/longitude coordinates. The layout is completed by adding a custom map title and a logo e.g. of the producing institution. Based on the <name> tag of the added KML files, entries are added in the map legend. A north arrow indicates the orientation of the map.

DATA SET DESCRIPTION

Image Data

For Legazpi a VHR satellite image from October 2007 is provided as background image layer. As data source GeoEye is declared. GeoEye is a company operating three satellites (Ikonos, Orbview, GeoEye). Google® has exclusive rights to use data from the GeoEye-1 satellite online. As the Geo-Eye-1 satellite was only launched in September 2008 and considering the spatial resolution of the data, the images are likely to be Quickbird which is provided by Digital Globe®. No further information about the radiometry of the data, sun illumination etc. are available. For visual change detection historic Quickbird imagery from May 2007 and November 2005 is available for Legaspi.

Figure 2. Green earthquake alert (6.4 Magnitude) for Northern Philippines (01.06.08) and NAKRI storm track (01/02.06.08) offered by GDACS network link. Global rainfall map by JAXA visualised in Google Earth™ (KMZ file to be loaded manually)

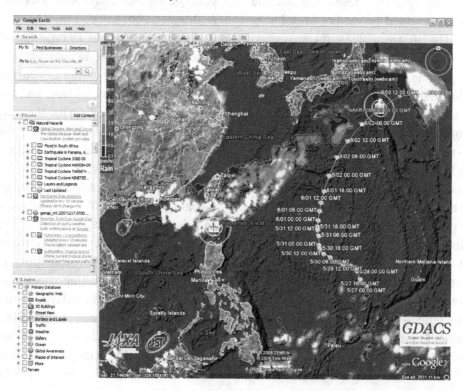

Near-Real-Time Hazard Monitoring

As described above Legazpi is exposed to various types of hazards. NetworkLinks were used to integrate information about tropical storms, floods, current seismic activity, and volcanoes (see Table 2 for details). The NetworkLinks are updated automatically and enable the user to get near-real-time information about hazards. Actual rainfall in near realtime is available on an hourly basis but has to be loaded manually. Figure 2 shows an example of a global rainfall map together with a tropical storm map provided by the Global Disaster Alert and Coordination System (GDACS)

integrated into Google Earth™. GDACS is a platform integrating web-based disaster information management systems with the aim to provide near real-time alerts about natural disasters around the world. The system facilitates the coordination of international response activities during the relief phase of a disaster (De Groeve, 2006; Vernaccini, 2007).

Topographic Map

A digital version of a topographic map 1:50.000 published by the National Mapping and Resources Authority (NAMRIA) was obtained from a map

Table 2. Hazard information provided as Google Earth™ NetworkLink

Hazards	Description	Provider,	Update Rate Server	URL
Hurricanes	Hurricanes live positions	Glooton JRC	10 min 5 min	http://www.glooton.fr/hurricanes.kmz http://www.gdacs.org
Tropical storms	Current tropical storm tracks and forecasted paths from Nat. Hurricane Center	GUI Weather JRC	30 min 5 min	http://www.guiweather.com/kml.html http://www.gdacs.org
Rainfall	Global Rainfall Map in near real time (~ four hours after observation) files to be loaded manually	EORC-JAXA	1 hour	http://sharaku.eorc.jaxa.jp/GSMaP/index.htm
Floods	Near real-time alerts about natural disasters around the world (Earthquakes, volcanoes, tropical cyclones, floods)	JRC	5 min	http://www.gdacs.org
Floods	24 hour real-time flood potential from merged satellite rainfall augmented by NWS GFS and NASA GEOS-5 forecast model data	NASA	5 min	http://trmm.gsfc.nasa.gov/trmm_rain/Events/trmm_google_24plus_hydro_model.kml http://trmm.gsfc.nasa.gov/trmm_rain/Events/trmm_google_24plusG5_hydro_model.kml
Volcano	Near real-time alerts about natural disasters around the world (Earthquakes, volcanoes, tropical cyclones, floods)	JRC	5 min	http://www.gdacs.org
Earth-quakes	Earthquakes with magnitude 1+ for the past 7 days	USGS	5 min	http://earthquake.usgs.gov
Fire hotspots	MODIS hotspot/active fire locations	FAO	1 hour	http://www.fao.org/nr/gfims/en/

provider. The file was transformed into SuperOverlay using GDAL to allow its draping over the Google Earth™ surface.

Static Hazard Maps

Hazard maps were obtained from the website of the Philippine Institute of Volcanology and Seismology (PHIVOLCS, 2010) for Mayon volcano. These include a lava flow hazard map, an ashfall hazard map and a lahar hazard map. The hazard maps were added as image SuperOverlays on the Google Earth™ terrain. The maps were available as JPG-files without georeference. Their geographic adjustment and positioning was done manually, prior to the SuperOverlay generation.

Population Map

Population figures were available from a printout provided by the local municipality. The 'Earthquakes and Megacities Initiative' provided barangay boundaries (smallest administrative unit in the Philippines) in SHP-format (SHP - standard GIS file format). Population figures were linked to barangay boundaries. As Google Earth™ does not support direct reading of the SHP-format the data was transposed into KML-format. Coordinates from the barangay boundary KML-file were

extracted and copied together with corresponding population figures into the E.M.A. GE Tools Excel sheet. The application allows to add various attributes and to adjust their visual representation. The data was converted back into the final population map in KML-format executing the macro.

Resources Map

The following feature classes of the study area were digitised in Google Earth™ to obtain maps of the infrastructural resources: roads were digitised and annotated with attributes about the road class and surface type. Building footprints were recorded and number of storeys added as known from the field. If available and depending on the requirements the number of residents and any other attribute could further be appended (e.g. age of building, construction- and roof type, use). Hospitals and evacuation centers were digitised as point features. Table 3 lists all spatial layers included.

Accuracy

The accuracy of Google Earth™ image data is not publicly documented by the software provider. By surprise one can find offsets between image tiles e.g. truncated or disjoint roads. A webbased

Table 3. Feature classes and attributes collected in Google Earth™

Layer	Type	Attributes
Roads	lines (digitised)	paved/unpaved road class (principal road, secondary road, minor road, track)
Buildings	polygons (digitised)	number of storey
Rivers and streams	lines (digitised)	
Barangay boundaries	polygons (converted from SHP into KML)	barangay ID
Population map	based on barangay boundaries	population Figure per barangay
Hospitals and evacuation centers	points (digitized)	type
Volcano hazard maps	SuperOverlay	see 5d
Dynamic hazard maps	NetworkLink	see 5b

'Data Problems Compendium' (GoogleEarth-Community, 2009) is listing data problems sorted by image, terrain and ancillary layer errors. In a recent paper Potere (2008) investigated the horizontal accuracy of Google Earth™ imagery in a bigger context. Based on 436 globally distributed control points he conducted a comparison with Landsat GeoCover data, an orthorectified product with absolute positional accuracy of less than 50 meters. The test resulted in an overall accuracy of 39.7 meters RMS (ranging from 0.4 meters to 171.6 meters). Higher accuracies were achieved for satellite imagery compared to aerial imagery as well as for developed countries compared to less developed countries.

As for the test area in Legazpi post-processed differential GPS data was available the RMS error based on ten selected GPS points was calculated. The resulting RMS of 6.29 m (x-direction) and 5.88 m (y-direction) was evaluated as acceptable. Apart from this accuracy measurement it is proposed that the relative accuracy between the single data layers is more relevant than the absolute accuracy.

RESULTS

Google Earth™ does not provide substantial analysis tools professional GIS offer. For example spatial and attribute queries are not supported. Nevertheless with the tools described in Sec. 4 it was possible to conduct several tasks related to disaster preparedness and response. Resulting data layers may be sufficient for taking decisions others may be only intermediate products and further conclusions will require a cognitive analysis. The strong capabilities of 3D visualization in Google Earth™ are an example for potential use of interactive analysis with respect to the terrain. The following exercises were successfully conducted:

With focus on storm surges:

1. Select all buildings in a buffer of 150 meters to the shoreline and which are located lower than 5 meter elevation: the shoreline was digitised and a buffer created using Geo Utilities buffering application. From the topographic map available as SuperOverlay the 5 meter contour line was digitised. By overlaying the building footprints with contours and buffer zone the buildings searched for could be determined. Having further information on the type and use of buildings as well as the number of inhabitants could increase the value of this analysis. The contour could also have been extracted from a digital elevation model like from Shuttle Radar Topographic Mission (SRTM) by applying the gdal_contour algorithm (Figure 3 a).

2. Select all barangays with highest population numbers along the shoreline: the population map previously created and based on the joined population figures and barangay boundaries was analysed for highest population figures (Figure 3 b).

With focus on floods:

1. Select all road segments potentially affected by river flooding (50 m buffer): rivers and creeks were digitised as visible from the Google Earth™ imagery. Buffers around the rivers were calculated with Geo Utilities buffering application. Roads previously created for the resources map were taken and intersected with the buffer polygons applying the Geo Utilities overlay 2D application. As result the intersection points between buffer polygons and road lines were calculated and hence the affected road segments could be determined (Figure 3 c). An example of the output of the printing engine, which shows the buffer around the river is shown in Figure 4.

Figure 3.

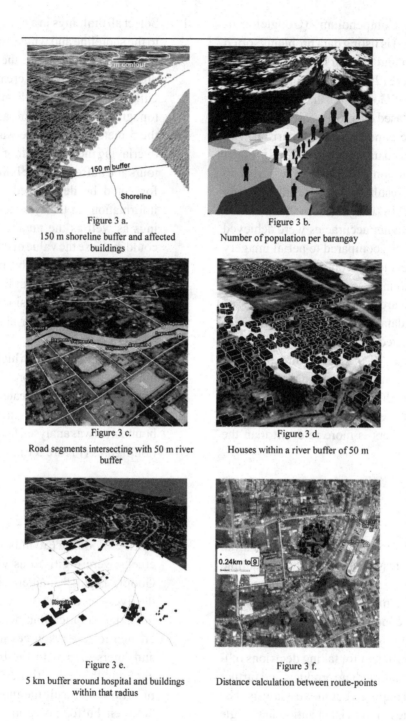

Figure 3 a.
150 m shoreline buffer and affected buildings

Figure 3 b.
Number of population per barangay

Figure 3 c.
Road segments intersecting with 50 m river buffer

Figure 3 d.
Houses within a river buffer of 50 m

Figure 3 e.
5 km buffer around hospital and buildings within that radius

Figure 3 f.
Distance calculation between route-points

2. Select all buildings within a 50 m buffer around rivers and streams: a similar calculation was applied as for storm surges. The river buffers created for the task above were taken and overlaid with building footprints.

Thus the affected buildings were found out. Having resident numbers on building level available would increase the value of this information (Figure 3 d).

Figure 4. Example of a resulting map from the developed printing engine

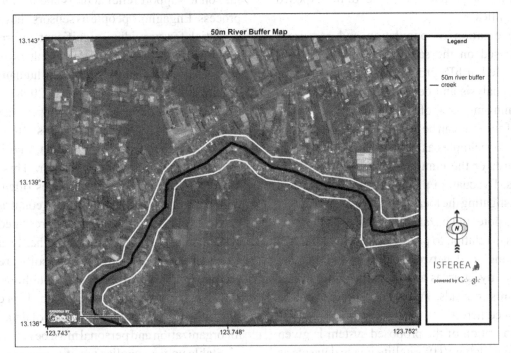

With focus on evacuation planning:

1. Select all buildings within a 5 km buffer around a selected evacuation center: in case of a disaster event schools and churches are taken as evacuation center. As example a hospital was selected. Another buffer was created and number of buildings were discovered. A comparison with the population map allowed conclusions on the proportion of people living in that area (Figure 3 e).

With focus on a fire emergency:

1. Calculate the shortest distance from the fire brigade station to a selected building: different roads from the fire brigade to a mall were taken from the resources map. The GE-Path software allows to calculate distances and to create routes between placemarks. Following the different roads important placemarks were set e.g. on junctions and crossroads.

After loading the resulting KML-file in the GE-Path software a path (line) was generated between the different placemarks and distances (in kilometers) calculated. The overall distances had to be summed up manually to determine the shortest route (Figure 3 f).

DISCUSSION

In this paper it is demonstrated that disaster managers can greatly benefit from the use of geoinformation. It is suggested to use publicly available geotools and data for achieving this aim. Using Google Earth™ as platform allows the replication to a range of other test cases. The near-real-time tracking of different hazards using NetworkLinks raises the awareness of the exposed communities and responsible stakeholders. It can function as early warning system and enables decision makers to assess the current hazard situation and helps enhancing the preparedness level of the exposed communities.

The creation of population and resources maps based on the satellite imagery provided by Google Earth™ provides sufficient detail for further analysis and decision making as well as for training purposes of the communities. Various types of analysis can be performed. This is demonstrated on examples as the exposure of buildings to hazards or the number of people exposed to hazards. Evacuation planning can be supported by investigating the location of evacuation centers towards potential hazard sites as well as their capacities in relation to people potentially affected. Integrating road networks allows studying the accessibility of areas and the impending impact of hazards to roads. Further questions could be formulated here.

A limitation of the proposed system is given by non-available VHR satellite image datasets as background reference in Google Earth™ which is still the case for some areas of the world. This could be overcome by integrating customized VHR imagery available at user side as SuperOverlay. General restriction of earth observation data is potential cloud coverage. Further constraint might occur due to the unavailability of ancillary datasets (baseline vector data, statistics, etc.).

The presented system is not limited to handle raster or vector data sets, but can be extended to visualize text based information from the web. In particular, Tomaszewski (2010) presents a system that extracts the geographic and thematic references from web-documents (e.g. RSS feeds from news about disasters) in order to visualize the information content geographically in Google Earth™. Using this approach the system could also be extended to integrate volunteered geographic information (VGI). Today, VGI became an important data source during and after disaster events and is considered having a high potential to enhance the overall understanding of disaster impacts. Online disaster-response communities are collecting, processing, and delivering geoinfor-

mation to support relief actions and the recovery process. Engaging "people as sensors" has a great potential for providing significant information timely and cost-effectively creating also synergies between governmental agencies and humanitarian organizations (Laituri & Kodrich, 2008).

The system described in this paper was setup within three days. Nevertheless this effort is dependent on the availability of data, digitization speed and capabilities of the user. This study demonstrates that several obstacles often mentioned for using GIS in developing countries can be overcome with the approach presented: The system setup requires no specific hardware but a standard personal computer. All software tools used are freely available and partly public domain. However, cost of data remains high. This can be substituted by personal digitization of data. Costs for organization and personal must be considered.

Stable power supplies are of course necessary to run the computer. An internet connection is necessary to access the Google Earth™ remote sensing data. In case of unreliable internet connection, which may be the case in developing countries or areas that are affected by an emergency event, the software can run in offline mode with cached imagery. If additional data are integrated via webservices, a dial-up internet connection for the duration of the synchronization of the data is sufficient.

Working with geographic information requires a general understanding of spatial concepts and spatial interrelations. Map reading capacity and an understanding of how the world looks from above on basis of a satellite image must be available. The use of Google Earth™ requires a general understanding of computer know how. However as its graphical interface and its use is intuitive, no in depth GIS expertise is necessary for using it. To ease the technical requirements needed to access the information (e.g. for decision makers), the map can be printed via a printing engine.

Setting up complex information systems require in depth analysis of user requirements, system design, coding, testing, and implementation which will span over a long time period. The test case presented here addresses selected key questions of disaster management and planning. It is believed that apart from the printing engine and clearly defined requirements assumed, a replication of the system described here can be setup within very short time. This however is dependent on the experience of the user, the size of the test case area, the availability of third party data, the time for data conversion, and personal digitization of data layers.

CONCLUSION

In this paper it is described how the use of publicly accessible geoinformation and tools can support disaster management. Based on an example from the Philippines the capabilities and power of Google Earth™ is demonstrated for this purpose. Several data layers were integrated from self-updating webservices providing near-real-time hazard information, to static SuperOverlays and vectorised features. The lack of specific tools for spatial analysis is overcome by using third party developments from the public domain. Basic analysis could be conducted by creating buffers, calculating distances and areas and analysing intersections. However, restrictions are clearly visible, e.g. limited data attribution, queries, analysis and storage capabilities. This could be overcome by integrating geodatabases for data storage and improved data analysis, which is a topic for our future research. Basic knowledge about spatial concepts, spatial data and their processing and analysis must be available by the user. The decision maker's in depth local knowledge and experience is essential for the interpretation and application of the created datasets.

Google Earth™ is not a full GIS but rather complementary to professional software packages. Nevertheless it gives the opportunity for non-spatial-experts to become spatially literate and to visualise and interactively analyse spatial phenomena. This may be a step to reduce obstacles against the implementation of new technologies within their professional environments which is not only a problem in the less developed world.

ACKNOWLEDGMENT

The main part of the research presented here was conducted during the authors' employment with the Geospatial Information Analysis for Global Security and Stability (ISFEREA) action which is part of the Global Security and Crisis Management Unit of the Joint Research Centre of the European Commission. This article is a revision of the paper "An efficient GIS concept for disaster management in developing countries based on virtual globes" which was originally published in the International Journal of Information Systems for Crisis Response and Management (IJISCRAM), Vol. 1, Issue 4, 2009.

REFERENCES

W3. (2009). *Extensible markup language* (XML). Retrieved Februrary 3, 2009, from http://www.w3.org/XML

Brunner, D., Lemoine, G., Thoorens, F. X., & Bruzzone, L. (2009). Distributed geospatial data processing functionality to support collaborative and rapid emergency response. *IEEE Journal of Selected Topics in Applied Earth Observations and Remote Sensing, 2*(1), 33–46. doi:10.1109/JSTARS.2009.2015770

Chow, E. T. (2008). The potential of maps APIs for Internet GIS applications. *Transactions in GIS, 12*(2), 179–191. doi:10.1111/j.1467-9671.2008.01094.x

Cova, T. J. (1999). GIS in emergency Management. In Longley, P., Goodchild, M. F., Maguire, D., & Rhind, D. (Eds.), *Geographical Information Systems. Principles, techniques, applications, and management* (2nd ed., pp. 845–858). New York, NY: John Wiley & Sons.

Currion, P. (2006). *Better the devil we know: Obstacles and opportunities in humanitarian GIS.* Retrieved September 20, 2010, from http://www.humanitarian.info/?page_id=35

Currion, P. (2009). Only connect: Problem sciences, information systems and humanitarian reform. *International Journal of Information Systems for Crisis Response and Management, 1*(1), 29–40. doi:10.4018/jiscrm.2009010103

Cutter, S. L. (2003). GI science, disasters, and emergency management. *Transactions in GIS, 7*(4), 439–446. doi:10.1111/1467-9671.00157

Daep, C. (2008). *Albay provincial coordinating council. Personal talk.* Legsapi City.

Dash, N. (1997). The use of Geographical Information Systems in disaster research. *International Journal of Mass Emergencies and Disasters, 15,* 135–146.

De Groeve, T., Vernaccini, L., & Annunziato, A. (2006). *Global disaster alert and coordination system.* Paper presented at the 3rd International ISCRAM Conference, Newark, New Jersey (United States of America).

De Longueville, B., Luraschi, G., Smits, P., Peedell, S., & De Groeve, T. (2010). Citizens as sensors for natural hazards. A VGI integration workflow. *Geomatica, 64*(1), 41–60.

EMDAT. (2008). *The OFDA/CRED international disaster database.* Université Catholique de Louvain, Brussels (Belgium). Retrieved September 20, 2010, from http://www.em-dat.net

FreeGeographyTools. (2009). *Using the Google Earth cache – Basics.* Retrieved September 20, 2010, from http://freegeographytools.com/2009/using-the-google-earth-cache-basics

FreeGeographyTools. (2010). *Xls2kml-Another Excel-to-kml converter with a few extras.* Retrieved November 10, 2010, from http://freegeographytools.com/2007/xls2kml-another-excel-to-kml-converter-with-a-few-extras

GDAL. (2008). *GDAL - Geospatial data abstraction library.* Retrieved September 20, 2010, from http://www.gdal.org

GeoUtilities. (2010). *GeoUtilities - Tools for Google Earth™.* Retrieved November 2, 2010, from http://geo-news.net/index_geof.html

Google. (2009a). *Google Earth™.* Retrieved from http://earth.google.com/

Google. (2009b). *KML documentation.* Retrieved February 5, 2009, from http://code.google.com/apis/kml/documentation/

Google. org. (2010). *Google crisis response - Haiti earthquake imagery.* Retrieved October 24, 2010, from http://www.google.com/relief/haitiearthquake/imagery.html

GoogleEarthCommunity. (2009). *Data problems compendium.* Retrieved February 9, 2009, from http://bbs.keyhole.com/ubb/showthreaded.php/Cat/0/Number/330340/an//page/2/vc/1

GoogleMaps. (2009). *Google Maps API.* Retrieved September 20, 2010, from http://code.google.com/apis/maps/

GoogleWebToolkit. (2009). *Google Web toolkit.* Retrieved September 20, 2010, from http://code.google.com/webtoolkit/

GVSIG. (2009). *gvSIG – Conselleria d'infrastructures i transport.* Retrieved November 10, 2010, from http://www.gvsig.org/web/home/gvsig-home/view?set_language=en

ISIS. (2003). Intelligent systems for humanitarian geo-infrastructure. User survey and requirements document.

Jones, M. T. (2005). *The autobiographical Earth*. Retrieved September 20, 2010, from http://video.google.com/videoplay?docid=1883812421992143014

Kaiser, R., Spiegel, P. B., Henderson, A. K., & Gerber, M. L. (2003). The application of Geographic Information Systems and Global Positioning Systems in humanitarian emergencies: Lessons learned, programme implications and future research. *Disasters, 27*(2), 127–140. doi:10.1111/1467-7717.00224

Laituri, M., & Kodrich, K. (2008). Online disaster response community: People as sensors of high magnitude disasters using internet GIS. *Sensors (Basel, Switzerland), 8*, 3037–3055. doi:10.3390/s8053037

Lemoine, G., & Brunner, D. (2007, 13-15. March 2007). *Integration of full resolution image coverages using SuperOverlays*. Paper presented at the FOSSGIS-Conference, Berlin.

Marincioni, F. (2007). Information technologies and the sharing of disaster knowledge: The critical role of professional culture. *Disasters, 31*(4), 459–476. doi:10.1111/j.1467-7717.2007.01019.x

Miller, C. C. (2006). A beast in the field: The Google Maps mashup as GIS/2. *Cartographica: The International Journal for Geographic Information and Geovisualization, 41*(3), 187–199. doi:10.3138/J0L0-5301-2262-N779

Mills, J. W. (2008). Understanding disaster: GI science contributions in the ongoing recovery from Katrina. *Transactions in GIS, 12*(1), 1–4. doi:10.1111/j.1467-9671.2008.01083.x

NOAA. (2010). *NOAA produces images of Haiti for first responders*. Retrieved September 20, 2010, from http://www.noaanews.noaa.gov/stories2010/20100119_haiti.html

Nourbakhsh, I., Sargent, R., Wright, A., Cramer, K., McClendon, B., & Jones, M. (2006). Mapping disaster zones. *Nature, 439*, 787–788. doi:10.1038/439787a

OGC. (2008). *OGC approves KML as open standard*. Retrieved from http://www.opengeospatial.org/pressroom/pressreleases/857

OpenStreetMap. (2010). *WikiProject Haiti*. Retrieved October 24, 2010, from http://wiki.openstreetmap.org/wiki/WikiProject_Haiti

PHIVOLCS. (2010). *Philippine Institute of Volcanology and Seismology*. Retrieved November 12, 2010, from http://volcano.phivolcs.dost.gov.ph/update_VMEPD/vmepd/vmepd/mayon-hazmaps.htm

Pisano, F. (2005). Using satellite imagery to improve emergency relief. *Humanitarian Exchange, 32*, 36-40. Retrieved from http://www.odihpn.org/documents/humanitarianexchange032.pdf

Potere, D. (2008). Horizontal positional accuracy of Google Earth's high-resolution imagery archive. *Sensors (Basel, Switzerland), 8*, 7973–7981. doi:10.3390/s8127973

Priyono, J. P., H., Dulbahri. (2007). Google Earth application to support disaster emergency response. *Jurnal Kebencanaan Indonesia, 1*(3).

Sgrillo. (2009). *GE-Path*. Retrieved November 10, 2010, from http://www.sgrillo.net/googleearth/gepath.htm

Stephenson, R., & Anderson, P. S. (1997). Disasters and the Information Technology revolution. *Disasters, 21*(4), 305–334. doi:10.1111/1467-7717.00065

Sui, D. Z. (2008). The wikification of GIS and its consequences: Or Angelina Jolie's new tattoo and the future of GIS. *Computers, Environment and Urban Systems, 32*, 1–5. doi:10.1016/j.compenvurbsys.2007.12.001

Tanser, F., & le Sueur, D. (2002). The application of geographical information systems to important public health problems in Africa. *International Journal of Health Geographics, 1*(4).

Tomaszewski, B. (2010). (in press). Situation awareness and virtual globes: Applications for disaster management. *Computers & Geosciences.*

Tran, P., Shaw, R., Chantry, G., & Norton, J. (2008). GIS and local knowledge in disaster management: A case study of flood risk mapping in Viet Nam. *Disasters, 33*(1), 152–169. doi:10.1111/j.1467-7717.2008.01067.x

UN-SPIDER. (2010). *United Nations platform for space-based information for disaster management and emergency response.* Retrieved October 20, 2010, from http://www.unoosa.org/oosa/unspider/index.html

Verjee, F. (2007). *An assessment of the utility of GIS-based analysis to support the coordination of humanitarian assistance.* Washington, DC: The George Washington University. Retrieved from http://www2.gwu.edu/~icdrm/publications/PDF/Verjee_Dissertation.pdf

Vernaccini, L., De Groeve, T., & Gadenz, S. (2007). *Humanitarian impact of tropical cyclones (EUR 23083 EN).* Luxembourg: JRC Scientific and Technical Reports.

Voigt, S., Kemper, T., Riedlinger, T., Kiefl, R., Scholte, K., & Mehl, H. (2007). Satellite image analysis for disaster and crisis-management support. *IEEE Transactions on Geoscience and Remote Sensing, 45*(6, Part 1), 1520–1528. doi:10.1109/TGRS.2007.895830

Wagner, M. J. (2006). *The view from Google Earth.* Retrieved November 10, 2010, from http://www.gpsworld.com/gis/integration-and-standards/the-view-google-earth-7434

Yarbrough, L., & Easson, G. (2005). Eye of the storm: Google Earth assists Katrina response and recovery. *Geomatica, 59*(4), 451–453.

Zonum. (2010). *Zonum solutions.* Retrieved October 29, 2010, from www.zonums.com

Chapter 16
Strategies to Prepare Emergency Management Personnel to Integrate Geospatial Tools into Emergency Management

Tricia Toomey
San Diego State University, USA

Eric Frost
San Diego State University, USA

Murray E. Jennex
San Diego State University, USA

ABSTRACT

Emergency management is a diverse field. Effective disaster management involves knowledge of various subjects as well as work experience in all aspects related to mitigation, planning, response, and recovery efforts. One field not being fully exploited by disaster management is the use of geospatial tools in the form of Geographic Information Systems (GIS), cartography, and geovisualization. One reason for this is that many emergency managers are not fully aware of the assistance GIS can lend to effectively manage disaster situations. All functions of emergency management have a strong geographic component. Where is the earthquake epicenter? Where is the damage? Where does the dam inundation run and who/what is in that path? Where is the area of road closures? The questions asking "where" are endless in effective emergency management and range from the mitigation stage through to the recovery stage. For example, a tsunami may inundate only a certain portion of the region, therefore, it is important to have mitigation and planning efforts concentrated in those regions. It is also important to know what businesses, housing, and populations are in the affected areas. The integration of geospatial tools for risk assessment, mitigation, planning, response, and recovery efforts is emerging as an effective and potentially invaluable resource for answering such questions in regards to emergency management.

DOI: 10.4018/978-1-60960-609-1.ch016

INTRODUCTION

Disasters impact every inch of the earth's surface. They can be tectonically driven such as earthquakes and tsunamis, weather driven as hurricanes or tornados, man-made terrorist events, technological disasters as in a chemical explosion, or fires that are part of the earth's natural process. According to Munich Re, the world's largest reinsurer, natural disasters killed at least 25,000 people in 2001 (Dahinten, 2002). No matter the disaster, effective emergency management can mitigate the effects of these disasters and save lives.

Modern civilizations have begun organizing attempts to protect life, property, and the environment. This is known as emergency management. Emergency management can be defined as the organization and management of resources and responsibilities for dealing with all aspects of emergencies, including risk assessment, mitigation, preparedness, response, and recovery.

Geospatial tools can lend aid in these disaster management functions. However, the wide-range of support geospatial tools have to offer is not always being used to its best advantage. This thesis will explore the strategies to prepare emergency management personnel to integrate geospatial tools, in the form of Geographic Information Systems (GIS), geovisualization, and cartography into the emergency management functions of risk assessment, mitigation, preparedness, response, and recovery.

BACKGROUND

After the terrorist attacks of September 11, 2001 killed nearly 3,000 people and the most destructive - and costly - natural disaster in U.S. history, Hurricane Katrina in August of 2005, killed over 1,800 people, emergency management began seeing fundamental structure changes and moved to the forefront of media and government (Dahinten, 2002; Koch, 2007). On February 28, 2003 President Bush released Homeland Security Presidential Directive (HSPD) 5 for the management of domestic incidents. HSPD-5 states:

"To prevent, prepare for, respond to, and recover from terrorist attacks, major disasters, and other emergencies, the United States Government shall establish a single, comprehensive approach to domestic incident management. The objective of the United States Government is to ensure that all levels of government across the Nation have the capability to work efficiently and effectively together, using a national approach to domestic incident management. In these efforts, with regard to domestic incidents, the United States Government treats crisis management and consequence management as a single, integrated function, rather than as two separate functions" (Bush, 2003a).

HSPD-5 set in place the National Incident Management System (NIMS) which is expected to provide a consistent nationwide approach for Federal, State, and local governments to work effectively and efficiently together to respond to crises (Bush, 2003a). NIMS will also "include a core set of concepts, principles, terminology, and technologies covering the incident command system; multi-agency coordination systems; unified command; training; identification and management of resources (including systems for classifying types of resources); qualifications and certification; and the collection, tracking, and reporting of incident information and incident resources." (Bush, 2003a)

The Interagency Geospatial Preparedness Team (IGPT) is a team of experts from FEMA, the National Imagery and Mapping Agency (NIMA), the U.S. Geological Survey (USGS), and the U.S. Department of Agriculture Forest Service. IGPT was created to help make geospatial information and technologies more readily available to the national community of emergency managers and responders. Susan Kalweit, former Chief of IGPT, believes the need for geospatial technology in homeland security is a necessity as when something occurs, the first questions asked include: where is it,' what does it look like, where are the assets necessary to respond, how do I get those assets from where they are to where I need them, and how do I get people safely out of harms reach? This makes the utility of geospatial information for preparedness, emergency response, and recovery is of utmost importance (Francica, 2004).

All phases of emergency management involve the collection, analysis, and dissemination of data in a logical manner. GIS can provide a mechanism to integrate and visually display all of this data (Johnson, 2000). GIS, geovisualization, and cartography can convey information quickly because comprehension doesn't require the extra mental processing required for text-based analysis (Krataoka, 2005, p.11). It has been shown that subjects respond faster to visual signals versus auditory signals as well (Chan & Chan, 2006). A viewer of a map-based product can understand a handful of facts about a given situation in one glance. It is this instantaneous understanding that gives geospatial tools a real advantage in the emergency management industry.

Geovisualization can allow hazards such as fire risk, earthquake fault lines, dam inundation pathways, and tsunami inundation zones to be overlaid and viewed with base map data such as census information, streets, critical facilities, and power grids, so that emergency managers can begin to see the inherent risk and formulate mitigation, preparedness, response, and even foresee recovery needs (Johnson, 2000). These risks can then be displayed in maps to effectively disseminate data. Geospatial tools in the form of GIS, geovisualization, and cartography can play an important role in risk assessment, mitigation, preparedness, response and recovery of disasters.

This claim that GIS can provide for more effective emergency response was tested by Björn Johansson and Jiri Trnka from the department of Computer and Information Science at Linköping

University and Rego Granlund, Rationella Datortjänster HB, Muggebo Fridensborg. Their experimental study of 132 persons, in 22 teams, compared command teams facing the task of extinguishing a simulated forest fire using GIS and paper-based systems. The results of their study showed that teams using GIS performed significantly better than teams with paper-based maps in terms of saved area and the study showed that communication volume was considerably reduced with the use GIS (Granlund, Johansson, & Trnka, 2007).

STATEMENT OF PROBLEM

With the implementation of NIMS, the government is strictly regulating emergency management. The processes of risk assessment, mitigation, preparedness, response, and recovery are streamlining to become more effective. One way to increase the effectiveness of all functions of emergency management is with the use of geospatial tools in the form of Geographic Information Systems (GIS), geovisualization, and cartography. However, many emergency managers are not familiar with the assistance geospatial tools can offer; therefore are less likely to use them.

GIS can aid in many disaster management functions. Careem, Bittner, and De Silva (2007) sum up this use of GIS when they noted that Hurricane Katrina could have been better responded too with a GIS that could have provided mapping of routes and locations of resources and shelters. Smart maps can provide crucial information to responders in a disaster situation. They can provide current information about locations and routes. Maps integrating satellite or aerial photographs can also help responders make decisions; for example, it may be necessary to find dry land to build a helicopter pad. Flooding increases the risk of certain types of infectious diseases, and images can display areas of standing water. Relief agencies may also need to estimate the population of a particular area, and GIS supports this as well (Careem, Bittner, and De Silva, 2007). However, years ago Davis, Bagozzi, and Warshaw (1989) noted that computer systems, such as GIS will not be able to improve performance if it isn't used.

As stated above, geospatial tools can play an important role in the emergency management phases. However, the wide-range of support geospatial tools have to offer is not always being used to its full advantage. This study will explore the question of how best to prepare emergency management personnel to integrate geospatial tools, in the form of Geographic Information Systems (GIS), geovisualization, and cartography into the emergency management functions of risk assessment, mitigation, preparedness, response, and recovery.

This article will begin by briefly defining geospatial tools and the functions of emergency management. To show the important role GIS tools can play in emergency management, examples of how geospatial tools are currently being integrated into emergency management functions and a literature review will demonstrate real-world case studies of how geospatial tools and emergency management are being integrated. This article will then explain two key strategies to prepare emergency management personnel to integrate geospatial tools into the emergency management field.

DEFINITION OF TERMS

Geospatial Analysis: Geospatial tools vary in analysis capability. What sets a GIS apart from cartography is geospatial analysis. Geospatial analysis involves the analysis of location based elements or geographic/spatial data. For example, the determination of spatial relationships, such as the measurable distance between objects on the globe. Geographic data can be described as data referencing places and events location on the earth's surface.

Geographic Information Systems (GIS): One major form of geospatial analysis is the use of GIS. Environmental Systems Research Institute (ESRI) explains a GIS as an arrangement of computer hardware, software, and geographic data that allow users to interact with, integrate, analyze, and visualize data spatially. A GIS can identify relationships, patterns, trends, and find solutions to spatial problems. It involves the input, manipulation, analyzing, and display of geographic data (Dent, 1999). GIS technology is used in many industries, especially within local governments. With established GIS communities and databases already in place in most local governments, the use of GIS in emergency management simply involves notifying emergency managers of its applications.

Cartography: Cartography can be defined as the science of map making (Rubenstein, 2002). While GIS offers a "flexible medium for the production of maps", cartography itself involves no geospatial analysis (Longley, Goodchild, Maquire, & Rhind, 2001, p. 253). Instead, cartography involves the creative symbolization and conveyance of spatial data, which in turn makes cartography and map-making more of an art than a science.

Geovisualization: Geovisualization is the visualization of geographic data and products. This may be in the form of 3D visuals of a geographic area of concern or visual representations of the earth's surface.

Common Operational Picture (COP): COP is the geographic display of all aspects of an incident. This may be in the form of response efforts and disaster related events. Its purpose is to provide situational awareness for the incident as a whole.

Incident: A natural or human-caused event or occurrence that requires an emergency response to protect life or property (Kataoka, 2005).

Emergency Management: The organization and management of resources and responsibilities for dealing with all aspects of emergencies, including risk assessment, mitigation, preparedness, response and recovery.

Risk Assessment: Risk assessment is the process or methodology used for evaluating the risk to disasters (Bullock & Haddow, 2006).

Mitigation: Long-term solutions to reducing the exposure to, probability of, or potential loss from hazards (Bullock & Haddow, 2006).

Preparedness: The preparation of plans, procedures, policies, training, and equipment necessary to respond to, and recover from incidents (Bush, 2003b).

Response: The short term, immediate activities intended to "save lives, protect property and meet the basic human needs" (Bullock & Haddow, 2006, p. 77). During this stage, local emergency managers and incident commanders support first responders, such as fire, law enforcement, and emergency medical teams.

Recovery: Recovery can be short-term projects that restore vital life-support systems to minimum operating standards such as cleanup, temporary housing, and providing access to food and water. However, recovery can also be long-term activities that may continue for a number of years after a disaster. Long-term recovery aims to return life to normal or an improved, safer level. Examples of long-term recovery projects include redevelopment loans, legal assistance, and community mitigation planning (Johnson, 2000).

National Incident Management System (NIMS): Released in March 2004 by the Department of Homeland Security (DHS), NIMS offers a standardized approach to incident management and response. NIMS was developed to allow first responders from different jurisdictions and disciplines to work together better in an effort to respond to natural disasters and emergencies. Benefits of NIMS include a unified approach to incident management, standard command and management structures, and emphasis on preparedness, mutual aid and resource management (NIMS, 2009).

Standardized Emergency Management System (SEMS): SEMS is a set of principles developed for coordinating state and local emergency response in California. SEMS provides the framework for a multi-level emergency response organization to facilitate the flow of information and resources. An example of a SEMS structure at a county emergency operations center can be seen in figure 1 (OES, 2007).

METHODOLOGY

Design of Investigation

The method of this study is action research. The author served as a GIS Analyst with the County of

Figure 1. Example of a SEMS compliant EOC organization

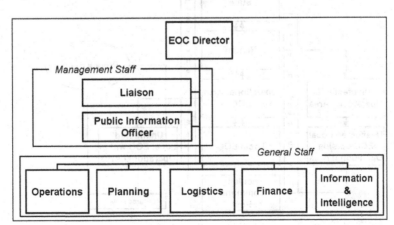

San Diego's Office of Emergency Services (OES) during the 2007 San Diego firestorm and through the period of this study. OES coordinates the overall response to disasters within the County of San Diego. When disaster strikes, OES is responsible for coordinating with all agencies that respond; ensuring resources are available and mobilized in times of disaster; and staffing the County of San Diego's Operational Area Emergency Operations Center (OAEOC). The OAEOC is a central facility that provides regional coordinated emergency response. Figure 2 provides a visual representation of the resource request and distribution process. OES is also responsible for developing plans and procedures for response to and recovery from disasters.

This research also draws from Davis' Technology Acceptance Model (TAM). TAM uses perceived usefulness and perceived ease of use as primary indicators of computer acceptance behaviors (Davis, Bagozzi, & Warshaw, 1989). This theory goes on to explain that in order for end-users to accept a new technology they need to perceive the technology will be useful and easy to use (Davis, Bagozzi, & Warshaw, 1989). A

literature review of various applications of geographic tools throughout the emergency management phases provides basis for the usefulness of geographic tools in the field of emergency management.

Data Collection

Data collection is from direct observation as a GIS Analyst in the OAEOC during the 2007 Firestorm, review of the 2003 Firestorm After Action Report, review of the 2007 Firestorm After Action Report and a literature review.

Data Analysis

The following literature review provides examples of how GIS, geovisualization, and cartography are being integrated into risk assessment, mitigation, preparedness, response and recovery of disasters. This provides useful insight into how one might effectively integrate these geospatial tools into the following emergency management processes. The literature review is also a collection of data to show emergency managers why geospatial

Figure 2. Emergency response resource request and distribution flowchart

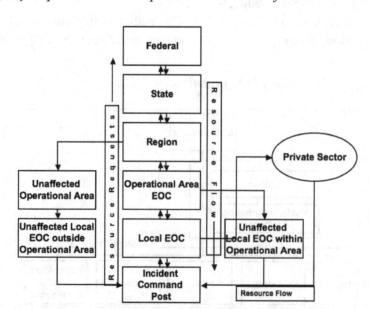

may be useful to them. According to TAM, this perceived usefulness is a key element in getting users to accept a new technology.

Limitations of Study

The limitation of this particular research and its conclusions are that this research pertains primarily to the operation of the County of San Diego OAEOC and the hazards associated with the County of San Diego and this research is primarily qualitative. These methods however may be implemented in other EOCs and jurisdictions with various hazards. This research relies heavily on the perceptions of the author and of the various general staff and management staff at the County of San Diego OAEOC.

LITERATURE REVIEW

Risk Assessment

The National Institute of Standards and Technology, NIST, defines risk as the net negative impact of the exercise of a vulnerability, considering both the probability and the impact of occurrence. Risk is traditionally represented by the formula:

R (risk) = p (probability of occurrence) * C (consequence of occurrence either represented by some value or by a loss function)

Risk management is the process of identifying risk, assessing risk, and taking steps to manage risk by reducing risks to an acceptable level (Stoneburner et al., 2001). Additionally, Smith et al. (2001) and Aubert et al. (1998) agree that IS managers and researchers traditionally define risk in terms of negative consequences describing risk as the possibility of loss or damage and the possibility of suffering harm or loss.

GIS can be used in three of the four steps laid out by Bullock and Haddow (2006) to effectively

assess the risk of disaster. Step two states to "evaluate each hazard for the severity and frequency" (Bullock & Haddow, 2006, p. 54). Geostatistical analysis can be performed within GIS to analyze the probability and severity of a hazard occurring. GIS is already used within the County of San Diego to assess the risk of fire hazards and is used in preparedness and mitigation planning. GIS can also be used to look at other factors that may be influencing the occurrence of a hazard.

Estimating the risk from a natural hazard is step three (Bullock & Haddow, 2006). By using GIS census data, one can quantify the number of people at risk to a particular disaster. GIS can also be used to identify critical facilities that may be in harms way.

Risk assessment can be difficult and require various analyses. Therefore, the Federal Emergency Management Agency (FEMA) developed a risk assessment software program. HAZUS (HAZards United States), as it is called, analyzes potential losses from floods, hurricane winds, and earthquakes. The software combines current scientific and engineering knowledge with GIS technology to estimate physical damage, economic loss and social impacts, step 4 of Bullock and Haddow's risk assessment steps. This tool can ease the burden of risk assessment to make way for mitigation, preparedness, and response efforts.

Mitigation

News and media outlets have capitalized on showing the costly and deadly damages from disasters. Hurricane Andrew crossed Southern Florida and the Louisiana coastline in August of 1992 (Abbott, 1998). Said to be the most destructive hurricane in United States history, Andrew caused $30 million in damages and killed 33 people in Florida and 15 in Louisiana (Abbott, 1998).

One way to prevent such damages and deaths is through mitigation. Mitigation actions involve long-term solutions to reducing the exposure to, probability of, or potential loss from hazards

(Bullock & Haddow, 2006). This can range from fire risk mitigation by land-use management and vegetation clearances in what is referred to as "defensible zones" to building zone restrictions for earthquake mitigation. FEMA's HAZUS software can be used to identify potential damages from floods, hurricanes, and earthquakes allowing for mitigation measures to be implemented in the correct geographic locations.

Year after year the costliest natural disaster to affect the United States is flooding. According to the National Oceanic and Atmospheric Administration (NOAA), flooding caused an average of $4.6 billion in damages during the 20-year period between 1983 and 2003 (Delmedico, 2007). In order to mitigate flood damages FEMA's Mitigation Division administers the National Flood Insurance Program (NFIP). The NFIP defines locations subject to a higher probability of flooding and distributes this data in the form of maps and GIS formats. These maps and the GIS formats give emergency managers flexibility in creating custom flood plain mapping to identify regions and facilities in need of mitigation efforts.

Preparedness

According to HSPD-8, "the term 'preparedness' refers to the existence of plans, procedures, policies, training, and equipment necessary at the Federal, State, and local level to maximize the ability to prevent, respond to, and recover from major events" (Bush, 2003b). Being prepared to respond to a major disaster is a big job. Two main factors in preparedness are the development of emergency operations plans and training in the form of preparedness exercises.

Once the risks of an area are assessed, emergency operations plans can be drawn. Operations plans can be defined as documents that describe policies and methods to be used when executing emergency operations. As HSPD-8 states, one major factor in preparedness plans is the locating of critical infrastructures (Bush, 2003b). GIS

can be used to inventory all critical infrastructure and resources to be deployed in disaster response activities.

Geospatial tools can also assist during emergency preparedness exercises. An emergency preparedness exercise is a simulation of an event in real-time. It is used to test current emergency response personnel and emergency response plans (Aspevig, 2006). As shown in Figure 3, the Montana Department of Public Health and Human Services used GIS and plume modeling to aid in the prediction a chemical release flow caused by a plane crash during the emergency preparedness exercise, Operation Last Chance One (Aspevig, 2006). GIS was then used to map resources and analyze demographics to show affected populations (Aspevig, 2006). These geospatial tools allowed the first responders and emergency management personnel of the Montana Public Health and Human Services to effectively plan for real disasters.

Response

When real disasters strike, the first responders to the event are local fire, police, and emergency medical personnel who are supported by local emergency management personnel and community government officials in an effort to save lives, protect property and meet the basic human needs (Bullock & Haddow, 2006). The emergency response stage immediately follows a disaster and is designed to provide emergency assistance to victims, stabilize the situation, reduce the probability of secondary damage, and speed recovery (Johnson, 2000).

On March 1, 2007 a deadly F3 tornado tore through Americus, Georgia. GIS was used to quickly and effectively "provide data to officials including information on coordinates for helicopters to land, numbers of houses in devastated areas, street location maps, and Red Cross shelter locations" (Butcher, 2007, p. 10). The next day, a FEMA crew was able to look at the damaged

Figure 3. Example of Montana Department of Public Health and Human Services Exercise Map (Aspevig, 2006)

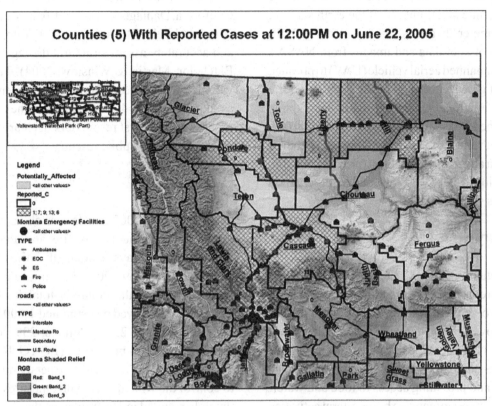

area via a helicopter and draw the tornado's path on a local map. This path was then digitized into a GIS and analyzed to compile a list of addresses of businesses and residences within the path of the tornado. It was this data that allowed emergency managers to begin evaluating damages.

Cartography and geovisualization can also play an important role in communicating with the public and other emergency response agencies during response situations. During the October 2007 wildfires that swept through San Diego, GIS, cartography, and geovisualization played an important role in communicating fire perimeters and evacuation areas amongst emergency management personnel and the public. Beginning on day one of the fires, the GIS Unit at the County of San Diego's Operational Area EOC (OAEOC) was able to construct fire perimeters using GIS

with data obtained from first responder radio traffic, the Sheriff's Astrea helicopter and Radio Amateur Civil Emergency Service (RACES). As evacuation areas were reported via WebEOC, a powerful emergency management communication tool, these too were mapped using GIS. Once this data was compiled, maps were constructed of fire perimeters and evacuation areas and sent to emergency management personnel, the media, and the public. As the fires progressed, perimeter data became more readily available from the California Department of Forestry and Fire Protection (CAL FIRE) and the San Diego City Fire Department via GIS formats.

Federal assets were also available. MODIS, Moderate Resolution Imaging Spectroradiometer, is a key instrument aboard the Terra and Aqua satellites that has the ability to detect hot spots on the earth's surface. NASA's Ikhana UAV flew at low altitude over Southern California to generate near-real time aerial images of the earth surface. Fire perimeter data was overlain with MODIS satellite hot-spot data and images from NASA's Ikhana unmanned aerial vehicle (UAV) to produce powerful geovisualization of the situation in the form of situational awareness maps. The Ikhana UAV helped to visually display the current surface of the earth and the current fire damage. Together, these data and maps were able to provide valuable information to emergency responders, emergency managers, and the public.

Recovery

Once a situation is stable, the recovery stage may begin to return all systems to normal. Recovery often involves two stages: short-term and long term-recovery. Short-term projects include restoration of vital life-support systems to minimum operating standards such as cleanup, temporary housing, and providing access to food and water. However, recovery can also be long-term activities that may continue for a number of years after a disaster. Long-term recovery aims to return life to normal or an improved, safer level. Examples of long-term recovery projects include redevelopment loans, legal assistance, and community mitigation planning (Johnson, 2000).

Geospatial tools can play a vital role in both of these stages. In the aftermath of the March 1, 2007 tornado in Americus, Georgia, GIS was used to query city and county properties available for recovery shelters (Butcher, 2007). GIS was also used to calculate the amount of square miles affected by the tornado. In the weeks following, maps were developed to track the clean-up process. Beverly Butcher, sole GIS Coordinator in the City of Americus, Georgia, stated: "As of March 31, 2007, I had printed more than 2,600 maps. All the information that was produced during this time benefited the community and raised awareness of the value of GIS" (Butcher, 2007, p. 12-13).

In the fall of 2003, San Diego was devastated by one of the worst wildfire disasters to hit California. Damage Assessment Teams, equipped with hand-held GPS units were able to quickly and accurately assess structural damage (Binge, Batchelor, Martin & Winslow, 2004). This data was then used to create damage assessment maps, as shown in Figure 4, to keep track of the recovery process and aid first responders in clearing areas to be opened for public re-entry.

Research

On October 21, 2007 two fires broke out in San Diego County, the Harris fire and the Witch fire. Within 10 days, a total of 7 fires burned approximately 369,000 acres, this equates to roughly 13% of the county's total land mass. These fires destroyed an estimated 1,600 homes, 800 outbuildings, 253 structures, 239 vehicles, and 2 commercial properties (EG&G Technical Services, 2007). Over 6,200 fire personnel fought to control the wind driven wild land fires that ultimately resulted in 10 civilian deaths, 23 civilian injuries, and 89 firefighter injuries.

The author responded on the GIS Unit to the County of San Diego's Operational Area Emergency Operation Center (OAEOC), which was responsible for coordinating and supporting the overall response to these active fires. Geospatial tools played an important role during the response to the 2007 firestorm. The 2007 Firestorm After Action Report states:

"Throughout the incident, the GIS Unit provided the common operating picture (COP) for the seven fires that were burning throughout the county, five of which were considered large in scope and size. The COP incident information included fire perimeters; active fire areas from the Modis Satellite; evacuated areas; evacuation shelters; road closures; and Local Assistances Centers (LACs). Other location information included community names; freeways and major roads; a

Figure 4. County of San Diego 2003 Cedar Fire Damage Assessment Map

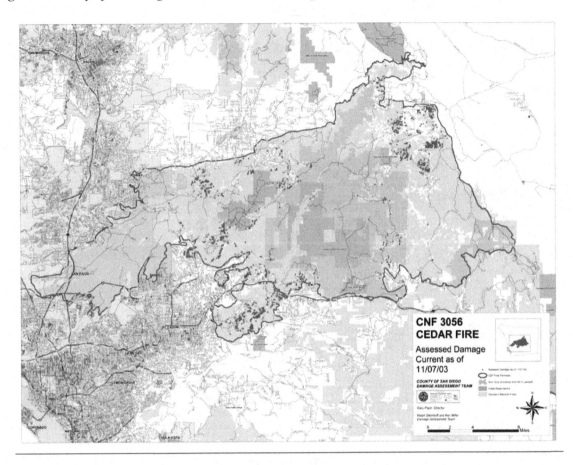

Thomas Brothers' page grid; Indian reservations; military lands; and U.S. Department of Agriculture (USDA) Forest Service lands." (EG&G Technical Services, 2007, p. 15 - 16)

An example of a COP map from the 2007 firestorm used in the San Diego OAEOC can be seen in Figure 5 and an example of a map, developed by the County of San Diego's Health and Human Services (HHSA), depicting the LAC's can be seen in Figure 6. These maps were both used by emergency managers and the public during the 2007 Firestorm. These maps provided situational awareness and offered a medium to convey vital information.

The 2007 AAR goes on to state,

"Incident geospatial information was used for a variety of purposes throughout the fires. Perimeter data was used to help determine evacuations; evacuation data was combined with demographic data to estimate the number of people evacuated, shelter sizes, and locations; the County Department of Environmental Health (DEH) used fire perimeter, evacuation data to identify hazardous materials in the path of the fires and used environmental health GIS layers to map and assess health issues in the area of active fire or power outages; evacuation boundaries were used to track repopulation of communities; government facilities data was overlaid with fire perimeters to determine potential impacts of services; parcel, assessor, and housing unit information was provided to incident teams in the field; and fire imagery

255

Figure 5. 2007 Firestorm COP map from the County of San Diego's OAEOC

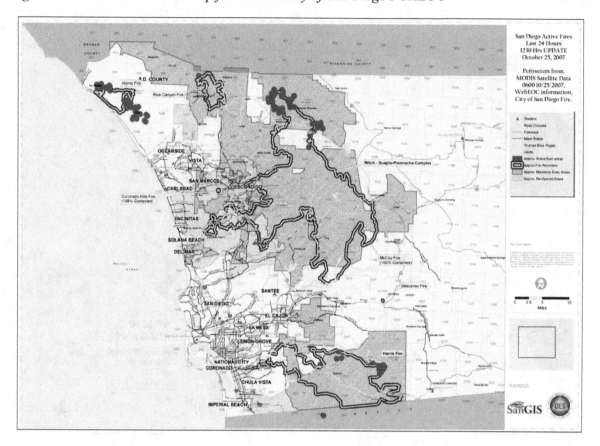

from different aerial platforms was provided to incident teams, policy members, and hazardous material teams. In addition, the county's Health and Human Services used the data to determine care facilities that were threatened or needed to be evacuated, and mapped health-related incidents." (EG&G Technical Services, 2007, p. 15 - 16)

An example of the aforementioned County of San Diego's HHSA's use of geospatial tools to map health-related incidents can be seen in Figure 7.

In fact, the GIS Unit at the County of San Diego OAEOC was recognized by Environmental Systems Research Institute (ESRI), the leading provider of GIS software, for their successful use of GIS in the 2007 wildfire response (Environmental Systems Research Institute, 2008).

The use of geospatial tools in this response was related to the integration of geospatial tools and emergency management functions at the County of San Diego's OAEOC, an example of which is shown in Figure 8. Before the incident occurred, the emergency managers understood and valued the usefulness and ease of use of geospatial tools. The emergency managers were familiar with what geospatial tools could offer, valued their use, and understood the process in which to request their use. This enabled them to request geospatial products and maps.

During the response efforts it was noticed that the various management and general staff of the EOC needed to understand the help that geospatial tools could offer in order to request such analysis and maps. In particular it was noted that staff needed to understand what types of analysis

Figure 6. 2007 Firestorm map depicting the LAC locations, developed by the County of San Diego's HHSA

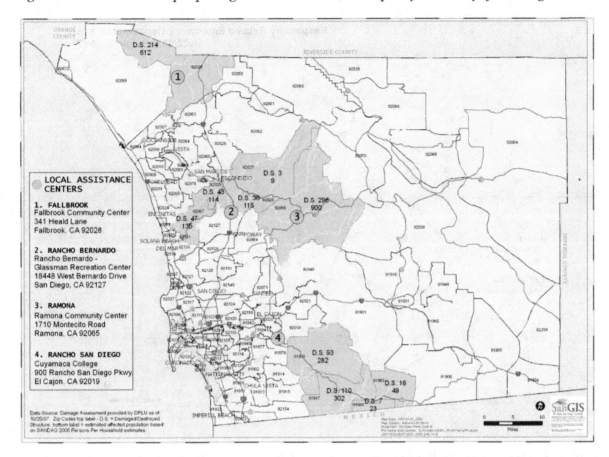

that could be conducted, types of data collected during the incident and available data collected pre-incident, how to request a map or analysis product, and at what scale maps could effectively portray data. This knowledge would provide for seamless geospatial integration and offer the OAEOC more geospatial products in which to more effectively respond to disasters.

Subsequent action research during day-to-day workings at the County of San Diego's OES resulted in similar findings. OES currently uses geospatial tools in many aspects of emergency management.

This was a great improvement over the use of GIS in past fire responses. During the 2003 firestorm, geospatial tools were not as widely used. Also, maps depicting the fire perimeter,

evacuation areas, local assistance centers, and shelters were not as widely available. The County of San Diego 2007 Firestorm After Action Report listed the following improvements since the 2003 fire response (EG&G Technical Services, 2007, p. 13 – 14):

- GIS positions were established within OES for day-to-day operations and OAEOC response during an incident. GIS staff and resources were established at departmental DOCs and the MOC.

- There was [GIS] participation in numerous county-level OAEOC disaster preparedness exercises."

Figure 7. HHSA map from the 2007 Firestorm depicting respiratory related emergency department visits.

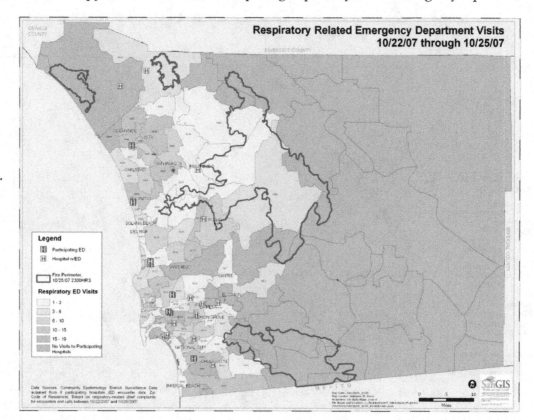

It was this integration of GIS prior to the 2007 Firestorm that enabled the emergency managers to become more familiar with and accepting of geospatial tools. This awareness and acceptance was needed to more fully integrate geospatial tools into emergency management.

FINDINGS

It is concluded that in order to integrate Geospatial tools in the form of Geographic Information Systems (GIS), geovisualization, and cartography into the fields of risk assessment, mitigation, preparedness, response, and recovery emergency managers need to be made aware of these geospatial tools in order to perceive their usefulness and ease of use. In the case of the County of San Diego OES this was done through employing a

GIS analyst during day-to-day operations prior to the 2007 Firestorm. This enabled the emergency managers to become more familiar with geospatial tools. The second way to integrate geospatial tools into the emergency management process is to train emergency managers on what geospatial tools have to offer.

According to TAM, two ways to gain user acceptance of a new computer system are through the user's perception of ease of use and usefulness. In order to show these two posits, a training session could encompass the collected data of this study and contain the following elements:

• **Definitions:** Explain what geospatial tools the GIS Unit uses, including the software names, how it is used, and a broad overview of the core concepts.

Figure 8. Example of day-to-day uses of geospatial tools in the County of San Diego OES.

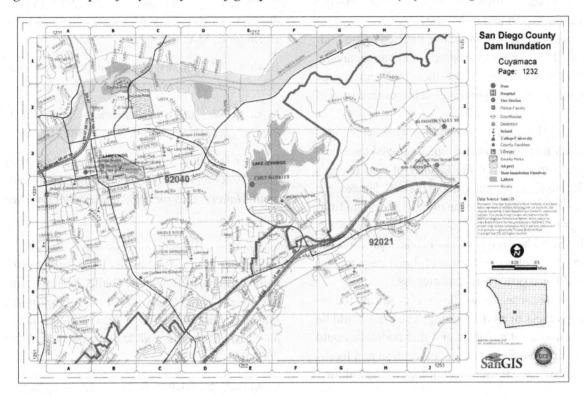

- **Explanation:** Give examples of how geospatial tools can aid emergency management functions. This may help to captivate the audience and help them relate more to the training content.
- **Data:** List and describe the types of data that could be collected during the incident as well as an overview of available data collected pre-incident.
- **Analysis:** Briefly explain the types of analysis that could be conducted to increase the effectiveness of emergency manager roles.
- **Map Requests:** This could be a "how-to" presentation on how emergency managers can request a map or analysis product including at what scale maps could effectively portray data, an overview of map sizes, and an explanation as to how the GIS unit would like to receive map requests (via paper forms, online forms, or verbal requests).

Providing this training to a group of emergency managers and testing the acceptance of this training was outside the timeframe of this study, however, it will be discussed in the conclusion.

CONCLUSION

The objective of this study was to identify strategies to prepare emergency management personnel to effectively integrate geospatial tools in the form of Geographic Information Systems (GIS), geovisualization, and cartography into the emergency management functions of risk assessment, mitigation, preparedness, response, and recovery.

To accomplish these objectives and address the research question, data collection was in the form of action research and direct observation as a GIS Analyst in the OAEOC during the 2007 Firestorm, review of the 2003 Firestorm After

Action Report, review of the 2007 Firestorm After Action Report and a literature review.

The analysis of the above data led to the findings that in order to prepare emergency management personnel to integrate these tools, emergency managers need to perceive usefulness and ease of use of geospatial tools.

Employing a GIS analyst to work with emergency management personnel allowed the emergency managers at the County of San Diego's OES to gain awareness about the tool. However, a training course providing the two important findings to integrate new technology with audiences that TAM laid out (the user needs to perceive the new technology will be useful and easy to use) could also provide this awareness.

Future research would involve testing the effectiveness of a GIS training. The class could be given to a set audience and that audience could be surveyed for their new perception and likelihood of using the new technology of the training.

REFERENCES

Abbott, P. L. (1998). *Natural Disasters 2e*. New Jersey: William C. Brown.

Aspevig, J. (2006 Spring). Hosted by Montana Department of Public Health and Human Services: Disaster Preparedness Exercise Uses GIS. *ArcNews Online*. Retrieved on January 3, 2008 from http://www.esri.com/news/arcnews/ spring06articles/ disaster-preparedness.html

Aubert, B., Patry, M., & Rivard, S. (1998). Assessing the Risk of IT Outsourcing. *Proceedings of the 31st Hawaii International Conference on Systems Sciences* (pp. 685-693). IEEE Publishing.

Binge, M. L., Batchelor, J., Martin, R. P., & Winslow, R. (2004). Using GIS As a Disaster Management Tool. *Proceedings of the ESRI User Conference 2004*. San Diego: ESRI.

Bullock, J. A., & Haddow, G. D. (2006). Introduction to Emergency Management. (2nd Ed.). Burlington, MA: Elsevier.

Bush, G. W. (2003a). *Homeland Security Presidential Directive/HSPD-5*. The White House.

Bush, G. W. (2003b). *Homeland Security Presidential Directive/HSPD-8*. The White House.

Butcher, B. (2007, Summer). GIS Helps Americus Quickly Respond to Tornado Damage. *Government Matters: GIS for State and Local Governement* (pp. 8-13).

Careem, M., Bittner, D., & de Silva, R. (2007). GIS Integration in the Sahana Disaster Management System. In B. Van de Walle, P. Burghardt, & C. Nieuwenhuis (Eds.), *Proceedings of the 4th International Conference on Information Systems for Crisis Response and Management ISCRAM 2007* (pp. 211-218).

Chan, A. H. S., & Chan, K. W. L. (2006). Synchronous and asynchronous presentations of auditory and visual signals: Implications for control console design. *Applied Ergonomics*, *37*(2), 131–140. doi:10.1016/j.apergo.2005.06.006

Dahinten, J. (2002, January 1). Natural disasters kill 25,000 worldwide in 2001. *Reuters*. Retrieved January 8, 2008, from http://www.planetark.org/ dailynewsstory.cfm/newsid/13886/newsDate/1-Jan-2002/story.htm

Davis, F. D., Bagozzi, R. P., & Warshaw, P. R. (1989). User acceptance of computer technology: A comparison of two theoretical models. *Management Science*, *35*, 982–1003. doi:10.1287/ mnsc.35.8.982

Delmedico, N. (2007 July-September). Take Advantage of New Floodplain Data: Understanding dFIRMs Necessary for Intelligently Mapping Hazards. *ArcUser* (pp. 22-25).

Dent, B. D. (1999). *Cartography: Thematic Map Design 5e*. Dubuque, Iowa: William C Brown.

EG&G Technical Services (Ed.) (2007). *County of San Diego 2007 Firestorms After Action Report*. Unpublished Manuscript.

Environmental Systems Research Institute. (2008, March 3). *ESRI Recognizes San Diego County Officials for GIS Work during Wildfires: GIS Use Improved Communications, Saved Infrastructure, and Assisted in Evacuations*. Press Release. Retrieved on March 4, 2008 from http://www.esri.com/news/releases/08_1qtr/san_diego_wildfires.html

Federal Emergency Management Agency (FEMA). (2009). *NIMS Resource Center*. Department of Homeland Security. Retrieved on May 17, 2009 from: http://www.fema.gov/emergency/nims/.

Francica, J. (2004, March 4). The Interagency Geospatial Preparedness Team (IGPT): An Interview with Susan Kalweit, Chief, IGPT. *Directions Magazine*. Retrieved January 3, 2008, from http://www.directionsmag.com/ article.php?article_id=324&trv=1

Granlund, R., Johansson, B., & Trnka, J. (2007). The Effects of Geographical Information Systems on a Collaborative Command and Control Task. In B. Van de Walle, P. Burghardt & C. Nieuwenhuis (Eds.), *Proceedings of the 4th International Conference on Information Systems for Crisis Response and Management ISCRAM 2007* (pp. 191-200).

Johnson, R. (2000). *GIS Technology for Disasters and Emergency Mangement*. Redlands, CA: ESRI Press.

Kataoka, M. (2005). *GIS for Homeland Security*. Redlands, CA: ESRI Press.

Koch, K. (2007, 29 August). *Katrina-ravaged Gulf Coast struggling 2 years later*. CNN.com/us. Retrieved on February 8, 2008, from http://www.cnn.com/2007/ US /08/29/katrina.day/index.html?iref=newssearch

Longley, P. A., Goodchild, M. F., Maquire, D. J., & Rhind, D. W. (2001). *Geographic Information Systems and Science*. New Jersey: John Wiley & Sons.

Office of Emergency Services. (2007). *Standardized Emergency Management System (SEMS) Guidelines*. Governor's Office of Emergency Services, State of California. Retrieved on May 15, 2009 from: http://www.oes.ca.gov/Operational/OESHome.nsf/Content/B49435352108954488256C2A0071E038?OpenDocument.

Rubenstein, J. (2002). *The Cultural Landscape: An Introduction to Human Geography 7e*. New Jersey: Prentice Hall

Smith, H. A., McKeen, J. D., & Staples, D. S. (2001). Risk Management in Information Systems: Problems and Potentials. *Communications of AIS*, 7, 13.

Stoneburner, G., Goguen, A., & Feringa, A. (2007). *NIST Special Publication 800-30, Risk Management Guide for Information Technology Systems*. United States National Institute of Standards and Technology.

This work was previously published in International Journal of Information Systems for Crisis Response and Management, Volume 1, Issue 4, edited by Murray E. Jennex, pp. 33-49, copyright 2009 by IGI Publishing (an imprint of IGI Global).

Chapter 17
Initial Requirements of National Crisis Decision Support System

Ahmad Kabil
Lawrence Technological University, USA

Magdy Kabeil
Sadat Academy for Management Sciences, Egypt

ABSTRACT

The National Crisis Decision Support System NCDSS represents special type of mission critical systems highly responsive enough to face a national crisis. The value of a NCDSS is assessed according to its impact on the value of surviving a national crisis. Such systems should have common initial requirements associated with their common conceptual design. A conceptual design representing basic modules of NCDSS is developed. The conceptual design provides a general foundation that can be transferred to a detailed design and implementation of an application. The proposed concept of NCDSS meets the initial specifications that are validated using a case scenario. The relative percentage of the total score that each module contributes to the design is evaluated using the Analytical Hierarchy Process (AHP) and the Quality Function Deployment (QFD) technique.

INTRODUCTION

National Crisis Decision Support System NCDSS represents special type of mission critical systems highly responsive enough to face a national crisis. The value of a NCDSS is assessed according to its impact on the value of surviving a national crisis. Such systems should have common initial requirements associated with their common conceptual design.

The performance of somebody facing danger is far different from his performance in the normal life, whatever the normal life challenges. A man avoiding bomb explosion is faster than himself in racetrack, no matter what prize of the race would be. At crisis situation the secretions of the pituitary gland stimulate the other endocrine glands, which activate the body subsystems to perform at full

DOI: 10.4018/978-1-60960-609-1.ch017

throttle with extraordinary effectiveness (Lewis, 2005). A measure of survivability of a living system is its flexibility to switch from maximum efficiency mode to maximum effectiveness mode according to the environmental dynamics (Miller, 1978).

Countries like human beings need some functioning system that can stimulate and leverage the relevant subsystems to perform at maximum effectiveness in crisis situation (Alpaslan, et al., 2009). Developing a National Crisis Management Center (NCMC) that can carry this responsibility has been an attractive idea on both governmental and corporate levels in many countries. "In times of crisis, communities and members of organizations expect their leaders to minimize the impact of the crisis at hand, while critics and bureaucratic competitors try to seize the moment to blame incumbent rulers and their policies" (Boin et al., 2006, p.151).

A measure of merit of a NCMC is its ability to allocate all relevant capabilities to be the most effective on the right points at the right times over all crisis phases (Kienzle, et al., 2010). The most critical factor in NCM processes is the high pace of events relative to the corresponding decision cycles (Schafer & Crichlow, 2002). However, if we record a crisis scenario on a video tape and replay it in slow motion, we will see it as a regular problem. On the other side, if the NCMIS can provide the crisis management team with the capabilities that make them feel, recognize, comprehend, analyze, structure, and decide faster, the NCM processes will be as manageable as the regular problem management processes. "Crisis management is all about the functional adaptation of communities, administrative agency, and political decision-making processes to the extreme conditions of crisis" (Hart & Boin, 2001, p. 30).

In most countries, crisis management is handled by a national security council consisting of key leaders of the country. Each member of the council has a different perspective based upon his own functioning MIS. There is no centralized NCMIS that can support integrating the different perspec-

tives of the different members of the council in one comprehensive decision structure. A National Center for Crisis Management is developed in some countries as an educational resource and advising body rather than an operational command center (Aini, 2001; Crisis-Navigator, 2008; ISSCM, 2008; NCCM, 2008; NCCMRT, 2008).

The NCMIS is more complex than regular systems because the solution sets are dynamic and reflect the changing nature of domains in crisis situations (Tiwana & Ramesh, 2001). Data requirements of NCMIS are different from regular MIS in several aspects: (1) data comes from different sources in different formats with different levels of timeliness; (2) the content of a data set is usually encountered in a mass of similar material relating to a variety of both relevant and irrelevant subjects; (3) critical data items need efficient methods of filtering, validating, referencing, cataloging, storing, and updating in limited time frame; (4) significant items of data when separated from other material surrounding it are often found to be fragmentary and incomplete; (5) detection of an important data item is usually followed by an intensive search for further complementary material; (6) much of the information is non-quantitative in nature and needs special techniques to incorporate it in the decision structure; (7) information is frequently highly subjective and consists of opinions and assessments rather than factual data; (8) information interpretation is often inseparable from that of acquisition of information; and (9) much of the work of information processing is concentrated on the search for clues from which assessment of present and potential future environmental conditions can be made (Radford, 1978).

The objective of this study is to define initial requirements of NCMIS that can be implemented into a specific detailed design for each particular application. A case scenario is used for testing the validity of NCMIS concept in meeting the initial requirements. A set of integrated requirements of expected crises is defined using the Analytical Hierarchy Process (AHP) and used as input to the

Quality Function Deployment (QFD) technique for evaluating the design modules (Akao, 1990).

The chapter is structured in seven sections. After this introduction, are discussed the levels of processing in a decision making cycle, which serve as a guide for addressing relevant modules of the conceptual design and workflow in the succeeding two sections. Next, design validation and a proof of concept (March & Smith, 1995) are presented in its application to a specific crisis scenario. In section six, the relative weight of each design module is evaluated. Finally, the contributions of the study and its limitations are discussed in the conclusion.

QUALITY FUNCTION IN DECISION CYCLE

The origin of the word "decide" is the Latin word "decidere", which means, literally, "to cut-off" ("de" means "off" and "cidere" means "to cut") (Stump, 2002). If all other conditions could be held equal, the quality of decision improves with time of thinking up to certain level and thereafter declines. A good practice in crisis management is to cut-off at a saddle point of the decision's quality-time curve within the available time limit as depicted in Figure 1.

The quality of decision is built from the very beginning all through the decision cycle (Herek et al., 1987; Keren & de-Bruin, 2004). The ge-

neric decision cycle in crisis management context starts with data gathering that is processed further to higher levels of information, knowledge, intelligence, wisdom, and decision (Figure 2). The decision is implemented through a Command, Control, Communication, Computer, and Intelligence (C4I) System to move a real-world-situation to be more suitable for the next decision or action. In this model, six layers of concepts require different levels of processing:

1. Data is defined as facts, symbols, or signals. The process of data gathering or acquisition is performed by employing several methods including general scanning, directed scanning, and active search (Radford, 1978).
2. Information is defined as useful data. Usefulness of data depends on the user, time and context of use (Shankaranarayanan & Cai, 2006; Shankaranarayanan et al., 2003). Transforming data to information starts with data cleansing and interpretation (Hernandez & Stolfo, 1998). Data interpretation helps assessing the usefulness of the data that is acquired and giving guidance feedback to the data acquisition process (Ballou et al., 1998; Fisher et al., 2003; Wang et al., 1998).
3. Knowledge is defined as the know-how of behavior. According to the Bureau for Crisis Prevention and Recovery (BCPR) of the United Nations Development Program (UNDP) (BCPR, 2007), knowledge management is defined as "the practice of capturing, storing and sharing knowledge so that we can learn lessons from the past and apply them in the future." (Lattimer et al., 2007, p. ix). Earl (2001) classifies knowledge management strategies into three categories: Technocratic, Behavioral, and Economic.
4. Intelligence is defined, in this context, as the capability of handling new situations. This definition considers intelligence as a complement of the capability of handling programmable situations. The definition is

Figure 1. Cut-off Points

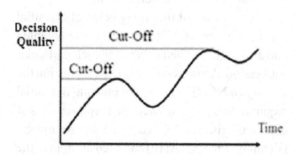

Figure 2. Levels of Processing in Decision Making

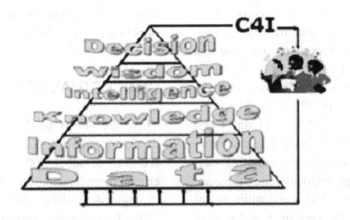

close to Merriam Webster's definition "the ability to learn or understand or to deal with new or trying situations" (MWD, 2008). Collective intelligence is a form of intelligence that emerges from the collaboration and competition of many individuals (MIT, 2008).

5. Wisdom is defined as the values and beliefs that form the preferences of a decision maker. Wisdom should reflect the philosophy and moral hierarchy of the group that the decision makers represent. The lack of representing group wisdom in a decision structure is a main source of mistakes in strategic decision making. Differences in wisdom and conflict of cultures are main factors in many international crises. Maris Martinsons (2001) has found that American, Japanese and Chinese leaders each exhibit a distinctive national wisdom in decision making.

6. Decision, the model's capstone, is defined as a selection of course of action among several alternatives to interact with a real-world-situation according to a set of preferences that reflect a specific wisdom. Human performance in decision making terms has been subject of active research from psychological, neurological, cognitive, and normative perspectives (Davern et al.,

2008; Hammond et al., 1980; Hammond et al., 1975; Post, 2004). From a psychological perspective, individual decisions are examined in the context of a set of needs, preferences and values (Curhan et al., 2004; Plous, 1993). From neuroscience perspective, decisions with uncertainty are aided by emotions (Greenberg & Safran, 1984; Kennerley et al., 2006; Naqvi et al., 2006). From a cognitive perspective, the decision making process is considered as a continuous process integrated in the interaction with the environment (Briggs, 1962). From a normative perspective, the analysis of individual decisions is concerned with the logic and rationality of decision making (Bell et al., 1988; Byrne, 2005; Kahneman & Tversk, 2000; Levin, 2006).

7. Some research using naturalistic methods show that in situations with higher time pressure and increased ambiguities experts use intuitive decision making rather than structured approaches (Zsambok & Klein, 1997). They follow recognition primed decision approach (Klein, 1998) to correlate a set of indicators to the expert's experience and directly arrive at a satisfactory course of action without weighing alternatives (Camerer & Johnson, 1991). Robust

decision-making extends the robust design philosophy (Fowlkes & Creveling, 1995) to general decision making approach by controlling what uncertainty possible and finding the best feasible solution that is as insensitive as possible to the remaining uncertainty (Ullman, 2006).

8. Katsenelinboigen (1997, p. 6) states that apart from the methods (selective or reactive) and sub-methods (programming, randomization, or predispositioning), there are two basic styles, which are combinational and positional. The combinational style is characterized by a clearly defined goal with outcomes linked to the initial position. The positional style is distinguished by a positional goal that allows making decisions in the unknown future using semi-complete linkages between the initial step and final outcome.

9. Most psychologists and political science scholars (Janis & Mann, 1977) believe that the main reason of defective decision making is "Groupthink". Groupthink is a type of thought exhibited by group members who try to minimize conflict and reach consensus without critically testing, analyzing, and evaluating ideas (Janis, 1982). Janis listed seven symptoms of the defective decision-making process which groupthink can produce: (1) incomplete survey of alternatives, (2) incomplete survey of objectives, (3) failure to examine risks of the preferred choice, (4) failure to reappraise initially rejected alternatives, (5) poor information search, (6) selective bias in processing available information, and (7) failure to develop contingency plans.

The quality of the decision layer is based upon the quality of wisdom layer and the quality and creativity of alternatives developed in lower layers of the model.

The C4I loop moves a real-world situation to the most appropriate position for the next decision or action (Harris, 1998).

CONCEPTUAL DESIGN OF NCMIS

There are numerous decisions associated with the development of NCMIS (Hevner et al., 2004; Klashner & Sabet, 2007). Conceptual design is crucial to understanding a new or complex MIS (Sprague & Carlson, 1982; Sprague & Watson, 1996). In engineering, conceptual design is defined as the creation, exploration, and presentation of ideas (Hudspeth, 2008). The conceptual design of the NCMIS identifies the very general type of solution that triggers and captures new ideas or opportunities to start with and identifies potential candidates for further development in each specific application case (Simitsis & Vassiliadis, 2008). It reflects the common requirements of NCMC in general terms that can be transferred later into detailed design (Austin, 1989; Bergman et al., 2000; Han et al., 2007; Treadgold, 2006; Turoff, 2002).

The decision making process consists of three main phases, intelligence, design and choice (Simon, 1977). Radford (1978) modifies Simon's model to take into account the interaction between participants. The NCMIS conceptual design consists of four main units, which are Intelligence Unit (NCMC-1), Design and Operations Unit (NCMC-2), Choice Unit (NCMC-3), and Integration and Display Unit (NCMC-4). Kabeil (2009) defines 15 modules that are included in the four main units as depicted in Figure 3 and as illustrated bellow.

NCMC-1. Intelligence Unit

Information relevant to the decision situation is gathered and maintained by the intelligence unit all through the crisis life cycle. This information is used to review courses of action that might be available to each of the participants and to construct possible future scenarios of the crisis (Hunt, 2001).

Information gathering is conducted at two levels, strategic and tactical. Strategic information is needed to formulate policies at the national levels. Tactical information is intended primarily to respond to the needs of crisis dynamics. The unit ensures that relevant data is readily timely accessible to the team members while still adhering to security standards such as security clearance and need-to-know principles. The unit includes the following seven modules.

NCMC-1.1. Monitoring Module

The Monitoring Module supports the production, dissemination, and display of crisis theater data. It consists of nodes that can create, receive, edit,

transmit, and store video clips as well as images, graphics, voice, and text data. Data can be either broadcasted in the operations room or shared interactively among system subscribers on a point-to-point or multi-point basis with a "push-pull" capability. The "pull" capability is designed to prevent communications circuit saturation by requesting and receiving only data relevant to the current phase of the crisis. On the other side, the "push" capability is designed to prompt time sensitive intelligence in near real time.

The module may use one or more of the following elements.

- NCMC-1.1.1. Video Element: the element is responsible for recording and sending online status of the crisis theater using sev-

Figure 3. Conceptual Design of the NCMIS

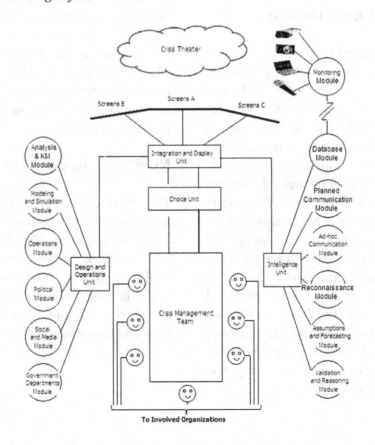

eral video channels according to the number of required views.

- NCMC-1.1.2. Imaging Element: the element is responsible for recording and sending batches of pictures depicting the status of the crisis theater whenever there is a meaningful situational change.
- NCMC-1.1.3. Sketching Element: the element is responsible for creating and sending batches of sketches depicting the status of the crisis theater whenever there is a meaningful situational change.
- NCMC-1.1.4. Audio Element: the element is responsible for reporting orally on the status of the crisis theater.

The crisis theater data is delivered interactively. So, the Monitoring Module can support the crisis management team with further clarification or simple interpretations.

NCMC-1.2. Database Module

Crisis management database is an integrated collection of NCMIS core data. The database structure corresponds to the needs of the expected crises and allows for access by multiple users and for use by several applications of the center. One of the basic principles of database management is to keep data where it is easily updated. So, while data is organized in a common structure, the sources of the data are quite diverse (Brooks, 2006). Data sources are organized in three categories. First category is internal data that is created and updated by the center itself including data-warehousing. Second category is preformatted data received on a regular basis from specific organizations based upon specific protocols. The third is ad-hoc data received from organizations in open format based upon the specialty. The timeliness and multitude of NCMC's data may need to be managed in distributed databases.

NCMC-1.3. Planned Communication Module

This module is responsible for building and managing a network of distributed databases belonging to several organizations and government departments. The coordination protocols between the NCMC and each one of these organizations and government departments include contents, structure, format, updating times, security, and error control of data exchange (Chen et al., 2008). The principles of Electronic Data Interchange (EDI) are applied to this module (Beckner, 2008; Fowler et al., 2007).

NCMC-1.4. Ad-Hoc Communication Module

This module is responsible for developing an index of data sources of different subjects and specialties. The coordination protocols between the NCMC and each one of these sources of data include only types of content, format, response time, security, and error control of data exchange. The module may include several intelligence cooperation frameworks on both international and regional levels which operate on a long-term institutional form.

NCMC-1.5. Reconnaissance Module

This module is responsible for conducting information gathering activities of strategic or operational significance. The module complements other intelligence modules by obtaining specific, well-defined and time-sensitive information. Tasks include environmental reconnaissance, armed reconnaissance, target and threat assessment and post-strike reconnaissance.

NCMC-1.6. Assumptions and Forecasting Module

The first responsibility of this module is to fill gaps of data in the decision structure (Ballou & Pazer, 2003; Fildes et al., 2006). A basic principle of handling missing data in decision structure is "assume don't ignore." There are several techniques for assuming missing data including statistics, regression, modeling, and simulation models.

The second responsibility of the module is to conduct forecasting activities including meteorological forecasts, prediction of decision consequences, and warning capabilities (NSCFM, 1984). A typology of uncertainty is developed and maintained in this module along with a framework for handling uncertainty at different stages in the crisis management processes (Refsgaard et al., 2007; Royes & Bastos, 2006).

NCMC-1.7. Validation and Reasoning Module

Reasoning is the process by which new information is derived from combinations of existing information. Reasoning allows crisis management team to rely on information as facts, even though they have not specifically verified this information in a physical manner (Browne et al., 1997). No decision in the crisis context is void of the need for reasoning (Brynielsson, 2007). However, the more structured a decision context is, the less reasoning necessary for a successful outcome.

After intelligence data is delivered, intelligence unit is responsible for supporting the analysts as they integrate the intelligence data into their decision making and planning processes. Data may require further clarification or the analysts may raise new issues that must be immediately addressed. Data may need to be related to a larger intelligence picture. Data may cause the user to consider new operational concepts that require the intelligence to be interpreted in a new context. Evaluation and feedback are continuously performed during every other phase of the intelligence cycle.

The main quality attributes of the unit are timely, accurate, usable (tailored to the specific needs), complete, relevant, objective (unbiased, undistorted, and free from political or other constraints), available (including appropriate security classification), understandable, concise, and synchronized with operations.

NCMC-2. Design and Operations Unit

The main responsibility of this module is to develop alternatives for decision making. Creativity in developing alternatives is a key factor in crisis decision making. Alternatives may include one or combinations of technological, industrial, diplomatic, economic, and/or military operations. Specifications of alternatives and possible courses of action are identified and clearly formulated. The unit includes the following six modules.

NCMC-2.1. Analysis and Knowledge Management Module

The module coordinates with the database module for maintaining the NCMC data-warehouse. Several techniques and tools are available to support decision-analysts in synthesizing the fragments of information, gleaning the most possible from their content, and forming a base of knowledge for decision making (DeRouen & Sprecher, 2004). Six analytic techniques are recommended by Global Security Organization (GSO, 2008).

- Matrix manipulation, from the simple use of associating people, events and objects to sophisticated use in multi-criteria multi-alternatives analysis and entities affinity analysis.
- Link analysis, where pictures and symbols are used to identify and show relationships among people, events and objects.

- Time-event charting (TEC), which is a method for placing actions in chronological form using symbols representing events, dates, and the flow of time.
- Visual investigative analysis (VIA) charting, which depicts the sequence of activities and events that lead up to carrying out a specific task.
- Program evaluation review technique (PERT) charting, which decomposes complex tasks into their component parts and identify the critical path, and probabilities of completion period within time constraints.
- Data-mining, which detects special patterns and clues from large volume of data maintained in the data-warehouse (Chen et al., 2008).

Each of these tools could be used for data analysis and creating tables, charts and graphs that interpret and clarify the results.

Knowledge in crisis management context includes domain-specific rules, heuristics, boundaries, constraints, previous outcomes, know-how, and entities behavior. The module is responsible for dealing with both explicit and tacit knowledge. Explicit knowledge is documented and easy to be programmed into the DSS by its own analysts, acquired by the DSS through repeated use, or distributed over specialized organizations. Tacit knowledge, on the other hand, is built in human beings as mental models and technical experiences. The tacit knowledge is managed in the NCMIS through a network of experts in different domains and protocols of communicating with them. Knowledge engineers in the module interview the domain experts and gather the information necessary for the DSS (Wang & Belardo, 2005; Zack, 1999). A variety of knowledge acquisition techniques such as interviewing, protocol analysis, brain storming, and modeling, among many others, are used to transfer tacit knowledge into explicit knowledge (Fischer & Mastaglio, 1991; Nevo & Chan, 2007; Turoff et.al. 2009).

NCMC-2.2. Modeling and Simulation Module

The first responsibility of this module is to develop and maintain the model-base of the NCMIS. Models and simulation are used for simplifying, normalizing, and documenting behavior of entities, events, processes, and phenomena relevant to expected crises. The module provides vehicles for estimating the possible outcomes of a decision problem over a wide range of possible conditions. The second responsibility of the module is to represent decision makers' preferences, to incorporate qualitative factors in decision structure, to integrate all models related to the crisis in consideration, and to develop the complete decision structure.

The model base contains both optimizing and satisfycing or heuristics models (Barkhi et al., 2005). The ability to run individual or combined models or to construct new models makes the NCMIS a powerful tool.

NCMC-2.3. Operations Module

Amongst the majority of security forces in a country there are usually small special task forces with unique ability to conduct military actions in crisis context. Despite the fact that these task forces belong to different line of command (such as DoD), the NCMC team (including the top commander of DoD) should be involved transparently in all details of crisis operations. Diverse military operations in crises context are a part of one or more of these missions (Holt & deVelde, 1961):

- Direct Action: It is a short duration strike or a small-scale offensive operation undertaken to seize, destroy, capture, recover or inflict damage on designated personnel or material in a crisis. Information requirements for direct actions include maps, weather, theater, weapons, and personnel. Most of the relevant data is maintained in the original department.

- Psychological Operation: It is conducted for conveying selected information to foreign audiences to influence their motives, emotions, objective reasoning and ultimately the behavior of crisis actors.

- Civil Affairs: It consolidates operational activities by assisting crisis management team in establishing, maintaining, influencing or exploiting relations between operation forces and civil authorities, both governmental and non-governmental, and the civilian population.

- Information Operations: It refers to actions taken place to affect the adversary's information systems while defending friendly information systems.

Despite the fact that each one of these missions uses its own DSS-C4I system, interfacing these systems to the crisis decision structure is the duty of the Operational Unit in the NCMIS.

NCMC-2.4. Social and Media Module

The Social and Media Module is responsible for communicating with the community and media at large. It represents the spokes person of the center. Regular newspaper conferences and official statements are prepared in the module in coordination with other modules. The module coordinates for crisis resilience in society (Boin & McConnell, 2007; Farnham et al., 2006; Hart et al., 1993).

NCMC-2.5. Political Module

In most national crises, one or more foreign countries may be direct actors or supportive actors. The Political Module is responsible for handling the political issues in crisis context.

NCMC-2.6. Government Departments Module

The Government Departments Module is responsible for communicating and coordinating with other ministries and administrations in their specialties in crisis management.

The main quality attributes of the unit outcomes are complete, innovative, practical, accurate, usable, secure, and synchronized alternatives. Each alternative is specified in terms of costs and benefits.

NCMC-3. Choice Unit

Crisis management decision problems are prime candidates for multiple criteria decision making (MCDM) techniques identified in Keen (1988). These problems involve multiple stakeholders, conflict in preferences, ethical choices, and trade-offs among economic, social, and environmental objectives. Addressing such problems require communication, team support, and increased emphasis on interactive MCDM methods.

The Choice Unit works as a one module that is responsible for developing a preferences structure of the decision makers in a crisis context (Limayem et al., 2006; Yates, 1990). Once the legitimate stakeholders, problem definition, objectives, and policy strategies are agreed upon, criteria hierarchy, and preferences structure are developed and used for ranking the alternatives and measuring the degree to which each objective is met. These criteria are analytically measurable, so it can objectively determine how well the objectives are met. In crisis management, the measurable criteria may change with time (Frijda, 2005).

The participants communicate in a way that often involves negotiation and bargaining. The unit provides models and techniques in the course of this interaction to help reaching an agreement on acceptable utility (Wilkenfeld et al., 1995). Utility refers to the scale on which preference is measured, thus the utilitarian definition of rationality is the maximization of utility (MIT, 2008).

The criteria for making the decision are refined, expanded, and weighted by interactions between the decision makers and the decision analysts. The preferences structure of a decision maker is a special mixture of three main ingredients: benefit-based preferences, image-based preferences, and doctrine-based preferences,

To incorporate the wisdom of decision makers and facilitate the choosing process, several functions are conducted in the Choice Unit including:

- 4.3.1. Organizing Complexity of choices: The greater the number of criteria and number of alternatives, the greater the complexity. The human brain is capable of consciously keeping track of 7 ± 2 interactions at one time; consequently, people often have difficulty predicting the behaviors of complex systems (Miller, 1956). The human brain and scientific analysis overcome the problem of complex interactions by grouping "activities" together in clusters and generalizing about their aggregate behavior (Saaty, 1982).

- 4.3.2. Checking Sensitivity of Decision to Assumed Data: The data received from the Assumptions and Forecasting Module of the Intelligence Unit needs to be incorporated in the decision structure. Sensitivity of the decision to assumed data is analyzed for deciding if the assumption is accepted or it needs further effort of validation.

- 4.3.3. Incorporating Qualitative Factors: Just as physical quantities could be distinguished and measured, the choice unit is able to do the same with perceptions of qualities, such as political and religious influences. The DSS is able to merge both quantitative and qualitative inputs into a single overall measure which allows determining the most desirable alternative.

- 4.3.4. Measuring Consistency in decision maker's preferences: If a decision maker considers safety of rescue team (SRT) is more important than safety of hostages (SH). He also considers safety of hostages is more important than releasing them (RH). At the same time, he considers releasing of hostages is more important than safety of rescue team, which represents inconsistency. The choice unit is able to determine inconsistency in preferences and judgments and is able to recommend adjustments using Eigen values of pairwise comparison matrices as illustrated in Saaty (1982).

- 4.3.5. Synthesizing Partial Judgments: the choice unit is able to consider all the information and judgments simultaneously and in relation to each other to reach a decision.

- 4.3.6. Comparing Consequences & Answer Questions of Type What-If: Implementing a decision by definition changes the dynamics of crisis situation. New actors, alternatives, and criteria may arise. Studying consequences is a main factor in the choice process.

- 4.3.7. Justifying the Rationale for a Decision: The unit gives full justification for each decision. It provides a "Road Map" of the analysis leading to the recommended decision.

A number of conceptual blocks may affect an individual's judgment. These blocks may include (a) perceptual blocks that tend to limit the area of investigation; (b) cultural and environmental blocks that are resulted from exposure to a particular set of cultural patterns or a particular social or physical environment; (c) emotional blocks that may arise from a fear of failure or loosing relatives; and (d) intellectual and expressive blocks due to the inability to generate ideas and to communicate them to others. The unit provides models and techniques to deal with the conceptual blocks of individuals through integrating their judgments horizontally with the team and vertically with their past history of judgments.

NCMC-4. Integration and Display Unit

The Integration and Display Unit works as a one module that is responsible for integrating all modules of the NCMIS and facilitating its team to access transparently the internal and external components of the system (Huang et al., 2002). The display function in the unit is concerned with making the information that is pertinent to the current status available to the team responsible for decisions in suitable format. The wide variety and scope of the information in a typical crisis context precludes displaying its entire content to all its users. The unit brings the details of the information available to the attention of the users with the least possible diversion of effort from their other tasks and responsibilities. The NCMIS team consists of decision makers, intermediary users, and system users. System users include operators and maintainers of the system (Alter, 1980).

The display function of the unit is responsible for creating and providing interface that minimizes the time of team comprehension. Shen-Hsieh and Schindler (2002) suggest approaches to use web-based interface technologies to create visual metaphors for data including visualizing time, collaborating, and modeling scenarios. They also demonstrate approaches to embedding more abstract constructs like decision theory, statistical analysis, and competitive advantage into these interfaces. Bharati (2004) discusses the quality of interface in web-based decision support systems.

The five modes of operation that need different types of interface are subscription, terminal, clerk, intermediary, and conference modes. In the subscription mode a decision-maker receives scheduled specific reports that are generated and submitted automatically by the system. In the terminal mode a decision-maker interacts directly with the MIS in an online manner for a specific inquiry. In the clerk mode, a decision-maker is using the system indirectly via input coding forms or other electronic batch submission processes. In the intermediary mode, a decision-maker interacts with the system through one or more intermediary users.

In the conference mode, the decision-makers interact comprehensively with the system as a group decision making process, which is the main mode of operation in the NCMIS. The conference room is a display room similar to military command centers. In the conference mode, as depicted in Figure 3, three sets of screens are used for displaying data to the crisis management team, which are Crisis Theater Screens (A), Alternatives Design Screens (B), and Choice Criteria Screens (C). Their purpose is to bring required strategic information, as well as relevant information from the internal system, to the notice of the decision makers in as comprehensive and expressive way as possible within the time limits. This is achieved by the use of display techniques that integrate information from a number of sources and allow concentration on specific issues and situations. The use of modern video display technology allows rapid and flexible movement through a number of subjects. It also facilitates continuous updating of the information displayed.

In the conference room, several boosts are prepared for subgroups and equipped with integration and display tools in attempt to avoid "Groupthink," which is a main reason of low quality decisions as defined in section 2 of the chapter. This arrangement helps setting up of several independent subgroups working on the same problem, inviting outside experts into meetings to discuss with and questioned by subgroups, and assigned the role of Devil's advocate to one of the subgroup members who should be a different person for each meeting (Baron, 2005; Janis, 1982).

The technical architecture of the unit should be supported by a network of integrated work stations, file servers, communication links, and encryption devices that insure the survivability, interoperability, security, compatibility, and capacity of the system (Goss, 2006; Graves, 2004). The detailed design must be as survivable as the team structure it supports. Assets that are vulnerable to damage or destruction must have alternative means of providing required data with minimal risk. Interoperability is a key factor for integrating several data sources and coordinating multiple command links. The technical architecture must be designed to be accommodated and integrated with both existing and projected involved systems. System security must be maintained according to a developed policy that permits widest possible access without compromising security. The level of compatibility must be capable of exchanging data and interacting with relevant applications, data bases, and communications protocols (Pine, 2007). The system capacity should make it possible to use applications that take advantage of multimedia technologies including video teleconferencing (Canós et al., 2004).

The MIS expertise, MIS design, and IT infrastructure affect the NCMIS use behavior and performance (Adkins et al., 2002; Benamati & Lederer, 2008; Lee et al., 2008; Moreau, 2006; Yuan & Detlor, 2005).

WORKFLOW IN THE NCMIS

While workflow systems have been proposed in literature for automating formal business procedures, some authors (Bui & Sankaran, 2001; Mak et al., 1999) present applications of workflow technology to disseminate and coordinate tasks and related information for crisis management support systems. An essential requirement for NCMIS is that response times must allow the decision maker time to appropriately react to an unfolding situation. Untimely delays in such context could negate the usefulness of even the most sophisticated system. Mak et al (1999) discuss the potential benefits of using a workflow approach for crisis management support systems, and de-

scribe the development of a suitable framework for an existing Swiss NCMC. They indicate that the ability of workflow technology to coordinate, monitor, organize and distribute specific tasks and the associated required information in a timely and efficient manner appears to make it an ideal tool for strategic crisis management systems.

On the level of conceptual design, a high level work flow is developed as depicted in Figure 4. The NCMC works in two modes, normal and operational. In the normal mode, the center is occupied in preparation for expected crises, following up potential crises, self development, and training.

Once the center realizes a warning for a national crisis, it switches to the operational mode. Based upon the level of preparedness and type of crisis, the communication networks are enabled and crisis situation is declared to all participants. The center units start conducting situation analysis and assessment, build decision structure and scale of available time frame. Cycles of decision making, Implementation, following up, and assessment are conducted until crisis resolution.

Post-crisis internal activities include process documentation, results analysis and assessment, process reporting, and learned-lesson discussions. The learned-lesson discussions among all people who were involved in the process improve the quality of process documentation, results analysis, and assessment. Post-crisis external activities include media and diplomatic reporting. The NCMC switches to the normal mode and continues archiving data, developing modules, and updating the Crisis Management Game, conducting self development and training activities (Kendall et al., 2005; Woltjer et al., 2006). "The key challenge in crisis termination is how to make an accurate and balanced assessment of the need to keep the crisis response infrastructure in place." (Hart & Boin, 2001, p. 31).

Figure 4. Workflow in NCMIS

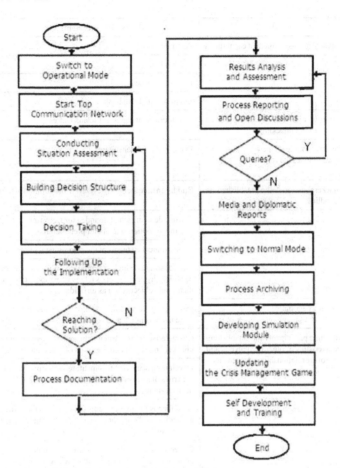

TESTING VALIDITY OF THE CONCEPTUAL DESIGN

The exercise suggested for testing validity of the conceptual design is to recall the scenario of a well documented crisis and define the needs for decision support throughout the crisis phases and the capability of NCMIS to provide these types of support. The selected case is the hijacking of an airplane as depicted in Radford (1978). Table 1 shows that the modules of the conceptual design support requirements of crisis management activities all through the crisis phases.

EVALUATION OF THE CONCEPTUAL DESIGN MODULES

The evaluation of the Conceptual Design Modules is based upon the Analytical Hierarchy Process (AHP) and QFD technique. The AHP is a mathematically rigorous, proven process for prioritization using pairwise comparison judgments (Saaty, 1982). Based on the pairwise comparison, a composite weight and relative priority are calculated for each item. The AHP is used in this study for structuring the relations and weighting the relative importance of the union of requirement items for all expected crises. A list of all expected crises is defined and prioritized according to the likely of occurrence and a relative loss-success value. A list

Table 1. Testing Validity of the Conceptual Design

Phase	Activity	Requirements	Supporting Module
1. Before Crisis	Development and assessment of capabilities	Potential crises	NCMC-1.6 NCMC-1.7
		Potential actors	
		Potential partners	NCMC-1.2
		Environmental databank	NCMC-1.2
2. when the initial news of the hijacking is received	High-ranking political officials received notification of the hijacking.	List of crisis management teams/cadres	NCMC-1.2 NCMC-4
	Forming a national-level special crisis-action team to coordinate the response.	List of national consultants	NCMC-1.2 NCMC-1.3 NCMC-1.4
	The hijackers' action-cadre established an initial deadline.	Building a time factor scale refers to the duration of the crisis	NCMC-2.1
	Evaluating available courses of action.	The first deadline schedule and its impact on initial responses in terms of option search and preparation.	NCMC-2.2
		Technological elements of the environment of the problem:	NCMC-2.1
		The constraints which are imposed on each of the participants by physical factors such as geography, climate, and man-made objects such as airfields	NCMC-2.1
3. Negotiations	Preparing for negotiations	Developing negotiations tactics for expanding the time dimension as much as possible.	NCMC-2.2
	Defining main participants and establishing the characteristics of other participants and the nature of the relationships between them.	Characteristics of participants and the organization the hijackers represent and the goals of that organization,	NCMC-1.5
		Developing scenarios to substitute the surprise element in the crisis that may reduce the alternatives examined by the decision-makers.	NCMC-1.6 NCMC-2.2
		Look for any factions existing within each of the participants and any possibility that these factions might come into conflict under the stress of the situation	NCMC-1.6 NCMC-1.7
		Governments which will cooperate in maintaining international law and agreements and which will not	NCMC-1.3 NCMC-2.5
		Governments and organizations which have a past history of involvement in such incidents and how have they behaved in the past under such circumstances	NCMC-1.4 NCMC-2.5
		The likely beliefs and value systems of the participants and the information which likely to be available to them at this time	NCMC-1.4 NCMC-1.5
		The commitments have been made by the participants and which of them are they likely to honor	NCMC-1.2 NCMC-2.1
		The likely preferences of the various participants for various possible outcomes of the situation	NCMC-1.5 NCMC-3
		The existence of individual leaders who might have had considerable influence on the situation	NCMC-1.5
		The possible involvement of potentially influential governments in other problems that might divert their attention from the hijacking problem.	NCMC-2.5
		Developing models for unstructured dual-track (military-political) approach.	NCMC-2.3 NCMC-2.5
		A continued search with new options and response reorientation, from a nonmilitary crisis resolution to a military crisis resolution and vise versa.	NCMC-2.3 NCMC-2.5

continued on following page

Table 1. continued

Phase	Activity	Requirements	Supporting Module
4. Take military action	Military planners, following automatic standard operating procedures, searched for viable military options to meet the deadline with reasonable probabilities of success.	Military operation cost/benefit analysis	NCMC-2.3
		The technological factors of the operation such as the range and capabilities of the airplane involved and where do facilities exist for handling, resupplying, and refueling such an aircraft	NCMC-1.4 NCMC-2.2
		The factors concerned with human capabilities, behavior, and endurance.	NCMC-2.1
		The natural elements of the environment:	NCMC-1.3
		The state of the weather at points within the range of the airplane.	NCMC-1.3
		The theater characteristics and logistics	NCMC-1.1
		Ensuring the highest level political-military interface to manage contingencies and participating in military decisions where there are perceived threats to significant national interests.	NCMC-2.3 NCMC-2.5
	Selecting a plan for military action	The possibility that using force would change the relative power of the participants significantly.	NCMC-2.2 NCMC-2.3
		The possibility that using force might cause potential participants to take a more active part in the existing situation or in a future situation linked to it	NCMC-2.1 NCMC-2.5
		The possibility that using force might cause world opinion to be a major participant, particularly if the operation failed.	NCMC-2.4 NCMC-2.5
		The possible interaction of the hijacking problem with other current and linked situations	NCMC-1.2 NCMC-2.5
		The constraints the world opinion posing on courses of action available to the participants.	NCMC-2.4 NCMC-2.5
		The possibility that the major powers would enter as active participants.	NCMC-2.5
		Recommended Decision	NCMC-3
5. After Crisis	Mobilize world opinion	Media Communications	NCMC-2.4
		Political Reconciliation	NCMC-2.5
	Internal Reconciliation	Internal programs	NCMC-2.6
	Analysis and development of experience package	Recall logging files	NCMC-1.2 NCMC-2.1
	Reporting and Documentation	Templates of documentations	NCMC-1.2
	Go back to the normal state	Upgrading instructions.	NCMC-4

of requirements is defined and relatively weighted for each one of crisis types. A set of integrated requirements representing the union of all requirement lists of all expected crises is developed with relative weights as depicted in Figure 5.

The set of Integrated Requirements is used as input for the QFD. The QFD is an overall concept that correlates design quality with user requirements (Sankaran et al., 2008; Slinger, 1992). It has been used in several domains including deci-

sion support and crisis management (Kara-Zaitri & Al-Daihan, 2008; Simitsis & Vassiliadis, 2008). The technique uses matrices to collect, analyze and manage goals towards a final product. However, 95% of the studies applying QFD so far use only the first matrix, called House of Quality (HoQ) (QFD-online, 2008). Basically, such matrix correlates requirements "what" to design modules "how" (Chan & Wu, 2002). The correlations between the integrated requirements and the design

Figure 5. Relative Weights of Requirements

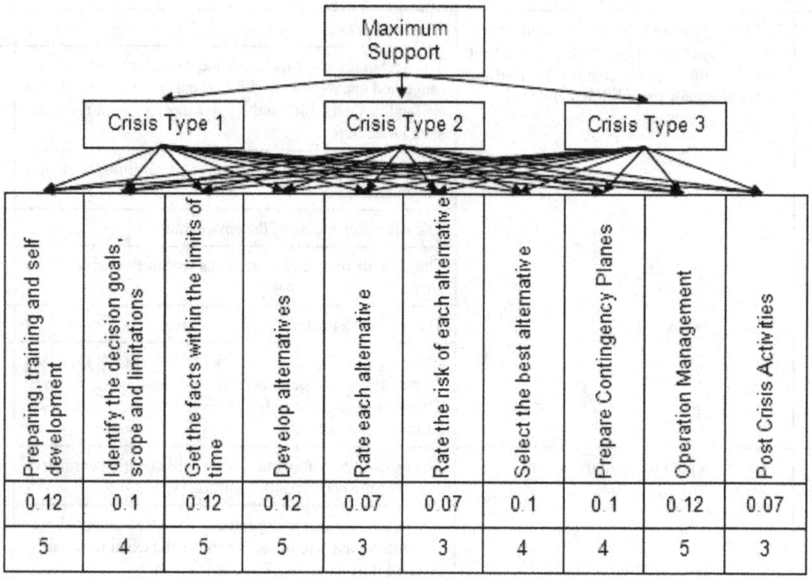
Maximum Support
Crisis Type 1
Crisis Type 2
Crisis Type 3
Preparing, training and self development
Identify the decision goals, scope and limitations
Get the facts within the limits of time
Develop alternatives
Rate each alternative
Rate the risk of each alternative
Select the best alternative
Prepare Contingency Planes
Operation Management
Post Crisis Activities
0.12
0.1
0.12
0.12
0.07
0.07
0.1
0.1
0.12
0.07
5
4
5
5
3
3
4
4
5
3

modules are specified using symbols of "strongly related," "moderately related," "weakly related," or "not related," which represent the corresponding numerical values 9, 3, 1, or 0 in the matrix calculations. The internal relationships between design modules are identified in the upper part of the HoQ matrix. The row score of design modules is the sum of the product between the relative weights of the integrated requirements and the correlations (between requirements and modules) as depicted in Figure 6.

The Relative % is the percentage of the total score that each component contributes in the design (Table 2). The results show that the conceptual design modules fulfill the integrated requirement of the NCMIS.

Table 2. Relative Weight (%) of the NCMIS Modules

Component	Rel. %
NCMC-1.1	7.6
NCMC-1.2	10.9
NCMC-1.3	5.9
NCMC-1.4	5.9
NCMC-1.5	6.2
NCMC-1.6	7.1
NCMC-1.7	5.9
NCMC-2.1	9.4
NCMC-2.2	9.1
NCMC-2.3	5.4
NCMC-2.4	3.2
NCMC-2.5	3.5
NCMC-2.6	4.7
NCMC-3	10.6
NCMC-4	4.5

CONCLUSION

National Crisis Decision Support System NCDSS represents special type of mission critical highly responsive systems. Initial requirements of a NCDSS are defined in a conceptual design of basic system modules. The conceptual design provides a general foundation that can be further developed up to a detailed design of a specific real application. The validity of the conceptual design is evaluated by measuring to how extend the design meets the

Figure 6. House of Quality Model

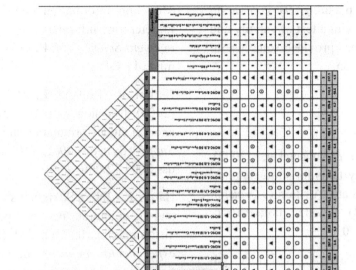

initial specifications of the system.. The relative importance of system modules are determined by calculating the relative percentage of the total score that each module contributes to the design using the Analytical Hierarchy Process AHP and the Quality Function Deployment QFD technique.

Basic modules of NCMIS are developed as a conceptual design, which provides a general foundation for the detailed design and implementation of an application. The concept of NCMIS meets the initial specifications that were validated using a case scenario. The relative percentage of the total score that each module contributes in the design is evaluated using the QFD approach. The conceptual design provides a system that is flexible and responsive to decision makers' needs in crisis management, while also supporting routine operational and administrative functions of the center.

The initial stages of the implementation of the NCMIS consist of the establishment of facilities and staffs to carry out the basic functions of the center. Once an initial allocation of resources has been made and the functions of the system have been established in an operating condition, the major task in the development of the system involves integrating the various and widespread strategic information activities already existing in the country.

As in any experimental work, this study has several limitations. The validation of the proposed conceptual design was conducted on a case work setting, and hence the internal validity is high, but the external validity has to be tested further with other types of crises. However, the use of airplane hijacking crisis, which is ranked high in representing national crises as a case study, was reasonable to test the validity of the conceptual design. Despite these limitations, the study indicates that the proposed conceptual design of the NCMIS is worth pursuing. By combining the conceptual design with a test of validity and evaluation, the study has provided some useful information to build upon.

REFERENCES

Adkins, M., Burgoon, M., & Nunamaker, J. (2002). Using group support systems for strategic planning with the United States Air Force. *Decision Support Systems*, *34*(3), 315–337. doi:10.1016/S0167-9236(02)00124-0

Aini, M., Fakharu'l-Razi, A., & Daude, M. (2001). Country report: Evolution of emergency management in Malaysia. *Journal of Contingencies and Crisis Management*, *9*(1), 46–53. doi:10.1111/1468-5973.00153

Akao, Y. (1990). *Quality function deployment: Integrating customer requirements into product design, English translation*. Cambridge, MA: Productivity Press.

Alpaslan, C. M., Green, S. E., & Mitroff, I. I. (2009). Corporate governance in the context of crises: Towards a stakeholder theory of crisis management. *Journal of Contingencies and Crisis Management*, *17*(1), 38–49. doi:10.1111/j.1468-5973.2009.00555.x

Alter, S. (1980). *Decision support systems: Current practice and continuing challenges*. Reading, MA: Addison-Wesley.

Austin, C. (1989). *National crisis management and technology* (p. 20319). Washington, DC: National Defense University, National War College Fort McNair.

Ballou, D., & Pazer, H. (2003). Modeling completeness versus consistency tradeoffs in information decision contexts. *IEEE Transactions on Knowledge and Data Engineering*, *15*(1), 240–243. doi:10.1109/TKDE.2003.1161595

Ballou, D., Wang, R., Pazer, H., & Tayi, G. (1998). Modeling information manufacturing systems to determine information product quality. *Management Science*, *44*(4), 462–484. doi:10.1287/mnsc.44.4.462

Barkhi, R., Rolland, E., Butler, J., & Fan, W. (2005). Decision support system induced guidance for model formulation and solution. *Decision Support Systems*, *40*(2), 269–281. doi:10.1016/j.dss.2003.12.006

Baron, R. (2005). So right it's wrong: Groupthink and the ubiquitous nature of polarized group decision making. In Zanna, M. (Ed.), *Advances in experimental social psychology* (pp. 219–253). San Diego, CA: Academic Press.

BCPR. (2007). *Knowledge management toolkit for the crisis prevention and recovery practice area. Bureau for Crisis Prevention and Recovery, United Nations Development Program*. UNDP.

Beckner, M. (2008). *Pro EDI in BizTalk server 2006 R2: Electronic document interchange solutions*. Berkeley, CA: Apress.

Bell, D., Raiffa, H., & Tversky, A. (1988). Descriptive, normative, and prescriptive interactions in decision making. In Bell, D., Raiffa, H., & Tversky, A. (Eds.), *Decision making: Descriptive, normative, and prescriptive interactions* (*Vol. 1*, pp. 9–32). Cambridge, UK: Cambridge University Press. doi:10.1017/CBO9780511598951.003

Benamati, J., & Lederer, A. (2008). (in press). Decision support systems infrastructure: The root problems of the management of changing IT. *Decision Support Systems.*.doi:10.1016/j.dss.2008.02.003

Bergman, M., King, J., & Lyytinen, K. (2000). Large scale requirements analysis as heterogeneous engineering. In Floyd, C., & Klischewski, R. (Eds.), *Social thinking—software practice*. Cambridge, MA: MIT Press.

Bharati, P., & Chaudhury, A. (2004). An empirical investigation of decision-making satisfaction in Web-based decision support systems. *Decision Support Systems, 37*(2), 187–197.

Boin, A., Hart, P., Stern, E., & Sundelius, B. (2006). *The politics of crisis management: Public leadership under pressure*. Cambridge, UK: Cambridge University Press.

Boin, A., & McConnell, A. (2007). Preparing for critical infrastructure breakdowns: The limits of crisis management and the need for resilience. *Journal of Contingencies and Crisis Management, 15*(1), 50–59. doi:10.1111/j.1468-5973.2007.00504.x

Briggs, I. (1962). *Introduction to type: A description of the theory and applications of the Myers-Briggs type indicator*. Palo Alto, CA: Consulting Psychologists Press.

Brooks, T. (2006). Affordable geospatial information technologies for disaster/ emergency response. *IAEM Bulletin, 23*(7), 1–6.

Browne, G., Curley, S., & Benson, P. (1997). Evoking information in probability assessment: Knowledge maps and reasoning-based directed questions. *Management Science, 43*(1), 1–14. doi:10.1287/mnsc.43.1.1

Brynielsson, J. (2007). Using AI and games for decision support in Command and Control. *Decision Support Systems, 43*(4), 1454–1463. doi:10.1016/j.dss.2006.06.012

Bui, T., & Sankaran, S. (2001). Design considerations for a virtual information center for humanitarian assistance/disaster relief using workflow modeling. *Decision Support Systems, 31*(2), 165–179. doi:10.1016/S0167-9236(00)00129-9

Byrne, R. (2005). *The rational imagination*. Cambridge, MA: The MIT Press.

Camerer, C., & Johnson, E. (1991). The process-performance paradox in expert judgment. How can experts know so much and predict so badly? In Ericsson, K., & Smith, E. (Eds.), *Toward a general theory of expertise - prospects and limits (Vol. 8)*. Cambridge, UK: Cambridge University Press.

Canós, J., Alonso, G., & Jaén, J. (2004). A multimedia approach to the efficient implementation and use of emergency plans. *IEEE MultiMedia, 11*(3), 106–110. doi:10.1109/MMUL.2004.2

Chan, L., & Wu, M. (2002). Quality function deployment: A literature review. *European Journal of Operational Research, 143*(3), 463–497. doi:10.1016/S0377-2217(02)00178-9

Chen, H., Reid, E., Sinai, J., & Silke, A. (2008). *Terrorism informatics: Knowledge management and data mining for homeland security. Integrated Series in Information Systems*. New York, NY: Springer.

Chen, R., Rao, H., Sharman, R., Upadhyaya, S., & Chakravarti, N. (2008). Emergency response Information System interoperability: Development of chemical incident response data model. *Journal of the AIS, 9*(3/4), 200–230.

Crisis-Navigator. (2008). *Index*. Retrieved on January 20, 2008, from http://www.crisisnavigator.org/index2.html

Curhan, J., Neale, M., & Ross, L. (2004). Dynamic valuation: Preference changes in the context of face-to-face negotiation. *Journal of Experimental Social Psychology, 40*(2), 142–151. doi:10.1016/j.jesp.2003.12.002

Davern, M., Mantena, R., & Stohr, E. (2008). Diagnosing decision quality. *Decision Support Systems, 45*(1), [REMOVED HYPERLINK FIELD]123-139.

DeRouen, K., & Sprecher, C. (2004). Initial crisis reaction and poliheuristic theory. *The Journal of Conflict Resolution, 48*(1), 56–68. doi:10.1177/0022002703260271

Earl, M. (2001). Knowledge management strategies: Toward a taxonomy. *Journal of Management Information Systems, 18*(1), [REMOVED HYPERLINK FIELD]215-233.

Farnham, S., Pedersen, E., & Kirkpatrick, R. (2006). Observation of Katrina/Rita groove deployment: Addressing social and communication challenges of ephemeral groups. *Proceedings of the 3rd International ISCRAM Conference*, (pp. 39-49). May 2006.

Fildes, R., Goodwin, P., & Lawrence, M. (2006). The design features of forecasting support systems and their effectiveness. *Decision Support Systems, 42*(1), 351–361. doi:10.1016/j.dss.2005.01.003

Fischer, G., & Mastaglio, T. (1991). A conceptual framework for knowledge-based critic systems. *Decision Support Systems, 7*(4), 355–378. doi:10.1016/0167-9236(91)90064-I

Fisher, C., Smith, I., & Ballou, D. (2003). The impact of experience and time on the use of data quality information in decision making. *Information Systems Research, 14*(2), 170–188. doi:10.1287/isre.14.2.170.16017

Fowler, K., Kling, N., & Larson, M. (2007). Organizational preparedness for coping with a major crisis or disaster. *Business & Society, 46*(1), 88–103. doi:10.1177/0007650306293390

Fowlkes, W., & Creveling, C. (1995). *Engineering methods for robust product design*. Reading, MA: Addison-Wesley.

Frijda, N. (2005). Dynamic appraisals: A paper with promises. *The Behavioral and Brain Sciences, 28*(2), 205–206. doi:10.1017/S0140525X05340040

Goss, K. (2006). Emerging technologies in emergency management. *IAEM Bulletin, 23*(7), 12–20.

Graves, R. (2004). Key technologies for emergency response. *Proceedings of the 1st International ISCRAM Conference*, (pp. 133-138). May 2004, Brussels.

Greenberg, L., & Safran, J. D. (1984). Hot cognition: Emotion coming in from the cold. *Cognitive Therapy and Research, 8*(6), 591–598. doi:10.1007/BF01173257

GSO. (2008). *Global Security Organization*. Retrieved on January 20, 2008, from http://www.globalsecurity.org/intell/library/ policy/dod/

Hammond, K., McClelland, G., & Mumpower, J. (1980). *Human judgment and decision making*. New York, NY: Praeger Publishers.

Hammond, K., Stewart, T., Brehmer, B., & Steinman, D. (1975). Social judgment theory. In Kaplan, M., & Schwartz, S. (Eds.), *Human judgment and decision processes* (pp. 271–312). New York, NY: Academic Press.

Han, T., Purao, S., & Storey, V. (2007). (in press). Generating large-scale repositories of reusable artifacts for conceptual design of Information Systems. *Decision Support Systems*. doi:. doi:10.1016/j.dss.2007.12.004

Harris, R. (1998). *Introduction to decision-making*. Virtual Salt. Retrieved from http://www.virtualsalt.com/crebook5.htm

Hart, P., & Boin, A. (2001). Between crisis and normalcy: The long shadow of post-crisis politics. In Rosenthal, U., Boin, R., & Comfort, L. (Eds.), *Managing crises: Threats, dilemmas, opportunities* (pp. 28–46). Springfield, IL: Charles C Thomas.

Hart, P., Rosenthal, U., & Kouzmin, A. (1993). Crisis decision making: The centralization thesis revisited. *Administration & Society, 25*(1), 12-45.

Herek, G., Janis, I., & Huth, P. (1987). Decision-making during international crises: Is quality of process related to outcome? *The Journal of Conflict Resolution, 31*(2), 203–226. doi:10.1177/0022002787031002001

Hernandez, M., & Stolfo, S. (1998). Real world data is dirty: Data cleansing and the merge/purge problem. *Journal of Data Mining and Knowledge Discovery, 2*(1), 9–37. doi:10.1023/A:1009761603038

Hevner, A., March, S., Park, J., & Ram, S. (2004). Design science in Information Systems research. *Management Information Systems Quarterly, 28*(1), 75–105.

Holt, R., & deVelde, R. (1961). Strategic psychological operations and American foreign policy. *The Journal of Political Economy, 69*(4), 397–399. doi:10.1086/258512

Huang, W., Wei, K., Watson, R., & Tan, B. (2002). Supporting virtual team-building with a GSS: An empirical investigation. *Decision Support Systems, 34*(4), 359–367. doi:10.1016/S0167-9236(02)00009-X

Hudspeth, M. (2008). *Conceptual design, technology for design engineering*. Desktop Engineering, 2008. Retrieved from http://www.deskeng.com/articles/aaagtm.htm

Hunt, E. (2001). The role of intelligence in modern society. *The American Scientist*. Retrieved from http://www.sigmaxi.org/amsci/articles/95articles/Hunt-full.html

ISSCM. (2008). *Institute for Safety, Security and Crisis Management*. Retrieved on January 20, 2008, from http://www.cot.nl/ english/

Janis, I., & Mann, L. (1977). *Decision making: A psychological analysis of conflict, choice, and commitment*. New York, NY: Free Press.

Janis, L. (1982). *Groupthink: Psychological studies of policy decisions and fiascos*. Boston, MA: Houghton Mifflin.

Kabeil, M. (2009). (in press). An AHP-QFD approach to developing DSS for crisis management. *International Journal of Management and Decision Making (IJMDM): Special issue on Decision Models. Decision Aids and Strategic Decision Making*.

Kahneman, D., & Tversk, A. (2000). *Choice, values, frames*. Cambridge, UK: The Cambridge University Press.

Kara-Zaitri, C., & Al-Daihan, S. (2008). *The application of augmented QFD to the evaluation of emergency plans*. QFD institute. Retrieved on January 20, 2008, from http://www.qfdi.org

Katsenelinboigen, A. (1997). *The concept of indeterminism and its applications: Economics, social systems, ethics, artificial intelligence, and aesthetics*. Westport, Connecticut: Praeger Publishers.

Keen, P. (1988). *Decision support systems: The next decade*. International Center for Information Technologies.

Kendall, K., Kendall, J., & Lee, K. (2005). Understanding disaster recovery planning through a theatre metaphor: Rehearsing for a show that might never open. *Communications of the AIS, 16*, 1001–1012.

Kennerley, S., Walton, M., Behrens, T., Buckley, M., & Rushworth, M. (2006). Optimal decision making and the anterior cingulate cortex. *Nature Neuroscience, 9*, 940–947. doi:10.1038/nn1724

Keren, G., & de-Bruin, W. B. (2004). On the assessment of decision quality: Considerations regarding utility, conflict and accountability. In Hardman, D., & Macchi, L. (Eds.), *Thinking: Psychological perspectives on reasoning, judgment and decision making*. Chichester, UK: John Wiley.

Kienzle, J., Guelfi, N., & Mustafiz, S. (2010). Crisis management systems: A case study for aspect-oriented modeling. *Transactions on Aspect-Oriented Software Development VII, LNCS, 6210*, 1–22. doi:10.1007/978-3-642-16086-8_1

Klashner, R., & Sabet, S. (2007). A DSS design model for complex problems: Lessons from mission critical infrastructure. *Decision Support Systems, 43*(3), 990–1013. doi:10.1016/j.dss.2005.05.027

Klein, G. (1998). *Sources of power: How people make decisions* (pp. 1–30). Cambridge, MA: MIT Press.

Lattimer, C., Meier-Ewert, G., & Watanabe, M. (2007). *Knowledge management toolkit: For the crisis prevention and recovery practice area*. United Nations Development Program (UNDP), Knowledge management in the Bureau for Crisis Prevention and Recovery (BCPR), March 2007. Retrieved from http://www.undp.org/ cpr/documents/whats_new/UNDP_Toolkit_ LowRes.pdf

Lee, Z., Wagner, C., & Shin, H. (2008). The effect of decision support system expertise on system use behavior and performance. *Information & Management, 45*(6)..doi:10.1016/j.im.2008.04.003

Levin, M. (2006). *Composite systems decisions*. New York, NY: Springer.

Lewis, M. (2005). Bridging emotion theory and neurobiology through dynamic systems modeling. *The Behavioral and Brain Sciences, 28*(2), 169–245. doi:10.1017/S0140525X0500004X

Limayem, M., Banerjee, P., & Ma, L. (2006). Impact of GDSS: Opening the black box. *Decision Support Systems, 42*(2), 945–957. doi:10.1016/j.dss.2005.08.004

Mak, H., Mallard, A., Bui, T., & Au, G. (1999). Building online crisis management support using workflow systems. *Decision Support Systems, 25*(3), 209–224. doi:10.1016/S0167-9236(99)00007-X

March, S., & Smith, G. (1995). Design and natural science research on Information Technology. *Decision Support Systems, 15*(4), 251–266. doi:10.1016/0167-9236(94)00041-2

Martinsons, M. (2001). Comparing the decision styles of American, Chinese and Japanese business leaders. *Best Paper Proceedings of Academy of Management Meetings,* Washington, DC, August 2001. SSRN: http://ssrn. com/abstract=952292

Miller, G. (1956). The magical number seven, plus or minus two: Some limits on our capacity for processing information. *Psychological Review, 63*(2), 81–97. doi:10.1037/h0043158

Miller, J. (1978). *Living systems*. New York, NY: McGraw-Hill.

MIT. (2008). *Handbook of collective intelligence*. The MIT Center for Collective Intelligence. Retrieved from http://scripts.mit.edu/~cci/HCI/index.ph

Moreau, E. (2006). The impact of intelligent decision support systems on intellectual task success: An empirical investigation. *Decision Support Systems, 42*(2), 593–607. doi:10.1016/j.dss.2005.02.008

MWD. (2008). *Merriam-Webster dictionary*. Retrieved June 19, 2008, from http://www.merriam-webster.com/dictionary

Naqvi, N., Shiv, B., & Bechara, A. (2006). The role of emotion in decision making: A cognitive neuroscience perspective. *Current Directions in Psychological Science, 15*(6), 327–328.

NCCM. (2008). *The National Center for Crisis Management*. Retrieved January 20, 2008, from http://www.nc-cm.org

NCCMRT. (2008). *The National Center for Crisis Management Research and Training*. Retrieved January 20, 2008, from http://www.crismart.org

Nevo, D., & Chan, Y. (2007). A Delphi study of knowledge management systems: Scope and requirements. *Information & Management, 44*(6), 583–597. doi:10.1016/j.im.2007.06.001

NSCFM. (2008). *National security crisis forecasting and management. GW Hopple, SJ.* Westview Press.

Pine, J. (2007). *Technology in emergency management.* Hoboken, NJ: John Wiley and Sons.

Plous, S. (1993). *The psychology of judgment and decision making.* New York, NY: McGraw-Hill.

Post, J. (2004). *Leaders and their followers in a dangerous world.* Ithaca, NY: Cornell University Press.

QFD-Online. (2008). *QFD-Online.* Retrieved January 20, 2008, from http://www.QFDOnline. com

Radford, K. (1978). *Information Systems for strategic decisions.* Reston, VA: Reston Publishing Company.

Refsgaard, J., Sluijs, J., Højberg, A., & Vanrolleghem, P. (2007). Uncertainty in the environmental modeling process - A framework and guidance. *Environmental Modelling & Software, 22*(11), 1543–1556. doi:10.1016/j.envsoft.2007.02.004

Royes, G., & Bastos, R. (2006). Uncertainty analysis in political forecasting. *Decision Support Systems, 42*(1), 25–35. doi:10.1016/j.dss.2004.09.009

Saaty, T. (1982). *Decision-making for leaders: The analytical hierarchy process for decisions in a complex world* (pp. 75–121). Belmont, CA: Lifetime Learning Publications.

Sankaran, R., Senthil, V., Devadasan, S., & Pramod, V. (2008). Design and development of innovative quality function deployment model. *International Journal of Business Innovation and Research, 2*(2), 203–222. doi:10.1504/IJBIR.2008.016653

Schafer, M., & Crichlow, S. (2002). The process-outcome connection in foreign policy decision making: A quantitative study building on groupthink. *International Studies Quarterly, 46*(1), 45–68. doi:10.1111/1468-2478.00222

Shankaranarayanan, G., & Cai, Y. (2006). Supporting data quality management in decision-making. *Decision Support Systems, 42*(1), 302–317. doi:10.1016/j.dss.2004.12.006

Shankaranarayanan, G., Ziad, M., & Wang, R. (2003). Managing data quality in dynamic decision environment: An information product approach. *Journal of Database Management, 14*(4), 14–32. doi:10.4018/jdm.2003100102

Shen-Hsieh, A., & Schindler, M. (2002). *Data visualization for strategic decision making* (pp. 1–17). American Institute of Graphic Arts Experience Case Study Archive.

Simitsis, A., & Vassiliadis, P. (2008). A method for the mapping of conceptual designs to logical blueprints for ETL processes. *Decision Support Systems, 45*(1), 22–40. doi:10.1016/j.dss.2006.12.002

Simon, H. (1977). *The new science of management decision.* Englewood Cliffs, NJ: Prentice Hall.

Slinger, M. (1992). *To practice QFD with success requires a new approach to product design.* Kontinuert Forbedring, Copenhagen, 20-21 February, 1992.

Sprague, R., & Carlson, E. (1982). *Building effective decision support systems.* Englewood Cliffs, NJ: Prentice Hall.

Sprague, R., & Watson, H. (1996). *Decision support for management.* Englewood Cliffs, NJ: Prentice Hall.

Stump, G. (2002). Effective decision making. *The Leadership News, 19.* Retrieved from http://www.uscg.mil/leadership/news/summer02/index.htm

Tiwana, A., & Ramesh, B. (2001). A design knowledge management system to support collaborative information product evolution. *Decision Support Systems, 31*(2), 241–262. doi:10.1016/S0167-9236(00)00134-2

Treadgold, G. (2006). Sahana: An open source disaster management system. *IAEM Bulletin, 23*(7), 7–16.

Turoff, M. (2002). Past and future emergency response Information Systems. *Communications of the ACM, 45*(4), 29–32. doi:10.1145/505248.505265

Turoff, M., Hiltz, S. R., White, C., Plotnick, L., Hendela, A., & Xiang, Y. (2009). The past as the future of emergency preparedness and management. *Journal of Information Systems for Crisis Response and Management, 1*(1), 12–28. doi:10.4018/jiscrm.2009010102

Ullman, D. (2006). *Making robust decisions.* Victoria, British Columbia, Canada: Trafford Publishing.

Wang, R., Lee, Y., Pipino, L., & Strong, D. (1998). Manage your information as a product. *Sloan Management Review, 39*(4), 95–105.

Wang, W., & Belardo, S. (2005). Strategic integration: A knowledge management approach to crisis management. *Proceedings of the 38th Hawaii International Conference on System Sciences,* (pp. 1-11).

Wilkenfeld, J., Kraus, S., Holley, K., & Harris, M. (1995). GENIE: A decision support system for crisis negotiations. *Decision Support Systems, 14*(4), 369–391. doi:10.1016/0167-9236(94)00027-P

Woltjer, R., Lindgren, I., & Smith, K. (2006). A case study of information and communication technology in emergency management training. *International Journal of Emergency Management, 3*(4), 332–347. doi:10.1504/IJEM.2006.011300

Yates, J. (1990). *Judgment and decision making.* Englewood Cliffs, NJ: Prentice Hall.

Yuan, Y., & Detlor, B. (2005). Intelligent mobile crisis response systems. *Communications of the ACM, 48*(2), 95–98. doi:10.1145/1042091.1042097

Zack, M. (1999). Developing a knowledge strategy. *California Management Review, 41*(3), 125–145.

Zsambok, C., & Klein, G. (1997). *Naturalistic decision making.* Mahwah, NJ: Lawrence Erlbaum Associates.

Compilation of References

Abbott, P. L. (1998). *Natural Disasters 2e*. New Jersey: William C. Brown.

Adelman, L. (1991). Experiments, quasi-experiments, and case studies: A review of empirical methods for evaluating decision support systems. *IEEE Transactions on Systems, Man, and Cybernetics*, *21*(2), 293–301. doi:10.1109/21.87078

Akrich, M. (1992). The description of technical objects. In Bijker, W. E., & Law, J. (Eds.), *Shaping technology/building society: Studies in socio-technical change* (pp. 206–224). Cambridge, MA: The MIT Press.

Akrich, M., & Latour, B. (1992). A summary of a convenient vocabulary for the semiotics of human and nonhuman assemblies. In Bijker, W. E., & Law, J. (Eds.), *Shaping technology/building society* (pp. 205–224). Cambridge, MA: MIT Press.

Alavi, M., & Leidner, D. E. (2001). Review: Knowledge Management and Knowledge Management Systems: Conceptual Foundations and Research Issues. *Management Information Systems Quarterly*, *25*(1), 107–136. doi:10.2307/3250961

Alter, S. (2003). 18 reasons why IT-reliant work systems should replace the IT artifact as the core subject matter of the IS field. *Communications of the AIS*, *12*(23), 365–394.

Alter, S. (2004b). *Making work system principles visible and usable in systems analysis and design*. Paper presented at the the Tenth Americas Conference on Information Systems, New York.

American Heritage Dictionary. (2000). *The American Heritage Dictionary of the English Language, Fourth Edition*. Houghton Mifflin Company.

American National Standards Institute. (1992). *Telecommunications, integrated services digital network (ISDN) multi-level precedence and preemption (MLPP) service capability*. (ANSI T1.619-1992- R1999).

Aminoff, H., Johansson, B., & Trnka, J. (2007). *Understanding coordination in emergency response*. Paper presented at the 26th European Annual Conference on Human Decision-Making and Manual Control, Lyngby, DK.

Andersen, P. (Ed.). (2007). Deliverable 54: Open architecture. Retrieved October 20, 2008 from http://www.ist-palcom.org/publications/deliverables/Deliverable-54-%5B2.2.3%5D-open-architecture.pdf

Ansell, C., Boin, A., & Keller, A. (2010). Managing transboundary crises: Identifying the building blocks of an effective response system. *Journal of Contingencies and Crisis Management*, *18*(4). doi:10.1111/j.1468-5973.2010.00620.x

Anton, H. (1988). *Calculus with Analitic Geometry, Third Edition*. John Weily and Sons, isbn 0-471-85045-4.

Appleby, M., Forlin, G., et al. (2003). The Law Relating to Emergencies and Disasters. *Tolley's Handbook of Disaster and Emergency Management: Principles and Practice*. R. Lakha and T. Moore, Butterworth-Heinemann, isbn 0-406-97270-2.

Artman, H. (2000). Team situation assessment and information distribution. *Ergonomics*, *43*(8), 1111–1128. doi:10.1080/00140130050084905

Artman, H., & Waern, Y. (2000). Distributed cognition in an emergency co-ordination center. *Cognition Technology and Work*, *1*(4), 237–246. doi:10.1007/s101110050020

Artman, H., & Persson, M. (2000). Old practices – New technology: Observations of how established practices meet new technology. In Dieng, R., Gibson, A., Kersenty, L., & De Michelis, G. (Eds.), *Designing cooperative systems* (pp. 35–49). Amsterdam, The Netherlands: Ios Press Ohmsha.

Aspevig, J. (2006 Spring). Hosted by Montana Department of Public Health and Human Services: Disaster Preparedness Exercise Uses GIS. *ArcNews Online.* Retrieved on January 3, 2008 from http://www.esri.com/news/arcnews/spring06articles/ disaster-preparedness.html

Asproth, V., & Håkansson, A. (2007). *Complexity Challenges of Critical Situations Caused by Flooding.* Emergence: Complexity & Organization, vol 9(1): 37-43, issn 1532-7000.

Aubert, B., Patry, M., & Rivard, S. (1998). Assessing the Risk of IT Outsourcing. *Proceedings of the 31st Hawaii International Conference on Systems Sciences* (pp. 685-693). IEEE Publishing.

Avgerou, C., Ciborra, C., & Land, F. F. (Eds.). (2004). *The social study of Information and Communications Technology: Innovation, actors and context.* Oxford, UK: Oxford University Press.

Avizienis, A., Laprie, J.-C., Randell, B., & Landwehr, C. (2004). Basic Concepts and Taxonomy of Dependable and Secure Computing. *IEEE Transactions on Dependable and Secure Computing, 1*(1), 11–33. doi:10.1109/TDSC.2004.2

Babb, E. M., Leslie, M. A., & Van Slyke, M. D. (1966). The potential of business-gaming methods in research. *The Journal of Business, 39*(4), 465–472. doi:10.1086/294887

Baker, F., & Polk, J. (2004). *Implementing MLPP for voice and video in the Internet protocol suite. Internet Engineering Task Force.* IETF.

Baker, F., & Polk, J. (2004). *MLEF without capacity admission does not satisfy MLPP requirements. Internet Engineering Task Force.* IETF.

Baker, F., & Polk, J. (2006). *Implementing an emergency telecommunications service for real time services in the Internet protocol suite (RFC 4542). Internet Engineering Task Force.* IETF.

Baldwin, C., & Clark, K. (1999). *Design rules: The power of modularity.* Cambridge, MA: MIT Press.

Barley, S. R. (1986). Technology as an Occasion for Structuring: Evidence from Observations of CT Scanners and the Social Order of Radiology Departments. *Administrative Science Quarterly, 31*(1), 78–108. doi:10.2307/2392767

Barrow, J. (1998). *Impossibility: The Limits of Science and the Science of Limits.* Oxford: Oxford University Press.

Baughman, Bruce. 2006. Testimony to US Senate Homeland Security and Government Affairs Committee Hearing: Hurricane Katrina—Recommendations for Reform. March 8 2006

Beers, M. (Ed.). (2003). *The Merck manual of medical information* (2nd ed.). Merck Research Laboratories.

Bellardo, S., Karwan, K. R., & Wallace, W. A. (1984). Managing the Response to Disasters Using Microcomputers. *Interfaces, 14*(2), 29–39. doi:10.1287/inte.14.2.29

Beredskabsstyrelsen. (2005). *Aftale om fremgangsmåden ved udsendelse af beredskabsmeddelelser* (in Danish). Retrieved from www.beredskabsstyrelsen.dk

Bergstrand, F., & Landgren, J. (2009). Information sharing using live video in emergency response work. *Proceedings of the 6ᵗʰ International ISCRAM Conference.*

Berners-Lee, T. (1999). *Weaving the Web: The original design and ultimate destiny of the World Wide Web.* New York, NY: HarperCollins Publishers, Inc.

Betts, B. J., Mah, R. W., Papasin, R., Del Mundo, R., McIntosh, D. M., & Jorgensen, C. (2005). Improving Situ-ational Awareness for First Responders via Mobile Computing. Published by *National Aeronautics and Space Administration Ames Research Center* Moffett Field, California. NASA/TM-2005-213470. Retrieved March 9, 2008 from http://ntrs.nasa.gov/archive/nasa/casi.ntrs.nasa.gov/20060000029_2005249624.pdf

Bigley, G. A., & Roberts, K. H. (2001). The incident command system: High-reliability organizing for complex and volatile task environments. *Academy of Management Journal, 44*(6), 1281–1299. doi:10.2307/3069401

Bijker, W. E., & Law, J. (1992). What catastrophe tells us about technology and society. In Bijker, W. E., & Law, J. (Eds.), *Shaping technology/building society*. Cambridge, MA: MIT Press.

Binge, M. L., Batchelor, J., Martin, R. P., & Winslow, R. (2004). Using GIS As a Disaster Management Tool. *Proceedings of the ESRI User Conference 2004.* San Diego: ESRI.

Black, S., Black, D., Carlson, M., Davies, E., Wang, Z., & Weiss, W. (1998). *An architecture for differentiated services (RFC 2475). Internet Engineering Task Force*. IETF.

Boden, D., & Molotch, H. (1994). The compulsion to proximity. In Friedland, R., & Boden, D. (Eds.), *NowHere. Space, time and modernity*. Berkeley: University of California Press.

Boehm, B., & Turner, R. (2004). *Balancing Agility and Discipline: A Giode fpr the Perplexed*. Boston, MA: Addison-Wesley, Pearson Education.

Boin, A., Kofman-Bos, C., & Overdijk, W. (2004). Crisis simulations: Exploring tomorrow's vulnerabilities and threats. *Simulation & Gaming, 35*(3), 378–393. doi:10.1177/1046878104266220

Bolt, B. A. (1993). *Earthquakes: Newly Revised and Expanded*. W.H. Freeman, New York, NY

Booth, S. A. S. (1993). *Crisis management strategy: competition and change in modern enterprises*. London, New York: Routledge.

Borgida, A., & Brachman, R. J. (1993). Loading data into description reasoners. In *Proceedings of the 1993 ACM SIGMOD International Conference on Management of Data*, (pp. 217–226). New York, NY: ACM Press.

Bos, N., Olsen, J. S., Nan, N., Shami, N. S., Hoch, S., & Johnston, E. (2006) 'Collocation Blindness' in Partially Distributed Groups: Is there a Downside to Being Collocated? *Proceedings of the CHI 2006*, Montreal, Quebec, 2006.

Bostrom, R., Anson, R., & Clawson, V. (1993). Group facilitation and group support systems. In Jessup, L., & Valacich, J. (Eds.), *Group Support Systems: New Perspectives* (pp. 146–168). New York, NY: Macmillan.

Braa, J. R., Monteiro, E., & Sahay, S. (2004). Networks of action: Sustainable health Information Systems across developing countries. *Management Information Systems Quarterly, 28*(3).

Bracken, P., & Shubik, M. (2001). War gaming in the information age: Theory and purpose. *Naval War College Review, 54*(2), 47–60.

Braden, R., Zhang, L., Berson, S., Herzog, S., & Jamin, S. (1997). *Resource reservation protocol (RSVP) (RFC 2205). Internet Engineering Task Force*. IETF.

Brahimi, L. (2000). *Report of the Panel on United Nations Peace Operations (United Nations A/55/305?S/2000/809)*. New York: United Nations.

Brannick, M. T., & Prince, C. (1997). An overview of team performance measurement. In Brannick, M. T., Salas, E., & Prince, C. (Eds.), *Team performance assessment and measurement* (pp. 331–355). Mahwah, NJ: Lawrence Erlbaum Associates.

Braunstein, B. (2006). Challenges in using distributed wireless mesh networks in emergency response. *Proceedings of the 3rd International ISCRAM Conference*, (pp 58-64). Newark, NJ, May.

Braverman, M. (2003). Managing the human impact of crisis. *Risk Management, 50*(5), 10–19.

Brehmer, B. (1992). Dynamic decision making: Human control of complex systems. *Acta Psychologica, 81*(3), 211–241. doi:10.1016/0001-6918(92)90019-A

Brehmer, B., & Svenmarck, P. (1995). Distributed decision making in dynamic environments: Time scales and architectures of decision making. In Caverni, J.-P., Bar-Hillel, M., Barron, F. H., & Jungermann, H. (Eds.), *Contributions to decision making – I* (pp. 155–174). Amsterdam, The Netherlands: Elsevier Science.

Brehmer, B. (1987). System design and the psychology of complex systems. In Rasmussen, J., & Zunde, P. (Eds.), *Empirical foundations of information and software science III* (pp. 21–32). New York, NY: Plenum Publishing.

Brehmer, B. (1991). Modern information technology: Timescales and distributed decision making. In Rasmussen, J., Brehmer, B., & Leplat, J. (Eds.), *Distributed decision making: Cognitive models for cooperative work* (pp. 193–200). New York, NY: John Wiley & Sons.

Brehmer, B., & Allard, R. (1991). Real-time dynamic decision making: The effects of task complexity and feedback delays. In Rasmussen, J., Brehmer, B., & Leplat, J. (Eds.), *Distributed decision making: Cognitive models for cooperative work* (pp. 319–334). New York, NY: John Wiley & Sons.

Briggs, R. O., Nunamaker, J. F., & Sprague, R. H. (1997/1998). 1001 unanswered research questions in GSS. *Journal of Management Information Systems, 14*(3), 3–21.

Brunner, D., Lemoine, G., Thoorens, F. X., & Bruzzone, L. (2009). Distributed geospatial data processing functionality to support collaborative and rapid emergency response. *IEEE Journal of Selected Topics in Applied Earth Observations and Remote Sensing, 2*(1), 33–46. doi:10.1109/JSTARS.2009.2015770

Bui, T., & Sivasankaran, T. R. (1990). *Relation between GDSS use and group task complexity.* Paper presented at the Proceedings of the Twenty-Third Hawaii International Conference on Systems Sciences, Hawaii

Bullock, J. A., & Haddow, G. D. (2006). Introduction to Emergency Management. (2nd Ed.). Burlington, MA: Elsevier.

Bunge, M. (1977). *Treatise on basic philosophy, the furniture of the world, ontology I* (*Vol. 3*). New York, NY: D. Reidel Publishing Co., Inc.

Bunge, M. (1979). *Treatise on basic philosophy: vol. 4, ontology II: A world of systems.* New York, NY: D. Reidel Publishing Co., Inc.

Burnell, L., Priest, J., & Durrett, J. (2004). Developing and Maintaining Knowledge Management System for Dynamic, Complex Domains. In Gupta, J., & Sharma, S. (Eds.), *Creating Knowledge Based Organizations.* London: IGP. doi:10.4018/9781591401629.ch010

Büscher, M., Kristensen, M., & Mogensen, P. (2008). Making the future palpable: Notes from a major incident Future Laboratory. *International Journal of Emergency Management, 5*(1/2), 145–163. doi:10.1504/IJEM.2008.019911

Büscher, M., Christensen, M., Hansen, K. M., Mogensen, P., & Shapiro, D. (2008). Bottom-up, top-down? Connecting software architecture design with use. In Voß, A., Hartswood, M., Ho, K., Procter, R., Rouncefield, M., Slack, R., & Büscher, M. (Eds.), *Configuring user-designer relations: Interdisciplinary perspectives.* New York: Springer Verlag.

Büscher, M. (2006). Interaction in motion: Embodied conduct in emergency teamwork. In: Mondada L. (ED.). Online Multimedia *Proceedings of the 2nd International Society for Gesture Studies Conference 'Interacting Bodies',* 15-18 June 2005, Lyon, France. Retrieved October 20, 2008 from http://gesture-lyon2005.ens-lsh.fr/article.php3?id_article=221

Bush, G. W. (2003a). *Homeland Security Presidential Directive/HSPD-5.* The White House.

Bush, G. W. (2003b). *Homeland Security Presidential Directive/HSPD-8.* The White House.

Butcher, B. (2007, Summer). GIS Helps Americus Quickly Respond to Tornado Damage. *Government Matters: GIS for State and Local Governement* (pp. 8-13).

Butts, C. T., Petrescu, M., & Cross, B. R. (2007). Responder communication networks in the World Trade Center disaster: Implications for modelling of communication within emergency settings. *The Journal of Mathematical Sociology, 31*(2). doi:10.1080/00222500601188056

Byrne, M. And Not a Drop to Drink, Water: an Alternative Test for Emergency Managers," *Homeland Security Affairs* IV, no. 2 (June 2008), http://www.hsaj.org/?article=4.2.2

Calamard, A. (2001). *Why humanitarian accountability? Contextual and operational factors.* Geneva: Humanitarian Accountability Project.

Callon, M. (1986b). Some elements of a sociology of translation: Domestication of the scallops and the fishermen in St. Brieuc's Bay. In Law, J. (Ed.), *Power, action and belief. A new sociology of knowledge?* (pp. 196–219). London, UK: Routledge & Kegan Paul.

Callon, M. (1991). Techno-economic networks and irreversibility. In Law, J. (Ed.), *A sociology of monsters. Essays on power, technology and domination* (pp. 132–161). London, UK: Routledge.

Capital Wireless Information Net (CapWIN). (2007). *Capital wireless information net.* Retrieved from http://www.capwin.org

Careem, M., Bittner, D., & de Silva, R. (2007). GIS Integration in the Sahana Disaster Management System. In B. Van de Walle, P. Burghardt, & C. Nieuwenhuis (Eds.), *Proceedings of the 4th International Conference on Information Systems for Crisis Response and Management ISCRAM 2007* (pp. 211-218).

Carley, K. M., & Harrald, J. R. (1997). Organizational Learning under Fire: Theory and Practice. *The American Behavioral Scientist, 40*(3), 310–332. doi:10.1177/0002764297040003007

Carlsson, S. A. (2001). *Knowledge management in network contexts.* Paper presented at the The 9th European Conference on Information Systems.

Carter, E., & French, S. (2005). *Nuclear emergency management in Europe: a review of approaches to decision making.* Paper presented at the ISCRAM 2005: Information Systems for Crisis Response and Management, Brussels.

Carver, L., & Turoff, M. (2007). Human Computer Interaction: The Human and Computer as a Team in Emergency Management Information Systems. *Communications of the ACM,* (March): 33–38. doi:10.1145/1226736.1226761

Caselli, F., & Coleman, W. J. (2001). *Cross-Country Technology Diffusion: The Case of Computers.* CEPR Discussion Paper No. 2744.

Cedergårdh, E., & Wennström, O. (2002). *The elements of command & control: The general principles of command & control in fire and rescue operations.* Karlstad, Sweden: Swedish Rescue Services Agency.

Cell broadcast Forum. (2007). *Cell broadcast in public warning systems.* Retrieved from www.cellbroadcastforum.org

Chan, A. H. S., & Chan, K. W. L. (2006). Synchronous and asynchronous presentations of auditory and visual signals: Implications for control console design. *Applied Ergonomics, 37*(2), 131–140. doi:10.1016/j.apergo.2005.06.006

Chandler, R., & Wallace, D. (2004). Business Continuity Planning After September 11. *Disaster Recovery Journal, 17*(3), 24–28.

Chen, R., Sharman, R., Rao, R., & Upadhyaya, S. (2008). Coordination in emergency response management. *Communications of the ACM, 51*(5), 66–73. doi:10.1145/1342327.1342340

Chen, R., Sharman, R., Rao, H. R., Upadhyaya, S. J., & Cook-Cottone, C. P. (in press) Coordination of Emergency Response: An Examination of the Roles of People, Process, and Information Technology, in Information Systems for Emergency Management, (Van de Walle, B., Turoff, M., and Hiltz S.R. eds) in the Advances in Management Information Systems monograph series (Zwass, V. editor-in-chief), Armonk, NY: M.E. Sharpe Inc. Anticipated 2009.

Cho, H., & Turoff, M. (2003). Delphi Structure and Group Size in Asynchronous Computer Mediated Communication. *Paper presented at the AMCIS 2003.*

Chow, E. T. (2008). The potential of maps APIs for Internet GIS applications. *Transactions in GIS, 12*(2), 179–191. doi:10.1111/j.1467-9671.2008.01094.x

Ciborra, C. (2002). *The labyrinths of information: Challenging the wisdom of systems.* Oxford, UK: Oxford University Press.

Ciborra, C. U. (1997). De profundis? Deconstructing the concept of strategic alignment. *Scandinavian Journal of Information Systems, 9*(1), 67–82.

Claessens, M., Lewyckyj, N., Biesemans, J., & Everarerts, J. (2005). Pegasus, a UAV project for disaster management. *Proceedings of the 2nd International ISCRAM Conference* (pp. 233-236).

Clark, H. H., & Brennan, S. (1991). Grounding in communication. In Resnick, L., Levine, J., & Teasley, S. (Eds.), *Socially shared cognition.* Washington, DC: American Psychological Association. doi:10.1037/10096-006

Clarke, K., Hardstone, G., Rouncefield, M., & Sommerville, I. (2006). *Trust in Technology: A Socio-Technical Perspective (Computer Supported Cooperative Work).* New York: Springer-Verlag.

Clemen, R. T., & Reilly, T. (1996). *Making Hard Decisions with Decision Tools* (2nd Edition ed.). Pacific Grove, CA: Duxbury, Thomson Learning.

Cohn, R. E. W. A. Wallace, and J. R. Harrald. 1991. "Organizing for Response: The Unresolved Problem. *Proceedings, 1991 International Oil Spill Conference*. American Petroleum Institute. Washington, DC. Pp 29-33.

Comfort, L. K. (1999). *Shared Risk: Complex Systems in Seismic Response*. Pittsburgh, PA: Pergamon Press.

Comfort, L. K. (2005). Risk, security, and disaster management. *Annual Review of Political Science*, *8*, 335–356. doi:10.1146/annurev.polisci.8.081404.075608

Comfort, L. K. (2007). Crisis management in hindsight: Cognition, communication, coordination, and control. *Public Administration Review*, *67*, 189–197. doi:10.1111/j.1540-6210.2007.00827.x

Comfort, L. K., & Haase, T. W. (2006). Communication, coherence, and collective action: The impact of Hurricane Katrina on communications infrastructure. *Public Works Management Policy*, *10*(4), 328–343. doi:10.1177/1087724X06289052

Comfort, L. K., Sungu, Y., Johnson, D., & Dunn, M. (2002). Complex systems in crisis: Anticipation and resilience in dynamic environments. *Journal of Contingencies and Crisis Management*, *9*(3), 144–158. doi:10.1111/1468-5973.00164

Comfort, L. K. 2005. "Fragility in Disaster Response: Hurricane Katrina, 29 August 2005" *The Forum*, Vol 3, Issue 3, Article 1.

Commfort, L. K., Sungu, Y., Johnson, D., & Dunn, M. (2001). Complex systems in crisis: Anticipation and resilience in dynamic environments. *Journal of Contingencies and Crisis Management*, *8*(4), 208–217.

Cook, M., Noyes, J. M., & Masakowski, Y. (2007). *Decision making in complex environments*. Aldershot, UK: Ashgate.

Cooper, D. F. (1978). On the design and control of crisis games. *Omega*, *6*(5), 460–461. doi:10.1016/0305-0483(78)90103-2

Coppola, N., Hiltz, S. R., & Rotter, N. (2004). Building Trust in Virtual Teams. *IEEE Transactions on Professional Communication*, *47*(2), 95–104. doi:10.1109/TPC.2004.828203

Cordella, A., & Shaikh, M. (2003). *Actor network theory and after: What's new for IS research?* Paper presented at the 11th European Conference on Information Systems.

Cova, T. J. (1999). GIS in emergency Management. In Longley, P., Goodchild, M. F., Maguire, D., & Rhind, D. (Eds.), *Geographical Information Systems. Principles, techniques, applications, and management* (2nd ed., pp. 845–858). New York, NY: John Wiley & Sons.

Coyle, D., & Childs, M. B. (2005). *The Role of Mobiles in Disasters and Emergencies*. GSM Association.

Crano, W. D., & Brewer, M. D. (2002). *Principles and methods of social research*. Mahwah, NJ: Lawrence Erlbaum Associates.

Crookall, D., & Saunders, D. (1998). Towards an integration of communication and simulation. In Crookall, D., & Saunders, D. (Eds.), *Communication and simulation* (pp. 2–32). Philadelphia, PA: Multilingual Matters.

Crookall, D., Oxford, R., & Saunders, D. (1997). Towards a reconceptualization of simulation: From representation to reality. *Simulation/Games for Learning*, *17*(4), 147-171.

Cross, R., Parker, A., Prusak, L., & Borgatti, S. P. (2001). Knowing what we know: Supporting knowledge creation and sharing in social networks. *Organizational Dynamics*, *30*, 100–120. doi:10.1016/S0090-2616(01)00046-8

Cummings, M. L. (2004). *Designing decision support systems for revolutionary command and control domains* (Unpublished doctoral dissertation). Charlottesville, VA: University of Virginia.

Currion, P. (2006). *Information and Technology Requirements Initiative: Assessment Report*. Washington, DC: Emergency Capacity Building Project.

Currion, P. (2009). Only connect: Problem sciences, information systems and humanitarian reform. *International Journal of Information Systems for Crisis Response and Management*, *1*(1), 29–40. doi:10.4018/jiscrm.2009010103

Currion, P. (2006). *Better the devil we know: Obstacles and opportunities in humanitarian GIS*. Retrieved September 20, 2010, from http://www.humanitarian.info/?page_id=35

Cutter, S. L. (2003). GI science, disasters, and emergency management. *Transactions in GIS, 7*(4), 439–446. doi:10.1111/1467-9671.00157

Daep, C. (2008). *Albay provincial coordinating council. Personal talk*. Legsapi City.

Dahinten, J. (2002, January 1). Natural disasters kill 25,000 worldwide in 2001. *Reuters*. Retrieved January 8, 2008, from http://www.planetark.org/ dailynewsstory. cfm/newsid/13886/newsDate/1-Jan-2002/story.htm

Danielsson, M., & Ohisson, K. (1999). Decision-making in emergency management: A survey study. *International Journal of Cognitive Ergonomics, 3*, 91–99. doi:10.1207/s15327566ijce0302_2

Dash, N. (1997). The use of Geographical Information Systems in disaster research. *International Journal of Mass Emergencies and Disasters, 15*, 135–146.

Davenport, T. H., & Prusak, L. (1998). *Working Knowledge*. Harvard Business School Press.

Davis, F. D. (1989). Perceived usefulness, perceived ease of use, and user acceptance of information technology. *Management Information Systems Quarterly, 13*(3), 319–339. doi:10.2307/249008

Davis, F. D., Bagozzi, R. P., & Warshaw, P. R. (1989). User acceptance of computer technology: A comparison of two theoretical models. *Management Science, 35*, 982–1003. doi:10.1287/mnsc.35.8.982

Davis, D. (2002). Fire commander. In Flin, R., & Arbuthnot, K. (Eds.), *Incident Command: Tales from the hot seat* (pp. 88–104). Burlington, VT: Ashgate Publishing Ltd.

De Groeve, T., Vernaccini, L., & Annunziato, A. (2006). *Global disaster alert and coordination system*. Paper presented at the 3rd International ISCRAM Conference, Newark, New Jersey (United States of America).

De Keyser, V., & Woods, D. D. (1990). Fixation errors: Failures to revise situation assessment in dynamic and risky systems. In Colombo, A. G., & Saiz de Bustamante, A. (Eds.), *Systems reliability assessment*. Dordrechts, The Netherlands: Kluwer Academic.

De Longueville, B., Luraschi, G., Smits, P., Peedell, S., & De Groeve, T. (2010). Citizens as sensors for natural hazards. A VGI integration workflow. *Geomatica, 64*(1), 41–60.

Dekker, S. W. A. (2002). *The field guide to human error investigations*. Burlington, VT: Ashgate Publishing Ltd.

Delmedico, N. (2007 July-September). Take Advantage of New Floodplain Data: Understanding dFIRMs Necessary for Intelligently Mapping Hazards. *ArcUser* (pp. 22-25).

Demchak, B., Chan, T. C., Griswold, W. G., & Lenert, L. (2006). Situation awareness during mass-casualty events: Command and control. *AMIA Annual Symposium Proceedings* (p. 905).

Demchak, B., Griswold, W. G., & Lenert, L. A. (2007). Data quality for situational awareness during mass-casualty events. *AMIA Annual Symposium Proceedings* (pp. 176-180).

Denef, S., Ramirez, L., Dyrks, T., & Stevens, G. (2008). Handy Navigation in Ever-Changing Spaces. An Ethnographic Study of Firefighting Practices. *Proceedings of DIS2008*. February 25–27, 2008. Cape Town, South Africa. forthcoming

Dennis, A. R., & Gallupe, R. B. (Eds.). (1993). *A history of GSS empirical research: Lessons learned and future directions*. New York: Macmillan.

Dennis, A. R., Valacich, J. S., & Nunamaker, J. F. (1990). An experimental investigation of small, medium and large groups in an electronic meeting system environment. *IEEE System. Man and Cybernetics, 25*, 1049–1057. doi:10.1109/21.59968

Dent, B. D. (1999). *Cartography: Thematic Map Design 5e*. Dubuque, Iowa: William C Brown. EG&G Technical Services (Ed.) (2007). *County of San Diego 2007 Firestorms After Action Report*. Unpublished Manuscript.

DeSanctis, G., & Gallupe, B. (1987). A foundation for the study of group decision support systems. *Management Science, 33*, 589–609. doi:10.1287/mnsc.33.5.589

DHS. (2001, last updated on). *Citizen Guidance on the Homeland Security Advisory System*. Retrieved 24 August, 2006, from http://www.dhs.gov/.

Di Maio, P. (2007). An open ontology for open source emergency response system. *Open Source Research Community*, January 2007.

Digital Combustion, Inc. (2004). *Fire Studio 3.0* (computer software).

Dixon, T. H. (1994, last updated on). *Sar Interferometry and Surface Change Detection*. Retrieved March 26, 2007, from http://southport.jpl.nasa.gov/scienceapps/dixon/index.html.

Downs, C. W., Jonhson, K. M., & Fallesen, J. J. (1987). *Analysis of feedback in after action reviews* (ARI Technical Report 745). Arlington, VA: U.S. Army Research Institute for Behavioral and Social Sciences.

Drabek, T. E., & McEntire, D. A. (2002). Emergent Phenomena and Multiorganizational Coordination in Disasters: Lessons from the Research Literature. *International Journal of Mass Emergencies and Disasters, 20*, 197–224.

Drabek, T. E., & McEntire, D. A. (2003). Emergent phenomena and the sociology of a disaster. *Disaster Prevention and Management, 12*(2), 97–112. doi:10.1108/09653560310474214

Driskell, J. E., Radtke, P. H., & Salas, E. (2003). Virtual teams: Effects of technological mediation on team performance. *Group Dynamics, 7*(4), 297–323. doi:10.1037/1089-2699.7.4.297

Dynes, R. R. (1994). Community Emergency Planning: False Assumptions and Inappropriate Analogies. *International Journal of Mass Emergencies and Disasters, 12*, 141–158.

Dynes, R. R., & Quarantelli, E. L. (1968). "Group Behavior under Stress" A Required Convergence of Organizational and Collective Behavior Perspectives. *Sociology and Social Research, 52*, 416–429.

Dynes, R. R., & Quarantelli, E. L. (1976). *Organizational Communications and Decision Making During Crises. Preliminary Paper #17*. Disaster Research Center. University of Delaware.

Earl, M. J. (1989). *Management strategies for information technology*. Prentice-Hall.

Eden, C., & Ackermann, F. (1998). *Making Strategy: the Journey of Strategic Management*. London: Sage.

Eden, C., & Radford, J. (Eds.). (1990). *Tackling Strategic Problems: the Role of Group Decision Support*. London: Sage.

Edgerton, D. (2007) *Creole technologies and global histories: rethinking how things travel in space and time*, in Journal of History of Science and Technology Vol.1, 75-112.

Elm, W., Potter, S., Tittle, J., Woods, D., Patterson, E., & Grossman, J. (2005). Finding decision support requirements for effective intelligence analysis tools. *Proceedings of the Human Factors and Ergonomics Society 49th Annual Meeting* (pp. 297-301).

EMDAT. (2008). *The OFDA/CRED international disaster database*. Université Catholique de Louvain, Brussels (Belgium). Retrieved September 20, 2010, from http://www.em-dat.net

Emergency Telecommunication Cluster, W. F. P. (2008). *Security Telecommunication Assessment Mission – Liberia*. Rome: World Food Programme.

Endsley, M., Bolté, B., & Jones, D. G. (2003). *Designing for Situation Awareness: An Approach to User-Centred Design*. London: Taylor & Francis.

Environmental Systems Research Institute. (2008, March 3). *ESRI Recognizes San Diego County Officials for GIS Work during Wildfires: GIS Use Improved Communications, Saved Infrastructure, and Assisted in Evacuations*. Press Release. Retrieved on March 4, 2008 from http://www.esri.com/news/ releases/08_1qtr/san_diego_wildfires.html

ETSI. (2006). *Analysis of the short message service (SMS) and Cell broadcast service (CBS) for emergency messaging applications*. Retrieved from www.etsi.org

Federal Communications Commission (FCC). (2007). *Summary: Auction 72*. Retrieved from http://wireless.fcc.gov/auctions/default.htm?job=auction_summary&id=73

Federal Communications Commission (FCC). (2010a). *FCC grants conditional approval of 21 petitions by cities, counties and states to build interoperable broadband networks for America's first responders*. Retrieved from http://fjallfoss.fcc.gov/edocs_public/attachmatch/DOC-298124A1.pdf

Federal Communications Commission (FCC). (2010b). *Implementing a nationwide, broadband, interoperable public safety network in the 700 MHz band* (DA 10-1494). Retrieved from http://fjallfoss.fcc.gov/edocs_public/attachmatch/DA-10-1494A1.pdf

Federal Communications Commission (FCC). (2010c). *Public safety and homeland security bureau approves long term de facto transfer spectrum lease agreements filed by conditional waiver recipients to establish 700 MHz interoperable public safety wireless broadband networks* (DA 10-1678). Retrieved from http://fjallfoss.fcc.gov/edocs_public/attachmatch/DA-10-1678A1.pdf

Federal Communications Commission (FCC). (2010d). *Public safety and homeland security bureau offers further guidance to conditional waiver recipients on completing the interoperability showing required by the 700 MHz waiver order* (DA 10-923). Retrieved from http://fjallfoss.fcc.gov/edocs_public/attachmatch/DA-10-923A1.pdf

Federal Communications Commission (FCC). (2010e). *The FCC's public safety bureau provides 700 MHz broadband waiver recipients additional time to more fully develop and finalize their network interoperability plans* (DA 10-1540). Retrieved from http://fjallfoss.fcc.gov/edocs_public/attachmatch/DA-10-1540A1.pdf

Federal Emergency Management Agency (FEMA). (2009). *NIMS Resource Center.* Department of Homeland Security. Retrieved on May 17, 2009 from: http://www.fema.gov/emergency/nims/.

Feltovich, P. J., Spiro, R. J., & Coulson, R. L. (1997). Issues of expert flexibility in contexts characterized by complexity and change. In Feltovich, P. J., Ford, K. M., & Hoffman, R. R. (Eds.), *Expertise in context: Human and machine.* Menlo Park, CA: AAAI/MIT Press.

FEMA. (2006, last updated on 27-Jul-2007). *Frequently Requested National Statistics Hurricane Katrina – One Year Later.* Retrieved 20 February, 2009, from http://www.fema.gov/hazard/hurricane/2005katrina/anniversary_factsheet.shtm.

FEMA. (2006, last updated on 09-Jun-2006). *Saffir-Simpson Hurricane Scale.* Retrieved December 12, 2006, from http://www.fema.gov/hazard/hurricane/hu_about.shtm.

FEMA. (2007, last updated on 27-Jul-2007). *Hurricane Katrina Information.* Retrieved 20 February, 2009, from http://www.fema.gov/hazard/hurricane/2005katrina/index.shtm.

FICORA. (2005). *Use of text messaging in public safety alerts.* (WG report 7/2005). Retrieved from www.ficora.fi

Fiedrich, F. (2000). An HLA-based multi-agent system for the search and rescue period after strong earthquakes. *Proceedings of the International Conference on Multiagent Systems* (ICMAS 2000) Workshop on RoboCup Rescue: Multi-Agent Approaches to the Simulation and Management of Major Urban Disasters, Boston, MA.

Fink, S. (1986). *Crisis Management. Planning for the Inevitable.* New York: American Management Association, AMACOM.

Fink, S. (2007, November). *The Science of Doing Good.* Scientific American Magazine.

Fjermestad, J., & Hiltz, S. R. (1998-1999). An assessment of group support systems experimental research: Methodology and results. *Journal of Management Information Systems, 15*(3), 127–149.

Francica, J. (2004, March 4). The Interagency Geospatial Preparedness Team (IGPT): An Interview with Susan Kalweit, Chief, IGPT. *Directions Magazine.* Retrieved January 3, 2008, from http://www.directionsmag.com/article.php?article_id=324&trv=1

FreeGeographyTools. (2009). *Using the Google Earth cache – Basics.* Retrieved September 20, 2010, from http://freegeographytools.com/2009/using-the-google-earth-cache-basics

FreeGeographyTools. (2010). *Xls2kml-Another Excel-to-kml converter with a few extras.* Retrieved November 10, 2010, from http://freegeographytools.com/2007/xls2kml-another-excel-to-kml-converter-with-a-few-extras

French, S., & Turoff, M. (2007). Decision Support Systems. *Communications of the ACM, 50*(3), 39–40. doi:10.1145/1226736.1226762

French, S., Carter, E., & Niculae, C. (2007). Decision Support in Nuclear and Radiological Emergency Situations: Are we too focused on models and technology? *Int. J. Emergency Management, 4*(3), 421–441. doi:10.1504/IJEM.2007.014295

French, S., Maule, A. J., & Papamichail, K. N. (2008). *Decision Making: Behaviour, Analysis and Support.* Cambridge: Cambridge University Press.

French, S., & Niculae, C. (2005). Believe in the Model: Mishandle the Emergency. *Journal of Homeland Security and Emergency Management, 2*(1). doi:10.2202/1547-7355.1108

French, S., Rios Insua, D., & Ruggeri, F. (2007). e-participation and decision analysis. *Decision Analysis, 4*(4), 1–16. doi:10.1287/deca.1070.0098

French, S., & Xu, D.-L. (2004). (in press). Comparison study of multi-attribute decision-analytic software. *Journal of Multi-Criteria Decision Analysis.*

Frey, L. R., Gouran, D. S., & Poole, M. S. (1999). *The handbook of group communication theory and research.* Thousand Oaks, CA: Sage Publications.

Fussell, S. R., Kraut, R. E., Lerch, F. J., Scherlis, W. L., McNally, M. M., et al. (1998). Coordination, overload, and team performance: Effects of team coordination strategies. In *Proceedings of the ACM Conference on Computer Supported Cooperative Work in Seattle, WA* (pp. 275-284). New York, NY: ACM.

Gallupe, R. B., Bastianutti, L., & Cooper, W. H. (1991). Unblocking brainstorms. *The Journal of Applied Psychology, 76*(1), 137–142. doi:10.1037/0021-9010.76.1.137

Garbis, C. (2002). The cognitive use of artifacts in cooperative process management: Rescue management and underground line control (Doctoral dissertation). *Linköping Studies in Art and Science, 258.* Linköping, SE: Linköping University.

Garshol, L. M., & Moore, G. (2006). *Information Technology - Document description and processing languages - Topic maps - XML syntax.* ISO. (ISO 13250-3).

Gaynor, M. (2003). *Network service investment guild: Maximizing ROI in uncertain markets.* Indianapolis, IN: Wiley Publishing, Inc.

Gaynor, M., & Bradner, S. (2004). *A real options metric to evaluate network, protocol, and service architecture.* Computer Communication Review. CCR.

Gaynor, M., & Bradner, S. (2008). *A statistical model to value network neutrality.* Media Law & Policy, New York Law School.

Gaynor, M., Pearce, A., Bradner, S., & Post, K. (2009). Open infrastructure for a nationwide emergency service network. [IJISCRAM]. *International Journal of Information Systems for Crisis Response and Management, 1*(2). doi:10.4018/jiscrm.2009040103

Gaynor, M. (2001). *The effect of market uncertainty on the management structure of network- based services.* Ph.D. Thesis, Harvard University.

Gaynor, M., & Bradner, S. (2001). Using real options to value modularity in standards. *Knowledge Technology and Policy, Special on IT Standardization, 14*(2).

Gaynor, M., Pearce, A., & Bradner, S. (2008). Open infrastructure for a nationwide emergency service network. *Proceedings of the 5th International ISCRAM Conference,* Washington, D.C.

GDAL. (2008). *GDAL - Geospatial data abstraction library.* Retrieved September 20, 2010, from http://www.gdal.org

GeoUtilities. (2010). *GeoUtilities - Tools for Google Earth™.* Retrieved November 2, 2010, from http://geonews.net/index_geof.html

Gestrelius, K. (1998). *Simulation and training games: Experimental learning.* Huskvarna, Sweden: SAAB Training Systems.

Gilchrist, I. (2000). *An analysis of the management of information on the fire service incident ground.* (Unpublished doctoral dissertation). University of Manchester, UK.

Gomez, E. A., Plotnick, L., et al. (2007). *Towards a Unified Public Safety Scale.* Hawaii International Conference on System Sciences (HICSS), Waikoloa, Hawaii.

Goodhue, D. L. (1995). Understanding user evaluations of information systems. *Management Science, 41*(12), 1827–1844. doi:10.1287/mnsc.41.12.1827

Goodhue, D. L., & Thompson, R. L. (1995). Task-technology fit and individual performance. *Management Information Systems Quarterly, 19*(2), 213–236. doi:10.2307/249689

Google. (2009a). *Google Earth™*. Retrieved from http://earth.google.com/

Google. (2009b). *KML documentation*. Retrieved February 5, 2009, from http://code.google.com/apis/kml/documentation/

Google. org. (2010). *Google crisis response - Haiti earthquake imagery*. Retrieved October 24, 2010, from http://www.google.com/relief/haitiearthquake/imagery.html

GoogleEarthCommunity. (2009). *Data problems compendium*. Retrieved February 9, 2009, from http://bbs.keyhole.com/ubb/showthreaded.php/Cat/0/Number/330340/an//page/2/vc/1

GoogleMaps. (2009). *Google Maps API*. Retrieved September 20, 2010, from http://code.google.com/apis/maps/

GoogleWebToolkit. (2009). *Google Web toolkit*. Retrieved September 20, 2010, from http://code.google.com/webtoolkit/

Gorry, A. G., & Scott-Morton, M. S. (1971). A framework for management information systems. *Sloan Management Review, 13*, 55–70.

Granger-Happ, E. (2001). *Wiring the Virtual Village*. Connecticut: Save the Children.

Granlund, R., Johansson, B., & Trnka, J. (2007). The Effects of Geographical Information Systems on a Collaborative Command and Control Task. In B. Van de Walle, P. Burghardt & C. Nieuwenhuis (Eds.), *Proceedings of the 4th International Conference on Information Systems for Crisis Response and Management ISCRAM 2007* (pp. 191-200).

Greater London Authority. (2006). *Report of the 7 July Review Committee*. ISBN 1 85261 8787.

Grohowski, R. B., McGoff, C., Vogel, D. R., & Martz, W. B., & F., N. J. (1990). Implementation of group support systems at IBM. *Management Information Systems Quarterly, 14*(4), 369–383. doi:10.2307/249785

Grossman, D. (2002). *New terminology and clarifications for Diffserv. Internet Engineering Task Force*. IETF.

Grossman, J., Trent, S., Patterson, E. S., & Woods, D. D. (2007). Supporting the cognitive work of information analysis and synthesis: A study of the military intelligence domain. *Proceedings of the Human Factors and Ergonomics Society 51st Annual Meeting* (pp. 348-352).

Gruber, T. R. (1993). A translation approach to portable ontologies. *Knowledge Acquisition, 5*(2). doi:10.1006/knac.1993.1008

Gu, Q., & Mendonça, D. (2005). Patterns of group information-seeking in a simulated emergency response environment. In B. Van de Walle, & B. Carlé (Eds.), *Proceedings of the 2nd International Conference on Information Systems for Crisis Response and Management in Brussels, Belgium* (pp. 109-116). Brussels, Belgium: SCK-CEN.

GVSIG. (2009). *gvSIG – Conselleria d'infrastructures i transport*. Retrieved November 10, 2010, from http://www.gvsig.org/web/home/gvsig-home/view?set_language=en

H.R. 5081: Broadband for First Responders Act of 2010, 111th Congress (2010).

Hackbarth, G. (1998, August 1998). The Impact of Organizational Memory on IT Systems, *paper presented at the Fourth Americas Conference on Information Systems*.

Hanseth, O. (2005). Beyond metaphysics and theory consumerism. *Scandinavian Journal of Information Systems, 17*(1), 159–166.

Harrald, J. R. (2006). Agility and discipline: Critical success factors for disaster response. *The Annals of the American Academy of Political and Social Science, 604*(1), 256–272. doi:10.1177/0002716205285404

Harrald, J. R. 2007. "Emergency Management Restructured: Intended and Unintended Consequences of Actions Taken Since 9/11/01", Chapter 6. *Emergency Management: The American Experience 1900-2005*. Claire B. Rubin, Editor. Public Entity Risk Institute, Fairfax, VA.

Harrald, J. R. and Linda Stoddart. 1998. "Scenario Based Identification and Structuring of Information Needs for the Response to Complex International Crises *Proceedings, Fifth Annual Conference of The Emergency Management Society*. Washington, D.C. pp. 295-306.

Harrald, John.R. and T. Mazzuchi "Planning for Success: A Scenario Based Approach to Contingency Planning Using Expert Judgment" 1993. *Journal of Contingencies and Crisis Management* 1:4. pp. 189-198

Hendela, A., Yao, X., Turoff, M., Hiltz, S. R., & Chumer, M. (2006) Virtual Emergency Preparedness Gaming: A follow up study, *Proceedings of ISCRAM 06*, May 14-17, NJIT, Newark NJ, ISBN 90-9020601-9

Hermann, C. F. (1965). Some consequences of crisis which limit the viability of organizations. *Administrative Science Quarterly*, 8(1), 61–82. doi:10.2307/2390887

Hester, N. C. J. Wilkinson, S.P. Horton, T. I Jefferson. 2008 "Integration of Information Systems for Port Earthquake Research Response. *Proceedings of the 5th International ISCRAM Conference*, F. Fiedrich and B. Van de Walle eds. pp. 362-367.

Hiltz, S. R., & Turoff, M. (1993). The Network Nation: Human Communication via [Addison Wesley, MIT Press.]. *Computer*, 1978.

Hiltz, S. R., Fjermestad, J., Ocker, R., & Turoff, M. (2006) Asynchronous Virtual Teams: Can Software Tools and Structuring of Social Processes Enhance Performance? In Volume II: Human-Computer Interaction in Management Information Systems: Applications, Dennis Galletta and Ping Zhang, editors, Armonk, NY: M. E. Sharpe, Inc., 119- 142.

Hinton, D., Klein, T. E., & Haner, M. (2005). An architectural proposal for future wireless emergency response networks with broadband services. *Bell Labs Technical Journal*, 10(2), 121–138. doi:10.1002/bltj.20097

Hipple, E. (1998). Economics of product development by user: The impact of sticky local information. *Management Science*, 44(5).

Hirokawa, R. Y., & Poole, M. S. (1996). *Communication and group decision-making* (2nd ed.). Thousand Oaks, CA: Sage Publications.

Hirschheim, R., Klein, H. K., & Lyytinen, K. (1996). Exploring the intellectual structures of Information Systems development: A social action rhetoric analysis. *Accounting Management & Information Technology*, 6(1/2), 1–64. doi:10.1016/0959-8022(96)00004-5

Hobijn, B. and Comin, D. (2003). *Cross-Country Technology Adoption: Making the Theories Face the Facts.* FRB NY Staff Report No.169.

Hollnagel, E., & Woods, D. D. (2005). *Joint cognitive systems: Foundations of cognitive systems engineering.* Boca Raton, FL: CRC Press. doi:10.1201/9781420038194

Hollnagel, E. (2006). Resilience: The challenge of the unstable. In Hollnagel, E., Woods, D. D., & Leveson, N. (Eds.), *Resilience engineering: Concepts and precepts* (pp. 9–14). Aldershot, UK: Ashgate.

Homer-Dixon, T. (2007). *The Upside of Down: Creativity, Catastrophe and the Renewal of Civilisation.* London: Souvenir Press.

Houghton, R. J., Barber, C., McMaster, R., Stanton, N. A., & Salmon, P. (2006). Command and control in emergency services operations: A social network analysis. *Ergonomics*, 49(12), 1204–1225. doi:10.1080/00140130600619528

HSE. (1996). *The chemical release and fire at the Associated Octel Company Ltd.* Sudbury, MA: HSE Books.

Huang, H., & Ocker, R. (2006) Preliminary Insights into the In-Group/Out-Group Effect in Partially Distributed Teams: An Analysis of Participant Reflections, *Proceedings of SIGMIS-CPR '06*, Claremont, California.

Hutchins, E. (2005). *Cognition in the wild.* Cambridge, MA: MIT Press.

Hygiene. (2008, October 15). In *Wikipedia, The Free Encyclopedia.* Retrieved October 15, 2008, from http://en.wikipedia.org/w/index.php?title=Hygiene&oldid=245367616

Hyslop, M. (2007). *Critical information infrastructures.* Heidelberg, Germany: Springer Verlag.

Iakovou, E., & Douligeris, C. (2001). An information management system for the emergency management of hurricane disasters. *International Journal of Risk Assessment and Management*, 2(3/4), 243–262. doi:10.1504/IJRAM.2001.001508

International Federation of Red Cross and Red Crescent Societies. (2005). *World Disasters Report 2005.* Geneva: IFRC.

Iocono, C. S., & Weisband, S. (1997) Developing Trust in Virtual Teams, IEEE Proceedings, 30th Hawaii International Conference on System Sciences (HICSS) Volume 2: Information Systems Track - Collaboration Systems and Technology. Washington DC: IEEE Computer Society.

Isenberg, D. S. (1998). The dawn of the stupid network. *ACM Networker, 2*(1), 24–31. doi:10.1145/280437.280445

ISIS. (2003). Intelligent systems for humanitarian geo-infrastructure. User survey and requirements document.

Jefferson, Theresa. and J. Harrald. (2007). Collaborative Technology: providing agility in response to extreme events. *International Journal of Electronic Governance, 1*(1), 79–93. doi:10.1504/IJEG.2007.014344

Jefferson, T. L. (2006). Evaluating the role of information technology in emergency and crisis management. *The Journal of Information and Knowledge Management Systems, 36*(3), 261–264.

Jennex, M. E. (2004). Emergency Response Systems: The Utility Y2K Experience. [JITTA]. *Journal of IT Theory and Application, 6*(3), 85–102.

Jennex, M. E. (2005). What is Knowledge Management? *International Journal of Knowledge Management, 1*(4), i–iv.

Jennex, M. E. (2006). Open Source Knowledge Management. *International Journal of Knowledge Management, 2*(4), i–iv.

Jennex, M. E., & Olfman, L. (2006). A Model of Knowledge Management Success. *International Journal of Knowledge Management, 2*(3), 51–68. doi:10.4018/jkm.2006070104

Jennex, M. E. (2008). A model for emergency response systems. In Janczewski, L., & Colarik, A. (Eds.), *Cyber warfare and cyber terrorism* (pp. 383–391). Hershey, PA: Idea Group.

Jennex, M. E. (2007). *Modeling emergency response systems.* Paper presented at the 40th Hawaii International Conference on System Sciences.

Jensen, R. (2007). *The Digital Provide: Information (Technology), Market Performance and Welfare in the South Indian Fisheries Sector*, in The Quarterly Journal of Economics, Vol.CXXII, Issue 3, 879-924.

Jiang, X., Hong, J. I., Takayama, L. A., & Landay, J. A. Ubiquitous computing for firefighters: Field Studies and prototypes of large displays for incident command. *Proceedings of the international conference on Computer-Human Interaction* (CHI) 2004, pp. 279-686.

Johannson, B., Hollnagel, E., & Granlund, A. (2002). The control of unpredictable systems. In C. Johnsson (Ed.) *Proceedings of the 21ˢᵗ European Annual Conference on Human Decision Making and Control.* GIST Technical Report G2002-1, Department of Computing Science, University of Glasgow, Scotland.

Johansson, B., Artman, H., & Waern, Y. (2000). Technology in crisis management systems – Ideas and effects. *Document Design (Amsterdam), 2*(3), 247–257.

Johansson, B. J. E., & Hollnagel, E. (2007). Pre-requisites for large scale coordination. *Cognition Technology and Work, 9*(1), 5–13. doi:10.1007/s10111-006-0050-z

Johansson, B. (2005). Joint control in dynamic situations (Doctoral dissertation). *Linköping Studies in Science and Technology, 972*. Linköping, Sweden: Linköping University.

Johnson, P. E., Moen, J. B., & Thompson, W. B. (1988). Garden path errors in diagnostic reasoning. In Bolec, L., & Coombs, M. J. (Eds.), *Expert system applications.* New York, NY: Springer-Verlag.

Johnson, R. (2000). *GIS Technology for Disasters and Emergency Mangement.* Redlands, CA: ESRI Press

Jones, P. E., & Roelofsma, P. H. M. P. (2000). The potential for social contextual and group biases in team decision-making: Biases, conditions and psychological mechanisms. *Ergonomics, 43*(8), 1129–1152. doi:10.1080/00140130050084914

Jones, M. T. (2005). *The autobiographical Earth.* Retrieved September 20, 2010, from http://video.google.com/videoplay?docid=1883812421992143014

Jul, S. (2007). Who's Really on First? A Domain-Level User, Task and Context Analysis for Response Technology. *Proceedings of the 4th International Conference on Information Systems for Crisis Response and Management ISCRAM2007* (Eds. B. Van de Walle, P. Burghardt & C. Nieuwenhuis), 2007, pp. 139-148.

Kaiser, R., Spiegel, P. B., Henderson, A. K., & Gerber, M. L. (2003). The application of Geographic Information Systems and Global Positioning Systems in humanitarian emergencies: Lessons learned, programme implications and future research. *Disasters, 27*(2), 127–140. doi:10.1111/1467-7717.00224

Kallinikos, J. (1992). The significations of machines. *Scandinavian Journal of Management, 8*(2), 113–132. doi:10.1016/0956-5221(92)90020-F

Kataoka, M. (2005). *GIS for Homeland Security*. Redlands, CA: ESRI Press.

Kendra, J., & Wachtendorf, T. (2002). *Preliminary Paper #324. Disaster Research Center, University of Delaware.* Creativity in Emergency Response After the World Trade Center Attack.

Kendra, J. M., & Wachtendorf, T. (2006). *Improvisation, creativity, and the art of emergency management (Disaster Research Center Preliminary Paper 357).* Newark, DE: University of Delaware.

Killian, L. M. (2002). An introduction to methodological problems of field studies in disaster research. In Stallings, R. A. (Ed.), *Methods of disaster research* (pp. 49–93). Philadelphia, PA: Xlibris.

Kincade, S., & Verclas, K. (2008). *Wireless Technology for Social Change: Trends in Mobile Use by NGOs. Washington, DC and Berkshire*. UK: UN Foundation – Vodafone Group Foundation Partnership.

Kitamato, A. (2005) Digital typhoon: Near real-time aggregation, recombination and delivery of typhoon-related information. Proceeding of the 4th International Symposium on Digital Earth. Retrieved October 26, 2005 from http://www.cse.iitb.ac.in/~neela/MTP/Stage1-Report.pdf

Kleiboer, M. (1997). Simulation methodology for crisis management support. *Journal of Contingencies and Crisis Management, 5*(4), 198–206. doi:10.1111/1468-5973.00057

Klein, G., Moon, B., & Hoffman, R. R. (2006, July/August). Making sense of sensemaking 1: Alternative perspectives. *IEEE Intelligent Systems*, 22–25.

Klein, G. A. (2007). Flexecution as a paradigm for replanning, part 1. *Intelligent Systems, 22*(5), 79–83. doi:10.1109/MIS.2007.4338498

Klein, G. A., & Thordsen, M. L. (1989). *Cognitive processes of the team mind*. Yellow Springs, OH: Klein Associates.

Klein, G. A., Calderwood, R., & Clinton-Cirocco, A. (1986). Rapid decision making on the fire ground. *Proceedings of the Human Factors Society 30th Annual Meeting*, (pp. 576-580).

Koch, K. (2007, 29 August). *Katrina-ravaged Gulf Coast struggling 2 years later.* CNN.com/us. Retrieved on February 8, 2008, from http://www.cnn.com/2007/ US /08/29/katrina.day/index.html?iref=newssearch

Koehler, G. A. (1995). *Fractals and Path Dependent Processes: A Theoretical Approach for Characterizing Emergency Medical Responses to Major Disasters*. What Disaster Response Management Can Learn From Chaos Theory California, USA, California Research Bureau.

Kolding Kommune. (2005). *Spoergeskemaundersoegelse* (in Danish). Retrieved from www.kolding.dk/printpage.asp?id=31377

Korolija, N., & Linell, P. (1996). Episodes: Coding and analyzing coherence in multiparty conversation. *Linguistics, 34*(44), 799–831. doi:10.1515/ling.1996.34.4.799

Korolija, N. (1998). Episodes in talk: Constructing coherence in multiparty conversation (Doctoral dissertation). *Linköping Studies in Arts and Science, 171*. Linköping, Sweden: Linköping University.

Kostman, J. T. (2004). 20 Rules for Effective Communication in a Crisis. *Disaster Recovery Journal., 17*(2), 20.

Kristensen, M., Kyng, M., & Palen, L. (2006). Participatory Design in Emergency Medical Service: Designing for Future Practice, *Proceedings of the ACM Conference on Human Factors in Computing Systems* (CHI 2006), 161-170.

Kyng, M. (Ed.). (2007). PalCom External Report no 52: Revised conceptual framework for palpable computing Section I. Retrieved October 20, 2008 from http://www.ist-palcom.org/publications/deliverables/Deliverable-37-%5B2.1.2%5D-palpability-revised-SectionI.pdf

Laituri, M., & Kodrich, K. (2008). Online disaster response community: People as sensors of high magnitude disasters using internet GIS. *Sensors (Basel, Switzerland), 8*, 3037–3055. doi:10.3390/s8053037

Lamb, R. (1999). *Using Intranets: Preliminary results from a socio-technical field study.* Paper presented at the 32nd Hawaii International Conference on System Sciences, Hawaii.

Landgren, J. (2005). Supporting fire crew sensemaking enroute to incidents. *International Journal of Emergency Management, 2*(3), 176–188. doi:10.1504/IJEM.2005.007358

Landgren, J., & Nuldén, U. (2007). A study of emergency response work: Patterns of mobile phone interaction. In M. R. Rosson, & D. Gilmore (Eds.), *Proceedings of the SIGCHI Conference on Human Factors in Computing Systems in San Jose, CA* (pp. 1323-1331). New York, NY: ACM.

Larsen, L. (2007). *Strengthening Humanitarian Information Management: A Status Report.* Geneva: OCHA Field Information Services Unit.

Latour, B. (2005). *Reassembling the social: An introduction to actor-network-theory.* Oxford, UK: Oxford University Press.

Law, J., & Hassard, J. (1999). *Actor network theory and after.* Blackwell Publishers/The Sociological Review.

Lee, J., & Moray, N. (1992). Trust and the allocation of function in the control of automatic systems. *Ergonomics, 35,* 1243–1270. doi:10.1080/00140139208967392

Lee, J. S., Lee, S. L., Damon, S. A., Geller, R., Janus, E. R., Ottoson, C., & Scott, M. J. (2006) Risk Communication needs in a chemical event, *Journal of Emergency Management,* 4, 2, 37-43, full report http://www.wetp.org/ wetp/ public/ has1_get_blob. cfm?ID=1051

Lee, J., & Bui, T. (2000). A Template-based Methodology for Disaster Management Information Systems. *Proceedings of the 33rd Hawaii International Conference on System Sciences.*

Lemoine, G., & Brunner, D. (2007, 13-15. March 2007). *Integration of full resolution image coverages using SuperOverlays.* Paper presented at the FOSSGIS-Conference, Berlin.

Li, W. (1999, last updated on 1999). *Zipf's Law.* Retrieved 24 august, 2006, from http://myhome.hanafos.com/~philoint/phd-data/Zipf's-Law-2.htm.

Lindblom, C. (1959). The Science of Muddling Through. *Public Administration Review, 79–88.* doi:10.2307/973677

Lindblom, C. (1965). *The Intelligence of Democracy.* Free Press.

Lindblom, C. (1979). Still muddling, not yet through. *Public Administration Review,* (November/December): 517–526. doi:10.2307/976178

Linell, P., & Korolija, N. (1997). Coherence in multi-party conversation. In Givon, T. (Ed.), *Conversation: Cognitive, communicative and social perspectives* (pp. 167–205). Amsterdam, The Netherlands: John Benjamins.

Linstone, H. A. (1973). On discounting the future. *Technological Forecasting and Social Change, 4,* 335–338. doi:10.1016/0040-1625(73)90074-7

Linstone, H.A., & Turoff, M. (1978). *The Delphi Method: Techniques and Applications.* London: Addison- Wesley.

Linstone, H., & Turoff, M. (1975) The Delphi Method: Techniques and Applications, Addison Wesley Advanced Book Program, 1975 (available online at http://is.njit.edu/turoff). Available at http://is.njit.edu/ turoff, last access 18 August 2007.

Lipton, E. (2006). The Katrina year: The next emergency: Despite steps, disaster planning still shows gaps. *The New York Times.* Retrieved from http://www.nytimes.com/

Livejournal. (2005). *The survival of New Orleans Weblog.* Retrieved from http://interdictor.livejournal.com

London Assembly. (2006). *Report of the 7th July review committee, Greater London authority.* Retrieved from www.london.gov.uk/assembly/reports/7july

Longley, P. A., Goodchild, M. F., Maquire, D. J., & Rhind, D. W. (2001). *Geographic Information Systems and Science.* New Jersey: John Wiley & Sons.

Lorincz, K., Malan, D.J., Fulford-Jones, T., Nawoj, A., Clavel, A., Shnayder, V., Mainland, G., Welsh, M. & Moulton, S. (2004). Sensor Networks for Emergency Response: Challenges and Opportunities. *Pervasive Computing* October - December 2004, pp. 16-23.

Macauley, L., & Alabdulkarim, A. (2005). *Facilitation of e-Meetings: State-of-the-Art Review.* Paper presented at the IEEE International conference on e-technology, e-commerce and e-service, Hong Kong.

Mackenzie, C., Hu, P. F.-M., Fausboll, C., Nerlich, M., & Benner, T. (2007). Challenges to remote emergency decision-making for disasters or Homeland Security. *Cognition Technology and Work, 9*(1), 15–24. doi:10.1007/s10111-006-0051-y

MacKenzie, C., Fu-Ming Hu, P., Fausboll, C., Nerlich, M., Benner, T., & Gagliano, D. (2007). Challenges to remote emergency decision-making for disasters or Homeland Security. *Cognition Technology and Work, 9*, 15–24. doi:10.1007/s10111-006-0051-y

Mallach, E. G. (2000). *Decision Support and Data Warehouse Systems.* Boston: McGraw Hill.

Malone, T. W. (1987). Modelling coordination in organizations and markets. *Management Science, 33*(10), 1317–1332. doi:10.1287/mnsc.33.10.1317

March, J. G., & Simon, H. A. (1958). *Organizations.* New York: John Wiley & Sons.

Marincioni, F. (2007). Information technologies and the sharing of disaster knowledge: The critical role of professional culture. *Disasters, 31*(4), 459–476. doi:10.1111/j.1467-7717.2007.01019.x

Martin, D., Bowers, J. & D. Wastell. The interactional affordances of technology: An ethnography of human-computer interaction in an ambulance control center. *Proceedings of HCI'97,* 263-281.

Maxwell, J. A. (1992). Understanding and validity in qualitative research. *Harvard Educational Review, 62*(3), 279–300.

McCann, C., & Pigeau, R. (2000). *The human in command: Exploring the modern military experience.* New York, NY: Kluwer Academic/Plenum Publishers.

McCurdy, N. J., Griswold, W. G., & Lenert, L. A. (2005). Reality fly through: Enhancing situational awareness for medical response to disasters using ubiquitous video. *AMIA Annual Symposium Proceedings* (pp. 510-514).

McDonald, S., & Sinha, R. (2008). Information communication technology: Reform of organisational crisis management during natural disasters. *International Journal of Management Practice, 3*(2), 131–149. doi:10.1504/IJMP.2008.018367

McGuirl, J. M., & Sarter, N. B. (2006). Supporting trust calibration and the effective use of decision aids by presenting dynamic system confidence information. *Human Factors, 48*(4), 656–665. doi:10.1518/001872006779166334

Meissner, A., Luckenbach, T., Risse, T., Kirste, T., & Kirchner, H. (2002). *Design challenges for an integrated disaster management communication and Information System.* Paper presented at The First IEEE Workshop on Disaster Recovery Networks (DIREN 2002), New York City.

Mendonca, D., & Wallace, W. A. (2004). Studying Organizationally-situated Improvisation in Response to Extreme Events. *International Journal of Mass Emergencies and Disasters, 22*(2), 5–29.

Mendonça, David., J. Harrald and T. Jefferson. (2007). Emergent Interoperability: Collaborative Adhocracies and Mix and Match Technologies in Emergency Management. *Communications of the ACM, 50*(3), 45–49. doi:10.1145/1226736.1226764

Mendonça, D. (2007). Decision Support for Improvisation in Response to Extreme Events. *Decision Support Systems, 43*(3), 952–967. doi:10.1016/j.dss.2005.05.025

Mendonça, D., & Fiedrich, F. (2006). Training for improvisation in emergency management: Opportunities and limits for information technology. *International Journal of Emergency Management, 3*(4), 348–363. doi:10.1504/IJEM.2006.011301

Mendonça, D., & Wallace, W. A. (2004). Studying organizationally-situated improvisation in response to extreme events. *International Journal of Mass Emergencies and Disasters, 22*(2), 5–29.

Mendonça, D., & Wallace, W. A. (2007). A cognitive model of improvisation in emergency management. *IEEE Transactions on Systems, Man and Cybernetics. Part A, 37*(4), 547–561.

Mendonça, D., Beroggi, G. E. G., & Wallace, W. A. (2003). Evaluating support for improvisation in simulated emergency scenarios. In *Proceedings of the 36th Hawaii International Conference on System Sciences (HICSS'03) – Track 8 – Volume 8*. Washington, DC: IEE Computer Society.

Miles, M. B., & Huberman, M. A. (1994). *Qualitative data analysis*. Sage Publications.

Miller, D. (2004). Exposing the Errors: An Examination of the Nature of Organizational Crisis. In *Responding to Crisis: A Rhetorical Approach to Crisis Communication*. Mahwah, NJ, London: Lawrence Erlbaum Associates.

Miller, C. C. (2006). A beast in the field: The Google Maps mashup as GIS/2. *Cartographica: The International Journal for Geographic Information and Geovisualization, 41*(3), 187–199. doi:10.3138/J0L0-5301-2262-N779

Mills, J. W. (2008). Understanding disaster: GI science contributions in the ongoing recovery from Katrina. *Transactions in GIS, 12*(1), 1–4. doi:10.1111/j.1467-9671.2008.01083.x

Miskel, J. (2008). *Disaster Response and Homeland Security: What Works, What Doesn't*. Stanford University Press.

Mitroff, I., & Turoff, M. (1973). Technological Forecasting and Assessment: Science and/or Mythology? *Journal of Technological Forecasting and Social Change, 5*, 13–134.

Moorman, C., & Miner, A. S. (1998). Organizational improvisation and organizational memory. *Academy of Management Review, 23*(4), 698–723. doi:10.2307/259058

Morison, A. (2009). Integrating diverse feeds to extend human perception into distant scenes. In McDermott, P. (Ed.), *Advanced decision architectures for the Warfighter: Foundation and technology*. Alion Science.

Morton, A., Ackermann, F., & Belton, V. (2003). Technology-driven and model-driven approaches to group decision support: focus, research philosophy, and key concepts. *European Journal of Information Systems, 12*(2), 110–126. doi:10.1057/palgrave.ejis.3000455

Mosier, K. L., & Skitka, L. J. (1996). Human decision makers and automated decision aids: Made for each other? In Parasuraman, R., & Mouloua, M. (Eds.), *Automation and human performance: Theory and applications* (pp. 201–220). Mahwah, NJ: Lawrence Erlbaum Associates, Inc.

Mostowfi, F., & Fotouhi, F. (2006) Improving quality of ontology: An ontology transformation approach. In *Proceedings of the 22nd International Conference on Data Engineering Workshops* (p. 61). Atlanta, GA.

Motro, A. (1997). Sources of uncertainty, imprecision, and inconsistency in Information Systems. In Motro, A., & Smets, P. (Eds.), *Uncertainty management in Information Systems: Needs and solutions*. Kluwer Academic Publishers.

Mowshowitz, A. (2002). *Virtual Organizations*. Quorum Books.

Moynihan, D. (2006) From forest fires to Hurricane Katrina: Case Studies of Incident Command Systems, Networks and Partnerships Series, IBM Center for The business of Government.

Muhren, W. G. Van Den Eede, B. Van de Walle. 2008. "Sensemaking as a Methodology for ISCRAM Research: Information Processing in an Ongoing Crisis. *Proceedings of the 5th International ISCRAM Conference*, F. Fiedrich and B. Van de Walle eds. pp. 315-323.

Munich Research Group. (2005). *Node 2*. Retrieved May 30, 2005, from http://www.lrz-muenchen.de/~ua352bm/webserver/webdata/Will/node2.html

Murhen, W., Van Den Eede, G., & Van de Walle, B. (2008). *Sensemaking as a methodology for ISCRAM research: Information processing in an ongoing crisis* Paper presented at the 5th International ISCRAM Conference Washington, DC, USA.

Murphy, T., & Jennex, M. E. (2006). Knowledge Management, Emergency Response, and Hurricane Katrina. *International Journal of Intelligent Control and Systems, 11*(4), 199–208.

Myers, N. (1999). *Manager's guide to contingency planning for disasters: protecting vital facilities and critical operations*. New York: Wiley.

NASA. (2005, last updated on 2007). *Hurricanes Katrina and Rita Storm Track Map and Animation*. Retrieved March 26, 2007, from http://www.nasa.gov/vision/earth/lookingatearth/h2005_katrina.html.

National Research Council. (2006). *Facing hazards & disasters: Understanding human dimensions*. Washington, DC: National Academy Press.

Network Reliability and Interoperability Council VII Focus Group 1D. (2005). *Communication issues for emergency communications beyond E911, final report – Properties, network architectures and transition issues for communications between emergency service organizations, including PSAPs.*

Niculae, C., French, S., & Carter, E. (2004). Emergency Management: Does it have a sufficiently comprehensive understanding of decision-making, process and context? *Radiation Protection Dosimetry, 109*, 97–100. doi:10.1093/rpd/nch257

NOAA. (2005, last updated on 2005). *The Fujita Scale.* Retrieved December 12, 2006, from http://www.crh.noaa.gov/glossary.php?letter=fujita.

NOAA. (2006, last updated on 2006). *Beaufort Wind Scale.* Retrieved January, 2007, from http://www.spc.noaa.gov/faq/tornado/beaufort.html.

NOAA. (2010). *NOAA produces images of Haiti for first responders.* Retrieved September 20, 2010, from http://www.noaanews.noaa.gov/stories2010/20100119_haiti.html

Norman, D. A. (1993). *Things that make us smart: Defending human attributes in the age of the machine.* Reading, MA: Addison-Wesley Publishing.

Norwegian public safety radio project. (2010). *Direktoratet for noedkommunikasjon*, Oslo. Retrieved from http://www.dinkom.no/default.asp?pub=0&sub=43

Nourbakhsh, I., Sargent, R., Wright, A., Cramer, K., McClendon, B., & Jones, M. (2006). Mapping disaster zones. *Nature, 439*, 787–788. doi:10.1038/439787a

Noy, N., & Klein, M. (2003). Ontology evolution: Not the same as schema evolution. *Knowledge and Information Systems, 5*.

Noy, F. N., & Musen, M. A. (2000) PROMPT: Algorithm and tool for automated ontology merging and alignment. In *Proceedings of the Seventeenth National Conference on Artificial Intelligence* (AAAI-2000), (pp. 450–455). Austin, TX.

Nunamaker, J. F., Briggs, R. O., Mittleman, D. D., Vogel, D. R., & Balthazard, P. A. (1996). Lessons from a Dozen Years of Group Support Systems Research: A Discussion of Lab and Field Findings. *Journal of Management Information Systems, 13*(3), 163–207.

Nunamaker, J. R., Weber, E. S., & Chen, M. (1989). Organizational crisis management systems: Planning for intelligent action. *Journal of Management Information Systems, 5*(4), 7–32.

O'Brian, F. A., & Dyson, R. G. (Eds.). (2007). *Supporting strategy: frameworks, methods and models.* Chichester: John Wiley and Sons, Ltd.

OCHA. (2007). *Operational Guidance on Responsibilities of Cluster / Sector Leads & OCHA in Information Management v2.0.* Geneva: OCHA Field Information Services Unit.

Office of Emergency Services. (2007). *Standardized Emergency Management System (SEMS) Guidelines.* Governor's Office of Emergency Services, State of California. Retrieved on May 15, 2009 from: http://www.oes.ca.gov/Operational/OESHome.nsf/Content/B494353521 08954488256C2A0071E038?OpenDocument.

OGC. (2008). *OGC approves KML as open standard.* Retrieved from http://www.opengeospatial.org/pressroom/pressreleases/857

OpenStreetMap. (2010). *WikiProject Haiti.* Retrieved October 24, 2010, from http://wiki.openstreetmap.org/wiki/WikiProject_Haiti

Orasanu, J., & Connolly, T. (1993). The reinvention of decision making. In Klein, G. A., Orasanu, I., Calderwood, R., & Zsambok, C. E. (Eds.), *Decision making in action: Models and methods* (pp. 3–20). Norwood, NJ: Ablex Publishing.

Orasanu, J., & Salas, E. (1993). Team decision making in complex environments. In Klein, G. A., Orasanu, J., Calderwood, R., & Zsambok, C. E. (Eds.), *Decision making in action: Models and methods* (pp. 327–345). Norwood, NJ: Ablex Publishing.

Orlikowski, W. J. (1992). The Duality of Technology: Rethinking the Concept of Technology in Organizations. *Organization Science, 3*(3), 398–427. doi:10.1287/orsc.3.3.398

Orlikowski, W., & Barley, S. (2001). Technology and institutions: What can research on Information Technology and research on organizations learn from each other. *Management Information Systems Quarterly*, *25*(2), 145–165. doi:10.2307/3250927

Orlikowski, W. J. (2007). Sociomaterial practices: Exploring technology at work. *Organization Studies*, *28*(9). doi:10.1177/0170840607081138

Orlikowski, W. J., & Gash, D. C. (1994). Technological frames: Making sense of information technology in organizations. *ACM Transactions on Information Systems*, *2*, 174–207. doi:10.1145/196734.196745

Orlikowski, W. J., & Iacono, C. S. (2001). Research commentary: Desperately seeking the "IT" in IT research - A call to theorizing the IT artifact? *Information Systems Research*, *12*(2), 121–134. doi:10.1287/isre.12.2.121.9700

Page, D. (2005). Seeing is believing. *Fire Chief*, September, 2005. Retrieved from http://firechief.com/tactics/command_camera_092305/

Palen, L., Hiltz, S. R., & Liu, S. (2007). Citizen Participation in Emergency Preparedness and Response. *Communications of the ACM*, *50*(special issue), 3, 54–58. doi:10.1145/1226736.1226766

Palen, L., & Liu, S. (2007). Citizen Communications in Crisis: Anticipating a Future of ICT Supported Participation, *Proceedings of the ACM Conference on Human Factors in Computing Systems* (CHI 2007), 727-736.

Palen, L., Vieweg, S., Sutton, J., Liu, S., & Hughes, A. 2007a. "Crisis Informatics: Studying Crisis in a Networked World". Proceedings of the Third International Conference on E-Social Science, Ann Arbor, MI, Oct 7-9, Palen, Leysia and Sophia B. Liu, 2007b. "Citizen Communications in Crisis: Anticipating a Future of ICT-Supported Participation", Proceedings of the ACM Conference on Human Factors in Computing Systems CHI 2007, 727-736.

Palm, J., & Ramsell, E. (2007). Developing local emergency management by co-ordination between municipalities in policy networks: Experiences from Sweden. *Journal of Contingencies and Crisis Management*, *15*(4), 173–182. doi:10.1111/j.1468-5973.2007.00525.x

Panko, R. R. (2003). SLAMMER: The First Blitz Worm. *Communications of the AIS, CAIS, 11*(12).

Parson, E. A. (1996). What can learn from a game? In Zeckhauser, R., Keeney, R. L., & Sebenius, J. K. (Eds.), *Wise choices: Decision, games, and negotiations* (pp. 233–252). Boston, MA: Harvard Business School Press.

Patterson, E. S., Cook, R. I., Woods, D. D., & Render, M. L. (2004). Examining the complexity behind a medication error: Generic patterns in communication. *IEEE SMC Part A, 34*(6), 749–756.

Patterson, E. S., Roth, E. M., & Woods, D. D. (2001). Predicting vulnerabilities in computer-supported inferential analysis under data overload. *Cognition Technology and Work*, *3*, 224–237. doi:10.1007/s10111-001-8004-y

Patterson, E. S., Roth, E. M., & Woods, D. D. (2010). Facets of complexity in situated work. In Patterson, E. S., & Miller, J. (Eds.), *Macrocognition metrics and scenarios: Design and evaluation for real-world teams*. Aldershot, UK: Ashgate.

Patton, D., & Flin, R. (1999). Disaster Stress: An Emergency Management Perspective. *Disaster Prevention and Management*, *8*(4), 261–267. doi:10.1108/09653569910283897

Payne, C. F. (1999). Contingency plan exercises. *Disaster Prevention and Management*, *8*(2), 111–117. doi:10.1108/09653569910266157

Pearce, A. (2006). An analysis of the public safety & homeland security benefits of an interoperable nationwide emergency communications network at 700 MHz built by a public-private partnership. *Media Law & Policy Journal. New York Law School, 16*(1), 41–61.

Pepper, S. (1999). Navigating haystacks, discovering needles. *Markup Languages: Theory and Practice, 1*(4). MIT Press.

Pepper, S., & Grønmo, G. O. (2001). *Towards a general theory of scope*. Retrieved from http://www.ontopia.net/topicmaps/materials/scope.htm

Perla, P. P. (1990). *The art of wargaming*. Annapolis, MD: U.S. Naval Institute.

Perrow, C. (1984). *Normal accidents: Living with high-risk technologies*. New York, NY: Basic Books.

Persson, M., & Worm, A. (2002). *Information experimentation in command and control*. Paper presented at the 2002 Command and Control Research Technology Symposium, Monterey, CA.

Persson, P.-A. (2000). Bringing power and knowledge together: Information Systems design for autonomy and control in command work (Doctoral dissertation). *Linköping Studies in Science and Technology, 639*. Linköping, SE: Linköping University.

Persson, P.-A. (2004). *Toward an understanding of the service-based command system*. Paper presented at the 9th ICCRTS Command and Control Research and Technology Symposium, Monterey, CA.

Peterson, D. M., & Perry, R. W. (1999). The impact of disaster exercise on participants. *Disaster Prevention and Management, 8*(4), 241–254. doi:10.1108/09653569910283879

Petrescu-Prahova, M. G., & Butts, C. T. (2005). *Emergent coordination in the World Trade Center disaster (Paper #36)*. Irvine, CA: Institute of Mathematical Behavioral Sciences/ University of California.

Phillips, L. D. (1984). A theory of requisite decision models. *Acta Psychologica, 56*, 29–48. doi:10.1016/0001-6918(84)90005-2

PHIVOLCS. (2010). *Philippine Institute of Volcanology and Seismology*. Retrieved November 12, 2010, from http://volcano.phivolcs.dost.gov.ph/update_VMEPD/vmepd/vmepd/mayonhazmaps.htm

Pierce, M., & Choi, D. (2004). *Architecture for assured service capabilities in voice over IP*. Internet Engineering Task Force (IETF) Internet draft.

Pierce, M., & Choi, D. (2004). *Requirements for assured service capabilities in voice over IP*. (Internet Engineering Task Force) IETF Internet draft.

Pisano, F. (2005). Using satellite imagery to improve emergency relief. *Humanitarian Exchange, 32*, 36-40. Retrieved from http://www.odihpn.org/documents/humanitarianexchange032.pdf

Plotnick, L., Gomez, E. A., & White, C. (2007) Furthering Development of a Unified Emergency Scale Using Thurstone's Law of comparative Judgment: A progress Report, *Proceedings of ISCRAM 2007, 4th International Conference on Information Systems for Crisis Response and Management*, Delft, the Netherlands, May 13-16, Brussels University Press.

Post, B. Q. (1992). *Building the business case for group support technology*. Paper presented at the the Twenty-Fifth Annual Hawaii International Conference on System Sciences., Los Alamitos, CA.

Potere, D. (2008). Horizontal positional accuracy of Google Earth's high-resolution imagery archive. *Sensors (Basel, Switzerland), 8*, 7973–7981. doi:10.3390/s8127973

Poynder, R. (2008), Open Access: Doing the Numbers http://poynder.blogspot.com/ 2008/ 06/ open-access-doing-numbers.html, Open and Shut Blog, Wednesday, 11 June 2008.

Premkumar, G. (2000). Inter-organizational systems and supply chain management: An information processing perspective. *Information Systems Management, 17*(3). doi:10.1201/1078/43192.17.3.20000601/31241.8

Priyono, J. P., H., Dulbahri. (2007). Google Earth application to support disaster emergency response. *Jurnal Kebencanaan Indonesia, 1*(3).

Public Safety Spectrum Trust (PSST). (2010). *Public safety spectrum trust*. Retrieved from http://www.psst.org/index.jsp

Raman, M., Ryan, T., & Olfman, L. (2006). Knowledge Management Systems for Emergency Preparedness: The Claremont University Consortium Experience. *International Journal of Knowledge Management, 2*(3), 33–50. doi:10.4018/jkm.2006070103

Rankin, W. J., Gentner, F. C., & Crissey, M. J. (1995). *After action review and debriefing methods: Technique and technology*. Paper presented at the 17th Interservice/Industry Training Systems and Education Conference, Albuquerque, NM.

Rantanen, J., Impiö, J., Karinsalo, T., Malmivaara, M., Reho, A., Tasanen, M. & Vanhala, J. Smart Clothing Prototype for the Arctic Environment, *Personal and Ubiquitous Computing*, Vol. 6, Issue 1, Jan. 2002. New York: Springer-Verlag.

Rasker, P. C., Post, W. M., & Schraagen, J. M. C. (2000). Effects of two types of intra-team feedback on developing a shared mental model in command & control teams. *Ergonomics*, *43*(8), 1167–1189. doi:10.1080/00140130050084932

Rasmussen, J., Brehmer, B., & Leplat, J. (1990). *Distributed decision making: Cognitive models for cooperative work*. New York, NY: John Wiley & Sons.

Reddy, M. C., Paul, S. A., Abraham, P. J., McNeese, M., DeFlitch, C., & Yen, J. (2009). Challenges to effective crisis management: Using information and communication technologies to coordinate emergency medical services and emergency department teams. *International Journal of Medical Informatics*, *78*(4), 259–269. doi:10.1016/j.ijmedinf.2008.08.003

Rice, R. E. (1987). Information, Computer Mediates Communications and Organizational Innovation. *The Journal of Communication*, *37*(4), 65–94. doi:10.1111/j.1460-2466.1987.tb01009.x

Rice, R. E. (1990). From Adversity to Diversity: Applications for Communication Technology to Crisis Management. *Advances in Telecommunications Management*, *3*, 91–112.

Rockhart, J. R. (1979). Chief Executives Define Their Own Data Needs. *Harvard Business Review*, *57*(2), 81–93.

Rockhart, J. R. (1981). The Changing Role of the Information System Executive: A Critical Success Factor Perspective. *Sloan Management Review*, 15–25.

Rockhart, J. R. C. V. Bullen, 1982. *A Primer on Critical Success Factors, MIT Center for Information Systems Research*, Cambridge, MA.

Rodriguez, P. A., Geckle, W. J., Barton, J. D., Samsundar, J., Gao, T., Brown, M. Z., & Martin, S. R. (2006). An emergency response UAV surveillance system. *AMIA Annual Symposium Proceedings* (p. 1078).

Rohn, E. (2007). *A Survey of Schema Standards and Portals for Emergency Management and Collaboration. The 4th International Conference on Information Systems for Crisis Response and Management (ISCRAM)*. B. Van de Walle, P. Burghardt et al. Delft, the Netherlands Retrieved Access 2007 from.

Romano, N. C., Nunamaker, J. F., Briggs, R. O., & Vogel, D. R. (1998). Architecture, design, and development of an HTML/JavaScript web-based group support system. *Journal of the American Society for Information Science American Society for Information Science*, *49*(7), 649–667. doi:10.1002/(SICI)1097-4571(19980515)49:7<649::AID-ASI6>3.0.CO;2-1

Rubel, R. C. (2001). War-gaming network-centric warfare. *Naval War College Review*, *54*(2), 61–74.

Rubenstein, J. (2002). *The Cultural Landscape: An Introduction to Human Geography 7e*. New Jersey: Prentice Hall

S. 3625: First Responders Protection Act of 2010, 111th Congress (2010).

S. 3756: Public Safety Spectrum and Wireless Innovation Act, 111th Congress (2010).

Salmon, P. M., Stanton, N. A., Walker, G. H., & Jenkins, D. P. (2009). *Distributed situation awareness: Theory, measurement and application to teamwork*. Aldershot, UK: Ashgate.

Saltzer, J., Reed, D., & Clark, D. (1984). End-to-end arguments in system design. *ACM Transactions on Computer Systems*, *2*(4), 277–288. doi:10.1145/357401.357402

Samarajiva, R. (2005) *Mobilizing information and communications technologies for effective disaster warning: lessons from the 2004 tsunami*, in New Media & Society, Vol 7(6): 731–747.

Schmidt, K., & Bannon, L. (1992). Taking CSCW seriously: Supporting articulation work. *Computer Supported Cooperative Work*, *1*(1), 7–40. doi:10.1007/BF00752449

Schraagen, J. M., Huis in 't, V. M., & de Koning, L. (2010). Information sharing during crisis management in hierarchical vs. network teams. *Journal of Contingencies and Crisis Management*, *18*(2). doi:10.1111/j.1468-5973.2010.00604.x

Scolaí, P. (2008). Materialising materiality. *Proceedings of the Twenty Ninth International Conference on Information Systems*, Paris.

Scott, T. D. (1983). *Tactical engagement simulation after action review guidebook (ARI Research Product 83-13)*. Arlington, VA: U.S. Army Research Institute for Behavioral and Social Sciences.

SECRICOM project. (2008-2012). Retrieved from www. secricom.eu

Seeger, M. W., Sellnow, T. L., & Ulmer, R. R. (2003). *Communication and Organizational Crisis.* Westport, CT: Praeger Publishers.

Segars, A. H., & Grover, V. (1999). Profiles of strategic Information Systems planning. *Information Systems Research, 10*(3), 199–232. doi:10.1287/isre.10.3.199

Segev, A., & Gal, A. (2008). Enhancing portability with multilingual ontology-based knowledge management. *Decision Support Systems, 45*(3). doi:10.1016/j. dss.2007.07.011

Segev, A., Leshno, M., & Zviran, M. (2007). Context recognition using Internet as a knowledge base. *Journal of Intelligent Information Systems, 29*(3). doi:10.1007/s10844-006-0015-y

Segev, A., & Gal, A. (2007). Puzzling it out: Supporting ontology evolution with applications to e-government. In *Proceedings of IJCAI - Workshop on Workshop on Modeling and Representation in Computational Semantics.*

Sgrillo. (2009). *GE-Path.* Retrieved November 10, 2010, from http://www.sgrillo.net/googleearth/gepath.htm

Shattuck, L., & Woods, D. D. (2000). Communication of intent in military command and control systems. In Mc-Cann, C., & Pigeau, R. (Eds.), *The human in command: Exploring the modern military experience* (pp. 279–292). New York, NY: Kluwer Academic/Plenum Publishers.

Shattuck, L. G., Graham, J. M., Merlo, J. L., & Hah, S. (2000). Cognitive integration: A study of how decision makers construct understanding in evolving contexts. In *Proceedings of the Human Factors Society 44thAnnual Meeting,* (pp. 478-482). Santa Monica, CA: Human Factors and Ergonomics Society.

Shepherd, R., Barker, G., French, S., Hart, A., Maule, J., & Cassidy, A. (2006). Managing food chain risks: integrating technical and stakeholder perspectives on uncertainty. *Journal of Agricultural Economics, 57*(2), 313–327. doi:10.1111/j.1477-9552.2006.00054.x

Shubik, M. (1972). On the scope gaming. *Management Science, 18*(5), 20–36. doi:10.1287/mnsc.18.5.20

Simon, H. (1960). *The New Science of Decision Making.* New York: Harper and Row.

Simonsen, P. (2007). *Katastrofevarsling til befolkningen via offentlige mobilnet* (in Danish). Cand.merc.dat thesis, Copenhagen Business school, Copenhagen.

Smith, P. J., McCoy, C. E., & Layton, C. (1997). Brittleness in the design of cooperative problem-solving systems: The effects on user performance. *IEEE Transactions on Systems, Man, and Cybernetics, 27*, 360–371. doi:10.1109/3468.568744

Smith, H. A., McKeen, J. D., & Staples, D. S. (2001). Risk Management in Information Systems: Problems and Potentials. *Communications of AIS, 7*, 13.

Smith, M. K., Welty, C., & McGuiness, D. L. (2004). *OWL Web ontology language guide.* W3C recommendation. Retrieved from http://www.w3.org/TR/owl-guide/

Soh, C., & Markus, M. L. (1995). *How IT creates business value: A process theory synthesis.* Paper presented at the 16th International Conference on Information Systems, Amsterdam, The Netherlands.

Souter, D. (2005). *The Economic Impact of Telecommunications on Rural Livelihoods and Poverty Reduction: A study of rural communities in India (Gujarat), Mozambique and Tanzania.* London: Commonwealth Telecommunications Organisation and Department for International Development.

Sphere Project. (2004). *Humanitarian charter and minimum standards in disaster response.* Geneva, Switzerland: The Sphere Project.

SSTI. (2005, last updated on). *Real Gross State Product by State, 2001-2005.* Retrieved March 2007, 2007, from http://www.ssti.org/Digest/Tables/061206t.htm.

Stallings, R. A. (2006). Methodological issues. In Rodríguez, H., Quarantelli, E. L., & Dynes, R. R. (Eds.), *Handbook of disaster research* (pp. 55–82). New York, NY: Springer.

Stanton, N. A., Baber, C., & Harris, D. (2008). *Modelling command and control: Event analysis of systemic teamwork.* Aldershot, UK: Ashgate.

STAPPA and ALAPCO. (2006, last updated on). *Air Quality Index (Aqi) - a Guide to Air Quality and Your Health.* Retrieved December 12, 2006, from http://airnow.gov/index.cfm?action=static.aqi.

State of California. (2003, last updated on 2003). *Modified Mercalli Intensity Scale*. Retrieved January, 2007, from http://www.abag.ca.gov/bayarea/eqmaps/doc/mmi.html.

Stephenson, R., & Anderson, P. S. (1997). Disasters and the Information Technology revolution. *Disasters, 21*(4), 305–334. doi:10.1111/1467-7717.00065

Stoneburner, G., Goguen, A., & Feringa, A. (2007). *NIST Special Publication 800-30, Risk Management Guide for Information Technology Systems*. United States National Institute of Standards and Technology.

Stout, R. J., Cannon-Bowers, J. A., Salas, E., & Milanovich, D. M. (1999). Planing, shared mental models, and coordinated performance: An empirical link is established. *Human Factors, 41*(1), 61–71. doi:10.1518/001872099779577273

Stroomer, S., & Van Oostendorp, H. (2003). Analyzing communication in team tasks. In van Oostendorp, H. (Ed.), *Cognition in a digital world* (pp. 175–204). Mahwah, NJ: Lawrence Erlbaum Associates.

Stumme, G., & Maedche, A. (2001). Ontology merging for federated ontologies on the Semantic Web. In *Proceedings of the International Workshop for Foundations of Models for Information Integration*. Viterbo, Italy.

Sui, D. Z. (2008). The wikification of GIS and its consequences: Or Angelina Jolie's new tattoo and the future of GIS. *Computers, Environment and Urban Systems, 32*, 1–5. doi:10.1016/j.compenvurbsys.2007.12.001

Sutton, J., Palen, L., & Shklovski, I. 2008. "Backchannels on the Front Lines: Emergent Use of Social Media in the 2007 Southern California Fires". *Proceedings of the 5th International ISCRAM Conference*, F. Fiedrich and B. Van de Walle eds. pp. 624-631.

Svenmarck, P., & Brehmer, B. (1991). D³Fire, an experimental paradigm for the study of distributed decision making. In B. Brehmer (Ed.), *Proceedings of the 3rd MOHAWC Workshop on Distributed Decision Making in Belgirate, Italy* (pp. 47-77). Roskilde, Denmark: Risö National Laboratory.

Svensson, S., Cedergårdh, E., Måstensson, O., & Winnberg, T. (2009). *Tactics, command, leadership*. Karlstad, Sweden: Swedish Civil Contingencies Agency.

Szerdy, J., & McCall, M. R. (1997). How to Facilitate Distributed Meetings Using EMS Tools. In Coleman, D. (Ed.), *Groupware: collaborative strategies for corporate LANs and intranets*. Upper Saddle River, NJ: Prentice Hall.

Tanser, F., & le Sueur, D. (2002). The application of geographical information systems to important public health problems in Africa. *International Journal of Health Geographics, 1*(4).

The White House/ 2006. *The Federal Response to Hurricane Katrina: Lessons Learned*. Washington, D.C. -06-32 March 2006

Thomas, L. C. (1984). *Games, theory and applications*. Mineola, NY: Courier Dover Publications.

Thurstone, L. L. (1927a). A Law of Comparative Judgment. *Psychological Review, 34*, 273–287. doi:10.1037/h0070288

Thurstone, L. L. (1928). Attitudes Can Be Measured. *American Journal of Sociology, XXXIII*(4), 529–554. doi:10.1086/214483

Thurstone, L.L., (1927b). The Method of Paired Comparisons for Social Values. Journal of Abnormal and Social Psychology, 21, 384:400.

Tierney, Kathleen J., C. Bevc, and E. Kuligowski. (2006). Metaphors Matter: Disaster Myths, Media Frames, and Their Consequences in Hurricane Katrina. *The Annals of the American Academy of Political and Social Science, 604*(March), 57–81. doi:10.1177/0002716205285589

Tierney, Kathleen. and C. Bevc. 2007. "Disaster as War: Militarism and the Social Construction of Disaster in New Orleans." In D. Brunsma and S. Picou (eds.) *The Sociology of Katrina: Perspectives on a Modern Catastrophe*. Lanham, MD: Rowman and Littlefield.

Tolk, A., Diallo, S. Y., & Turnitsa, C. D. (2007). Applying the levels of conceptual interoperability model in support of integratability, interoperability, and composability for system-of-systems engineering. *Journal of Systemics. Cybernetics and Informatics, 5*(5), 65–74.

Tomaszewski, B. (2010). (in press). Situation awareness and virtual globes: Applications for disaster management. *Computers & Geosciences*.

Torgerson, W. S. (1958). *Theory and Methods of Scaling*. John Wiley & Sons, Inc.

Townsend, F. F. (2006). *The Federal Response to Hurricane Katrina, Lessons Learned*. United States of America: Department of Homeland Security.

Tran, P., Shaw, R., Chantry, G., & Norton, J. (2008). GIS and local knowledge in disaster management: A case study of flood risk mapping in Viet Nam. *Disasters, 33*(1), 152–169. doi:10.1111/j.1467-7717.2008.01067.x

Transport and Energy Ministry. (2006). *Key figures catalogue for use for techno-economic analyses in the transport area*, 4th ed, (in Danish). Retrieved from www.trm.dk/graphics/Synkron-Library/trafikministeriet/Publikationer/Rapporter/Noegletalskatalog%20juni%202006.pdf

Trnka, J., & Jenvald, J. (2006). Role-playing exercise – A real-time approach to study collaborative command and control. *International Journal of Intelligent Control and Systems, 11*(4), 218–228.

Trnka, J., Rankin, A., Jungert, E., Lundberg, J., & Granlund, R. (2009). *Information support in modern crisis and disaster response operations (Project Report)*. Linköping, Sweden: Linköping University.

Trnka, J. (2009). Exploring tactical command and control: A role-playing simulation approach (Doctoral dissertation). *Linköping Studies in Science and Technology, 1266*. Linköping, Sweden: Linköping University.

Trnka, J., Granlund, H., & Granlund, R. (2008). Using low-fidelity simulations to support design of decision-support systems for command and control applications. In M. Hirakawa, & E. Jungert (Eds.), *Proceedings of the 14th International Conference on Distributed Multimedia Systems in Boston, MA* (pp. 158-163). Skokie, IL: Knowledge Systems Institute.

Turoff, M. (2002). Past and Future Emergency Response Information Systems. *Communications of the ACM, 45*(4), 29–33. doi:10.1145/505248.505265

Turoff, M., Chumer, M., Van de Walle, B., & Yao, X. (2004). The design of a dynamic emergency response management information system (DERMIS). *Journal of Information Technology Theory and Application, 5*(4), 1–36.

Turoff, M. (1972). Delphi Conferencing: Computer Based Conferencing with Anonymity. *Journal of Technological Forecasting and Social Change, 3*(2), 159–204. doi:10.1016/S0040-1625(71)80012-4

Turoff, M. (2002). Past and Future Emergency Response Information Systems. *Communications of the ACM, 45*(4), 29–32. doi:10.1145/505248.505265

Turoff, M., & Hiltz, S. R. (1995). Computer Based Delphi Processes. In Adler, M., & Ziglio, E. (Eds.), *Gazing Into the Oracle: The Delphi Method and Its Application to Social Policy and Public Health* (pp. 56–88). London: Kingsley Publishers.

Turoff, M., Van de Walle, B., & Hiltz, S. R. (2010). Emergency response Information Systems: Past, present, and future. In Turoff, M., Van de Walle, B., & Hiltz, S. R. (Eds.), *Information Systems for emergency management* (pp. 369–388). New York, NY: M.E. Sharpe Inc.

Turoff, M., and Hiltz, S. R., (2008) Information Seeking Behavior and Viewpoints of Emergency Preparedness and Management Professionals Concerned with Health and Medicine, Report to the National Library of Medicine, February, 2008. (Will be Web accessible)

Turoff, M., Chumer M., Hiltz, R., Klashner, R., Alles, M., Vararheyi, M., and Kogan, A., (2004b) Assuring Homeland Security: Continuous Monitoring, Control & Assurance of Emergency Preparedness, *Journal of Information Technology Theory and Application, (JITTA)*, 6, 3, 1-24.

Turoff, M., Chumer, M., & Hiltz, S. R. (2006) Emergency Planning as a Continuous Game. *Proceedings of the 3rd International ISCRAM Conference, Newark, NJ.*

Turoff, M., Chumer, M., Van de Walle, B., and Yao, X., (2004). The Design of a Dynamic Emergency Response Management Information System (DERMIS). *The Journal of Information Technology Theory and Application (JITTA)*, 5:4, 2004, 1-35.

Turoff, M., Hiltz, S. R., Cho, H.-K., Li, Z., & Wang, Y. (2002) Social Decision Support Systems. *Proceedings of the 35th Hawaii International Conference of System Sciences.*

U.S. Department of Homeland Security Inspector General. (2006). *A Performance Review of FEMA's Disaster Management in Response to Hurricane Katrina.* Washington, D.C.

U.S. Senate Homeland Security and Government Affairs Committee. 2006. *Hurricane Katrina: A Nation still Unprepared.* Washington, DC

Uhr, C. (2007). *Behind the charts – Exploring conditions for high level emergency response management in a complex environment (Report 1037).* Lund, Sweden: Institute of Fire Safety Engineering.

United Nations and EU Civil Protection Commission. (2009, last updated on 20 Feb 2009). *The Global Disaster Alert and Coordination System* Retrieved 20 February, 2009, from http://www.gdacs.org/.

UN-SPIDER. (2010). *United Nations platform for space-based information for disaster management and emergency response.* Retrieved October 20, 2010, from http://www.unoosa.org/oosa/unspider/index.html

Urban, J. M., Bowers, C. A., Monday, S. D., & Morgan, B. B. Jr. (1995). Workload, team structure, and communication in team performance. *Military Psychology, 7*(2), 123–139. doi:10.1207/s15327876mp0702_6

USEPA. (2008, last updated on April 22, 2008). *Air Quality Index: A Guide to Air Quality and Your Health.* Retrieved 20 July, 2008, from http://airnow.gov/index.cfm?action=aqibroch.index.

USGS. (2006, last updated on 2006). *The Richter Magnitude Scale.* Retrieved January, 2007, from http://pubs.usgs.gov/gip/earthq4/severitygip.html.

Vaccari, L., Marchese, M., Giunchiglia, F., McNeill, F., Potter, S., & Tate, A. (2006). *OpenKnowledge deliverable 6.5: Emergency response in an open Information Systems environment.*

van de Walle, B., & Turoff, M. (Eds.). (2007). Special issue: Emergency response Information Systems: Emerging trends and technologies. *Communications of the ACM, 50*(3), 28–65.

Van de Walle, B., Turoff, M., & Hiltz, S. R. (in press). (expected 2009). Information Systems for Emergency Management. In the Advances in Management Information Systems monograph series (Editor-in-Chief: Vladimir Zwass). Armonk, NY. *M.E. Sharpe Inc.*

Van de Walle, B., & Turoff, M. (2008). Decision support for emergency situations. *Information Systems and E-Business Management, 6*(3), 295–316. doi:10.1007/s10257-008-0087-z

Van de Walle, B., & Turoff, M. (2008). Decision Support for Emergency Situations. In Burstein, F., & Holsapple, C. (Eds.), *Handbook on Decision Support Systems, International Handbook on Information Systems Series, Springer-Verlag, (This chapter will be open on the Web).*

Vera, D., & Crossan, M. (2005). Improvisation and innovative performance in teams. *Organization Science, 16*(3), 203–224. doi:10.1287/orsc.1050.0126

Verjee, F. (2007). *An Assessment of the Utility of GIS-based Analysis to Support the Coordination of Humanitarian Assistance.* Washington: The George Washington University, Dept. of Engineering Management and Systems Engineering.

Verjee, F. (2007). *An assessment of the utility of GIS-based analysis to support the coordination of humanitarian assistance.* Washington, DC: The George Washington University. Retrieved from http://www2.gwu.edu/~icdrm/publications/PDF/Verjee_Dissertation.pdf

Vernaccini, L., De Groeve, T., & Gadenz, S. (2007). *Humanitarian impact of tropical cyclones (EUR 23083 EN).* Luxembourg: JRC Scientific and Technical Reports.

Vettore, A., Ponte, S., et al. (2003). *Space-Based Surface Change Detection with Differential Synthetic-Aperture Radar (Sar) Interferometry: Potentialities and Preliminary Investigations.* Geomatica, vol 57(3): 326-334, issn 1195-1036

Vickery, B. C. (1966). *Faceted classification schemes.* Graduate New Brunswick, NJ: School of Library Service, Rutgers, the State University.

Voigt, S., Kemper, T., Riedlinger, T., Kiefl, R., Scholte, K., & Mehl, H. (2007). Satellite image analysis for disaster and crisis-management support. *IEEE Transactions on Geoscience and Remote Sensing, 45*(6, Part 1), 1520–1528. doi:10.1109/TGRS.2007.895830

Von Krogh, G. (1998). Care in Knowledge Creation. *California Management Review, 40*(3), 133–153.

W3. (2009). *Extensible markup language* (XML). Retrieved Februrary 3, 2009, from http://www.w3.org/XML

W3C. (2005, last updated on 2008). *Emergency Information Interoperability Framework*. Retrieved 20 February, 2009, from http://www.w3.org/2005/Incubator/eiif/charter-20071203.

Wachtendorf. T. & Kendra, J.M. (2005). Improvising disaster in the city of jazz: Organizational response to hurricane Katrina. Understanding Katrina: Perspectives from the social sciences, Retrieved October 20, 2008 from http://understandingkatrina.ssrc.org

Wade, M., & Holland, J. (2004). The resource-based view and Information Systems research: Review, extension, and suggestions for future research. *Management Information Systems Quarterly, 28*(1), 107–142.

Wagner, M. J. (2006). *The view from Google Earth*. Retrieved November 10, 2010, from http://www.gpsworld.com/gis/integration-and-standards/the-view-google-earth-7434

Walker, P., & Minear, L. (2004). *Ambiguity and Change: Humanitarian NGOs Prepare for the Future*. Massachusetts: The Feinstein International Famine Center, Tufts University.

Wall, I. (2006). *The Right to Know: The Challenge of Public Information and Accountability in Aceh and Sri Lanka*. New York: Office of the UN Secretary General's Special Envoy for Tsunami Recovery.

Walsham, G. (1997). Actor-network theory and IS research: Current status and future prospects. In Lee, A., Liebenau, J., & DeGross, J. (Eds.), *Information Systems and qualitative research* (pp. 466–480). London, UK: Chapman Hall.

Ward, J., & Peppard, J. (2002). *Strategic planning for information systems*. Wiley.

Warfield, J. N. (2003). A Proposal for Systems Science. *Systems Research and Behavioral Science, 20*(6), 507–520. doi:10.1002/sres.528

Warfield, J. N. (2002). *Understanding Complexity: Thought and Behavior*. AJAR Publishing Company, Palm Harbor, Florida, isbn 0-971-6962-0-9.

Webb, G. R. (2004). Role Improvising during Crisis Situations. *International Journal of Emergency Management, 2*, 47–61. doi:10.1504/IJEM.2004.005230

Weick, K. (1995). *Sensemaking in Organizations*. CA: Sage Publications.

Weick, K. (1996). Prepare your organization to fight fires. *Harvard Business Review*, (May): 1.

Weick, K. E. (1996). Drop Your Tools: An Allegory for Organizational Studies. *Administrative Science Quarterly, 41*, 301–313. doi:10.2307/2393722

Weick, K. E. (1998). Improvisation as a Mindset for Organizational Analysis. *Organization Science, 9*(5), 543–555. doi:10.1287/orsc.9.5.543

Weick, K. E., & Sutcliffe, K. M. (2001). *Managing the Unexpected: Assuring High Performance in an Age of Complexity*. San Francisco: Jossey-Bass.

Wenger, E., McDermott, R., & Snyder, W. (2002). *Cultivating communities of practice: a guide to managing knowledge*. Boston, Mass.: Harvard Business School Press.

Wertsch, J. V. (1997). *Mind in action*. New York, NY: Oxford University Press.

White, C., Plotnick, L., Aadams-Moring, R., Turoff, M., & Hiltz, S. R. (2008) Leveraging a Wiki to Enhance Virtual Collaboration in the Emergency Domain, Proceedings *of the 41ˢᵗ HICSS*.

White, C., Plotnick, L., Turoff, M., & Hiltz, S. R. (2007b) A Dynamic Voting Wiki, *Proceedings of 13ᵗʰ Americas Conference on Information Systems*.

White, C., Turoff, M., & Van de Walle, B. (2007a). A Dynamic Delphi Process Utilizing a Modified Thurstone Scaling Method: Collaborative Judgment in Emergency Response. *Proceedings of 4th Information Systems on Crisis Response Management*.

Whitt, R. (2007). The promise of open platforms in the upcoming spectrum auction. [Web log post]. Retrieved from http://googlepublicpolicy.blogspot.com/2007/07/promise-of-open-platforms-in-upcoming.html

Woltjer, R., Lindgren, I., & Smith, K. (2006). A case study of information and communication technology in emergency management training. *International Journal of Emergency Management*, 3(4), 32–347. doi:10.1504/IJEM.2006.011300

Woltjer, R. (2009). Functional modeling of constraint management in aviation safety and command and control (Doctoral dissertation). *Linköping Studies in Science and Technology, 1249*. Linköping, Sweden: Linköping University.

Wood, M. (2006). *Proposed request for comments on international cell alert via cell broadcasting channelization codes*, v3. CEASA. Retrieved from www.ceasa-int.org/channel_codes_v3.htm

Woods, D. D., Dekker, S. W. A., Cook, R. I., Johannesen, L. L., & Sarter, N. B. (2010). *Behind Human Error* (2nd ed.). Aldershot, UK: Ashgate.

Woods, D. D., & Hollnagel, E. (2006). *Joint cognitive systems: Patterns in cognitive systems engineering*. Boca Raton, FL: Taylor & Francis. doi:10.1201/9781420005684

Woods, D. D., & Sarter, N. B. (2010). Capturing the dynamics of attention control from individual to distributed systems. *Theoretical Issues in Ergonomics*, 11(1), 7–28. doi:10.1080/14639220903009896

Woods, D. D., & Dekker, S. (2000). Anticipating the effects of technological change: A new era of dynamics for human factors. *Theoretical Issues in Ergonomics Science*, 1(3), 272–282. doi:10.1080/14639220110037452

Woods, D. D., & Branlat, M. (2010). How adaptive systems fail. In Hollnagel, E., Paries, J., Woods, D. D., & Wreathall, J. (Eds.), *Resilience engineering in practice*. Aldershot, UK: Ashgate.

Woods, D. D. (1993). Process-tracing methods for the study of cognition outside the experimental psychology laboratory. In Klein, G. A., Orasanu, J., Calderwood, R., & Zsambok, C. E. (Eds.), *Decision making in action: models and methods* (pp. 228–251). Norwood, NJ: Ablex Publishing Corporation.

Wybo, J. L., & Lonka, H. (2002). Emergency management and the information society: How to improve the synergy? *International Journal of Emergency Management*, 1(2), 183–190. doi:10.1504/IJEM.2002.000519

Yao, X., & Turoff, M. (2007) Using Task Structure to Improve Collaborative Scenario Creation, *Proceedings of ISCRAM 2007, 4th International Conference on Information Systems for Crisis Response and Management*, Delft, the Netherlands, May 13-16, Brussels University Press.

Yarbrough, L., & Easson, G. (2005). Eye of the storm: Google Earth assists Katrina response and recovery. *Geomatica*, 59(4), 451–453.

Yin, R. (1994). *Case study research*. Sage Publications Inc.

Zelik, D. Patterson. E. S., & Woods, D. D. (2010). Measuring attributes of rigor in information analysis. In E. S. Patterson & J. Miller (Eds.), *Macrocognition metrics and scenarios: Design and evaluation for real-world teams*. Aldershot, UK: Ashgate.

Zhang, N., Bayley, C., & French, S. (2008). *Use of Web-based Group Decision Support for Crisis Management*. Paper presented at the ISCRAM2008, Washington DC.

Zhao, S., Addams-Moring, R., & Kekkonen, M. (2005). Building mobile emergency announcement systems in 3G networks. *Proceedings of the Communications and Computer Networks Conference*, (pp 141-148). Calgary, Canada: ACTA Press.

Ziesche, S. (2007). Social-networking Web systems: Opportunities for humanitarian information management. *Journal of Humanitarian Assistance*.

Zonum. (2010). *Zonum solutions*. Retrieved October 29, 2010, from www.zonums.com

About the Contributors

Murray E. Jennex is an Associate Professor at San Diego State University, editor in chief of the International Journal of Knowledge Management, editor in chief of Idea Group Publishing's Knowledge Management book series, co-editor in chief of the International Journal of Information Systems for Crisis Response and Management, and president of the Foundation for Knowledge Management (LLC). Jennex specializes in knowledge management, system analysis and design, IS security, e-commerce, and organizational effectiveness. Jennex serves as the knowledge management systems track co-chair at the Hawaii International Conference on System Sciences. He is the author of over 100 journal articles, book chapters, and conference proceedings on knowledge management, end user computing, international Information Systems, organizational memory systems, ecommerce, security, and software outsourcing. He holds a BA in chemistry and physics from William Jewell College, an MBA and an MS in software engineering from National University, an MS in telecommunications management and a PhD in Information Systems from the Claremont Graduate University. Jennex is also a registered professional mechanical engineer in the state of California, a certified Information Systems security professional (CISSP), and a certified secure software lifecycle professional (CSSLP).

* * *

Clare Bayley is a Research Associate at Manchester Business School currently working on stakeholder involvement and participation for societal risk management. With a degree in chemistry and PhD on multi-criteria perspectives of environmental policy, Bayley has worked on a number of interdisciplinary research projects combining natural and social science. Bayley has interests in science policy, nuclear sustainability, human reliability analysis, group decision making, and the psychology of how people make decisions.

Denis Blackmore, PhD, is a full Professor at the department of mathematical sciences at NJIT. His academic genealogy can be traced all the way to Newton. His research is primarily in the theory and applications of dynamical systems (nonlinear dynamics) and closely related fields. He has studied a plethora of applications in such areas as automated assembly, biological populations, computer aided geometric design, fluid mechanics, granular flows, plant growth, relativistic and quantum physics, and rough surface analysis.

Scott Bradner has been involved in the design, operation and use of data networks at Harvard University since the early days of the ARPANET. He was involved in the design of the original Harvard data networks, the Longwood Medical Area network (LMAnet) and New England Academic and Research Network (NEARnet). He was founding chair of the technical committees of LMAnet, NEARnet, and the Corporation for Research and Enterprise Network (CoREN). Mr. Bradner served in a number of roles in the IETF. He was the co-director of the Operational Requirements Area (1993-1997), IPng Area (1993-1996), Transport Area (1997-2003), and Sub-IP Area (2001-2003). He was a member of the IESG (1993-2003) and was an elected trustee of the Internet Society (1993-1999), where he currently serves as the Secretary to the Board of Trustees. Scott is also a trustee of the American Registry of Internet Numbers (ARIN). Mr. Bradner is the University Technology Security Officer in the Harvard University Office of the Provost. He tries to help the University community deal with technology-related privacy and security issues. He also provides technical advice and guidance on issues relating to the Harvard data networks and new technologies to Harvard's CIO. He founded the Harvard Network Device Test Lab, is a frequent speaker at technical conferences, a weekly columnist for Network World, and does a bit of independent consulting on the side.

Dominik Brunner received a Diploma in technical computer science from the University of Applied Sciences Hof, Germany, in 2004, and his Ph.D. in information and communication technologies from the University of Trento, Italy, in 2009. From 2006 to 2009 he was with the European Commission - Joint Research Centre, Ispra, Italy, where he investigated novel damage assessment methods for very high resolution SAR imagery to support emergency response after natural disasters. Currently, he is working at the Fraunhofer Institute of Optronics, System Technologies, and Image Exploitation in Karlsruhe, Germany. There, his main research interests are in the fields of image processing and pattern recognition for spaceborne and ground based radar images.

Monika Büscher, Senior Lecturer at the Centre for Mobilities Research, Sociology and Imagination Lancaster, Lancaster University, co-director of mobilities.lab. She studies people's everyday material and epistemic practices - on the move or in situ, including practices of place-making and (distributed) collaboration. Her approach is ethnographic, rooted in ethnomethodology and science and technology studies. Her work critically informs collaborative, interdisciplinary socio-technical innovation in different settings.

Nong Chen received her Bachelor's of Science degree in industrial engineering in 2001 from the school of Economics and Management, Beijing University of Technology, China. She further studied at University of Southern Denmark. She obtained her Master's in technical informatics and her Ph.D. from the Delft University of Technology. Her research interests are personalized information seeking and retrieval, systems modeling and architectures, crisis response and management, geographic information systems, and location based services.

Paul Currion runs a consultancy specializing in information management for humanitarian operations. He was an initiative manager for the Emergency Capacity Building Project, developing ways of improving NGO use of technology; WFP Regional Information Manager for the Indian Ocean Tsunami response; manager and liaison for Humanitarian Information Centres (HICs) in Kosovo, Afghanistan, Iraq, and Liberia; and is a board member for the Sahana disaster management software project. In addition to working with governments, UN agencies, NGOs and the Red Cross movement, he has researched and written extensively on information management issues, including the UN ICT Task Force publication ICT For Peace, and maintains a blog dedicated to these issues at humanitarian.info.

Ajantha Dahanayake is full Professor of Information Systems of the Information Technology and Marketing department at Georgia College and State University. Dr. Dahanayake served at Delft University of Technology's Computer Science department as well as at the Technology Policy and Management school. She was also the chair of the Information Systems and Software Engineering department of the Open University (the Netherlands). She served as the director of the BETADE research program of the Delft University of Technology; funding research in component based systems development with Euro 3M research grants. Dr. Dahanayake's current research is focused on ICT enabled services.

Simon French is Professor of information and decision science at Manchester Business School. He has interests in decision and risk analysis, Bayesian statistics, Information Systems, and knowledge management. He was a member of the International Chernobyl Project, leading the decision conferences; it was this experience on the Chernobyl Project that led him to realise the paramount importance of good information management and communication as an integral part of risk management. He has been involved in the development of RODOS, a decision support system for nuclear emergency management. Recently he has worked risk communication, stakeholder involvement and e participation, particularly in relation to societal risk management.

Sarah Friedeck is currently a graduate Research Assistant under Dr. Gaynor and Master of Health Administration graduate student in the Health Management and Policy Department at Saint Louis University's School of Public Health. She received her Bachelor of Arts in Psychology from the University of Nevada, Las Vegas in 2009.

Eric Frost is co-director of the Center for Homeland Security Technology Assessment, the Visualization Center, and the Center for Information Technology and Infrastructure. He also directs a center on Central Asia. All these roles come together in humanitarian and homeland security efforts to use technology and geospatial imagery to help solve difficult problems in difficult circumstances. Frost and his colleagues use many new technologies and protocols that are enhanced and tested during exercises such as Strong Angel III (http://www.strongangel3.net/) and Operation Golden Phoenix. Frost and colleagues work with satellite imagery and GIS, sensor networks, wireless and optical communication, data fusion, visualization, and decision support for first responders and humanitarian groups, especially crossing the civilian-military boundary. His work on computer visualization, fiber optics, and oil-and-gas exploration in places such as Indonesia, Kazakhstan, Australia, and Mexico are often involve major interactions with companies, governments, and universities in many other countries.

Mark Gaynor, PhD, MS, ME, MA is an Associate Professor of Health Management, School of Public Health at Saint Louis University. Mark's PhD in Computer Science is from Harvard University. His research interests include distributed sensor networks for medical applications, innovation with distributed architecture, IT/healthcare standardization, designing network based-services, IT for healthcare, and emergency medical services. He is CTO and member of the board of directors at 10Blade, a small company building EMRs for NASA. His first book, *Network Services Investment Guide: Maximizing*

ROI in Uncertain Markets, is in press with Wiley (2003). He has been a PI and Co-PI on several grants from NSF, NIH, NSBI, and the U.S. Army.

Dan Harnesk is Assistant Professor at the Division of Information System Science at Lulea University of Technology (LTU), Sweden. His research concerns information security and crisis management, and he is the manager of the Information Security Group – InfoSec@LTU. He has particular interest in socio-technical aspects of Information Systems/security design. Dan is a member of the editorial board of the Journal of Information Systems Security. He obtained his doctoral degree in computer and systems science at LTU, introducing a concept for social, transaction, and IT alignment in SME interfirm relationships. His teaching duties at the university currently consist of Master level courses in Strategic Management of Information Security and Research Methods.

John Harrald is a Research Professor at the Virginia Tech Center for Technology, Security and Policy and is an Emeritus Professor at George Washington University's School of Engineering and Applied Science where he was co-founder and co-director of The GWU Institute for Crisis, Disaster, and Risk Management. He is the executive editor of the Journal of Homeland Security and Emergency Management, a member of the Board of Scientific Counselors for the Center for Disease Control's Coordinating Officer for Terrorism Preparedness and Emergency Response, and a member of the National Research Council Disasters Roundtable Steering Committee. He received a BS from the U.S Coast Guard Academy, a MS from MIT and his PhD from Rensselaer Polytechnic Institute.

Art Hendela is the Owner, Founder, and President of Hendela System Consultants, Inc. of Little Falls, NJ, a consulting firm specializing in Web database applications. He holds a BS in chemical engineering and an MS in computer science, both from New Jersey Institute of Technology. As a part-time PhD student at NJIT, Hendela works in the area of serious games with an emphasis on planning systems for computer security. His research interests include mathematical modeling, database systems, and computer security. Hendela has been married 20 years to Vega and has two sons, Martin, 16, and Karl, 11. In his limited spare time, Hendela enjoys coaching soccer and baseball and playing basketball and softball.

Starr Roxanne Hiltz, a sociologist and computer scientist whose work focuses on "human centered" information systems, is currently distinguished Professor Emerita, Information Systems department, College of Computing Sciences, NJIT. For 2008-2009 she has been chosen to be the Fulbright/ University of Salzburg distinguished chair in communications and media. Her research interests include group support systems (virtual teams and online communities), evaluation research methods, asynchronous learning networks, emergency management Information Systems, pervasive computing, and the applications and impacts of "social computing" ("Web 2.0") systems.

Björn Johansson is deputy research director at the Swedish Defense Research Agency and Assistant Professor at Linköping University. He has a Ph.D. in Cognitive Systems (2005). His research concerns cognitive systems engineering, command and control, temporal characteristics of control tasks, crisis management, resilience engineering, mixed reality, and human communication. He has produced more than 30 publications in scientific journals and edited books, including conference proceedings. He is member of several different academic and industrial networks concerned with safety and crisis management.

Magdy Kabeil is an Emeritus Professor at Sadat Academy for Management Sciences, Egypt, a US Fulbrighter to UC Berkeley 1995/96, and a former Director Manager of the National Operations Research Center of Egypt. He holds a PhD in Information Systems Quality Assurance from the College of Engineering, Ain Shams University, Egypt, and a MS in Operations Research from the Air Force Institute of Technology, Dayton OH, USA. He teaches undergraduate and graduate courses in Decision Support Systems (DSS), Modeling and Simulation, System Dynamics, and Business Process Reengineering (BPR). In addition, he has published over 35 articles in professional publications. His research interests include DSS, crisis management, BPR, and IT planning, education, and diffusion in developing countries.

Ahmad Kabil is a graduate student at the Lawrence Technological University, MI. He works as a teaching assistant in the fields of Database Management Systems, Management Information Systems, and Decision Support Systems (DSS). His research interest is in DSS. He also has some practical experience in the IT industry. After getting his Bachelor degree in Management Information Systems, he worked in the field of software development. He worked also as a summits and conferences organizer at the World Development Forum (WDF). The company offers focused integrated marketing channels for the IT decision-makers along with IT Vendors/ IT solution providers and relevant experts.

Margit Kristensen, head of innovation, pervasive healthcare at Alexandra Institute A/S in Aarhus, Denmark has a professional background as registered nurse and a Master's degree in informatics, with specialization in health informatics. She was, from 2004-2008, part of the EU project PalCom as part of management and workpackage leader in the workpackage addressing prototypes for emergency response. Her research interest concerns use of Information Technologies in healthcare to support collaboration, coordination, and communication.

John Lindström is a Researcher at the Division of Computer Aided Design and a member of the Information Security Group at Lulea University of Technology. John has prior to joining the academia worked for about 15 years with product and service development, and technical and management consulting in the information security business. John's main research interests are within information security, crisis and emergency management, as well as product development. John holds a doctoral degree within computer and systems science on strategic information security.

John McGuirl is a researcher at Decision Systems Analytics, a research and consulting group based in Columbus, Ohio. He received his PhD in Industrial Systems Engineering, specializing in cognitive systems engineering at The Ohio State University in 2008. He is interested in developing new ways to support decision-making in hi-tempo, uncertain environments: assessing and improving the resilience of teams and organizations, and studying how complex adaptive systems emerge and behave. His most recent work has focused on team coordination in the operating room and improving patient safety during perioperative care.

Preben Holst Mogensen, Associate Professor at the Computer Science Department, University of Aarhus, and CEO, partner, and co-founder of 43D ApS. Coordinating, managing, and participating in several EU projects since 1990, most recently as co-coordinator in the EU Integrated Project PalCom, his research interests concern tools and techniques for active user involvement in system development (participatory/cooperative design); pervasive computing; cooperative analysis; prototyping; CSCW; object oriented approaches to system developments.

L-F Pau is Adjunct Professor at the Copenhagen Business School and Professor at the Rotterdam School of Management, in the field of Mobile Business. He was, until recently, CTO of L.M. Ericsson's Network Systems division with worldwide responsibilities, which he joined from a prior position as CTO for Digital Equipment / Hewlett Packard Europe; he was earlier or in parallel on the faculties of Danish Technical University, Ecole Nationale Supérieure des Télécommunications (Paris), M.I.T., and University of Tokyo. He has been on the Boards of IEEE Standards, Rapid IO Forum, OMG and more. He is a Fellow of IEEE (USA), BCS (UK), JSPS (Japan). He holds an MSc from ENS Aéronautique et espace, MBA from Institut d'études politiques, Dr.Ing from Univ. Paris 9, and DSc from Univ. Paris 6.

Alan Pearce founded Information Age Economics in 1979 after a senior-level policy career in the U.S. Government from 1971 to 1979. In his position as Chief Economist, he was one of the prime architects of public policies at the Federal Communications Commission, the U.S. House of Representatives Committee on Communications, and the Office of Telecommunications Policy in the Executive Office of the President that laid the foundation of a new information era in the telecommunications-information-entertainment industry. Since leaving the government, Dr. Pearce has provided services to telecommunications, wireless, satellite, cable TV, movie and program production companies, and broadcasting corporations, along with software and equipment manufacturers. He has also consulted with, and conducted research for, a wide variety of government organizations at the international, federal, state, and local levels. In the past several years, Dr. Pearce conducted the economic research that persuaded the U.S. government to approve Cingular's $41 billion all-cash acquisition of AT&T Wireless, and that led the European Union and the U.S. Government to deny MCI-WorldCom's attempted $129 billion acquisition of Sprint. He also pioneered the concept of improving first responder support by economically justifying an adequate amount of spectrum at 700 MHz in order to enable a nationwide public safety and homeland security network, and also worked on research that measured the effects of accelerated broadband deployment in the U.S. on Gross Domestic Product and employment for President-elect Obama's Transition Team. Dr. Pearce has Bachelor's and Master's degrees from The London School of Economics and a Ph.D. from Indiana University.

Linda Plotnick is a PhD candidate (ABD) in the Information Systems department at the New Jersey Institute of Technology. Her dissertation examines leadership and trust issues in partially distributed teams that are engaged in software development in the emergency domain. A partially distributed team is a hybrid team comprised of collocated subteams that are distant from one another and communicate primarily through electronic media. She also conducts research in the emergency management domain with special interest in public warning and in mitigating threat rigidity. Linda has presented conference papers at ISCRAM, AMCIS, and HICSS. She has a BA, MSE, and MBA from the University of Pennsylvania.

Kendall Post has Electrical Engineering degree from the University of Wisconsin and 30 years of applied engineering and engineering management experience. His work has involved biomedical, telecommunications, radio-communications, radio-navigation, and space instrumentation. Ken is the principle investigator of a 10-year, private sector study of public warning, mass mobilization, and other problems in disaster management communications. The study sought to understand what it would take to attain sustained readiness for all national planning scenarios. It arose from an introduction to adjunct faculty of FEMA's Emergency Management Institute & Fire Service Academy. It included market research, gap analysis, focus group, and technical feasibility activities. The study found 4 fundamental barriers – 3 policy / leadership, 1 performance - to sustained readiness. It identified the key criteria for overcoming the performance barrier, and the stakeholder preferred enterprise model for correcting the policy / leadership barriers. The technical feasibility efforts showed that "smart" device methods are key to solving long-standing public warning and mass mobilization problems. The overall effort provided a roadmap for closing the 25+ year gap in applied science and engineering to the vital infrastructure underlying disaster preparedness and management.

Murali Raman received his PhD in Management Information Systems from the School of IS & IT, Claremont Graduate University, USA. Murali is a Rhodes Scholar and a Fulbright Fellow. His other academic qualifications include an MBA from Imperial College of Science Technology and Medicine, London, an MSc in HRM from London School of Economics. Raman is currently an academician attached to Multimedia University Malaysia, where he teaches and conducts research in the area of management Information Systems, project management and e-business models. He has published in more than fifty papers in international journals and conference proceedings. His corporate experience includes working with Maybank Malaysia (2 years) and Accenture Consulting (5 years) before embarking on an academic path. He has consulted with numerous companies including several based in the USA (Claremont University Consortium), Ghana (GIMPA), Singapore (AsiaOne, Kepple bank), Australia (Monash Supply Chain and Logistics Center), and Malaysia (Panasonic, OUM, RHB Bank, Intan, MAKPEM, Malaysian Association of Social Workers, CDC Consulting among others). His research interests are mainly in the area of knowledge management systems and its application in an institutional context.

Eli Rohn, PhD, CISA, CGEIT is a former Adjunct Professor at the department of Information Systems at NJIT and an active member of ISCRAM.ORG. He is currently the managing partner of the consulting firm Cognimax LLC, and a commercial pilot at Aerial Operations LLC, both located in NJ. He is a certified Information Systems auditor (CISA) and certified in the governance of enterprise IT (CGEIT). His research interests include complex adaptive systems and their application to Information Systems.

Nadine Sarter is an Associate Professor in the Department of Industrial and Operations Engineering and the Center for Ergonomics at the University of Michigan. She received her PhD in industrial and systems engineering, with a specialization in cognitive ergonomics/cognitive systems engineering, from Ohio State University in 1994. Sarter's primary research interests include a) the design and evaluation of multimodal HCI and CSCW interfaces (including sight, sound, and touch), b) support for attention and interruption management through adaptive notifications and preattentive reference, c) the design of decision aids that support trust calibration and adaptive function allocation, and d) human error and error management in a variety of complex domains, including aviation, the military, and the automotive industry.

Aviv Segev is an Assistant Professor at the Knowledge Service Engineering Department at KAIST - Korea Advanced Institute of Science and Technology. His research interests include classifying knowledge using the Web, mapping context to ontologies, knowledge mapping, and implementations of these areas as expert systems in the fields of Web services, medicine, and crisis management. He has published over 30 papers in scientific journals and conferences. In 2004 he received his Ph.D. from Tel-Aviv University in Management Information Systems in the field of context recognition. Previously, Aviv was a simulation project manager in the Israeli Aircraft Industry.

P. Simonsen is a Consultant with Accenture Denmark specializing in test and emergency systems. He is a Cand. Merc. Dat graduate from the Copenhagen Business School.

Tricia Toomey is a Geographic Information Systems (GIS) specialist with the San Diego State University Research Foundation, Homeland Security Research Technology Center where she specializes in integrating GIS into the public safety/emergency management community. Toomey holds a BA in geography with an emphasis in methods of geographical analysis and a MSc in homeland security with an emphasis in communication and Information Systems. She has been involved in the emergency management/homeland security community in San Diego for over three years.

Jiri Trnka is Scientist at the Swedish Defence Research Agency. He has a Ph.D. in Informatics (2009). His research focuses on information support for collaborative command and control in emergency and crisis response operations. He has participated in a number of projects concerned with command and control, decision-support systems, simulations, and training. Besides research he has expertise in the area of planning, execution, and evaluation of major crisis and emergency management exercises.

Murray Turoff is an Information Scientist who has been involved in the design and application of group oriented computer mediated communication (CMC) Systems since 1970. In 1971, he designed and implemented the "Emergency Management Information System and Reference Index" as a nationwide EMISARI to the hundreds of professionals around the US managing the 1971 wage-price-freeze. This system continued to be used by the federal government for emergency operations until the mid 1980's. After 9/11 he turned back to focus again on the emergency applications of CMC systems after developing applications in many other areas (project management, online learning, group decision support, online Delphis, etc). He was and is of the view that the government has very little "organizational or community memory" of some of its earlier major accomplishments in emergency preparedness and management and particularly of the Office of Emergency Preparedness in the Executive Office of the President.

Connie White is an Assistant Professor in the Department of Emergency Administration and Management at Arkansas Tech University. She is also a PhD candidate (ABD) at the New Jersey Institute of Technology and conducts her graduate work under the direction of Murray Turoff. White's doctoral research is focused on the emergency domain. She has recent research and publications relating to new applications of technology for emergency and crisis management. White studies fast decision-making amongst groups of experts where there is uncertainty in the information and only a subgroup (fraction) of the experts may be available when the decision needs to be made. White creates, works with, and studies virtual communities of practice and swift trust amongst team members in the emergency response environment domain. She conducts research using as subjects emergency domain professionals, where the exercises are coordinated with various levels of government officials and real world practitioners.

David Woods is Professor of Cognitive Systems Engineering and Human Systems Integration at Ohio State University, and Director of the university's campus wide initiative on complexity in natural, social, and engineered systems. He studies how people cope with complexity in time pressured situations such as critical care medicine, aviation, space missions, intelligence analysis, and crisis management, including multiple accident investigations. He designs new systems to help people find meaning in large data fields when they are under pressure to diagnose anomalies and re-plan activities. His latest work on safety concerns models and measures of the adaptive capacities of organizations to determine how they are resilient and if they are becoming too brittle in the face of change. Past-President of Human Factors and Ergonomics Society, won Laurel Award from Aviation Week and Space Technology, advisor to the Columbia Accident Investigation Board, founding board member of the National Patient Safety Foundation, member of several National Academy of Science committees, most recently on Dependable Software, he is author or editor of 8 books, including Behind Human Error, Resilience Engineering, and Resilience Engineering in Practice.

Xiang Yao is a PhD candidate in the Information Systems department at New Jersey Institute of Technology (NJIT). He got his BA in computer science and engineering from Beijing University of Astronautics and Aeronautics in 1995. He joined NJIT to conduct research in developing and evaluating group support systems for emergency management. He initiated and developed a collaborative scenario creation system being able to support virtual table-top exercises (TTX) and knowledge sharing.

Gunter Zeug graduated as Geographer from Ludwig-Maximilians University Munich, Germany in 2000. Shortly after, he joined GAF AG, an internationally renowned consulting company for remote sensing and geoinformation, as technical expert. There he was mainly involved in the design and implementation of agricultural GIS tools related to the EU-Common Agricultural Policy. From 2006 to 2009 Gunter worked with the ISFEREA action at the Joint Research Centre of the European Commission as geomatics and remote sensing specialist. His main research interests were in the field of urban hazard risk assessment and more general challenges of urbanization in the developing world including population growth, environmental impact and hazard risk. In 2010, Gunter joined the European Environment Agency in Copenhagen. There he is involved in the coordination of the in-situ component of the Global Monitoring for Environment and Security (GMES) program of the European Union.

Nan Zhang is a PhD student at Manchester Business School. With both her first degree and MSc in Information Systems, she is currently focusing her research on evaluation of e-participation. She has also worked on a few interdisciplinary research projects on stakeholder involvement and e-participation.

Index

A

9/11 terrorism attack 1, 6, 134
access overload control (ACCOLC) 192-193
acoustic messaging 188
Actor Network Theory (ANT) 140, 143-146, 149, 151-153
agility 1-2, 4, 8-9, 103, 153
Air Quality Index (AQI) 217, 226
alarm congestion analysis 188
Amazon 100
ambient technologies 72
Analytical Hierarchy Process (AHP) 262-263, 275, 279, 285
automatic identification systems (AIS) 75, 152, 212, 261, 281, 283

B

Base system controller (BSC) 193
Beaufort Wind Scale 215, 226
blogs 27, 37, 39, 85-88, 92-93, 232
Boxing Day tsunami crisis 85-86
Bureau for Crisis Prevention and Recovery (BCPR) 264-265, 280, 284

C

California Department of Forestry and Fire Protection (CAL FIRE) 253
Capital Wireless Information Net (CapWIN) 97, 107
cartography 245-248, 250, 253, 258-259, 261
cell broadcast (CB) 188, 190, 192-196
cell broadcast (CB) technology 192
cell broadcast center (CBC) 190, 193
Clean Air Act 217
closed-circuit TV (CCTV) 72
collaborative improvisation 74, 79, 82
command centers 55-57, 67, 124, 263, 273

Common Alerting Protocol (CAP) 224

Common Alerting Protocol (CAP) 224
Common Operational Picture (COP) 248, 254-256
communication modelling 112, 119, 121
communicative roles 112-113, 119, 121, 127-129, 132
computer scientists 77
Control, Communication, Computer, and Intelligence (C4I) System 264, 266
control event (CE) 207
Core Meta-Model 158, 164, 181
cost-benefit analysis 191, 194, 196
crisis information flow management 94
crisis information mapping 85
crisis management 1, 9, 41, 43-46, 52, 54, 56, 87, 94-95, 97, 117, 134-135, 139-154, 159, 185, 197, 202-207, 211-212, 214, 227-228, 241, 246, 262-264, 268-271, 273-275, 277, 279-281, 283-284, 286
crisis management information systems 139-140, 142-145, 148-151, 206
crisis management organization 214
crisis management systems 141, 146, 205
crisis organizations 139-140, 142, 145, 148, 151
crisis relief-response process 156
crisis response 11, 27-28, 40, 52, 54, 83-84, 87, 97, 108, 134, 156-161, 163-165, 168-170, 173-175, 181-184, 201-202, 204-211, 213, 226, 229-230, 241-242, 260-261, 275, 286
crisis response systems 158, 161, 165, 204-205, 209-210, 286
criterion of key communication agent 120, 122-127
Cyclone Nargis 34

D

damage assessment maps 254
DARPA Agent Markup Language (DAML) 89
data gathering 56, 99, 204, 207, 264
data packets 80